Money, Banking, and Financial Markets

The building on this book's cover is the Second Bank of the United States, located in Philadelphia. It operated from 1816 to 1836, serving some of the functions of the modern Federal Reserve. President Andrew Jackson vetoed legislation to extend the Bank's charter because he believed it served "moneyed interests" at the expense of common people (see Chapter 8).

To the right of the Second Bank, the central photo shows a specialist (in a blue coat) and traders at work on the floor of the New York Stock Exchange (see Chapter 5). They are flanked by two currencies. At the top is a gold certificate, a type of money used in the United States in the late nineteenth and early twentieth centuries (see Chapter 2); at the bottom are Japanese yen.

SECOND EDITION

Money, Banking, and Financial Markets

Laurence M. Ball
Johns Hopkins University

WORTH PUBLISHERS

Senior Publisher: Catherine Woods

Executive Editor: Charles Linsmeier

Senior Acquisitions Editor: Sarah Dorger

Executive Marketing Manager: Scott Guile

Senior Development Editor: Marie McHale

Development Editor: Barbara Brooks

Associate Media Editor: Jaclyn Castaldo

Editorial Assistant: Mary Walsh

Associate Managing Editor: Tracey Kuehn

Project Editor: Kerry O'Shaughnessy

Photo Editor: Cecilia Varas

Photo Researcher: Julie Tesser

Art Director: Babs Reingold

Senior Designer, Cover Designer: Kevin Kall

Production Manager: Barbara Anne Seixas

Composition: MPS Limited, a Macmillan Company

Printing and Binding: Quad Graphics, Versailles

Cover Photos: *Second Bank of the United States PHILADELPHIA USA:* © Aflo Co. Ltd./
Alamy; *Stock brokers:* AP Photo/Richard Drew; *Gold certificate and gold coins:*
© Corbis Premium RF/Alamy

Library of Congress Control Number: 2011920626

ISBN-13: 978-1-4292-4409-1

ISBN-10: 1-4292-4409-7

Printed in the United States of America

First printing 2011

Worth Publishers

41 Madison Avenue

New York, NY 10010

www.worthpublishers.com

www.wortheconomics.com

Laurence Ball is Professor of Economics at Johns Hopkins University. He holds a Ph.D. in economics from the Massachusetts Institute of Technology and a B.A. in economics from Amherst College. Professor Ball is a Research Associate of the National Bureau of Economic Research and has been a visiting scholar at the Federal Reserve, the Bank of Japan, the Central Bank of Norway, the Reserve Bank of Australia, and the Hong Kong Monetary Authority. His academic honors include the Houblon-Norman Fellowship (Bank of England), a Professorial Fellowship in Monetary Economics (Victoria University of Wellington and Reserve Bank of New Zealand), the NBER Olin Fellowship, and the Alfred P. Sloan Research Fellowship. He is the coauthor with N. Gregory Mankiw of *Macroeconomics and the Financial System* (Worth Publishers). Professor Ball lives in Baltimore with his wife, Patricia, and their son, Leverett.

To Patricia

brief contents

contents

🏛 *indicates coverage of financial crises.*

Online Case Study
An Update on the
Stock Market

PART III BANKING

Chapter 7 Asymmetric Information in the Financial System 189

Online Case Study
An Update on the
Mortgage Crisis

Students have a natural interest in money, banking, and financial markets, and instructors have felt the buzz around their money and banking courses rise dramatically in recent years. Students of business and economics come to class perplexed by the financial crisis of 2007–2009, the deep recession, and the controversies about how the government and Federal Reserve responded and should respond.

Heightened student interest creates a golden opportunity for us instructors. We have a chance to show students how economic analysis can help them understand the critical events of the day. Our courses can cut through the cacophony of media sound bites to reveal the basic forces at work in the financial system and in the overall economy.

In writing this book, I was guided by two principles:

1. *To explain core ideas of economic theory simply yet rigorously.* I emphasize foundational topics such as asset-pricing theory, the effects of asymmetric information on the financial system, and the causes of aggregate economic fluctuations.

2. *To apply theory as directly as possible to real-world issues.* Plentiful examples, accompanied by graphs, charts, tables, and photos, reinforce the text, and 80 Case Studies discuss current and historical events in detail.

FROM THE FIRST EDITION TO THE SECOND

Events have occurred since the first edition of this book was published that demonstrate its topical relevance. Innovative coverage in the first edition included a capstone chapter that analyzed financial crises. This approach—originally aimed at explaining past events such as the Great Depression—is a natural way to build student understanding of the crisis of 2007–2009.

Other innovations in the first edition included coverage of such topics as the causes and effects of asset-price bubbles, the zero bound on interest rates, the growth of securitization and subprime lending, and the costs and benefits of Europe's currency union. All these topics have proved critical for understanding the U.S. and world economies today.

While validating many of the first edition's topic choices, recent events also gave me lots of work to do on this second edition. Momentous changes have occurred in the financial system, economy, and policymaking. I have strived to keep up with these changes and to keep the book's material on the cutting edge of economic analysis. To this end, I have thoroughly revised the case studies—half either are new (15) or are significantly updated or refocused (24)—and I thoroughly updated the text.

Second edition updates address topics ranging from adjustable rate mortgages, which have plummeted in popularity since the first edition, to Warren Buffett, whose legend has grown with his purchase of Goldman Sachs stock, to Walmart's interest in banking: it has opened a bank in Canada. Many new topics can be grouped into broad categories:

- *The behavior of asset prices:* New coverage updates the growth and collapse of the U.S. housing bubble and the 50 percent fall in the Dow Jones stock index during the financial crisis.

- *Troubles at financial institutions:* Among them, crises at the top-five investment banks in 2008 and AIG's disastrous losses on credit default swaps. I also examine the various channels through which the subprime mortgage crisis hurt commercial banks.

- *Financial controversies and scandals:* New case studies address the role of credit rating agencies in the subprime crisis, banks' use of Structured Investment Vehicles (SIVs) to avoid capital requirements, and Bernard Madoff's shocking Ponzi scheme.

- *Government regulation:* The text surveys the many proposals for financial reforms and those enacted in the Dodd-Frank Act of 2010, and it details recent legislation concerning credit card fees and student loans.

- *The financial crisis and the economy:* I analyze the spread of the crisis from Wall Street to Main Street, the sharp rise in unemployment alongside the near-disappearance of inflation, and prospects for the future.

- *The new world of economic policy:* Topics include the unprecedented interventions in the financial system by the Treasury Department and Federal Reserve over 2007–2009, the Fed's efforts to stimulate the economy with interest rates at the zero bound, the debate over fiscal stimulus, and how the money multiplier has become a divider.

 The timeline in Figure 18.3 tracks significant financial and economy-wide events and policy actions leading up to, during, and in the aftermath of the crisis.

As in the first edition, Chapter 18 analyzes financial crises. I have expanded it to review the history of the 2007–2009 crisis and its aftermath in detail. To emphasize how the final chapter builds on earlier ones, material on financial crises throughout the book is flagged, as here, with an icon—a broken bank.

While this second edition devotes much attention to recent events in the United States, it also retains a broad historical and international scope. The book contains discussions of money and banking in the days of Alexander Hamilton, William Jennings Bryan, and Richard Nixon. It discusses banking in Japan, the debt crisis in Greece, hyperinflation in Zimbabwe, and tulip bulbs in Holland.

ONLINE CASE STUDIES KEEP THE BOOK CURRENT

We can hope that changes in the financial system and economy during the life of this edition are not as dramatic as those of the last few years. Yet surely there will be breaking news as the aftermath of the crisis continues to play out and unexpected events occur. To keep each chapter's coverage fresh, a set of 18 online case studies is available through the EconPortal.

These regularly updated cases supplement the text and cover such topics as the U.S. economic recovery (or lack thereof); implementation of the Dodd-Frank Act; unwinding of the Federal Reserve's emergency policies; and the fate of European economies grappling with high government debt. The EconPortal also provides lecture PowerPoint slides and assessment to accompany each online case study. A complete, chapter-by-chapter list of text and online case studies appears inside the front cover.

AN OVERVIEW OF THE TEXT

This book addresses a vast range of economic issues, but I have strived to make it as concise as possible. Students often report that textbooks overwhelm them with masses of detail that obscure essential concepts. My approach is to exposit key topics as clearly as I can, to strip away outdated material and unimportant details, and to produce a student-friendly book. Focusing on the key material has produced a book of 18 chapters in five parts that is about 100 pages shorter than a standard money and banking text.

PART I: Foundations

Chapters 1 and 2 outline the basic purposes of the financial and monetary systems and introduce the concept of a financial crisis. Chapter 1 describes how the financial system channels funds from savers to investors, its role in economic growth, the problem of asymmetric information in financial markets, and how banks help to reduce this problem. Chapter 2 introduces students to money—what it is, why we need it, and how it's changing—and to the major functions of central banks.

PART II: Financial Markets

Chapters 3–6 describe markets for stocks, bonds, derivatives, and currencies. Who participates in these markets? What are these players trying to do? What determines asset prices, interest rates, and exchange rates? These financial markets chapters emphasize important controversies and apply theory to recent events.

Chapter 3's detailed, updated treatment of asset pricing retains such topics as Campbell and Shiller's evidence for bubbles in stock prices. New material includes the Gordon growth model of stock prices. Chapter 4 features updated coverage on yield curves and a new case study on Greece's debt crisis.

Another key topic, the debate over the efficient markets hypothesis and the ability of stock pickers to beat the market, is joined in Chapter 5 by

This icon directs students to online resources.

ECON P⊕RTAL

▶ EconPortal is the digital gateway to *Money, Banking, and Financial Markets.* Details on the EconPortal and other supplements and media follow on p. xxxiii.

an explanation of credit default swaps and their role in crippling AIG. Chapter 5 also chronicles the upheaval in investment banking during 2008, and Chapter 6 reports on how Europe's debt crisis has affected the euro.

PART III: Banking

Chapters 7–10 discuss the roles of banks and other financial intermediaries. Chapter 7 explains why banks exist, Chapter 8 describes the structure of the banking industry, Chapter 9 explains how banks seek profits, and Chapter 10 discusses why and how they are regulated.

Part III starts with a detailed treatment of asymmetric information in Chapter 7, where precise numerical examples demonstrate how moral hazard and adverse selection can cause loan markets to break down. The chapter then ties these problems to practical topics such as the Madoff scandal and the rating of mortgage-backed securities.

The banking discussion in the following three chapters emphasizes the long-term trend toward deregulation and the moves toward re-regulation in response to the financial crisis. I also include detailed analyses of securitization and of subprime lending as background for understanding the crisis.

PART IV: Money and the Economy

I believe that students need to see how the Fed affects the economy before discussing what the Fed ought to do. Thus, one innovation of this book is to present basic theories of money and economic fluctuations before turning to monetary policy debates. Chapters 11–14 analyze fluctuations—booms and recessions, inflation and deflation. I emphasize topics critical for understanding recent history, including the effects of asset-price declines and the zero bound on interest rates.

Economic fluctuations and Federal Reserve policy involve the interplay of interest rates, output, and inflation. The framework used by modern macro theorists, in which the interest rate is the Fed's policy instrument, suggests a model for analyzing fluctuations in the short run. In this model of the economy, an aggregate expenditure curve graphs the relationship between the interest rate and output and a Phillips curve the relationship between output and inflation.

The Online Appendix to Chapter 12 compares the AE/PC model to the more traditional model of aggregate demand and aggregate supply.

This AE/PC model is a natural fit, both with academic research and with real-life discussions of economic events. In Chapter 12, an extended case study uses the model to interpret U.S. economic history from 1960 to the present.

PART V: Monetary Policy

Chapters 15–18 survey central banking, debates about monetary policy and institutions, and the mechanics of financial crises. In the last two decades, central banks around the world have become more independent, their policymaking has become more transparent, and many have adopted inflation targeting. A major motivation for these changes has been academic research on the dynamic consistency problem in monetary policy.

The policy discussion in Part V starts with a theoretical analysis of the dynamic consistency problem and then moves to a wide range of practical questions. How does the FOMC decide when to change interest rates? Why did Ben Bernanke advocate inflation targeting when he was a professor, and what will he do about it as Fed chair? What policy mistakes produced the economic instability of the 1970s? Why did European countries abolish their national currencies and create the euro? How and why have central banks sought to increase political support for their policies?

To understand financial crises, students need to apply what they know about financial markets, banks, monetary policy, and the overall economy—all the major subjects of this book. By illuminating financial crises, especially the most recent episode, Chapter 18 delivers the payoff from taking a course on money, banking, and financial markets.

CHOICES FOR COURSE EMPHASIS AND COVERAGE

This book contains just 18 chapters but covers more than enough material for a money and banking course. Most instructors will want to emphasize some parts of the text and touch more lightly on others.

I suggest that any course cover Chapters 1–2, the book's foundation, and Chapters 3–4, which present the core concepts about interest rates and asset prices. Most instructors will also want to delve into Chapter 7, which models asymmetric information to explain why banks exist; Chapters 11–12, the core theory on money and economic fluctuations; and Chapter 18 on financial crises.

Otherwise, the best chapters to cover depend on the emphasis of a course. Here are a few examples:

The financial system The key material for this emphasis is Chapter 5 on securities markets and Part III (Chapters 7–10) on banking. I also recommend Chapter 13, which examines the interactions of the financial system, monetary policy, and economic fluctuations.

The behavior of the aggregate economy Cover Part IV (Chapters 11–14) on money and the economy and as much of Part V (Chapters 15–18) on monetary policy as possible.

Monetary policy Cover Part V in detail.

An international perspective The key material is Chapter 6 on foreign exchange markets and Chapter 17 on international monetary policy. I also recommend two chapters that emphasize cross-country comparisons: Chapter 14 on inflation and Chapter 16 on monetary institutions.

TOOLS TO AID LEARNING

Each chapter in this book and its accompanying Web site features a variety of aids to student learning:

- *Case Studies* The 80 Cases in the text and 18 Online Case Studies bridge the gap between economic theory and real events as told from the viewpoints of financial firms, aggregate economies, policymakers, and individuals.

- *Illustrations* More than 200 tables and graphs help students visualize theory and trends in real data on the economy and financial system. Photographs, recent and historical, reinforce the ties between theory and real events.

- *Key Terms* To help students learn the language of money, banking, and financial markets, key terms appear in **boldface** when they are introduced in the text and repeated with their definitions in the margin. An alphabetical list of Key Terms, referenced by page number, appears at the end of each chapter. At the end of the book, a Glossary lists the definitions of all 300 terms.

- *Margin Notes* These sidelights expand on points in the text and refer students to related coverage, for example, coverage of financial crises, in other parts of the book. Some margin notes include Web pointers that direct the student to further information on the text Web site and elsewhere.

- *Chapter Summaries* Each chapter ends with a section-by-section, bullet-point Summary that helps students absorb and review the material.

- *Questions and Problems* Each chapter concludes with a set of Questions and Problems designed for homework assignments. A set of Online and Data Questions asks students to research information on the Internet or to examine data at the text Web site and elsewhere.

- *Chapter Appendixes* The Chapter 1 Appendix reviews background material on measuring real GDP, and the Chapter 12 Appendix ties together two explanations for the long-run behavior of interest rates. Online Appendices cover advanced theoretical topics related to coverage in Chapters 12, 14, and 15.

ACKNOWLEDGMENTS

Scores of people provided invaluable help as I wrote and revised this book, from research assistants and students who commented on draft chapters to academic colleagues and practitioners in the world of money and banking to the exceptional team, named on page iv, at Worth Publishers. To thank everyone properly in this preface would grossly compromise my goal of writing a concise book. I must, however, single out my development editor, Barbara Brooks, for service beyond the call of duty.

I also want to acknowledge the economics teachers who shaped the book's second edition by using and offering comments on the first edition, by reviewing chapters for both editions, and by participating in focus groups:

Burton Abrams
University of Delaware

Douglas Agbetsiafa
Indiana University at South Bend

Francis Ahking
University of Connecticut at Storrs

Ehsan Ahmed
James Madison University

Jack Aschkenazi
American InterContinental University

Cynthia Bansak
San Diego State University

Clare Battista
California Polytechnic State University

Peter Bondarenko
University of Chicago

Michael Brandl
University of Texas at Austin

James Butkiewicz
University of Delaware

Anne Bynoe
Pace University

Tina Carter
Florida State University

Jin Choi
DePaul University

Peter Crabb
Northwest Nazarene University

Evren Damar
Pacific Lutheran University

Ranjit Dighe
State University of New York at Oswego

Aimee Dimmerman
George Washington University

Ding Du
South Dakota State University

John Duca
Southern Methodist University

Fisheha Eshete
Bowie State University

Robert Eyler
Sonoma State University

Imran Farooqi
University of Iowa

David Flynn
University of North Dakota

Yee-Tien Fu
Stanford University

Doris Geide-Stevenson
Weber State University

Ismail Genc
University of Idaho

Rebecca Gonzalez
University of North Carolina, Pembroke

David Hammes
University of Hawaii at Hilo

Jane Himarios
University of Texas at Arlington

David Hineline
Miami University

Aaron Jackson
Bentley College

Nancy Jianakoplos
Colorado State University

Frederick Joutz
George Washington University

Bryce Kanago
University of Northern Iowa

John Kane
State University of New York at Oswego

Elizabeth Sawyer Kelly
University of Wisconsin

Kathy Kelly
University of Texas at Arlington

Faik Koray
Louisiana State University

John Krieg
Western Washington University

Kristin Kucsma
Seton Hall University

Gary Langer
Roosevelt University

Mary Lesser
Iona College

David Macpherson
Florida State University

Michael Marlow
California Polytechnic State University

W. Douglas McMillin
Louisiana State University

Perry Mehrling
Barnard College

Jianjun Miao
Boston University

John Neri
University of Maryland

Rebecca Neumann
University of Wisconsin at Milwaukee

Robert Pennington
University of Central Florida

Ronnie Phillips
Colorado State University

Dennis Placone
Clemson University

Ronald Ratti
University of Missouri

Robert Reed
University of Kentucky

Joseph Santos
South Dakota State University

Mark Siegler
California State University at Sacramento

Robert Sonora
Fort Lewis College

Richard Stahl
Louisiana State University

Frank Steindl
Oklahoma State University

James Swofford
University of South Alabama

Behrouz Tabrizi
Saint Francis College

Sven Thommesen
Auburn University

Brian Trinque
University of Texas at Austin

Kristin Van Gaasbeck
California State University at Sacramento

Rubina Vohra
New Jersey City University

John Wade
Eastern Kentucky University

Qingbin Wang
University at Albany

Charles Weise
Gettysburg College

Raymond Wojcikewych
Bradley University

Paul Woodburne
Clarion University

Bill Yang
Georgia Southern University

Most of all, I want to thank my family, whose support made this book possible.

Laurence M. Ball
Baltimore, January 2011

Worth Publishers has crafted an exciting and useful supplements and media package to accompany the second edition of Ball's *Money, Banking, and Financial Markets*. The package helps instructors teach their Money and Banking courses, and it helps students grasp concepts more readily.

Accuracy is so critically important that all the *MBFM* supplements have been triple-checked—by members of the supplements team, reviewers, and a separate, additional team of accuracy checkers. The time and care that have been put into the supplements and the media ensure a seamless package.

EconPortal

ECON P⊕RTAL

EconPortal is the digital gateway to Ball's *Money, Banking, and Financial Markets*. Designed to enrich your course and improve your students' understanding of economics. EconPortal is a powerful, easy-to-use, complete, and completely customizable teaching and learning management system.

Interactive eBook with Embedded Learning Resources The eBook's functionality allows for highlighting, note-taking, graph and example enlargements, a full searchable glossary, as well as a full text search. You can customize any eBook page with comments, external Web links, and supplemental resources.

A Personalized Study Plan for Students Featuring Diagnostic Quizzing Students will be asked to take the PSP: Self-Check Quiz after they have read the chapter and before they come to the lecture that discusses that chapter. Once they've taken the quiz, they can view their Personalized Study Plan based on the quiz results. The PSP will guide them to the appropriate eBook materials and resources for further study and exploration.

***The Economist* News Feed** This real-time feed automatically pulls articles on money and banking topics and allows one click assigning of news articles from *The Economist*.

Online Case Studies One per chapter (see the Table of Contents), to update and extend a case study or other timely coverage beyond the text's publication date. Prepared by John Duca (Southern Methodist University).

A Fully Integrated Learning Management System EconPortal is your one stop for all the teaching, learning, and media resources tied to *Money, Banking, and Financial Markets*. The system carefully integrates these resources into an easy-to-use system, the Assignment Center. The system organizes preloaded assignments centered on a comprehensive course outline and offers you flexibility—from adding your own assignments from a variety of question types to preparing self-graded homework, quizzes, or tests. Assignments may be created from the following:

- **End-of-Chapter Quiz Questions** *MBFM* 2e end-of-chapter problems are available in a self-graded format—perfect for quick in-class quizzes or homework assignments. The questions have been carefully edited to ensure that they maintain the integrity of the text's end-of chapter problems.

- **Graphing Questions** Pulled from our graphing tool engine, EconPortal can provide electronically gradable graphing-related problems. Students will be asked to draw their response to a question, and the software will grade that response. These graphing exercises are meant to replicate the pencil-and-paper experience of drawing graphs—with the bonus to you of not having to hand-grade each assignment!

- **Test Bank Questions** Generate assignments by drawing from the pool of *MBFM* 2e Test Bank questions.

Using EconPortal's Assignment Center, you can select your preferred policies for scheduling, maximum attempts, time limitations, feedback, and more. You will be guided through the creation of assignments, and you can assign and track any aspect of your students' interaction with practice quizzes. The Gradebook captures your students' results and allows for easily exporting reports. The ready-to-use course can save you many hours of preparation time. It is fully customizable and highly interactive.

eBooks can be purchased through www.courses.bfwpub.com.

INSTRUCTOR SUPPLEMENTS

INSTRUCTOR'S MANUAL WITH SOLUTIONS MANUAL

Prepared by Jane Himarios (University of Texas–Arlington), for each chapter in the textbook the Instructor's Manual provides:

- **Brief Chapter Summary:** summarizing the contents of the chapter.

- **Detailed Section Summaries:** detailed lecture notes including coverage of all case studies and references to online case studies.

- **Inside and Outside the Classroom Activities:** problems, exercises, and discussion questions relating to lecture material, designed to enhance student learning.

- **Detailed Solutions:** to all end-of-chapter questions and problems; prepared by Doris Geide-Stevenson (Weber State University).

PRINTED TEST BANK

Prepared by Robert Sonora (Fort Lewis College), Joann Weiner (George Washington University), and Martin Pereyra (University of Missouri–Columbia). The Test Bank provides questions ranging in levels of difficulty and format to assess students' comprehension, interpretation, analysis, and synthesis skills. Containing over 100 questions per chapter, the Test Bank offers a variety of multiple-choice, true/false, and short-answer questions.

COMPUTERIZED TEST BANK

The printed Test Bank will be available in CD-ROM format for both Windows and Macintosh users. With this flexible, test-generating software, instructors can easily create and print tests as well as write and edit questions.

STUDENT SUPPLEMENTS

STUDY GUIDE

Prepared by Richard Stahl (Louisiana State University), the Study Guide complements the textbook by providing students additional opportunities to develop and reinforce lessons learned in the money and banking text. For each chapter of the textbook, the Study Guide provides:

- *Brief Chapter Summary:* summarizing the contents of the chapter.
- *Key Terms:* listed and defined, with space for students to write in the definitions in their own words.
- *Detailed Section Summaries with Student Tips and Concept-Related Questions:* including coverage of all case studies, tips to help students with difficult concepts, and 3–5 questions per section to reinforce learning of key concepts.
- *Self-test End-of-Chapter Questions:* 15–20 application-oriented, multiple- choice questions.
- *Worked-out Solutions:* including solutions to all Study Guide review questions.

COMPANION WEB SITE FOR STUDENTS AND INSTRUCTORS

www.worthpublishers.com/ball2

The companion site is a virtual study guide for students and an excellent resource for instructors. For each chapter in the textbook, the tools on the site include:

Student Tools

- *Practice Quizzes:* a set of 20 questions with feedback and page references to the textbook. Student answers are saved in an online database that can be accessed by instructors.
- *Key Economic Data and Web Links to Relevant Research:* related to chapter content and end-of-chapter questions.
- *Key Term Flashcards:* Students can test themselves on the key terns with these pop-up electronic flashcards.

Instructor Resources

- *Quiz Gradebook:* The site gives instructors the ability to track students' interaction with the practice quizzes via an online gradebook. Instructors may choose to have student results e-mailed directly to them.

- *PowerPoint Lecture Presentations:* These customizable PowerPoint slides, prepared by James Butkiewicz (University of Delaware), are designed to assist instructors with lecture preparation and presentation by providing learning objectives, animated figures, tables, and equations from the textbook, key concepts, and bulleted lecture outlines.

- *Illustration PowerPoint Slides:* A complete set of figures and tables from the textbook in JPEG and PowerPoint formats.

- *Images from the Textbook:* Instructors have access to a complete set of figures and tables from the textbook in high-res and low-res JPEG formats.

eBOOK

Students who purchase the *Money, Banking, and Financial Markets* eBook have access to interactive textbooks featuring:

- quick, intuitive navigation

- customizable note-taking

- highlighting

- searchable glossary

With the Ball eBook, instructors can:

- Focus on only the chapters they want. You can assign the entire text or a custom version with only the chapters that correspond to your syllabus. Students see your customized version, with your selected chapters only.

- Annotate any page of the text. Your notes can include text, web links, and even photos and images from the book's media or other sources. Your students can get an eBook annotated just for them, customized for your course.

eBooks can be purchased through http://ebooks.bfwpub.com/

COURSE MANAGEMENT SYSTEM

The Ball Course Cartridge allows you to combine your Course Management System's most popular tools and easy-to-use interface with the text-specific, rich Web content, including preprogrammed quizzes, links, activities, and a whole array of other materials. The result: an interactive, comprehensive online course that allows for effortless implementation, management, and use. The Worth electronic files are organized and prebuilt to work within your CMS software and can be easily downloaded from the CMS content showcases directly onto your department server. You can also obtain a CMS formatted version of the book's test bank.

chapter one

The Financial System

Schott Solar

The financial system is part of your daily life. You buy things with debit or credit cards, and you visit ATMs to get cash. You may have borrowed money from a bank to buy a car or pay for college. You see headlines about the ups and downs of the stock market, and you or your family may own shares of stock. If you travel abroad, you depend on currency markets to change your dollars into local money at your destination.

The financial system is also an important part of the overall economy. When the system works well, it channels funds from people who have saved money to people, firms, and governments with investment projects that make the economy more productive. For example, companies obtain loans from banks to build factories that provide new jobs for workers and produce new goods for consumers. By increasing an economy's productivity, the financial system helps the economy to grow and the living standards of its citizens to rise.

At times, however, the financial system malfunctions, damaging the economy. In the United States, the most traumatic example is the Great Depression. In October 1929, the stock market fell by more than 25 percent in one week, wiping out many fortunes. After the stock market crash, people lost confidence in the financial system. They rushed to

The financial system channels funds to investment projects that make the economy more productive. An example is the Schott Solar factory in Albuquerque, New Mexico. Here a quality-control technician examines a solar energy panel before it is shipped.

their banks to withdraw money, and banks ran out of cash. Nearly half of all U.S. banks were forced out of business in the early 1930s.

These events triggered an economic disaster. The nation's output fell by 30 percent from 1929 to 1933, and the unemployment rate rose to 25 percent. Millions of Americans were impoverished.

In 2007, the United States was struck by its worst financial crisis since the Great Depression. This time, the crisis began with a fall in house prices, which produced a rash of defaults on home-mortgage loans. Over the next two years, the effects spread through the financial system: U.S. stock prices fell dramatically, and many large banks failed or came close to failing. Financial turmoil produced a sharp contraction in the economy as consumption and investment plummeted and the unemployment rate doubled between 2007 and 2010.

This book explores financial systems and financial crises in the United States and around the world. We discuss the different parts of these systems, such as banks and stock markets, and their economic functions. We discover how a healthy financial system benefits the economy, why the system sometimes breaks down, and what a government can do to strengthen a country's financial system.

This book also discusses money. Money is another part of your daily life: you may have dollar bills in your pocket right now. Like the financial system, money is critical to an economy's health. A sharp fall in the U.S. money supply prolonged the 1930s' Depression. Throughout the book we discuss the effects of the money supply and how economic policymakers determine this variable.

Part I lays a foundation for discussing all these topics. We begin with an overview of the financial system's two main parts: financial markets and banks.

▶ Chapter 1 introduces the financial system. Chapter 2 introduces money and describes how a central bank can control the money supply.

1.1 FINANCIAL MARKETS

In economics, a market consists of people and firms who buy and sell something. The market for shoes includes the firms that manufacture shoes and the consumers who buy them. The market for labor includes workers who sell their time and firms that buy that time. **Financial markets** are made up of people and firms that buy and sell two kinds of assets. One type of asset is currencies of various economies, such as dollars and euros. In this chapter, we focus on the second type of asset: securities.

A **security** is a claim on some future flow of income. Traditionally, this claim was recorded on a piece of paper, but today most securities exist only as records in computer systems. The most familiar kinds of securities are stocks and bonds.

Financial market a collection of people and firms that buy and sell securities or currencies

Security claim on some future flow of income, such as a stock or bond

Bonds

A **bond**, also called a *fixed-income security*, is a security issued by a corporation or government that promises to pay the buyer predetermined amounts of money at certain times in the future. Corporations issue bonds to finance investment projects such as new factories. Governments issue bonds when

Bond (*fixed-income security*) security that promises predetermined payments at certain points in time. At *maturity*, the bond pays its *face value*. Before that, the owner may receive *coupon payments*

they need funds to cover budget deficits. When a corporation or government issues bonds, it is borrowing money from those who buy the bonds. The issuer receives funds immediately and pays the buyers back in the future. Because bond issuers owe money to bond purchasers, bonds are also called *debt securities*.

For example, you might pay $100 for a bond that pays you $6 a year for 10 years and then pays back the $100 at the end of the tenth year. To introduce some terms, the *face value* of this bond is $100, and the *coupon payment* is $6; the bond's *maturity* is 10 years. Almost always, the total payments promised by a bond—the face value plus all coupon payments—exceed the price that a buyer pays for the bond. This means that bonds pay **interest**: the issuer pays buyers for the use of their funds.

Bonds differ in their maturities, which range from a few months to 30 years or more. Bonds with maturities of less than a year have special names: they are called *commercial paper* when issued by corporations and *Treasury bills* when issued by the U.S. government. Bonds also differ in the stream of payments they promise. For example, a *zero-coupon bond* yields no payments until it matures. To attract buyers, it sells for less than its face value. You might pay $90 for a zero-coupon bond that pays $100 at maturity.

In our world, promises—including promises to make payments on bonds—are not always kept. Sometimes a bond issuer **defaults**: it fails to make coupon payments or to pay the face value at maturity. A corporation defaults on its bonds if it declares bankruptcy. A government defaults if it doesn't have enough revenue to make bond payments.

Risks of default vary greatly for different bonds. This risk is small for bonds issued by the U.S. government or by well-established, highly successful corporations. Default risk is larger for new corporations with unknown prospects or corporations that are losing money, because these companies may go bankrupt and stop making bond payments. The greater the risk of default, the higher the interest rate that a bond must pay to attract buyers.

Stocks

A **stock**, or *equity*, is an ownership share in a corporation. As of 2010, Exxon Mobil Corporation had issued about 5 billion shares of stock. If you own 50 million of these shares, you own 1 percent of Exxon Mobil and its oil refineries and are entitled to 1 percent of the company's future profits.

Companies issue stock for the same reason they issue bonds: to raise funds for investment. Like a bond, a share of stock produces a flow of income—but a different kind of flow. A bondholder knows exactly how much the bond will pay (unless the issuer defaults). The earnings from a company's stock are a share of profits, and profits are unpredictable. Consequently, buying stocks is usually riskier than buying bonds. People buy stocks despite the risk because stocks often produce higher returns.

Because stock is an ownership share, stockholders have ultimate control over a corporation. Stockholders elect a corporation's board of directors, which oversees the business and hires a president to run its day-to-day

Interest payment for the use of borrowed funds

Default failure to make promised payments on debts

Stock (equity) ownership share in a corporation

Bond holders
no control

operations. In contrast, bondholders have no control over a corporation; a bond is simply a corporation's promise of future payments to the bond's buyer.

Stock and bond markets generate many challenging questions: How do firms decide how many bonds and shares of stock to issue, how do people decide which bonds and stocks to buy, and what determines the prices of these securities? Before we answer these questions, let's address a larger issue. What is the purpose of stock and bond markets: why do people participate in them, and why are they important for the economy?

▶Chapters 3 through 5 analyze the behavior of security market participants and the determination of security prices.

1.2 ECONOMIC FUNCTIONS OF FINANCIAL MARKETS

① *Channel funds*
② *Risk sharing.*

Stock and bond markets are important to the economy for two reasons. First, these securities markets exist to channel funds from savers to investors with productive uses for the funds. Second, securities markets help people and firms share risks. ②

Matching Savers and Investors ① *Channel funds.*

We can illustrate the first role of securities markets with an example. Consider a young man named Britt. Unlike most people, Britt can throw a baseball 95 miles an hour—and he has a good curve ball, too. For these reasons, a baseball team pays him $10 million a year to pitch. Britt happens to be a thrifty person, so he does not spend all his salary. Over time, he accumulates a lot of savings and wonders what he should do with it.

Inflation causes
monetary value to fall

If he just accumulates cash and puts it in a safe, Britt knows his savings will not grow. In fact, if there is inflation, the value of his money will fall over time. Britt wonders how he can use his wealth to earn more wealth.

In another city, Harriet, the owner of a software company, is pondering her future. Harriet is a person of great vision and has an idea that could make her rich: an application that sends smells from one smartphone to another.

Harriet wants to develop this app, which will let people send perfumes to their sweethearts and rotten-egg smells to their enemies. She knows this product, iSmells, will be highly profitable. Unfortunately, it is expensive to buy the computers and hire the programmers needed for Harriet's project. Because her current business does not generate enough profits to finance this investment, Harriet fears that she won't be able to develop her great idea.

Financial markets can help both Harriet and Britt solve their problems. Harriet can obtain the funds for her investment from Britt (and people like him). Her company can issue new stock, which people like Britt will buy in the hope of sharing in Harriet's future profits. Harriet can also raise funds by selling bonds and using part of her future profits to make the payments promised by the bonds.

This is a win–win outcome. Harriet develops the exciting new software she has dreamed of. Britt earns large returns on the stocks and bonds that he buys. Harriet's workers earn the high wages that a profitable business can afford to pay. People around the world have fun exchanging iSmells.

This simple example captures the primary role of all the trillion-dollar financial markets in the real world. At any point in time, some people consume less than they earn and save the rest. Other people know how to use these savings for investments that earn profits and benefit the economy. When they work well, financial markets transfer funds from the first group of people to the second, allowing productive investments to take place.

A note on terminology: we will use the word **savers** for people like Britt who accumulate wealth by spending less than they earn. We will use the word **investors** for people like Harriet who start or expand businesses by building factories, buying equipment, and hiring workers.

How investors and savers interact?

> **Savers** people who accumulate wealth by spending less than they earn
>
> **Investors** people who expand the productive capacity of businesses

This terminology is standard among economists, but in common parlance, people often use the term *investor* differently. Britt might say he is "investing" when he buys stocks or bonds from Harriet. But for us, purchasing securities is a form of saving. Harriet does the investing when she buys computers and hires programmers. With this terminology, the primary role of financial markets is to move funds from savers to investors.

Risk Sharing

Financial markets have a second important role in the economy: they help people share risks. Even if investors could finance their projects without financial markets, the markets would exist to perform this risk-sharing function alone.

To see this point, let's suppose Harriet is wealthy. If she uses most of her wealth, she could finance the expansion of her business without getting funds from anyone else. She would not have to sell stocks or bonds in financial markets. She would retain full ownership of her firm and keep all the profits from iSmells.

Sole owner without investor.

Because the software business, like any industry, is risky, this strategy is probably unwise. Harriet's new software might be profitable, but there is no guarantee. It's possible that another firm will produce a better version of the software or that consumers will tire of smartphone gimmicks and move on to the next technological toy.

In these cases, Harriet might not sell much software, and she could lose the funds she invested. Because of this risk, putting her money in a safe instead of into her company starts to look like a better idea. This strategy means giving up a chance for high software profits, but it is less risky.

Fortunately, Harriet does not have to choose between hoarding money and risking everything on her company. Thanks to financial markets, she can fund her new investment, at least in part, by issuing stocks and bonds. This approach reduces the amount of her own wealth that Harriet must put into the firm and makes it possible for her to share the risk from her business with the buyers of her securities.

How sharing risk works?

Harriet can use the wealth she doesn't spend on iSmells to buy stocks and bonds issued by other companies. She is likely to earn money on these assets even if her own business fares poorly. Harriet can also buy bonds issued by the U.S. and other governments. Such behavior is an example of **diversification**, the distribution of wealth among many assets.

Diversification the distribution of wealth among many assets, such as securities issued by different firms and governments

Why is diversification desirable? Most of the time, some companies do well and others do badly. The software industry might boom while the steel industry loses money, or vice versa, and one software company may succeed while another fails. If a person's wealth is tied to one company, he loses a lot if the company is unsuccessful. If he buys the securities of many companies, bad luck and good luck tend to average out. Diversification lets savers earn healthy returns from securities while minimizing the risk of financial disaster.

This book discusses some sophisticated ideas about diversification. At its core, however, the idea of diversification is common sense. The late James Tobin won the Nobel Prize in Economics in 1981 largely for developing theories of asset diversification. When a newspaper reporter asked Tobin to summarize his Nobel-winning ideas, he said simply, "Don't put all your eggs in one basket."

But just because a principle is commonsense doesn't mean that people follow it. The following case study offers an example of people who failed to heed James Tobin's advice, with disastrous consequences.

CASE STUDY

The Perils of Employee Stock Ownership

Many Americans save for their retirement through *401(k) plans*, named for the congressional act that created them. A 401(k) plan is a savings fund administered by a company for its workers. Saving through a 401(k) plan is appealing because any income contributed to the plan is not taxed. In addition, some companies match employee contributions to 401(k) plans.

Mutual fund financial institution that holds a diversified set of securities and sells shares to savers

A person who puts money in a 401(k) plan may choose among a variety of assets to purchase. Usually the choices include shares in **mutual funds**. A mutual fund is a financial firm that buys and holds a large number of different stocks and bonds. Buying mutual fund shares is a relatively easy way to diversify your eggs into more than one basket.

A company's 401(k) asset offerings often include stock in the company itself, and some employees choose to put most of their 401(k) savings into company stock. As a result, their assets are not diversified. There seem to be several reasons for this behavior. Some employers encourage it, believing that workers are more loyal if they own company stock. Many workers are confident about their companies' prospects, so they view company stock as less risky than other securities. People are influenced by success stories such as Microsoft, where employees grew rich from owning company stock.

But putting all your eggs in one basket is disastrous if someone drops the basket. A poignant example is Enron, the huge energy company that went bankrupt in 2001. At Enron, 58 percent of all 401(k) funds—and all the savings of some workers—was devoted to Enron stock. During 2001, as an accounting scandal unfolded, Enron's stock price dropped from $85 to 30 cents. This wiped out the retirement savings of many employees. One 59-year-old man saw his 401(k) account fall from $600,000 to $11,000.

The disaster was even worse because Enron laid off most of its employees. Workers lost their life savings at the same time they lost their jobs. Many suffered hardships such as the loss of their homes.

Since the Enron disaster, financial advisors have urged greater diversification in 401(k) plans. Many people have taken this advice to heart. One study estimates that, averaging over all companies, the percentage of 401(k) funds in company stock fell from 19 percent in 1999 to 10 percent in 2008.

The government has encouraged this trend through the Pension Reform Act of 2006, which limits companies' efforts to promote employee stock ownership. Before the act, some companies contributed their stock to 401(k) plans on the condition that workers hold on to the stock. Now employees must be allowed to sell company stock after 3 years of service.

Despite these changes, economists worry that far too much 401(k) wealth remains in company stock. Company stock accounts for more than half of 401(k) assets at some large firms, including Procter & Gamble, Pfizer, and General Electric. In 2008–2009, GE employees saw their 401(k) balances plummet when GE Capital, a subsidiary that lends to consumers and businesses, suffered large losses. GE's stock price fell from $37.49 in December 2008 to $5.73 in March 2009, a decrease of 85 percent. In this case, the price recovered somewhat—it was $18.94 in March 2010—but the GE episode illustrates the perils of employees holding their company's stock.

Some economists think the government should take stronger action to address this problem. They propose a cap on the percentage of 401(k) money that goes to company stock. At this writing, however, no new laws appear imminent.[*]

[*] For more on Enron's workers, see "Workers Feel Pain of Layoffs and Added Sting of Betrayal," *The New York Times*, January 20, 2002. For recent trends in 401(k) plans, see Sarah Holden and Jack VanDerhei, "401(k) Plan Asset Allocation, Account Balances, and Loan Activity in 2008," Issue Brief No. 335, Employee Benefit Research Institute, October 2009.

1.3 ASYMMETRIC INFORMATION

When financial markets work well, they channel funds from savers to investors, and they help people reduce risk. But financial markets don't always work well. Sometimes they break down, harming savers, investors, and the economy. The problems of financial markets can be complex, but many have the same root cause: **asymmetric information**, a situation in which one participant in an economic transaction has more information than the other participant. In financial markets, the asymmetry generally occurs because the sellers of securities have more information than the buyers.

Two types of asymmetric information exist in financial markets, *adverse selection* and *moral hazard*. **Figure 1.1** outlines both concepts. Let's discuss them in turn.

> **Asymmetric information**
> situation in which one participant in an economic transaction has more information than the other participant

FIGURE 1.1 Asymmetric Information in Financial Markets

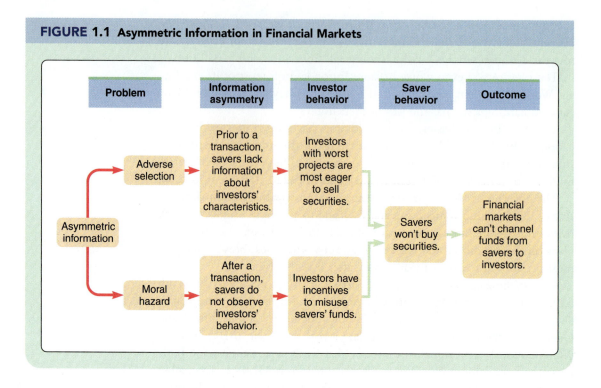

Adverse Selection

In general, **adverse selection** means that the people or firms that are most eager to make a transaction are the least desirable to parties on the other side of the transaction. In securities markets, a firm is most eager to issue stocks and bonds if the values of these securities are low. That is the case if the firm's prospects are poor, which means that earnings on its stock are likely to be low and default risk on its bonds is high. Adverse selection is a problem for buyers of securities because they have less information than issuers about the securities' value. Because of their relative ignorance, buyers run a risk of overpaying for securities that will probably produce low returns.

To illustrate adverse selection, let's return to the story of Harriet and Britt and add a third character, Martha. Like Harriet, Martha runs a software firm, and she would like to develop i-smells technology. But Martha is not as gifted as Harriet. Not only are there technical glitches in Martha's plans for the software but she is also a terrible manager. She is disorganized, and her abrasive personality results in high employee turnover. For all these reasons, if Martha invests in i-smells technology, she is less likely than Harriet to develop a successful product.

Both Martha and Harriet would like to finance their investments by selling securities to Britt. If Britt knew that Harriet is more talented than Martha, he would realize that Harriet's stock will probably produce higher earnings than Martha's and that Harriet is less likely to go bankrupt and default on her bonds. In short, he would prefer to buy Harriet's securities over Martha's.

But remember: Britt's expertise is baseball, not software or business. He doesn't know Martha or Harriet, and he can't evaluate their talents. The two women have equally glib sales pitches for their products, so both businesses seem like good bets to him. Britt doesn't know the value of either woman's securities because he doesn't know the likelihood that each will succeed.

The story gets worse. Martha and Harriet understand their own businesses, so they *do* know the value of their securities. They have more information than Britt. This information asymmetry produces adverse selection: Martha, the more-inept businessperson, wants to issue more securities than Harriet. Why? Harriet knows that shares in her company are worth a lot. Therefore, while she wants to diversify by selling some stock to others, she wants to keep a relatively large amount for herself. Martha, on the other hand, knows her stock is not worth much because there's a good chance her company will fail. She wants to unload all her stock onto other people and keep little or none for herself.

Britt doesn't understand software, but he does understand adverse selection. He realizes that when somebody is extremely eager to sell something, it is probably not worth much. When firms offer securities for sale, then, Britt worries that most are a bad deal. So he decides after all to put his money in a safe—he won't earn anything, but at least he won't get ripped off. Consequently, neither Harriet nor Martha can finance investment. In Martha's case, this is no great loss. But Harriet's inability to obtain financing harms the many people who would benefit from her project: Harriet, savers such as Britt, Harriet's workers, and consumers.

Moral Hazard

The second asymmetric information problem prevalent in financial markets arises after a transaction has been made. **Moral hazard** is the risk that one party to a transaction will act in a way that harms the other party. Issuers of securities may take actions that reduce the value of those securities, harming their buyers. The buyers can't prevent this because they lack information on the issuers' behavior.

> **Moral hazard** the risk that one party to a transaction will act in a way that harms the other party

To understand moral hazard, let's once again change the Britt-and-Harriet story. In this version, there is no adverse selection: Harriet is the only one looking for funding (there is no Martha), and everyone in securities markets, including Britt, knows that Harriet can produce great software. Britt would do well to buy Harriet's securities as long as Harriet performs as everyone expects her to and wisely uses the funds for software development.

But what if Harriet doesn't do what she's supposed to do? Software is a tough, competitive industry. Harriet has the skills to succeed, but she must work hard and keep costs low to earn profits. Unfortunately, as a human being, Harriet faces temptations. She wants to pay high salaries to herself and the friends who work for her. She wants some nice Postimpressionist paintings on her office wall. And she thinks it would be fun to leave work at 2 P.M. every Friday to party at trendy clubs.

If Harriet succumbs to these temptations, costs rise, productivity falls, and her firm is less profitable. If the problems get out of hand, iSmells could even go bankrupt. If Harriet had financed her business with her own wealth, she would have incentives to work hard and behave prudently because the cost of artwork and parties would come out of her own pocket. But these incentives disappear if Harriet's firm is financed by Britt. If Britt buys the firm's stock, then it is he, not Harriet, who loses if profits are low. If Britt buys bonds, then it is he who loses if the firm goes bankrupt and defaults.

Asymmetric information underlies this example of moral hazard. Harriet knows how she runs her business and Britt doesn't, but he does know the fickleness of human nature. Before buying securities, Britt might make Harriet promise to work hard and spend his money wisely. But this promise would be meaningless, because Britt lives on the other side of the country and has no way of knowing whether Harriet is keeping her promise.

If Britt could somehow see everything Harriet does, he could demand his savings back the first time she leaves work early. He could cancel her account at the art dealer and her reservations at the trendy clubs. But Britt is busy on the pitcher's mound and can't keep track of what happens at Harriet's office. So he refuses to buy Harriet's securities. Once again, Harriet cannot finance investment, even though she has a great idea for a new product.

1.4 BANKS

The story of Britt and Harriet has taken a bad turn. Because of asymmetric information, financial markets have failed to channel funds from savers to investors. But now a hero arrives on the scene: a bank. Britt deposits his money in the bank and earns interest. The bank lends money to Harriet for her investment. Ultimately, Britt's savings find their way to Harriet, and not only do both people benefit but also the economy as a whole benefits.

Why can Harriet get money from a bank if she can't get it from financial markets? The answer is that banks reduce the problems that stem from asymmetric information. We'll discuss how banks address asymmetric information later in this section. First, we need to understand some basics about banks.

What Is a Bank?

Financial institution (*financial intermediary*) firm that helps channel funds from savers to investors

Bank financial institution that accepts deposits and makes private loans

A bank is one kind of **financial institution**. A financial institution, also called a *financial intermediary*, is any firm that helps channel funds from savers to investors. A mutual fund is another example of a financial institution, because it sells shares to savers and uses the proceeds to purchase securities from a number of firms.

A **bank** is a financial institution defined by two characteristics. First, it raises funds by accepting deposits, including savings deposits and checking deposits that people and firms use to make payments. Both types of deposits earn interest; savings deposits earn more than checking. The second characteristic of a bank is that it uses its funds to make loans to companies and individuals. These are **private loans**: each is negotiated between one lender and one borrower. In this way, they differ from the borrowing that occurs when companies sell bonds to the public at large in financial markets.

There are several types of banks. For example, *savings and loan associations* are usually small, and much of their lending is to people buying homes. *Commercial banks* can be very large, and they lend for many purposes. In the past, banks were restricted to accepting deposits and making loans, but today banks engage in many financial businesses. They trade securities, sell mutual funds and insurance, and much more. Still, what makes them banks are their deposits and loans.

Another note on terminology: in everyday language, people use the term *bank* more broadly than we have defined it. Some institutions are called banks even though they don't accept deposits or make loans. One example is an *investment bank*, a financial institution that helps companies issue new stocks and bonds. An investment bank is not really a bank in economists' sense of the term.

Banks Versus Financial Markets

Like financial markets, banks channel funds from savers to investors. Funds flow through a bank in a two-step process: savers deposit money in the bank, and then the bank lends the deposited money to investors. In financial markets, savers provide funds directly to investors by buying their stocks and bonds. For these reasons, channeling funds through banks is called **indirect finance**, and channeling them through financial markets is called **direct finance**. **Figure 1.2** illustrates these concepts.

Private loan loan negotiated between one borrower and one lender

▶ We discuss the various types of banks in Chapter 8.

Indirect finance savers deposit money in banks that then lend to investors
Direct finance savers provide funds to investors by buying securities in financial markets

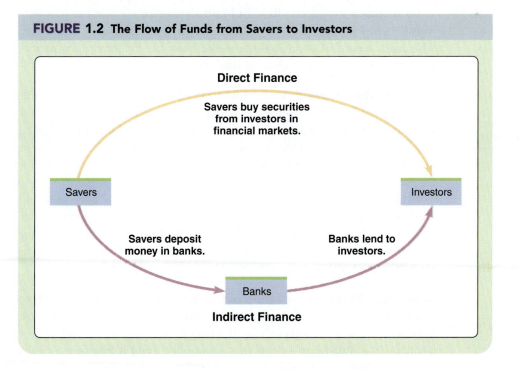

FIGURE 1.2 The Flow of Funds from Savers to Investors

Direct Finance

Savers buy securities from investors in financial markets.

Savers

Investors

Savers deposit money in banks.

Banks lend to investors.

Banks

Indirect Finance

Why Banks Exist

Indirect finance is costly. To cover their costs and earn some profit, banks charge higher interest on loans than they pay on deposits. In effect, banks take a cut of the funds they transfer to investors. Nonetheless, people like Britt and Harriet use banks because of the asymmetric information problems that hinder direct finance.

Banks help Harriet to expand her business, and they also help Britt because they pay him interest on his savings. The interest that Britt earns from his bank account may be less than the return on a security, but it's more than Britt would earn by putting his money in a safe.

Banks can help Britt and Harriet because they lessen the problems of asymmetric information that hobble securities markets. Banks overcome these problems by producing information about the investors that borrow from them. Greater information reduces both adverse selection and moral hazard in financial transactions.

Reducing Adverse Selection
Banks reduce adverse selection by screening potential borrowers. If both Harriet and Martha want money, Britt can't tell who has a better investment project. But a good banker can figure it out.

When the two investors apply for loans, they must provide information about their business plans, past careers, and finances. Bank loan officers are trained to evaluate this information, along with information from independent sources such as credit-reporting agencies, and decide whose project is likely to succeed. A firm with a bad project may go bankrupt, and bankrupt firms default not only on any bonds they've issued but also on bank loans they've taken out.

Loan officers may detect flaws in Martha's plans or see that her past projects have lost money. They turn down Martha and lend money to Harriet, who has a record of success. Because the bank has gathered information, funds flow to the most productive investment.

Reducing Moral Hazard
To combat moral hazard once a loan is made, banks include covenants in their loan contracts. A **covenant** is a statement about how the bank expects the borrower to behave, and it must be agreed on by both the bank and the borrower. For example, Harriet's lender might include a covenant requiring that she spend her loan on computers and not on parties at trendy clubs.

> **Covenant** provision in a loan contract that restricts the borrower's behavior

Banks monitor their borrowers to make sure they obey covenants and don't waste money. Harriet must send her bank periodic reports on her spending. If she misuses her loan—thereby increasing the risk of bankruptcy and default—the bank can demand its money back. With this monitoring in place, it is safe for the bank to finance Harriet's investment.

Who Needs Banks?
Some firms can raise funds by issuing securities; those that can't depend on bank loans to fund their investments. The asymmetric information problem explains why. If a firm is large and well established—a Microsoft or Wal-Mart—savers may know a lot about it from news media

or the security analysis industry. With all this information, savers will believe they know enough to make a good decision about buying the firm's securities. Savers know less about newer or smaller firms, however, and are less willing to buy their securities. For this reason, startups and small businesses need to finance their investments with bank loans.

Individuals also rely on banks for funding. Again, the reason is asymmetric information. If one day you buy a house, you won't be able to finance your purchase by issuing bonds because it is likely that no one would buy them. Most savers have heard of Microsoft but probably know little or nothing about you, so they would not be willing to risk giving you their money by purchasing your bonds. Fortunately, individuals can borrow from banks. Banks lend to home buyers after gathering information on their incomes and credit histories.

1.5 THE FINANCIAL SYSTEM AND ECONOMIC GROWTH

We have seen how the financial system helps individual savers such as Britt and investors such as Harriet. Financial markets and banks also benefit the economy as a whole. When funds flow to good investment projects, the economy becomes more productive and living standards rise. A strong financial system spurs this **economic growth**.

Saving and Economic Growth

If you have studied macroeconomics, you learned about economic growth. Economists define it as the growth of **real gross domestic product (real GDP)**, the measure of an economy's total output of goods and services. If economic growth is 3 percent in 2020, this means that real GDP is 3 percent higher in 2020 than it was in 2019. If you need more review on how economists measure GDP, see the Appendix on page 24.

When real GDP rises, an economy produces more goods and services, and the people in the economy can consume more. Therefore, a high level of economic growth causes living standards to rise rapidly.

In your macro class, you probably learned that economic growth depends on saving rates. The more people save, the more funds are available for investment. With high saving, companies can build factories and implement new technologies. They produce more, leading to higher profits and higher wages for workers.

Differences in saving rates help explain why some economies grow faster than others. One famous example is the "East Asian miracle," the rapid growth of countries such as Taiwan, Singapore, and South Korea. In 1960, these countries were among the world's poorest; by the 1990s, their living standards approached those in the most-developed countries. A major reason was high saving. In South Korea, for example, saving averaged more than 20 percent of GDP over the period 1960–1995. In the United States, by contrast, saving averaged 7 percent of GDP over that period.

Economic growth increases in productivity and living standards; growth in real GDP

Real gross domestic product (real GDP) the measure of an economy's total output of goods and services

The Allocation of Saving

Your macro course was right to stress the benefits of saving. However, it likely ignored the issues discussed in this chapter. Basic macro theories assume that saving flows automatically to investors with productive projects. In fact, the right investors get funds only if the economy has a strong financial system that functions well. An economy can save a lot and still remain poor if saving is not channeled to its best uses.

Financial systems vary across countries. Some, including the United States, have large stock and bond markets and banks that usually have ample funds. In these countries, it is relatively easy for individuals and firms with good investment projects to raise funds. In other countries, the financial system is underdeveloped: it is difficult for firms to issue securities, and bank loans are scarce. When a financial system cannot work properly, investors have trouble financing their projects and economic growth slows.

What explains these differences? One factor is government regulation. Some governments regulate securities markets to reduce the problem of asymmetric information. In the United States, for example, companies that issue securities must publish annual reports on their investments and earnings. This information lessens adverse selection, and savers are more willing to buy securities. Some countries lack such regulations.

▶ Chapter 10 discusses governments' involvement in banking in detail.

Government policies also affect banks. In the United States, the government provides deposit insurance that compensates people who lose deposits because a bank fails, thereby encouraging savers to channel funds through banks. Not all countries have such insurance.

Evidence on the Financial System and Growth

Many economists have studied the effects of financial systems on economic growth. Much of this research has occurred at the World Bank, a large international organization that promotes economic development. The research finds that differences in financial systems help explain why some countries are richer than others.

Figure 1.3 presents a portion of World Bank data drawn from 155 countries between 1996 and 2007. Figure 1.3A shows *stock market capitalization* in several groups of countries. This variable is the value of all stocks issued by corporations, expressed as a percentage of GDP. For example, a figure of 50 percent means the total value of stocks is half a year's output. Stock market capitalization measures investors' success in raising funds through the stock market. Figure 1.3B shows total *bank loans*, again as a percentage of GDP. This variable measures banks' success in channeling funds from savers to investors.

The figure divides countries into four groups based on their real GDP per person. The high-income group contains a quarter of all countries, those with the highest real GDP per person. Upper-middle-income countries make up the next quarter, and so on. For each group, the figure shows the average levels of stock market capitalization and bank loans.

Figure 1.3 has a simple message. Richer countries—those with higher real GDP per person—tend to have stronger financial systems than poorer countries.

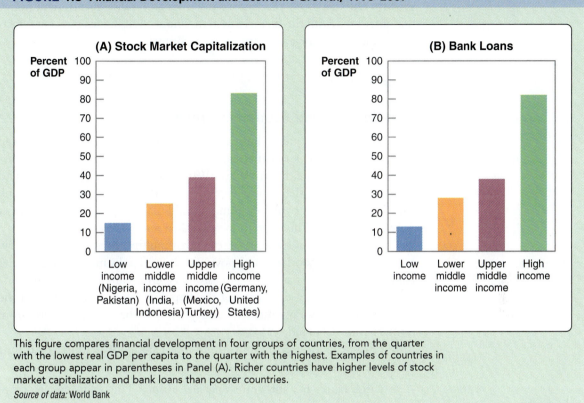

FIGURE 1.3 Financial Development and Economic Growth, 1996–2007

This figure compares financial development in four groups of countries, from the quarter with the lowest real GDP per capita to the quarter with the highest. Examples of countries in each group appear in parentheses in Panel (A). Richer countries have higher levels of stock market capitalization and bank loans than poorer countries.

Source of data: World Bank

Rich countries have larger stock markets and more bank loans. These facts support the view that financial development aids economic growth.

By themselves, these graphs are not conclusive. They show a correlation between financial development and income levels, but correlation does not prove causation. Financial development could cause economic growth, but the opposite is also possible: perhaps countries grow rich for some other reason, such as good educational systems or robust foreign trade, and this growth causes them to develop stronger financial systems. Or perhaps some third factor causes both economic growth and financial development.

Much of the World Bank's research addresses the question of causality. One strategy is to compare countries with strong and weak financial systems in some past period, such as the 1960s. Researchers find that countries with stronger systems during the 1960s had faster economic growth in the decades *after* the 1960s. This suggests that financial development comes first and causes growth, rather than vice versa.[1]

---

[1] Much of this research is summarized in Asli Demirguc-Kunt and Ross Levine, "Finance, Financial Sector Policies, and Economic Growth," World Bank Policy Research Working Paper 4469, January 2008.

Let's examine two cases that illustrate how the financial system affects growth. The first, from U.S. history, discusses an unwise government policy that interfered with the financial system. The second discusses recent efforts to expand the financial systems of poor countries.

CASE STUDY

Unit Banking and Economic Growth

Today, large banks conduct business throughout the United States. You can find branches of Bank of America, for example, in most U.S. cities. This has not always been true. Before World War II, federal law allowed a bank to operate in only one state. Some states went further and restricted each bank to a single branch. A bank's customers could make deposits or seek loans at only one location. This restriction was called *unit banking*.

Proponents of unit banking believed that multiple branches would allow banks to become too large and powerful. Large banks might drive smaller banks out of business and exploit customers. Unit banking was most common in the Midwest, the home of the Populist political movement of the nineteenth century. Populists were angry at banks for seizing property from farmers who defaulted on loans.

In retrospect, most economists think unit banking was a mistake. It hurt both banks and their customers, for several reasons:

- Large banks benefit from *economies of scale*. They can operate more efficiently than small banks because they can offer services at a lower cost per customer. Unit banking increased banks' costs by keeping them small.

- With unit banking, a bank operated in only one town. If the town's economy did poorly, many borrowers defaulted on loans. The bank lost money and might be forced out of business. Having branches in different towns is a form of diversification: it reduces risk.

- Under unit banking, many small towns had only one bank, which operated as a monopoly. Customers had nowhere else to go if the bank charged high interest rates on their loans or provided poor service. In states that allowed multiple branches, banks from throughout the state could enter a town and increase competition.

For all these reasons, unit banking reduced the number of banks and their efficiency. The policy impeded the flow of funds from savers to investors. The result was lower economic growth.

Economists Rajeev Dehejia of Columbia University and Adriana Lleras-Muney of Princeton University analyzed the effects of unit banking. Their 2007 study compares states with unit banking to states that allowed multiple branches during the period from 1900 to 1940. As you might expect, the volume of bank loans was higher in states that permitted branching, confirming that branching helps move funds from savers to investors.

The Dehejia–Lleras-Muney study's most important findings reveal the effects of unit banking on the overall economy, including both the agricultural and manufacturing sectors. In states with branching, farm acreage was larger, and the value of farm machinery per acre was higher. Apparently, the less-constrained banking systems provided more funds for farmers to expand their farms and make them more productive. States with branching had higher employment in manufacturing industries and higher manufacturing wages. Again this suggests that, when allowed branching, banks were better able to channel funds to investors, in this case to firms that wanted to build new and more productive factories. The study provides a concrete example of how policies that promote banking can contribute to a prosperous economy.*

* Rajeev Dehejia and Adriana Lleras-Muney, "Financial Development and Pathways of Growth: State Branching and Deposit Insurance Laws in the United States from 1900 to 1940," *Journal of Law and Economics*, 50 (2007) 239–272.

CASE STUDY

Microfinance

Poor countries have severe shortages of jobs that pay decent wages. As a consequence, many people seek to support themselves by starting rudimentary businesses—making furniture or clothes, running small restaurants or shops. In many countries, women are especially likely to start businesses because discrimination limits their other opportunities.

A business requires an initial investment; for example, a furniture maker must buy tools and raw materials. Often the necessary funds are small by the standards of high-income countries but still exceed the wealth of would-be entrepreneurs. Most banks shy away from lending to the very poor, because they fear high default rates and the interest payments on tiny loans do not cover the costs of screening and monitoring borrowers. Discrimination can make it especially difficult for women to get loans.

Without bank loans, many people are unable to start businesses that might lift them out of poverty. Others borrow from village moneylenders at exorbitant interest rates—sometimes 10 to 20 percent per *day*.

Microfinance, or *microlending*, seeks to fill this gap in developing countries' banking systems by providing small loans to poor people. The idea was pioneered by Muhammad Yunus, an economics professor in Bangladesh, who founded the Grameen Bank in the village of Jobra in 1974. Since then, microfinance institutions (MFIs) have sprung up in Africa, Asia, Latin America, Eastern Europe, and even in the United States.

MFIs are initially funded by governments, international organizations such as the World Bank, or private foundations. Their loans can be as small as $25, but they are large enough to fund simple businesses. Microfinance has grown spectacularly since its beginnings in a single village. As of 2010, MFIs had close to 100 million borrowers around the world.

MFIs try to overcome the problems that make conventional banks wary of lending to the poor. For example, some MFIs require that people

Microfinance (*microlending*) small loans that allow poor people to start businesses

borrow money in groups. The Grameen Bank lends to five would-be entrepreneurs at a time. This practice reduces the bank's costs per loan. In addition, it reduces the problem of moral hazard—the risk that borrowers will squander their loans and default. Credit is cut off to all five borrowers if any one of them defaults, creating peer pressure to use loans prudently.

Many MFIs lend primarily to women. In part this reflects the institutions' desire to serve a group that faces discrimination elsewhere. But MFIs also cite their self-interest: they report that women default on loans less often than men. Overall, default rates on microloans are low—less than 2 percent at many institutions.

Muhammad Yunus, the founder of Grameen Bank, discusses microfinance during a 2004 visit to Kalampur village in Bangladesh.

Many people think that microfinance has helped reduce poverty. In 2006, Muhammad Yunus and the Grameen Bank were awarded the Nobel Peace Prize. Yunus is the first economist to win a Nobel Prize in an area other than economics. In explaining its choice, the Nobel committee said that "loans to poor people without any financial security had appeared to be an impossible idea," but "Yunus and Grameen Bank have shown that even the poorest of the poor can work to bring about their own development."

The microfinance industry is changing as it grows. Most MFIs are non-profit organizations supported by donations. In recent years, however, for-profit commercial banks have taken an interest in microfinance. These banks have observed the success of MFIs, especially the low default rates on their loans, and decided that microfinance can be profitable. Commercial banks have started making microloans in countries such as India, Colombia, and Senegal. Elsewhere, commercial banks support microfinance indirectly by lending money to MFIs.

Mexico's Compartamos ("Let's Share" in Spanish) is one of Latin America's largest microlenders, with a million borrowers. In 2006, it transformed itself from a nonprofit organization into a commercial bank. In 2007, it raised $500 million by issuing stock that is now traded on Mexico's stock exchange. Compartamos no longer relies on donations or government funding.

Many supporters of microfinance welcome the involvement of commercial banks because it increases the availability of microloans. Others, however, criticize the "commercialization" of microfinance. They allege that for-profit lenders charge excessive interest rates and deny loans to the poorest of the poor. Muhammad Yunus has criticized Compartamos, saying it is "raking in money off poor people desperate for cash."*

* For more on this controversy, see "Microfinance's Success Sets Off a Debate in Mexico," *The New York Times*, April 5, 2008, page C1; and Robert Cull, Asli Demirguc-Kunt and Jonathan Morduch, "Microfinance Meets the Market," *Journal of Economic Perspectives* (Winter 2009): 167–192.

Markets Versus Central Planning

Another way to grasp the importance of the financial system is to ask what happens if an economy lacks one entirely. Imagine a country with an economy run by the government. No private firms exist; everybody works for the government, which decides what goods and services to produce and who receives them. The government also decides what investment projects are worthwhile and orders that they be undertaken. No one raises funds for investment through financial markets or private banks.

This is not a fanciful idea but rather a basic description of a **centrally planned economy**, also known as a *command economy*. This was the economic system under Communist governments in the Soviet Union and Eastern Europe that held power until the early 1990s. The economies of Cuba and North Korea are still based primarily on central planning.

If you have studied microeconomics, you learned that its central idea is the desirability of allocating resources through free markets. Market prices provide signals about what firms should produce and consumers should buy, guiding the economy to efficiency. Microeconomists take a dim view of central planning, because a modern economy is too complicated for government officials to run without the help of markets.

The basic principles of free markets also apply to the financial system. Prices in financial markets, such as stock prices and interest rates, help channel funds to the most productive investments. This process does not work perfectly, but it beats the alternative of central planning. History shows that government officials do a poor job of choosing investment projects. To illustrate this point, the next case examines history's most famous example of central planning.

Centrally planned economy
(*command economy*)
system in which the government decides what goods and services are produced, who receives them, and what investment projects are undertaken

CASE STUDY

Investment in the Soviet Union

In 1917, a Communist revolution led by V. I. Lenin overthrew Czar Nicholas II of Russia. Lenin established the Soviet Union, which eventually grew to include Russia and 14 other "republics" from Ukraine in the west to Uzbekistan in Central Asia. The economy of the Soviet Union was centrally planned.

Initially, the Soviet economy was mainly agricultural, and most of its people were poor. After Lenin's death in 1924, Josef Stalin took control of the government and began a push to "industrialize." Stalin and the leaders who succeeded him hoped to achieve rapid economic growth through investment in factories and modern technologies. Because Soviet planners controlled the economy's resources, they could dictate high levels of investment. From the 1930s to the 1980s, investment as a percentage of GDP was more than twice as high in the Soviet Union as in the United States and Western Europe.

At first, high investment did produce rapid economic growth. In the 1950s and 1960s, Soviet planners predicted—and Western leaders feared—that the Soviet Union would become the world's most productive economy. But growth slowed in the 1970s and 1980s. Despite high investment, the Soviet Union fell further and further behind the West. Partly because of economic failure, the Soviet Union broke apart in the early 1990s. Russia and the other former republics shifted to economic systems based on free markets.

What went wrong with the Soviet Union? Although many factors led to its downfall, in retrospect it is clear that an important factor was a misallocation of investment. Soviet planners chose projects poorly, so high investment did not lead to high output. Economic historians point to a number of mistakes:

- Planners put too many resources into prestige sectors of the economy that symbolized economic development, mainly heavy industry. The Soviets built too many factories to produce steel and too few to produce consumer goods. They invested in an unsuccessful effort to develop large airplanes. Starting in the 1950s, they spent heavily on their space program, which boosted national pride but strained the economy.

- Soviet planners overemphasized *short-run* increases in productivity. They were too hasty in trying to reach Western output levels. In 1931, Stalin said, "We are fifty or a hundred years behind the advanced countries. We must make good the distance in ten years. Either we do it or they will crush us." This attitude caused planners to neglect investments that were important for the long term. For example, they skimped on maintenance of roads and other infrastructure. This had little immediate effect, but over time the crumbling infrastructure became a drag on productivity.

- A related problem was that factory managers were evaluated based on annual production quotas. Managers focused on meeting current quotas rather than increasing long-run productivity. For example, they were reluctant to retool factories to use new technologies because this might disrupt production temporarily.

- The power of government bureaucrats reduced efficiency. Plant managers were rewarded for following orders, not for thinking of innovative ways to raise output. In addition, managers competed for investment funds by lobbying the government. Those who were well connected or talented at lobbying received more resources than they needed, while other managers received too few.[*]

---

[*] For more on Soviet investment, see Gur Ofer, "Soviet Economic Growth, 1928–1985," *Journal of Economic Literature* 25 (December 1987) 1767–1833. This article was published shortly before the breakup of the Soviet Union.

1.6 FINANCIAL CRISES

This chapter has stressed the benefits of a well-functioning financial system. Financial markets and banks help funds flow to productive investment projects, they reduce risk, and ultimately they contribute to economic growth. But financial systems don't always work well, and when they malfunction an economy can experience a **financial crisis**, a major disruption of the financial system, typically involving sharp drops in asset prices and failures of financial institutions. Financial crises often harm the whole economy, reducing output and raising unemployment.

The U.S. financial crisis that began in 2007 is a dramatic example of such a malfunction. Losses on subprime mortgages (home loans to people with weak credit histories) led to the failure or near-failure of many large banks. Bank lending contracted severely, and the disruption in lending resulted in lower consumption and investment throughout the economy. The Dow Jones Index of stock prices fell 55 percent from 2007 to early 2009, shaking confidence in the economy and further reducing consumption and investment. Financial turmoil pushed the U.S. economy into the worst recession since the 1930s: the unemployment rate rose from less than 5 percent in 2007 to more than 10 percent late in 2009.

Governments may respond dramatically to financial crises. The Great Depression of the 1930s led to President Franklin Roosevelt's New Deal. The recent crisis was met by measures that would have been almost unthinkable a few years earlier. The government became a partial owner of the nation's largest banks. The Federal Reserve, the central bank of the United States, expanded the money supply massively through loans to financial institutions. The Fed also pushed short-term interest rates close to zero.

Financial crises are complex events that involve the interplay of securities markets, banks, the overall economy, and government and central bank policies. We discuss all these topics in the chapters that follow, returning to analyze financial crises in the United States and around the world at the end of the book. A better understanding of crises is one payoff from studying money, banking, and financial markets.

> **Financial crisis** major disruption of the financial system, typically involving sharp drops in asset prices and failures of financial institutions

> In the coming chapters, you will see this icon when we discuss topics related to financial crises. These topics are building blocks for an in-depth analysis of financial crises in Chapter 18.

> ▶ We introduce the Federal Reserve and its functions in Chapter 2.

Summary

- The financial system has two central parts: financial markets and banks.

1.1 Financial Markets

- Financial markets are markets for currencies and for securities, such as stocks and bonds.
- A bond is a fixed-income security: it promises predetermined payments at certain times. When a corporation or government issues bonds, it is borrowing money from those who buy the bonds.

- A stock or equity is an ownership share in a corporation. A stockholder receives a share of the corporation's earnings.

1.2 Economic Functions of Financial Markets

- The primary function of financial markets is to channel funds from savers to investors with productive uses for those funds.
- Financial markets also help people diversify their asset holdings. This reduces risk. People who don't

diversify, such as employees who hold too much of their companies' stock, can suffer disaster.

1.3 Asymmetric Information

- Financial markets can malfunction because of asymmetric information: sellers of securities (investors) know more than buyers (savers).

- Adverse selection arises from asymmetric information about investors' characteristics. Investors with low chances for success are the most eager to sell securities.

- Moral hazard arises from asymmetric information about investors' actions. Investors have incentives to misuse the funds they receive from savers.

1.4 Banks

- Financial institutions such as banks and mutual funds are firms that help channel funds from savers to investors.

- Banks raise funds by accepting deposits and use the funds to make private loans.

- Banks reduce adverse selection and moral hazard by gathering information to screen borrowers, putting covenants into loan agreements, and monitoring borrower behavior. These activities make it possible for investors who cannot issue securities to raise funds for their investments.

1.5 The Financial System and Economic Growth

- Saving can spur economic growth—but only if the financial system channels savings into productive investment.

- Differences in financial systems help explain why some countries are richer than others. Rich countries tend to have stronger financial systems than poor countries do, with higher stock market capitalization and more bank loans.

- Poorly conceived government policies can hinder the financial system's operation and reduce economic growth. An example from U.S. history is unit banking. Programs that expand the financial system, such as microfinance, can spur growth and alleviate poverty.

- Central planning is a poor system for allocating investment funds, as illustrated by the history of the Soviet Union.

1.6 Financial Crises

- Economies sometimes experience financial crises in which asset prices plummet and financial institutions fail. Crises can harm the overall economy, reducing output and raising unemployment. A major financial crisis began in 2007 in the United States.

Key Terms

Questions and Problems

1. When financial markets channel funds from savers to investors, who benefits? Explain.

2. Suppose an owner of a corporation needs $1 million to finance a new investment. If his total wealth is $1.2 million, would it be better to use his own funds for the investment or to issue stock in the corporation? What if the owner's wealth is $1 billion?

3. Suppose you were required to put all your retirement savings in the securities of one company. What company would you choose, and why? Would you choose the company you work for? Would you buy stock or bonds?

4. Suppose there are two investors. One has a project to build a factory; the other has a project to visit a casino and gamble on roulette. Which investor has a greater incentive to issue bonds? Which investor's bonds are a better deal for savers?

5. Suppose a company raises funds by issuing short-term bonds (commercial paper). It uses the funds to make private loans. Such a firm is called a *finance company*. Is a finance company a type of bank?

6. Firms such as Moody's and Standard & Poor's study corporations that issue bonds. They publish "ratings" for the bonds—evaluations of the likelihood of default. Suppose these rating companies went out of business. What effect would this have on the bond market? What effect would it have on banks?

7. National credit bureaus collect information on people's credit histories. They are likely to know whether you ever defaulted on a loan. Suppose that a new privacy law makes it illegal for credit bureaus to collect this information. What effect would this have on the banking industry?

8. When a bank makes a loan, it sometimes requires borrowers to maintain a checking account at the bank until the loan is paid off. What is the purpose of this requirement?

9. Microfinance institutions argue that (a) many traditional banks discriminate against women in lending and (b) women have lower default rates than men on loans from MFIs. Discuss how point (a) could explain point (b).

▶ Online and Data Questions
www.worthpublishers.com/ball

10. The text Web site contains World Bank data on financial development. Using these data, compare bank loans as a percentage of GDP in two groups of countries: those in East Asia (8 countries) and those in sub-Saharan Africa (16 countries). For each group, compute the average of the bank-loan variable for three time periods: 1976–1985, 1986–1995, and 1996–2007.

    a. Which of the two regions has a higher level of bank loans? How has the level of loans changed over time in each region?

    b. What might explain the differences between East Asia and Africa that you found in part (a)? How do you think these differences have affected the economies of the two regions?

11. In the World Bank data, examine bank loans as a percentage of GDP in the United States, Germany, and Japan. Is the level of bank loans relatively high or low in the United States? What might explain this fact? (*Hint*: see the data on stock market capitalization in the three countries.)

12. Link through the text Web site to the site of Planet Rating, a French organization that calls itself "the global microfinance rating agency." What is the main function of Planet Rating? How might its work help the microfinance industry to grow?

A Small Research Project

13. Do you know someone (such as a parent) who is working and saving for retirement? Does he or she have money in a 401(k) plan? What securities does the person hold through the plan? Does he or she follow the principle of diversification?

APPENDIX: MEASURING OUTPUT AND THE PRICE LEVEL

This appendix reviews the basic macroeconomic concept of real GDP. To derive this variable, we must first define nominal GDP and the aggregate price level.

Nominal GDP is the total value of all final goods and services produced in an economy in a given period. For example, in the United States, nominal GDP was $14 trillion in 2009. If we add up all the $20,000 cars produced in 2009, all the $5 hamburgers, $15 haircuts, and so on, the total is $14 trillion.

The **aggregate price level** is an average of the prices of all goods and services. It is a weighted average: some prices have a bigger influence than others. The weights are based on the amount of spending on each item. For example, car prices have a large weight because consumers spend a lot on cars. Toothpick prices have a small weight because relatively little is spent on toothpicks.

There are several different measures of the price level. The best known are the *consumer price index* (CPI) and the *GDP deflator*. These variables differ in subtle ways, such as the methods for choosing weights. The details are not important for our purposes: we will simply interpret the aggregate price level as an average of all prices.

The **inflation rate** is one of the best-known economic variables. It is the percentage change in the aggregate price level over a period of time, typically a year. As measured by the GDP deflator, for example, the inflation rate over 2009 was 0.7 percent. This means the price level was seven tenths of a percent higher at the end of 2009 than at the beginning.

We can now define real GDP as nominal GDP divided by the aggregate price level:

$$\text{real GDP} = \frac{\text{nominal GDP}}{\text{aggregate price level}}$$

As we discuss in Section 1.5, economists use this variable to measure an economy's output of goods and services. Economic growth is the growth of real GDP.

Real GDP is defined in this way to produce a measure of output that is not distorted by inflation. Suppose the prices of all goods and services double but there is no change in what the economy produces. Nominal GDP doubles because everything is worth twice as much in dollars. The aggregate price level also doubles. In the formula for real GDP, both the numerator and the denominator double, so real GDP does not change. The constancy of real GDP captures the fact that output has not changed.

Nominal GDP the total value of all final goods and services produced in an economy in a given period

Aggregate price level an average of the prices of all goods and services

Inflation rate percentage change in the aggregate price level over a period of time

Money and Central Banks

Mark Gertler is an economics professor at New York University. Although he is well respected in academic circles, he usually receives little attention in the mass media. Yet on the afternoon of October 24, 2005, Gertler received phone calls from NBC, CBS, ABC, CNN, and more than 50 print journalists, all seeking interviews. What was the occasion?

On that day, President George W. Bush had appointed Ben Bernanke, formerly an economics professor at Princeton University, as chair of the Federal Reserve System. Everyone was eager to learn about Bernanke's beliefs and character, but the Bush administration had asked him not to speak to the media. So reporters sought out anyone who knew him. Gertler was a leading target because he had coauthored several research papers with Bernanke and briefly shared a house with him.

Reporters were not the only people who reacted quickly to Bernanke's appointment. At the New York Stock Exchange, traders responded by bidding up stock prices. When the president made his announcement, the Dow Jones Index of stock prices was at 10,216. Within a few minutes, traders pushed the Dow to 10,333, a rise of more than 1 percent. The value of stocks in U.S. corporations jumped by billions of dollars.

PBS

July 26, 2009: Fed Chairman Ben Bernanke (left) fields questions about the economy and the financial crisis at the Federal Reserve Bank of Kansas City. PBS news anchor Jim Lehrer (right) moderated the town hall–style meeting.

Federal Reserve System (the Fed) central bank of the United States

Central bank institution that controls an economy's money supply

Why was Ben Bernanke's appointment such big news? Why did it cause stock prices to jump? The short answer is that the **Federal Reserve System**, or **Fed**, is the central bank of the United States. A **central bank** controls an economy's *money supply*, and the money supply has strong effects on the financial system and the economy. The central bank also influences the financial system through such actions as making emergency loans to troubled banks. These functions give Bernanke and other Fed officials great economic power. Their decisions help determine the levels of output, unemployment, and inflation in the U.S. economy.

What is the money supply? How does it affect the economy? How do central banks control the money supply, and what else do they do? These questions are major topics in this book, and this chapter introduces them. Our main focus here is money—what it is, how it's measured, how people use it, and its economic functions.

2.1 WHAT IS MONEY?

Money is a word that economists use differently from most people. In everyday speech, *money* is often used as a synonym for income or wealth. Someone might remark that "neurosurgeons make a lot of money," meaning their annual incomes are high. Or you might hear that "Bill Gates has a lot of money" because his wealth—the total value of his assets—is $50 billion. Gates's wealth includes assets such as Microsoft stock, other securities, and real estate.

For economists, by contrast, **money** is a narrow class of assets with special properties. Money serves the economy as the medium of exchange, the unit of account, and a store of value.

Money class of assets that serves as an economy's medium of exchange

What is money?

Properties of Money.

The Medium of Exchange

Although money serves several functions, it is defined by its primary role: people use it as the **medium of exchange**. That is, people use money to purchase goods and services. Money is whatever a grocery store or movie theater accepts as payment.

In today's economy, dollar bills are one form of money. The balances in people's checking accounts are also money, because many goods and services can be bought by writing a check or debiting an account electronically. Stocks and bonds are *not* money because you can't walk into a store and trade them for groceries.

People with wealth must choose what assets to hold—how to divide their wealth among stocks and bonds, real estate, money, and other assets. People with substantial wealth usually hold only a small fraction of it in money. The reason is that money yields a poor return compared to other assets, such as bonds. A dollar bill pays no interest. Some checking accounts pay interest, but the interest rates are usually lower than those on bonds.

Medium of exchange whatever people use to purchase goods and services

Nonetheless, everybody holds *some* wealth in the form of money because of its unique role as the medium of exchange. Rich people keep most of their wealth in securities and real estate, but they keep enough in cash and checking accounts to buy groceries, pay for haircuts, and otherwise purchase the goods and services they desire. The amount of wealth that people choose to hold in money is called **money demand**. To see the benefits of holding money, let's discuss how an economy would operate if money didn't exist.

Money Versus Barter

In any economy, people produce goods and services and trade them for other goods and services. In the absence of money, this trade occurs through **barter**, in which one good or service is traded directly for another. Barter was the means of trade in early societies. Often it took place in a village market. A dairy farmer might bring milk to the market and trade it to a weaver for cloth or to a potter for a bowl. *for Barter to cccur*

Barter is cumbersome. For it to work, individuals must experience a **double coincidence of wants**. This means I have something that you want *and* you have something I want. If a dairy farmer wants a piece of cloth, it is not enough to find a weaver; he must find a weaver who is thirsty for milk. If the weavers he encounters are looking for other things, the farmer cannot make the trade he desires.

Probably a dairy farmer in a simple village will eventually find a thirsty weaver. The farmer can trade for what he wants because many people need milk. The double-coincidence problem is more severe in highly developed economies with large numbers of goods and services, many of which are consumed by small parts of the population. Economic specialization makes barter more difficult.

To see this point, consider Tom the music teacher. Tom produces a specialized service: viola lessons. One day Tom notices his hair is getting long and decides to get a haircut. Let's suppose Tom lives in an economy without money and therefore must acquire his haircut through barter. He must offer the barber a deal: "If you give me a haircut, I'll teach you the viola part in Mozart's Quartet Number 1 in G major."

You may see the problem. Some people, including some barbers, don't want music lessons. Even if they do, their instrument may be the clarinet, not the viola. Tom's proposal is likely to be turned down by many barbers. Tom might spend the whole day traveling around town before he finds a hair-cutting viola student.

Tom's life is easier if his economy has money. Tom can give lessons to anyone who wants to learn the viola. His students may not know how to cut hair, but that doesn't matter. They pay Tom with money, and Tom uses the money to buy a haircut. Even if the barber hates stringed instruments, he knows he can spend Tom's money on things he does like. Trade no longer requires a double coincidence of wants: the people Tom teaches and the people who give him haircuts need not be the same.

Money demand amount of wealth that people choose to hold in the form of money

▶ In Chapter 4, we examine the factors that determine money demand, such as the interest rates that other assets pay.

Barter system of exchange in which goods and services are traded directly, with no money involved

Double coincidence of wants condition needed for barter: each party to a transaction must have something the other wants

Nineteenth-Century Visitors to Barter Economies

Probably no one has really tried to trade a viola lesson for a haircut. However, William Stanley Jevons—the nineteenth-century economist who coined the term "double coincidence"—recorded some true stories about the inconveniences of barter. These stories involve Europeans who were accustomed to using money but visited Pacific islands in which barter was the means of exchange.

One of Jevons's anecdotes concerns Mademoiselle Zelie, a well-known French singer on a world tour. In the Society Islands, near Tahiti, she agreed to give a concert in return for one-third of the receipts from tickets. Jevons reports, "When counted, her share was found to consist of three pigs, twenty-three turkeys, forty-four chickens, five thousand cocoa nuts, besides considerable quantities of bananas, lemons, and oranges." These were the commodities exchanged for concert tickets under the local barter system.

In Parisian markets, these livestock and fruits could have sold for around 4000 francs—a good payment for a concert. However, nobody in the Society Islands had money to buy the goods. Mlle. Zelie had no means of shipping her possessions to France, and she did not have time during her visit to eat much of the pork, poultry, or fruit. She had to leave them behind and therefore gained little from her singing. (Before leaving, she fed the fruit to the pigs and chickens.)

Jevons also tells of a Mr. Wallace, who traveled in the Malay archipelago. People there did not use money, so Mr. Wallace had to barter for his dinner each night. Unfortunately, sometimes the people with food did not desire any of Mr. Wallace's possessions: there was no double coincidence of wants. To reduce the risk of going hungry, Mr. Wallace began traveling with a collection of goods, such as knives, cloth, and liquor, that he hoped would appeal to the local people. This made his suitcase heavier, but it raised the odds that he could make a trade.

Fortunately, in the twenty-first century, money is used almost everywhere. Thanks to money, touring singers can be paid, and travelers can buy dinner wherever they go.[*]

[*] Jevons tells the stories of Mlle. Zelie and Mr. Wallace in his book *Money and the Medium of Exchange*, D. Appleton and Company, 1875.

The Unit of Account

Unit of account measure in which prices and salaries are quoted

In addition to serving as the medium of exchange, money has another related role in the economy. Money is the **unit of account**. This means that prices, salaries, and levels of wealth are measured in money. Dollar bills are money in the United States, and so prices are quoted in dollars.

To see why this measurement function is important, think again of an economy without money. In this world, prices would have to be set in units of goods or services. Different prices might be set in different units, making it hard to compare them.

For example, suppose you live in this economy and need a new washing machine. You want to buy it as inexpensively as possible. You see that one store sells a machine for 500 loaves of bread. Another store sells the same model for 30 pairs of men's loafers. It would be hard to figure out which deal is better—you would have to know the prices of bread and shoes. To make matters worse, you might find that bread prices are quoted in apples and shoe prices in oranges. You literally would have to compare apples and oranges!

Once again, money makes life easier. If dollars are the unit of account, you will see that one store charges $500 for the washing machine and the other charges $400. You know immediately that the second price is lower. You can shop wisely for a washer without researching the prices of other goods.

A Store of Value

Traditionally, economists have cited a third function of money, one beyond its roles as the medium of exchange and unit of account. Money is a **store of value**—a form in which people can hold wealth.

Store of value form in which wealth can be held

To understand this function, think again about a dairy farmer. If his farm is unusually productive one year, he may want to set something aside for the next year when times could be harder. The farmer can't save the extra milk he produces—it will spoil, making it worthless. Milk is not a good store of value. The solution is to sell the milk for money. If the farmer keeps the money in a safe place, he will have it next year when he needs it.

Money's store-of-value function has become less important in advanced economies. We have already discussed why: the financial system has produced assets with returns higher than money. In most economies today, holding money is better than holding milk, but holding bonds is better still, because bonds pay more interest. People with financial savvy use money as a medium of exchange, but they hold most of their wealth in other assets.

Exceptions occur, mainly in poor countries. In some places the financial system functions so poorly that few assets are more attractive than money. People hold much of their wealth in cash. But there is a twist: most of this cash is foreign currency—U.S. dollars or euros—rather than the local money. This currency switch results from inflation, as we discuss later in this chapter.

2.2 TYPES OF MONEY

Money is defined by what it does, not by what it is. Money is whatever people use as the medium of exchange. Today, certain greenish pieces of paper are money because people use them to buy goods and services. But money could be anything else that people use to buy things.

Types of Money

Over human history, many objects have served as money—everything from seashells to whiskey to animal skins. (That is why we still call our dollars "bucks," for buckskins, which once served as money on the American frontier.) Regardless, all kinds of money fall into two broad categories: commodity money and fiat money.

① Commodity Money

Commodity money valuable good that serves as the medium of exchange

Commodity money is a valuable good that also becomes the medium of exchange. Think again of a village of farmers and artisans. Even in this village, barter is cumbersome. A dairy farmer who wants a shirt must find a thirsty weaver, and a shoemaker who wants chicken must find a barefoot poultry farmer.

So the village adopts a better system. When someone trades her product, she does not insist on receiving what she wants at the moment. Instead, everyone provides goods and services in return for a particular commodity—grain, for example. People accept grain even if they don't need it because they know others will accept it. The shirtless dairy farmer trades milk for grain and then uses the grain to acquire a shirt.

In this system, grain becomes the medium of exchange, just as dollar bills are a medium of exchange today. People also start setting prices in grain—a shirt might cost two bushels. So grain becomes the unit of account. A commodity has taken on the key functions of money.

This example is not fanciful. Grain really was used as money in ancient Egypt. Another agricultural product—tobacco—served as money in the British colonies of Maryland and Virginia.

Precious Metals

Although many goods have been used as money, the most common commodity moneys are gold and silver. These metals are used for purposes such as jewelry making. They are also good choices for money because they are durable—they don't fall apart or go sour. In addition, precious metals have high value relative to weight. Pieces of gold or silver can purchase a lot of goods and services while still being light enough to carry.

Coins At first, the precious metals used as money were unmarked lumps of various sizes. Coins appeared in China around 1000 BCE and in Greece around 700 BCE. Governments produced metal coins with standard weights and purities. This made it easier to buy and sell things, because people exchanging coins didn't have to weigh them or examine them carefully.

Coins had markings stamped on them for identification. For example, the city-state of Athens issued silver coins with the goddess Athena on the front and an owl on the back. Alexander the Great, who had a large ego, decreed that his likeness be stamped on his empire's coins. This started the tradition of money with pictures of political leaders.

Gold and silver coins circulated throughout the world until the middle of the twentieth century. But today, they have been replaced by other kinds of money.

Origins of Paper Money Paper money appeared around the year 1000 in China and between 1500 and 1700 in Europe. Originally, it was a version of commodity money, because it was backed by commodities. A piece of paper money was essentially an ownership certificate for a certain amount of gold or silver—or, in Maryland and Virginia, a certain amount of tobacco.

People carried paper money because it was more convenient than coins. In Europe, paper money was issued first by private banks and later by governments. Anyone who held money could turn it in to the issuer and demand the commodity that the money represented, which limited the amount of paper money that banks or governments could create.

One hundred years ago in the United States, money was backed by gold. Paper money looked fairly similar to the currency of today, but the phrase "Gold Certificate" was printed on each bill. This meant that the money could be exchanged for gold coins. A $20 bill, for example, could be traded for 20 gold dollar coins, each weighing 0.0484 ounces.

In an economy with commodity money, people may trade goods or services for something they do not wish to use. They accept gold or gold certificates even if they have no interest in making jewelry. However, the money they accept has value for someone. Today, we use a different kind of money.

Fiat Money

Money is no longer backed by gold. In the United States, the "Gold Certificate" label on paper money has been replaced by "Federal Reserve Note." What does that mean?

No longer backed by gold.

Fiat money money with no intrinsic value

It means that today's currency is **fiat money**—money with no intrinsic value. Fiat money cannot be made into jewelry, baked into bread, or otherwise

ANA Money Museum

The $20 bill on the top, a Gold Certificate from 1928, is commodity money; the $20 bill on the bottom, a Federal Reserve Note from 2006, is fiat money. The two bills appear similar but differ in their fine print. Look carefully at the Gold Certificate, and you may be able to make out a complete sentence. It begins at the top of the bill with "This certifies that there have been deposited in the Treasury of" and continues in the banner, "The United States of America," then picks up at the bottom, "twenty dollars" and below that, "in gold coin payable to the bearer on demand." The Federal Reserve Note features the phrase "twenty dollars," but it doesn't mention anything payable to the bearer.

put to use. And fiat money is *not* backed by any commodity. No government or bank has promised to exchange anything for your $20 bills. These bills are money "by fiat," which means the government has simply declared them money. "Gold Certificate" means that money can be traded for gold, but "Federal Reserve Note" doesn't really mean anything. It's just a label for a worthless piece of paper.

From one point of view, it might seem odd that people trade goods and services for fiat money. Take your textbook author, for example. I work hard all day on writing and teaching and endure long meetings of faculty committees. And what do I get in return? Nothing I can eat or wear or play with. All my university gives me is a bunch of worthless pieces of paper. Why do I bother to work?

The answer, of course, is that I can trade my worthless pieces of paper for things I value. The grocer will give me bread for my worthless paper because he knows that others will accept the paper from him. With commodity money, people accept a commodity they might not want because everybody else accepts it. With fiat money, people accept paper that is worthless to *everyone* because everybody else does. Thanks to this behavior, dollar bills serve their purpose as a medium of exchange.

From Commodity Money to Fiat Money

Fiat money evolved out of the original paper money, which was backed by commodities. Governments realized that people were happy to use paper money and rarely demanded the commodities behind it. So they started cheating, in a sense. They promised to redeem money for commodities, but they issued more money than they had in commodities to back it up. This was possible as long as people didn't try to trade in all the money at once.

Once people became accustomed to paper money, governments took the next step and stopped promising to redeem the money for commodities. Thus, paper money became fiat money. The pioneers in this area were countries that needed to pay for wars, such as Britain during the Napoleonic Wars. Because money was not backed by anything, governments could print as much as they needed.[1]

In the United States, the nature of money has evolved through twists and turns. The dollar has sometimes been commodity money, sometimes fiat money, and sometimes in between, as we discuss in the next case study.

CASE STUDY

The History of the U.S. Dollar

Before the American Revolution, each colony issued its own money. The first national currency was created by the Continental Congress in 1776, shortly after it declared independence from Britain. This money was the Continental dollar.

---

[1] For more on the development of money, see Glyn Davies, *A History of Money from Ancient Times to the Present Day,* University of Wales Press, 1994.

The Continental Dollar The new currency was fiat money. Like other governments, Congress printed large amounts to pay for the Revolutionary War.

Congress worried that people would think the dollar worthless, as it was not backed by anything. To encourage acceptance of the money, a congressional resolution appealed to patriotism:

> *Any person who shall hereafter be so lost to all virtue and regard for his country as to refuse Bills or obstruct and discourage their currency or circulation shall be deemed published and treated as an enemy of the country. . . .*

This appeal didn't work for long. When governments print money rapidly, inflation is the inevitable outcome. During the revolution, prices rose so much that Continental dollars became almost worthless.

▶The causes and costs of inflation are major topics in Chapter 14.

Money in the New Republic Alexander Hamilton became the first secretary of the treasury in 1789. He earned his current spot on the $10 bill through wise economic policies. Hamilton wanted American money to have a stable value, so he created dollar coins. A dollar was either 0.056 ounces of gold or 0.84 ounces of silver. The government allowed people to trade in 100 Continental dollars for one of the new dollar coins, which was generous to the holders of Continentals.

Paper money also developed, but unevenly. At times the government established a national bank, a precursor to the modern Federal Reserve. The First Bank of the United States operated from 1791 to 1810, and the Second Bank from 1816 to 1836. One function of the banks was to issue "national bank notes," which were paper money backed by gold and silver coins.

▶Section 8.2 discusses the politics that led to the opening and closing of the First and Second Banks of the United States.

Private banks also issued notes. These banks, like the national banks, promised to redeem the notes for coins. However, private banks sometimes went out of business, reneging on their promises. Because of this risk, people refused notes issued by some banks and accepted others for less than their face value.

This system ended with the Civil War in the 1860s. Once again, war prompted the government to issue large amounts of fiat money. This paper currency was called "Greenbacks," because it was the first American money of that color. As usual, rapid creation of money caused high inflation.

The Classical Gold Standard In 1879, the government reestablished commodity money. It set the value of a dollar at 0.0484 ounces of gold. To say the same thing a different way, the government declared that an ounce of gold was worth $1/(0.0484) = 20.67$ dollars. The primary type of money was gold certificates like the one pictured on page 31.

During this period, the government did not control the amount of money in the economy. It passively issued gold certificates to anyone who turned in gold and gave back gold to anyone who turned in the certificates. This system lasted until 1913, when the Federal Reserve System was established.

To the Present Today, dollars are fiat money—there is no link to gold. The tight link under the gold standard was relaxed in several steps, beginning in 1913 when Congress instructed the Fed to create an "elastic currency."

The Fed was required to hold gold reserves equal to at least 40 percent of the money it created. However, as long as it obeyed this constraint, the Fed could expand or contract the money supply as it chose. The gold standard was still in effect in the sense that people could trade dollars for gold, or vice versa.

The next big step occurred during the Great Depression of the 1930s. In 1933, President Franklin Roosevelt temporarily broke the link between the dollar and gold. It was reestablished in 1934 but with major changes. The value of a dollar was reduced from 0.0484 ounces of gold to 0.0286 ounces, allowing more dollars to be printed.

▶ Before 1971, governments traded dollars for gold as part of the world system for fixing exchange rates between currencies. We discuss this system in Chapter 17.

Most important, Americans could no longer exchange money for the gold that theoretically backed it. Only foreign governments had the right to trade dollars for gold. Indeed, it became illegal for private citizens to own gold, except small amounts for uses such as jewelry making. All other gold had to be sold to the government. This restriction lasted until 1974.

In 1945, the Fed's required gold reserves were reduced from 40 percent of the money it issued to 25 percent. In 1965, the minimum was abolished entirely. The final step came in 1971, when President Nixon eliminated the right of foreign governments to trade dollars for gold. Since then, gold and dollars have had no connection to one another.

Alternatives to a National Currency

In most countries, a central bank issues fiat money, which serves the economy as a medium of exchange, unit of account, and store of value. Exceptions of several kinds exist, however.

Dollarization In some countries, the national currency is replaced by foreign currency. Most often this currency is the U.S. dollar, so this phenomenon is called **dollarization**.

Dollarization use of foreign currency (often U.S. dollars) as money

Dollarization sometimes arises informally, without any action by the government. People and businesses decide to use dollars rather than the local money. Usually the reason is high inflation, which makes local currency lose value rapidly. Informal dollarization was common in Latin America in the 1980s and in former Soviet republics in the 1990s. Inflation rates in these countries often exceeded 100 percent—or even 1000 percent—per year.

One aspect of dollarization is that people in other nations use U.S. currency as a store of value. Often this practice continues even after the country has reduced its inflation rate, because people fear that inflation could return. Today, roughly half of U.S. currency is held abroad, mostly in $100 bills. Banks in some countries even offer accounts in which people can deposit dollars rather than local money. The value of these deposits is not affected by local inflation.

Sometimes the dollar replaces the local currency as the unit of account, and prices are quoted in dollars. In the 1980s, for example, many stores in Argentina set prices in dollars rather than Argentine pesos. Dollar prices were easier to understand, because the value of the peso was changing rapidly during those inflationary times. Sometimes, people paid for things with pesos—dollar prices were converted to pesos using the current exchange rate. Other times, people paid with dollars, meaning that dollars became the medium of exchange as well as the unit of account.

More recently, some countries have "officially" dollarized. This means the government steps in and completely abolishes the local currency, making dollars the only money throughout the country. Ecuador dollarized in 2000 and Zimbabwe in 2009. Officials in these countries acted out of frustration with escalating inflation. Unable to stabilize their currencies, they got rid of them.

Zimbabwe + Ecuador.

Currency Boards Another variation on money is created when a government establishes a **currency board**, an institution that issues money backed by a foreign currency. If the foreign currency is U.S. dollars, for example, then people can trade their money for dollars at a fixed rate. The currency board must hold enough dollars to buy back all the money it has created.

Currency board
institution that issues money backed by a foreign currency

Economies with currency boards include Bulgaria, where each Bulgarian lev can be traded for 0.515 euros; and Hong Kong, where each Hong Kong dollar can be traded for 0.115 U.S. dollars. (Hong Kong has maintained this arrangement despite its political integration into China.) Argentina established a currency board in 1991, but it broke down amid a financial crisis in 2001.

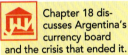 Chapter 18 discusses Argentina's currency board and the crisis that ended it.

Like dollarization, currency boards are usually prompted by high inflation rates. Inflation erodes the value of a country's money. A currency board seeks to preserve this value by tying the money to a stable currency.

Inflationary measures

A currency board is the closest thing to commodity money in the world today: it issues money that is exchangeable for something of value. The twist is that this something is not a commodity but a well-respected fiat money issued by another country.

Currency Unions A group of countries may form a **currency union**: they agree to abolish their national monies and create a single currency for the group. They also create a central bank to issue the common currency. Note that this arrangement differs from dollarization, when one country unilaterally adopts the money of another.

Currency union group of countries with a common currency

Currency unions exist in several parts of the world, including West Africa and the Caribbean. The best known is in Europe. In 1999, 11 European countries abolished their national currencies, including the French franc and German mark, and created a new currency, the euro. In 2011, Europe's currency union had 17 members, and it is likely to grow further as Eastern European countries join. Euros are issued by the European Central Bank (ECB) in Frankfurt, Germany.

Why a currency union? Briefly, the hope is to increase trade and other economic links within the union. It is easier to travel and do business if everyone uses the same currency. In the case of the euro, a single currency is also a symbol of political unity.

 ▶Chapter 17 surveys the pros and cons of currency unions.

Online Case Study
Alternative Currencies in
the United States

We have seen the great diversity in money. The next case study, based on a personal experience, offers an odd twist on dollarization, one that helps us understand the nature of fiat money.

CASE STUDY

Clean and Dirty Money

We have discussed the puzzle of fiat money: people provide goods and services in return for worthless pieces of paper. The resolution of this puzzle is that people accept fiat money because everybody else accepts it.

Economic theorists have pointed out that such a system might break down. If everybody else *refuses* to accept money, then you will too: you won't work for green pieces of paper if the grocer won't take them from you, and the grocer won't take them if people won't accept them from her. A common belief that nobody will accept money implies that nobody does accept it, just as a belief in acceptance produces acceptance.

The idea of people refusing money may seem far-fetched, but it has actually happened. In 1996, I visited Uzbekistan, a country in central Asia, to help teach an economics course for young government officials. At the time, Uzbekistan suffered from high rates of inflation, and this led to substantial dollarization. For example, the stipends for students in the course were paid in U.S. dollars, and people used dollars for major purchases.

However, an odd custom developed. Uzbeks would accept U.S. currency for goods and services only if it was clean and unwrinkled. A $100 bill that looked worn out or smudged could not be used to buy things. I was surprised by this behavior. Often people refuse to buy goods if they are in poor condition; you wouldn't buy shoes if the soles were worn out. But we usually think that money is money, even if it is wrinkled. Why did people in Uzbekistan turn down certain bills?

The answer is that each person turned down worn bills because everybody else did. Once the custom of refusing certain bills somehow got started, it was self-perpetuating. This is a real example of how the acceptance of fiat money can break down if people expect it to break down.

A student in our course had a $100 bill in his pocket, along with a pen. The pen broke, producing a large ink spot next to the picture of Benjamin Franklin. This flaw meant that people were unlikely to accept the bill. The student was crestfallen—it was as if his $100 had disappeared—$100 is a lot of money, especially in a poor country like Uzbekistan.

But there is a happy ending. I had a clean, new $100 bill in my wallet, and I knew that nobody in the U.S. cares about inkspots on money. So I traded my $100 bill for the student's $100 bill, which I took home and spent. This made the student happy and cost me nothing. (I thought about offering only $90 for the imperfect $100 bill but managed to resist this greedy impulse.)

2.3 MONEY TODAY

Let's leave Uzbekistan and focus on money in the United States today. We introduce how the Federal Reserve measures the **money supply**, which is the total amount of money in the economy. We also discuss the ways that people use money to purchase goods and services. The ways that we spend money are evolving rapidly.

> **Money supply** total amount of money in the economy

Measuring the Money Supply: M1

Each month the Federal Reserve reports data on the **monetary aggregates**, which are measures of the money supply. The Fed reports on two different aggregates called M1 and M2. **M1** is the Fed's primary measure of the money supply and the measure we use most often in this book.

The idea behind M1 is that money is the medium of exchange—it's what people use to purchase goods and services. Today, people purchase things mainly with two assets: currency and the deposits in their checking accounts. So these two assets are the major components of M1. Currency is included in M1 only if it is held by the nonbank public. Currency sitting in bank vaults or ATMs isn't part of the money supply.

M1 also includes a third component: traveler's checks. These are dying out because travelers can get cash from ATM networks worldwide, but the Fed still keeps track of them.

To summarize,

$$M1 = \text{currency} + \text{checking deposits} + \text{traveler's checks}$$

In May 2010, total currency held by the nonbank public was about $882 billion. Deposits in checking accounts were $823 billion, and traveler's checks were $5 billion. Adding these three numbers, M1 totaled $1710 billion, or $1.7 trillion.

$1.7 trillion is about 12 percent of U.S. GDP. That may sound like a lot, but the level of M1 is small compared to other assets. The total value of the stock of U.S. companies, for example, is more than 100 percent of GDP. As we've discussed, people hold relatively little of their wealth in money because it yields low returns. Nonetheless, changes in the money supply have big effects on the economy because of money's role as the medium of exchange.

> **Monetary aggregate** measure of the money supply (M1 or M2)
>
> **M1** the Federal Reserve's primary measure of the money supply; the sum of currency held by the nonbank public, checking deposits, and traveler's checks

> ▶ A small detail: as measured by the Fed, the traveler's check component of M1 includes only traveler's checks issued by institutions other than banks. Traveler's checks issued by banks are included in checking deposits. Don't ask me why.

How We Spend Money

There is only one way to spend currency—hand it over at the register. But there are several ways to spend the money in checking accounts. The traditional way is to write a paper check—that's how checking accounts got their name. As you probably know from experience, though, people can also spend checking deposits electronically. Funds are taken from your checking account when you swipe a debit card at a store. You can also transfer funds over the Internet, commonly to pay monthly bills such as utilities. Many firms make electronic payments, such as direct deposits of paychecks.

Electronic payments are becoming more common. In the United States, the volume of payments made by paper check peaked in the mid–1990s and has declined since then. **Figure 2.1** presents data on payment methods from a survey that the Federal Reserve conducts every 3 years. The number of payments made by check was 42 billion in 2000 and 31 billion in 2006. Over the same period, electronic payments rose from 15 billion to 41 billion. Economists debate whether check usage will level off in the future or checks will eventually disappear.

Is this trend important for the economy? Yes and no. It is important in reducing costs for banks, because processing electronic payments is less expensive than sending checks through the banking system. Electronic payments are one of the many ways computers have made the economy more efficient.

On the other hand, these technological innovations don't really change the nature of money. M1 is still defined as currency and checking deposits, regardless of how the deposits are spent. And changes in payment methods have little effect on the principles we will discuss that govern what determines the money supply and how it affects the economy.

[Handwritten margin notes: "Efficiency ↑ → Electronic Payments, Costs ↓" and "M1 not really affected by electronic payments"]

[Margin box:] Online Problem 12 at the end of the chapter asks you to examine the Fed's payments data for 2009 to discover whether the trend toward electronic payments is continuing.

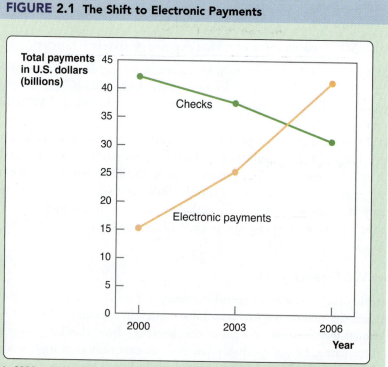

FIGURE 2.1 The Shift to Electronic Payments

In 2000, payments by paper check were almost three times as common in the United States as were electronic payments. By 2006, electronic payments exceeded checks. Electronic payments, made with debit cards or over the Internet, do not include credit card purchases, which are not final payments.

Source: 2007 Federal Reserve Payments Study

What About Credit Cards?

At this point, you may think we have left something out. When you make purchases, you don't use just cash and checking accounts. Probably you also use credit cards. A credit card looks similar to a debit card, but it works differently. Nothing is taken directly from your checking account; instead, you receive a credit card bill each month.

Even though people buy things with credit cards, economists ignore them in measuring the money supply. The rationale is that you don't really pay for something when you use a credit card. Instead, you buy the item on credit—that is, by borrowing. You pay for your purchase later, when you pay your credit card bill. And you use the funds in your checking account to pay this bill, either by writing a check or by electronic transfer. Your checking account is the ultimate way you pay for your purchase, just as when you write a check at the store.

Credit Card's seen as borrowing not included,

The Payments System

Now that we've discussed how people pay for goods and services, let's discuss how sellers of goods and services receive payment. This might sound like the same topic, but it's not. Suppose you give your landlady a rent check, for example. From your point of view, you've paid money. But your check is not money for the landlady: she can't trade it for groceries. Somehow the check must be transformed into money that the landlady can spend.

This happens through the **payments system**. A purchase sets off a series of transactions that ends with the seller receiving money. The details depend on the initial method of payment. Let's start with paper checks.

Payments system
arrangements through which money reaches the sellers of goods and services

Check Clearing Suppose your rent is $500. You give your landlady, Julia, a check for that amount, and she deposits it in *her* checking account. Then different things can happen. The story is simplest if you and Julia happen to have accounts at the same bank. When the bank receives the check, it reduces your balance by $500 and adds that amount to Julia's balance. Julia has received $500 that she can spend.

Now suppose that you and Julia have accounts at different banks. For Julia to receive payment, your check must travel from her bank, where she deposits it, to yours. This trip usually includes a stop at another institution—one where both your bank and Julia's have accounts. This could be a third private bank, but most often it is a branch of the Federal Reserve. All banks hold accounts at the Fed and use them for processing checks.

Figure 2.2 shows what happens. You give your check to Julia (step 1) and she deposits it in her bank account (step 2). Then Julia's bank deposits the check in *its* account at the Federal Reserve (step 3). The Fed adds $500 to this account and deducts $500 from your bank's account. The Fed also sends the check to your bank (step 4). When your bank receives the check, it deducts $500 from your account.

When Julia deposits your check (step 2), her account balance does not rise immediately. Her bank waits until it knows that the check is good—that

How it works.

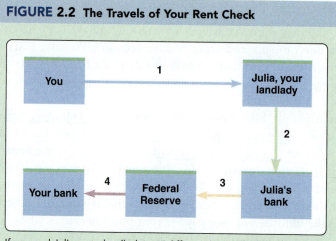

FIGURE 2.2 **The Travels of Your Rent Check**

If you and Julia, your landlady, use different banks, paying your rent triggers a series of transactions. You give your rent check to Julia (step 1), and she deposits it in her bank (step 2). Julia's bank deposits the check in its account at the Federal Reserve (step 3), and the Fed debits your bank's account. Finally, the Fed sends the check to your bank (step 4), and your bank debits your account.

you have at least $500 in your account. Julia's bank learns this at the end of the process, after the check reaches your bank and your account is debited (step 4). At that point, Julia's checking account balance rises by $500. Julia has finally received money that she can spend.

The Shift to Check Imaging Traditionally, paper checks traveled through the payments system by truck and airplane. This was a legal requirement in many states: to debit your account for a check you wrote, your bank had to receive the original check. Transportation accounted for much of the cost of check processing.

All this changed under a 2004 federal law called Check21, which allows digital imaging of checks. Now a merchant who receives a paper check can scan it and send it to his bank electronically. Or, if he sends in the paper check, the bank can convert it to an image at that point. The check image travels between the computers of banks and the Federal Reserve; no costly airplane transport is needed.

Following the enactment of Check21, banks quickly adopted the technology for check imaging; by 2009, it was used for virtually all checks. Because of this change, the total cost of processing a check has fallen from about a dollar to 25 cents. This cost saving may slow the decline of checks as a means of payment.

Processing Electronic Payments Electronic deposits and withdrawals also trigger a series of transactions among banks and the Federal Reserve. These occur through networks that link computers at the different institutions.

Suppose you swipe your debit card at the grocery store. The machine that reads your card first checks with your bank to ensure that you have sufficient funds for your purchase—or that the bank allows overdrafts on your account. If the purchase is approved, your bank debits your account by the amount of the purchase. It also sends a message to the Fed asking that funds be transferred from its Fed account to that of the grocer's bank. (The same transfer would occur if the Fed were processing a check from you to the grocer.) When the grocer's bank receives the funds, it credits the grocer.

▶ Chapter 9 explores the growth of overdraft programs, which are controversial because of the fees that banks charge.

Debits when you spend money credits the person rec money.

New Kinds of Money

As technology evolves, so does money. Two new ways of purchasing goods and services, *stored-value cards* and *e-money*, are less common than electronic transfers from checking accounts. But they are potentially more important in the sense that they may change what counts as money in the definition of M1.

Two ways of purchasing goods.

Ⓐ **Stored-Value Cards** A **stored-value card** looks like a debit or credit card. The difference is that it is "prepaid." For example, you might pay $100 in cash and receive a card with that balance. When you buy things with the card, the balance is reduced. Some cards can be "reloaded"—you make additional payments to increase the balance.

Stored-value card card issued with a prepaid balance that can be used for purchases

Many stored-value cards can be used for only one purpose. Common examples include calling cards issued by telephone companies, gift cards issued by stores, and fare cards issued by transit systems.

Banks issue multipurpose stored-value cards. Since 1999, many of these cards have been associated with the Visa and MasterCard networks. They can be used for purchases anywhere that accepts these credit cards. Stored-value cards can be bought at many locations, such as convenience stores and Western Union offices; in some places, machines dispense them.

Banks charge fees for stored-value cards. Their customers include people without checking accounts and parents who buy the cards to budget their teenagers' spending. (Stored-value cards are sometimes called "teen cards.") Cards can be replaced if lost, an advantage over cash.

In the United States, the use of stored-value cards is rising but is still low compared to debit and credit cards. Stored-value cards are popular in Asia—except they are not always cards. In countries such as Japan, you can load money on your cell phone and buy things by waving the phone over a reader, as shown in the accompanying photo. It's not yet clear whether this technology will catch on in the United States.

We can think of stored-value cards as electronic versions of traveler's checks.

A new way to buy things.

AP Photo/Itsuo Inoure

[handwritten margin note: Store Value cards ignored in M1 calculation.]

[handwritten margin note: Same for e-money.]

E-money funds in an electronic account used for Internet purchases

▶ Unlike PayPal, online purchases made through Google Checkout and Amazon Payment (created in 2006 and 2009, respectively) do not involve e-money. Rather, Google and Amazon store information on credit and debit cards and make it easier to use these cards online.

Liquidity ease of trading an asset for money

[handwritten margin note: More easily for money + inexpensively.]

Traveler's checks are also prepaid, usable for purchases, and replaceable if lost. Recall that traveler's checks are included in the M1 measure of the money supply. By the same logic, M1 should include the balances on stored-value cards—or at least multipurpose cards. These balances are mediums of exchange.

Currently, the Federal Reserve ignores stored-value cards when it measures money. It doesn't matter much today, because card balances are small compared to total M1. However, this could change.

Electronic Money **E-money** is yet another variation on the medium of exchange. Currently, the main issuer of e-money is PayPal, a subsidiary of eBay. You can establish a PayPal account and deposit money electronically either by transferring it from a bank account or by charging a credit card. To purchase goods, you transfer funds from your PayPal account to the account of the online merchant.

As with stored-value cards, there is an argument for adding e-money to M1, but this has not happened so far. Some economists doubt that e-money will become a major means of payment. It is not essential for Internet commerce, as people can use credit and debit cards online. As of 2010, PayPal was used for only 10 percent of online purchases.

2.4 LIQUIDITY AND BROAD MONEY

Now that we've introduced money, we can define another of this book's key concepts: **liquidity**. An asset is liquid if it can be traded for money easily and inexpensively.

The Need for Liquidity

To see why liquidity is important, recall Britt, the star pitcher we met in Chapter 1. Britt has considerable wealth, and he must decide how to divide it among various assets. Britt would be unwise to keep a large part of his wealth in money because, as we discussed earlier, other assets yield higher returns. Britt decides to hold only the minimal amount of money he needs to purchase goods and services.

But Britt has a problem: he doesn't know how much money he will need. He has a monthly budget, but he doesn't always follow it. Sometimes Britt sees a new electronic toy that he must have and spends an extra $200. His car's transmission failed one time, producing an unexpected expense of $1000. And there's always the risk of an emergency, such as a medical problem, that would cost much more.

So Britt faces a dilemma. If he holds enough money for any possible spending, much of his wealth will be diverted from higher-earning assets. On the other hand, if he holds too little money, he may run out if he has large bills to pay.

Liquid assets are the solution to Britt's dilemma. Many liquid assets produce higher returns than money. These assets can't be spent but can be traded quickly for assets that *can* be spent if necessary. If Britt holds a substantial level of liquid assets, he can earn good returns on his wealth and still be ready for unexpected expenses.

Degrees of Liquidity

The liquidity of assets varies widely. **Figure 2.3** illustrates this point by comparing several types of assets.

By definition, the most liquid assets are money that people can spend directly, including currency and checking deposits. Some other kinds of bank deposits, such as savings deposits, are almost as liquid. You can't spend the balance in a savings account, but it takes just a few minutes at an ATM to withdraw these funds or transfer them to a checking account. Thus, savings deposits can easily be turned into money. For this reason, savings deposits are sometimes called *near money*.

Securities are less liquid than savings deposits. If you own a stock or bond, you can't trade it for cash at an ATM. To sell the security, you must call a broker or contact one online. You must pay a fee, and you may not get your money until the next day.

Still, securities are more liquid than many assets. Real estate, for example, is illiquid. A house can be traded for money, but the process is time consuming and expensive. The seller must hire a real estate agent, show the house to prospective buyers, and negotiate a price. It can take months to make a deal. If a house must be sold quickly, the seller may have to accept less than the house is really worth.

Sometimes a trade-off exists between the returns on assets and their liquidity. For example, checking deposits earn less interest than savings deposits, or even no interest, but they are more liquid. Savings deposits earn less interest than bonds. Given this trade-off, many people hold a mixture of assets with different degrees of liquidity.

Britt, for example, keeps money in a checking account for routine spending, such as trips to the grocery store. He also maintains a savings

▶ We discuss how securities are traded in Chapter 5.

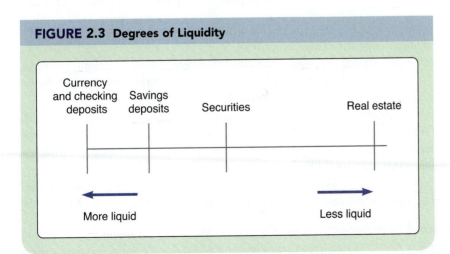

FIGURE 2.3 Degrees of Liquidity

| Currency and checking deposits | Savings deposits | Securities | Real estate |

◀ More liquid   Less liquid ▶

account. If he wants to make a special purchase, he transfers funds from savings to checking—this is not hard, but it would be a nuisance to do it every time he visits a store.

Britt keeps most of his wealth in securities. He usually doesn't touch these assets, but he can sell some in an emergency—or when he buys a new Land Rover. It is worth paying occasional broker's fees to earn the high potential returns on securities.

Measuring Broad Money: M2

M1 plus other liquid assets

M2 broad measure of the money supply that includes M1 and other highly liquid assets (savings deposits, small time deposits, and retail money-market mutual funds)

The Federal Reserve's primary measure of the money supply, M1, is based on money as the medium of exchange. The concept of liquidity helps us understand the Fed's other measure, **M2**. This monetary aggregate includes the assets in M1 plus other assets that are highly liquid, such as savings deposits. M2 is sometimes called *broad money* because it includes more than M1.

To see the idea behind M2, remember the definition of money: it can be used to purchase goods and services. Only the assets in M1—mainly currency and checking deposits—are used *directly* for purchases. For practical purposes, however, liquid assets such as savings deposits are almost as useful as M1 for making purchases. To spend the funds in your savings account, you need only stop at an ATM on the way to the store. Thus, some economists think that a measure of money should include savings deposits and assets with similar liquidity. The M2 aggregate is such a measure.

The Federal Reserve's definition of M2 includes several types of assets listed in **Table 2.1**. Notice that the level of M2 is about five times the level of M1. Besides the assets in M1, M2 has three components: savings deposits, small time deposits, and retail money-market mutual funds.

TABLE 2.1 The Monetary Aggregates

Levels in May 2010 (Billions of dollars)	
Components of M1	
Currency	882.0
Checking deposits	823.4
Traveler's checks	4.9
Total M1	1710.3
Components of M2 = M1 +	
Savings deposits	5069.2
Small time deposits	1063.6
Retail money-market mutual funds	735.8
Total M2	8578.9

Source: Federal Reserve Bank of St. Louis

Savings Deposits This component is about 60 percent of M2. As we've discussed, savings deposits earn higher interest than checking deposits. Usually savings deposits can't be spent directly, but they can be withdrawn at any time. *Example*

One kind of savings account is a *money-market deposit account* (MMDA). The existence of MMDAs blurs the line between checking and savings deposits because it is possible to write checks on MMDAs. However, depositors are limited to six checks a month, and people don't make purchases with MMDAs very often. The Fed treats MMDAs as savings rather than checking accounts, so they are included in M2 but not in M1.

Small Time Deposits A time deposit is also known as a *certificate of deposit (CD)*. A CD is like a savings account except that deposits are made for a fixed period (usually between 6 months and 3 years). There is a penalty for early withdrawal from a time deposit.

"Small" time deposits are those worth less than $100,000. This covers most CDs held by individuals. Larger-denomination time deposits, which are held mainly by firms and financial institutions, are not included in M2.

Some economists think that *no* time deposits should be included in a measure of the money supply. The restriction on withdrawals reduces the liquidity of time deposits, limiting their usefulness for purchasing goods and services. However, the Federal Reserve has judged that small time deposits are liquid enough to belong in M2.

Retail Money-Market Funds This is the only component of M2 that is not a bank account. A money-market fund is a mutual fund that holds bonds with maturities of less than a year: Treasury bills and commercial paper. The "retail" part of money-market funds covers shares that are purchased for less than $50,000. Once again, this restriction is meant to capture assets held by individuals.

Shares in money-market funds are highly liquid; they can be cashed in quickly without a fee. Some funds allow limited check writing, like money-market deposit accounts at banks.

> As detailed in Section 18.3, the problems of money-market funds played a dramatic role in the financial crisis of 2007–2009.

CASE STUDY

Sweep Programs

Most of the assets included in M1 and M2 are bank accounts, so innovations in banking influence these aggregates. An important example is **sweep programs** in which banks shift funds between customers' checking accounts and their money-market deposit accounts. This practice is invisible to consumers, but it has greatly reduced the levels of M1 calculated by the Federal Reserve.

Sweep programs began in 1994, when a change in Federal Reserve regulations made them legal. In a sweep program, computer software identifies funds in people's checking accounts that they are not likely to spend soon, based on their past behavior. This money is automatically "swept" into MMDAs. Funds are periodically moved back to the checking accounts to cover withdrawals and checks written on the accounts.

The motivation for sweep programs arises from Fed regulations. The Fed requires banks to hold reserves equal to a certain percentage of their total checking deposits. A bank's reserves consist of the cash in its vault and deposits it makes at the Fed. MMDAs have no reserve requirements, so moving funds from checking accounts to MMDAs reduces a bank's required level of reserves. This benefits the bank because reserves pay little interest: sweep programs free up funds for more profitable uses.

Checking deposits are part of M1, and MMDAs are not; as a type of savings deposit, MMDAs count only in M2. Therefore, when banks sweep funds from checking accounts to MMDAs, M1 falls. We can see this effect

> **Sweep program** banking practice of shifting funds temporarily from customers' checking accounts to money-market deposit accounts

FIGURE 2.4 Sweep Programs and M1

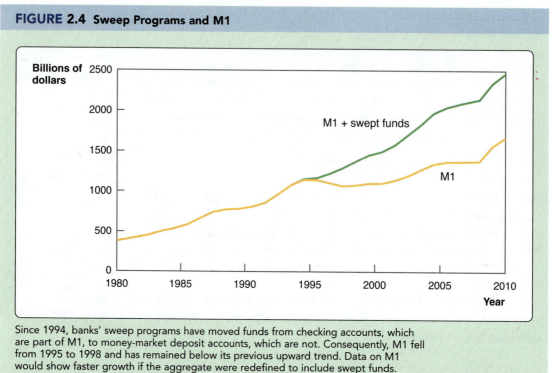

Since 1994, banks' sweep programs have moved funds from checking accounts, which are part of M1, to money-market deposit accounts, which are not. Consequently, M1 fell from 1995 to 1998 and has remained below its previous upward trend. Data on M1 would show faster growth if the aggregate were redefined to include swept funds.

Source: sweepmeasures.com (maintained by Barry E. Jones, Binghamton University)

in **Figure 2.4**, which shows the behavior of M1 over time. Normally, M1 rises, because people hold more money as the economy grows. But M1 fell for several years after 1994, when sweep programs started.

Most consumers are unaware that their checking deposits may be swept into other accounts. Bank brochures mention this only in the fine print. Consumer ignorance of the practice doesn't matter, as funds that are swept out of checking accounts are always swept back in when they are needed.

Recall that M1 is meant to measure mediums of exchange—the funds available to buy goods and services. People can spend all the money they deposit in checking accounts, even funds that have moved temporarily to MMDAs. Therefore, a growing number of economists argue that the definition of M1 should be revised to include funds swept out of checking accounts.

Changing the definition of M1 would make a big difference. In Figure 2.4, the green line shows M1 plus swept funds—what M1 would total if its definition were changed. With this adjustment, M1 grows steadily rather than dipping after 1994. In early 2010, M1 was 48 percent higher with swept funds included than without.[*]

[*] The Federal Reserve does not collect data on swept funds, but economists have produced estimates of this variable, which we use in Figure 2.4. For the method behind these estimates, see Donald Dutkowsky, Barry Z. Cynamon, and Barry E. Jones, "U.S. Narrow Money for the 21st Century," *Economic Inquiry*, January 2006.

2.5 FUNCTIONS OF CENTRAL BANKS

To complete our introduction to money, let's discuss the institution that controls the money supply: the central bank. As defined in the chapter introduction, the central bank of the United States is the Federal Reserve System, which includes 12 Federal Reserve Banks spread across the country. Overseeing the system is a Board of Governors in Washington, D.C. The most powerful individual at the Fed is the Chair of the Board of Governors—currently, Ben Bernanke.

A central bank has many roles in the economy. Let's outline the most important functions, which are summarized in **Table 2.2**.

> **TABLE 2.2 Major Functions of Central Banks**
>
> 1. Clearing checks and electronic payments
> 2. Monetary policy (managing the money supply)
> 3. Emergency lending
> 4. Financial regulation

Clearing Payments

We mentioned this role of central banks in our discussion of the payments system. Every private bank has an account at the Federal Reserve Bank for its region. Banks use these accounts to clear checks and process electronic payments (see Figure 2.2). Because banks have accounts there, the Fed is sometimes called the "banks' bank."

Monetary Policy

The best-known function of central banks is **monetary policy**, or management of the money supply. These policy decisions, which we discuss at many points in the book, have strong effects on the economy.

How does a central bank control the money supply? After all, M1 is mainly currency and deposits in checking accounts. A central bank chooses how much currency to issue, but it does not directly determine checking deposits, which are created by banks and their customers. Nonetheless, central banks have developed ways to manipulate how much money is created.

Monetary policy central banks' management of the money supply

▶ You will learn how central banks control the money supply in Chapter 11.

Emergency Lending

Central banks have long lent money to private banks. This lending occurs primarily during financial crises, which threaten banks with failure. During crises, banks need loans to survive, and they cannot get funds from private sources. So the central bank steps in as the **lender of last resort**.

During the financial crisis of 2007–2009, the Federal Reserve greatly expanded its lending role. Previously it had lent only to deposit-taking banks, but during the crisis it also lent to nondepository institutions such as investment banks and the insurance conglomerate American International Group (AIG). The Fed even lent to corporations in nonfinancial industries, such as manufacturing, by purchasing their short-term bonds (commercial paper).

Lender of last resort central bank's role as emergency lender to financial institutions

Financial Regulation

In most countries, central banks regulate private banks. Regulators try to reduce the risk of bank failure by restricting banks' activities. For example, banks are discouraged from making loans with high default risk. In the

United States, the Federal Reserve shares bank regulation duties with other government agencies.

The regulatory role of the Federal Reserve, like its lending role, is changing as a result of the financial crisis. A 2010 law, the Consumer Protection and Wall Street Reform Act, increases the Fed's authority over various kinds of financial institutions.

We discuss the policies of central banks throughout this book. As a preview, the next case study reviews the actions of the Federal Reserve following the terrorist attacks on September 11, 2001. In addition to the direct human cost, the attacks threatened America's financial system and economy. The Fed, under then-Chairman Alan Greenspan, responded quickly to contain these threats and to minimize the economic trauma. Its actions involved all four central bank functions.

We discuss bank regulation in Chapter 10. Chapters 11 and 18 examine the Federal Reserve's responses to the 2007–2009 crisis and the new regulatory powers it gained after the crisis.

CASE STUDY

The Fed and September 11

The attacks on the World Trade Center and the Pentagon immediately interrupted the payments system. Because airplanes were grounded, checks stopped traveling among banks. In addition, the attacks knocked out electronic communications in Manhattan's financial district. Many banks could not make electronic payments that they had promised.

Consequently, some banks did not receive payments they expected and ran short of money. This could have had a domino effect. When banks are worried about a money shortage, they are reluctant to send money elsewhere; they delay payments and refuse to make loans. This means that other banks don't receive expected funds. Everybody starts hoarding money, and the payments system can break down.

Without a payments system, people can't buy or sell goods and services. So a serious breakdown in payments could have disrupted the whole economy, slowing growth and raising unemployment. The Fed took several actions to prevent this outcome.

- The Fed adjusted the rules governing payments. Normally, the Fed charges overdraft fees to banks with negative balances in their Fed accounts. These fees were suspended from September 11 to September 21. This policy encouraged banks to keep making payments even if incoming funds were delayed, pushing their balances negative.

- The Fed acted as a lender of last resort. At 11:45 AM on September 11, 3 hours after the initial attack, it issued a press release saying, "The Federal Reserve System is open and operating" and ready with emergency loans. Lots of those loans were needed: on September 12 the Fed had $45 billion of loans out to banks, about 200 times the normal level for the early 2000s.

- The Fed relaxed bank regulations, allowing loans that it would normally prohibit. For example, the Fed encouraged banks to lend to securities dealers, which it usually considers risky. Many dealers needed money because, like banks, they didn't receive expected payments.

Besides disrupting payments, the 9/11 attacks threatened the economy in other ways. A higher demand for money raises interest rates. Banks' scramble for money could have raised rates, which in turn would have slowed economic growth. However, starting on September 11, the Fed increased the money supply to match money demand. This action kept interest rates stable.

On Monday, September 17, the Fed went a step further. It decided the economy needed not stable interest rates, but *lower* rates. It decided to push short-term rates from 3.5 percent to 3 percent, which it accomplished by increasing the money supply.

The Fed acted because it feared a decline in economic growth. Growth was threatened by problems in certain industries, such as airlines and travel, and by reduced consumer spending overall caused by general uncertainty in the aftermath of 9/11. Lower interest rates encouraged consumers and firms to begin spending again and helped offset the factors that threatened to reduce economic growth.

2.6 THE REST OF THIS BOOK

We have now completed Part I of this book. Chapter One introduced the central parts of the financial system—financial markets and banks—and their roles in the economy. Chapter Two has discussed money—what it is, how it is measured, how it is spent—and how central banks can manage the money supply.

The rest of the book expands on this foundation. Before diving into the details, let's look at where we're going. The balance of the book is divided into four parts: financial markets, banking, money and the economy, and monetary policy.

Financial Markets

Part II examines financial markets in detail. We first discuss the prices and returns on securities, such as stocks and bonds. Why do stock prices sometimes rise and sometimes fall? Why are some interest rates high and some low?

We then discuss firms' decisions to issue securities and savers' decisions about which securities to buy. When you accumulate wealth, should you buy stocks or bonds? Which firms' securities are the best buy?

Part II also discusses the markets for "derivative" securities, including futures, options, and credit-default swaps. We will see how some people and firms use these markets to reduce risk while others use them to gamble. Finally, we discuss the markets for foreign currencies and explain why currency values fluctuate and how these fluctuations affect the economy.

Banking

In Part III we turn to the banking industry and expand on the primary reason that banks exist: to reduce the problem of asymmetric information in the financial system. We discuss changes in banking over recent decades, including the growth of subprime lending and the creation of securities backed by bank loans.

Part III also discusses the business of banking—how banks earn profits from accepting deposits, making loans, and other activities. We will see that banking can be a risky business and that bank failures are costly to the economy. This leads to the topic of government regulation, which aims to reduce the risk of bank failure.

Money and the Economy

Part IV returns to the topic of money. We discuss how central banks such as the Federal Reserve control the money supply. We then discuss economic fluctuations—the ups and downs of output, inflation, and unemployment. Central banks' decisions about the money supply are a central factor in these fluctuations.

This discussion builds on the earlier parts of the book. We will see that central banks' power stems from their influence on the financial system. Changes in the money supply affect financial variables such as interest rates, asset prices, and the level of bank lending, which in turn affect the rest of the economy.

Monetary Policy

Part V turns to monetary policy. How should central banks use their power? We examine the strategies that central banks pursue to stabilize the economy and their successes and failures.

Part V also explores financial crises. The discussion builds on earlier parts of the book, because crises involve interactions among financial markets, banks, and central banks. We examine crises ranging from the Great Depression to exchange rate crises in emerging economies, with special emphasis on the U.S. crisis of 2007–2009. We will see that financial crises can devastate economies and that preventing crises is one of the most controversial issues in economic policy.

Summary

- An economy's money supply is controlled by the central bank. The Federal Reserve System is the central bank of the United States.

2.1 What Is Money?

- Money is, first, the medium of exchange: the assets people use to purchase goods and services.
- Money offers an alternative to barter as a means of trading goods and services. Barter is inefficient because it requires a double coincidence of wants: when two people trade, each must have something the other wants.

- Money serves as the unit of account—that is, the measure in which prices are quoted. Money is also a store of value, a form in which wealth can be held.

2.2 Types of Money

- Commodity money is a medium of exchange with intrinsic value, such as gold coins or paper money exchangeable for gold.
- Fiat money, the kind of money used today, is intrinsically worthless pieces of paper. Each person accepts fiat money only because others do.

- Fiat money evolved from commodity money over time. The U.S. dollar has sometimes been commodity money, sometimes fiat money, and sometimes in between.

- Dollarization occurs when a country adopts a foreign currency as its money. A currency board issues a local money backed by a foreign currency. A currency union, such as the euro area, is a group of countries that creates a common money.

2.3 Money Today

- M1 is a measure of the money supply based on the idea that money is the medium of exchange. It includes assets that people use to purchase goods and services: cash, balances in checking accounts, and traveler's checks. New forms of money, such as stored-value cards and e-money, are not currently included in M1.

- Technology is rapidly changing how money is spent. Debit cards and Internet payments are replacing paper checks.

- Sellers of goods and services receive money through the payments system, a series of transactions among banks and the Federal Reserve.

2.4 Liquidity and Broad Money

- An asset's liquidity is the ease of trading it for money. The liquidity of assets ranges from high (e.g., savings accounts) to medium (e.g., securities) to low (e.g., real estate).

- Holders of liquid assets can earn higher returns than they would from money while still being ready for unexpected spending.

- M2 is a broad measure of the money supply. It includes the components of M1 and other highly liquid assets, such as savings deposits.

- Banks' sweep programs have shifted funds out of checking accounts, reducing the measured level of M1.

2.5 Functions of Central Banks

- The Federal Reserve System is the central bank of the United States. This system includes 12 Federal Reserve Banks located around the country and a Board of Governors in Washington, D.C.

- The primary functions of central banks are payments processing, monetary policy, emergency lending, and financial regulation.

2.6 The Rest of This Book

- By building on the foundation laid in Chapters One and Two, the four remaining parts of this book detail the workings of financial markets and the banking system, how money influences the economy, and the policies that central banks pursue to stabilize the economy.

Key Terms

barter, p. 27

central bank, p. 26

commodity money, p. 30

currency board, p. 35

currency union, p. 35

dollarization, p. 34

double coincidence of wants, p. 27

e-money, p. 42

Federal Reserve System, p. 26

fiat money, p. 31

lender of last resort, p. 47

liquidity, p. 42

M1, p. 37

M2, p. 44

medium of exchange, p. 26

monetary aggregate, p. 37

monetary policy, p. 47

money, p. 26

money demand, p. 27

money supply, p. 37

payments system, p. 39

store of value, p. 29

stored-value card, p. 41

sweep program, p. 45

unit of account, p. 28

Questions and Problems

1. The U.S. government owns more than 8000 tons of gold, stored mainly at Fort Knox in Kentucky. Why did the government accumulate this gold? Should it continue to hold the gold or sell it?

2. In the 1964 movie *Goldfinger*, the title character schemes to increase the price of gold. He plans to drop an atomic bomb on Fort Knox, making the gold there radioactive. His operation is financed by North Korea, which hopes to make the dollar worthless, disrupting the U.S. economy. If James Bond hadn't thwarted Goldfinger's plan, what effects might it have had on the monetary system and economy in 1964?

3. Scientists believe that the Sun will explode some billions of years from now. According to some economic theorists, this means that nobody should accept money today. What is the logic behind this idea?

4. The U.S. population is approximately 300 million. Using the information in Table 2.1, calculate the average amount of U.S. currency per citizen. Do most Americans hold that much cash? If not, where is it?

5. Suppose that technology completely eliminates the use of cash. People buy newspapers by putting debit cards in the newspaper box. They use the Internet to pay babysitters. With no cash, does the nature of money change? Should the Federal Reserve change the definition of M1?

6. Explain how each of these events affects the amount of M1 that people hold:
   a. ATMs are invented.
   b. Credit cards are invented.
   c. Debit cards are invented.
   d. Stored-value cards are invented.
   e. Interest rates on bonds rise.

7. Is your checking account a sweep account? Find out from your bank. How much of the money you deposit is actually in the account on a typical day, and how much has been swept into an MMDA?

8. Recall the transactions that are triggered when you pay your rent (see Figure 2.2). Now suppose your check bounces because you don't have enough funds in your account. How does this change the series of transactions?

9. For a citizen of the United States, how liquid is each of the following assets? Explain each answer.
   a. Bonds issued by the U.S. government
   b. Bonds issued by corporations
   c. Postimpressionist paintings
   d. British pounds

▶ Online and Data Questions
www.worthpublishers.com/ball

10. Using the data on the text Web site, compute the ratio of M1 to GDP and the ratio of M2 to GDP. These ratios show how much money people hold relative to total spending in the economy. Plot these ratios over the last 40 years. Have the ratios been steady, or have they risen or fallen? What might explain these trends?

11. Figure 2.4 shows that sweep programs have reduced the level of M1. How do you think sweeps have affected M2? Do the M2 data on the text Web site support your answer?

12. Link through the text Web site to the 2010 Federal Reserve Payments Study. From 2006 to 2009, did the shift to electronic payments shown in Figure 2.1 slow down, continue at the same pace, or speed up? Explain why.

13. The text Web site has links to several sites with information about stored-value cards. Some are maintained by card issuers, others by government agencies or consumer advocates. After visiting some of these sites, discuss the pros and cons of multipurpose stored-value cards. Who, if anybody, would be wise to use them?

Asset Prices and Interest Rates

AP Photo/Rechard Drew

August 10, 2010: A television screen on the floor of the New York Stock Exchange shows the latest news on stock prices, interest rates, and Federal Reserve policy.

A t any time of the day, you can tap into financial news on your TV, computer, iPhone, or BlackBerry. You may learn, for example, that the interest rate on 3-month Treasury bills is currently 2.1 percent, and the rate on 30-year Treasury bonds is 3.4 percent. You may also see that the price of Microsoft stock has risen from $35 per share to $37, while Exxon is unchanged at $81. A dollar can buy 110 yen or 0.85 euros in foreign currency markets.

As this information scrolls across your television or iPhone screen, it may raise questions in your mind. As an inquisitive student, you wonder what determines the various interest rates, asset prices, and exchange rates you hear about. What economic forces cause these numbers to move around?

As someone who hopes to be wealthy or at least will need to manage a personal retirement account, you wonder about which assets you should buy. Which is a better deal: 2.1-percent interest on a 3-month Treasury bill or 3.4 percent on a 30-year bond? Is $37 a good price for Microsoft? Should you look into Japanese or European securities?

Part II of this book helps you answer questions like these about financial markets. This chapter discusses how the prices of assets are determined, why these prices fluctuate, and how they are related to interest rates. We outline some general principles and apply them to different types of assets, such as stocks and bonds. Economists' approach to asset pricing rests on a fundamental concept: the present value of an income stream. So our first task is to understand what present value means.

3.1 VALUING INCOME STREAMS

A financial asset yields a stream of income in the future. The owner of a bond receives a payment when the bond matures and may receive coupon payments before then. The owner of a firm's stock receives part of the firm's future earnings. To find the value of an asset, we must determine the value of these income streams.

In making such valuations, the key principle is that payments have different values depending on when they are received. A dollar today is worth more than a dollar in the future, because you can take today's dollar, put it in the bank, and earn interest on it. This process transforms one dollar today into more than one dollar in the future.

Future Value

To compare payments at different times, economists begin with the concept of **future value**. The future value of a dollar is how many dollars it can produce in some future year. To understand this concept, suppose that banks pay an interest rate of 4 percent. If you deposit a dollar today, it grows to $1.04 in a year. Thus, the future value of a dollar today is $1.04 in 1 year.

If you keep your money in the bank for a second year, it grows by another 4 percent. When $1.04 grows by 4 percent, it becomes $(1.04) (1.04), or $(1.04)^2 = \$1.082$. So a dollar today is worth $(1.04)^2$ in 2 years. If you keep the money in the bank for a third year, it grows by 4 percent again, becoming $(1.04)^3 = \$1.125$.

You should see the pattern. With a 4–percent interest rate, a dollar left in the bank for n years, where n is any number, grows to $(1.04)^n$. A dollar today is worth $(1.04)^n$ in n years.

The same principle applies to interest rates other than 4 percent. Let i be any interest rate expressed in decimal form. (In decimal form, 4 percent is 0.04). A dollar today grows to $(1 + i)$ in a year, $(1 + i)^2$ in 2 years, and $(1 + i)^n$ in n years. So the future value of a dollar is given by

FUTURE VALUE

$$\$1 \text{ today} = \$(1 + i)^n \text{ in } n \text{ years} \qquad (3.1)$$

Present Value

We've seen how much a dollar today is worth in the future. Now let's turn this relation around to see how much a *future* dollar is worth *today*. This is the **present value** of the future dollar.

We can understand present value (PV) with a little algebra. We start by turning around Equation (3.1) for future value:

$$\$(1 + i)^n \text{ in } n \text{ years} = \$1 \text{ today}$$

> **Future value** value of a dollar today in terms of dollars at some future time; $1 today = $(1 + i)^n$ in n years

> **Present value** value of a future dollar in terms of today's dollars; $1 in n years = $1/(1 + i)^n$ today

[Handwritten margin notes:]
Earn interest on a dollar.
what is future value
$1 = \$(1 + i)^n$
Future Value
Present Value
$\$1 \frac{1}{(1 + i)^n}$

Now divide both sides of the equation by $(1 + i)^n$:

$$\frac{\$(1 + i)^n}{(1 + i)^n} \text{ in } n \text{ years} = \frac{\$1}{(1 + i)^n} \text{ today}$$

The left side of this equation simplifies, giving us a key formula:

PRESENT VALUE

$$\$1 \text{ in } n \text{ years} = \frac{\$1}{(1 + i)^n} \text{ today} \qquad \textbf{(3.2)}$$

To do FV to PV.

$(1 + i)^\wedge = \$1$

then $\dfrac{(1 + i)^n}{(1 + i)^\wedge} = \dfrac{\$1}{(1 + i)^n}$

$PV = \dfrac{\$1}{(1 + i)^n}$

A dollar n years from today is worth $1/(1 + i)^n$ dollars today.

With a 4-percent interest rate, the present value of a dollar in n years is $\$1/(1.04)^n$. For example, the present value of a dollar in 3 years is $\$1/(1.04)^3 = \$0.889$. The present value of a dollar in 20 years is $\$1/(1.04)^{20} = \$0.456$.

↑i ↓PV of money!

Equation (3.2) holds a key implication: *a higher interest rate reduces the present value of future money.* Mathematically, a higher i reduces present value because it raises the denominator in the formula. The economic explanation is that a higher interest rate means a saver can trade a dollar today for more future dollars. Turning this around, at a higher interest rate, a future dollar is worth less today. For example, if the interest rate rises from 4 percent to 6 percent, the present value of a dollar in 3 years falls from $\$0.889$ to $\$1/(1.06)^3 = \$0.840$. The present value of a dollar in 20 years falls from $\$0.456$ to $\$0.312$.

Economic explanation ✳

A Series of Payments We can extend our reasoning to value a flow of money over multiple years. Suppose someone promises you $3 in 2 years and $5 in 4 years. Each dollar in 2 years is worth $\$1/(1 + i)^2$, so the $3 are worth $\$3/(1 + i)^2$. The $5 in 4 years are worth $\$5/(1 + i)^4$. Altogether, the present value of the future payments is $\$3/(1 + i)^2 + \$5/(1 + i)^4$.

PV of future payments

To get a general formula for a series of payments, suppose you receive $\$X_1$ in one year, $\$X_2$ in two years, and so on up to $\$X_T$ in T years. The present value of this flow of money is

$$\text{present value} = \frac{\$X_1}{(1 + i)} + \frac{\$X_2}{(1 + i)^2} + \cdots + \frac{\$X_T}{(1 + i)^T} \qquad \textbf{(3.3)}$$

To practice using this formula, let's calculate the present value of a contract signed by baseball star C. C. Sabathia, a left-handed pitcher. After the 2008 season, the New York Yankees agreed to pay Sabathia $23 million per year for seven years (from 2009 through 2015). The total payments over the life of this contract are $7 \times \$23 = \$161$ million. To calculate the present value of the payments, let's assume an interest rate of 4 percent. In this case, the present value in 2008 was

$$\$23 \text{ million}/(1.04) + \$23 \text{ million}/(1.04)^2 + \cdots + \$23 \text{ million}/(1.04)^7$$

If you plug these numbers into a calculator, you will find that the present value of Sabathia's salary in 2008 was about $138 million.

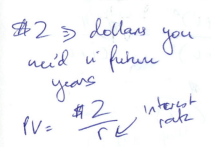

Payments Forever Some assets provide income indefinitely—there is no year T when the last payment is made. For example, a share of stock entitles the holder to a stream of earnings with no endpoint. A rare type of bond called a *perpetuity* pays interest forever.

In some cases, we can derive simple formulas for the present value of a perpetual income stream. One such case is a constant annual payment. If you receive a payment of $\$Z$ in all future years, the present value is

$$\text{present value} = \frac{\$Z}{(1+i)} + \frac{\$Z}{(1+i)^2} + \frac{\$Z}{(1+i)^3} + \cdots$$

where the "..." at the end means the series continues forever. This equation simplifies to

$$\text{present value} = \frac{\$Z}{i} \tag{3.4}$$

Deriving the last equation requires complicated algebra, but the equation itself is simple. For perpetual payments, a higher annual payment means a higher present value. And, as always, a higher interest rate means a lower present value. For example, if the interest rate is 4 percent, a payment of $100 per year forever has a present value of $100/(0.04) = $2500. If the interest rate falls to 2 percent, the present value of payments rises to $100/(0.02) = $5000.

Another kind of perpetual income stream is a payment that grows over time at a constant rate. To analyze this case, let $\$Z$ be the payment in one year, and let g be the annual rate at which the payment grows. Each year, the payment is $(1+g)$ times the previous payment: it is $\$Z(1+g)$ in 2 years, $\$Z(1+g)^2$ in 3 years, and so on. We assume the growth rate of payments is less than the interest rate ($g < i$). In this case, the present value of all payments is

▶ If $g > i$, then payments grow so quickly that their present value is infinite. Nobody in the real world receives income with an infinite present value.

$$\text{present value} = \frac{\$Z}{(1+i)} + \frac{\$Z(1+g)}{(1+i)^2} + \frac{\$Z(1+g)^2}{(1+i)^3} + \cdots$$

This equation simplifies to[1]

$$\text{present value} = \frac{\$Z}{(i-g)} \tag{3.5}$$

Once again, the present value of payments depends on the initial payment Z and the interest rate i. In addition, present value depends on the growth rate g. When payments grow at a higher rate, their present value is higher. Mathematically, a higher g raises present value because it reduces $i - g$, the denominator in the formula.

---

[1] Here is the algebra behind Equations (3.4) and (3.5). Let $X = Z/(1+i)$ and let $a = (1+g)/(1+i)$. With this notation, the equation that precedes (3.5) can be written as PV = $X(1 + a + a^2 + ...)$. Multiplying this equation by a gives us $a(\text{PV}) = X(a + a^2 + ...)$. Notice that $X(a + a^2 + ...) = \text{PV} - X$, so we can write $a(\text{PV}) = \text{PV} - X$. Rearranging this equation yields PV $= X/(1-a)$. Substituting the definitions of X and a into the last equation and simplifying yields PV $= Z/(i-g)$, which is Equation (3.5). Equation (3.4) is a special case of (3.5) in which $g = 0$, which means the annual payment is constant.

TABLE 3.1 Present Values of Some Common Types of Payments

Payment (Dollars)	Present Value (Dollars)	Equation
$1 in n Years	$\dfrac{\$1}{(1+i)^n}$	(3.2)
A series of annual payments: $\$X_1, \$X_2, \ldots, \$X_T$	$\dfrac{\$X_1}{(1+i)} + \dfrac{\$X_2}{(1+i)^2} + \cdots + \dfrac{\$X_T}{(1+i)^T}$	(3.3)
An annual payment of Z forever	$\dfrac{\$Z}{i}$	(3.4)
An annual payment that equals Z in the first year and grows at rate g	$\dfrac{\$Z}{(i-g)}$	(3.5)

Suppose again that $Z = \$100$ and $i = 4$ percent. If $g = 2$ percent, the present value of payments is $\$100/(0.04 - 0.02) = \$100/(0.02) = \$5000$. If g rises to 3 percent, the present value rises to $\$100/(0.04 - 0.03) = \$100/(0.01) = \$10,000$.

Table 3.1 summarizes the key principles about present values that we have derived.

3.2 THE CLASSICAL THEORY OF ASSET PRICES

Now that we understand the concept of the present value of an income stream, we can use this concept to answer the question we raised earlier in this chapter: what factors determine the price of an asset, such as a stock or bond? Economists usually answer this question with a theory based on several ideas involving present values.

The Present Value of Income

An asset produces a flow of income. This flow might be a series of fixed payments (in the case of bonds) or a share of a company's profits (in the case of stock). According to the **classical theory of asset prices**, the price of an asset equals the present value of the income that people expect to receive from the asset:

Classical theory of asset prices the price of an asset equals the present value of expected income from the asset

asset price = present value of expected asset income

Notice the word *expected* in the theory. In many cases, nobody knows exactly how much income an asset will produce. For example, nobody is certain of a company's future profits, which determine the income from stock. Given this uncertainty, the classical theory says that asset prices depend on people's expectations, or best guesses, of asset income.

The rationale for the classical theory is simple. People purchase an asset because it yields a future stream of income. The present value tells us how much this income stream is expected to be worth and thus how much we should be willing to pay for the asset.

Suppose an asset's price were *below* the present value of its expected income. Say the present value is $100 and the asset price is $80. This situation wouldn't last long. At a price of $80, the asset is a great deal: buyers pay less than the asset is worth. Lots of savers will purchase the asset, and high demand will push up the price until it rises to $100.

Conversely, if an asset price exceeds the present value of expected income, then sellers receive more than the asset is worth. In this situation, the asset's owners will rush to sell, and the increase in supply will push down the price.

The classical theory applies to many types of assets. For example, it says that the price of an apartment building equals the present value of net rental income from the building. Let's look more closely at the theory's implications for two classes of assets: bonds and stocks.

Bond Prices The income from a bond includes the periodic coupon payments (if any) and the face value received at maturity. Let's say a bond has a maturity of T years, a face value of F, and an annual coupon payment of C. Assuming no chance of default, bondholders expect to receive all the promised payments. The payments are C in years 1 through $T-1$ and $C + F$ in year T. The bond price is the present value of these expected payments. Using Equation (3.3), this present value is

$$\frac{\text{bond}}{\text{price}} = \frac{C}{(1 + i)} + \frac{C}{(1 + i)^2} + \cdots + \frac{C}{(1 + i)^{T-1}} + \frac{(C + F)}{(1 + i)^T} \quad (3.6)$$

For example, suppose a bond's maturity is 4 years, so $T = 4$. Annual coupon payments are $5 ($C = 5), the face value F is $100, and the interest rate is 4 percent. In this case, Equation (3.6) tells us

$$\text{bond price} = \frac{\$5}{1.04} + \frac{\$5}{(1.04)^2} + \frac{\$5}{(1.04)^3} + \frac{\$105}{(1.04)^4} = \$103.63$$

Stock Prices Someone who owns a firm's stock owns a share of the firm. However, firms' earnings do not flow directly to their stockholders. Instead, firms periodically make payments to stockholders called **dividends**. If a company with 1 million shares announces a dividend of $2 per share, it will pay stockholders a total of $2 million in dividends.

Dividend payment from a firm to its stockholders

Because dividends are the income from stock, a stock's price is the present value of expected dividends. If expected dividends per share are D_1 in the next year, D_2 in the year after that, and so on, then

$$\text{stock price} = \frac{D_1}{(1 + i)} + \frac{D_2}{(1 + i)^2} + \frac{D_3}{(1 + i)^3} + \cdots \quad (3.7)$$

In any year, a firm's dividends can differ from its earnings. Indeed, some firms earn healthy profits yet pay no dividends at all. Instead, they might use their earnings to finance investment projects such as new factories or new-product development.

Over the long run, however, dividends are tied closely to earnings. If a firm uses its current earnings for investment rather than dividends, the investment boosts future earnings. These future earnings allow the firm to pay higher future dividends. Therefore, any rise in earnings raises dividends at some point in time. The present value of dividends increases, raising the firm's stock price. Because of these connections, expectations about companies' earnings have strong effects on stock prices.

What Determines Expectations?

people's expectations are the best forecast for the asset

An asset price depends on the present value of *expected* asset income. What determines what people expect? The classical theory assumes that people's expectations are the best possible forecasts of asset income based on all available information. This assumption is called **rational expectations**.

To understand the implications of rational expectations, let's revisit Harriet's software company, iSmells. The price of the company's stock depends on people's expectations of its future earnings, which will determine the dividends the company can pay. Rational expectations of earnings are based on all available information about the company. For example, if Harriet announces a new product, expected earnings rise to reflect the product's likely impact. If the economy enters a recession, expected earnings adjust based on how Harriet's firm will be affected. Expected earnings also take into account the costs of producing software, the number of competitors the firm faces, and all other factors that affect how successful Harriet's firm is likely to be.

It is important to realize that rational expectations are not always accurate or correct. Unpredictable events—changes in production costs or consumer demand, successes and failures in developing new products, to name a few—can cause a firm's actual earnings to differ from the earnings people expect. If people have incorporated all relevant, available information into their expectations, however, their expectations will be as accurate as possible, and the differences between expected and actual earnings will be as small as possible.

> **Rational expectations** theory that people's expectations of future variables are the best possible forecasts based on all available information

▶ We introduced Harriet, the entrepreneur investor, in Chapter 1.

Earnings

What Is the Relevant Interest Rate?

In addition to depending on expectations about earnings, asset prices depend on interest rates, which determine the present value of asset income. What interest rates should we use in present value formulas? In the classical theory, different interest rates are relevant for different assets. The riskier an asset—that is, the more uncertainty about the income flow from the asset—the higher the interest rate.

↑ risk
↑ IR
greater uncertainty

To understand this effect of risk, recall our initial discussion of present value, where we saw that a dollar today is worth $1 + i$ dollars in a year. In this discussion, i is an interest rate that savers receive for sure—say, from a safe bank account. From now on, we will call this rate the **safe interest rate**, or *risk-free rate*, i^{safe}. With this notation, a dollar today is worth a certain $\$(1 + i^{\text{safe}})$ in a year. Conversely, a certain dollar in a year is worth $\$1/(1 + i^{\text{safe}})$ today.

> **Safe interest rate (i^{safe})** interest rate that savers can receive for sure; also known as *risk-free rate*

Same applies for
FV and PV

When determining asset prices, however, we often have to value uncertain payments. For example, suppose the expected dividend in some year from a share of stock is $10. This is the best forecast, but the dividend could range between $8 and $12 per share. People dislike such risk. With this uncertainty, the expected dividend from the stock is worth less than a certain $10.

How does risk affect present values? A dollar today is worth $1 + i^{safe}$ certain dollars next year. This means a dollar today is worth *more* than $1 + i^{safe}$ risky dollars next year, because risky dollars are less valuable than certain dollars. To put it differently, a dollar today is worth $1 + i^{safe} + \varphi$ risky dollars in a year, where φ (the Greek letter phi) is a **risk premium**. A risk premium is a payment on an asset that compensates the owner for taking on risk.

> **Risk premium (φ)** payment on an asset that compensates the owner for taking on risk
>
> **Risk-adjusted interest rate** sum of the risk-free interest rate and the risk premium on an asset, $i^{safe} + \varphi$

The same reasoning applies to risky income at any point in the future. A dollar today is worth $(1 + i^{safe} + \varphi)^n$ risky dollars in n years. Turning this around, the present value of a risky dollar in n years is $1/(1 + i^{safe} + \varphi)^n$. In our equations for asset prices, the interest rate is the sum of the safe rate and the risk premium, $i = i^{safe} + \varphi$. We call this sum the **risk-adjusted interest rate**.

Assets carry varying degrees of risk. The greater the risk, the higher the risk premium. For example, stocks have higher risk premiums than bonds because, as we discuss in Section 3.6, the income from stocks is more volatile. A higher risk premium raises the risk-adjusted interest rate in the present value formula, reducing the present value of expected income. Therefore, a higher risk premium reduces an asset's price.

Table 3.2 summarizes the ideas behind the classical theory of asset prices.

↑ risk ↑ i
Stocks have higher risk premiums than bonds
↑ φ ↓ AP.

The Gordon Growth Model of Stock Prices

Stock prices are among the most closely watched asset prices in an economy. The classical theory says a stock price is the present value of expected dividends per share. Using this idea to value stocks can be cumbersome, however, as it requires year-by-year forecasts of dividends into the distant future. Therefore, economists have sought easier ways to calculate stock prices.

One approach was proposed by Myron Gordon in 1959. Gordon pointed out that many firms raise dividends fairly steadily over time. To capture this behavior in a simple way, he assumed that expected dividends grow at a constant rate g. If expected dividends next year are D_1, expected dividends in the following years are $D_1(1 + g)$, $D_1(1 + g)^2$, and so on.

Stock Price
According to CT of AP
$$PV = \frac{D}{(1+i)^n}$$

Assumption than D grows.

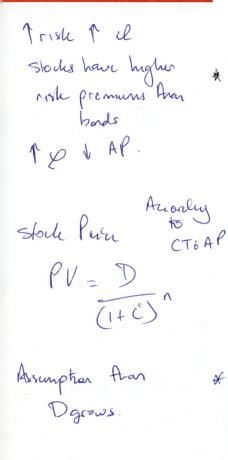

TABLE 3.2 The Classical Theory of Asset Prices

- An asset price equals the present value of expected income from the asset.
- Expectations about income are rational. Expected income is the best possible forecast based on all available information.
- The interest rate in the present value formula is a risk-adjusted rate. It equals the safe interest rate plus a risk premium: $i = i^{safe} + \varphi$.

with g

With the assumption of constant dividend growth, we can derive a firm's stock price from Equation (3.5), in which the present value of any steadily growing income stream is $Z/(i - g)$, where Z is the first payment and g is the payment growth rate. In Gordon's analysis, the first payment Z equals D_1, the first expected dividend, implying the following:

i is the adjusted IR for stock -

Calculation

GORDON GROWTH MODEL

$$\text{stock price} = \frac{D_1}{(i - g)} \qquad (3.8)$$

where i is the risk-adjusted interest rate for the stock. Equation (3.8) is called the **Gordon growth model** because it emphasizes the expected growth rate of dividends as a determinant of stock prices.

> **Gordon growth model**
> theory in which a stock price *P* is determined by an initial expected dividend, the expected growth rate of dividends, and the risk-adjusted interest rate: $P = D_1/(i - g)$

3.3 FLUCTUATIONS IN ASSET PRICES

If you follow the financial news, you will notice that asset prices move around a lot. Stock and bond prices rise and fall, providing ample subject matter for TV and Internet analysts. What are the basic forces behind these price movements?

Why Do Asset Prices Change?

The classical theory says an asset price is the present value of expected income from the asset. This present value changes if expected income changes or if interest rates change.

In CT why do AP change

① D is expected

+ the relation between exp + assess income

Stock prices change frequently because of changes in expected income from the stock. These changes occur when there is news, good or bad, about a company's prospects. If a drug company patents a new wonder drug that helps people lose weight without changing their eating habits, rational expectations of the company's earnings rise. Higher expected earnings mean larger expected dividends for stockholders, so the stock price rises accordingly. If a car company's new model is recalled because of safety defects, its expected earnings and stock price fall. If there are signs that the whole economy is entering a recession, expected earnings and stock prices are likely to fall for many companies.

② Δ in IR.

Expectations
↑ Expectations
↑ Dividends.
↑ Price Rise.

↓ Expectations
↓ Dividends
↓ Price falls.

Such news has less effect on bond prices than on stock prices because the income from a bond is fixed as long as the issuer does not default. As a result, news about companies' prospects often has little effect on the expected income from bonds.

Changes in interest rates, however, affect the prices of both stocks and bonds. A higher interest rate reduces asset prices because it reduces the present value of any income flow. Recall that the relevant interest rate is the risk-adjusted rate, the economy's safe rate plus a risk premium ($i^{\text{safe}} + \varphi$). An asset price falls if the safe rate rises or the risk premium rises. The risk premium might rise because of greater uncertainty about income from the asset. For example, uncertainty about a firm's stock could rise if competitors enter its industry and people are unsure about how much business the firm will lose.

IR affect S+B.

AP ↓ / i^{safe} ↑ or α ↑

CASE STUDY

The Fed and the Stock Market

In Chapter 2, we described the excitement around Ben Bernanke's appointment as Federal Reserve chair in 2005. We can now see one reason the Fed is so important: monetary policy has strong influences on asset prices. When the Fed adjusts the money supply to push interest rates up or down, asset prices often react within minutes. Let's use the classical theory of asset prices to examine the reaction of stock prices. When the Fed raises interest rates, the stock market is affected in several ways, summarized in **Figure 3.1**:

- One rate determined by the Fed is the economy's safe interest rate. A higher safe rate reduces the present value of dividends received by stockholders, which decreases stock prices.

- Higher interest rates reduce spending by consumers and firms. The economy slows, reducing expected earnings for many companies. As a result, expected dividends for these companies fall, which again reduces stock prices.

- Some economists think there is a third effect when interest rates rise: higher risk premiums. A slower economy not only reduces expected earnings but also raises uncertainty, because it is hard to predict how badly companies will be hurt by the slowdown. Greater uncertainty means higher risk premiums, which raise risk-adjusted interest rates and decrease present values and stock prices.

FIGURE 3.1 The Fed and the Stock Market

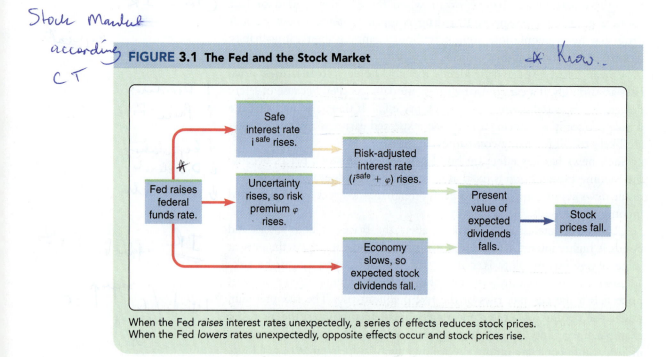

When the Fed *raises* interest rates unexpectedly, a series of effects reduces stock prices. When the Fed *lowers* rates unexpectedly, opposite effects occur and stock prices rise.

When the Fed raises interest rates, all three effects reduce the present value of dividends, pushing stock prices down. If the Fed reduces rates, the three effects work in reverse, and stock prices rise.

A qualification: Fed actions have large effects *only when they are unexpected*. If people know the Fed is going to change interest rates, stock prices are likely to adjust in advance, and nothing happens when the Fed moves. In contrast, surprise rate changes cause sharp jumps in stock prices.

Ben Bernanke understands all this, because he studied the effects of Fed policies during his career as an economics professor. He estimated the effects of interest rate changes on the stock market in a 2005 paper with Kenneth Kuttner of Williams College.

Bernanke and Kuttner examined the period from 1989 to 2002. They measured changes in stock prices on days when the Fed made surprise announcements about interest rates. On average, a rise in rates of 0.25 percent—say, from 4.0 percent to 4.25 percent—caused stock prices to drop suddenly by about 1 percent. A decrease in interest rates had the opposite effect: a cut of 0.25 percent *raised* stock prices by 1 percent.[*]

[*] See Ben Bernanke and Kenneth Kuttner, "What Explains the Stock Market's Reaction to Federal Reserve Policy?" *Journal of Finance* (June 2005): 1221–1257.

Which Asset Prices Are Most Volatile?

All asset prices change over time, but some fluctuate more than others. Let's discuss why some asset prices are especially volatile.

Long-Term Bond Prices Changes in interest rates are the primary reason for changes in bond prices. (As noted earlier, expected income flows are constant unless default risk changes.) If interest rates in an economy rise, then all bond prices fall. But the size of the effect differs depending on bond maturities. *A change in interest rates has a larger effect on prices of long-term bonds than on prices of short-term bonds.*

The reason for this difference is that short-term bonds provide income only in the near future, whereas most payments on long-term bonds come later. The present value of payments is affected more strongly by the interest rate if the payments come later.

To illustrate this point, **Table 3.3** compares bonds with maturities ranging from 1 year to 30 years. Each bond has a face value of $100 and coupon payments of $5 per year. The table shows the prices of the bonds when the interest rate is 4 percent and when it is 6 percent. The longer a bond's maturity, the greater the percentage fall in the price when the interest rate rises.

For example, the owner of a 1-year bond receives a single coupon payment of $5 plus the face value of $100, both paid after 1 year. When the interest rate rises from 4 percent to 6 percent, the present value of these payments, and thus the bond's price, falls from $100.96 to $99.06. This decrease is only 1.89 percent of the bond's initial price. In contrast, the owner of a 30-year bond receives a series of coupon payments over 30 years plus the face value at the end of 30 years. When the interest rate rises, the

TABLE 3.3 Bond Prices, Maturity, and Interest Rates

This table shows how much bond prices fall when the interest rate (*i*) rises from 4% to 6%. All bonds have a face value of $100 and annual coupon payments of $5. The change in the interest rate has larger effects on prices of long-term bonds than on prices of short-term bonds.

Years to Maturity	Price if $i = 4\%$	Price if $i = 6\%$	Percentage Fall in Price from Increase in i
1	$100.96	$99.06	1.89
2	101.89	98.17	3.65
3	102.78	97.33	5.30
4	103.63	96.53	6.85
5	104.45	95.79	8.29
10	108.11	92.64	14.31
15	111.12	90.29	18.75
20	113.59	88.53	22.06
25	115.62	87.22	24.57
30	117.29	86.24	26.48

price of this bond falls from $117.29 to $86.24, a decrease in of 26.48 percent. Because the bond's payments are stretched over a long period, a rise in the interest rate can wipe out a large part of the bond's value.

Stock Prices Prices for stocks are more volatile than prices for bonds, even long-term bonds. Stock prices fluctuate greatly for two reasons. First, like long-term bonds, stocks yield income far into the future: a firm's earnings continue indefinitely. Changes in interest rates have large effects on the present value of this long-term income. Second, as we've discussed, news about firms and the economy causes changes in expected earnings and dividends and thus in stock prices. Fluctuations in stock prices caused by changes in expected earnings add to the fluctuations caused by changes in interest rates.

3.4 ASSET-PRICE BUBBLES

The classical theory of asset prices says an asset price equals the present value of expected income from the asset. Is this just a theory, or does it explain asset-price movements in the real world?

The answer to this question is controversial. Clearly there are elements of truth in the theory. We have seen, for example, that it helps explain how stock prices react to Federal Reserve policies. However, many economists believe that changes in asset prices can occur for reasons outside the classical theory—reasons other than changes in interest rates or expected income.

Sometimes, for example, asset-price increases are part of an **asset-price bubble**. In a bubble, asset prices rise rapidly even though there is no change in interest rates or expected income to justify the rise. Let's discuss how bubbles can occur and the debate over their relevance to the asset-price movements that we observe in the economy.

> **Asset-price bubble** rapid rise in asset prices that is not justified by changes in interest rates or expected asset income

How Bubbles Work

When a bubble occurs, an asset price rises simply because people *expect* it to rise. To see how this might happen, suppose a famous stock analyst announces that the stock of Acme Corporation is hot: the stock price is likely to rise rapidly in the future. Let's assume the expert doesn't really have a good reason for this view; he is just trying to get attention with a bold prediction. Nonetheless, many people believe the expert and rush to buy Acme. This increased demand pushes up the price of the stock. The expert looks smart, and a bubble has begun.

Once a bubble begins, it feeds on itself. When Acme's price starts rising, more and more people decide the stock is hot. They buy Acme stock, pushing the price higher still. The stock looks even hotter, more buyers rush in, and so on.

As the bubble expands, Acme's price rises far above the level dictated by the classical theory: the present value of earnings per share. People pay more for the stock than it is really worth. They buy it because they expect the price to rise even higher in the future, and therefore they expect to be able to sell the stock for a profit.

The problem with bubbles is that they eventually pop. At some point Acme's price will rise so high that people begin to doubt whether price increases can continue. They stop buying the stock and start to sell what they have. This fall in demand for the stock and increase in supply cause the price to fall back toward the level dictated by the classical theory. Many people who bought Acme at the height of the bubble will lose a lot when the bubble bursts.

Bubbles can arise in many kinds of asset prices. From January 2002 to July 2006, for example, the price of the average house in the United States rose 71 percent. During that period, many people bought second homes or rental properties, believing that prices would continue to rise and that they would make lots of money when they sold their property. The bubble was also fueled by an increase in the availability of home-mortgage loans. Lenders relaxed their standards for borrowers' incomes and credit histories, allowing more people to enter the housing market. This development increased housing demand and pushed up prices.

The peak of the housing bubble occurred in July 2006. Between then and April 2009, the average house price fell 33 percent. The losses to homeowners produced a surge of defaults on mortgage loans, which triggered the U.S. financial crisis of 2007–2009.

In addition to stocks and houses, history has seen bubbles in the prices of bonds, foreign currencies, precious metals, and commodities such as coffee and sugar. The next case study discusses one famous bubble.

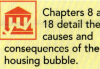 Chapters 8 and 18 detail the causes and consequences of the housing bubble.

Tulipmania

A dramatic asset-price bubble occurred in Holland in the 1630s. Oddly enough, the asset was tulip bulbs. Holland was growing wealthy from foreign trade. Merchants showed off their new wealth by building estates, which included fancy gardens. The tulip, originally from Turkey, reached Holland in 1593, and its dramatic colors made it the most popular flower. Certain rare varieties were especially prized for their intricate patterns. These tulips became status symbols.

The supply of tulips was limited, as they reproduce slowly; a tulip yields only one or two new bulbs in a year. The combination of high demand and low supply meant that bulb prices rose rapidly. In 1633, someone traded three rare bulbs for a house. In 1634, someone offered 3000 guilders, roughly the annual income of a wealthy merchant, for one bulb. The offer was turned down.

Initially, such prices reflected the true value of tulips, in the sense that people were willing to pay that much to plant bulbs in their gardens. But at some point—historians differ on when—a bubble emerged. People without gardens started buying bulbs. They planned to make money by reselling the bulbs after prices rose even higher.

In 1636, tulipmania swept Holland. Word spread that tulip bulbs were the way to get rich quickly. People mortgaged their property to borrow money and buy bulbs. Groups met regularly in taverns to trade bulbs.

The bubble started in prices of rare bulbs but then spread to common tulips, which had previously been inexpensive. Prices for common bulbs exploded in the winter of 1636–37. The price of one variety, the Switser tulip, rose from 1 guilder in January 1637 to 30 guilders in February.

February 1637 was the peak of the bubble. At that point, the government started discussing measures to end it, such as giving tulip buyers the right to renege on contracts. This development shook people's confidence in tulips, and they stopped buying. Prices for many bulbs fell by more than 90 percent in February and stayed low. In 1722, a Switser bulb cost one-twentieth of a guilder.[*]

[*] For more on this episode, see Mike Dash, *Tulipmania: The Story of the World's Most Coveted Flower and the Extraordinary Passions It Aroused*, Weidenfeld and Nicholson Publishers, 1999.

Looking for Bubbles

Economists often debate whether bubbles are occurring in asset prices. Discussions of stock prices sometimes focus on **price–earnings (P/E) ratios**, the price of stock divided by earnings per share. Using earnings over the recent past, economists compute P/E ratios for individual companies and the average P/E ratio for the stock market. Some think that high P/E ratios are evidence of bubbles.

Price–earnings ratio (P/E ratio) a company's stock price divided by earnings per share over the recent past

How P/E determine bubbles.

P ↑ then PE ↑

To see why, recall the classical theory: a stock price equals the present value of expected dividends per share, which depends on expected earnings. It is difficult to test this theory, because we can't directly measure expectations of future earnings. But some economists argue that earnings in the recent past are a good guide to future earnings. If a stock price is unusually high compared to past earnings—if the P/E ratio is high—then the price is probably high relative to future earnings, meaning it is higher than it should be under the classical theory. A bubble may be underway.

According to the classical theory, high P/E ratios could be explained by low interest rates. Low rates raise the present value of future income, pushing up stock prices. In practice, however, stocks' P/E ratios sometimes rise without changes in interest rates. These cases may be explained by bubbles.

It is important to note that a high P/E ratio indicates a bubble *only* if recent earnings are a good predictor of future earnings. If earnings are expected to grow rapidly, then recent earnings are not a good predictor of future earnings. For example, suppose a company is developing a promising new product. The company's current earnings are low, but earnings are expected to rise a lot when the product is introduced. According to the classical theory, high expected earnings imply a high stock price. With current earnings low, the classical theory predicts a high P/E ratio.

Economists have tried to determine the correct interpretation of P/E ratios. Do high ratios usually signal a bubble? Or are they more likely to reflect expectations of high earnings growth? Some researchers address this issue by examining what happens to stock prices *after* a period of high P/E ratios. Remember that bubbles eventually end. If a bubble has pushed up the P/E ratio, stock prices are likely to fall later. In contrast, if a high P/E ratio reflects high expected earnings, there is no reason to expect stock prices to fall. Examining later price movements helps to isolate the reasons why the P/E ratio was high.

This approach was introduced in a 1997 paper by John Campbell of Harvard University and Robert Shiller of Yale University. Campbell and Shiller examined the P/E ratio for a large group of companies, the S&P 500. For a given year, they defined P as the average stock price for the group and E as average earnings per share over the previous 10 years. Campbell and Shiller then compared the P/E ratio to the change in stock prices over the following 10 years.

Figure 3.2 illustrates Campbell and Shiller's comparison for the period from 1918 through 2000. In this graph, the horizontal axis is the P/E ratio, and the vertical axis is the average percentage change in stock prices over the next 10 years. We see a negative relationship: when the P/E ratio is high, stock prices are likely to fall. Campbell and Shiller concluded that high P/E ratios are usually caused by bubbles that dissipate in the future.

Campbell and Shiller's research was stimulated by a rapid rise in stock prices during the 1990s. The following case study discusses this period and stock-price fluctuations since then.

FIGURE 3.2 **Evidence for Bubbles?**

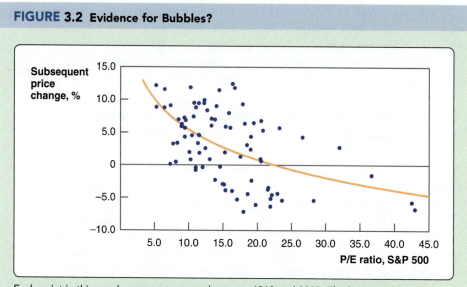

Each point in this graph represents a year between 1918 and 2000. The horizontal axis is the price–earnings ratio for stocks in the S&P 500, based on average earnings over the previous 10 years. The vertical axis is the average percentage change in S&P prices over the following 10 years, adjusted for inflation. (The 10-year change following 2000 is estimated with data through 2009.) The orange "best fit" line through the data points indicates a negative relationship between these two variables: when the P/E ratio is high, stock prices are likely to grow slowly or fall over the following 10 years.

Source: Robert Shiller, Yale University (www.econ.yale.edu/~shiller/data.htm)

CASE STUDY

The U.S. Stock Market, 1990–2010

Figure 3.3 charts the Dow Jones Index of stock prices from 1990 through 2010. We see large swings in prices, which the ideas in this chapter can help us understand. Let's examine stock-price movements over three periods: 1990 to 2003, 2003 to 2007, and 2007 to 2010.

1990–2003: The Tech Boom and Bust The 1990s were a boom period for the stock market. The Dow Jones Index rose from about 2500 at the start of the decade to above 6000 in 1997, when Campbell and Shiller wrote their paper. The index continued to rise after that, peaking at 11,497 in the summer of 2000.

Companies' earnings rose during the 1990s, but not as fast as stock prices. This meant rising P/E ratios. From 1960 to 1995, the average P/E ratio for the Dow Jones Index was about 15. This ratio rose above 40 in 2000. P/E ratios were especially high for stocks of "tech" companies—those involved with computers, software, and the Internet. Many of these companies had P/E ratios above 100.

During the 1990s, many economists argued that a stock market bubble was underway. Federal Reserve Chair Alan Greenspan supported this idea

FIGURE 3.3 U.S. Stock Prices, 1990–2010

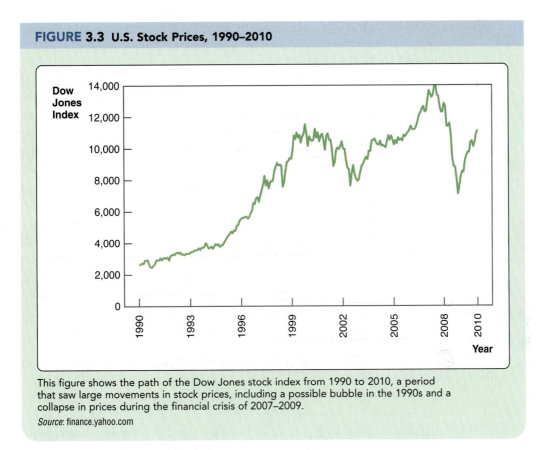

This figure shows the path of the Dow Jones stock index from 1990 to 2010, a period that saw large movements in stock prices, including a possible bubble in the 1990s and a collapse in prices during the financial crisis of 2007–2009.

Source: finance.yahoo.com

in a famous 1996 speech. Greenspan suggested that stock prices had been "unduly escalated" by "irrational exuberance," meaning prices had risen above the levels dictated by the classical theory.

Others argued that the high P/E ratios were in line with the classical theory. They pointed to the rapid spread of computer and Internet use in the 1990s. These technologies raised productivity and reduced costs in many industries, making it rational to expect rapid growth in companies' earnings. As we've discussed, expectations of high earnings growth imply a high P/E ratio in the classical theory.

Stock prices peaked in 2000 then fell for the next 3 years. The Dow Jones Index fell below 8000 in 2003. Believers in a stock market bubble claimed vindication. They interpreted the price declines as the bursting of the bubble and evidence that stocks were never really worth the prices of the late 1990s.

But again, not all analysts agree with this interpretation. Believers in the classical theory point to the effects of several bad-news stories between 2000 and 2003: the terrorist attacks of September 11, 2001; the discovery of false accounting at companies such as Enron; and the recession of 2001. These events reduced companies' expected earnings, possibly explaining the fall in stock prices. So the debate over stock bubbles continues.

2003–2007: Recovery

As we see in Figure 3.3, stock prices started rising again in 2003. The Dow passed its 2000 peak in 2006 and reached 14,000 in mid-2007.

Initially, the rise in stock prices was driven by low interest rates. The Federal Reserve pushed rates down in 2003 because the economy remained weak after the 2001 recession. In 2004, the Fed started raising rates, but an economic recovery sustained the stock market boom. In contrast to the 1990s, the P/E ratio for the Dow was stable in the mid-2000s, suggesting that rising prices reflected increases in companies' earnings rather than a bubble.

2007–2010: The Financial Crisis and Its Aftermath

Stock prices started falling in late 2007 as the housing bubble burst and disrupted financial markets. The decline accelerated after the failure of Lehman Brothers, a major investment bank, in September 2008. The Dow reached a trough of 6547 in March 2009.

The financial crisis reduced stock prices through two channels. First, it reduced expectations of companies' future earnings and dividends. Initially, expected earnings fell for financial firms hit directly by the crisis. As the effects of the crisis spread through the economy, earnings forecasts also fell for nonfinancial firms.

Second, the financial crisis increased risk premiums. Unprecedented events created uncertainty about how bad the crisis would get. This uncertainty was reflected in large day-to-day swings in stock prices as traders reacted to the latest news. In the last four months of 2008, the Dow Jones Index rose or fell by 5 percent or more on nine different days. Uncertainty about companies' prospects raised risk premiums for their stocks.

In response to the financial crisis, the Federal Reserve pushed down the economy's safe interest rate (i^{safe}). As measured by the rate on 3-month government bonds (Treasury bills), the safe interest rate fell below 0.1 percent at the end of 2008. However, the decrease in the safe rate was smaller than the increases in risk premiums for stocks (φ). This difference implied an increase in risk-adjusted interest rates ($i^{safe} + \varphi$), which reduced the present value of future income. The combination of this effect and lower expected income caused stock prices to fall sharply.

In March 2009, the fall in stock prices ended. The Dow Jones Index rose over the next year and reached 11,000 in April 2010. Rising stock prices reflected a growing belief that the worst of the financial crisis was over, largely because of government and Federal Reserve efforts to save financial institutions from failure. This optimism raised earnings forecasts for companies and reduced risk premiums, partially reversing the fall in stock prices during the crisis. At the end of 2010, however, the Dow remained far below the 14,000 level it had reached in 2007.

3.5 ASSET-PRICE CRASHES

Believers in asset-price bubbles think that bubbles eventually end and prices fall. Sometimes this occurs gradually over a period of months or years. The bubble in U.S. stock prices was reversed over the period 2000–2003 and the

Chapters 5 and 18 discuss the failure of Lehman Brothers and its impact on financial markets.

Online Case Study
An Update on the Stock Market

housing bubble over 2006–2009. At other times, however, a bubble ends with an **asset-price crash** as prices plummet over a very short period.

We saw earlier that Holland's tulip bubble ended with a crash in 1637. In U.S. history, the most famous crashes have occurred in the stock market. In both 1929 and 1987, stock prices fell dramatically *within a single day*. Crashes can have disastrous effects on the economy if policymakers do not handle them well. Let's discuss how crashes occur.

How Crashes Work

In CT of AP

Crashes are hard to explain with the classical theory of asset prices. Under that theory, prices fall sharply only if there is a large drop in the present value of expected asset income. This requires either a rise in interest rates or bad news about future income, and crashes often occur without such events. For example, when the stock market crashed on October 19, 1987, prices fell by 23 percent, yet interest rates were stable on that day, and there was no significant news about companies' earnings or dividends.

A crash is easier to explain if it is preceded by an asset-price bubble. At some point during a bubble, people start worrying that it will end. They would like to hold assets as long as prices rise but sell before the bubble bursts. So they watch alertly for the end of the bubble.

At some point, a few asset holders get especially nervous and decide to start selling. Others notice this and fear that the bubble may be ending. They sell, too, hoping to dump their assets before prices fall too much. These actions push down prices, causing more people to sell. Pessimism about prices is self-fulfilling, just as optimism is self-fulfilling during a bubble.

Once a crash starts, it can accelerate rapidly. As prices fall, panic sets in, many asset holders try to sell at the same time, and prices plummet. Eventually, prices fall far enough to make the assets attractive again. At this point, prices may be *below* the present value of expected income, so it is more profitable to hold assets than to sell them. The rush to sell abates, and prices stabilize.

According to this reasoning, a crash is a risk whenever an asset-price bubble is underway. However, nobody knows how to explain why crashes occur on particular days. Sometimes there is a small piece of news, such as a report of low company earnings, that makes asset holders more nervous. But often the timing of a crash appears arbitrary. Even in retrospect, we do not know why the 1987 crash occurred on October 19 rather than some other day.

CASE STUDY

The Two Big Crashes

Stock prices rose rapidly during the Roaring Twenties: the Dow Jones stock index climbed from 70 in 1921 to 365 in September 1929. This performance reflected excitement about new technologies, such as cars, radios, and electric appliances. The demand for stocks was also fueled by people's ability to "buy on margin," that is, to buy stock on credit, with only a small down payment.

Asset-price crash large, rapid fall in asset prices

▶ The decline in stock prices over 2007–2009 does not qualify as a crash by our definition. Unlike the 1929 and 1987 episodes, it was not concentrated in a very short time period. A related difference is that it's easy to identify bad news about the economy that contributed to the 2007–2009 price decline.

Price

P < PV so more profitable to hold than sell.

In retrospect, the 1920s' experience looks like a classic bubble, but economists did not recognize this at the time. On October 17, 1929, economist Irving Fisher of Yale University commented that "stock prices have reached what looks like a permanently high plateau."

It is not clear why the crash occurred just when it did. Increases in interest rates in early 1929 may have made stockholders nervous, because they reduced the present values of company earnings. In any case, the stock market fluctuated erratically for several months and then plummeted. The largest one-day decline occurred on "Black Monday," October 28, when the Dow dropped by 13 percent. This crash was followed by a series of smaller declines. In July 1932, the Dow reached a low of 41.

October 19, 1987: Traders at the New York Stock Exchange work frantically as stock prices plummet.

The 1987 crash was in some ways a repeat of 1929. It followed a rapid rise in prices: the Dow climbed from 786 in 1980 to 2655 in August 1987. Some observers suggested that a bubble was underway, but again the crash was unexpected. The market started falling on October 14, and the bottom fell out on October 19, the second Black Monday. That day the Dow dropped 23 percent, easily beating the 1929 record for a one-day drop.

The 1987 crash was exacerbated by the use of computers to trade stocks. Computers sped up trading, so prices fell more quickly than in 1929. Moreover, in 1987 large stockholders such as mutual funds had systems of *program trading* in which computers automatically sold stock if the market fell by a certain amount. These systems were designed to get rid of stocks quickly if a crash was underway. When the crash occurred, program trading worsened the vicious circle of falling prices and heavy selling.

Despite the similarities between the two crashes, their aftermaths differed. After October 1929, stock prices stayed depressed. The Dow did not climb back to its precrash level until 1954. In 1987, the market bounced back quickly. The Dow reached its precrash level in 1989 and kept rising through the 1990s.

The two crashes also had different effects on the overall economy. The 1929 crash contributed to the Great Depression of the 1930s, whereas economic growth was strong after the 1987 crash. Part of the explanation is the different responses of the Federal Reserve. The Fed responded passively to

Chapters 11 and 18 discuss the causes of the Great Depression.

the 1929 crash and the bank panics that followed. In 1987, the Fed lent money to financial institutions threatened by the crash, thus preventing a major disruption of the financial system.

Crash Prevention

How to Prevent crashes.

Is there any way to prevent asset-price crashes? Both the federal government and stock exchanges have imposed rules for stock trading to make crashes less likely. Let's discuss two rules, one adopted after the 1929 crash and one after the 1987 crash.

Margin Requirements After the 1929 crash, Congress gave the Federal Reserve authority to establish **margin requirements**. These are limits on the amount that people can borrow to buy stock. Margin requirements have varied over time, but in recent years they have been around 50 percent. This means that stock purchasers must pay at least 50 percent of the cost with their own money.

This regulation tries to curtail the buildup of stock price bubbles that precede crashes. As we have discussed, the practice of buying on margin helped fuel the stock market boom of the 1920s. Margin requirements make such a price run-up less likely. When prices don't rise as high, there is less danger they will fall sharply.

> **Margin requirements**
> limits on the use of credit to purchase stocks

Circuit Breakers After the 1987 crash, some securities exchanges established **circuit breakers**, requirements to shut down trading temporarily if prices fall sharply. These rules are motivated by the view that crashes are a vicious circle of panic and falling prices. A circuit breaker stops this process; it gives people time to calm down and assess the true value of their assets. If the circuit breaker works, the rush to sell subsides and prices stabilize when the exchange reopens. (In other words, panicky asset traders are like naughty 4-year-olds: they behave more rationally after a time-out.)

At the New York Stock Exchange, current rules mandate a suspension of trading if the Dow Jones Index falls 10 percent within a day. The length of the suspension depends on the size of the fall and the time of day. For example, trading halts for an hour if prices fall 10–20 percent before 2 PM. Larger decreases can halt trading for the rest of the day.

So far, trading on the New York Stock Exchange has been interrupted only once—on July 27, 1997. At that time the rules set smaller price declines as triggers for circuit breakers. The Dow Jones Index fell 7 percent, which was enough to shut down the exchange for the rest of the day.

> **Circuit breaker**
> requirement that a securities exchange shut down temporarily if prices drop by a specified percentage

3.6 MEASURING INTEREST RATES AND ASSET RETURNS

In the previous sections, we have studied how asset prices are determined and why they change over time. With this background, we can define two concepts that are closely related to asset prices: a bond's yield to maturity and the rate of return on a stock or bond. We will use these concepts frequently as we discuss stock and bond markets in future chapters.

Yield to Maturity

Buying a bond means lending money to the company or government that issues the bond. In deciding whether to buy a bond, people compare the interest the bond pays to the interest they could receive on other bonds or on deposits in a bank account.

Comparing interest is not as straightforward as it might seem, however. Unlike the stated interest rate on a bank account, the interest rate on a bond is not always obvious. Consider a bond with a $100 face value, 4 years to maturity, coupon payments of $5 per year, and a price of $95. If you buy this bond, what interest rate will you earn?

Economists answer this question by calculating the bond's **yield to maturity**. This concept is based on the classical theory of asset prices. Earlier, we used this theory to derive Equation (3.6), which gives the price of a bond:

> **Yield to maturity** interest rate that makes the present value of payments from a bond equal to its price

$$\text{bond price} = \frac{C}{(1+i)} + \frac{C}{(1+i)^2} + \cdots + \frac{C}{(1+i)^{T-1}} + \frac{(C+F)}{(1+i)^T}$$

where C is the coupon payment, F is the face value, T is the maturity, and i is the interest rate. This equation tells us that a bond's price equals the present value of payments from the bond. We can use it to calculate the price if we assume a certain interest rate.

To measure yield to maturity, we turn this calculation around. We know the payments on a bond and the bond's price, and we use the previous equation to derive an interest rate. This interest rate is the bond's yield to maturity, the rate that makes the present value of the bond's payments equal to its price.

Recall the example of a bond with a 4-year maturity, a $100 face value, and $5 coupon payments. If the bond's price is $95, our bond-price equation implies

$$95 = \frac{5}{(1+i)} + \frac{5}{(1+i)^2} + \frac{5}{(1+i)^3} + \frac{105}{(1+i)^4}$$

The yield to maturity is the interest rate i that solves this equation. Here, the solution is $i = 0.065$, or an interest rate of 6.5 percent.

A technical note: Usually, there is no easy way to solve equations like the last one. You have to use trial and error, plugging in different values for i until you find one that makes the right side equal to the 95 on the left. Fortunately, a computer or financial calculator can do this for you quickly.

Recall that the classical theory implies that asset prices move inversely with interest rates. In the case of bonds, this principle is true by definition: it follows from how we measure the yield to maturity. If the price on the left side of our equation goes up, the interest rate on the right must go down for the equation to hold.

In our example of a 4-year bond, if the price rises from $95 to $98, the yield to maturity falls from 6.5 percent to 5.6 percent. If this happens, you might hear on the news that "bond prices rose" or that "interest rates on bonds fell." These are two ways of saying the same thing.

[handwritten: $\frac{P_1 - P_0}{P_0} + \frac{X}{P_0}$]

The Rate of Return

Suppose you buy a stock or bond and hold onto it for a year. How much have you earned by holding the security? You have potentially increased your wealth in two ways: *[handwritten: Ways to increase your wealth]*

1. The security may pay you directly. A bond may yield a coupon payment. If you own a company's stock, you do not directly receive the company's profits, but you may receive a dividend. *[handwritten: Coupon or Dividend.]*

2. The price of the security may change. If the price rises, you own a more valuable asset, so your wealth rises. This is called a **capital gain**. Of course the price may also fall, causing a **capital loss**.

The total amount you gain from holding the security is the capital gain or loss plus any direct payment you receive. This total is called the **return** on the security:

$$\text{return} = (P_1 - P_0) + X$$ *[handwritten: Coupon / Dividend]*

where P_0 is the initial price of the security, P_1 is the price after you hold it for a year, and X represents a direct payment. (X can be a coupon payment, C, or a dividend, D.)

The **rate of return** on a security is the return expressed as a percentage of the initial price. It is calculated by dividing the return by the price:

AN ASSET'S RATE OF RETURN *[handwritten: RoR.]*

$$\text{rate of return} = \frac{\text{return}}{P_0} = \frac{(P_1 - P_0)}{P_0} + \frac{X}{P_0} \tag{3.9}$$

The rate of return has two parts. The first is the percentage change in the security price, and the second is the direct payment divided by the initial price.

Suppose in 2020 you buy a bond for $80. In 2021, the bond makes a coupon payment of $4 and the price rises to $82. Plugging these numbers into Equation (3.9), the rate of return is

$$\frac{(82 - 80)}{80} + \frac{4}{80} = 0.075, \text{ or } 7.5\%$$ *[handwritten: Profit / Gain.]*

If the bond makes a coupon payment of $4 but the price falls from $80 to $75, the rate of return is

$$\frac{(75 - 80)}{80} + \frac{4}{80} = -0.013, \text{ or } -1.3\%$$ *[handwritten: Loss]*

As this example illustrates, the rate of return can be negative if there is a large enough capital loss.

Capital gain increase in an asset holder's wealth from a change in the asset's price

Capital loss decrease in an asset holder's wealth from a change in the asset's price

Return total earnings from a security; the capital gain or loss plus any direct payment (coupon payment or dividend); return = $(P_1 - P_0) + X$

Rate of return return on a security as a percentage of its initial price; rate of return = $(P_1 - P_0)/P_0 + X/P_0$

▶ In the case of a bond, the second term in the rate-of-return formula is the coupon payment divided by the initial price, C/P_0. This variable is called the *current yield* on the bond.

Returns on Stocks and Bonds

Figure 3.4 traces some data on rates of return. It shows the average rates of return on U.S. stocks and Treasury bonds from 1900 through 2009. You can see immediately that stock returns are more volatile than bond returns. This reflects the fact that stock prices fluctuate more than bond prices, as we discussed in Section 3.3. Changes in stock prices cause large swings in the rate of return.

RoR ↑ for Stocks.

While returns on stock are more volatile than those on bonds, the average rate of return is higher for stocks. For the period from 1900 through 2009, the average rate of return was about 11 percent for stocks and 5 percent for bonds. This difference should make sense. As we discussed earlier, savers choose assets with more uncertain, or volatile, income only if they are compensated with a risk premium—a higher average return.

Rate of Return Versus Yield to Maturity

People are often confused about the difference between the rate of return on a bond and the yield to maturity. Both variables tell us something about how much you earn by holding the bond. But they can behave quite differently. For example, a decrease in a bond's price can simultaneously cause

FIGURE 3.4 Stock and Bond Returns, 1900–2009

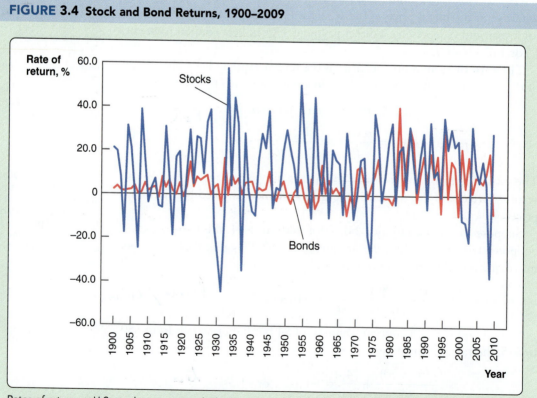

Rates of return on U.S. stocks are more volatile than rates of return on Treasury bonds.

Source: Jeremy Siegel, University of Pennsylvania (jeremysiegel.com)

an increase in the yield to maturity (because a bond's price and its yield are inversely related) and a *negative* rate of return (because bondholders suffer capital losses). If you are thinking of buying a bond, which variable should you care about?

The answer depends on how long you are likely to hold the bond. If you hold the bond until it matures, the yield to maturity tells what interest rate you receive. Fluctuations in the bond's price, which affect the rate of return, are irrelevant if you never sell the bond.

On the other hand, if you sell the bond after a year, you will receive the rate of return for the year. The yield to maturity does not matter if you don't hold the bond to maturity.

3.7 REAL AND NOMINAL INTEREST RATES

We now introduce a crucial distinction between two kinds of interest rates, *nominal interest rates* and *real interest rates*. The rates we have discussed so far are nominal interest rates, but we'll see that real rates are more important for economic decisions. What is the difference?

A **nominal interest rate** is the interest rate offered by a bank account or a bond. If a sign at your bank says "savings accounts now paying 4.2%," then 4.2 percent is a nominal interest rate. If you calculate that a bond's yield to maturity is 5.8 percent, that is also a nominal rate.

The **real interest rate** is the nominal rate minus the inflation rate. Economists use the letter *r* for the real rate, *i* for the nominal rate, and π for the inflation rate. Thus we can write   *Fisher equation.*

$$r = i - \pi \qquad\qquad (3.10)$$

> **Nominal interest rate (i)**
> interest rate offered by a bank account or bond
>
> **Real interest rate (r)**
> nominal interest rate minus the inflation rate;
> $r = i - \pi$

If your bank pays a 5-percent nominal interest rate and the inflation rate is 3 percent, then the real interest rate is $5\% - 3\% = 2\%$.

What's the meaning of the real interest rate? Suppose again that the nominal rate is 5 percent and the inflation rate is 3 percent. You put $100 in the bank and it grows to $105 after a year. Does that mean you are 5 percent richer? Not really, because the value of your money has been eroded by inflation.

A 3-percent inflation rate means that each of your dollars is worth 3 percent less than a year ago. The bank has paid you 5 percent of your initial deposit, but inflation has taken away 3 percent of its value. Subtracting your loss from your gain, the value of your deposit has risen 2 percent. This 2 percent is the real interest rate.

Generally, economists think the behavior of consumers and firms depends on real interest rates, not nominal rates. For example, real rates help determine how much people save out of their incomes. Savers care how much their wealth will grow after accounting for the losses from inflation.

Figure 3.5 graphs real and nominal interest rates from 1960 through 2010. The green line shows a nominal rate, the yield to maturity on 3-month Treasury bills. The orange line shows the real rate, measured as the nominal rate minus inflation over the previous year.

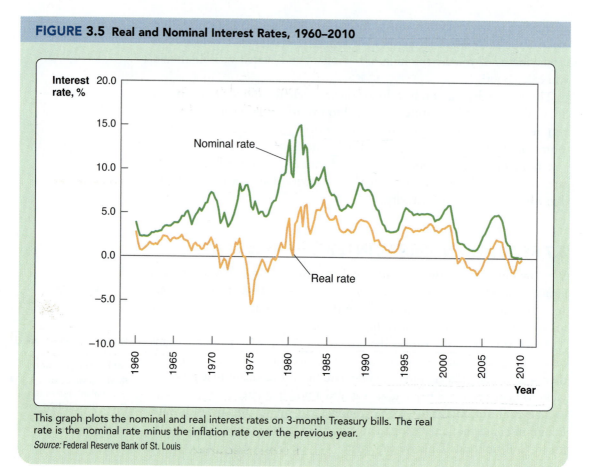

FIGURE 3.5 **Real and Nominal Interest Rates, 1960–2010**

This graph plots the nominal and real interest rates on 3-month Treasury bills. The real rate is the nominal rate minus the inflation rate over the previous year.

Source: Federal Reserve Bank of St. Louis

The graph shows that real and nominal interest rates can move quite differently. In the 1970s, nominal rates were high, but inflation was also high, so real interest rates were low or negative. Since the 1980s, low inflation has kept nominal and real rates closer to one another.

In addition to distinguishing between nominal and real interest rates, economists also define nominal and real versions of asset returns. The rate of return in Equation (3.9) is the *nominal rate of return*. The *real rate of return* is the nominal rate minus the inflation rate. For example, if the nominal rate of return on a stock is 10 percent and inflation is 3 percent, the stock's real rate of return is 10% − 3% = 7%.

Real Interest Rates: Ex Ante Versus Ex Post

Let's now make our definition of the real interest rate more precise. Suppose in 2020 you buy a bond with a 10-year maturity and a nominal interest rate (the yield to maturity) of 7 percent. To find the real interest rate, you must subtract the inflation rate from 7 percent. This raises a question: over what time period should you measure the inflation rate?

The relevant time period is the life of the bond. For a 10-year bond issued in 2020, this is the period from 2020 to 2030. Inflation over this period determines how much of the earnings on the bond are eroded in real terms.

You should see a problem. If you are thinking about buying a bond in 2020, you would like to know the real interest rate that it pays. You can calculate the nominal rate, but you don't have a crystal ball to foretell what inflation will be from 2020 to 2030. What, then, is the real interest rate?

Economists answer this question in two different ways. They define two versions of the real interest rate: *ex ante* and *ex post*. In Latin, *ex ante* means "from before," and *ex post* means "from after." The **ex ante real interest rate** is the nominal rate minus the inflation rate that people *expect* when a bond is sold:

Ex ante real interest rate ($r^{\text{ex ante}}$) nominal interest rate minus expected inflation over the loan period; $r^{\text{ex ante}} = i - \pi^{\text{expected}}$

$$\text{Ex Ante Real Interest Rate}$$
$$r^{\text{ex ante}} = i - \pi^{\text{expected}} \qquad (3.11)$$

In our example, suppose that people's best guess is that inflation will average 2 percent per year over the period 2020–2030. In this case, the ex ante real interest rate is the nominal rate of 7 percent minus 2 percent, or 5 percent.

The **ex post real interest rate** is the nominal rate minus the *actual* inflation rate:

Ex post real interest rate ($r^{\text{ex post}}$) nominal interest rate minus actual inflation over the loan period; $r^{\text{ex post}} = i - \pi^{\text{actual}}$

$$\text{Ex Post Real Interest Rate}$$
$$r^{\text{ex post}} = i - \pi^{\text{actual}} \qquad (3.12)$$

Suppose people expect inflation of 2 percent per year over 2020–2030, but unexpected events cause actual inflation to average 4 percent. The ex post real interest rate is $7\% - 4\% = 3\%$.

When people borrow or lend funds, their decisions depend on the ex ante real interest rate; they don't yet know the ex post rate. In the end, however, the ex post rate determines what borrowers really pay and lenders receive. The ex post rate is lower than the ex ante rate if inflation turns out higher than expected:

$$\pi^{\text{actual}} > \pi^{\text{expected}} \rightarrow r^{\text{ex post}} < r^{\text{ex ante}}$$

The reverse happens if inflation is lower than expected:

$$\pi^{\text{actual}} < \pi^{\text{expected}} \rightarrow r^{\text{ex post}} > r^{\text{ex ante}}$$

In our example, actual inflation turns out to be 4 percent, higher than the expected level of 2 percent. This means the ex post real rate is 3 percent, lower than the ex ante rate of 5 percent.

The difference between ex ante and ex post real interest rates can cause problems for the financial system. The next case study recounts a famous example.

CASE STUDY

Inflation and the Savings and Loan Crisis

In the early 1960s, U.S. inflation rates averaged less than 2 percent per year. This situation appeared stable, so people expected low inflation to continue in the future. However, inflation rose rapidly in the late 1960s and 1970s.

Because actual inflation over this period was higher than expected, ex post real interest rates were lower than ex ante rates. In real terms, lenders received less from borrowers than they expected to receive when they made the loans.

Losses to lenders were greatest for long-term loans, especially home mortgages. In 1965, the nominal interest rate on 30-year mortgages was less than 6 percent. This rate was locked in until 1995. Because inflation was expected to be less than 2 percent, the ex ante real interest rate was positive. However, the inflation rate averaged 7.8 percent over the 1970s, implying negative ex post rates.

Negative real interest rates on mortgages were a great deal for homeowners. But they caused large losses for banks that specialized in mortgages, such as savings and loan associations. These losses were one reason for the so-called S&L crisis of the 1980s, when many savings and loans went bankrupt.

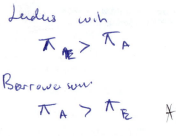
We return to this episode in Chapters 9 and 10.

Inflation-Indexed Bonds

The preceding case study illustrates a general point: *uncertainty about inflation makes it risky to borrow or lend money.* This is true for bank loans, and also when firms borrow by issuing bonds. In both cases, borrowers and lenders agree on a nominal interest rate but gamble on the ex post real rate. Borrowers win the gamble if inflation is higher than expected, and lenders win if inflation is lower than expected.

Can borrowers and lenders avoid this gamble? One tool for reducing risk is **inflation-indexed bonds**. This type of bond guarantees a fixed ex post real interest rate. Unlike a traditional bond, it does not specify a nominal interest rate when it is issued. Instead, the nominal rate adjusts for inflation over the life of the bond, eliminating uncertainty about the real rate.

Inflation-indexed bond bond that promises a fixed real interest rate; the nominal rate is adjusted for inflation over the life of the bond

For example, an indexed bond might promise an ex post real interest rate of 2 percent. This means the nominal rate (i) is 2 percent plus the average inflation rate over the life of the bond, π^{actual}. If the inflation rate turns out to be 3 percent, the nominal interest rate is 5 percent. If the inflation rate is 4 percent, the nominal interest rate is 6 percent. Either way, the ex post real rate, $i - \pi^{\text{actual}}$, is 2 percent. Higher inflation doesn't benefit borrowers at the expense of lenders, or vice versa.

Economists have long advocated the creation of inflation-indexed bonds. The government of the United Kingdom began issuing indexed bonds in 1975, and the U.S. Treasury followed in 1997. The U.S. bonds are called TIPS, for Treasury Inflation Protected Securities.

Yet indexed bonds have not proved very popular. Currently, TIPS account for less than 10 percent of Treasury securities, as most savers prefer to buy traditional bonds. No corporations issue inflation-indexed bonds. Economists find this situation puzzling, since indexed bonds reduce risk, both for borrowers and for lenders. Some economists suggest that savers simply don't understand the benefits of indexation.

Summary

3.1 Valuing Income Streams

- The future value of a dollar is how many dollars it can produce in some future year. The future value of a dollar in n years is $\$(1 + i)^n$, where i is the interest rate.

- The present value of a future dollar is its worth in today's dollars. The present value of a dollar in n years is $\$1/(1 + i)^n$. We can use this formula to find the present value of a stream of income.

- A perpetual payment of $\$Z$ per year has a present value of $\$Z/i$. A perpetual payment that equals $\$Z$ in the first year and grows annually at rate g has a present value of $\$Z/(i - g)$.

3.2 The Classical Theory of Asset Prices

- The classical theory says an asset price equals the present value of expected future income from the asset.

- The price of a company's stock is the present value of expected dividends per share. Expected dividends are influenced strongly by the company's expected earnings.

- The classical theory assumes that expectations are rational: expected asset income is the best possible forecast, given all available information.

- The interest rate used to compute an asset price is a risk-adjusted rate. It equals the safe rate (i^{safe}) plus a risk premium (φ). The risk premium rises with uncertainty about asset income.

- In the Gordon growth model, the price of stock is $D_1/(i - g)$, where D_1 is the expected dividend in 1 year, i is the risk-adjusted interest rate, and g is the expected growth rate of dividends.

3.3 Fluctuations in Asset Prices

- A rise in expected asset income raises asset prices. A rise in interest rates reduces asset prices.

- Actions by the Federal Reserve have strong effects on stock prices because they influence companies' earnings, the safe interest rate, and risk premiums.

- The prices of long-term bonds are more volatile than those of short-term bonds because they respond more strongly to changes in interest rates. Stock prices are more volatile than bond prices because they respond strongly to both interest rate changes and changes in expected company earnings.

3.4 Asset-Price Bubbles

- Some economists believe that asset prices are influenced by bubbles. This means that prices rise above the present value of asset income. People pay high prices for assets because they expect prices to rise even higher.

- Bubbles occur in many types of asset prices, including stock prices and real estate prices. In the seventeenth century, Holland experienced a bubble in the prices of tulip bulbs.

- Some economists think that high price–earnings ratios signal bubbles in the stock market. When P/E ratios are high, returns on stocks are usually low over the next decade.

- Stock prices in the United States rose rapidly in the 1990s and then fell from 2000 to 2003. Some economists interpret this episode as a bubble and its collapse. Prices rose again from 2003 to mid-2007 and then fell greatly during the financial crisis of 2007–2009. The crisis reduced companies' expected earnings and increased risk premiums.

3.5 Asset-Price Crashes

- An asset-price bubble may end with a crash: prices plummet in a short period of time. A crash occurs when asset holders lose confidence, sparking a vicious circle of selling and declining prices.

- U.S. stock prices crashed on two "Black Mondays": October 28, 1929, and October 19, 1987.

- To reduce the risk of crashes, the government has established margin requirements that limit borrowing to buy stock. Securities exchanges have created circuit breakers: trading is suspended if prices fall by large amounts.

3.6 Measuring Interest Rates and Asset Returns

- The interest rate on a bond is measured by the yield to maturity, the interest rate that makes the present value of the bond's payments equal to its price.

- The return on an asset is the change in its price plus any current payment (a coupon payment or stock dividend). The rate of return is the return as a percentage of the initial price.

- The rate of return on stocks is more volatile than the rate of return on bonds, but it is higher on average.

■ A bond's rate of return shows what someone earns by holding the bond for a year and then selling it. The yield to maturity shows the earnings from holding the bond to maturity.

3.7 Real and Nominal Interest Rates

■ The interest rates we observe in financial markets are nominal rates (i). A real interest rate (r) is a nominal rate minus the inflation rate (π).

■ The ex ante real interest rate on a loan or bond is the nominal rate minus the inflation rate *expected* over the life of the loan or bond. The ex post real rate is the nominal rate minus the *actual* inflation rate over the period.

■ When inflation is higher than expected, ex post real interest rates are lower than ex ante rates, benefiting borrowers at the expense of lenders. The reverse occurs when inflation is lower than expected. The rise in inflation in the 1970s produced negative ex post rates, which helped cause the savings and loan crisis of the 1980s.

■ Inflation-indexed bonds guarantee fixed real interest rates. The nominal interest rate adjusts for inflation, eliminating the effect of inflation on the ex post real rate.

Key Terms

asset-price bubble, p. 65

asset-price crash, p. 71

capital gain, p. 75

capital loss, p. 75

circuit breaker, p. 73

classical theory of asset prices, p. 57

dividend, p. 58

ex ante real interest rate, $r^{\text{ex ante}}$, p. 79

ex post real interest rate, $r^{\text{ex post}}$, p. 79

future value, p. 54

Gordon growth model, p. 61

inflation-indexed bond, p. 80

margin requirements, p. 73

nominal interest rate, i, p. 77

present value, p. 54

price–earnings (P/E) ratio, p. 66

rate of return, p. 75

rational expectations, p. 59

real interest rate, r, p. 77

return, p. 75

risk premium, φ, p. 60

risk-adjusted interest rate, p. 60

safe interest rate, i^{safe}, p. 59

yield to maturity, p. 74

Questions and Problems

1. Suppose you win the lottery. You have a choice between receiving $100,000 a year for 20 years or an immediate payment of $1,200,000.

   a. Which should you choose if the interest rate is 3 percent? If it is 6 percent?

   b. For what range of interest rates should you take the immediate payment?

2. Suppose a bond has a maturity of 3 years, annual coupon payments of $5, and a face value of $100.

   a. If the interest rate is 4 percent, is the price of the bond higher or lower than the face value? What if the interest rate is 6 percent?

   b. For what range of interest rates does the price exceed the face value? Can you explain the answer?

3. Suppose that people expect a company's earnings to grow in the future at the same rate they have grown in the past. Does this

behavior satisfy the assumption of rational expectations? Explain.

4. Describe how each of the following events affects stock and bond prices.

   a. The economy enters a recession.

   b. A genius invents a new technology that makes factories more productive.

   c. The Federal Reserve raises its target for interest rates.

   d. People learn that major news about the economy will be announced in a few days, but they don't know whether it is good news or bad news.

5. Consider two stocks. For each, the expected dividend next year is $100 and the expected growth rate of dividends is 3%. The risk premium is 3% for one stock and 8% for the other. The economy's safe interest rate is 5%.

   a. What does the difference in risk premiums tell us about the dividends from each stock?

   b. Use the Gordon growth model to compute the price of each stock. Why is one price higher than the other?

   c. Suppose the expected growth rate of dividends rises to 5% for both stocks. Compute the new price of each. Which stock's price changes by a larger percentage? Explain your result.

6. Consider two bonds. Each has a face value of $100 and matures in 10 years. One has no coupon payments, and the other pays $10 per year.

   a. Calculate the price of each bond if the interest rate is 3 percent and if the interest rate is 6 percent.

   b. When the interest rate rises from 3 percent to 6 percent, which bond price falls by a larger percentage? Explain why.

7. Suppose a bond has a face value of $100, annual coupon payments of $4, a maturity of 5 years, and a price of $90.

   a. Write an equation that defines the yield to maturity on this bond.

   b. If you have the right kind of calculator or software, calculate the yield to maturity.

8. Suppose the price of the bond in problem 7 falls from $90 to $85 over a year. Calculate the bond's rate of return over the year.

9. Suppose the yield to maturity on a 1-year bond is 6 percent. Everyone expects inflation over the year to be 3 percent, but it turns out to be 5 percent. What is the nominal interest rate on the bond, the ex ante real rate, and the ex post real rate?

10. "I just bought my first house. Economists are predicting low inflation in the future, but I sure hope they're wrong!" Why might it make sense for someone to say this?

11. "Buying an inflation-indexed bond is risky. If I buy a conventional bond, I know what interest rate I will receive. With an indexed bond, the rate can rise or fall depending on inflation. Risk-averse savers should prefer conventional bonds." Discuss.

▶ Online and Data Questions

www.worthpublishers.com/ball

12. The text Web site contains data from the Bernanke–Kuttner paper on the Fed and the stock market (see p. 63). The data cover 68 days from 1995 through 2002 when the Fed either changed interest rates or decided not to change them. For each of these days, the data include the change in a short-term interest rate and the percentage change in stock prices. The data also include the interest rate change that participants in financial markets expected before the Fed acted. (The expected change is measured using data from futures markets, which we discuss in Chapter 5).

   a. Make a graph with the change in the interest rate on the horizontal axis and the percentage change in stock prices on the vertical axis. Plot a point for each day in the data set.

   b. Now compute the *unexpected* change in the interest rate—the actual change minus the expected change. Redo the graph in part (a) with this variable on the horizontal axis.

c. Which has a stronger effect on stock prices, the change in the interest rate or the unexpected change? Explain your finding.

13. The text Web site links to bloomberg.com, which provides daily data on the Dow Jones stock index. Find a day within the last year when the index rose or fell by at least 2 percent. Consult news reports for that day and discuss why stock prices might have changed. Was the change consistent with the classical theory of asset prices?

14. The text Web site contains data on interest rates for Treasury bonds. For the most recent data, compare the rates on 10-year conventional bonds and 10-year inflation-indexed bonds. What do these rates tell us about expectations of future inflation?

chapter four

What Determines Interest Rates?

Low interest rates help families buy new homes.

Low interest rates have helped American citizens. It's helped them buy a home. It's helped them refinance if they own a home. It's put more money in circulation, which is good for job creation.

—*George W. Bush, 2003*

Lower interest rates have made it easier for businesses to borrow and to invest and create new jobs. Lower interest rates have brought down the cost of home mortgages, car payments, and credit cards to ordinary citizens.

—*Bill Clinton, 1996*

I think that if the interest rates had been lowered more dramatically that I would have been reelected President. . . .

—*George H. W. Bush, 1998*

These statements from three former presidents illustrate the importance of interest rates. These rates affect the lives of individuals and the growth of the overall economy. They can help determine election outcomes.

Chapter 3 discussed how real and nominal interest rates are measured. This chapter asks, what factors determine interest rates? Why do some bonds and bank loans have higher rates than others? Why do rates rise in some time periods and fall in others?

Figure 4.1 on page 86 illustrates the behaviors that we want to understand. For the period from 1960 to 2009, the figure shows the paths of several interest rates: the rates on 90-day Treasury bills, 10-year

FIGURE 4.1 U.S. Real Interest Rates, 1960–2009

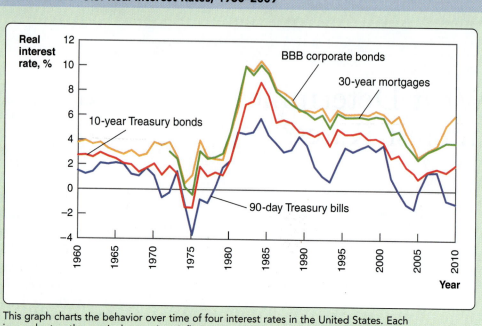

This graph charts the behavior over time of four interest rates in the United States. Each is a real rate—the nominal rate minus inflation over the previous year. The broad movements in the four interest rates are similar over time.

Source: Federal Reserve Bank of St. Louis

Treasury bonds, moderate-risk corporate bonds, and 30-year home mortgages. Each interest rate is a real rate (r), defined as the nominal rate (i) minus inflation (π) over the previous year (review Equation 3.10).

The various interest rates in the figure usually move together. Rates fell in the 1970s, rose sharply in the early 1980s, and have mostly fallen since then. This chapter presents two theories that help explain these movements. In one theory, interest rates are determined by the supply and demand for loans. In the other, rates are determined by the supply and demand for money.

Figure 4.1 reveals differences among individual interest rates. Notice, for example, that the corporate bond rate is always higher than the Treasury bond rate. The Treasury bond rate is usually higher than the Treasury bill rate, but it dips below the T-bill rate occasionally. In 2008–2009, the corporate bond rate rose sharply while the Treasury bill rate fell. This chapter reviews the reasons behind such differences in interest rates. It turns out that two factors are most important: the term of a bond or loan and the risk of default by the borrower.

4.1 THE LOANABLE FUNDS THEORY

Loanable funds theory
real interest rates are determined by the supply and demand for loans

The first theory of interest rates that we'll examine is the **loanable funds theory**, which states that the real interest rate is determined by the supply and demand for loans. Recall that the financial system channels funds from savers to investors. The loanable funds theory assumes that funds are transferred in a simple way. An economy's savers and investors meet in a market for loans, where the savers lend to the investors.

A   The interest rate is the price of a loan—what investors pay savers for using their funds. Economists generally believe that prices are determined by supply and demand, and the loan market is no exception. The interest rate is determined by the supply and demand for loans.

Like all economic models, the loanable funds theory simplifies reality. The theory assumes only one type of loan and one interest rate; it ignores the diversity of rates illustrated in Figure 4.1. The theory also assumes that savers lend directly to investors, which ignores the role of banks. Nonetheless, the loanable funds theory offers us many insights into the forces that determine interest rates.

▶ Chapter 1 explains how the financial system channels funds from savers, who accumulate wealth, to investors, who expand the productive capacity of the economy.

Saving, Investment, and Capital Flows

What determines the supply and demand for loans? We have assumed that loans are used to finance investment. Therefore, the demand for loans is the level of investment in the economy. If investors decide to undertake more projects, they must borrow more:

↑I ↑ Demand.

$$\text{demand for loans} = \text{investment}$$

The supply of loans is a bit more complicated. Investors borrow from savers, which suggests that the supply of loans equals the level of saving. This is the end of the story if the economy is "closed"—that is, it does not interact with the economies of other countries. However, real-world economies are open, with loans flowing across national borders. An economy's supply of loans depends on these flows as well as on its level of saving.

Closed economy   *S = Saving.*

Loans can flow in two directions. First, a country's investors can borrow from abroad. For example, a U.S. company that wants to build a new factory can sell bonds to Europeans as well as to Americans. Funds raised from foreign savers are called **capital inflows**. An economy's supply of loans includes these inflows as well as saving within the economy. Conversely, a country's savers can lend to foreign investors. U.S. savers might buy bonds issued by European companies. Funds sent abroad are called **capital outflows**. These funds are a part of a country's saving that is *not* lent to that country's investors.

Capital inflows funds provided to a country's investors by foreigners
Capital outflows funds provided to foreign investors by a country's savers

To summarize, an economy's total supply of loans is its saving *plus* capital inflows *minus* capital outflows. Economists use the term **net capital inflows** for capital inflows minus outflows. The supply of loans can be written as

Net capital inflows capital inflows minus capital outflows

Open economy
$$\text{supply of loans} = \text{saving} + \text{capital inflows} - \text{capital outflows}$$
$$= \text{saving} + \text{net capital inflows}$$

Capital inflows can be greater or less than outflows, so net capital inflows can be either positive or negative. Positive net inflows raise the supply of loans above the level of saving, while negative net inflows do the reverse.

+ve NCF   Supply of loans above Saving.
−ve NCF   Supply of loans below saving

Effects of the Real Interest Rate

Now that we know what constitutes the demand and supply for loans, let's discuss how these variables are affected by the price of loans—the interest rate. The relevant interest rate here is the ex ante real rate—the nominal interest rate minus expected inflation over the loan period (Equation 3.11). The real rate measures the true cost of borrowing and the true earnings from lending. Loan decisions depend on the ex ante real rate, not the ex post rate, because only the ex ante rate is known when loans are made.

Effects on Loan Demand The demand for loans equals the level of investment. To see how the real interest rate affects this variable, consider a firm with a possible investment project—say, a new factory. In deciding whether to build the factory, the firm compares the costs to the revenues the factory is likely to produce. The costs include the interest payments on the loans that finance the project. A rise in the real interest rate means higher costs, making it less likely the firm will decide to build the factory.

This reasoning applies to investment projects throughout the economy. A higher real interest rate makes investment more costly, so fewer projects are undertaken. Lower investment means that investors want fewer loans.

LOAN DEMAND

↑ real interest rate → ↓ investment → ↓ quantity of loans demanded

Effects on Supply The real interest rate affects both components of loan supply: saving and net capital inflows. A higher interest rate means higher returns to savers. Saving becomes a better deal: the money you put aside grows more rapidly. Thus, a higher interest rate encourages people to save more:

↑ real interest rate → ↑ saving

To see how the interest rate affects capital flows, consider a foreign saver who plans to purchase bonds and is choosing among bonds issued in different countries. For example, a French saver is choosing between bonds issued by French corporations and U.S. corporations. If the real interest rate rises in the United States, then U.S. bonds become more attractive. Everything else equal, the saver will buy more U.S. bonds. Thus the higher interest rate increases capital inflows to the United States.

A higher U.S. interest rate also influences U.S. savers. It encourages them to buy bonds in their own country rather than send money abroad. So a higher interest rate decreases capital outflows. The combination of higher inflows and lower outflows raises net capital inflows:

↑ real interest rate → ↑ capital inflows and ↓ capital outflows

→ ↑ net capital inflows

To summarize, a higher real interest rate raises both saving and net capital inflows. Both effects raise the quantity of loans supplied:

LOAN SUPPLY

↑ real interest rate → ↑ saving and ↑ net capital inflows

→ ↑ quantity of loans supplied ✱

The Equilibrium Real Interest Rate

Figure 4.2 summarizes our analysis with a graph. It shows how the quantity of loans supplied and the quantity demanded depend on the real interest rate. The graph gives specific numbers as examples.

In the figure, the downward-sloping line is the demand curve. This curve shows how investment falls as the real interest rate rises, reducing the quantity

Movement along the curve when i changes.

FIGURE 4.2 The Loan Market

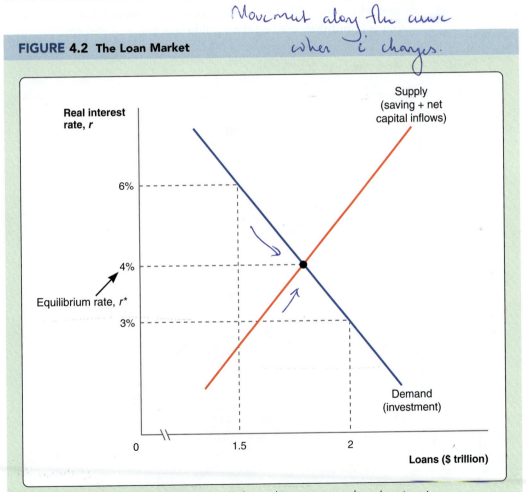

The demand for loans equals investment. A higher real interest rate reduces investment and therefore reduces the quantity of loans demanded. The supply of loans equals saving plus net capital inflows. A higher interest rate raises both factors and therefore raises the quantity of loans supplied. Here the equilibrium real interest rate, r*, where the supply and demand curves intersect, is 4 percent.

of loans demanded. If the interest rate is 3 percent, investment is $2 trillion. If the rate rises to 6 percent, investment falls to $1.5 trillion in this example.

The upward-sloping line is the supply curve. It shows that a higher interest rate raises the sum of saving and net capital inflows and therefore raises the quantity of loans supplied.

In this market, what interest rate will be charged for loans? The answer is the interest rate at which the supply and demand curves intersect. This is the *equilibrium* real interest rate, r^*. In our graph, the curves intersect at a rate of 4 percent, so this is the equilibrium rate.

To understand why the interest rate is 4 percent, suppose it were higher—say, 7 percent. This rate would attract high levels of saving and net capital inflows but discourage investment. As shown in **Figure 4.3**, the quantity of loans supplied would exceed the quantity demanded. As a result, not all lenders would be able to find borrowers to take their funds. In competing to attract borrowers, lenders would start offering lower interest rates. Rates would fall until they reached the equilibrium rate of 4 percent.

FIGURE 4.3 Adjustment to Equilibrium

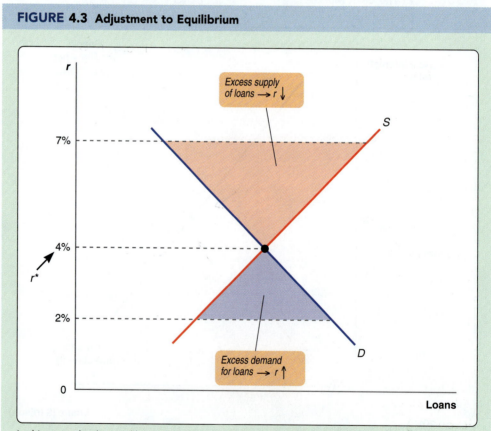

In this example, the equilibrium real interest rate, r^*, is 4 percent. A higher interest rate—say, 7 percent—creates an excess supply of loans: not all lenders can find borrowers. In this situation, lenders offer lower interest rates to attract borrowers, pushing rates down toward 4 percent. A real interest rate lower than the equilibrium level—say, 2 percent—creates an excess demand for loans: not all borrowers can find lenders. In this case, borrowers offer higher rates to attract lenders, pushing rates up toward 4 percent.

Conversely, if the interest rate were 2 percent, the quantity of loans demanded would exceed the quantity supplied. Borrowers would compete to acquire scarce loans, pushing the interest rate up to 4 percent.

4.2 DETERMINANTS OF INTEREST RATES IN THE LOANABLE FUNDS THEORY

Shifts in L FT.

Now let's put the loanable funds theory to work. We can use the theory to analyze the effects of various events and economic policies on the real interest rate. The theory says that the interest rate changes when there is a shift in the supply or demand for loans.

Economists distinguish between shifts in supply and demand curves and movements *along* the curves. Changes in the real interest rate cause movements along the curves; a higher rate raises the quantity of loans supplied and reduces the quantity demanded. A curve shifts when supply or demand changes for a reason *besides* changes in the interest rate. Such an event affects the equilibrium interest rate.

↑ IR ⟨ ↑ qty of loans supplied / ↓ qty of loan demanded.

Supply and demand for loans are determined by investment, saving, and net capital inflows. A number of factors cause these variables to change, shifting the supply and demand curves. **Table 4.1** lists some important factors detailed in the following sections.

Shifts in Investment

The demand for loans shifts if a change occurs in the level of investment at a given interest rate. For example, suppose someone invents a machine that makes factories more productive. Many firms want to buy this new machine, so investment rises.

Figure 4.4 illustrates this shift in the demand curve. Before the machine was invented, investment was $2 trillion if the interest rate was 3 percent. Now, because of the invention, a 3 percent interest rate produces $2.3 trillion of investment. Before, a 6-percent interest rate produced $1.5 trillion of investment; now it produces $1.8 trillion. After the invention, investment still depends negatively on the interest rate but is higher at each rate. In Figure 4.4, the demand curve for loans shifts to the right, from D_1 to D_2.

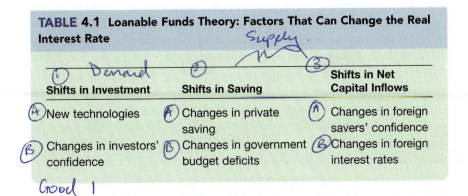

TABLE 4.1 Loanable Funds Theory: Factors That Can Change the Real Interest Rate

Supply.

① Demand Shifts in Investment	② Shifts in Saving	③ Shifts in Net Capital Inflows
Ⓐ New technologies	Ⓐ Changes in private saving	Ⓐ Changes in foreign savers' confidence
Ⓑ Changes in investors' confidence	Ⓑ Changes in government budget deficits	Ⓑ Changes in foreign interest rates

Good !

FIGURE 4.4 An Increase in Investment

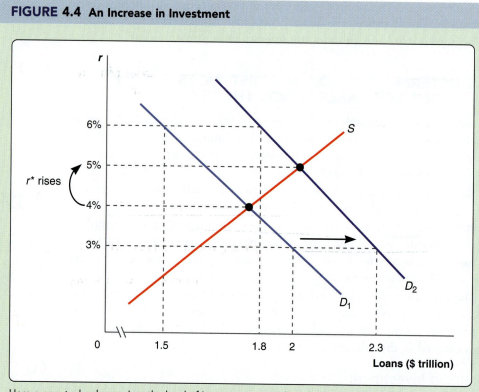

Here a new technology raises the level of investment at each real interest rate. A rise in investment shifts the demand for loans from D_1 to D_2, and r^* rises from 4 percent to 5 percent.

Understanding this shift makes it easy to see what happens to the equilibrium interest rate. Before the new machine was invented, supply and demand intersected at a real interest rate of 4 percent. After the shift, the intersection occurs at 5 percent, the new equilibrium interest rate.

Generally, any event that encourages investment shifts the demand curve for loans to the right, raising the equilibrium interest rate. Any event that makes investment less attractive does the reverse: the demand curve shifts to the left, and the interest rate falls.

In real economies, why might investment change for a given interest rate? The example of a new machine is not fanciful: sometimes investment shifts because new technologies are invented. One example is the development of the Internet and related computer applications in the late 1990s. These innovations led to a surge in investment as companies bought new computers and software.

Another factor is investors' confidence in the economy—their expectations about future economic growth. Strong growth raises the demand for companies' products, making it profitable to increase output. To produce more, companies invest in new factories and machines. Therefore, if good economic news raises expected growth, investment rises for a given interest

rate. The demand curve for loans shifts to the right. The opposite happens
if bad news reduces expected growth.

Shift to right → Good News.
Shift to left → Bad News

Shifts in Saving

The supply of loans shifts when a change occurs in the behavior of saving
or net capital inflows. Let's consider saving first. Suppose people become
more thrifty: they save more at a given interest rate. This change raises the
sum of saving and net capital inflows at a given interest rate, shifting
the supply curve for loans to the right.

Figure 4.5 graphs an example. If the real interest rate is 3 percent, a
higher level of saving raises the quantity of loans supplied from $1.6 trillion
to $1.8 trillion. At a rate of 6 percent, the quantity supplied rises from
$2 trillion to $2.2 trillion. The shift in the supply curve reduces the equilibrium interest rate from 4 percent to 3.5 percent.

Why might the level of saving change for a given interest rate? An economy has two kinds of saving: **private saving**, or saving by individuals and
firms, and **public saving**, or saving by the government. Total saving is the
sum of the two:

In domestic economy 2 types of

saving = private saving + public saving

Private saving saving
by individuals and firms

Public saving saving by
the government (tax
revenue minus government
spending)

FIGURE 4.5 An Increase in Saving

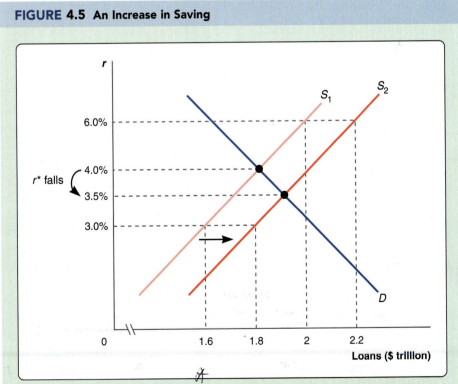

Ppl who are thriftier save more.

When people become thriftier, they save more at each real interest rate, increasing the
supply of loans. In this example, the supply curve for loans shifts from S_1 to S_2, and r^*
falls from 4 percent to 3.5 percent.

To understand changes in saving, let's examine the two components in turn.

Private Saving The level of private saving can change considerably over time. In the first half of the 1980s, private saving in the United States averaged 20 percent of GDP. Then saving started to decline, and from 2000 to 2007 it averaged 14 percent of GDP. Low saving shifted the supply curve for loans to the left, causing interest rates to be higher than they otherwise would be. Possible reasons for the fall in saving include the spread of credit cards through the economy and the increasing availability of home-equity loans, which allow people to borrow against the equity they build up in their houses. In short, easier access to credit may have encouraged people to spend more and save less.

Private saving rose during the financial crisis to 17 percent of GDP in 2009. Higher saving shifted the supply of loans to the right and helped produce low interest rates. One factor behind higher saving was the fall in house prices during the crisis, which made consumers feel less wealthy and reduced the availability of home-equity loans. Another factor was uncertainty about the economy's future, which motivated consumers to save for rainy days.

Public Saving The government saves if it takes in tax revenue and doesn't spend it all; that is,

$$\text{public saving} = \text{tax revenue} - \text{government spending}$$

This component of saving is determined by political decisions about taxing and spending.

Public saving can be either positive or negative. A **budget surplus** occurs when public saving is positive (tax revenue exceeds government spending) and a **budget deficit** when it is negative (spending exceeds revenue). Deficits have been the norm in recent history. Since 1970, the U.S. government has run surpluses in only four years.

Economists often advise governments to reduce budget deficits. The loanable funds theory captures one reason why: deficits raise the real interest rate. Suppose, for example, that the government starts with a deficit and then cuts taxes. The tax cut raises the deficit, which means it reduces public saving—that component of saving becomes more negative. Assuming no big change in the rate of private saving, total saving falls for a given interest rate. As illustrated in **Figure 4.6**, the supply curve for loans shifts to the left, and the equilibrium real interest rate rises.

To understand the consequences of this increase in the interest rate, recall the quotations from past presidents at the start of this chapter. Higher interest rates make it harder for people to buy houses, borrow for college, or pay off their credit cards. Higher rates also reduce investment in factories and machines, hurting the future productivity of the economy. Lower productivity reduces the incomes of both workers and firms.

Budget surplus a positive level of public saving

Budget deficit a negative level of public saving

FIGURE 4.6 A Rise in the Government Budget Deficit

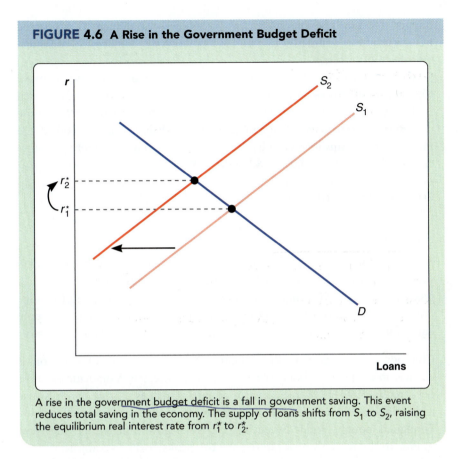

A rise in the government budget deficit is a fall in government saving. This event reduces total saving in the economy. The supply of loans shifts from S_1 to S_2, raising the equilibrium real interest rate from r_1^* to r_2^*.

CASE STUDY

Budget Deficits and Interest Rates

The loanable funds theory tells us that budget deficits raise interest rates, but it does not tell us the size of this effect. For example, U.S. budget deficits averaged around 4 percent of GDP over the period 2005–2009. How does a budget deficit of that size affect interest rates?

A 2009 study by Thomas Laubach of Goethe University in Germany estimates the effects of U.S. budget deficits. Laubach, a former Fed economist, examines forecasts of deficits made by two government agencies, the Office of Management and Budget (OMB) and the Congressional Budget Office (CBO), over the period 1976–2006. Laubach focuses on forecasts of the deficit five years into the future (e.g., forecasts in 2000 of the deficit in 2005). The goal is to capture long-term movements in the deficit, which are likely to have larger effects than year-to-year fluctuations.

Laubach estimates the effects of deficits on the interest rate for 10-year Treasury bonds. He finds that, on average, a rise in the forecasted deficit of 1 percent of GDP raises the interest rate by about 0.25 percent. Therefore, the total effect of a 4-percent deficit, compared to a balanced budget, is to raise the interest rate by $4 \times 0.25 = 1.0$ percent. If a balanced budget produces an interest rate of, say, 5 percent, the deficit raises the interest rate to 6 percent.

We've seen that different interest rates in the economy tend to move together (see Figure 4.1). If Laubach's results are accurate, the budget deficit is likely to raise many interest rates by similar amounts. To get a sense of the cost, suppose you have a student loan with a balance of $20,000. If the interest rate on this loan rises by 1.0 percent, your current interest charges rise by $200 per year ($0.01 \times \$20,000 = \$200$).[*]

[*] See Thomas Laubach, "New Evidence on the Interest Rate Effects of Budget Deficits and Debt," *Journal of the European Economic Association*, 7 (June 2009): 858–885.

Shifts in Capital Flows

A final factor that causes changes in interest rates is shifts in net capital inflows. **Figure 4.7A** shows what happens if net capital inflows rise for a given interest rate. The effects are similar to those of higher saving (see Figure 4.5). The sum of saving and net capital inflows rises, shifting the supply curve for loans to the right. This shift reduces the equilibrium interest rate.

Changes in Confidence Why might capital flows shift? One reason is changes in confidence about an economy's performance. A dramatic example occurred in 1997–1998 in East Asian countries such as Taiwan, South Korea, and Indonesia. These countries had previously received large capital inflows. Foreigners bought bonds issued by East Asian governments, and they lent money to the region's banks to finance the banks' loans to companies.

FIGURE 4.7 **Shifts in Capital Flows**

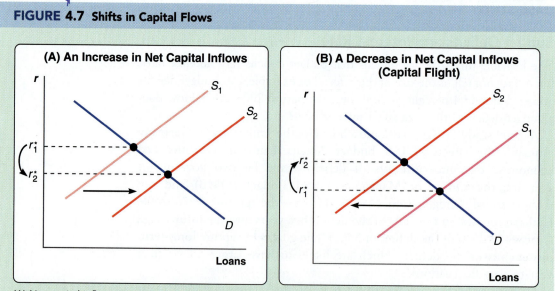

(A) Net capital inflows rise at each real interest rate, shifting the supply of loans from S_1 to S_2. The equilibrium real interest rate falls from r_1^* to r_2^*. (B) Net capital inflows fall at each real interest rate, shifting the supply of loans from S_1 to S_2. The equilibrium real interest rate rises from r_1^* to r_2^*.

In the late 1990s, these economies and banking systems experienced problems, and foreign savers began to fear that their loans would not be repaid. This led to a sharp drop in capital inflows. Net capital inflows (inflows minus outflows) shifted from positive to negative. A shift of this type is called **capital flight**.

The fall in net capital inflows meant the supply of loans in East Asian countries shifted to the left, as shown in **Figure 4.7B**. These shifts raised interest rates sharply. In South Korea, for example, short-term rates jumped from 12 percent in November 1997 to 31 percent in December.

Foreign Interest Rates Another factor behind a country's capital flows is interest rates in *other* countries. Let's think about net capital inflows to the United States. A saver choosing between U.S. bonds and those of another country—say, France—compares interest rates in the two countries. If the French interest rate rises, French bonds become more attractive. Savers in France buy more French bonds and fewer U.S. bonds, reducing capital inflows to the United States. U.S. savers also buy more French bonds, raising capital outflows from the United States. Lower inflows and higher outflows both reduce net capital inflows.

Once again, a fall in net capital inflows reduces the supply of loans at a given U.S. interest rate. The supply curve shifts to the left, raising the equilibrium real interest rate, as shown in Figure 4.7B.

This analysis implies that interest rates in different countries are connected: they tend to move in the same direction. An event that raises the interest rate in one country, such as a higher budget deficit, reduces net capital inflows to other countries. The supply of loans falls in the other countries, so their interest rates rise too.

Figure 4.8 presents evidence that supports our analysis. The figure shows the real interest rates on short-term government bonds in the United States, Canada, and France for the period 1960–2009. From year to year, these rates bounce around in different ways. But they all follow the broad pattern that we saw in Figure 4.1 for U.S. real rates: a fall in the 1970s, a rise in the 1980s, and a downward drift since then.

Nominal Interest Rates

The loanable funds theory helps us understand the ex ante real interest rate. Let's now return to the subject of nominal interest rates—the rates posted at banks and the bond yields reported in financial media. What determines these rates?

To answer this question, we start with the definition of the ex ante real interest rate: $r = i - \pi^e$, where r is the real interest rate, i is the nominal rate, and π^e is expected inflation. If we turn this equation around, we get the

FISHER EQUATION

$$i = r + \pi^e \tag{4.1}$$

so called because it was developed by the economist Irving Fisher.

> **Capital flight** sudden decrease in net capital inflows that occurs when foreign savers lose confidence in an economy

> ▶ In Section 3.5, we discuss Fisher's failure to foresee the 1929 stock crash.

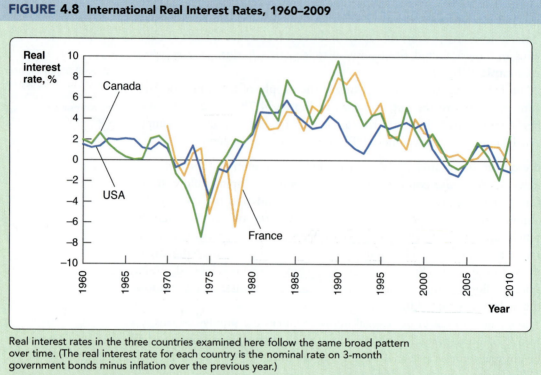

FIGURE 4.8 International Real Interest Rates, 1960–2009

Real interest rates in the three countries examined here follow the same broad pattern over time. (The real interest rate for each country is the nominal rate on 3-month government bonds minus inflation over the previous year.)

Source: International Monetary Fund

Fisher equation the nominal interest rate equals the real rate plus expected inflation: $i = r + \pi^e$

Adaptive expectations theory that people's expectations of a variable are based on past levels of the variable; also, *backward-looking expectations*

▶ We made a different assumption, rational expectations, in analyzing asset prices in Section 3.2. Chapters 12 and 16 discuss economists' debate over the behavior of expectations.

According to the **Fisher equation**, a rise in the real interest rate (r) raises the nominal rate (i). So the various factors that shift real rates—the items in Table 4.1 on page 91—shift nominal rates too. In addition, for a given real rate, the nominal rate rises and falls with expected inflation, π^e. A rise in π^e of one percentage point raises i by one percentage point.

What determines expected inflation? Economists have not settled this question, but many think a reasonable assumption is **adaptive expectations**. This means that expected inflation is based on inflation rates in the recent past. If annual inflation has run at 3 percent recently, people expect inflation near 3 percent in the future. If inflation rises to 4 percent, people start expecting 4 percent. This assumption is also called *backward-looking expectations*.

With adaptive expectations, observed inflation rates influence nominal interest rates. An increase in inflation raises expected inflation, which raises the interest rate implied by the Fisher equation.

This *Fisher effect* explains much of the behavior of nominal interest rates. **Figure 4.9** presents data on nominal rates and inflation for 41 countries during the 1990s. As the Fisher effect implies, countries with higher inflation have higher interest rates.

FIGURE 4.9 Inflation and Nominal Interest Rates Across Countries

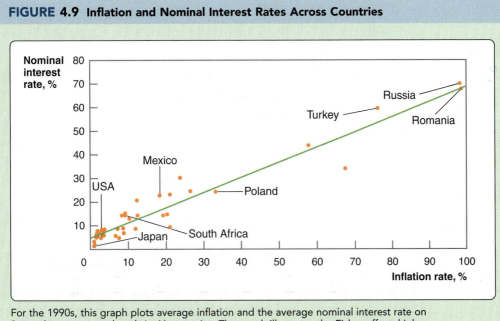

For the 1990s, this graph plots average inflation and the average nominal interest rate on 3-month government bonds in 41 countries. The graph illustrates the Fisher effect: higher inflation raises the nominal interest rate.

Source: International Monetary Fund

4.3 THE LIQUIDITY PREFERENCE THEORY

In the loanable funds theory, interest rates are determined by the supply and demand for loans. We now turn to the **liquidity preference theory**, where interest rates are determined by the supply and demand for money. The demand for money is sometimes called *liquidity preference* because money is the most liquid asset.

In the liquidity preference theory, the supply and demand for money determine the *nominal* interest rate. This is one difference from the loanable funds theory, which explains the *real* interest rate; when we use that theory, we must use the Fisher equation to find the nominal rate. We'll compare our different theories of interest rates after we develop the liquidity preference theory.

In the liquidity preference theory, the key simplifying assumption is that only two kinds of assets exist: money and bonds. All wealth is held in one of these forms. The assets differ in two ways:

1. Money is the medium of exchange. People use money to purchase goods and services; they can't use bonds.

2. Bonds pay interest but money does not. This assumption is fairly realistic. In modern economies, money consists mainly of cash and checking accounts. Cash doesn't pay interest. Some checking accounts do pay interest, but only small amounts.

> **Liquidity preference theory** the nominal interest rate is determined by the supply and demand for money

▶ Figure 2.3 compares the degrees of liquidity of different types of assets.

▶ Section 2.1 defines money and discusses its role as the medium of exchange.

The Market for Money

Using these assumptions, let's discuss the key concepts in the liquidity preference theory: money supply and money demand.

Control by CB

Money Supply The money supply is the total amount of money in the economy. The central bank—in the United States, the Federal Reserve—controls the money supply. For our current purposes, we can assume the central bank exerts its control in a simple way. If it wants to increase the money supply, it first prints new money. It uses this money to purchase bonds, putting the money into circulation in the economy. If the central bank wants to reduce the money supply, it takes in money by selling some of the bonds that it owns and puts this money in a paper shredder.

▶ In reality, central banks control the money supply through a more complicated process that we discuss in Chapter 11.

Money Demand In the liquidity preference theory, people choose how to split their wealth between the economy's two assets: money and bonds. Money demand is the amount of wealth that people choose to hold in the form of money.

When people choose their money holdings, they face a trade-off. Because money is the medium of exchange, holding a large amount makes life more convenient. If you carry lots of cash and keep a high balance in your checking account, you can buy things whenever you want. If you hold less cash, a purchase may require a trip to an ATM. If your checking balance is low, you may have to sell bonds to buy something expensive.

On the other hand, holding money reduces your interest income. Each dollar of wealth held in money is a dollar less in interest-bearing bonds. This means that a key determinant of money demand is the nominal interest rate on bonds. Because money pays a nominal rate of zero, the interest rate on bonds tells us how much you give up by holding money. If bonds pay 5 percent, you lose 5 percent by holding money. In economic language, the nominal interest rate on bonds is the *opportunity cost* of holding money.

Money or dollars # do not accumulate interest when cash on hand.

When the interest rate rises, the opportunity cost of money rises. This leads people to hold less money and to place more of their wealth in bonds. Holding less money makes it more cumbersome to buy things, but people accept this inconvenience if bonds pay high interest rates. Therefore,

$$\uparrow i \rightarrow \downarrow \text{ quantity of money demanded}$$

The Equilibrium Interest Rate

Figure 4.10 summarizes our discussion. It shows how money supply and money demand are related to the nominal interest rate. Money demand is captured by a downward-sloping curve: a higher interest rate reduces the quantity of money demanded. The money supply is fixed at a level chosen by the central bank, regardless of the interest rate. This means the money supply curve is vertical. We use the symbol $\overline{M}$ to denote the money supply chosen by the central bank.

The equilibrium nominal interest rate, i^*, is the rate where the supply and demand curves intersect. Market forces push the interest rate to i^*. To

FIGURE 4.10 The Market for Money

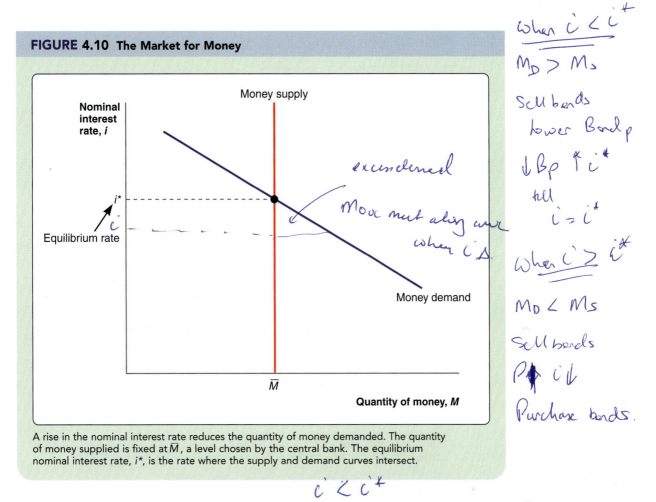

Handwritten margin notes:
When $i < i^*$
$M_D > M_s$
Sell bonds
lower Bond p
$\downarrow Bp \uparrow i^*$
till
$i = i^*$
when $i > i^*$
$M_D < M_s$
Sell bonds
$P \uparrow i \downarrow$
Purchase bonds.

Graph labels: Money supply; Nominal interest rate, i; i^*; Equilibrium rate; excess demand; Move must along curve when $i \downarrow$; Money demand; $\overline{M}$; Quantity of money, M

Handwritten below figure: $i < i^*$

A rise in the nominal interest rate reduces the quantity of money demanded. The quantity of money supplied is fixed at $\overline{M}$, a level chosen by the central bank. The equilibrium nominal interest rate, i^*, is the rate where the supply and demand curves intersect.

understand this process, suppose the interest rate is below i^*. In this case, the quantity of money demanded exceeds the quantity supplied. In other words, the amount of money that people want to hold is greater than the amount the central bank has created.

In this situation, people try to get more money. They do so by selling bonds, which pushes down the price of bonds. Lower bond prices mean higher interest rates, so i rises toward i^*. Conversely, if the interest rate is above i^*, the quantity of money demanded is less than the quantity supplied. People try to reduce their money holdings by purchasing bonds, which pushes bond prices up and the interest rate down.

▶ Section 3.6 describes the inverse relationship between bond prices and interest rates.

Changes in Interest Rates

In the liquidity preference theory, changes in equilibrium interest rates are caused by shifts in money supply and money demand. **Table 4.2** lists some reasons for these shifts.

Shifts in Money Supply The central bank can choose to change the money supply, $\overline{M}$. **Figure 4.11** shows what

TABLE 4.2 Liquidity Preference Theory: Factors That Can Change the Nominal Interest Rate

Shifts in Money Supply
Decisions by the central bank

Shifts in Money Demand
Changes in aggregate spending
Changes in transaction technologies

FIGURE 4.11 An Increase in the Money Supply

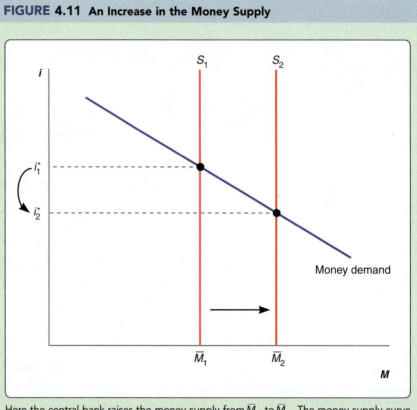

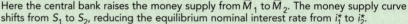

Here the central bank raises the money supply from $\overline{M}_1$ to $\overline{M}_2$. The money supply curve shifts from S_1 to S_2, reducing the equilibrium nominal interest rate from i_1^* to i_2^*.

ms ↑
    ms curve shifts right
ms ↓ ms curve shifts left

happens when $\overline{M}$ increases. The money supply curve shifts to the right, reducing the equilibrium nominal interest rate.

This effect on i is often the motive for changes in the money supply. Central banks act when they believe that changes in interest rates would benefit the economy. For example, after the 9/11 terrorist attacks in 2001, the Federal Reserve raised the money supply to reduce interest rates and stimulate the economy. From 2007 to 2009, the Fed pushed interest rates down repeatedly to counter the recession caused by the financial crisis.

▶ The case study in Section 2.5 reviews the Fed's response on 9/11 in detail.

Shifts in Money Demand The money demand curve shifts if people change the level of money they hold at a given interest rate. **Figure 4.12** illustrates an increase in money demand. The demand curve shifts to the right, raising the equilibrium interest rate.

Mo shifts when
    ppl want to spend
or save.

Why might money demand shift? One reason is a change in aggregate spending on goods and services. Because the purpose of money is to facilitate purchases, people hold more money when they spend more. A person planning a shopping spree needs more cash and checking deposits than a more frugal person. For the economy as a whole, the demand for money rises when total spending rises.

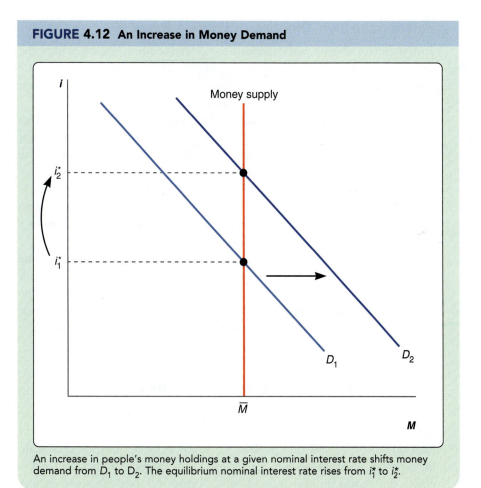

FIGURE 4.12 An Increase in Money Demand

An increase in people's money holdings at a given nominal interest rate shifts money demand from D_1 to D_2. The equilibrium nominal interest rate rises from i_1^* to i_2^*.

An economy's total spending is nominal GDP. This variable is the product of real GDP and the aggregate price level:

$$\text{nominal GDP} = \text{real GDP} \times \text{aggregate price level}$$

Real GDP measures the quantity of goods and services purchased, and the price level measures the cost of these items. An increase in nominal GDP can result *either* from a rise in real GDP (economic growth) or from a rise in the price level (inflation). In either case, higher spending shifts money demand to the right, raising the equilibrium interest rate, as shown in Figure 4.12.

Another source of money-demand shifts is changes in *transaction technologies*. This term refers to the methods that people use to obtain money and spend it. Transaction technologies evolve over time, changing the amount of money that people wish to hold.

For example, as ATMs spread to more locations, people may decide to carry less cash in their wallets, because cash is easily available at ATMs. This change reduces the quantity of money demanded at a given interest rate. The money demand curve shifts to the left, which reduces the equilibrium nominal interest rate.

►To review the concepts of real GDP and the aggregate price level in detail, see the appendix to Chapter 1.

Relating the Two Theories of Interest Rates

Earlier in this chapter we described the loanable funds theory, where the real interest rate is determined by the supply and demand for loans. The nominal rate is determined by the Fisher equation: it is the equilibrium real rate plus expected inflation [see Equation (4.1)].

In the liquidity preference theory, the nominal interest rate is determined by the supply and demand for money. It is natural to ask how this theory relates to the loanable funds theory. Which is more relevant for the interest rates we see in the real world?

The full answer to this question is complex. We will return to the question in Part IV of this book, which includes some necessary background on economic fluctuations. We'll see that the two theories complement one another, capturing different aspects of interest rate behavior.

A brief preview: For explaining the *long-run* behavior of interest rates, the loanable funds theory is the best framework. The supply and demand for loans determines the average real interest rate over periods of, say, 5 or 10 years. The liquidity preference theory is most useful for explaining the *short-run* behavior of interest rates—the ups and downs from year to year. These movements mainly reflect central banks' decisions about the money supply.

4.4 THE TERM STRUCTURE OF INTEREST RATES

TABLE 4.3 Factors That Explain Differences Among Interest Rates

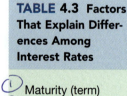

- Maturity (term)
- Default risk
- Liquidity
- Taxation

Term structure of interest rates relationships among interest rates on bonds with different maturities

Both the loanable funds theory and the liquidity preference theory assume that an economy has a single interest rate. In reality, there are many different rates on different bonds and bank loans. At any point in time, some rates are higher than others, as we saw in Figure 4.1. The balance of this chapter discusses differences among interest rates. **Table 4.3** lists the main factors behind these differences.

One factor is the term of a bond or a loan. *Term* means time to maturity. Bond maturities range from a few months to 30 years or more. Different maturities usually imply different interest rates, even for bonds issued by the same borrower. Similarly, banks charge different interest rates on loans of different durations.

The relationships among interest rates on bonds with different maturities are called the **term structure of interest rates**. Let's discuss what determines the term structure—why interest rates differ across maturities and how these differences change over time.

The Term Structure Under Certainty

To understand the term structure, we analyze savers' decisions about what bonds to buy. For now, let's make a major simplifying assumption: savers know the interest rates on all bonds, both today and in the future. For example, they know the rates on bonds that will be issued today, a year from now, and 5 years from now. We derive a theory of the term structure under this assumption of certainty, and then we look at what happens when savers are uncertain about future interest rates.

We start with an example involving 1-year and 2-year bonds. Suppose it is 2020, and Barbara plans to save money for two years, until 2022. Barbara is considering two ways to save: by purchasing 1-year bonds and by purchasing 2-year bonds. Let's compare the interest that Barbara the saver receives in the two cases.

Suppose first that Barbara buys 2-year bonds, and let $i_2(2020)$ denote the annual interest rate—the yield to maturity—on 2-year bonds issued in 2020. Barbara receives this interest rate for two years, for a total of $2i_2(2020)$. For example, if the interest rate is 4 percent, Barbara receives a total of $2(4\%) = 8\%$ of her initial wealth.[1]

Now suppose Barbara buys 1-year bonds. She purchases these bonds in 2020, and they mature in 2021. At that point she can use the proceeds to buy new 1-year bonds that mature in 2022. The interest rates on 1-year bonds purchased in 2020 and 2021 are $i_1(2020)$ and $i_1(2021)$, so Barbara receives total interest of $i_1(2020) + i_1(2021)$. Recall that we're assuming certainty, so Barbara knows both 1-year rates in advance.[2]

From this information, we can derive a relationship between 1- and 2-year interest rates. The interest earnings from a 2-year bond issued in 2020 must equal the total earnings from 1-year bonds issued in 2020 and 2021; that is,

$$2i_2(2020) = i_1(2020) + i_1(2021)$$

This equation must hold if borrowers issue both 1- and 2-year bonds. If the 2-year bonds offered more interest, savers like Barbara would buy only 2-year bonds. Issuers of 1-year bonds would have to raise interest rates to attract buyers. If 2-year bonds paid less, issuers of these bonds would have to raise rates. When savers know current and future interest rates for certain, competition to sell bonds equalizes the interest payments for different maturities.

If we divide the last equation by 2, we get a formula for the 2-year interest rate:

$$i_2(2020) = \frac{1}{2}\left[i_1(2020) + i_1(2021)\right]$$

The 2-year rate is the average of the current 1-year rate and the 1-year rate in the following year. For example, if the 1-year rate is 3 percent in 2020 and 5 percent in 2021, the 2-year rate in 2020 is 4 percent.

---

[1] This calculation uses an approximation. To see this, let's compute the earnings on a 2-year bond exactly. If someone saves a dollar at an interest rate i_2, his wealth grows to $1 + i_2$ dollars after a year. His wealth after two years is $(1 + i_2)^2$ (see the discussion of future value in Section 3.1). The quantity $(1 + i_2)^2$ equals $1 + 2i_2 + (i_2)^2$. Subtracting off the saver's initial dollar yields his total earnings: $2i_2 + (i_2)^2$.

We've assumed that the earnings on a 2-year bond are simply $2i_2$, which means we ignore the $(i_2)^2$ term. Economists often use this approximation because $(i_2)^2$ is small. For an interest rate of 4 percent (or 0.04 in decimal form), $(i_2)^2$ is 0.16% (0.0016). The total earnings on a 2-year bond are $2i_2 + (i_2)^2 = 8\% + 0.16\% = 8.16\%$. Our approximation yields 8 percent, which is accurate enough for present purposes.

[2] Once again we've used an approximation. The exact earnings from the 1-year bonds are $i_1(2020) + i_1(2021) + [i_1(2020)] \times [i_1(2021)]$. We ignore the last term (the product of the two rates), which is small.

This logic applies to any year. If $i_2(t)$ is the interest rate on a 2-year bond issued in year t, $i_1(t)$ the rate on a 1-year bond issued in year t, and $i_1(t + 1)$ the 1-year rate in the following year, then

$$i_2(t) = \frac{1}{2} [i_1(t) + i_1(t + 1)]$$

The 2-year rate in year t is the average of the 1-year rates in years t and $t + 1$.

This formula also holds for periods other than a year. If t is a *month* and $t + 1$ is the following month, the formula says that the 2-month interest rate is the average of two 1-month rates.

Our logic extends beyond one- and two-period bonds to longer-term bonds. If $i_3(t)$ is the interest rate on a *three*-period bond, then

$$i_3(t) = \frac{1}{3} [i_1(t) + i_1(t + 1) + i_1(t + 2)]$$

The three-period interest rate is the average of the one-period rates in the current period, t, and the next two periods, $t + 1$ and $t + 2$.

The rationale for this equation is similar to our reasoning about two-period bonds. Someone saving for three periods can buy either a three-period bond or a series of three one-period bonds. These strategies must produce the same earnings if savers buy both kinds of bonds. Equal earnings implies our formula for $i_3(t)$.

Finally, we can write a general formula for any maturity. Let $i_n(t)$ be the interest rate on an n-period bond in period t, where the maturity n can be four periods, five periods, or anything else. This interest rate is

$$i_n(t) = \frac{1}{n} [i_1(t) + i_1(t + 1) + \ldots + i_1(t + n - 1)] \tag{4.2}$$

The n-period interest rate is the average of one-period rates in the current period and the next $n - 1$ periods. For example, the 10-year interest rate in 2020 is the average of the 1-year rates in 2020 and the next nine years, 2021 through 2029.

The Expectations Theory of the Term Structure

So far, we have assumed that savers know the interest rates on all bonds, current and future. This simplifying assumption is not realistic. In 2020, savers know the current interest rates for all maturities, but they do not know with certainty what rates will be in 2021 or later.

To account for this fact, economists analyze the term structure with the **expectations theory of the term structure**. In this theory, savers do not know the future with certainty, but they have expectations about future interest rates. These expectations are rational: they are the best possible forecasts given all available information. Savers choose among bond maturities based on their rational expectations about future interest rates.

In the expectations theory of the term structure, bonds of different maturities must produce the same *expected* earnings. If they don't, nobody

Expectations theory of the term structure the n-period interest rate is the average of the current one-period rate and expected rates over the next $n - 1$ periods

will buy the bonds with lower expected earnings. This reasoning leads to the

EXPECTATIONS THEORY OF THE TERM STRUCTURE

$$i_n(t) = \frac{1}{n} [i_1(t) + Ei_1(t + 1) + \cdots + Ei_1(t + n - 1)] \qquad (4.3)$$

where E means "expected." This equation is the same as Equation (4.2), except it replaces actual future interest rates with expected rates. The n-period interest rate is the average of the current one-period rate and expected rates from $t + 1$ to $t + n - 1$.

▶ See Section 3.2 to review rational expectations.

Accounting for Risk

The expectations theory of the term structure assumes that savers choose bonds based only on expected interest rates. This assumption ignores the role of uncertainty. Modifying the theory to account for risk makes it more realistic, because savers are risk averse. When asset returns are uncertain, savers demand higher expected returns as compensation.

To see the implications of risk for the term structure, recall that long-term bond prices respond more strongly to changes in interest rates and are therefore more volatile than short-term bond prices. This means that holders of long-term bonds may experience large capital gains or losses, and this risk makes the bonds less attractive to savers.

▶ Table 3.3 illustrates the relative volatility in short- and long-term bond prices.

Therefore, once we take risk into account, it is *not* true that long- and short-term bonds yield the same expected earnings, as the basic expectations theory assumes. If they did, savers would buy only short-term bonds, which are less risky. To attract buyers, long-term bonds must offer higher expected earnings.

Economists capture this idea by modifying the expectations theory of the term structure to include a **term premium** for long-term interest rates. This premium, denoted by τ (the Greek letter tau), is the extra return that compensates the holder of a long-term bond for the bond's riskiness. Equation (4.3) becomes

Term premium (τ) extra return on a long-term bond that compensates for its riskiness; τ_n denotes the term premium on an n-period bond

THE EXPECTATIONS THEORY WITH A TERM PREMIUM

$$i_n(t) = \frac{1}{n} [i_1(t) + Ei_1(t + 1) + \cdots + Ei_1(t + n - 1)] + \tau_n \qquad (4.4)$$

where τ_n is the term premium for an n-period bond. This equation says that the n-period interest rate is the average of expected one-period rates *plus* the term premium.

Bonds of different maturities have different term premiums. The quantity τ_2 is the premium for two-period bonds, τ_3 is the premium for three-period bonds, and so on. The longer a bond's maturity, the higher its term premium—for example, $\tau_3 > \tau_2$ and $\tau_4 > \tau_3$. A longer maturity means a more variable bond price, requiring greater compensation for risk.

The Yield Curve

Yield curve graph comparing interest rates on bonds of various maturities at a given point in time

The term structure of interest rates can be summarized in a graph called the **yield curve**. The yield curve shows interest rates on bonds of various maturities at a given point in time. **Figure 4.13** shows a hypothetical yield curve for January 1, 2020. On that day, bonds with longer maturities have higher interest rates. For example, the 3-month interest rate is 4 percent, the 1-year rate is 5 percent, and the 10-year rate is 6 percent.

Yield Curve Shapes The yield curve looks different at different points in time. The shape of the curve depends on expectations about future interest rates. **Figure 4.14** shows four possibilities. All assume the same one-period rate but reflect different expectations about future rates, and these expectations produce different interest rates at longer maturities.

Suppose that people expect the one-period interest rate to stay constant. The expected future rates—$Ei_1(t + 1)$, $Ei_1(t + 2)$, and so on—all equal the current rate, $i_1(t)$. Substituting this assumption into the formula for the n-period rate, Equation (4.4), yields

$$i_n(t) = \frac{1}{n} [i_1(t) + i_1(t) + \cdots + i_1(t)] + \tau_n$$

FIGURE 4.13 Hypothetical Yield Curve for January 1, 2020

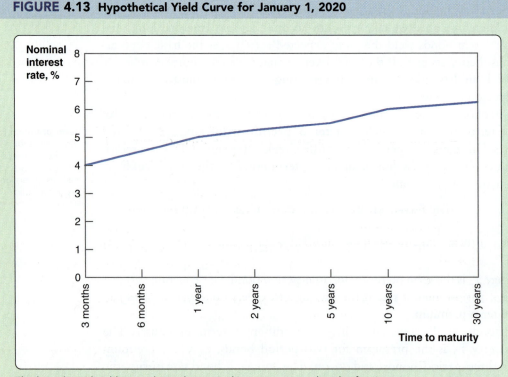

This hypothetical yield curve shows the nominal interest rates on bonds of various maturities on January 1, 2020. On that day, the 3-month interest rate is 4 percent, the 1-year rate is 5 percent, and the 10-year rate is 6 percent.

FIGURE 4.14 Four Possible Yield Curves

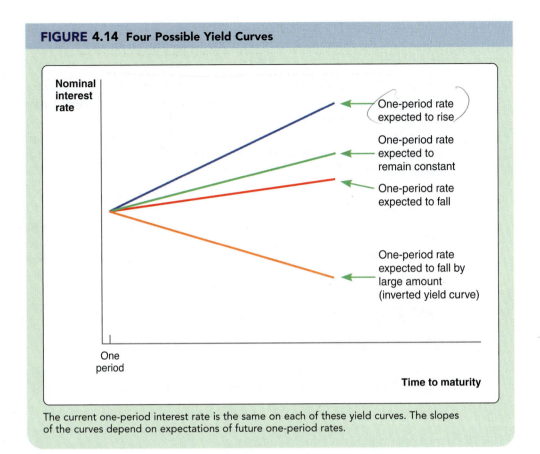

The current one-period interest rate is the same on each of these yield curves. The slopes of the curves depend on expectations of future one-period rates.

which simplifies to

$$i_n(t) = i_1(t) + \tau_n$$

With the one-period rate expected to stay constant, the average of expected future rates equals the current one-period rate. The n-period rate is the one-period rate plus a term premium.

Recall that the term premium τ_n rises with a bond's maturity, n. Therefore, the last equation implies that the interest rate $i_n(t)$ rises with n. This case is captured by the green line in Figure 4.14. Rising term premiums cause the yield curve to slope upward.

The other lines in the figure illustrate cases where the one-period interest rate is *not* expected to stay constant. The blue line is an example in which people expect the one-period rate to rise in the future. The average of expected future rates exceeds the current rate, pushing up long-term interest rates: they exceed the one-period rate by more than the term premium. In our graph, the yield curve is steep.

The red line is an example in which people expect the one-period interest rate to fall. The average of expected future rates is less than the current rate, reducing long-term rates and flattening the yield curve.

Finally, the orange line is an example of an **inverted yield curve**, a curve that slopes downward. This situation arises when people expect an

Inverted yield curve
downward-sloping yield curve signifying that short-term interest rates exceed long-term rates

unusually large fall in the one-period interest rate. This expectation reduces long-term rates by more than term premiums raise them, so long-term rates lie below the current one-period rate.

Forecasting Interest Rates The expected path of interest rates determines the shape of the yield curve. Turning this relation around, the yield curve tells us about the expected path of rates. An unusually steep curve, such as the blue line in Figure 4.14, means that short-term interest rates are expected to rise. An inverted curve, such as the orange line in Figure 4.14, means rates are expected to fall sharply.

These facts imply a use for the yield curve: to forecast interest rates. If you are thinking of borrowing money in the future, you would like to know future interest rates. You can't know these rates for sure, but you can estimate them with the yield curve. The yield curve reveals the expectations of people who trade bonds. These are good forecasts, because bond traders are well informed about interest rates.

CASE STUDY

Some Historical Examples of Yield Curves

To better understand the yield curve, let's look at some historical examples. **Figure 4.15** graphs the yield curves for U.S. Treasury bonds in January 1981,

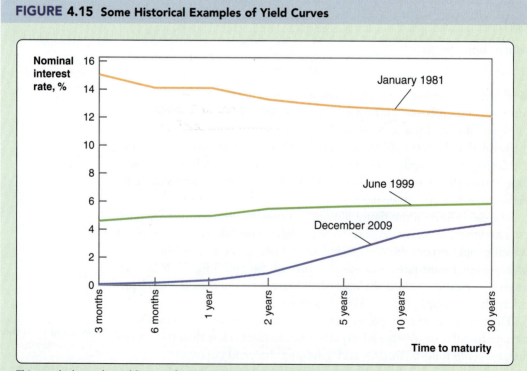

FIGURE 4.15 Some Historical Examples of Yield Curves

This graph shows the yield curves for U.S. Treasury bonds at three points in time.
Source: Federal Reserve Board

June 1999, and December 2009. These cases illustrate some of the possible yield curves that we've discussed.

Notice first that interest rates were highest at all maturities in 1981. Inflation was high at that time, producing high nominal interest rates through the Fisher equation, $i = r + \pi^e$. Interest rates were lowest in 2009, when inflation was very low.

The key features of the yield curves are their slopes. The yield curve for June 1999 has a common shape—a moderate upward slope. The interest rate is 4.6 percent at a maturity of 3 months, 5.6 percent at 2 years, and 6.0 percent at 30 years. The curve for December 2009 is steeper than usual, rising from less than 0.1 percent at 3 months to 4.5 percent at 30 years. Finally, the yield curve for January 1981 is inverted: interest rates fall with maturity over most of the curve. Let's discuss why the 2009 and 1981 yield curves had uncommon shapes.

December 2009 At this time, the Federal Reserve was fighting a deep recession. It had expanded the money supply, which reduced short-term interest rates as predicted by the liquidity preference theory (see Figure 4.11). The Fed hoped that low interest rates would stimulate spending by consumers and firms and help the economy recover.

The situation in December 2009 was extraordinary: the 3-month Treasury bill rate had not been so close to zero since the 1930s. Participants in bond markets expected that the economy would eventually recover, and the Fed would raise interest rates to more normal levels. Because expected future short-term rates exceeded the current short-term rate, the yield curve had a steep upward slope.

January 1981 At this time the Fed's primary concern was inflation, which was running at a rate of about 10 percent. To contain inflation, the Fed had slowed the growth of the money supply, raising the 3-month Treasury bill rate from 10 percent in September 1980 to 15 percent four months later. This policy was intended to slow economic growth temporarily, which in turn would reduce inflation.

As in 2009, bond market participants viewed the Fed's policy as temporary: they expected short-term interest rates to fall once inflation was under control. Indeed, they expected interest rates to end up lower than they were before the Fed started raising them, because lower inflation would reduce rates through the Fisher effect. Therefore, in January 1981 expected future interest rates were far below the current rate of 15 percent. This difference was large enough to outweigh term premiums and invert the yield curve.

As it happened, expectations of falling interest rates proved correct. The 3-month Treasury bill rate fell to 8 percent in 1983 and to 6 percent in 1986.

▶ Chapter 12 details the effects of monetary policy on economic growth and inflation.

4.5 DEFAULT RISK AND INTEREST RATES

The governments and corporations that issue bonds sometimes default: they don't make the payments they have promised. The risk of default varies across bonds, leading to differences in interest rates, with higher-risk bonds paying higher rates. The reason is simple. Default risk makes bonds less attractive to savers, so if bonds with different risk promised the same interest rate, savers would buy only the bonds with lowest risk. Issuers of high-risk bonds must offer high interest rates to attract buyers.

Default Risk on Sovereign Debt

Many national governments issue bonds to cover their budget deficits. These bonds are called **sovereign debt**. Default risk on these bonds varies greatly across countries.

Sovereign debt bonds issued by national governments

The U.S. government has never defaulted on its bonds. People generally assume this record will continue, so the bonds' default risk is close to zero. As a consequence, the interest rates on U.S. government bonds are always among the lowest for a given maturity.

The story is different in countries where governments have defaulted on bonds. Two examples are Russia in 1998 and Argentina in 2001. In both cases, the government ran up debt through years of high spending, and weak economies made it difficult to collect enough taxes to pay off the debt. Eventually, the government stopped making promised payments on its bonds.

Because of such experiences, purchasers of sovereign debt pay close attention to default risk. They are assisted by **bond-rating agencies**, such as Moody's Investor Service and Standard & Poor's (S&P). These firms study the political and economic situations in different countries and estimate the chances that governments will default.

Bond-rating agencies firms that estimate default risk on bonds

Rating agencies summarize their judgments with a grade for each country's debt. For example, Standard & Poor's gives ratings from AAA (triple A, the highest) to D (the lowest). Sometimes a plus or minus is added to the letter grade. **Table 4.4** shows the different S&P ratings, the corresponding ratings from Moody's, and examples of countries with these ratings in 2010. A low rating usually means that a country must offer high interest rates to sell its debt.

Sovereign debt from the richest countries, such as the United States and Germany, usually receives a AAA rating. A few rich countries slip to AA or A because of high government debt. For example, Italy's rating in 2010 was A+, or slightly above A, reflecting a debt of 107 percent of a year's GDP, one of the higher levels in Europe.

TABLE 4.4 Sovereign Debt Ratings, June 2010

Standard & Poor's	Moody's	Risk	Examples
AAA	Aaa	Lowest risk	United States, Germany
AA	Aa	Low risk	Chile, Japan
A	A	Low risk	Italy, China
BBB	Baa	Medium risk	Colombia, India
BB, B	Ba, B	High risk	Nigeria, Venezuela
CCC, CC, C	Caa, Ca, C	Highest risk	Ecuador
D	C	In default	

Poorer countries usually have lower debt ratings. Such countries have defaulted in the past, and analysts worry that economic or political crises will produce future defaults. Colombia's rating in 2010 was BBB+ and Venezuela's was BB−.

The bottom of the ratings scale covers countries with serious problems. In 2010, Ecuador had the world's lowest rating, CCC+. Ecuador's problems with budget deficits led it to default on parts of its debt in 1994, 2001, and 2008, and rating agencies think the risk of future defaults is high.

CASE STUDY

Greece's Debt Crisis

Early in 2010, reports that the Greek government might default on its debt dominated the international financial news. Greece had long run large budget deficits for reasons that range from tax evasion to high spending on retirement benefits. In 2007, Greece's debt was 106 percent of its GDP, and its bond rating was a mediocre A.

In 2009 and 2010, Greece's debt problem worsened dramatically. A recession reduced tax revenue, raising the debt to 126 percent of GDP in 2009, and this figure appeared likely to rise further in 2010 and beyond. This trend increased worries that Greece might default. As shown in **Figure 4.16A**, Standard & Poor's lowered Greece's debt rating three times, and the rating reached BB+ in April 2010.

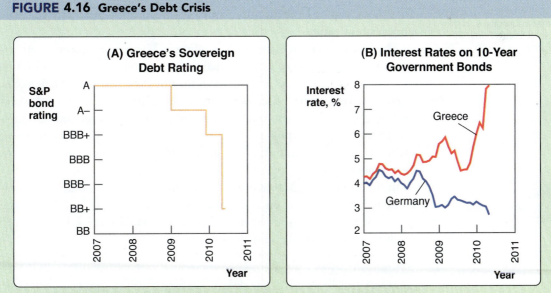

FIGURE 4.16 Greece's Debt Crisis

Over 2009–2010, fears that the Greek government might default on its debt caused the country's bond rating to fall (A) and interest rates on its bonds to rise relative to rates on bonds issued by other European governments (B).

Sources: Standard & Poor's; OECD

Of course, rising default risk produced rising interest rates. **Figure 4.16B** shows the yield to maturity on 10-year Greek government bonds; for comparison, it also shows yields on German bonds, which had a steady rating of AAA. From November 2009 to May 2010, the German interest rate fell from 3.2 percent to 2.7 percent, but the Greek rate rose from 4.8 percent to 8.0 percent.

Greece's deteriorating situation became a crisis in May 2010. Like many bond issuers, the Greek government needed to *roll over* its debt: when bonds reached maturity, it needed to raise funds to pay them off by issuing new bonds. A large number of bonds matured in May 2010, but with growing fears of default, it was not clear whether anyone would buy new Greek bond issues. Without bond buyers, the Greek government would run out of money and be forced to default immediately on its maturing bonds.

The debt crisis threatened other European countries. Many analysts predicted that a Greek default would shake confidence in the debt of Portugal, Spain, and Ireland, where debt levels were also rising, although not as fast as in Greece. These countries might be unable to roll over their debt, and they also would default. A wave of government defaults would shake confidence in the entire European economy, causing capital flight, reducing consumption and investment, and potentially causing a severe recession across the continent.

In an effort to prevent this outcome, the European Union (EU), an organization of 27 member countries, and the International Monetary Fund (IMF) agreed to lend Greece 110 billion euros (equivalent to $134 billion) over three years. The first installment, in May 2010, allowed Greece to pay off the bonds maturing that month and thus to avoid immediate default.

The loan to Greece came with conditions. The loan agreement sets targets for reducing Greece's budget deficit, and the lenders can cancel future disbursements of money if the targets are not met. To reduce deficits, the Greek government has raised taxes, frozen the salaries of government workers, and proposed further austerity measures, including reductions in retirement benefits. These policies have provoked strong opposition, however, including violent demonstrations in the streets of Athens and strikes by Greek labor unions.

In the summer of 2010, Greece's fate was uncertain. Would the government reduce its deficit enough to secure the rest of the EU–IMF loan? Even if it did receive the balance of the loan, would Greece have enough funds to avoid a default on its bonds?

 Chapter 18 details how default on sovereign debt damages a country's economy, how the effects spread to other countries, and the role of the IMF in debt crises.

 Online Case Study
An Update on European Debt

Default Risk on Corporate Debt

Corporations sometimes declare bankruptcy and default on their bonds. Bond-rating agencies study corporations and estimate default risk using the same grading scale as for sovereign debt (see Table 4.4).

AAA ratings go to well-known corporations with successful track records. Examples include ExxonMobil, Microsoft, and Johnson & Johnson. Bonds issued by these companies are considered safe—but not quite as safe as U.S. government bonds. In recent years, AAA corporate bonds have paid interest rates about one or two percentage points above Treasury bonds.

Companies with problems receive lower bond ratings. For example, in 2010 the media conglomerate Time Warner's bonds had a rating of BBB (medium risk). The rating reflected a high level of debt accumulated from purchasing other companies; an unsuccessful merger with AOL, which Time Warner bought in 2000 and sold in 2009; and the increasing availability of entertainment on the internet, which threatened Time Warner subsidiaries in the movie and television industries.

Corporate bonds with ratings below BBB are called **junk bonds** to indicate their high risk. In 2010, this category included many airlines. Continental and Delta had ratings of B, and United and US Airways had ratings of B–.

> **Junk bond** corporate bond with an S&P rating below BBB

Like countries, corporations can see their bond ratings change over time. General Motors is a dramatic example. Long considered one of the strongest U.S. companies, GM had a bond rating of AAA from 1953 (when it was first rated) until 1981. Over the 1980s and 1990s, however, GM's rating fell repeatedly as competition from Japanese carmakers cut into the company's sales, and GM did a poor job of containing costs.

> For current bond ratings on thousands of companies, link through the text Web site to the Standard & Poor's site.

GM's rating was AA– in 1990, A in 2000, and B in 2005. In 2008, as vehicle sales plummeted during the deepening U.S. recession, GM suffered large losses. Worries that the company might go bankrupt pushed its rating down to CC.

In June 2009, General Motors did declare bankruptcy. The U.S. government provided funds for a restructuring that continued the company's operations, but payments stopped on "old GM" bonds. The bankruptcy court ruled that holders of these bonds could eventually trade them for stock in the "new GM." In early 2010, GM bonds were selling at about 30 cents for each dollar of face value: bondholders had lost most of the money they lent to the company.

CASE STUDY

The High-Yield Spread

Bond ratings affect the interest rates that corporations must pay. How big is this effect? How much extra interest do savers demand as compensation for default risk? The answers vary over time, depending on the state of the economy.

> Chapter 18 elaborates on the high-yield spread's role in the financial crisis of 2007–2009 and in the recession that followed.

To illustrate, **Figure 4.17** presents data on the **high-yield spread**. This variable is the difference between two interest rates: the rates on corporate bonds with BBB ratings and with AAA ratings (both with maturities of 10 years). AAA bonds are safe, whereas BBB bonds have significant

> **High-yield spread** difference between interest rates on BBB and AAA corporate bonds with 10-year maturities

FIGURE 4.17 **The High-Yield Spread, 1960–2010**

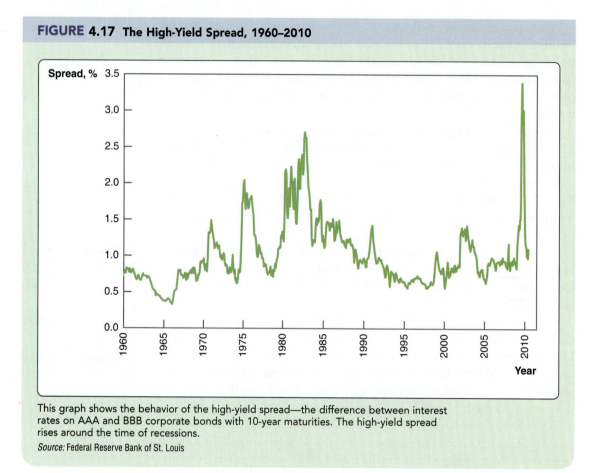

This graph shows the behavior of the high-yield spread—the difference between interest rates on AAA and BBB corporate bonds with 10-year maturities. The high-yield spread rises around the time of recessions.

Source: Federal Reserve Bank of St. Louis

default risk; a BBB rating is just above junk-bond level. The high-yield spread is the extra interest that compensates for default risk on BBB bonds.

In many years, the high-yield spread is 1 percentage point or less, but the spread has risen sharply in certain periods. Figure 4.17 reveals spikes in the 1970s and 1980s, smaller increases in the early 1990s and early 2000s, and a large increase over 2008–2009.

What causes these peaks is no mystery: they all occur near recessions, when the economy's output falls. When a recession occurs, many firms see their earnings fall. Firms with AAA ratings are strong enough to survive these episodes, but BBB firms, which were shaky to start with, may be driven into bankruptcy. Default risk rises, for BBB bonds, so savers demand greater compensation for this risk.

Economists monitor the high-yield spread because of its relation to recessions. The spread often starts rising near the beginning of a downturn and signals trouble to come. For example, the spread started shooting up in October 2008, suggesting that the ongoing financial crisis would cause major damage to the economy. This prediction was borne out as the unemployment rate rose from 6.6% in October 2008 to 10.1% in October 2009.

4.6 TWO OTHER FACTORS

We have discussed the two biggest reasons for differences in interest rates, maturity and default risk. Two other factors listed in Table 4.3 on page 104, liquidity and taxes, are worth a mention.

Liquidity

Remember the concept of liquidity: an asset's liquidity is the ease of converting it to money. Asset holders value liquidity because they might need to raise money quickly in an emergency.

Bonds vary in their liquidity. U.S. government bonds are highly liquid, because bond dealers trade large quantities every day. People can sell government bonds in this market whenever they want.

Corporate bonds are less liquid. A particular company—say, Johnson & Johnson—issues far fewer bonds than the government, and the bonds are not traded as often. Someone who wants to sell a Johnson & Johnson bond may not find a buyer quickly.

Recall that corporate bonds pay higher interest rates than U.S. government bonds. One reason is default risk, as we have discussed. Another is liquidity: savers demand an extra return on corporate bonds to compensate for the difficulty of selling them. The interest rate spread between government bonds and the highest-rated corporate bonds (AAA) largely reflects liquidity, because default risk on AAA corporate bonds is almost as low as default risk on government bonds.

Taxes

Taxation affects interest rates. This factor is most relevant for interest rates on **municipal bonds**—bonds issued by state and local governments in the United States. Interest income from Treasury bonds issued by the federal government is taxed at the same rate as wages and salaries, but interest on municipal bonds is tax-free.

This tax difference encourages savers to buy municipal bonds. As a result, these bonds usually pay lower interest rates than Treasury bonds. In the early 2000s, rates on municipal bonds were about half a percentage point below rates on Treasury bonds with the same maturity.

The behavior of municipal-bond interest rates changed during the financial crisis of 2007–2009. These rates rose *higher* than the rates on Treasury bonds during the crisis and stayed about the same as Treasury rates in 2010. These developments reflected budget crises in many states and cities, a result of falling tax revenue as the economy slumped. Bondholders started to fear default on municipal bonds and demanded higher interest rates as compensation. This effect offset the tax advantages that reduce municipal bond rates.

Municipal bonds bonds issued by state and local governments

Summary

- This chapter surveys the determinants of interest rates. It analyzes the overall level of interest rates and differences among rates on different bonds and loans.

4.1 The Loanable Funds Theory

- In the loanable funds theory, the real interest rate is determined by the supply and demand for loans.
- The demand for loans equals investment. A higher interest rate reduces the quantity of loans demanded.
- The supply of loans equals saving plus net capital inflows. A higher interest rate raises both parts of this sum, so it increases the quantity of loans supplied.
- The equilibrium real interest rate, r^*, is the rate at which the supply and demand for loans intersect.

4.2 Determinants of Interest Rates in the Loanable Funds Theory

- Shifts in the supply and demand for loans cause changes in the equilibrium real interest rate. These shifts result from changes in investment, saving, and net capital inflows.
- The causes of investment shifts include new technologies and changes in investor confidence. Shifts in saving arise from changes in private saving and public saving (the budget surplus or deficit). Net capital inflows shift because of changes in confidence and changes in foreign interest rates.
- The nominal interest rate is the equilibrium real interest rate plus expected inflation. Countries with high inflation have high nominal interest rates.

4.3 The Liquidity Preference Theory

- In the liquidity preference theory, the nominal interest rate is determined by the supply and demand for money.
- The supply of money is the amount created by the central bank. The demand for money is the amount that people choose to hold. A rise in the nominal interest rate reduces the quantity of money demanded.
- The equilibrium nominal interest rate, i^*, is the rate at which money supply and money demand intersect. It changes when the central bank changes the money supply, or when money demand shifts. Shifts in money demand arise from changes in aggregate spending or changes in transaction technologies.

4.4 The Term Structure of Interest Rates

- The term structure is the relationship among interest rates on bonds of different maturities (terms).
- According to the expectations theory of the term structure, the interest rate on an n-period bond is the average of the current one-period rate and the expected rates for the next $n - 1$ periods.
- The interest rates on long-term bonds include term premiums that compensate for the risk of price changes. Term premiums rise with a bond's maturity.
- The yield curve summarizes the term structure at a point in time. The yield curve usually slopes upward, is steeper than usual when short-term interest rates are expected to rise, and is inverted when interest rates are expected to fall by a large amount. Economists use the yield curve to forecast future interest rates.

4.5 Default Risk and Interest Rates

- Interest rates on bonds increase with the level of default risk. This risk is low for bonds issued by the U.S. government but high for some other governments. Default risk also varies for corporate bonds.
- Agencies such as Moody's and Standard & Poor's rate the default risk on countries' and corporations' bonds.
- The high-yield spread is the difference between interest rates on BBB and AAA corporate bonds. This spread rises in recessions.

4.6 Two Other Factors

- Corporate bonds are less liquid than U.S. government bonds. This fact helps explain why corporate bonds pay higher interest rates than government bonds do.
- Interest income from municipal bonds is not taxed, which reduces interest rates on these bonds.

Key Terms

adaptive expectations, p. 98

bond-rating agencies, p. 112

budget deficit, p. 94

budget surplus, p. 94

capital flight, p. 97

capital inflows, p. 87

capital outflows, p. 87

expectations theory of the term structure, p. 106

Fisher equation, p. 98

high-yield spread, p. 115

inverted yield curve, p. 109

junk bond, p. 115

liquidity preference theory, p. 99

loanable funds theory, p. 86

municipal bonds, p. 117

net capital inflows, p. 87

private saving, p. 93

public saving, p. 93

sovereign debt, p. 112

term premium, τ, p. 107

term structure of interest rates, p. 104

yield curve, p. 108

Questions and Problems

1. Using the loanable funds theory, show in a graph how each of the following events affects the supply and demand for loans and the equilibrium real interest rate:

   a. A war leads the government to increase spending on the military. (Assume taxes do not change.)

   b. Wars in *other* countries lead to higher government spending in those countries.

   c. Someone invents a new kind of computer that makes firms more productive. Many firms want to buy the computer. Higher productivity also increases people's confidence in the economy, so consumers see less need to save.

   d. The same things happen as in part (c). In addition, increased confidence in the economy raises net capital inflows.

2. Suppose the real interest rate rises. Using the loanable funds theory, discuss whether this event is likely to reflect good economic news or is a sign of trouble.

3. Comment on this statement: "People care about real interest rates, not nominal rates. Therefore, money demand should depend on the difference between the real rates on money and bonds, *not* the nominal rate on bonds."

4. Suppose that discount brokers make bonds more liquid. It becomes quick and inexpensive to sell bonds. In the liquidity preference theory, how does this development affect money demand and the interest rate?

5. Suppose again that discount brokers make bonds more liquid. What should the central bank do if it doesn't want the interest rate to change? Explain your answer.

6. Suppose it is 2020 and the 1-year interest rate is 4 percent. The expected 1-year rates in the following four years (2021 to 2024) are 4 percent, 5 percent, 6 percent, and 6 percent.

   a. Assume the expectations theory of the term structure, with no term premiums.

Compute the interest rates in 2020 on bonds with maturities of 1, 2, 3, 4, and 5 years. Draw a yield curve.

b. Redo part (a) with term premiums. Assume the term premium for an *n*-year bond, τ_n, is $(n/2)$ percent. For example, the premium for a 4-year bond is $(4/2)\% = 2\%$.

7. Suppose it is 2020, the 1-year interest rate is 8 percent, and the 10-year rate is 6 percent.

   a. Draw a graph showing a likely path of the 1-year rate from 2020 through 2029.

   b. Why might people expect such a path for the 1-year rate?

8. Using the expectations theory without term premiums, derive a formula giving the 4-year interest rate in 2020 as a function of *2-year* rates in 2020 and the future.

9. Suppose that some event has no effect on expected interest rates, but raises uncertainty about rates. What happens to the yield curve? Explain.

10. Suppose a Treasury bond costs $100 and promises a payment of $105 in one year. A bond from the Acme Corporation costs $100 and promises $107 in a year. Assume that Acme pays the $107 with probability *p*. With probability $1 - p$, Acme defaults and pays nothing. What are likely values of *p*? Explain.

▶ Online and Data Questions
www.worthpublishers.com/ball

11. From the text Web site, link to the site of the Federal Reserve Bank of St. Louis; also, see the "Guide to St. Louis Fed Data." Get data on the inflation rate and the interest rate on 90-day Treasury bills. Compute the average T-bill rate and average inflation for each decade from the 1960s to the 2000s. Graph the relationship between the two variables across decades, and explain your results.

12. From the text Web site, link to the St. Louis Fed site for data on the high–yield spread and on the unemployment rate.

    a. Graph unemployment on the horizontal axis and the spread on the vertical axis, with a point for each year from 1970 to the present. What do you learn from this graph?

    b. Graph the recent behavior of unemployment and the high–yield spread, with time on the horizontal axis. Plot the two variables for every *month* from January 2007 to the present. What do you learn from this graph that you didn't learn from the graph in part (a)?

13. Link through the text Web site to the "Ratings" page of the Standard & Poor's Web site. Find a country or corporation whose debt rating has recently changed and explain why S&P made the change.

Securities Markets

UPI Photo/Monika Graff/Landov

If you are a college student, you may not be a saver right now. But someday you probably will be. Perhaps your brilliance and hard work will make you rich. Even if your income is modest, you will probably set some of it aside for retirement. Either way, you will have to choose what to do with your savings.

Should you put your money in a bank? Should you buy securities such as stocks and bonds? Which securities are best? Should you buy individual securities or buy shares of a mutual fund that owns many different securities?

People around the world face the problem of **asset allocation**, as do financial institutions that hold assets, such as banks and pension funds. Decisions about asset allocation produce the activity that we see in financial markets—the daily trading of securities worth billions of dollars.

This chapter discusses securities markets. We first meet the participants in these markets, including a variety of financial institutions. Then we discuss how the markets work—how governments and firms issue securities and how securities are traded. Much securities trading occurs at exchanges such as the New York Stock Exchange, pictured here.

Traders conduct business on the floor of the New York Stock Exchange on July 17, 2007, when the Dow Jones stock index rose above 14,000 for the first time.

Asset allocation decisions by individuals or institutions about what assets to hold

Next we analyze the key choices facing securities market participants. These include firms' decisions about what securities to issue and savers' choices about allocating their assets. Savers must decide how to split their wealth among broad classes of assets, such as stocks and bonds. They must also choose among individual securities, such as the stocks of different companies.

We turn last to another class of securities: *derivatives*, securities with payoffs tied to the prices of other assets. Markets for derivatives have grown rapidly in the last few decades. We discuss what derivative securities are, why they are traded, and the risks they can create.

The behavior of securities markets is a vast subject. This chapter's overview highlights key issues and ideas. If you take courses in finance, you will study some of these topics in detail. The goal here is to give you a broad understanding of what happens in securities markets.

5.1 PARTICIPANTS IN SECURITIES MARKETS

The players in securities markets include individual savers like you and me and many kinds of financial institutions. The key institutions are listed in Table 5.1. Some own large quantities of securities, some help people and firms to trade securities, and some do both.

TABLE 5.1 Major Institutions in Securities Markets

Securities Firms
Mutual funds
Hedge funds
Brokers
Dealers
Investment banks
Other Financial Institutions
Pension funds
Insurance companies
Commercial banks

Before diving into the details, let's review our terminology. In the financial world, the purchase of securities is often called *investment*. People who buy securities are *investors*, and institutions that buy securities are *institutional investors*. You will encounter this terminology in the media, and you will hear it if you talk to a stockbroker.

In economics, however, *investment* means the production of physical capital, such as factories and machines. When Exxon builds an oil well, it is investing. When you buy Exxon's securities, you are saving, *not* investing. We will stick with this economic terminology throughout the book.

Individual Owners

Some securities are owned by individual people. In 2007 (the latest year with data available), U.S. citizens directly owned 28 percent of the stock of U.S. companies. They also owned most shares in mutual funds, which held another 25 percent of U.S. corporate stock.

Over time, stock ownership has spread to a larger fraction of the U.S. population. In 1983, only 19 percent of households owned any stock, either directly or indirectly through mutual funds. In 2008, 47 percent of households owned stock. One reason for this trend is the growth of 401(k) plans that channel workers' retirement savings into securities.

Although many people own stock, a few hold disproportionately large amounts. In 2007, the wealthiest 1 percent of U.S. households owned 38 percent of stock held by individuals. The top 10 percent in wealth owned 80 percent.

Securities Firms

Among the financial institutions that participate in securities markets, one broad category is **securities firms**. These companies' primary purpose is to hold securities, trade them, or help others trade them. There are several types of securities firms: mutual funds, hedge funds, brokers and dealers, and investment banks.

Mutual Funds **A mutual fund** is a financial institution that holds a diversified set of securities and sells shares to savers. In effect, each shareholder owns a small part of all the securities in a fund. Buying mutual fund shares is an easy way for savers to diversify their assets, which reduces risk.

About 8000 separate mutual funds exist in the United States. Most are run by large mutual fund companies such as Fidelity, Vanguard, and American Funds. Each company offers a menu of funds that feature different sets of securities.

Some funds hold a wide variety of stocks and bonds; others specialize. For example, some funds hold only Treasury bonds, and some hold only corporate bonds. Some specialize in stocks issued by large firms, and some specialize in small firms' stock. Some funds hold only U.S. securities, and some hold foreign securities.

Hedge Funds Like mutual funds, **hedge funds** raise pools of money to purchase securities. Unlike mutual funds, they cater only to wealthy people and institutions. Most hedge funds require clients to contribute $1 million or more.

A key difference between hedge funds and mutual funds involves government regulation. To protect small savers, the government limits the risks that mutual funds can take with shareholders' money. Hedge funds are largely unregulated, because the government assumes that the funds' rich customers can look out for themselves. Light regulation means that hedge funds can make risky bets on asset prices. These bets sometimes produce large earnings and sometimes large losses.

One common tool of hedge funds is **leverage**: funds borrow money from banks and use it to increase their security holdings. Larger security holdings magnify the funds' gains and losses when security prices change. Mutual funds aren't allowed to use leverage to buy securities because of the risk of large losses. Another risky practice of hedge funds, one forbidden for mutual funds, is trading derivative securities (discussed in detail in Section 5.6).

Money flowed into hedge funds in the early 2000s, and their total assets reached $3 trillion in 2007. During the financial crisis of 2007–2009, asset values fell and savers withdrew money from hedge funds. In 2009, total hedge-fund assets had fallen to $1.5 trillion.

Brokers and Dealers These firms help securities markets operate. A **broker** buys and sells securities on behalf of others. For example, if you want to acquire a share of Microsoft, a broker will buy it for you in a stock market. You pay a fee to the broker for this service.

Securities firm company whose primary purpose is to hold securities, trade them, or help others trade them; includes mutual funds, hedge funds, brokers and dealers, and investment banks

Mutual fund financial institution that holds a diversified set of securities and sells shares to savers

Hedge fund variant of a mutual fund that raises money from wealthy people and institutions and is largely unregulated, allowing it to make risky bets on asset prices

Leverage borrowing money to purchase assets

Broker firm that buys and sells securities for others

You can choose between two types of brokers. A *full-service broker* has advisors who help clients choose which securities to buy. Leading full-service brokers include Merrill Lynch, Smith Barney, and Dean Witter. A *discount broker* provides less advice, or none at all; customers must choose securities on their own. This category includes Charles Schwab, TD Ameritrade, and online brokers such as E*Trade.

Dealer firm that buys and sells certain securities for itself, making a market in the securities

A **dealer** buys securities for itself, not others, and earns profits by reselling them at higher prices. Typically, a dealer firm specializes in a narrow set of securities, such as Treasury bills or the stocks of certain companies. It holds an inventory of these securities and "makes a market" for them. The dealer stands ready to buy the securities when someone else wants to sell and to sell when someone else wants to buy.

Investment Banks This type of securities firm includes well-known names such as Goldman Sachs, Morgan Stanley, and Credit Suisse. An **investment bank** is not really a bank in economists' sense of the term, because it does not take deposits. Instead, investment banks have several functions in securities markets.

Investment bank financial institution that serves as an underwriter and advises companies on mergers and acquisitions

Underwriter financial institution that helps companies issue new securities

A traditional function is underwriting, a process we discuss in Section 5.2. As an **underwriter**, an investment bank helps companies issue new stocks and bonds. It advises the companies and markets the securities to potential buyers.

Investment banks also advise companies on *mergers and acquisitions*, or M&A. In these deals, two companies are combined or one company buys another. Investment banks research their client companies' potential profits from M&A and advise their clients about which deals to make and what prices to pay.

Although underwriting and advising are their core functions, investment banks have developed other ways to earn profits. Many investment banks buy and sell securities. Like hedge funds, they try to make money through risky bets on asset prices.

Investment banks also practice *financial engineering*, the development and marketing of new types of securities. One such security is the *junk bond*, a bond issued by a corporation with a low credit rating. Junk bonds were the brainchild of investment banker Michael Milken, whose firm, Drexel Burnham, started underwriting junk bonds in 1977. This innovation allowed more corporations to raise money in bond markets. More recently, investment banks have invented new derivative securities and securities backed by home-mortgage loans, as discussed in upcoming case studies.

Other Financial Institutions

In addition to securities firms, several other financial institutions are important participants in securities markets, because they buy large quantities of stocks and bonds.

Pension Funds Employers, both private firms and governments, establish pension funds to provide income to retired workers. Employers contribute money to the funds, and sometimes workers also make contributions. Pension funds use this money to purchase securities, and earnings from the securities provide retirement benefits.

Insurance Companies These companies sell life insurance and insure property, such as houses and cars. Purchasers of insurance pay premiums, which the companies use to buy securities. Earnings from the securities pay for insurance claims.

Commercial Banks In contrast to investment banks, commercial banks are institutions that accept deposits and make loans. Their primary assets are those loans—the money they are owed by borrowers. However, commercial banks also own securities, mainly government bonds. Banks hold bonds for liquidity: they can sell the bonds easily if they need cash.

Financial Industry Consolidation

In practice, the various types of institutions that participate in securities markets overlap, because many firms engage in more than one business. For example, Merrill Lynch has long been a leader in both investment banking and brokerage. Over the last 20 years, mergers have produced large securities firms with multiple functions.

Two major events have contributed to consolidation in the financial industry. One was the 1999 repeal of the *Glass-Steagall Act*, which forbade commercial banks from merging with investment banks. With Glass-Steagall gone, mergers created conglomerates such as Citigroup and JPMorgan Chase, which own commercial banks and also perform most functions of securities firms.

▶ Chapter 8 discusses the reasons behind the repeal of Glass-Steagall and the mergers that followed.

The financial crisis of 2007–2009 is the second major event that has contributed to financial industry consolidation. During the crisis, financial institutions that were relatively healthy bought institutions in danger of failing. The next case study discusses two of these deals: the takeovers of the investment banks Bear Stearns and Merrill Lynch.

CASE STUDY

The Upheaval in Investment Banking

At the start of 2008, the five largest investment banks in the United States were Goldman Sachs, Morgan Stanley, Merrill Lynch, Lehman Brothers, and Bear Stearns. Over the course of the year, all these institutions faced crises that threatened their survival.

Chapter 18 revisits the 2008 crisis in investment banking. We discuss the impact on the U.S. economy and detail the responses of the Federal Reserve and the federal government.

The story begins in the early 2000s, when the five investment banks started issuing *mortgage-backed securities* (MBSs). To create these securities, they purchased home-mortgage loans from the original lenders and bundled them together. The buyers of the securities became entitled to shares of the interest and principal payments that borrowers made on the underlying mortgages.

▶ Chapter 8 details how mortgage-backed securities are created, the growth of subprime lending, and the causes of rising default rates.

Investment banks were not the first financial institutions to issue mortgage-backed securities. But the novel feature of their MBSs was that the mortgages backing them were *subprime*: they were loans to people with weak credit histories. Subprime borrowers must pay higher interest rates than traditional mortgage borrowers pay. As a result, securities backed by subprime mortgages promised high returns to their owners—as long as borrowers made their mortgage payments.

The investment banks sold some of their mortgage-backed securities to customers, but they kept others for themselves. Unfortunately, the decline in house prices that started in 2006 caused a rash of defaults on subprime mortgages, because many borrowers couldn't afford their payments and couldn't sell their houses for enough to pay off their debts. As defaults rose, participants in financial markets realized that securities backed by subprime mortgages would produce less income than previously expected. Lower expected income reduced the prices of the securities, causing large losses to the investment banks and other owners of MBSs.

Eventually, mounting losses created crises at the investment banks. In early 2008, rumors spread that Bear Stearns might go bankrupt. Other financial institutions stopped lending to Bear or buying its bonds because they feared that Bear would default on its obligations. Bear ran out of money to pay off its existing loans and commercial paper that was maturing.

In March 2008, lawyers for Bear Stearns started preparing a bankruptcy filing. At the last minute, the Federal Reserve intervened. The Fed brokered a deal in which JPMorgan Chase purchased Bear Stearns. As a result, Bear did not default on its debts. The firm ceased to exist, but many of its operations continued under the management of JPMorgan Chase.

Six months later, Lehman Brothers faced a similar crisis: doubts about its survival led other institutions to cut off lending to the firm. But in contrast to Bear's fate, nobody stepped in to save Lehman, and it declared bankruptcy on September 15. It went out of business and defaulted on its outstanding bonds and bank loans.

Lehman's failure shocked participants in financial markets, creating fears that other investment banks would fail. On the same day as Lehman's bankruptcy, Bank of America purchased Merrill Lynch. Like Bear Stearns, Merrill was absorbed into a healthier institution.

Goldman Sachs and Morgan Stanley held fewer mortgage-backed securities than the other investment banks. They lost less and were able to remain independent but needed to reassure other financial institutions that they would survive. To do so, both firms became *financial holding companies (FHCs)* on September 21. This reorganization gave them the right to open commercial banks and to receive emergency loans from the Fed. In return, Goldman and Morgan accepted greater Fed regulation of their activities.

Despite these dramatic events, large investment banks still exist in the United States. As FHCs, Goldman Sachs and Morgan Stanley remain independent and continue to conduct investment-banking activities, including underwriting and securities trading. Merrill Lynch still operates as a broker and investment bank, albeit as a subsidiary of Bank of America. After losses in 2008, both Merrill and Goldman (but not Morgan Stanley) returned to profitability in 2009.

Online Case Study
An Update on Investment Banks

5.2 STOCK AND BOND MARKETS

Now that the players in securities markets have been introduced, let's discuss how they interact with one another. Savers and financial institutions participate in two kinds of markets. Firms and governments issue new securities in **primary markets**, and existing securities are traded in **secondary markets**.

> **Primary markets** financial markets in which firms and governments issue new securities
>
> **Secondary markets** financial markets in which existing securities are traded

Primary Markets

When a firm is founded, it can get funds from the owners' personal wealth and from bank loans. It may also attract funds from *venture capital firms*, which finance new companies in return for ownership shares. Up to this point, the firm is a *private company* with a small number of owners.

The Process of Issuing Securities As a firm grows, it may need more funds than it can raise as a private company. At that point, it turns to securities markets. It becomes a **public company**, a firm that issues securities that are traded in financial markets. A firm becomes public by making a first sale of stock, which is called an **initial public offering**, or **IPO**. Purchasers of the stock receive ownership shares in the firm. In return, the firm receives funds that it can use for investment.

> **Public company** firm that issues securities that are traded in financial markets
>
> **Initial public offering (IPO)** sale of stock when a firm becomes public

Typically, a company's IPO is underwritten by investment banks. The company initiates this process by hiring a lead investment bank, which enlists other investment banks to form a *syndicate*. The syndicate members purchase the company's stock and resell it immediately to financial institutions, such as mutual funds and pension funds. Shares are not offered to individual savers. Typically, investment banks sell the stock for 5 to 10 percent more than they pay for it.

A company announces an IPO in a formal document called a *prospectus*, which describes the stock being offered and the price. The prospectus also provides detailed information on the company, including financial statements and biographies of managers. The company's investment banks help prepare the prospectus. They also market the stock by sending their representatives around the country on *road shows*, presentations about the stock to potential purchasers, such as mutual fund managers.

After a firm goes public, it returns to securities markets periodically to raise funds for investment. The firm can issue new stock, spreading ownership of the firm across additional buyers. It can also borrow money by issuing bonds. Investment banks underwrite these security issues, just as they underwrite IPOs.

▶Section 1.3 explains how asymmetric information affects financial markets.

The Need for Underwriters Investment banks earn large profits from underwriting. They receive a significant chunk of the money that firms raise by issuing securities. Why can't firms cut out investment banks and sell securities directly to the final purchasers?

The answer is that investment banks reduce the asymmetric information problem of adverse selection—that is, the problem that firms may be most eager to issue securities when the value of the securities is low. Adverse selection prevents brand-new companies from issuing securities. To go public, a firm needs a track record to help people judge the value of its stock. Even then, potential purchasers of securities are wary because they know less about the firm's business than the firm does. They fear that potentially unprofitable companies will try to sell securities at inflated prices.

Investment banks reduce this worry when they underwrite a firm's securities. They research the firm and try to ensure that it is sound and that its securities are priced reasonably. Investment banks convince other institutions of the securities' value by putting their own reputations on the line. If the Acme Corporation hires Goldman Sachs to underwrite its IPO, it has a better chance of selling its securities. Mutual fund managers may not have heard of Acme, but they've heard of Goldman Sachs, and they know that Goldman has a history of underwriting good securities.

Because reputation is so important, underwriting is a concentrated industry dominated by a small number of institutions. Since 2000, 10 investment banks have underwritten more than half the securities issued around the world. It is hard for lesser-known underwriters to enter the business. If your friend Joe started Joe's Discount Investment Bank, he would probably have trouble selling securities. Mutual fund managers don't know Joe, so they would fear a ripoff.

We can better understand the role of underwriters by examining Google's IPO in 2004—one of the few that did *not* involve traditional underwriting. Instead, Google sold shares through an auction in which any institution or person could submit bids. Google hired Morgan Stanley and Credit Suisse to run the auction, but these firms did not research the company's finances or market Google's stock to possible buyers. As a result, they received only 3 percent of the IPO revenue, not the usual 5 to 10 percent charged by underwriters.

Google was able to modify the traditional IPO because it was an unusually well-known, successful company. Its reputation reduced the adverse selection problem. Many people were eager to buy Google stock, so the company didn't need the usual help from investment banks.

One issuer of securities has never hired an investment bank: the U.S. government. The government is even better known than Google, so it can sell bonds directly to savers and financial institutions. Most government bonds are issued through auctions run by the Treasury Department and designed to produce the highest possible prices for the bonds. Many details of Google's auction were patterned after Treasury auctions. The next case study describes how some of these auctions work.

CASE STUDY

Treasury Bill Auctions

Every Monday, the U.S. Treasury auctions T-bills with maturities of 13 weeks and 26 weeks. Each T-bill has a face value of $1000, which it pays at maturity. It is a zero-coupon security, meaning it pays nothing before maturity.

A few days before each auction, the Treasury examines its needs for cash and decides how many bills to issue. It announces this figure and invites bids, which are due by 1 PM on the auction day.

There are two kinds of bidders: noncompetitive and competitive. Non-competitive bidders simply state how many T-bills they wish to buy without specifying a price. These bidders are mainly small savers. Any saver can establish an account with the Treasury and submit bids through the TreasuryDirect Web site. The minimum purchase is a single $1000 T-bill.

Competitive bidders are bond dealers and other financial institutions that often buy millions of dollars worth of T-bills. Each competitive bidder states a desired quantity of bills *and* the price it is willing to pay. Many bids are submitted just seconds before the 1 PM deadline.

Once all the bids are in, the Treasury determines who gets the available T-bills. First, T-bills are allocated to all the noncompetitive bidders. Then the competitive bidders are ranked by the prices they submitted. The bidder with the highest price is awarded the number of bills it wants, then the bidder with the second-highest price, and so on until no bills are left.

All the T-bills are sold for the same price—the lowest price offered by any bidder who receives bills. Bidders who submitted higher prices pay less than they bid. This system is called a *unitary price auction*.

Let's look at a specific example. On Monday, January 25, 2010, the Treasury auctioned $23 billion worth of 13-week T-bills. It received approximately $2.3 billion in noncompetitive bids and $97.0 billion in competitive bids. The noncompetitive bidders received their requested $2.3 billion, leaving $20.7 billion for the competitive bidders with the highest bids.

The median of successful bids was $999.90 (half the successful bids were above this level and half below). The lowest successful bid was $999.86, so all the bills were sold for that price. A price of $999.86 for a $1000 T-bill implies a yield to maturity of 0.014 percent over 13 weeks. This is equivalent to an annual yield of about 0.056 percent.

Before 1998 the Treasury used a different system called a *discriminatory auction*. Each bidder paid whatever price it bid. In our example, an institution that submitted the median bid of $999.90 would have paid that price rather than $999.86.

It might appear that discriminatory auctions raise more revenue for the government than uniform price auctions. However, economists believe that uniform price auctions produce higher bids. A bidder is less leery of overpaying, because it won't pay its full bid if the bid is unusually high. The Treasury experimented with different kinds of auctions during the 1990s and decided that uniform price auctions raise the most money.

Link through the text Web site to the TreasuryDirect site to see how individuals bid for T-bills. If you have a spare $1000, you can buy a T-bill next Monday.

▶ The tiny yield on T-bills in January 2010—less than a tenth of a percent—reflected a decision by the Federal Reserve to keep interest rates near zero. The Fed was trying to help the economy recover from a deep recession, as we discuss in Chapter 12.

Secondary Markets

After securities are issued in primary markets, their buyers often resell them in secondary markets. Then the securities are traded repeatedly among institutions and individual savers.

▶ Secondary markets can also be categorized as *money markets* or *capital markets*. Money markets are markets for bonds with maturities less than 1 year (T-bills and commercial paper). Capital markets are markets for longer-term bonds and for stocks.

To understand this process, we first discuss how brokers help people enter securities markets. Then we discuss the main types of secondary markets: *exchanges* and *over-the-counter (OTC) markets*. OTC markets can be divided into *dealer markets* and *electronic communication networks (ECNs)*.

The Role of Brokers

A financial institution can buy securities directly from other institutions. Individual savers can buy bonds directly from the government in auctions. However, to buy stocks or corporate bonds, individuals need assistance from brokers.

If you want to buy securities, the first step is to establish an account with a broker. You can use a traditional broker, such as Merrill-Lynch, or an online broker, such as E*Trade. You deposit money in your account so it is available to buy the securities you choose.

When you want to buy or sell, you contact your broker by phone or over the Internet. You place an order—let's say you want to buy 100 shares of Boeing, the aircraft manufacturer. You can place a *market order,* which tells the broker to buy Boeing for the best price he can find. Or you can place a *limit order*, telling him to buy only if the price reaches a certain level. The broker fills your order in different ways, depending on which type of secondary market he uses.

Exchange physical location where brokers and dealers meet to trade securities

Exchanges

Your broker may fill your order at an **exchange**, a physical location where brokers and dealers meet. Exchanges are used mostly to trade stocks, not bonds. The world's largest securities exchange is the New York Stock Exchange (NYSE), located on Wall Street in lower Manhattan. The stocks of roughly 3000 companies are traded on the NYSE. Other cities with large stock exchanges include London, Frankfurt, Tokyo, and Sao Paolo.

Figure 5.1 illustrates how stocks are traded on the NYSE. You have asked your broker, Merrill-Lynch, to buy 100 shares of Boeing. Merrill has a *seat* on the exchange, allowing it to trade there. The person you contact at Merrill sends your order to one of the firm's *commission brokers,* who works on the floor of the exchange.

Specialist broker–dealer who manages the trading of a certain stock on an exchange

The commission broker walks to the *trading post* for Boeing stock. The trading post is a desk staffed by a broker–dealer called a **specialist**. The NYSE chooses one securities firm to provide a specialist for each stock (the specialist for Boeing works for Spear, Leeds, and Kellogg). The specialist manages the trading of that stock.

Brokers tell the specialist how many shares of Boeing they want to buy or sell and what prices they will accept. The specialist records this information and arranges trades. Sometimes the specialist matches a broker who wants to buy stock with another who wants to sell. Other times, the specialist acts as a dealer, trading with brokers on behalf of her own firm. Either way, her job is to help brokers make the trades ordered by their customers.

Link through the text Web site to the NYSE's Web site for more information on stock trading.

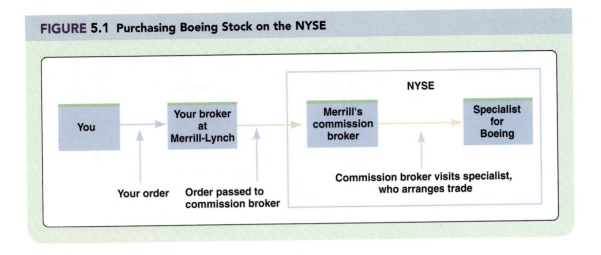

FIGURE 5.1 Purchasing Boeing Stock on the NYSE

Dealer Markets A secondary market that has no physical location—one that is not an exchange—is an **over-the-counter (OTC) market**. One type of OTC market is a **dealer market** in which all trades are made with dealers. A computer network connects the dealers to brokers and other financial institutions that want to trade. Each dealer posts *bid* prices at which it will buy certain securities and *ask* prices at which it will sell.

The largest dealer market for stocks is the NASDAQ network. The initials stand for National Association of Securities Dealers Automated Quotation. Roughly 3000 stocks are traded on the NASDAQ, the same number as on the NYSE. NASDAQ companies tend to be smaller, and many are in high-tech industries. Within the NASDAQ network, 20 or more firms may be dealers in a particular stock. All the dealers post bid and ask prices. If you tell your broker to trade a stock for you, he looks for the dealer with the best price.

Most corporate and government bonds are traded on dealer markets. Again, computer networks link dealers with other financial institutions that want to make trades. The biggest bond dealers are divisions of financial conglomerates such as Citigroup and JPMorgan Chase.

Dealers make profits from the **bid–ask spread**—the gap between the prices at which they buy and sell a security. The size of these spreads varies greatly. Spreads are smaller for more liquid securities—those that are easy to trade because there are many buyers and sellers. For the most liquid Treasury securities, spreads are well under 0.1 percent of the price. Dealers can profit from small spreads by purchasing great numbers of securities and reselling them immediately.

Bid–ask spreads are higher for stocks, and higher still for corporate bonds. Spreads on these bonds can be several percentage points. The bond of a particular company may not be traded frequently. If a dealer buys the bond, it might take awhile to sell it, and the price could fall in the meantime. The bid–ask spread compensates the dealer for this risk.

Over-the-counter (OTC) market secondary securities market with no physical location

Dealer market OTC market in which all trades are made with dealers

Link through the text Web site to the NASDAQ Web site for more information on that market.

Bid–ask spread gap between the prices at which a dealer buys and sells a security

Electronic communications network (ECN)
OTC market in which financial institutions trade securities with one another directly, rather than through dealers

ECNs An alternative to exchanges and dealer markets is an **electronic communications network**. An **ECN** is an over-the-counter market in which financial institutions such as brokers and mutual funds trade directly with one another, a process that doesn't require dealers. Institutions that want to trade submit offers to the ECN. They say what securities they want to buy or sell and the prices they will accept. The electronic system automatically matches buyers and sellers who submit the same price. Traders pay a small fee for each transaction.

The advantage of trading through an ECN is that there is no bid–ask spread. The seller of a security receives the full price paid by the ultimate buyer. Dealers don't take a cut.

The first ECN, Instinet, was created in 1969. As of 2010, about a dozen ECNs operated in the United States, including Instinet, Island, and Archipelago. Trading has grown rapidly since the mid-1990s, especially for NASDAQ stocks. More than half of all trades in these stocks occur through ECNs rather than the NASDAQ dealer network.

Finding Information on Security Prices

Suppose you are adding up your wealth and want to know the current prices of the stocks and bonds you own. Daily newspapers such as the *Wall Street Journal* report prices from the previous day. A number of Web sites provide information that is updated more frequently. One popular site is bloomberg.com. The Bloomberg company was founded in 1981 by Michael Bloomberg (currently mayor of New York City). Its Web site reports prices for many types of U.S. and foreign stocks and bonds. It also reports prices of shares in leading mutual funds.

 The text Web site has a link to bloomberg.com and a guide to using the site.

Figure 5.2A presents a page from the Bloomberg site, one that covers the 30 stocks in the Dow Jones Index. During the trading day, this page is updated about every 20 minutes. It reports the price of each stock, the change in the price since the start of the day, and the number of shares traded. Clicking on a company symbol leads to more detailed information on the company, including past movements in its stock price, the price–earnings ratio, and dividend payments. **Figure 5.2B** shows this information for Boeing.

Each day the prices of some stocks rise and others fall. The overall behavior of prices is measured by **stock market indexes**, which average the prices for a group of stocks.

Stock market index an average of prices for a group of stocks

The Dow Jones is the oldest and most famous stock index. However, because the Dow covers only 30 stocks, it may not capture the movements of the whole market. The Standard & Poor's (S&P) 500 index is better for this purpose, because it covers the 500 largest U.S. companies. The Wilshire 5000 index is even broader. The NASDAQ index covers all the companies that are traded in that market and is influenced strongly by the prices of tech stocks.

Web sites such as bloomberg.com provide data on a variety of stock market indexes. In Figure 5.2A, information on the Dow appears above the prices of individual stocks. The Bloomberg site also provides indexes for sectors of the economy, such as transportation and utilities, and indexes for foreign stocks.

FIGURE 5.2 **Stock Prices on Bloomberg.com**

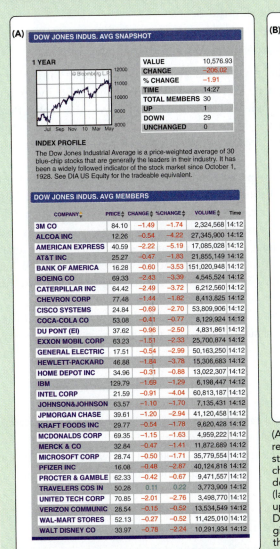

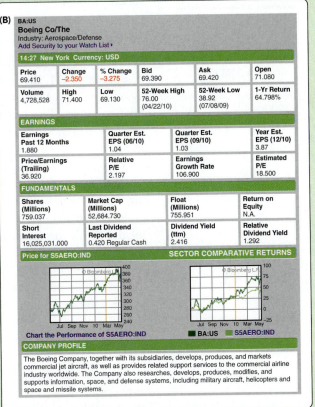

(A) A page downloaded from bloomberg.com on May 14, 2010 reports data on the 30 stocks in the Dow Jones Index. For each stock, the page shows the current share price (in dollars), the change in the price since the start of the day (both the change in dollars and the percentage change), the number of shares traded (labeled *volume*), and the time at which these numbers were last updated. The top of the page provides information on the overall Dow index. (B) Clicking on "BOEING CO" leads to a page that gives detailed information on Boeing, including past movements in the stock price, the price–earnings ratio, and dividends. Visit the "Guide to Bloomberg" on the text Web site for detailed definitions of the variables on these pages.

5.3 CAPITAL STRUCTURE: WHAT SECURITIES SHOULD FIRMS ISSUE?

So far we've discussed the mechanics of securities trading. Now we turn to the behavior of market participants—their decisions about which securities to sell and buy. We start with firms' decisions about issuing new securities.

The basic reason that firms issue securities is to raise funds for investment. A firm can raise funds by issuing either stocks or bonds. How does it choose between the two?

Capital structure mix of stocks and bonds that a firm issues

The mix of stocks and bonds that a firm issues is called its **capital structure**. Economists have long debated which capital structure is best. Let's discuss some of the key ideas in this debate.

Is Capital Structure Irrelevant?

Modigliani–Miller theorem (MM theorem) proposition that a firm's capital structure doesn't matter

The starting point for analyzing capital structure is the **Modigliani–Miller theorem (MM theorem)**. This idea was proposed in 1958 by Franco Modigliani and Merton Miller, who both went on to win the Nobel Prize in Economics. Their view of capital structure is simple: capital structure doesn't matter. Stocks and bonds are equally good ways for firms to raise funds.

In making their argument, Modigliani and Miller assume that firms operate for the benefit of their stockholders. Stockholders give something up when a firm issues securities. If the firm issues new stock, current stockholders lose part of their ownership of the firm. They receive smaller shares of the firm's future earnings. If the firm issues bonds, stockholders retain full ownership, but part of their earnings goes to interest payments. When firms issue securities, Modigliani and Miller argue, they should choose the type that minimizes the costs to current stockholders.

▶To review the classical theory in detail, see Section 3.2.

To determine these costs, Modigliani and Miller use the classical theory of asset prices. The classical theory says that the price of any security, whether a stock or a bond, equals the present value of expected income from the security.

The classical theory leads quickly to the conclusion that capital structure doesn't matter. Suppose a firm sells a share of new stock for $100. The present value of expected earnings that the buyer receives—and current stockholders give up—is $100. If the firm sells a bond for $100, the future payments again have a present value of $100. Either way, it costs $100 in present value to raise $100. Stocks and bonds are equally good deals for their issuers.

Why Capital Structure Does Matter

The MM theorem implies that firms shouldn't care which securities they issue. However, few people take this idea literally. The theorem ignores several practical differences between stocks and bonds. Some of these factors encourage firms to issue stocks, and some favor bonds. As a result, most firms issue a mixture of the two.

Taxes Corporations pay taxes on their profits at rates up to 35 percent (as of 2010). In computing profits, corporations can deduct interest payments on bonds. Therefore, the more bonds a firm issues, the lower its taxes. In contrast, issuing stock does not affect corporate taxes.

These tax rules change the relative costs of securities. Ignoring taxes, the MM theorem says it is equally costly to issue stocks and bonds. But the costs of issuing bonds are partly offset by their tax benefits, making them a cheaper way to raise funds.

Bankruptcy Although issuing bonds has tax benefits, it also has a disadvantage: the risk of bankruptcy. When a firm sells bonds, it promises certain payments to bondholders. If the firm's earnings are low, it may not be able to make the payments. If it does not make the payments, it defaults, leading to bankruptcy. The more bonds a firm issues, the greater this risk.

Bankruptcy is costly. It triggers a legal process that requires expensive lawyers and accountants. Sometimes a bankrupt firm is forced to shut down, eliminating opportunities for future profits. Sometimes the firm continues to operate and eventually emerges from bankruptcy, but only after its business is disrupted.

Firms can reduce bankruptcy risk by issuing stocks rather than bonds. If a firm's earnings are low, then stockholders receive low returns. The stockholders are disappointed, but the firm has not defaulted. Stocks don't require payments that the firm might have trouble making.

Adverse Selection As we discussed earlier, savers fear that firms will try to sell securities for more than their true value. This adverse selection problem affects capital structure because it is more severe for stocks than for bonds.

To see why, remember that adverse selection is caused by asymmetric information: buyers of securities know less than sellers. This asymmetry may be small when firms issue bonds. Buyers know exactly how much a bond pays as long as the issuer doesn't default, and they may know that default is unlikely. In contrast, stock purchasers are always uncertain about how much they will earn. This uncertainty creates scope for adverse selection.

The consequence is that some firms can issue bonds more easily than stock. To sell stock to nervous savers, these firms would have to accept low prices—less than the stock is really worth. In addition to the tax advantages, then, adverse selection is another reason to issue bonds.

Debt Maturity

When firms issue bonds, they must also choose the bonds' maturity. Firms can issue long-term bonds, which typically have maturities of 5 or 10 years, or commercial paper, with maturities under a year.

Generally, firms choose bond maturities based on their ability to pay off the bonds. A long-term investment project, such as a new factory, takes years to produce revenue. Firms finance these projects with long-term bonds, which they can pay off after revenue starts coming in.

Firms issue commercial paper when they need to borrow for short periods. This need often arises from the time lag between production and sales. For example, a swimwear company might produce bathing suits in the winter and sell them in the spring. It can issue 3-month commercial paper to cover its winter production costs until it receives revenue in the spring.

5.4 ASSET ALLOCATION: WHAT ASSETS SHOULD SAVERS HOLD?

We now turn from the issuers of securities to the buyers. Savers and institutions must choose their asset allocation—that is, how they split their wealth among different types of assets. We discuss the main factors in these decisions, focusing on the choice between stocks and bonds. We also touch on bank deposits, another asset held by savers.

The Risk–Return Trade-Off

▶ Figure 3.4 compares the rates of return on stocks and on bonds from 1900 through 2009.

Stocks have a higher average rate of return over time than bonds do. From 1900 through 2009, the nominal rate of return averaged about 11 percent for U.S. stocks and 5 percent for Treasury bonds. We can find average *real* returns by subtracting the inflation rate, which averaged 3 percent over 1900–2009. The real rate of return averaged 8 percent for stocks and 2 percent for bonds.

▶ These disastrous years for the stock market occurred during the worst year of the Great Depression and at the height of the 2007–2009 financial crisis.

The disadvantage of stocks is that their returns are more volatile than bond returns: a saver can earn a lot on stocks, but she can also lose a lot. In 17 of the 110 years from 1900 through 2009, for example, nominal stock returns were less than −10 percent. In 2 years, 1932 and 2008, returns were nearly −40 percent. In contrast, returns on Treasury bonds have never been less than −10 percent.

When a saver chooses between stocks and bonds, she chooses between average return and safety. The choice is not all-or-nothing, however. The saver can split her wealth between the two assets, seeking a high return on part of it and keeping the rest safe. A key decision is the fraction of wealth to put into stocks. Raising this fraction raises the average return on total assets, but it also increases risk.

Calculating the Trade-Off Suppose that bonds have a real return of 2 percent (the actual average since 1900). Assume that this return is constant, so bonds are safe assets. (In reality, bond returns vary somewhat, but we assume this variation is small enough to ignore.) Stocks, by contrast, have variable returns. Assume that half the time the real return is 22 percent, and half the time it is −6 percent. The average return on stocks is

$$\frac{1}{2}[22\% + (-6\%)] = 8\%$$

This average exceeds the return on bonds, but stocks are risky.

You have some wealth—say, $100—to split between stocks and bonds. We'll use the letter s to denote the fraction of wealth you put in stocks. The fraction in bonds is $1 - s$. If $s = 0.6$, for example, you put $60 in stocks and $40 in bonds. The overall return on your wealth is a weighted average of stock and bond returns with weights of s and $1 - s$. In other words,

$$\text{return on wealth} = s(\text{return on stocks})$$

$$+ (1 - s)(\text{return on bonds}) \quad \textbf{(5.1)}$$

As long as you hold some stock (s is positive), the return on your wealth is variable. If stock returns are high (22 percent), Equation (5.1) becomes

return on wealth if stock returns high

$$
\begin{aligned}
&= s(22\%) + (1 - s)(2\%) \\
&= s(22\%) + 2\% - s(2\%) \\
&= 2\% + s(20\%)
\end{aligned}
\tag{5.2}
$$

If stock returns are low (-6 percent)

return on wealth if stock returns low

$$
\begin{aligned}
&= s(-6\%) + (1 - s)(2\%) \\
&= s(-6\%) + 2\% - s(2\%) \\
&= 2\% - s(8\%)
\end{aligned}
\tag{5.3}
$$

Using Equations (5.2) and (5.3), we can see how the choice of s, the fraction of wealth in stock, affects your average return and risk. Given that high and low stock returns occur with equal probability, the average return is the simple average of (5.2) and (5.3):

average return on wealth

$$
\begin{aligned}
&= \frac{1}{2} [2\% + s(20\%)] + \frac{1}{2} [2\% - s(8\%)] \\
&= 1\% + s(10\%) + 1\% - s(4\%) \\
&= 2\% + s(6\%)
\end{aligned}
\tag{5.4}
$$

The last line shows that a rise in s raises your average return.

Risk can be measured in several ways, but we will use one simple measure: the difference between the overall return on your wealth when stock returns are high, Equation (5.2), and the overall return when stock returns are low, Equation (5.3). This difference shows how much your wealth can vary, based on stock returns:

difference between high and low returns on wealth

$$
\begin{aligned}
&= [2\% + s(20\%)] - [2\% - s(8\%)] \\
&= s(28\%)
\end{aligned}
\tag{5.5}
$$

▶ Economists often use another measure of risk, the standard deviation of returns. You know what this means if you have studied statistics. In our example, the standard deviation of the return on wealth is $s(14\%)$. An increase in s raises this standard deviation, as well as raising the difference in returns that we use to measure risk.

A rise in the fraction s raises this measure of risk.

Figure 5.3 shows the trade-off you face in this example. It shows the risk and average return that result from different levels of stock ownership s. If $s = 0$ (you buy no stock), your average return is only 2 percent, but you face no risk. Both risk and return rise as s rises, reaching their highest levels at $s = 1$ (you buy only stock).

Saving in a Bank Account Buying stocks and bonds isn't the only way to save. Many people deposit some or all their wealth in bank accounts. What role do bank accounts play in asset allocation?

FIGURE 5.3 The Risk–Return Trade-Off

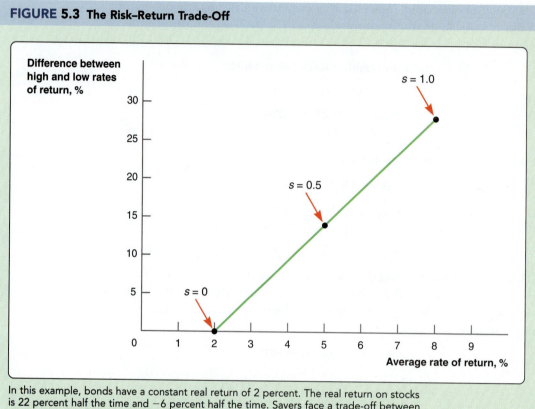

In this example, bonds have a constant real return of 2 percent. The real return on stocks is 22 percent half the time and −6 percent half the time. Savers face a trade-off between the average return on wealth and risk, measured here by the difference between the returns on wealth when stock returns are high and low. An increase in s, the fraction of wealth in stock, raises both the average return and risk.

For present purposes, the answer is that bank accounts are similar to bonds. Bank accounts produce lower average earnings than stocks, but they are safe. In the example we just discussed, you can think of your holdings of "bonds" as your total safe assets, including both bonds and bank accounts. Your key decision is how to split your wealth between these safe assets and risky stock.

In reality, bank accounts and bonds are not exactly the same. Bonds pay somewhat higher interest rates than bank accounts do but are less liquid. For now we ignore these differences and lump bonds and bank accounts together as safe assets.

▶ Chapter 7 expands on the differences for savers between bank accounts and bonds.

Choosing the Mix

How should you respond to the risk–return trade-off? Should you put a large fraction of your wealth in stock, accepting risk to seek high returns? Or should you play it safe and put most of your wealth in bonds and bank accounts?

These questions do not have absolute answers. The right asset allocation depends partly on personal preferences about risk. Some people are highly *risk averse:* they worry a lot about worst-case scenarios and find it painful to lose money. These individuals should hold most of their wealth in safe assets and accept low returns to avoid risk. Individuals who can better tolerate risk should put most of their wealth in stocks.

Despite this role for personal preference, most economists think that a typical individual—someone with an average level of risk aversion—should hold more stocks than bonds. Financial planners who advise savers say the same thing. A common rule of thumb is that savers should hold two-thirds of their wealth in stocks and one-third in bonds. Some advisors say the share in stocks should be even higher than two-thirds.

Two basic factors underlie this advice. First, historically, average returns are not just higher for stocks than for bonds—they are *much* higher. Over long periods, the differences in returns add up. If you put $100 in bonds and they produce their average real return of 2 percent, your wealth grows to $181 in 30 years. If you put $100 in stocks and they earn 8 percent, you end up with $1006.

Second, stocks are not really as risky as they first appear. We've seen that the returns on stock vary greatly from year to year. However, these fluctuations tend to average out over time, as good years offset bad years. People who hold stock for long periods—say, 20 or 30 years—are quite likely to do well overall.

This point was popularized by a 1994 book, *Stocks for the Long Run,* by Jeremy Siegel of the Wharton Business School at the University of Pennsylvania. Siegel compared stock and bond returns over every 30-year period since 1871 (1871–1901, 1872–1902, and so on). He found that stocks had higher returns than bonds over every 30-year period, a fact that has continued to hold true since the book was published.

Some people follow Siegel's advice to hold stock, but many don't. Although stockholding has grown, about half of U.S. savers still own no stock. Many of these people have significant wealth in safe assets.

Economists debate the reasons for this behavior. Many think that savers who avoid stock are simply making a mistake—that they don't understand the true risks and returns from stock holding. Yet some economists suggest that savers might have good reasons to avoid stocks because they really *are* risky. So far, stockholders haven't lost money over any 30-year period, because bad years have been followed by good years. But the future might differ from the past, and a run of bad luck could produce large losses for stockholders. Such losses might result from an unprecedented national disaster, such as a war that destroys much of the economy.[1]

Economists' usual advice to hold stocks has one important qualification, which we discuss in the next case study.

---

[1] This idea is discussed by Robert Barro of Harvard University in "Rare Disasters and Asset Markets in the Twentieth Century," *Quarterly Journal of Economics* 121 (August 2006): 823–866.

CASE STUDY

Age and Asset Allocation

Economists such as Jeremy Siegel argue that stocks are not very risky. However, the risks from stockholding grow with age, so older people should hold less stock than younger people.

Recall Siegel's point: stocks are safe because high and low returns average out over time. This argument applies to people who hold stocks for long periods. An older person has a shorter saving horizon: he is likely to start selling his assets soon to finance retirement. If this person holds stock, a few bad years can reduce his wealth significantly, and he won't have a chance to recoup these losses.

Another difference between young and old savers is that the young can expect more future income from working. This prospect reduces the risk of holding stock. To see this point, suppose a 30-year-old puts all his savings in stock and the market crashes. Even if this person's wealth is wiped out, this event is not a disaster. The 30-year-old has several decades to earn money, rebuild his savings, and finance retirement. In contrast, a current retiree who loses his wealth is in trouble, because he has no future earnings.

For these reasons, financial advisors tell savers to change their asset allocation as they age. You should start by holding mostly stock and then shift gradually toward bonds. One rule of thumb is that the percentage of your wealth in stocks should be at least 100 minus your age—at least 70 percent at age 30, 60 percent at age 40, and so on.

5.5 WHICH STOCKS?

We have discussed the allocation of wealth among broad asset classes such as stocks and bonds, but a saver must also choose specific assets within each class. We now consider this decision, focusing on the choice among stocks issued by different companies.

One key principle is *diversification*. Holding too much of one company's stock can be disastrous if the company does badly. To reduce risk, savers should split their wealth among a sizable number of stocks. One way to do this is to buy shares in a mutual fund.

▶ A case study in Section 1.2, The Perils of Employee Stock Ownership, highlights some consequences of nondiversification.

By itself, the principle of diversification does not pin down which stocks to buy. A saver can achieve diversification with around 30 or 40 stocks; with that many, one company's misfortune can't hurt too much. Thousands of companies issue stock, so the possible combinations of 30 or 40 are vast. Someone—either you or a mutual fund manager—must choose which stocks to buy.

The Efficient Markets Hypothesis

Suppose you graduate from college and get a job at a mutual fund. Your boss asks you to recommend stocks for the fund to purchase. With little experience, you're not sure what to suggest. Fortunately, you remember a friendly finance professor. You decide to consult her, reasoning that a finance professor must know how to pick stocks.

You may be surprised at the professor's advice. She is likely to tell you that it doesn't matter which stocks you pick. Rather than sweating over your decision, you can choose stocks randomly. Write the names of companies on pieces of paper, put them in a hat, close your eyes, and pull out your selections.

Is your professor joking? Is she hiding her true secrets for stock picking? No, her advice is probably sincere, because she believes in the **efficient markets hypothesis**. The **EMH** says that no stock is a better buy than any other, a conclusion that justifies random choices. The EMH is a central tenet of finance theory.

The EMH follows from another finance principle: the classical theory of asset prices. To see the connection, think about how you would choose stocks if you *don't* draw names from a hat. You would look for good deals—stocks that are worth a lot relative to their prices. A stock's worth is the present value of expected dividends, so you should buy stocks with prices below this level. In Wall Street lingo, you should buy stocks that are **undervalued assets**.

But the classical theory says that a stock price always equals the present value of expected dividends and that expected dividends are the best possible forecasts because of rational expectations. Thus, the price of a stock always equals the best estimate of the stock's value. This equality implies that undervalued stocks do not exist, so it's futile to look for them.

Prices Follow Random Walks To understand the efficient markets hypothesis in another way, let's think about movements in stock prices. When you pick stocks, you might try to forecast future price changes. If you can identify stocks with prices that are likely to rise, you can buy these stocks and earn capital gains when the increases occur. If your forecasts are correct, your returns will exceed those on a random selection of stocks.

Once again, the EMH says your strategy won't work. A stock price reflects expectations of a firm's dividends based on all available information. The price changes when expectations change in response to new information. For this information to matter, it must be a surprise—say, an announcement that the firm's recent earnings were higher than anticipated. If the information were known in advance, it would already be accounted for in expected dividends.

By definition, you can't predict surprises. Because only surprise information affects stock prices, changes in these prices are unpredictable. In statistical language, each price follows a **random walk**. You never know which prices are likely to rise, so once again stock picking is futile.

The Critique of Stock Picking The efficient markets hypothesis is controversial. It is popular among finance professors, but there are many doubters at securities firms. Analysts for mutual funds and brokers think they can do what the EMH says is impossible: identify undervalued stocks.

Efficient markets hypothesis (EMH) the price of every stock equals the value of the stock, so no stock is a better buy than any other

Undervalued asset asset with a price below the present value of the income it is expected to produce

Random walk the movements of a variable whose changes are unpredictable

The dividends a company can pay depend on its earnings. Therefore, in looking for undervalued stocks, analysts produce forecasts of future earnings. These forecasts are based on many factors: companies' past performances, their current investment projects, competition in their industries, and so on. When forecasts for a company's earnings are high compared to its stock price, analysts recommend the stock. The securities firms they work for buy the stock or recommend it to clients.

Thousands of firms perform this analysis, and they put considerable resources into it. They pay high salaries to attract talented, hardworking analysts who gather lots of data and use sophisticated statistical techniques. They monitor companies continuously, so their forecasts always take into account the latest news.

Analysts argue that this effort pays off with good stock picks. But EMH supporters disagree, pointing out that the analysts' research and the resulting stock trades actually are forces that make the market efficient.

We can best see this point with an example. Assume that, initially, the price of Boeing stock equals the present value of expected dividends. The stock is neither undervalued nor overvalued. Then Boeing announces some good news: United Airlines has ordered 50 new planes. Analysts who follow Boeing read its news release and realize that the order will raise the company's earnings. Higher earnings will lead to higher dividends, so Boeing is undervalued at its current price. Analysts tell their firms to buy the stock.

This scenario plays out at many firms, creating a surge in demand for Boeing. High demand causes the stock price to rise and quickly reach a level that equals the new present value of dividends, a valuation that incorporates the news about the United order. At this point, Boeing stock is no longer undervalued. Analysts' efforts to identify an undervalued stock have caused the undervaluation to disappear.

Choosing Between Two Kinds of Mutual Funds

The efficient markets hypothesis is relevant to a decision facing many savers: the choice among stock mutual funds. There are two types of funds. An **actively managed fund** employs analysts who do the kind of research on companies that we have discussed. These funds buy and sell stocks frequently based on the analysts' recommendations.

In contrast, an **index fund** doesn't try to pick stocks. Instead, it buys *all* the stocks in a broad market index, such as the S&P 500. An index fund doesn't hire analysts to study companies—someone just looks up which stocks are in the index. The fund buys these stocks and then holds onto them, so it doesn't trade as often as an actively managed fund.

If you believe the EMH, you should prefer index funds. The EMH says that stocks picked by analysts will do no better, on average, than an index. And actively managed funds have the disadvantage of high fees. To pay analysts and traders, the funds usually charge shareholders 1 percent or more of their assets each year. Many index funds charge around a quarter of a

Actively managed fund mutual fund that picks stocks based on analysts' research

Index fund mutual fund that buys all the stocks in a broad market index

percent. Once fees are deducted, returns are likely to be higher for index funds than for actively managed funds.

Many economists have examined returns on mutual funds. Generally, their data support the view that index funds produce higher returns, on average, than actively managed funds. This finding suggests that the EMH has a large element of truth.

For example, about 1300 actively managed stock funds operated over the decade 1995–2005. Averaging these funds together, the rate of return was 8.2 percent. Over the same period, the return on the S&P 500 was 10.0 percent. Of the individual actively managed mutual funds, 15 percent had a higher return than the S&P 500, and 85 percent had a lower return.

Notice that *some* funds beat the S&P index. What accounts for this success? There are two possible answers. One is that the managers of successful funds—the top 15 percent—are unusually talented. They can identify undervalued stocks even though the average manager can't. Given this interpretation, it might make sense to buy shares in actively managed funds if you can figure out which funds have the best managers.

Believers in the EMH have a different view: successful fund managers are lucky. Different funds buy different sets of stocks. There is no good reason to prefer one portfolio to another. Nonetheless, over any period, news about companies will cause some stocks to perform better than others. Mutual funds that happen to own these stocks will have above-average returns.

According to this view, it's impossible to predict which mutual funds will beat a market index. You can see which funds have done so in the past. But because these funds were just lucky, there is no reason to think their success will continue. You should reject all managed funds and put your wealth in a low-cost index fund.

Once again, research supports the predictions of the efficient markets hypothesis. A number of studies have examined mutual funds with above-average returns over periods of 1 to 5 years. The studies ask whether these funds beat an index in subsequent years, and generally find that they don't.

Can *Anyone* Beat the Market?

Some economists interpret the EMH as an absolute law: anyone who tries to beat a stock market index is wasting his time. Yet other economists have a less extreme view. They think that beating the market is difficult but not impossible, because exceptions to market efficiency exist. In any case, people keep trying to beat the market—to succeed where the average mutual fund fails. Many would-be market beaters fall into one of three categories: fast traders, behaviorists, and perhaps geniuses.

Fast Traders One strategy for beating the market relies on speed. To understand this approach, recall the logic behind the EMH. If there is good news about a company, demand rises for the company's stock. Higher demand pushes the stock price to a level that reflects current expectations about earnings and dividends.

The EMH assumes that stock prices respond instantly to news. In reality, price adjustment takes a little time. For example, suppose good news breaks about a NASDAQ stock. This news prompts buy orders to dealers who trade the stock. These dealers see decreases in their inventories, realize that demand has risen, and raise their ask prices for the stock.

This process may not take long. Dealers can respond to demand shifts within minutes or even seconds. But there is a brief period before a stock price adjusts to news when the stock is undervalued. Traders can profit from this undervaluation if they get their orders in quickly.

Many investment banks have departments that specialize in fast trading. Much of the work is done by powerful computers rather than by humans. The computers are programmed to react to news that will affect security prices, such as announcements of economic statistics. When triggered by such news, some computers can buy or sell securities within 3 milliseconds (0.003 second).

Behaviorists Fast trading exploits brief deviations from market efficiency. Another strategy is based on the view that inefficiencies persist, making some stocks undervalued for long periods. People who identify these stocks can beat the market even if they aren't especially fast. This view is held by believers in **behavioral finance**.

Behavioral finance
field that uses ideas from psychology to study how deviations from rational behavior affect asset prices

Recall that stock prices depend on expectations about companies' future earnings and dividends. The EMH assumes rational expectations: people who forecast earnings, such as stock analysts, do as well as they can given their information. Behaviorists dispute this assumption. They argue that forecasters regularly make certain kinds of mistakes, leading to over- or undervaluation of stocks.

This idea has become popular over the past quarter century. One leader of the behavioral school is Richard Thaler of the University of Chicago. Researchers such as Thaler try to identify common mistakes in earnings forecasts. They base their work on theories from psychology as well as finance.

One mistake stressed by behaviorists is "anchoring" of stock analysts' forecasts: analysts form opinions about companies and then are reluctant to change them. If analysts have predicted that a company will do badly, they resist evidence to the contrary. If the company reports good news, analysts grudgingly raise their earnings forecasts, but not as much as they should. With earnings forecasts too low, the company's stock is undervalued.

Some hedge funds use behavioral theories to try to identify undervalued stocks and beat the market. (Thaler and others founded one of the first in 1993.) Some behavioral funds have performed well in recent years, but we need more data to tell whether this record reflects good strategies or good luck.

Geniuses? Many stock pickers are neither fast traders nor behaviorists. They just study companies, forecast earnings, and decide which stocks are undervalued. We have seen that most people who follow this approach can't beat the market. But maybe a few can.

In recent history, a handful of stock pickers have gained notoriety for beating the market repeatedly. One is Peter Lynch, who ran Fidelity's Magellan Fund from 1978 to 1990. Magellan's average return during this period was 29 percent. Also famous is William Miller of Legg Mason, whose fund beat the S&P 500 for 15 straight years, from 1991 through 2005.

Hard-core believers in the EMH say that Lynch and Miller were lucky. If so, they were *very, very* lucky for a long time. The EMH implies that a mutual fund has no better than a 1/2 probability of beating an index each year. The probability of winning 15 years in a row is at most $(1/2)^{15} = 0.00003$. Many observers doubt that anyone beats these odds through luck alone. They conclude that people such as Lynch and Miller really can pick stocks.

How do they do it? EMH supporters stress that everyone has the same information about companies. Lynch and Miller read the same annual reports as other mutual fund managers and receive the same news releases. But perhaps some people have unusual skill in *interpreting* information. If a company creates a new product, for example, everyone hears about it. But a few geniuses have special insights about the product's likely success. They can forecast earnings better than the rest of the market.

When people name the best stock pickers, Peter Lynch and William Miller are often on the list. But one man is always at the top: Warren Buffett.

CASE STUDY

The Oracle of Omaha

Warren Buffett was born in Omaha, Nebraska, in 1930, the son of a stock-broker. He earned a master's degree in economics and then worked in New York for Benjamin Graham, a famous stock picker of the 1940s and 1950s. In 1957, Buffett returned to Omaha and started a fund, Buffett Partnership, Ltd. Its initial wealth was $105,000 from family and friends plus $100 of Buffett's own money. Buffett bought stocks through this company and a successor, Berkshire Hathaway.

The rest is history. From 1965 through 2009, the return on Berkshire Hathaway stock averaged 20.3 percent, compared to 9.3 percent for the S&P 500. If you had put $10,000 in an S&P index fund in 1965, you would have had about $540,000 in 2009. If you put $10,000 in Berkshire Hathaway in the same year, you would have had $43 million in 2009.

As of 2009, Buffett owned about 30 percent of Berkshire Hathaway's stock, and his total wealth was $40 billion. In March 2010, *Forbes* magazine declared Buffett the world's third-richest person (Bill Gates ranked second with $50 billion, and, at $53.5 billion, Mexican business tycoon Carlos Slim ranked first). Despite his success, Buffett still lives in a house that he bought for $32,000 in 1957. At age 79, he was still running Berkshire Hathaway full-time.

How does Buffett pick stocks? He says he buys "great companies" with high earnings potential. In looking for such companies, Buffett "sticks with businesses we think we understand. That means they must be relatively

AP Photo/Nati Harnik

Standing before a mockup of a Burlington Northern locomotive, Warren Buffett greets a journalist at an annual Berkshire Hathaway shareholders meeting.

simple and stable in character." This principle leads Buffett to avoid tech companies such as Microsoft, whose businesses change rapidly.

Buffett assigns great weight to the quality of companies' managers. He looks for people who are smart and dedicated to making money for shareholders. He is leery of "empire builders"—managers who maximize their companies' size rather than profits. Buffett likes to meet managers personally to judge their abilities.

Over the years, Berkshire Hathaway has purchased large stakes in many companies, including the *Washington Post* (in 1973), GEICO (1976), Coca-Cola (1988), and Gillette (1989). Most of these acquisitions have proved profitable. For example, Coca-Cola's stock price in 1988 was $11. The company's recent earnings had been mediocre, and analysts predicted that its business would stagnate. Buffett realized that Coke had untapped potential for expanding overseas, using its world-famous brand name. After he bought the company's stock, Coke did expand overseas, and analysts raised their earnings forecasts. By 1993, Coca-Cola's stock price was $75.

Buffett's reputation for brilliance grew during the financial crisis of 2007–2009. Berkshire Hathaway's stock fell 10% in 2008, but it fared much better than the S&P 500, which fell 37%. In September 2008, at the height of the crisis, Berkshire Hathaway bought $5 billion in Goldman Sachs stock. As the crisis diminished over 2009, Goldman's stock rose and Buffett earned large profits.

In November 2009, Berkshire Hathaway made the largest acquisition in its history: it purchased Burlington Northern railroad for $34 billion. This deal reflected Buffett's preference for traditional, stable industries. Buffett also knew Burlington Northern well, because Berkshire had owned 23% of the company since 2006.

In explaining the 2009 purchase, Buffett said he expected the demand for freight-train service to rise as the economy grows and high oil prices make trucking more expensive. It's too early to judge the success of the Burlington deal, but Buffett's record suggests that, once again, he was quicker than others to recognize a company's potential.

For more on Warren Buffett's stock picking, link through the text Web site to Berkshire Hathaway's Web site and to buffettsecrets.com.

5.6 DERIVATIVES

Derivatives securities with payoffs tied to the prices of other assets

So far, this chapter has emphasized two kinds of securities: stocks and bonds. We now turn to a more recently developed asset class—**derivatives**. The payoffs from these securities are tied to the prices of other assets; that is, the securities are "derived" from the other assets. Common types of derivatives include *futures*, *options*, and *credit default swaps*.

We first define these types of derivatives and describe how they are traded; then we discuss their uses. As you will see, some savers and financial institutions use derivatives to reduce risk. Others use derivatives to make risky bets on asset prices.

Futures

A **futures contract** is an agreement to trade an asset for a certain price at a future point in time, the *delivery date*. One party agrees to sell the asset and another agrees to buy. The oldest futures contracts are those for agricultural products, such as grain and cotton. Farmers have traded these contracts for centuries.

Futures also exist for nonagricultural commodities, such as oil and natural gas, and for securities, such as bonds and stocks. These *financial futures* were invented in the 1970s. The most common are futures for Treasury bonds and for stock indexes.

Some futures contracts, such as those for Treasury bonds, literally require the seller to deliver securities to the buyer. Other contracts specify cash payments based on security prices. For example, a seller of futures on the S&P 500 does *not* deliver shares of the 500 stocks. Instead, for each future, she pays an agreed-upon *multiplier* times the S&P index on the delivery date. If the multiplier is $10 and the index is 1000, she pays ($10) $\times$ (1000) = $10,000.

Trading futures can produce either gains or losses. Generally, one side of a contract earns money at the expense of the other. Who wins depends on the price in the futures contract and the current price of the asset on the delivery date.

Let's consider an example. On January 1, 2020, Jack sells a futures contract for a Treasury bond to Jill. Jack promises to deliver the bond on July 1, and Jill promises to pay $100 on that date. When July 1 arrives, it turns out that Treasury bonds are trading for $110. Jill is in luck. She pays Jack the $100 they agreed on 6 months earlier, receives a bond, and can resell it for the current price of $110. These transactions yield Jill a profit of $10. Jack, on the other hand, receives only $100 for a bond worth $110. He loses $10.

Now let's change the story. Jack and Jill make the same deal on January 1, but the price of Treasury bonds on July 1 is $90. In this case, Jack wins: he receives $100 for a bond worth $90, gaining $10. Jill pays $100 for a $90 bond, losing $10.

Futures are traded on exchanges such as the Chicago Board of Trade and the Chicago Mercantile Exchange. People who want to trade hire brokers who work at the exchanges. A broker whose client wants to sell a certain contract looks for a broker whose client wants to buy. When the brokers meet, they arrange a trade.

When a trade occurs, both buyer and seller must post deposits with the futures exchange. These deposits are called *margins*. The purpose is to ensure

Futures contract agreement to trade an asset for a certain price at a future point in time

that both parties fulfill their contract on the delivery day. A typical margin is 10 percent of the futures price. On January 1, when Jack and Jill trade a $100 bond future, each must deposit $10 with the exchange.

Options

Option the right to trade a security at a certain price any time before an expiration date

Call option an option to buy a security

Put option an option to sell a security

A futures contract requires a transaction at the delivery date. An **option**, as the name suggests, may or may not produce a later transaction. If Jack sells Jill an option, she gains the right to trade a security with him—but not an obligation. Jill pays Jack a fee to receive the option.

A **call option** allows its owner to *buy* a security at a certain price, called the *strike price*. The option holder can make this purchase at any point before the option's expiration date, which is set in the contract. If he buys the security, he is said to *exercise* the option. A **put option** allows its owner to *sell* a security. Like a call option, it specifies a strike price and an expiration date.

▶ The options we discuss are known as *American* options, the most common type in the United States. A *European* option can be exercised only on a single day in the future rather than at any time before an expiration date.

Call and put options for stocks and bonds are traded on exchanges such as the Chicago Board of Options Exchange. As on futures exchanges, brokers for buyers and sellers meet to make deals. An option buyer immediately pays a fee to the seller. The seller makes a margin deposit to guarantee his performance if the buyer exercises the option.

Options also come from another source. Many companies create call options on their own stock and give them to executives as part of their pay. Options are valuable if stock prices rise, as the following example illustrates.

It is January 1, 2020. The current price of Google stock is $400. You buy a call option on one share of Google, with a strike price of $450 and an expiration date of July 1. You pay $20 for this option.

As long as Google's price is below $450, you don't exercise the option. You don't choose to buy the stock for more than it's worth. If July 1 arrives and the price is still below $450, the option expires. The $20 you paid for the option is a loss.

On the other hand, suppose that Google's stock rises to $500 on April 1. At that point, you might exercise the option. You can buy the stock for $450 and resell it for $500. You come out $30 ahead after accounting for the $20 you paid initially.

▶ Problem 5.11 explores the dilemma of when to exercise an option.

It is tricky to choose when to exercise an option. In our example, you earn a profit by exercising on April 1. But you might do even better by waiting. If the stock reaches $600 on May 1, you will earn more by exercising then. On the other hand, the stock might fall after April 1. If that happens, you will wish you had cashed in when the stock was high.

Credit Default Swaps

Credit default swap (CDS) derivative with payouts triggered by defaults on certain debt securities

A **credit default swap (CDS)** is a derivative tied to debt securities, such as bonds and mortgage-backed securities, that promises certain future payments. A CDS buyer pays premiums, and payments on the CDS are triggered by defaults on the original securities. For example, Jack might sell Jill a CDS on bonds issued by the Acme Corporation. In this deal, Jill agrees to pay a series of premiums over some time period—say, the next 5 years. In return, Jack promises to make payments to Jill if Acme defaults on its bonds.

We can sometimes interpret a CDS as an insurance policy. Jill may buy a CDS on Acme bonds because she owns some of the bonds and therefore stands to lose if Acme defaults. With the CDS, she has "swapped" her default risk to Jack. Jack will compensate Jill for losses, just as her auto insurance company will compensate her for an accident.

Yet a CDS differs from a conventional insurance policy in an important way. Jill can buy insurance on her car, but she *cannot* buy insurance on her neighbor Joan's car. Allstate won't agree to pay Jill for Joan's accidents, because they don't cost Jill anything. In contrast, Jill *can* buy credit default swaps on Acme bonds even if she doesn't own the bonds. She will receive money if Acme defaults even though the default does not affect her directly.

The first CDSs were issued in 1997 by Chase Manhattan Bank (now part of JPMorgan Chase). They were tied to municipal bonds, but soon others were created for corporate bonds and mortgage-backed securities. The CDS market grew explosively from 2000 to 2007: the total payments promised in case of default grew from less than $1 trillion to $62 trillion.

In contrast to futures and options, credit default swaps are *not* traded on exchanges. Each CDS is negotiated privately between a buyer and a seller, with no margin deposit by either. CDSs are traded by many financial institutions, including commercial banks, investment banks, and insurance companies.

Hedging with Derivatives

Why do people trade derivatives? One purpose is to reduce risk through **hedging**. To hedge is to purchase an asset that is likely to produce a high return if another of one's assets produces a low or negative return. Hedging was the original purpose of credit default swaps: a security holder can reduce his default risk by purchasing a CDS on the security. Futures and options can also be used for hedging; let's look at some examples.

Hedging reducing risk by purchasing an asset that is likely to produce a high return if another of one's assets produces low or negative returns

Hedging with Futures
Hedging was the original purpose of agricultural futures. Imagine a farmer growing wheat and a miller who will buy the wheat when it is harvested in 6 months. Both parties face risk from fluctuations in the price of wheat. If the price is high in 6 months, the farmer will earn extra income, but the miller's costs will rise. The reverse happens if the price is low.

Wheat futures eliminate this risk. The farmer can sell a contract for wheat in 6 months, and the miller can buy this contract. The contract locks in a price for both parties.

Like commodities futures, financial futures can reduce risk. The owners of securities experience gains and losses when security prices change. To hedge, security holders make derivatives trades that produce profits if they suffer losses elsewhere.

For example, commercial banks hold large quantities of Treasury bonds. They stand to lose a lot if bond prices fall. A bank can reduce this risk by selling Treasury bond futures. If bond prices do fall, the bank earns profits from its sale of futures (like Jack in our earlier example). The profits on futures cancel the losses on bonds. If prices rise, the bank loses on futures but gains from its bond holdings. Either way, the bank's total profits are insulated from bond-price movements.

Other institutions hedge by *buying* futures rather than selling them. Suppose a pension fund expects a large contribution in 3 months and plans to use this money to buy Treasury bonds. The pension fund faces risk because it doesn't know how much the bonds will cost. It can lock in a price by purchasing T-bond futures with a delivery date in 3 months, just as a miller can use futures to lock in a price for wheat.

Hedging with Options Security holders can also reduce risk by trading options. One hedging strategy is a *protective put*, which means a purchase of put options on securities you own. It protects against big losses on the securities.

For example, suppose you own shares in a mutual fund that holds the S&P 500. The current level of the S&P index is 1000. The index is likely to rise, but you worry about the possibility of a stock market crash. You might sleep better if you buy puts on the index—say, with a strike price of 900. In effect, this option lets you sell stocks for 90 percent of their current value, even if prices fall lower. Your potential losses are limited.

You must pay for the put options, but you never use them if the S&P index stays above 900. Nonetheless, it may be prudent to purchase the puts: it is worth paying fees to reduce risk.

Speculating with Derivatives

Speculation using financial markets to make bets on asset prices

Derivatives are also useful for **speculation**. This practice is the opposite of hedging, which reduces risk: speculators use financial markets to make risky bets on asset prices. Speculators earn a lot if they are right and lose a lot if they are wrong.

Suppose the current price of a Treasury bond is $100. Most people expect this price to stay constant, so the 6-month futures price is also $100. You, however, are more insightful than most people. You realize that the Federal Reserve is likely to lower its interest rate target, pushing up bond prices. You can bet on this belief by purchasing the $100 Treasury bond futures. You will profit if T-bonds are selling for more than $100 in 6 months.

You can also bet on Treasury bonds simply by purchasing the bonds themselves. However, buying futures has the advantage that you need less money up front. You need only post margin, not pay full price, for the bonds you bet on. As a result, you can make larger bets.

For example, suppose you have $1000 available to bet on bond prices. At the current price of $100, you can buy 10 bonds. If the price in 6 months is $110, you earn $10 per bond, for a total of $100. Your initial $1000 rises by 10 percent. If the bond price is $120, you earn $200, a return of 20 percent.

Now suppose that you buy bond futures. If the margin requirement is 10 percent, you must deposit $10 for every $100 future. Depositing your $1000 lets you buy 100 futures. Now if the bond price in 6 months is $110, you earn $10 per future, for a total of $1000. The return on your initial $1000 is 100 percent. If the price in 6 months is $120, your return is 200 percent. Thanks to futures, you have profited greatly from your understanding of the Fed and bond prices.

You can also use options to bet on T-bonds. If you think the price will rise, you might sell put options on the bonds—say, with a strike price of $100. As long as the actual price stays above $100, nobody exercises the options. The fees you receive for the options are pure profit.

The catch, of course, is that speculation requires you to predict asset prices better than other people, something the efficient markets hypothesis says is impossible. If it's really likely that the Fed will lower interest rates, then everyone else also knows this information, and the prices of futures and options have already adjusted to it, thus eliminating profit opportunities. According to the EMH, speculation is pure gambling; you might as well play the slots.

Nonetheless, many financial institutions speculate with derivatives. Leading players include investment banks and hedge funds. The term *hedge fund* is a misnomer, because hedge funds don't hedge, they speculate.

As you might expect, some speculators have made large profits and others have lost a lot. *Rogue traders* are responsible for some losses. These low-level employees make unauthorized trades, gambling with their firms' money in the hope that large gains will advance their careers.

Nick Leeson is one infamous rogue trader. Leeson worked in the Singapore office of Barings LLC, a prestigious British bank. Starting in 1992, when he was 25, Leeson speculated on Japan's Nikkei stock index. One of his strategies was to sell "straddles" on the index: he sold call options with a strike price above the current level of the index *and* sold put options with a strike price below the current level. His bet was that the index would stay between the two strike prices, so neither the calls nor the puts would be exercised.

For awhile, Leeson's strategy worked, and he produced large profits for Barings. Unfortunately, in February 1995 an earthquake in the Japanese city of Kobe triggered a sharp fall in the Nikkei. At that point, the put options that Leeson had sold were exercised, meaning Barings was forced to buy stock for prices well above the current market. Leeson lost more than $1 billion through this and similar strategies, and Barings went bankrupt. Leeson went to jail for trying to cover up his losses.

Speculating with derivatives produced large gains and losses during the financial turmoil of 2007–2009. Credit default swaps played a major role in the story, as we see in the next case study.

CASE STUDY

Credit Default Swaps and the AIG Fiasco

Many credit default swaps issued in the 2000s were tied to subprime mortgage-backed securities, which we discussed in the case study on investment banks (Section 5.1). These CDSs differed somewhat from the type we've discussed before. A traditional CDS yields a payoff if the issuer of some security defaults on payments that it owes. In contrast, the sellers of CDSs on mortgage-backed securities promised to pay CDS buyers if the market prices of the underlying securities fell, even if the securities' issuers had not yet defaulted. This feature proved important over 2006–2008, when prices of mortgage-backed securities fell rapidly and triggered payments on CDSs.

Some firms had used credit default swaps to hedge the risk on mortgage-backed securities. In 2006, for example, analysts at Goldman Sachs started worrying that house prices might fall. Goldman saw that it could lose money on the mortgage-backed securities it owned, so it started buying CDSs to hedge against this possible loss. It did so sooner than other investment banks, and this strategy helped limit its losses during the crisis.

Other firms used credit default swaps to speculate. Like Goldman Sachs, some hedge funds foresaw trouble in the housing market. They bet against mortgage-backed securities by purchasing CDSs on securities they didn't own. These bets paid off handsomely: researchers estimate that one hedge fund, run by John Paulson, earned $15 billion on CDSs.

If hedgers and speculators were buying credit default swaps, who was selling them? The answer in many cases was the American International Group, a conglomerate that primarily owns insurance companies. AIG's swaps promised payments of hundreds of billions of dollars if prices of mortgage-backed securities fell far enough.

AIG management thought the company was getting a good deal. It received a steady flow of fees from the sale of CDSs, and managers didn't expect to pay out much in return. They didn't anticipate the fall in house prices and its effects on mortgage-backed securities. In 2006, an AIG report to government regulators said the likelihood of losses on CDSs was "remote, even in severe recessionary market scenarios."

This view was refuted spectacularly over the next two years. As the mortgage crisis unfolded, AIG had to make larger and larger payments to holders of its CDSs. In September 2008, when Lehman Brothers went bankrupt, it seemed likely that AIG would suffer the same fate.

At that point, the Federal Reserve stepped in. The Fed feared that a collapse of AIG would magnify the financial crisis, so it kept the company afloat with more than $100 billion in loans. The Treasury Department also aided AIG by purchasing its stock. AIG survived, but the Fed and Treasury were widely criticized for their use of taxpayers' money.

Summary

5.1 Participants in Securities Markets

- Securities firms are companies whose primary purpose is to hold, trade, or help others trade securities. These firms include mutual funds, hedge funds, brokers, dealers, and investment banks.

- Other financial institutions that own large quantities of securities include pension funds, insurance companies, and commercial banks.

- In 2008, U.S. investment banks suffered major losses on mortgage-backed securities. As a consequence, the five largest investment banks either failed, were bought by other institutions, or became financial holding companies.

5.2 Stock and Bond Markets

- Corporations and governments issue securities in primary markets. Investment banks underwrite corporations' securities, reducing the problem of adverse selection. The U.S. government sells bonds through auctions.

- After securities are issued, they are traded in secondary markets. These markets include exchanges, such as the New York Stock Exchange, and over-the-counter markets, which have no physical location. OTC markets include dealer markets and electronic communications networks.

- Information on securities prices is available in newspapers such as the *Wall Street Journal* and on Web sites such as bloomberg.com.

5.3 Capital Structure: What Securities Should Firms Issue?

- Firms can finance investment by issuing either stocks or bonds. The mix of the two that a firm chooses is called its *capital structure*.

- The Modigliani–Miller theorem states that a firm's capital structure is irrelevant. Stocks and bonds are equally good ways for firms to raise funds.

- In reality, issuing bonds rather than stock reduces a firm's taxes. It also lessens the adverse selection problem. On the other hand, issuing bonds raises the risk of bankruptcy. Because of these trade-offs, most firms issue a mixture of stock and bonds.

5.4 Asset Allocation: What Assets Should Savers Hold?

- Savers must choose how to split their wealth among different classes of assets, such as stocks and bonds.

Stocks have higher average returns than bonds, but they are also riskier.

- Economists and financial planners advise savers to hold most of their wealth in stock, arguing that gains in average return outweigh the risk. Yet many people ignore this advice: they hold most of their wealth in safe assets, including bonds and bank accounts.

- Financial planners advise savers to shift their wealth from stock to safe assets as they grow older.

5.5 Which Stocks?

- According to the efficient markets hypothesis, every stock's price equals the best estimate of its value, so no stock is a better buy than any other. It is futile to look for stocks that will produce higher-than-average returns.

- Actively managed mutual funds employ analysts who select stocks; index funds hold all the stocks in a broad market index. Most actively managed funds underperform index funds, a fact that supports the efficient markets hypothesis.

- The EMH may not be completely true: some stock traders may be able to beat the market. Some try to do so by reacting quickly to news, some employ behavioral theories of finance, and some try to predict companies' prospects better than others can. Warren Buffett has been hugely successful with the last approach.

5.6 Derivatives

- Derivative securities include futures contracts, options, and credit default swaps. A futures contract is an agreement to trade an asset for a certain price at a future point in time. An option is a right (but not an obligation) to trade a security at a certain price before an expiration date. A credit default swap is a derivative that yields a payment if the issuer of some debt security defaults.

- Some people and institutions use derivatives to hedge. They purchase derivatives that will produce high returns if other assets they own produce low or negative returns.

- Other people and institutions use derivatives to speculate. They make bets on asset prices that sometimes produce large profits and sometimes large losses. AIG suffered disastrous losses on credit default swaps in 2008 during the financial crisis.

Key Terms

actively managed fund, p. 142

asset allocation, p. 121

behavioral finance, p. 144

bid-ask spread, p. 131

broker, p. 123

call option, p. 148

capital structure, p. 134

credit default swap (CDS), p. 148

dealer, p. 124

dealer market, p. 131

derivatives, p. 146

efficient markets hypothesis (EMH), p. 141

electronic communications network (ECN), p. 132

exchange, p. 130

futures contract, p. 147

hedge fund, p. 123

hedging, p. 149

index fund, p. 142

initial public offering (IPO), p. 127

investment bank, p. 124

leverage, p. 123

Modigliani–Miller theorem, p. 134

mutual fund, p. 123

option, p. 148

over-the-counter (OTC) market, p. 131

primary markets, p. 127

public company, p. 127

put option, p. 148

random walk, p. 141

secondary markets, p. 127

securities firm, p. 123

specialist, p. 130

speculation, p. 150

stock market index, p. 132

undervalued asset, p. 141

underwriter, p. 124

Questions and Problems

1. When investment banks underwrite IPOs, they typically sell stock for 5–10 percent more than they pay for it. When they underwrite new stock for companies that are already public, the typical markup is 3 percent. What explains this difference?

2. As in Section 5.4, assume that bonds pay a real return of 2 percent. Stocks pay 22 percent half the time and −6 percent half the time. Suppose you initially have wealth of $100, and let X be your wealth after 1 year. What fraction of your wealth should you hold in stock under each of the following assumptions?

   a. You want to maximize the average value of X.

   b. You want to maximize the value of X when the return on stocks is −6 percent.

   c. You want to be certain that X is at least $100 (that is, you don't lose any of your initial wealth). Subject to that constraint, you maximize the average value of X.

3. Suppose two people are the same age and have the same level of wealth. One has a high-paying job and the other has a low-paying job. Who should hold a higher fraction of his or her wealth in stock? Explain.

4. Chapter 3 presented the classical theory of asset prices. In this chapter, we discussed two

Summary

5.1 Participants in Securities Markets

- Securities firms are companies whose primary purpose is to hold, trade, or help others trade securities. These firms include mutual funds, hedge funds, brokers, dealers, and investment banks.

- Other financial institutions that own large quantities of securities include pension funds, insurance companies, and commercial banks.

- In 2008, U.S. investment banks suffered major losses on mortgage-backed securities. As a consequence, the five largest investment banks either failed, were bought by other institutions, or became financial holding companies.

5.2 Stock and Bond Markets

- Corporations and governments issue securities in primary markets. Investment banks underwrite corporations' securities, reducing the problem of adverse selection. The U.S. government sells bonds through auctions.

- After securities are issued, they are traded in secondary markets. These markets include exchanges, such as the New York Stock Exchange, and over-the-counter markets, which have no physical location. OTC markets include dealer markets and electronic communications networks.

- Information on securities prices is available in newspapers such as the *Wall Street Journal* and on Web sites such as bloomberg.com.

5.3 Capital Structure: What Securities Should Firms Issue?

- Firms can finance investment by issuing either stocks or bonds. The mix of the two that a firm chooses is called its *capital structure*.

- The Modigliani–Miller theorem states that a firm's capital structure is irrelevant. Stocks and bonds are equally good ways for firms to raise funds.

- In reality, issuing bonds rather than stock reduces a firm's taxes. It also lessens the adverse selection problem. On the other hand, issuing bonds raises the risk of bankruptcy. Because of these trade-offs, most firms issue a mixture of stock and bonds.

5.4 Asset Allocation: What Assets Should Savers Hold?

- Savers must choose how to split their wealth among different classes of assets, such as stocks and bonds.

Stocks have higher average returns than bonds, but they are also riskier.

- Economists and financial planners advise savers to hold most of their wealth in stock, arguing that gains in average return outweigh the risk. Yet many people ignore this advice: they hold most of their wealth in safe assets, including bonds and bank accounts.

- Financial planners advise savers to shift their wealth from stock to safe assets as they grow older.

5.5 Which Stocks?

- According to the efficient markets hypothesis, every stock's price equals the best estimate of its value, so no stock is a better buy than any other. It is futile to look for stocks that will produce higher-than-average returns.

- Actively managed mutual funds employ analysts who select stocks; index funds hold all the stocks in a broad market index. Most actively managed funds underperform index funds, a fact that supports the efficient markets hypothesis.

- The EMH may not be completely true: some stock traders may be able to beat the market. Some try to do so by reacting quickly to news, some employ behavioral theories of finance, and some try to predict companies' prospects better than others can. Warren Buffett has been hugely successful with the last approach.

5.6 Derivatives

- Derivative securities include futures contracts, options, and credit default swaps. A futures contract is an agreement to trade an asset for a certain price at a future point in time. An option is a right (but not an obligation) to trade a security at a certain price before an expiration date. A credit default swap is a derivative that yields a payment if the issuer of some debt security defaults.

- Some people and institutions use derivatives to hedge. They purchase derivatives that will produce high returns if other assets they own produce low or negative returns.

- Other people and institutions use derivatives to speculate. They make bets on asset prices that sometimes produce large profits and sometimes large losses. AIG suffered disastrous losses on credit default swaps in 2008 during the financial crisis.

Key Terms

Questions and Problems

1. When investment banks underwrite IPOs, they typically sell stock for 5–10 percent more than they pay for it. When they underwrite new stock for companies that are already public, the typical markup is 3 percent. What explains this difference?

2. As in Section 5.4, assume that bonds pay a real return of 2 percent. Stocks pay 22 percent half the time and −6 percent half the time. Suppose you initially have wealth of $100, and let X be your wealth after 1 year. What fraction of your wealth should you hold in stock under each of the following assumptions?

   a. You want to maximize the average value of X.

   b. You want to maximize the value of X when the return on stocks is −6 percent.

   c. You want to be certain that X is at least $100 (that is, you don't lose any of your initial wealth). Subject to that constraint, you maximize the average value of X.

3. Suppose two people are the same age and have the same level of wealth. One has a high-paying job and the other has a low-paying job. Who should hold a higher fraction of his or her wealth in stock? Explain.

4. Chapter 3 presented the classical theory of asset prices. In this chapter, we discussed two

ideas that follow from the classical theory: the Modigliani–Miller theorem, and the efficient markets hypothesis. How well do these two ideas fit real-world financial markets? Where does each fit on a spectrum from literally true to completely unrealistic?

5. Suppose everyone in the world becomes convinced that the efficient markets hypothesis is true. Will it stay true? Explain.

6. Research around 1980 showed that stocks of small firms had higher average returns than stocks of large firms. This finding gained much attention, as it seemed to contradict the efficient markets hypothesis. It suggested a simple way to beat the market: purchase only small-firm stocks.

   a. Can you explain this deviation from market efficiency? (*Hint:* Think about the behavior in financial markets that leads to efficiency, and why this behavior might not occur.)

   b. Would you guess that small stocks have done better than large stocks since 1980? Why or why not?

7. Recall that U.S. mutual fund companies offer about 8000 separate funds. Suppose each fund has a 50-percent chance of beating the S&P 500 each year.

   a. Over a 5-year period, how many funds will beat the market in every year? How about a 15-year period?

   b. Based on the performance of William Miller's mutual fund from 1981 through 2005, would you say Miller is a genius? Explain.

8. In 1989, the economist Paul Samuelson rated Warren Buffett the greatest stock picker in the country. Yet Samuelson warned against buying Berkshire Hathaway stock. He wrote that "knowledge of Buffett's skills may be already fully discounted in the marketplace. Now that BH has gone up more than a hundredfold, it is at a premium."

   a. Explain Samuelson's reasoning in your own words.

   b. People who followed Samuelson's advice have regretted it, because the returns on BH stock since 1989 have been similar to earlier returns. What does this tell us about Buffett or the efficient markets hypothesis?

9. On its Web site, one mutual fund company describes its "disciplined and sophisticated investment strategies." (The term *investment* is used to mean the choice of securities.) Let's change the company's name to "Smith." With this alteration, the site says:

   At the center of Smith's investment process is the Smith Investment Committee. It consists of a select group of senior investment professionals who are supported by an extensive staff. This staff provides multilevel analyses of the economic and investment environments, including actual and projected corporate earnings, interest rates, and the effect of economic forecasts on market sectors, individual securities, and client portfolios.

   Does this statement convince you to buy Smith mutual funds? Why or why not?

10. Suppose you hold most of your wealth in stock. What kinds of options should you buy or sell in each of the following circumstances?

    a. You think the stock market will probably do well, but you worry about a crash.

    b. You want to get a steady return on your assets. You don't care whether you get rich from a big rise in the market.

    c. You think there will soon be big news about firms' earnings, but you don't know whether the news will be good or bad.

11. Suppose you buy call options on Microsoft stock. Each option costs $2 and has a strike price of $40 and an expiration date of July 1. Discuss whether you would exercise the options in each of the following situations, and why:

    a. It is March 1, and Microsoft's stock price is $30.

b. It is March 1, and the stock price is $40.10.

c. It is March 1, and the stock price is $50.

d. It is June 30, and the stock price is $50.

e. It is June 30, and the stock price is $40.10.

12. Suppose company A has a stable stock price. The price is not likely to change much in the next year. Company B has an uncertain stock price: it could either rise or fall by a lot. Would you pay more for a call option on A's stock or B's stock? Explain.

▶ Online and Data Questions

www.worthpublishers.com/ball

13. Use bloomberg.com to answer the following questions:

a. Which has done better over the last year—the U.S. stock market or the Brazilian stock market?

b. Which have done better over the last year—the stocks in the Dow Jones Index or the NASDAQ index?

c. What is the rate of return on Boeing stock over the last year?

14. The text Web site provides data on rates of return for selected mutual funds. Choose 20 actively managed funds and rank them by their average returns over the period 2000–2004. Then rank the same funds by their average returns over 2005–2009. What is the relationship between the two rankings? Are the results surprising? Explain.

15. Link through the text Web site to buffettsecrets.com and study Warren Buffett's principles for choosing stocks. Do you think you could beat a stock index by following these principles? Explain.

chapter six

Foreign Exchange Markets

ALASTAIR MILLER/BLOOMBERG NEWS/Landov

The currency of South Africa is the *rand*. **Figure 6.1** on p. 158 shows the value of this currency as measured by the *exchange rate* between the rand and the U.S. dollar. This variable, known more formally as the **nominal exchange rate (*e*)**, is the price of one currency in terms of another.

In recent years, the value of the rand has fluctuated a lot. At the start of 2000, 1 rand was worth about 0.16 dollars (16 cents). The exchange rate fell rapidly over the next two years, reaching a low of 0.09 in 2002. Then the trend reversed, and the exchange rate climbed to 0.17 in 2005. It bounced up and down over the following 5 years but fell overall during that period. The exchange rate was 0.13 in early 2010, as South Africa prepared to host soccer's World Cup that summer.

Why does the rand lose value in some periods and gain value in others? Can we predict future movements in South Africa's exchange rate? And why do these movements matter? Is it better for South Africans if the exchange rate rises or if it falls?

This 100-rand note features Cape buffaloes and the name of South Africa's central bank in English and Afrikaans. At the beginning of 2010, 100 rand were worth about 13 U.S. dollars.

FIGURE 6.1 South Africa's Nominal Exchange Rate, 2000–2010

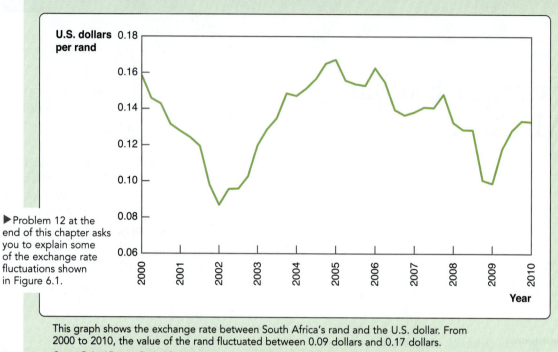

Problem 12 at the end of this chapter asks you to explain some of the exchange rate fluctuations shown in Figure 6.1.

This graph shows the exchange rate between South Africa's rand and the U.S. dollar. From 2000 to 2010, the value of the rand fluctuated between 0.09 dollars and 0.17 dollars.
Source: Federal Reserve Bank of St. Louis

Nominal exchange rate (e) price of one unit of a currency in terms of another currency

Economists ask similar questions about exchange rates around the world. This chapter tackles these issues. We start by discussing the markets in which currencies are traded. Then we discuss how exchange rates affect economies, the factors that cause exchange rates to fluctuate, and how speculators try to profit from exchange rate movements.

6.1 CURRENCY MARKETS AND EXCHANGE RATES

Every day, people and firms exchange trillions of dollars worth of currencies. They need foreign currencies to make two kinds of transactions. One is purchasing goods and services from other countries. For example, some Americans like to buy French wine, which French vineyards sell for euros. To buy this wine, American importers must first trade dollars for euros.

The other kind of transaction is purchases of foreign assets, which are called *capital outflows* (review Section 4.1). For example, some U.S. mutual funds buy stock in European as well as American companies. The European stock is sold for euros, so the funds must trade dollars for euros before buying the stock.

The Trading Process

How does someone trade dollars for euros? It depends who you are and how much you are trading.

The Interbank Market Large currency trades occur in the "interbank" market. As the name suggests, participants are large commercial banks, such as JPMorgan Chase, and investment banks, such as Deutsche Bank. These institutions are dealers, trading currencies for themselves, and they also act as brokers for companies and individuals. The minimum trade on the interbank market is $1 million worth of currency.

The interbank market is an over-the-counter market—it has no physical location. Most trades occur through two electronic networks—Reuters and Electronic Broking Services (EBS)—where dealers post bid and ask prices for currencies. Dealers are located in many time zones, so trading goes on 24 hours a day. (The trading week starts at 3 PM on Sunday, Eastern Time, which is Monday morning in Sydney, Australia, and ends at 4:30 PM on Friday.)

More than 100 currencies are traded in the interbank market. In most trades, the U.S. dollar is exchanged for one of the other currencies. Traders use dollars because this currency is highly liquid—there are many buyers and sellers. Institutions buy dollars even if they ultimately want a different currency. If a bank wants to exchange South African rand for Swiss francs, the easiest way is to trade rand for dollars and then trade the dollars for francs.

▶ Notice that the word *rand* is like the word *sheep*: the plural form is the same as the singular, with no "s" added.

As you might imagine, currency traders do not ship bundles of cash around the world. Instead, they exchange bank deposits. If an institution trades dollars for euros, it receives a credit in an account holding euros. It also has an account holding dollars, which is debited.

The Retail Market Most companies and individuals can't trade in the interbank market. If they want foreign currency, they must use a bank as a broker.

Suppose a clothing store in the United States needs euros to buy dresses from a French designer. The store has an account at JPMorgan Chase. It asks the bank to take dollars from its account and use them to purchase euros. The euros are either deposited in another account or paid directly to the French clothier. JPMorgan profits by charging the store a bit more for the euros than it pays on the interbank market.

Recall that only large banks trade in the interbank market. Small banks trade currencies through accounts at large banks. Say your business has an account at First Bank, a small bank in your town. First Bank has an account at JPMorgan Chase. If you need euros, First Bank transfers funds from your account to its account at JPMorgan, and JPMorgan buys the euros.

Your Week in Paris You encounter small-scale currency markets when you travel abroad. Dealers have offices in airports and tourist spots where you can trade dollars for foreign currency. However, these trades are expensive. Dealers set large spreads between their bid and ask prices—often about 10 percent. So the exchange rates you get are significantly worse than interbank rates.

It is less expensive to get currency from ATMs. ATMs in many countries accept U.S. bank cards. You receive foreign currency, and dollars are deducted from your account based on the interbank rate. You pay a small fee to the bank that owns the ATM.

If you use your credit card in foreign countries, charges are converted to dollars on your bill. The exchange rate is the interbank rate, but your card issuer is likely to add a 1–2 percent fee for foreign purchases. It's usually cheaper to buy your souvenirs with cash from ATMs.

Measuring Exchange Rates

An exchange rate involves two currencies. A nominal exchange rate can be expressed as the price of either currency in terms of the other. For example, the dollar–rand exchange rate on March 1, 2010 can be stated as 0.130 dollars per rand. It can also be stated as 7.692 rand per dollar. The second version of the exchange rate is the inverse of the first (7.692 = 1/0.130).

Throughout this book, we express each exchange rate as the amount of foreign currency that buys one unit of the local currency. When we analyze South Africa, for example, we treat the United States as a foreign country. We state the exchange rate as 0.130, because it takes that fraction of a dollar to buy 1 rand.

South Africa has other exchange rates with currencies such as the euro and the Japanese yen. Again, when we study South Africa, we state these rates as foreign currency per rand. On March 1, 2010, the rates were 0.096 euros per rand and 11.613 yen per rand.

When we study the U.S. economy, we state exchange rates as foreign currency per dollar. The rates are euros per dollar, yen per dollar, and so on. In this case, the exchange rate with South Africa is stated as 7.692 rand per dollar.

Appreciation rise in a currency's price in terms of foreign currency

Depreciation fall in a currency's price in terms of foreign currency

Changes in Exchange Rates An **appreciation** of a currency is a rise in its price. Each unit of the currency is worth more foreign currency. For example, the rand appreciates against the dollar if the exchange rate rises from 0.15 dollars per rand to 0.20. A **depreciation** is a fall in a currency's price. The rand depreciates if the exchange rate falls from 0.15 dollars per rand to 0.10.

When people discuss exchange rates, they often use the terms *strong* and *weak*. Saying that a currency has become stronger means that it has appreciated. A currency is weaker if it has depreciated.

Information on Exchange Rates Exchange rates fluctuate from minute to minute, just like stock and bond prices. Many newspapers and Web sites report nominal exchange rates. One good source is bloomberg.com. Bloomberg's main currency page, shown in **Figure 6.2**, reports exchange rates between the U.S. dollar and six major currencies, along with the changes in these rates since the beginning of the day. The exchange rates come from the interbank market and are updated every 15 minutes. Other Bloomberg pages give exchange rates between the dollar and 33 other currencies.

FIGURE 6.2 Exchange Rates on bloomberg.com

Currencies				
Benchmark Currency Rates				
CURRENCY	VALUE	CHANGE	% CHANGE	TIME
EUR-USD	1.2695	0.0033	0.2575%	14:02
GBP-USD	1.5347	-0.0115	-0.7436%	14:03
USD-JPY	84.1320	-0.4862	-0.5746%	14:02
AUD-USD	0.8903	-0.0015	-0.1679%	14:03
USD-CAD	1.0641	0.0041	0.3825%	14:03
USD-CHF	1.0169	-0.0094	-0.9130%	14:03

This page, downloaded from bloomberg.com on July 18, 2010, shows exchange rates between the U.S. dollar (USD) and six foreign currencies: the euro (EUR), British pound (GBP), Japanese yen (JPY), Australian dollar (AUD), Canadian dollar (CAD), and Swiss franc (CHF). When USD precedes the label for the foreign currency, the exchange rate is expressed as units of foreign currency per U.S. dollar (for example, 84.132 yen per dollar). When the label for the foreign currency comes first, the exchange rate is expressed as U.S. dollars per unit of foreign currency (for example, 1.2695 dollars per euro). The table shows current exchange rates, changes since the start of the trading day, and the time this information was last updated.

6.2 WHY EXCHANGE RATES MATTER

Exchange rates get a lot of attention. The financial media highlight fluctuations in the dollar along with stock prices and interest rates. Why do we care about exchange rates?

Effects of Appreciation

Suppose the dollar appreciates against the euro. The exchange rate rises from 0.8 euros per dollar to 0.9. This event is neither entirely good nor entirely bad for the United States. Some Americans benefit from the appreciation, and others are hurt. These mixed effects can make exchange rates a controversial topic.

Table 6.1 summarizes the effects of a dollar appreciation on Americans. As the following sections detail, the effects fall on consumers, firms and their workers, and owners of foreign assets.

Cheaper Imports The first effect is beneficial. When the dollar appreciates against the euro, European goods and services become less expensive for American consumers.

Suppose you visit Paris and stay in a hotel that costs 100 euros per night. You have dollars and trade them for euros to pay your bill. If a dollar buys 0.8 euros, then a full euro costs 1/0.8 dollars, or $1.25. To get 100 euros to pay the hotel, you need $125. If the dollar appreciates to 0.9 euros, you

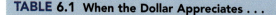

TABLE 6.1 When the Dollar Appreciates . . .

Imports become less
expensive $\longrightarrow$ benefits U.S. consumers

$\longrightarrow$ hurts U.S. firms that compete
with imports

U.S. goods become more
expensive to foreigners $\longrightarrow$ hurts U.S. firms that export

Foreign assets become
less valuable in dollars $\longrightarrow$ hurts U.S. owners of foreign assets

need only 1/0.9 dollars, or about $1.11, for each euro. The hotel room costs $111, so the appreciation saves you money on your trip.

You don't need to travel to benefit from a dollar appreciation. A stronger dollar means that American wine importers need fewer dollars to buy wine from French vineyards. Lower costs to importers lead to lower prices at your local wine store. You can more often afford a nice chardonnay with dinner.

Lower Sales for Domestic Firms Although an appreciation is good for consumers, it hurts many U.S. firms because it becomes harder to sell their goods and services. In popular jargon, an appreciation hurts the firms' "competitiveness." Two types of firms are hurt.

One type is firms whose products compete with imports. We saw that a dollar appreciation makes French wine less expensive for Americans. This price change causes consumers to switch from California wines to French wines, reducing the sales of California vineyards. Similarly, hotels in Florida lose business when a strong dollar attracts tourists to Paris.

The other type of firms hurt by an appreciation is exporters. U.S. goods become more expensive for Europeans, reducing sales in Europe. Suppose a U.S. company exports clothes to France. It sells a pair of jeans for $50. If the exchange rate is 0.8 euros per dollar, a French consumer must pay $(0.8)(50) = 40$ euros for the jeans. If the exchange rate is 0.9, the cost of the jeans rises to $(0.9)(50) = 45$ euros. Fewer jeans are sold.

When U.S. firms lose sales, their profits fall, hurting stockholders. The firms' employees are also hurt, because lower sales can lead to wage cuts or layoffs.

Losses to Holders of Foreign Assets A final group affected by the exchange rate is Americans who own foreign assets. An appreciation hurts this group because it reduces the dollar value of the assets.

Suppose you own a bond issued by the French government that will soon pay 100 euros. You plan to trade the euros for dollars to spend in your hometown. If the exchange rate is 0.8 euros per dollar, the 100 euros will buy you $100/0.8 = 125$ dollars. If the rate rises to 0.9 before you receive the bond payment, you end up with only $100/0.9 = 111$ dollars.

CASE STUDY

The Politics of the Dollar

A strong dollar has both pluses and minuses for the United States. Most economists believe that, overall, a weaker dollar is desirable in some circumstances. These situations include recessions, when firms' sales are low and unemployment is high. A depreciation increases the competitiveness of U.S. firms, so they sell more goods and hire more workers.

Nonetheless, government officials rarely admit that a weak dollar can be good. Robert Rubin, for example, who served as President Clinton's treasury secretary from 1995 to 1999, was often asked his views on exchange rates. He would say only, "A strong dollar is in our nation's interest." Journalists started calling this statement a "mantra."

Since Rubin's tenure, most treasury secretaries have echoed his views. In 2007, Secretary Henry Paulson, appointed by President George W. Bush, responded to a question about exchange rates by repeating Rubin's mantra. In 2009, Timothy Geithner, appointed by President Obama, said, "I believe very deeply that it's very important for the U.S. and the economic health of the U.S. that we maintain a strong dollar."

Deviating from this viewpoint has proven perilous. In 2001, President Bush's first treasury secretary, Paul O'Neill, surprised observers by declaring, "We are not pursuing, as it is often said, a policy of a strong dollar." This comment provoked widespread criticism. The *Wall Street Journal* charged that O'Neill had "tried to trash the value" of his country's currency. O'Neill responded that he had been misinterpreted. A week after his initial comment, he said, "I believe in a strong dollar and I'm not ever going to change." But the damage was done. O'Neill's waffling on the dollar contributed to a reputation for unwise remarks, and he lost his job in 2002.

What's wrong with questioning the strong dollar? The answer involves terminology rather than substance. The word *strong* has positive connotations, and *weak* has negative connotations. The public wouldn't like a defense secretary who advocated a weak military. They wouldn't like a U.S. Olympic coach who promised to field a weak team. Noneconomists often assume that a weak dollar must somehow be bad for the nation's well-being or pride.

▶ The stock market likes a weaker dollar: it helps U.S. exporters and gives them a boost when they convert profits from abroad to dollars.

Secretary O'Neill's successor, John Snow, took a novel approach to this issue. In 2003, he said he didn't mind a recent depreciation of the dollar. That attitude made sense, as unemployment was high and the Bush administration was trying to reduce it. Snow cited the fact that "when the dollar is at a lower level, it helps exports."

Snow denied, however, that he was abandoning support for a strong dollar. Instead, he invented a new definition of the term. He declared that a currency is "strong" if it is "a good medium of exchange . . . something people are willing to hold . . . hard to counterfeit, like our new $20 bill." The dollar can be strong by this definition even if the exchange rate is low.

Economic policymaking will become easier if Snow's definition catches on and people start interpreting a "strong dollar" policy as opposition to counterfeiting. Then treasury secretaries could support depreciations when necessary without appearing wimpy.

Hedging Exchange Rate Risk

Table 6.1 shows that an appreciation of the dollar helps some groups and hurts others. A depreciation has the opposite effects: it hurts American consumers and helps firms and holders of foreign assets. Overall, fluctuations in exchange rates create risk. Anyone affected by exchange rates can win or lose, depending on whether the dollar "strengthens" or "weakens."

As we stress throughout this book, people generally dislike risk. They can reduce the risk arising from exchange rate fluctuations by trading futures contracts for currencies.

Currency Futures and Hedging Currency futures work in a way similar to futures contracts for stocks and bonds. Two parties agree to trade currencies at a certain exchange rate on a future delivery date. Currency futures are traded on the Reuters and EBS networks, where the underlying currencies are also traded.

Firms use currency futures to hedge exchange rate risk. The basic method is the same as hedging in security markets: firms make futures trades that produce profits if they suffer losses elsewhere. For example, a firm that exports to Europe can hedge exchange rate risk by selling euro futures. Let's say the firm agrees to sell euros at a rate of 0.8 per dollar in 6 months. If the exchange rate in 6 months turns out to be 0.9, the firm profits. Under the futures contract, it trades 0.8 euros for dollars that are now worth 0.9. The gains from this transaction offset losses from the strong dollar, which hurts the firm's European sales.

If the exchange rate in 6 months is 0.7, the firm loses on its futures trades. But these losses are offset by profits from higher European sales. The firm is protected against both rises and falls in the dollar.

Asset holders also hedge exchange rate risk. A U.S. mutual fund that holds French securities is likely to sell euro futures. Once again, this transaction produces profits if the dollar strengthens, offsetting the fall in the dollar value of the securities.

> ▶Section 5.6 discusses stock and bond futures—for example, how banks trade Treasury bond futures to hedge against fluctuations in interest rates.

Limits to Hedging Hedgers can't eliminate exchange rate risk entirely. The use of currency futures is limited because contracts rarely have delivery dates more than 6 months in the future. Hedgers can protect themselves against short-lived movements in exchange rates, but not changes that last more than 6 months.

Suppose it is January and the exchange rate is 0.8 euros per dollar. The rate is expected to stay at this level. To guard against unexpected changes, an exporter has sold euro futures at 0.8, with delivery dates ranging from February to July. In February, something happens that raises the exchange rate to 0.9, and now this rate is expected to persist. The stronger dollar reduces the exporter's sales and profits. Until July, these losses are offset by gains on futures contracts, but not after that.

The exporter can keep selling 6-month euro futures. In February it can sell contracts for delivery in August, and in March it can sell contracts for September. However, with the exchange rate at 0.9 and expected to stay there, the futures rate also rises to 0.9. The exporter doesn't profit from futures unless the dollar rises even more. It can't undo the damage from the appreciation from 0.8 to 0.9.

Changes in exchange rates often last longer than 6 months. We saw in Figure 6.1, for example, that South Africa's exchange rate rose throughout the period from 2002 to 2005. South Africa's exporters couldn't have hedged against this appreciation.

Real Versus Nominal Exchange Rates

We've outlined the major effects of exchange rates on people and firms. To make our analysis precise, we must discuss a nuance that we've ignored so far: the distinction between nominal and real exchange rates.

We defined the nominal exchange rate, e, in the introduction to this chapter. It is the price of a unit of currency in terms of a foreign currency. The **real exchange rate (ε)** is a more subtle concept. It measures the relative prices of domestic and foreign goods.

> **Real exchange rate (ε)** measure of the relative prices of domestic and foreign goods ($\varepsilon = eP/P^*$)

Defining the Real Exchange Rate To understand the real exchange rate, remember why exchange rates matter: they affect the costs of goods and services in different countries. If the dollar appreciates against the euro, a Paris hotel room costs Americans less.

The costs of goods and services also depend on the prices that firms charge in their local currencies. If the Paris hotel cuts its room rate from 100 euros to 90, American tourists save 10 percent on their lodging costs. The effect is the same as if the dollar appreciated by 10 percent.

The real exchange rate measures the relative prices of goods in different countries, accounting both for the nominal exchange rate *and* for local prices. The definition of the real exchange rate uses the concept of the aggregate price level. An economy's price level is an average of prices of all its goods and services. We denote a country's price level by P and the foreign price level by P^*.

> ▶The appendix to Chapter 1 reviews the concept of the aggregate price level.

For now, let's focus on the U.S. real exchange rate against the euro. When we calculate this variable, the nominal exchange rate e is measured in euros per dollar. P is the U.S. price level, and P^* is the European price level. Each economy's price level is measured in its own currency: P is in dollars, and P^* is in euros.

To find the real exchange rate ε, we must compare the prices of American and European goods. This requires that we measure these prices in the same currency. Let's measure them in euros. Suppose first that someone wants to buy American goods with euros. She must trade the euros for dollars and then use the dollars to buy the goods. Each dollar costs e euros (the nominal exchange rate), and the goods cost P dollars (the U.S. price level). The cost of the goods in euros is e times P:

$$\text{cost of American goods in euros} = eP$$

If someone wants to buy European goods with euros, she doesn't need to trade currencies. The cost of the goods is simply P^*, the European price level:

$$\text{cost of European goods in euros} = P^*$$

The real exchange rate is the ratio of the two costs:

$$\varepsilon = \frac{\text{cost of U.S. goods}}{\text{cost of European goods}} = \frac{eP}{P^*} \qquad (6.1)$$

Suppose the nominal exchange rate (e) is 0.8. The U.S. price level (P) is 150, and the European price level (P^*) is 100. Then the real exchange rate (ε) is $(0.8)(150)/(100) = 1.2$. This means that U.S. goods are 1.2 times as costly as European goods.

Changes in Real Exchange Rates The formula for the real exchange rate shows that this variable rises if the nominal rate rises. Holding price levels constant, a nominal appreciation raises the cost of American goods relative to European goods. Suppose again that $P = 150$ and $P^* = 100$. If $e = 0.8$, the real exchange rate is 1.2. If e rises to 0.9, the real exchange rate rises to $(0.9)(150)/(100) = 1.35$.

The real exchange rate also changes if P or P^* changes. For example, a rise in P^*, the European price level, reduces the real exchange rate. The dollar becomes weaker in real terms. Say that P^* rises from 100 to 110. In other words, Europe experiences 10-percent inflation. Assume that e stays constant at 0.8 and P stays at 150. In this case, the U.S. real exchange rate falls from 1.2 to $(0.8)(150)/(110) = 1.09$.

To understand why the dollar weakens, think of an American who buys euros. As long as e is constant, he gets the same number of euros for each dollar. But a higher European price level means the euros have less purchasing power. A dollar is worth less in terms of the foreign goods it can buy.

Which Exchange Rate Matters? Earlier we discussed how an appreciation affects American consumers and firms. Now we can be more precise: these effects follow from a rise in the real exchange rate. The real rate determines the costs of imports. It also determines the costs of American goods in Europe and, hence, the competitiveness of U.S. exports.

In our earlier examples, we asked, what happens if the nominal exchange rate rises from 0.8 to 0.9? These examples implicitly assume that price levels are constant, which means a higher nominal rate raises the real rate as well. This assumption is fairly realistic for the United States and Europe today, because the price levels in these two economies are stable. We return to this issue in Section 6.5.

The Trade-Weighted Real Exchange Rate

The United States has many real exchange rates. In addition to the dollar–euro rate, there are rates between the dollar and the yen, the dollar and the British pound, and so on. These rates can move in different directions. Sometimes the dollar appreciates against one currency while depreciating against another.

Economists often summarize a country's exchange rates with a **trade-weighted real exchange rate**. This variable is a weighted average of real exchange rates with all foreign currencies. The weight on each country's currency is proportional to the level of trade with that country.

In the trade-weighted real exchange rate for the United States, the dollar–euro rate has the largest weight. In 2009, this weight was 0.18, because 18 percent of U.S. trade was with euro countries. The weight means that a 1 percent rise in the dollar–euro exchange rate raises the trade-weighted rate by 0.18 percent. Other weights include 0.09 for the dollar–yen rate and 0.05 for the rate between the dollar and the British pound. The trade-weighted exchange rate measures the overall strength of the dollar.

Figure 6.3 shows U.S. real exchange rates from 1980 through 2009. It includes the U.S. rates against several currencies and the trade-weighted rate (the thick black line). The figure shows that real exchange rates fluctuate considerably over time.

> **Trade-weighted real exchange rate** weighted average of a country's real exchange rates, with weights proportional to levels of trade

FIGURE 6.3 U.S. Real Exchange Rates, 1980–2009

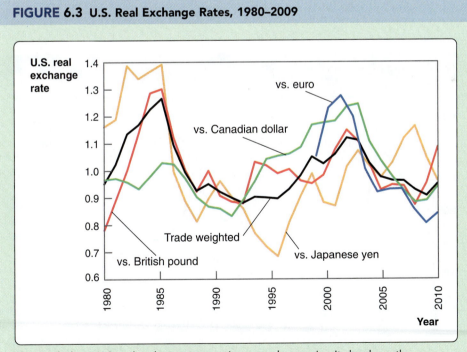

This graph shows U.S. real exchange rates against several currencies. It also shows the trade-weighted real exchange rate, which measures the overall strength of the U.S. dollar. (The scale of each series is adjusted so the average value from 1980 through 2009 is 1.0.)

Sources: OECD; Bank for International Settlements

CASE STUDY

Exchange Rates and Steel

U.S. companies are hurt by a strong dollar if they export their products or compete with imports. Steel companies do both. They compete with foreign firms both at home and abroad, so exchange rates have large effects on their sales.

Figure 6.4 shows the total output of the U.S. steel industry from 1980 through 2009. The figure also shows the U.S. trade-weighted real exchange rate from Figure 6.3. Fluctuations in the exchange rate help explain the ups and downs of the steel industry over the 30 years covered by the figure.

In the 1980s, the U.S. steel industry faced a crisis. Its annual output fell from 110 million tons in 1981 to an average of 77 million over 1982–1986. Steel companies laid workers off, and some economists suggested the industry was dying.

The initial fall in steel output reflected the U.S. recession of 1981–1982. However, output stayed low as the rest of the economy recovered in the mid-1980s. Exchange rates were the main reason. The trade-weighted real exchange rate rose by 33 percent from 1980 to 1985, hurting the competitiveness of U.S. steel.

Then the situation improved. Steel output started rising in 1987, and this trend continued for a decade (except for an interruption during the recession of 1990–1991). A 1996 book on the industry was called *The Renaissance*

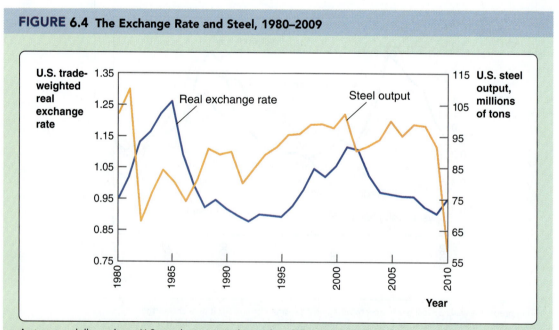

FIGURE 6.4 The Exchange Rate and Steel, 1980–2009

A stronger dollar reduces U.S. steel output, and a weaker dollar increases steel output.

Sources: Bank for International Settlements; World Steel Association

of American Steel. This turnaround resulted partly from innovations in manufacturing. U.S. steel companies moved from large factories to "mini-mills" where costs were lower. However, exchange rates also helped revive the industry. The dollar fell over the late 1980s and then stabilized at a moderate level in the first half of the 1990s.

The so-called renaissance was followed by another troubled period. Steel output leveled off in the late 1990s despite a booming economy, and output fell sharply from 2000 to 2002. Once again, layoffs were widespread, and more than 30 steel companies went bankrupt.

As in previous periods, the exchange rate helps explain the steel industry's fortunes. The trade-weighted rate rose by 25 percent from 1995 to 2001, as shown in Figure 6.4. And once again, the crisis passed when the appreciation was reversed: the dollar started falling in 2003 and steel output recovered.

In tough times, the steel industry often seeks help from the government. To protect their sales, companies advocate restrictions on imports of foreign steel. Such policies are controversial. Typically, they are supported by congressional members from steel-producing areas but opposed by economists who believe in free trade.

During the 1980s steel crisis, the Reagan administration negotiated "voluntary restraint agreements" with European countries and Japan. Under pressure, these countries agreed to reduce their sales of steel in the United States. The agreements were allowed to lapse in the early 1990s as U.S. steel companies recovered.

In the late 1990s, the Clinton administration again tried to reduce steel imports by negotiating with foreign governments. In March 2002, at the height of another steel crisis, the Bush administration imposed tariffs on steel. *Tariffs* are taxes on imports; in this case, foreign steel was taxed at rates as high as 30 percent.

The steel tariffs angered foreign governments as well as U.S. companies, such as auto firms, that purchase steel. The recovery of the domestic steel industry after 2002 reduced support for the tariffs, and they were rescinded in December 2003.

In the years after 2004, the U.S. steel industry faced new problems. Output stagnated from 2004 to 2007, largely because of China's growing steel industry. The dollar weakened against most currencies but was strong against the Chinese yuan, making U.S. steel producers uncompetitive with Chinese producers. In 2008–2009, U.S. steel output plummeted as a deep recession devastated steel-consuming industries such as construction and autos.

▶ Chapter 17 discusses the dollar–yuan exchange rate, its effects on the U.S. steel industry, and the resulting political controversy.

6.3 THE LONG-RUN BEHAVIOR OF EXCHANGE RATES

So far we've focused on how exchange rates affect people and firms. The rest of the chapter discusses the factors that determine exchange rates and why they change over time.

When economists ask, "What determines variable X?" they often give two sets of answers—one for the long run and one for the short run. Exchange rates behave differently over these two time horizons, so we start with the long-run theory. Economists don't define the long run as a precise time span. But roughly speaking, you can think of long-run exchange rate movements as trends over a decade or more, not year-to-year fluctuations.

Purchasing Power Parity

Purchasing power parity (PPP) theory of exchange rates based on the idea that a currency purchases the same quantities of goods and services in different countries; implies that real exchange rates are constant over time

Law of one price theory that an identical good or service has the same price in all locations

The leading theory of long-run exchange rates is called **purchasing power parity (PPP)**. Its key idea is that a currency can purchase the same quantities of goods and services in different countries. Let's discuss this idea and its implications for exchange rates.

The Law of One Price PPP starts with a basic idea from microeconomics: the **law of one price**. This law says that an identical good or service should sell for the same price everywhere. If a certain kind of hammer costs $10 at a hardware store in Boston, it should also cost $10 at a store in Kansas City or San Diego.

To see the rationale for this idea, suppose it's not true. A hammer costs $10 in Boston but $11 in San Diego. This difference creates opportunities for people to make money. Someone can buy hammers for $10 in Boston, ship them to San Diego, sell them for $11, and earn profits. This strategy is called *arbitrage*.

Arbitrage eliminates price differences. It raises the demand for hammers in Boston, pushing up the price in that city. It raises supply in San Diego, pushing down the price there. This process continues until the two prices reach the same level, perhaps $10.50.

You can probably see that the law of one price is not completely realistic. But let's assume for the moment that the law holds and see where it leads us.

The Law Across Borders PPP applies the law of one price across national borders. The price of a hammer should be the same not only in Boston and San Diego but also in Paris. Otherwise, someone could make money shipping hammers across the Atlantic. Suppose again that a hammer costs $10 in Boston. If the nominal exchange rate is 0.8 euros per dollar, then $10 is worth 8 euros. The law of one price says a hammer must cost 8 euros in Paris.

Under PPP, what's true for hammers is true for all goods and services. Everything costs the same in the United States and Europe. Remember that we measure the overall cost of goods and services with the aggregate price level. The cost in Europe, measured in euros, is P^*. The cost in the United States is P in dollars and eP in euros, where e is the nominal exchange rate. So

$$eP = P^*$$

This equation has strong implications for exchange rates. If we divide both sides by P^*, we get

$$\frac{eP}{P^*} = 1$$

Here, the left side is the real exchange rate. PPP says this variable must always equal 1. It is constant. The law of one price rules out changes in the relative prices of U.S. and European goods.

Rearranging again, we get an expression for the nominal exchange rate:

$$e = \frac{P^*}{P} \qquad\qquad (6.2)$$

Under PPP, the nominal exchange rate equals the ratio of price levels in Europe and the United States.

How Reasonable Is PPP?

Purchasing power parity is not exactly true. In reality, goods can sell for different prices in different countries. And the real exchange rate changes over time, as we saw in Figure 6.3.

PPP can fail because arbitrage isn't perfect. It is costly to ship hammers around the world. If hammer prices vary by modest amounts, the earnings from arbitrage may be less than the shipping costs. In this case, differences in hammer prices can persist.

The limits to arbitrage are clear if we look beyond hammers. Some things are very hard to transport, especially services. If a haircut costs more in Paris than in Boston, the law of one price says someone will hire Boston barbers and fly them to Paris. This doesn't really happen.

On the other hand, PPP contains a large grain of truth. The assumption of arbitrage captures the idea that market forces push prices toward each other. Differences in prices produce flows of goods that cause the differences to diminish.

Suppose U.S. goods are more expensive than European goods. In other words, the U.S. real exchange rate is high. Imports are cheap for Americans, so goods flow from Europe to the United States. The demand for U.S. products is low, putting pressure on U.S. firms to reduce their prices. Across the ocean, the strong dollar means booming sales for European firms. In this environment, the firms are likely to raise prices. Over time, falling American prices and rising European prices reduce the real exchange rate, pushing it toward the PPP level.

Evidence for PPP

Now that we've discussed the logic behind purchasing power parity, let's turn to evidence that supports it. We'll see that long-run movements in exchange rates fit well with the theory.

PPP says the nominal exchange rate equals a ratio of price levels: $e = P^*/P$. To study exchange rate movements over time, we take percentage changes:

$$\% \text{ change in } e = \% \text{ change in } \frac{P^*}{P}$$

The right side of this equation can be rewritten using a common approximation: the percentage change in a ratio equals the change in the numerator minus the change in the denominator. This implies

$$\% \text{ change in } e = (\% \text{ change in } P^*) - (\% \text{ change in } P)$$

▶Note to math majors: We are using a first-order Taylor approximation.

To interpret this equation, recall that the percentage change in a country's price level defines its inflation rate. The percentage change in the foreign price level, P^*, is the foreign inflation rate. So we can write

$$\% \text{ change in } e = \pi^* - \pi \qquad \textbf{(6.3)}$$

where π stands for the inflation rate. The percentage change in a country's exchange rate is the difference between foreign inflation and domestic inflation. For example, if $\pi^* = 5\%$ and $\pi = 3\%$, the exchange rate rises by $5 - 3 = 2\%$.

Equation (6.3) fits exchange rate movements over long periods. **Figure 6.5** shows changes in the U.S. exchange rate against 43 foreign currencies

---

FIGURE 6.5 Inflation and Nominal Exchange Rates

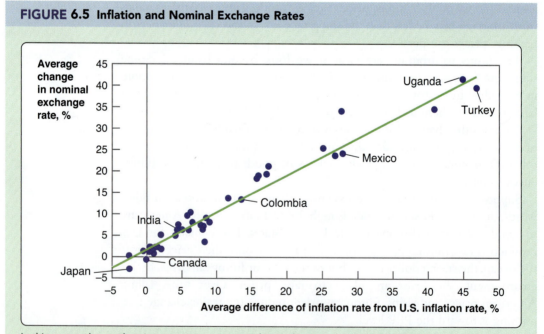

In this scatterplot, each point represents a country during the period 1980–2009. The horizontal axis is the average difference between the country's annual inflation rate and the U.S. inflation rate, and the vertical axis is the average percentage change in the U.S. exchange rate against the country's currency. As predicted by PPP, inflation differences explain changes in nominal exchange rates.

Source: International Monetary Fund

over the period 1980–2009. For each currency, the figure plots the average annual change in the nominal exchange rate, e, against the difference between foreign and U.S. inflation.

For example, the point in the lower left is the Japanese yen. Over 1980–2009, the dollar's value in yen changed by -2.7 percent per year. The average difference between the Japanese and U.S. inflation rates was -2.5 percent. (Inflation averaged 1.2 percent in Japan and 3.7 percent in the United States.)

Figure 6.5 confirms a close relationship between inflation and changes in nominal exchange rates. Japanese inflation was lower than U.S. inflation, so the dollar depreciated against the yen. The difference between Canadian and U.S. inflation was close to zero, implying little change in the U.S.–Canada exchange rate. In contrast, Uganda and Turkey had high inflation, so the dollar appreciated strongly against Uganda's shilling and Turkey's lira.

6.4 REAL EXCHANGE RATES IN THE SHORT RUN

Although purchasing power parity explains long-run changes in exchange rates, it doesn't fit the short-run picture well. Contrary to PPP, real exchange rates fluctuate considerably from year to year. We now develop a theory of these short-term fluctuations. For the moment, let's focus on the overall level of the U.S. real exchange rate as measured by the trade-weighted rate.

This exchange rate is determined in the currency markets we discussed in Section 6.1. It is the price of a dollar in these markets. Economists generally believe that prices are determined by supply and demand, and the exchange rate is no exception.

Net Exports and Capital Flows

The supply of dollars comes from Americans who trade dollars for foreign currencies. Recall that Americans sell dollars for two reasons: to buy foreign goods and services and to buy foreign assets. Purchases of foreign goods and services are imports, and purchases of assets are capital outflows. The supply of dollars is the total amount that must be sold for these purposes:

$$\text{supply of dollars} = \text{imports} + \text{capital outflows}$$

The demand for dollars comes from foreigners. They buy dollars to purchase American goods and services and to purchase American assets. Foreign purchases of goods and services are exports for the United States, and the purchases of assets are capital inflows. Therefore,

$$\text{demand for dollars} = \text{exports} + \text{capital inflows}$$

We assume the exchange rate adjusts to equalize supply and demand:

$$\text{supply of dollars} = \text{demand for dollars}$$

Substituting in the previous equations, we get

imports + capital outflows = exports + capital inflows

To understand the last equation, it helps to rearrange the terms. We can rewrite the equation as

exports − imports = capital outflows − capital inflows

Net exports (NX) exports minus imports

Net capital outflows (NCO) capital outflows minus capital inflows

The left side of this equation, exports minus imports, is called **net exports (NX)**. The right side, capital outflows minus capital inflows, is **net capital outflows (NCOs)**. Using these terms, we can write the equation more compactly:

$$NX = NCO \qquad\qquad (6.4)$$

Net exports can be either positive or negative. NX is positive if exports exceed imports, creating a *trade surplus,* and negative if imports exceed exports, creating a *trade deficit.* Similarly, net capital outflows can be either positive or negative. Either way, net exports and net capital outflows must be equal to balance the supply and demand for dollars.

In Section 4.1 we defined net capital *inflows* as capital inflows minus capital outflows. The term we use here, *net capital outflows,* is the reverse. In Equation (6.4), we could replace net capital outflows with − (net capital inflows), and the equation would say the same thing.

Effects of the Real Exchange Rate

Now the real exchange rate enters the story. Remember that a rise in this variable means that U.S. goods become more expensive compared with foreign goods. This change leads foreigners to buy fewer U.S. goods, so U.S. exports fall. Americans also switch from U.S. to foreign goods, so imports rise. Both lower exports and higher imports reduce net exports:

$$\uparrow \varepsilon \rightarrow \downarrow \text{exports, } \uparrow \text{imports}$$
$$\rightarrow \downarrow \text{net exports}$$

We assume that the exchange rate does *not* affect net capital outflows. This variable is determined by factors such as interest rates and confidence in the economy.

The Equilibrium Exchange Rate

Figure 6.6 summarizes our discussion. This graph shows the relationships among net exports, net capital outflows, and the real exchange rate. Net exports and net capital outflows are measured in dollars. The downward-sloping curve shows the behavior of net exports. A higher real exchange rate reduces net exports. The vertical line captures the behavior of net capital outflows, which do not change as the real exchange rate changes.

We have seen that net exports must equal net capital outflows. This happens only if the real exchange rate is at the level marked ε^* in the

FIGURE 6.6 The Real Exchange Rate in the Short Run

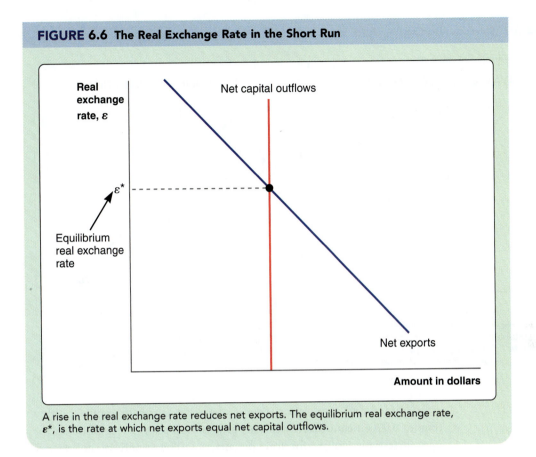

A rise in the real exchange rate reduces net exports. The equilibrium real exchange rate, ε^*, is the rate at which net exports equal net capital outflows.

graph, where the two curves intersect. This level is the equilibrium real exchange rate. Supply and demand in currency markets push the exchange rate to equilibrium.

6.5 FLUCTUATIONS IN EXCHANGE RATES

We can use Figure 6.6 to explain short-run fluctuations in the real exchange rate. These movements are caused by shifts in the two curves in the figure: net exports and net capital outflows. The main reasons for such shifts are summarized in **Table 6.2**.

Shifts in Net Capital Outflows

Many changes in exchange rates are caused by shifts in net capital outflows. **Figure 6.7A** shows what happens when NCO rises. The vertical curve in our graph shifts to the right, reducing the equilibrium exchange rate. **Figure 6.7B** shows the opposite case: a fall in NCO raises the exchange rate.

TABLE 6.2 Why Do Real Exchange Rates Fluctuate?

Shifts in net capital outflows because of . . .
Changes in real interest rates (causes include changes in monetary policy or in budget deficits)
Changes in confidence
Changes in expected future exchange rates

Shifts in net exports because of . . .
Foreign recessions
Changes in commodity prices

FIGURE 6.7 Shifts in Net Capital Outflows

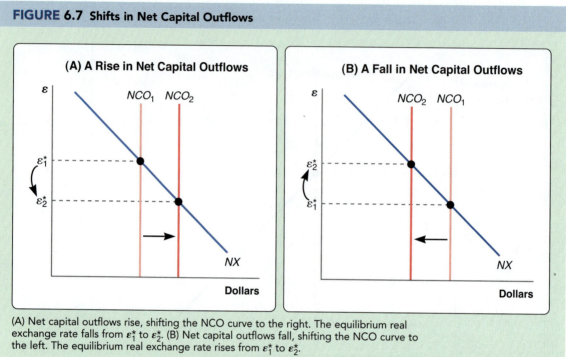

(A) Net capital outflows rise, shifting the NCO curve to the right. The equilibrium real exchange rate falls from ε_1^* to ε_2^*. (B) Net capital outflows fall, shifting the NCO curve to the left. The equilibrium real exchange rate rises from ε_1^* to ε_2^*.

To understand these effects, remember that a rise in capital outflows (Figure 6.7A) means that Americans buy more foreign assets. To do so, they must first trade dollars for foreign currency. The supply of dollars rises, pushing down the price of the dollar.

Chapter 4 discussed several reasons that capital flows can fluctuate, including changes in interest rates and changes in confidence. Let's review these factors and examine their effects on exchange rates.

Changes in Interest Rates A key factor is the real interest rate, r. If r rises in the United States, U.S. assets become more attractive. Capital outflows fall as Americans keep more of their wealth at home, and capital inflows rise. Both effects reduce net capital outflows. In Figure 6.7B, the vertical line shifts to the left, raising the real exchange rate.

This analysis tells us that *factors that influence the real interest rate also affect the real exchange rate.* For example, a tightening of monetary policy raises the real interest rate in the short run. This action raises the real exchange rate as well.

The real interest rate is also influenced by government budget deficits. For example, large deficits during the presidency of Ronald Reagan contributed to high real interest rates in the mid-1980s, which in turn caused an appreciation of the dollar. We saw the effects of this appreciation on the U.S. steel industry in the case study in Section 6.2.

Changes in Confidence Another key factor is confidence in the economy. A drop in confidence can provoke capital flight—a shift toward foreign assets. This means a rise in net capital outflows. In Figure 6.7A, the vertical line shifts to the right, reducing the real exchange rate.

East Asian countries, for example, were hit by capital flight in 1997–1998. Applied to this episode, our short-run theory predicts decreases in East Asian exchange rates—depreciations against the dollar and other currencies outside the region. This prediction is correct. In Korea, for example, the value of the won fell from 0.11 dollars in October 1997 to 0.06 the following January.

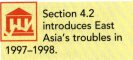 Section 4.2 introduces East Asia's troubles in 1997–1998.

Changes in Expected Exchange Rates A final factor is expectations about future exchange rates. Suppose the real exchange rate is low, but people learn it is likely to rise in the future. For example, the central bank indicates it will tighten monetary policy, pushing up the exchange rate. The expectation of this event shifts capital flows, changing the exchange rate immediately. The exchange rate reacts before the central bank actually does anything.

To see why, recall that an appreciation hurts the owners of foreign assets, because it reduces the value of these assets in domestic currency. When people expect the exchange rate to rise in the future, they expect losses on foreign assets. This discourages them from buying the assets, so net capital outflows fall. As usual, a decrease in net capital outflows raises the real exchange rate.

This effect helps explain the volatility of exchange rates—why they jump up and down so frequently. Exchange rates can jump without changes in the variables that affect them directly, such as interest rates. It is enough for news to arrive that changes expectations about the future.

CASE STUDY

The Euro Versus the Dollar

The euro was created on January 1, 1999, and at the beginning of 2011 it was the currency for 17 European countries. Since the euro was launched, its value has been a subject of intense interest to European economists, politicians, and ordinary citizens. This interest partly reflects the importance of a "strong" euro to European pride.

Figure 6.8 shows the European real exchange rate against the U.S. dollar from 1999 to 2010. The exchange rate is defined from the European point of view, so an increase means the euro is more valuable and the dollar less valuable. The figure shows that the euro fell from 1999 to 2001, rose from 2001 to 2008, and then fell again.

At least two factors help explain the initial fall in the euro. One was the attitude of policy makers at the European Central Bank (ECB). When the euro was created, Wim Duisenberg, the ECB president, stated that he was mainly concerned with controlling inflation and did not have any "exchange rate aim." Commentators interpreted this statement to mean the ECB might allow the exchange rate to fall. As we have discussed, expectations of a lower exchange rate cause higher capital outflows, and hence an immediate fall in the exchange rate.

▶ Chapters 16 and 17 discuss the workings of the European Central Bank.

FIGURE 6.8 The Euro Versus the Dollar

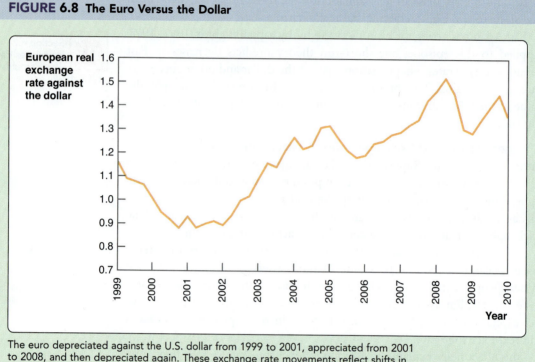

The euro depreciated against the U.S. dollar from 1999 to 2001, appreciated from 2001 to 2008, and then depreciated again. These exchange rate movements reflect shifts in capital flows.

Source: OECD

Online Case Study
An Update on Exchange Rates

Another factor was growing confidence in the U.S. economy. The late 1990s were the "new economy" period in which U.S. productivity grew rapidly and the stock market soared. U.S. assets became more attractive, raising net capital outflows from Europe. This shift exacerbated the fall in the euro.

Events in the United States also partly explain the euro's turnaround in 2001. In the early 2000s, new-economy euphoria ebbed as the stock market fell and the United States entered a recession. Net capital outflows from Europe decreased and the euro rose. In addition, the Federal Reserve responded to the 2001 recession by easing monetary policy. It reduced real interest rates and kept them low until 2004, while interest rates in Europe stayed relatively high. This difference made European assets more attractive. It was another reason for lower net capital outflows and a stronger euro.

The euro fell modestly during 2005 then resumed its upward path. Over 2006–2008, confidence in the U.S. economy fell, first from concern over large government budget deficits, then as the housing bubble burst and a recession began. In addition, the Fed reduced interest rates in response to the weakening economy while the ECB raised rates to contain inflation. All these developments made European assets more attractive compared with American assets. Europe's net capital outflows fell and the euro rose.

The rise in the euro ended abruptly in the fall of 2008, when the financial crisis exploded after the failure of Lehman Brothers and it became clear that both the European and the U.S. economies would be hit hard. In the flight to safety, financial institutions around the world bought U.S. Treasury securities. The flow of capital to the U.S. strengthened the dollar, which meant a weaker euro. The euro also fell because the crisis finally led the ECB to cut interest rates.

The euro recovered briefly in 2009 as financial panic subsided, but then another blow occurred: the Greek debt crisis. Fears that governments in Greece and elsewhere might default shook confidence in Europe's economies, pushing the euro down.

> Section 4.5 discusses the flight to safety and the Greek debt crisis. We return to the dramatic events of 2008–2010 throughout the book.

Shifts in Net Exports

Another source of exchange rate fluctuations is shifts in net exports. For example, suppose U.S. goods become more fashionable in Europe. Everyone in France and Germany wants the latest American clothes and electronic gadgets. For a given exchange rate, U.S. net exports are higher. **Figure 6.9A** shows what happens in the U.S. economy. The NX curve shifts to the right, raising the real exchange rate. Once again, this result makes sense if we think about currency markets. To buy more U.S. goods, foreigners need more dollars. Higher demand for the dollar pushes up its price.

Figure 6.9B shows the opposite case. Here, European goods become more popular, reducing U.S. net exports. The NX curve shifts to the left, reducing the real exchange rate.

Shifts in preferences for countries' goods are one reason net exports might shift. Let's discuss two other reasons that are often important: foreign recessions and changes in commodity prices.

FIGURE 6.9 Shifts in Net Exports

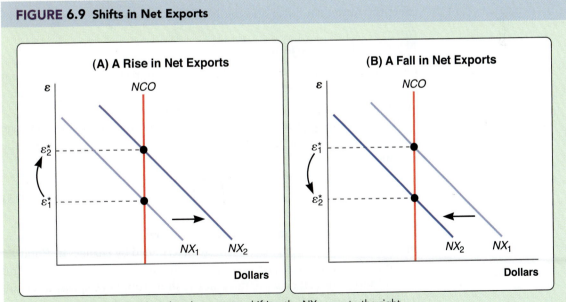

(A) Net exports rise for each real exchange rate, shifting the NX curve to the right. The equilibrium real exchange rate rises from ε_1^* to ε_2^*. (B) Net exports fall for each real exchange rate, shifting the NX curve to the left. The equilibrium real exchange rate falls from ε_1^* to ε_2^*.

Foreign Recessions Net exports depend on the strength of foreign economies. Suppose that Europe and Japan enter recessions. Incomes fall in those economies, so people reduce their spending, including spending on U.S. goods. From the U.S. point of view, net exports fall at any exchange rate. As in Figure 6.9B, the NX curve shifts to the left, reducing the real exchange rate.

The effect of a foreign recession is largest when the level of trade with the foreign country is high. Consider Canada, which exports roughly 30 percent of its GDP to the United States. When the United States enters a recession, Canadian exports are hit hard, pushing down the exchange rate. For example, during the financial crisis of 2007–2009, the U.S. recession contributed to the Canadian dollar's drop from 1.00 U.S. dollars in March 2008 to 0.79 in March 2009. In contrast, the United States exports less than 3 percent of its GDP to Canada. So fluctuations in Canada's economy do not greatly affect the United States.

Commodity Prices The main exports from some countries are commodities such as oil or agricultural products. For these countries, changes in the real exchange rate arise largely from fluctuations in commodity prices.

Norway, for example, exports oil from its North Sea wells. These exports are 15–20 percent of Norwegian GDP. The price of oil in U.S. dollars is determined by world supply and demand. If oil prices rise, Norway's net exports rise for a given exchange rate. Norway may ship the same quantity of oil, but it counts as higher exports because the oil is more valuable. The NX curve shifts to the right, raising the value of the Norwegian kroner.

Similarly, copper is a large part of Chile's exports. So fluctuations in the world price of copper affect the value of Chile's peso. Australia and New Zealand have large agricultural exports, so fluctuations in agricultural prices affect the Australian dollar and the New Zealand dollar.

Nominal Rates Again

Our short-run theory explains fluctuations in real exchange rates, but remember that the exchange rates reported in the news are nominal rates. What determines the short-run behavior of these rates?

To answer this question, we start with the definition of the real exchange rate: $\varepsilon = (eP)/P^*$. Rearranging this equation yields an expression for the nominal rate:

$$e = \varepsilon\left(\frac{P^*}{P}\right) \tag{6.5}$$

Our long-run theory, purchasing power parity, assumes that ε is constant. So changes in the nominal exchange rate are determined by changes in P and P^*.

We've seen, however, that the real rate fluctuates in the short run. And often P and P^* do *not* change much in the short run. These price levels are stable if domestic and foreign inflation rates are low. In this case, fluctuations in real exchange rates produce parallel fluctuations in nominal rates.

For example, **Figure 6.10A** compares real and nominal exchange rates between the euro and the dollar. From 1999 to 2010, Europe and the

FIGURE 6.10 Real and Nominal Exchange Rates Against the Dollar, 1999–2010

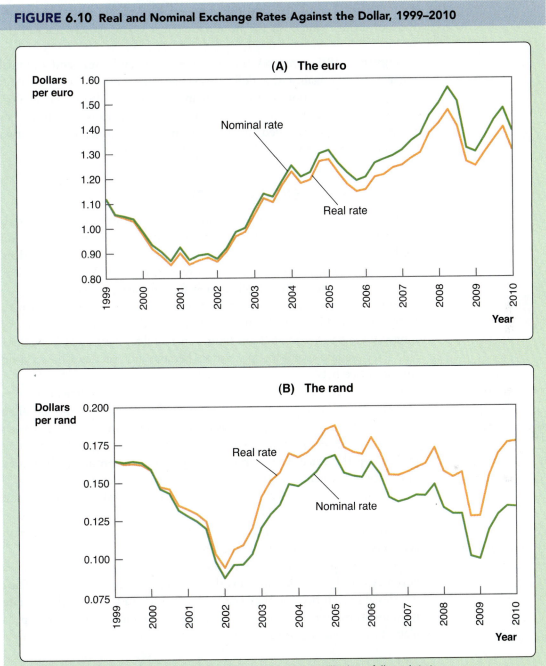

(A) Real and nominal exchange rates between the euro and the dollar have followed similar paths, because the European and U.S. price levels have been fairly stable. (B) Real and nominal exchange rates have diverged somewhat more for South Africa. South Africa's inflation rate has exceeded the U.S. inflation rate, raising South Africa's real exchange rate relative to its nominal rate.

Sources: Federal Reserve Bank of St. Louis; OECD; Statistics South Africa

United States had similar, low inflation rates. The ratio of price levels, P^*/P, did not change much, so the nominal exchange rate closely tracked the real rate.

Figure 6.10B compares the South African rand's real and nominal exchange rates against the dollar over the same period. The two rates diverge somewhat more in this case than they do for Europe. Since 2002, the real rate has risen compared to the nominal rate because South Africa's inflation rate has exceeded the U.S. inflation rate. Nonetheless, the two exchange rates have followed the same broad pattern.

6.6 CURRENCY SPECULATION

Now that we've discussed how exchange rates are determined, let's turn to another aspect of currency markets: speculation. Speculators place bets on exchange rates, just as they bet on movements in stock and bond prices. They forecast changes in rates, buy currencies they think will appreciate, and then resell them. They profit if their forecasts are correct.

Currency speculators include commercial banks, investment banks, hedge funds, and individuals. Speculators trade both currencies and currency futures. We saw in Section 6.2 that futures are useful for hedging exchange rate risk. They are also useful for speculation, because little money is needed up front to place bets.

Of course, it's not easy to predict exchange rates. The efficient markets hypothesis (EMH) applies to currencies as well as to stocks and bonds. The EMH says there can't be good reasons to expect profits from a currency purchase. If there were, traders would already have bought the currency, pushing up the price. The market quickly eliminates profit opportunities, just as the stock market eliminates undervaluation of companies.

▶ Consult Section 5.5 to review the efficient markets hypothesis. Section 5.6 describes how speculators use derivative securities to bet on stock and bond prices.

Speculators do not fully believe the EMH. They think they can forecast exchange rates well enough to earn profits. Banks and hedge funds stake large amounts of money on this belief. Observers estimate that speculation accounts for more than half of all currency trades.

Much speculation occurs over short time periods. Speculators buy a currency and then resell it in a few days, or even within the same day. They use this approach because they think they can forecast daily exchange rate movements better than longer-term changes. In addition, short-term speculation can produce profits quickly.

Forecasting Methods

How do speculators forecast exchange rates? Typically they use a blend of several methods. Widely used approaches include economic analysis, monitoring of order flows, and technical analysis.[1]

---

[1] For more on these methods, see Callum Henderson, *Currency Strategy: A Practitioner's Guide to Currency Trading, Hedging and Forecasting,* 2nd ed., Wiley, 2006. Henderson is a former analyst for Citigroup.

Economic Analysis Major speculators such as banks employ economists who forecast exchange rates using theories like the ones we've studied in this chapter. The economists try to predict the variables in these theories, such as interest rates and net exports, and to derive the implications for exchange rates.

For many speculators, however, economic analysis is not the primary forecasting tool. The reason is speculators' focus on very short time periods. Economic theories, even theories of the "short run," try to explain exchange rate movements over months or years. Usually the theories don't explain the wiggles in rates that occur from day to day or hour to hour.

Order Flow Many currency speculators examine **order flows**. Order flow is a concept that arises in dealer markets, which include currency markets as well as some stock and bond markets. Dealers hold inventories of currencies and accept both "buy" and "sell" orders from other traders. A currency's order flow is the difference between total buy orders and sell orders over some period.

> **Order flow** in a dealer market, the difference between total buy orders and sell orders over some period

A positive order flow means that buy orders exceed sell orders. Traders are purchasing more of a currency from dealers than they are selling to dealers, so dealers' inventories of the currency are falling. A negative order flow means sales to dealers exceed purchases, so inventories are rising.

When some circumstance causes exchange rates to change, order flows are part of the process. For example, suppose confidence in South Africa's economy increases. The demand for South African assets rises, so people want more rand. Dealers start receiving more buy orders for rand than sell orders; that is, order flow is positive. Dealers see their inventories of rand fall, and they respond by raising the price of rand. This means the rand appreciates.

Because of this chain of effects, speculators can use order flow to predict exchange rate movements. If they see a rising order flow, they know this is part of a process that will soon cause a currency to appreciate. Large banks have an advantage here, because they act as currency dealers as well as speculators. They are the first to see buy and sell orders from their customers. They can identify shifts in order flow before other traders do and before exchange rates adjust.

Technical Analysis **Technical analysis** encompasses a variety of techniques for predicting prices in financial markets, including exchange rates. The common feature is that past movements in prices are used to predict future prices. The underlying idea is that financial prices repeatedly follow certain patterns. Technical analysts try to recognize a pattern while it is occurring. If they succeed, they can predict where prices will go as the pattern continues.

> **Technical analysis** set of methods for forecasting prices in financial markets based on the past behavior of prices

Many currency speculators use technical analysis: they forecast exchange rates based on the past behavior of rates. Yet technical analysis is controversial; many economists say it doesn't work. The next case study explores this issue.

CASE STUDY

More on Technical Analysis

The first methods of technical analysis were developed by stock traders a century ago. These traders used graphs of past stock prices to predict future prices. Today, however, technical analysis is not very popular in the stock market. Most analysts pick stocks by studying companies and forecasting their earnings.

Technical analysis is more popular in currency markets: according to industry surveys, most commercial banks and investment banks use it to help forecast exchange rates. Technical analysis comes in many flavors. Some methods are complex, but we'll discuss two that are relatively simple.

Comparing Averages In one approach, technical analysts compute averages of an exchange rate over different periods. They compare an average over the recent past to an average over a longer period. If the recent average is higher, this signals that the exchange rate is following an upward trend. This trend is likely to continue, so the exchange rate should rise in the near future.

Specifically, many traders compare the average exchange rate over the past 12 days and the past 26 days. If the 12-day average is higher, the exchange rate is trending up. (The difference between the two averages has a fancy name: the 12/26-day moving average convergence divergence indicator.)

Support and Resistance Levels Another idea is that an exchange rate is likely to stay in a certain range above and below its current level. The bottom of this range is the exchange rate's *support level.* and the top is the *resistance level.* If the rate falls to the support level, it is likely to bounce back up rather than fall farther. If it rises to the resistance level, it is likely to bounce back down.

To exploit this behavior, speculators wait until an exchange rate moves near a support or resistance level. At that point, they know which way the rate is likely to bounce, so they can make profitable trades. The trick, of course, is to identify support and resistance levels. Again, speculators use a variety of methods. One view is that support and resistance are tied to an exchange rate's previous highs and lows. For example, if the highest value of the dollar over the last 3 months was 0.9 euros, then 0.9 may be a resistance level.

It's not obvious why support and resistance levels exist. Speculators' profit-taking strategies are one possible source of resistance. Traders often plan to sell a currency if it rises to a certain level in order to lock in their gains. A trader may choose an exchange rate's past high as the level for profit taking. If many traders make this choice, the past high becomes a resistance level. When the exchange rate reaches the past high, a large number of sell orders are triggered, pushing the rate down.

Does It Work? Many economists don't believe in technical analysis. Indeed, some supporters of the efficient markets hypothesis ridicule the approach.

Burton Malkiel of Princeton University says that "technical analysis is about as useful as going to a fortune teller."

Economists have compared the performance of stock mutual funds that employ different strategies. Some studies examine funds that use technical analysis, and they support the view that this approach doesn't work. These findings are one reason that most stock pickers eschew technical analysis.

It is not clear, however, that technical analysis is ineffective in currency markets. There is less research on this topic, and some of the studies that exist suggest that technical analysis *can* predict exchange rates. One example is a 2000 study by Carol Osler of the Federal Reserve Bank of New York, who examined support and resistance levels estimated by several large banks.[*] The banks publish these levels each day for the benefit of traders who use the banks as brokers. Osler examined exchange rates between the dollar and three currencies: the pound, the yen, and the deutschmark (Germany's currency before the euro).

Osler's results suggest that support and resistance are useful concepts. She found that exchange rates often bounce as predicted by technical analysis when they hit published support or resistance levels. This doesn't always happen, but it happens more often than it would by chance if the published levels were meaningless.

[*] See Carol Osler, "Support for Resistance: Technical Analysis and Intraday Exchange Rates," Federal Reserve Bank of New York *Economic Policy Review,* July 2000.

▶ Malkiel is famous for a 1973 book promoting the EMH: *A Random Walk Down Wall Street.*

▶ Section 5.5 discusses research on mutual fund performance.

Summary

- The nominal exchange rate, e, is the price of one unit of a currency in terms of another currency.

6.1 Currency Markets and Exchange Rates

- People and firms buy foreign currency so they can purchase foreign goods and services and foreign assets.

- Financial institutions trade currencies on the interbank market, which consists of electronic networks. Large banks are dealers in this market. Banks also serve as brokers for firms and individuals that trade currencies.

- A rise in a currency's price in terms of foreign currency is an appreciation, and a fall in a currency's price is a depreciation.

6.2 Why Exchange Rates Matter

- An appreciation of the dollar helps U.S. consumers by making imports less expensive. It hurts U.S. firms by making their products more expensive compared with foreign goods. It hurts holders of foreign assets by reducing the dollar value of the assets.

- Overall, the U.S. economy sometimes benefits from a depreciation of the dollar. But politicians usually advocate a strong dollar because *strong* sounds better than *weak*.

- Firms and asset holders can hedge part of their exchange rate risk by trading futures contracts for currencies. They can't protect against persistent changes in exchange rates, because contract delivery dates are for 6 months or less.

- A country's real exchange rate, ε, is the relative price of domestic and foreign goods. This variable is eP/P^*, where e is the nominal exchange rate, P is the domestic price level, and P^* is the foreign price level.

- A country's trade-weighted real exchange rate is an average of its exchange rates against different countries' currencies, with weights proportional to its levels of trade with those countries.

- Exchange rates explain many ups and downs in the U.S. steel industry. In both the 1980s and the early 2000s, a strong dollar reduced steel output and spurred protectionist trade policies.

6.3 The Long-Run Behavior of Exchange Rates

■ Purchasing power parity (PPP) is a theory based on the assumption that goods and services have the same prices in all locations. It implies that the real exchange rate is constant. The nominal exchange rate is P^*/P, the ratio of the foreign and domestic price levels.

■ PPP explains the long-run behavior of exchange rates. As the theory predicts, long-run changes in nominal rates are closely related to countries' inflation rates.

6.4 Real Exchange Rates in the Short Run

■ In the short run, a country's real exchange rate is determined by the supply and demand for its currency. For supply and demand to balance, net exports must equal net capital outflows: NX = NCO.

■ Net exports depend negatively on the real exchange rate: as ε rises, NX falls. The equilibrium exchange rate, ε^*, is the level at which net exports equal net capital outflows.

6.5 Fluctuations in Exchange Rates

■ A rise in net capital outflows reduces the real exchange rate. NCO can shift because of changes in interest rates, confidence, or expectations about future exchange rates.

■ Since the euro was created in 1999, its exchange rate against the dollar has fluctuated because of statements by the European Central Bank, shifts in confidence about the U.S. and European economies, and changes in U.S. and European interest rates.

■ A rise in net exports at a given real exchange rate raises the equilibrium exchange rate. NX can shift because of foreign recessions or changes in commodity prices.

■ In the short run, nominal and real exchange rates move together if countries' price levels are stable.

6.6 Currency Speculation

■ Speculators, including banks and hedge funds, account for more than half of currency trading. Speculators forecast exchange rates over the near future and buy currencies they think will appreciate. Their forecasting methods include economic analysis, monitoring of order flows, and technical analysis.

■ Technical analysts compare averages of exchange rates over different periods and estimate support and resistance levels.

■ Many economists argue these methods don't work, but most speculators use them, and some research suggests they have merit.

Key Terms

appreciation, p. 160

depreciation, p. 160

law of one price, p. 170

net capital outflows (NCO), p. 174

net exports (NX), p. 174

nominal exchange rate (e), p. 158

order flow, p. 183

purchasing power parity (PPP), p. 170

real exchange rate (ε), p. 165

technical analysis, p. 183

trade-weighted real exchange rate, p. 167

Questions and Problems

1. Suppose it takes $1.05 to buy 1 euro. What is the U.S. nominal exchange rate against the euro? What is the European nominal exchange rate against the U.S. dollar?

2. Recall from Section 6.1 that most currency trades involve the U.S. dollar. How would William Stanley Jevons explain this fact? (*Hint:* We met Jevons in Section 2.1)

3. Suppose the U.S. dollar appreciates for a period of time and then returns to its initial level. Compare a 10-percent appreciation that lasts for 2 years and a 50-percent appreciation that lasts 6 months.

   a. Which of these events hurts U.S. exporters more? Explain.

   b. How would the answer be different if currency futures did not exist?

4. On July 15, 2002, a CNN headline reported, "Euro tops dollar." The value of a euro had risen from slightly below $1.00 to slightly above $1.00. Discuss the importance of this event.

5. Suppose it takes $1.05 to buy 1 euro, the U.S. price level is 120, and the European price level is 125.

   a. Calculate the U.S. real exchange rate against the euro.

   b. Suppose the U.S. price level rises to 130. Calculate the real exchange rate again and explain why it has risen or fallen.

6. Section 6.2 defined the U.S. real exchange rate against the euro as the price of American goods divided by the price of European goods. We measured both prices in euros. Suppose we measured both prices in dollars instead of euros. Would this change the definition of the real exchange rate? Explain.

7. For decades, 1 British pound has been worth more than 1 U.S. dollar. One Japanese yen has been worth less than 0.01 U.S. dollars (1 cent). So a pound is more than 100 times as valuable as a yen. Does this difference matter for the British and Japanese economies? Explain.

8. Suppose that, at a certain real exchange rate, a country's net exports exceed its net capital outflows. Is the equilibrium exchange rate higher or lower than this level? Explain both in words and with a graph.

9. Suppose country A sends most of its exports to country B. It gets most of its imports from country C. If A's currency appreciates against B's currency and depreciates against C's, what happens to A's imports, exports, and net exports?

10. Using graphs, show how each of the following events affects a country's net capital outflows, net exports, and equilibrium real exchange rate.

    a. A rise in foreign interest rates

    b. A fad for buying foreign goods

    c. An announcement that a tax cut will occur in the future

    d. Rising ethnic tensions that threaten to cause a civil war

11. Suppose a country's central bank wants to keep the real exchange rate constant. What should it do to the real interest rate if foreign economies enter recessions? Explain your answer with a graph.

12. Events in South Africa between 2000 and 2010 included the following:

    a. At the start of the decade, a corruption scandal hurt the government's reputation, and the AIDS epidemic intensified.

    b. From 2002 to 2005, the government budget deficit and the inflation rate both fell.

    c. In 2007–2008, a shortage of electricity forced some of South Africa's mines to shut down.

    d. In 2009, the world prices of metals mined in South Africa rose rapidly.

    According to the theories in this chapter, how should each of these events have affected South Africa's exchange rate? Are these predictions confirmed by the data in Figure 6.1? Explain.

13. Suppose the U.S. real exchange rate against the British pound rises by 6 percent from one year to the next. The U.S. inflation rate is 2 percent, and the British inflation rate is 3 percent. What is the change in the nominal exchange rate?

14. We discussed three techniques for speculating on exchange rates: economic analysis, monitoring of order flows, and technical analysis. Assume a key part of the efficient markets hypothesis: it is impossible to predict exchange rate movements based on any publicly available information. Under this assumption, could any of the three techniques succeed? Explain.

▶ Online and Data Questions
www.worthpublishers.com/ball

15. Compute the changes in the U.S. trade-weighted real exchange rate from 2008 to 2009 and from 2009 to 2010. Use data on exchange rates, price levels, and trade shares from the text Web site. What economic forces might explain the changes in the exchange rate?

16. For 43 countries, Figure 6.5 plots the difference between a country's inflation rate and the U.S. inflation rate, and the percentage change in the U.S. exchange rate against the country's currency. The inflation rates and exchange rate changes are averages over 1980–2009. Redo the figure using inflation rates and exchange rate changes in a single year, 2010. (Data are available at the text Web site.) How does the figure change when it is based on a single year rather than 30 years? What explains the differences?

17. Using data from the text Web site, compute the real exchange rate for the Russian ruble against the U.S. dollar for each year from 1992 through 2009.

    a. Do a bit of Internet research on Russia and try to explain the movements in the real exchange rate.

    b. Do movements in Russia's real exchange rate explain most of the movements in its nominal exchange rate? Explain.

chapter seven

Asymmetric Information in the Financial System

Stan Honda/AFP/Getty Images

March 10, 2009: Flanked by federal marshals, Bernard Madoff leaves Federal District Court in New York after agreeing to plead guilty to operating a massive Ponzi scheme.

We are in the midst of studying how the financial system channels funds from savers to investors. Let's step back for a moment and review the big picture, summarized in **Figure 7.1** [on page 190], where we see that funds can flow directly from savers to investors in financial markets or indirectly through banks. Part II analyzed direct finance via financial markets. Part III, which covers Chapters 7–10, focuses on indirect finance via banks.

This part-opening chapter bridges financial markets and banking by closely examining the harmful effects of information asymmetries. The need for banks stems from asymmetric information in financial markets, where investors who sell securities know more than savers who buy the securities, creating *adverse selection* and *moral hazard*.

After exploring both of these problems, we survey efforts by private firms and by government regulators to reduce information asymmetries. Such efforts help financial markets work better, but they don't eliminate the markets' problems entirely. As a result, some investors can't raise funds in financial markets.

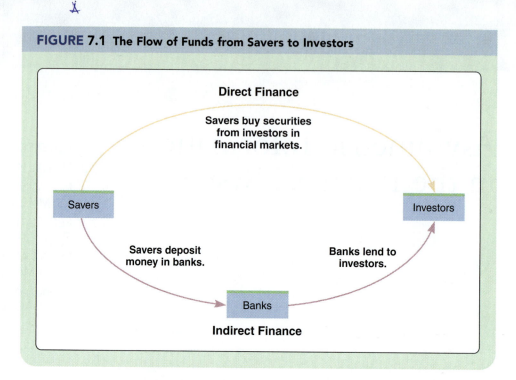

FIGURE 7.1 The Flow of Funds from Savers to Investors

The chapter then details how banks reduce asymmetric information problems. Banks gather information about borrowers and add provisions to loan contracts that reduce moral hazard and adverse selection. Because of these safeguards, banks can provide funds to investors who can't sell securities in financial markets.

Finally, we discuss another function of banks: reducing transaction costs. Bank accounts make it easy for people to save and to purchase goods and services. When investors need funds, borrowing from a bank can be less expensive than issuing securities. Along with asymmetric information, transaction costs help explain the existence of indirect finance.

▶Chapter 8 surveys the banking industry and how it is changing. Chapter 9 discusses the banking business: how bank managers seek to earn profits and contain risk. Chapter 10 discusses government regulation of banks.

7.1 ADVERSE SELECTION

Often the people or firms on one side of an economic transaction know more than those on the other side. This information asymmetry leads to *adverse selection*: among the informed parties, those who are most eager to make a deal are the least desirable to parties on the other side. Adverse selection is a big idea in economic theory, because the problem arises in many types of markets.

The Lemons Problem

In 1970, George Akerlof of the University of California, Berkeley, published the classic paper on adverse selection; he won the Nobel Prize in Economics in 2002. Akerlof presented a folksy example about used cars to show how adverse selection causes markets to malfunction.

Consider the market for 2010 Honda Accords. These cars vary in quality: some are good, and some are "lemons" that are constantly in the repair shop. If everyone knew the quality of each Accord, the used-car market would work well. The price of each car would reflect its quality. Good cars would sell for more than lemons, so every seller would get what his car is worth.

The market would also function all right if *nobody* knew the quality of each Accord. All cars would look alike, so there would be a single price for any Accord. This price would reflect the *average* quality of Accords. It would be below the price of a car that people knew to be good but above the price of a known lemon.

Akerlof, however, considers an intermediate case in which information is asymmetric. The seller of a car knows its quality because she has experience driving it. But the buyer does not know the quality: to him, all Accords look alike.

Buyers' ignorance means there will be a single price for all Accords, as in the case when nobody observes quality. One might guess that this price will reflect the average quality of all Accords. But now there is a problem. If owners of good cars see a price based on average quality, they will realize that this price is less than their top-notch cars are worth. They will hold onto the cars rather than sell them. In contrast, owners of lemons will eagerly dump their cars for a price based on average quality. At this price, the market will be flooded with lemons.

The story gets worse from there. Buyers would pay a price based on average quality if both good and bad cars were sold. But when only lemons are available, buyers realize they will end up with one, and so the price falls. Indeed, the market can unravel.

To see this, suppose some lemons are mediocre cars and some are really terrible. A low price leads the owners of so-so cars as well as good cars to refuse to sell. With only terrible cars on the market, the price falls farther. It becomes a vicious circle: a lower price reduces the average quality of cars for sale, and lower quality reduces the price. In the end, we may find that no cars are sold—or only the very worst. Most owners can't sell their cars for what they're worth, and buyers can't find a decent car.

The problem of adverse selection affects many markets besides used cars—the market for health insurance, for example. People know more about their own health than insurance companies do. Relatively sick people are likely to buy the most health insurance, because it is a good deal for them. This fact discourages companies from selling insurance and pushes up the price.

Lemons in Securities Markets

Seller knows more than buyer.

When a firm sells a security, it knows more than buyers do about the security's likely returns, because it knows its business. Just as in the used-car market, this asymmetry leads to adverse selection, a problem that plagues both stock and bond markets.

▶Section 3.2 presents the classical theory of asset prices.

Lemons in Stock Markets Suppose a firm wants to raise funds by issuing stock. According to the classical theory of asset prices, the value of the stock depends on the firm's future earnings. Savers can forecast these earnings based on the firm's past performance and its announcements about future plans.

But the firm has more information than savers have. The firm's managers can predict future sales by talking to the sales force. They learn from the research department whether new products are on the way. Engineers tell them whether factories are working smoothly.

This asymmetry causes the same adverse-selection problem as in the used-car market. Suppose the price of each firm's stock is based on the public's forecast of its earnings. Some firms will know their stock is undervalued: it is worth more than the selling price, because earnings are likely to be higher than the public expects. Others will know their stock is overvalued. Firms with overvalued stock will issue lots of it: like the owners of crummy cars, they are eager to sell something for more than it's worth. Firms with undervalued stock will hold back.

Savers understand this behavior. They realize that the stocks offered for sale are likely to be lemons. This belief pushes down stock prices. More firms stop issuing stock, so prices fall farther. As with used cars, a vicious circle can cause the market to break down.

Lemons in Bond Markets Adverse selection is not *always* a problem when firms issue bonds. The buyer of a bond knows exactly what income he will receive as long as the issuer doesn't default—and default risk is low for some issuers, such as highly successful corporations. When someone buys a safe bond, he need not worry that it's a lemon. An absence of adverse selection helps explain why corporations sometimes issue bonds rather than stock when they need funds.

Adverse selection *is* a problem in bond markets when default risk is significant. In this case, the "quality" of a bond is the probability of default. The interest rate on a bond reflects the public's assessment of this risk. A firm may know that its true default risk is higher or lower than the public thinks. If it is higher, then issuing bonds is a good deal, because the firm pays an interest rate below what it should pay given the true risk. Once again, low-quality securities can flood the market, causing it to break down.

Adverse selection is exacerbated by a fact about investment projects: those with a high risk of failure often have high returns if they succeed. Risky firms are eager to issue bonds, worsening adverse selection. Suppose, for example, that a drug company decides to make a big, risky investment. It will spend lots of money to develop a drug that cures cancer. This project might well fail, in which case the company will go out of business. But if the project succeeds, it will produce huge profits.

▶Section 5.3 discusses firms' decisions about issuing stocks and bonds.

This company will be eager to sell bonds, even if it must pay a high interest rate. It can easily cover the interest payments if the project succeeds. If the project fails, the company defaults, making the interest rate irrelevant. Because of such scenarios, firms will try to issue lots of low-quality bonds.

Adverse Selection: A Numerical Example

To clarify the concept of adverse selection, let's consider a numerical example, which is summarized in **Figure 7.2**.

FIGURE 7.2 Adverse Selection: An Example

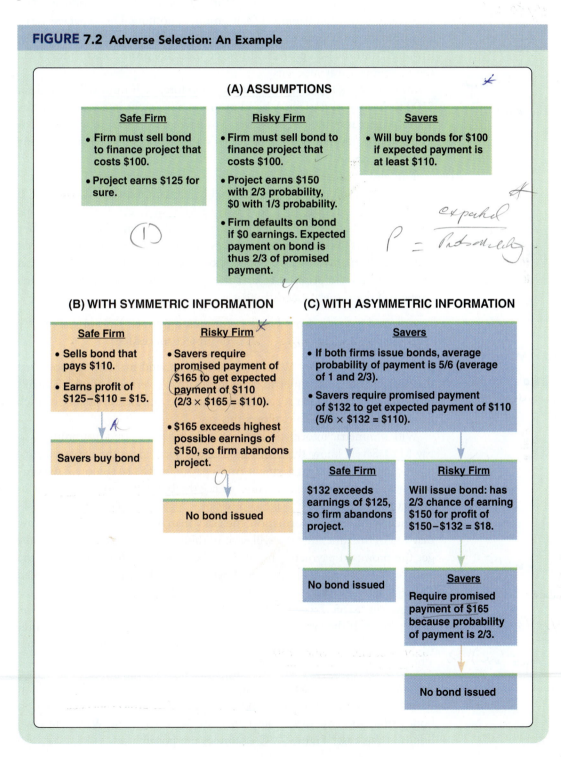

[Handwritten margin notes:]

Project costs $100.

Safe   Risky.

$125 (1) $150 (2/3)
revenue $0 (1/3)
*   Revenue.*

Expected Earnings (risky)
= 2/3 × 150 = $100.

Buy bond if payment is
at least $110.

Symmetric Info. Market
is savers have info.
is which bonds are risky and
*   which aren't*

expected = promise (safe)
*   safe*

risky
Expected payment is 110.
so savers buy only if
$110 = pp × 2/3 (success)
$165 > $150 (project loss)

Assumptions Figure 7.2A sets up the example. Two firms have potential investment projects. Each project costs $100 to undertake. One firm's project is safe. In a year, it produces $125 in revenue for sure.

The other firm's project is risky. With probability 2/3, it produces $150 in a year, but with probability 1/3, it produces nothing. The expected earnings from the risky project are 2/3 × ($150) = $100, which is less than the earnings from the safe project. However, the risky project earns more than the safe project if it succeeds.

Initially, neither firm has any funds. Therefore, each must sell a bond for $100 to finance its project. A bond promises a payment in a year, when the firm's project is complete. However, this payment is made only if the project produces revenue; if the project fails, the firm defaults. Will savers buy the firms' bonds?

The answer depends on what other options savers have. Let's assume savers can buy some other asset that yields a certain return of 10 percent. If they put $100 into this asset, they receive $110 in a year. Let's also assume savers buy the assets with the highest expected income. This means they will buy a firm's bond if the expected payment is at least $110, the payment from the alternative asset. A bond's expected payment is the payment it promises times the probability that the payment is actually made—which happens if the project succeeds; that is,

expected payment from bond = (promised payment) × (probability *(only if project succeeds)* of project success)

Symmetric Information What happens in the bond market? Suppose first that information is symmetric. This means that savers know which firm's project is safe and which is risky. As a result, they know the quality of each firm's bond. Figure 7.2B explores this case.

With symmetric information, the safe firm can sell a bond that promises to pay $110. Savers know the firm's project will succeed, so the expected payment equals the promised payment. And a payment of $110 is enough to compete with the alternative asset. After selling the bond, the firm carries out its project and earns $125. It makes a profit of $15 after paying off the bond.

Under symmetric information, the risky firm is out of luck. Savers know that 1/3 of the time the firm will earn nothing and default on its bond; they get the promised payment only 2/3 of the time. Therefore, savers buy the bond only if 2/3 times the promised payment is at least $110. The promised payment must be at least $165, because (2/3) × ($165) = $110.

However, $165 exceeds $150, the highest possible earnings from the risky project. If the risky firm promises $165, it cannot make a profit after paying off the bond, even if its project succeeds. Therefore, it does not issue a bond or undertake the project.

Asymmetric Information Now suppose that information is asymmetric. If both firms issue bonds, savers can't tell which is safe and which is risky. So bonds from the two firms must offer the same payment. Who will issue bonds in this case? Figure 7.2C examines the possibilities.

Suppose both firms issue bonds. If a saver buys a bond, it might be from the risky firm, with a success probability of 2/3, or the safe firm, with a probability of 1. Averaging these two numbers, the overall probability of success is 5/6.

Once again, savers will buy bonds if the expected payment is at least $110. This requires a promised payment of $132, because then the expected payment is (5/6) × ($132) = $110.

But now adverse selection rears its ugly head. If bonds must promise $132, the safe firm won't issue one. It would earn only $125, so it can't make a profit after paying off the bond. In contrast, the risky firm will be delighted to sell a bond promising $132. If its project works, the firm earns $150 and keeps $150 − $132 = $18. If the project fails, the firm defaults and loses nothing.

You may see how the story ends. Savers realize that only the risky firm will sell a bond with a promised payment of $132. Thus, the probability of repayment is really 2/3, the probability for the risky firm, not 5/6. With this probability, savers won't accept a promised payment of $132; they will require $165, as in the symmetric-information case. But that drives the risky firm out of the market. In the end, neither firm issues bonds.

7.2 MORAL HAZARD

Like adverse selection, moral hazard arises in many areas of economics. Once again, the underlying cause is an information asymmetry: one party in an economic relationship can't observe the actions of others. Therefore, it's impossible to ensure that everyone behaves in a desirable way. There is a "hazard" of harmful behavior.

The classic example comes from the insurance industry. (The term *moral hazard* was invented by insurers before it was adopted by economists.) Suppose I buy auto insurance. The insurance company would like me to behave in a way that minimizes the claims it must pay. I should drive carefully, never talking on my cell phone, and park only in safe neighborhoods. However, once I have insurance, I may become careless. I don't worry much about fender benders or theft, because insurance will pay most of the costs.

This moral hazard hurts both insurance companies and drivers. Frequent accidents lead to higher insurance premiums. Drivers would be better off if they could promise to be careful in return for lower premiums. Unfortunately, asymmetric information makes such an agreement impossible. I know whether I talk on my cell phone while driving, but the insurance company does not. If I have an accident, I can blame it on bad luck. There is no way to enforce a promise to drive safely.

This kind of moral hazard is also called the **principal–agent problem**. One person or company, the agent, does something that affects another, the principal. Both parties would benefit if they could agree that the agent behave a certain way. But such an agreement is impossible, because the principal does not observe what the agent does. In the insurance example,

Handwritten margin notes:
safe firm (3/3)
risky firm (2/3)
Total 5/6

Adverse selection?
safe firm loss no bond
risky firm profit issue bond
however.

Since it is only the risky firm.
They don't want 2/3
but 5/6 prob.

Insurance is example of PAP.

Principal–agent problem
moral hazard that arises when the action of one party (the agent) affects another party (the principal) that does not observe the action

the company is the principal, the driver is the agent, and his care in driving is the unobserved action.

Another example of moral hazard concerns workers' effort at their jobs. My boss (the principal) would like me (the agent) to work hard. If I do, my firm will be profitable and wages will rise. However, once I close my office door, I would rather peruse the ESPN Web site than tire myself out with work. Moral hazard arises because my boss is busy in his office and does not see what I'm doing.

Moral hazard arises in financial markets because savers who buy securities do not observe the actions of firms that issue securities. Here, savers are the principals and firms are the agents. Let's examine the moral hazard problem in stock markets and in bond markets.

Moral Hazard in Stock Markets

The moral hazard problem can be severe when firms issue stock. The ownership of a corporation may be spread across many shareholders. Often the managers who run a firm own only a small part of it. Yet their actions determine the profits that go to all shareholders.

In theory, a firm's managers work for its shareholders. Their job is to maximize profits. However, managers may be tempted to do things that benefit themselves but reduce profits. They may pay themselves huge salaries and decorate their offices with expensive art. They may head for the golf course at 3 PM rather than stay late to build up the business.

Moral hazard can make it difficult for firms to sell stock. If savers fear that managers will misuse their funds, they won't provide the funds in the first place. Because of this mistrust, even firms with good investment projects may have trouble financing the projects through the stock market.

Moral hazard often involves behavior that is perfectly legal. It's not against the law to earn $20 million a year or to skip work for golf, even if shareholders suffer. In egregious cases, moral hazard may include crimes such as embezzlement. In 2005, Dennis Kozlowski, the former president of Tyco, a manufacturing conglomerate, was convicted of larceny and fraud for appropriating Tyco's funds for his own use. According to prosecutors, Kozlowski and another Tyco executive received $600 million in improper payments from the company, including bonuses that were kept secret from shareholders and loans that were later forgiven.

Managers work for shareholders is objective to maximize profits.

what shareholders fear.

AP Photo/HO/New York district attorney

Moral hazard in Sardinia, 2001. Tyco CEO Dennis Kozlowski hired models in togas for his wife's extravagant birthday party.

Prosecutors also alleged that Kozlowski charged Tyco for extravagant personal expenses, such as the $5.7 million cost of decorating his apartment on Fifth Avenue in New York. The decorations included a shower curtain that cost $6,000, a $2,200 wastebasket, and $2,900 worth of coat hangers. In 2001, Kozlowski charged Tyco for half of his then-wife Karen's fortieth birthday party—a $2.1 million toga party on the Mediterranean island of Sardinia.

The jury in Kozlowski's case found that these expenditures amounted to theft from Tyco's shareholders. He was sentenced to 8 to 25 years in prison.

Moral Hazard in Bond Markets

Like adverse selection, the moral hazard problem is less severe in bond markets than in stock markets. Bondholders don't care if a firm's managers waste money on salaries and parties, as long as the firm makes the promised payments on its bonds. But moral hazard arises when firms issue bonds with significant default risk. Managers may increase this risk by misusing funds, so savers are wary of buying the bonds.

Recall that some investment projects combine a high risk of failure with large returns if they succeed. We have seen that this fact worsens the adverse-selection problem in bond markets. It also worsens moral hazard. Once a firm obtains funds, it has different options for how to use them, including some with high risk and high return. A drug company, for example, can divert funds from its normal investments to gamble everything on a cancer drug. Such a gamble is attractive if financed with borrowed money.

Savers understand the drug company's incentive to gamble and therefore ascribe a high default risk to its bonds. They may refuse to buy the bonds, preventing the company from financing any investment. The company would be better off if it could promise to invest in safe projects. Unfortunately, such a promise is unenforceable, because bondholders don't see what the company does.

The Numerical Example Again for Moral Hazard

We can illustrate the moral hazard problem in bond markets by varying our example of adverse selection (see Figure 7.2). Assume again that two investment projects cost $100 each; one produces $125 for sure, and one produces $150 with probability 2/3. However, let's no longer assume the two projects belong to different firms. Instead, a single firm has the option of pursuing either the safe project or the risky project.

Once again, assume the firm can sell a bond for $100 if the expected payment is at least $110. If the firm could guarantee that it will pursue the safe project, then the expected payment would equal the promised payment. In that case, the firm could sell a bond promising $110. It would undertake the project, earn $125, and make a profit of $125 − $110 = $15.

Unfortunately, this won't happen if information is asymmetric. Suppose the firm sells a bond that promises $110. At that point, whatever the firm has promised, it can pursue either project. Bondholders can't control the firm's decision because they don't see what it does. The firm will consider its options.

As we have seen, the safe project yields a certain profit of $15. The risky project produces $150 if it succeeds. In this case, the firm pays off the bond and its profit is $150 − $110 = $40. If the risky project fails, the firm defaults on the bond and earns nothing. Because the risky project succeeds 2/3 of the time, the expected profit is (2/3) × ($40) = $26.67. This exceeds the profit from the safe project, so the firm chooses the risky project.

Once again, the bond market unravels. Savers know the firm will choose the risky project, so they won't buy bonds promising $110. With a 2/3 chance of success, they need a promised payment of $165 to get an expected payment of $110. But the firm can't profit from either project if it promises $165. So no bond is sold and neither project is funded.

CASE STUDY

Ponzi Schemes

Some savers directly purchase securities issued by firms. Others put their money in mutual funds or hedge funds that purchase securities on their behalf. Turning your wealth over to a fund creates a moral hazard problem: the fund manager may misuse your money. One method for large-scale theft is a century-old practice that recaptured the national attention after hedge-fund manager Bernard Madoff was arrested in November 2008.

Madoff was running a **Ponzi scheme**, a swindle in which an asset manager persuades people to give him their money by presenting a crafty-sounding plan that promises unusually high financial returns. Often the plan details are "secret"; invariably, the plan doesn't really exist.

The schemer sends clients false statements showing that their wealth is growing rapidly. In reality, growth is financed by new clients who give more money. The scam works as long as clients do not ask the manager for too much cash back. The manager uses some new money to pay clients who make withdrawals and siphons off the rest for his own use. Success breeds further success, because the appearance of high returns convinces more and more people to entrust their money to the dishonest manager.

Ponzi schemes got their name from Charles Ponzi, an Italian who immigrated to the United States in 1903. Ponzi pursued a criminal career but hid his past when he formed the Old Colony Foreign Exchange Company in Boston in 1920. Ponzi claimed he could earn huge profits through a complex scheme involving purchases of foreign postage stamps. Starting with a few friends, he raised money by promising incredible returns—in some cases, 50 percent in 45 days.

Initially Ponzi made good on these promises, making him famous. Money flooded into his company. But before a year had passed, Massachusetts bank regulators became suspicious, investigated Ponzi's finances, and uncovered

Ponzi scheme swindle in which an asset manager falsely claims to earn high returns and pays clients who ask for cash by raising money from new clients

the truth. Ponzi was jailed, and his company was closed. Clients received 30 cents for each dollar they supposedly had in their accounts.

Many swindlers have emulated Ponzi. In the 1980s, savers lost millions of dollars on schemes run by real estate developers in Michigan and currency traders in California. But Bernard Madoff's was by far the largest Ponzi scheme in history. When it collapsed in 2008, clients' accounts at his hedge fund totaled $36 billion, but the fund's true assets were about half that amount.

Madoff ran his scheme for more than two decades without getting caught. He used his clients' money to fund a lavish lifestyle as well as make large, influential donations to charity. Many factors contributed to Madoff's success. Before beginning his fraud, he was highly successful as a legitimate stock broker. He helped to establish the NASDAQ exchange and served as its chair. This background helped convince people that Madoff was capable of producing the profits he promised. Unlike Charles Ponzi, he promised good but not spectacular returns—he reported steady returns of 10–15 percent per year—so his dishonesty was not obvious.

Madoff recruited many customers socially, through networking with wealthy people. His clients occasionally asked for details on his money-making methods but accepted his replies that the methods were too complex to understand or were secret. Madoff also received large sums from not-for-profit institutions such as universities and charitable foundations that typically spend only a small part of their endowment each year. These clients didn't ask for much cash. In the 1990s and 2000s, Madoff kept his Ponzi scheme going by expanding his fundraising from the United States to Europe and then to the Middle East.

If not for the financial crisis of 2007–2009, Madoff might still be running his Ponzi scheme. During the crisis, worried savers made large withdrawals from hedge funds around the country to put into safe assets. This proved Madoff's downfall: he faced unexpected demands for cash that he couldn't meet, making it clear that his business was fraudulent.

Individuals and institutions that trusted Madoff with their money were hurt badly when his scheme collapsed. Yeshiva University lost more than $100 million of its endowment, several charitable foundations were forced to close, and a number of hospitals experienced large losses. Elie Wiesel, a winner of the Nobel Peace Prize, lost his life savings. In the end, the scheme also proved disastrous for Madoff, pictured on page 189. In 2009, at age 70, he was sentenced to 150 years in prison. During his incarceration at a federal prison in North Carolina, he has suffered from depression and been injured in fights with other inmates.

The Madoff scandal led to greater scrutiny of asset managers who reported suspiciously high returns. In 2009, the federal government filed criminal charges related to 60 different Ponzi schemes, including a multi-billion dollar scheme run by Stanford Financial Associates of Houston.[*]

---

[*] For more on Charles Ponzi and Bernard Madoff, see Mitchell Zuckoff, *Ponzi's Scheme: The True Story of a Financial Legend*, Random House 2005; and Diana B. Henriques, "Madoff Scheme Kept Rippling Outward, Across Borders," *New York Times*, December 19, 2008 (available at www.nytimes.com).

7.3 REDUCING INFORMATION ASYMMETRIES

We have painted a bleak picture of asymmetric information causing securities markets to break down. Can this problem be solved? Market participants work to reduce adverse selection and moral hazard and to make it possible for some firms to issue securities. Their solutions to information problems are imperfect, however, so other firms are shut out of securities markets.

Information Gathering

Adverse selection arises because savers lack information about firms. At a broad level, it is obvious how to reduce this problem: savers should get more information. They should examine firms' past earnings and financial condition. They should learn the details of firms' projects and estimate the chances of success. They should find out which managers have reputations for skill and honesty. Such research can help savers determine which firms' securities are valuable and which are lemons.

Moral hazard can also be reduced if savers gather information—in this case, information about firms' uses of funds. Before buying securities, savers should make firms promise to undertake safe projects and not to waste money. Then they should visit the firms' offices frequently to check that the promises are kept. They should monitor firms' expenditures and raise questions about parties in Sardinia.

The Free-Rider Problem

Unfortunately, this information gathering often doesn't happen. It takes time and effort to learn about firms. And many securities are held by small savers, who lack sufficient incentives to incur these costs. If I have $1000 to save, I would like to learn about the firms offering securities so I can avoid lemons. But I can't afford to quit my job and spend my time studying firms. Similarly, once I buy a firm's security, I don't have time to visit the firm frequently, and I can't afford an accountant to monitor its finances.

Suppose a thousand savers have $1000 each, for a total of $1 million. With that much money at stake, it's worth having someone gather information about firms. One might think that savers would band together to study firms, sharing the trouble and expense. Each saver could donate a few hours of time or pay a fee to help hire an accountant. Together, savers could learn which securities are lemons and which firms are misusing their funds.

However, this may not occur because of a concept you may recall from your first economics course. This **free-rider problem** arises when people can benefit from a good without paying for it; as a result, nobody pays and the good isn't produced. In financial markets, the free-rider problem arises in the production of information.

To see the problem, suppose someone started a group to study firms. A saver would have an incentive *not* to join this group. If he doesn't join, he can simply watch what securities the group buys and buy the same ones. This strategy provides the benefits of information gathering without the

Free-rider problem people can benefit from a good without paying for it, leading to underproduction of the good; in financial markets, savers are free riders when information is gathered

costs of joining the group. Similarly, a smart saver will let others do the work of monitoring firms' uses of funds. If everyone thinks this way, the savers' group never gets off the ground.

The situation mirrors free-rider problems in other contexts. The residents of a town would benefit if they got together Saturday mornings to clean up the public park. However, each individual would rather sleep in and let others do the work. So the park stays dirty. In the same way, all savers would benefit if they gathered information, but free riding prevents this from happening.

Information-Gathering Firms

The free-rider problem limits information gathering in financial markets. However, some types of firms do gather information on the value of securities. Two examples are investment banks and bond-rating agencies. These firms overcome the free-rider problem by charging fees to savers and investors who benefit from their work.

How to overcome free rider problem.

Investment Banks These institutions reduce the problem of adverse selection in primary securities markets, especially by underwriting initial public offerings of stock. Investment banks assuage fears that shares in a company are lemons by researching the company and providing information to buyers of the stock. They build reputations that lead people to trust their assessments of companies. As we've seen, investment banks earn high fees because most companies need their help to issue securities.

▶ Investment banks are introduced in Section 5.1, and Section 5.2 describes the underwriting process.

Rating Agencies These firms research companies and rate the default risk on their bonds. In the United States, the three leading rating agencies are Moody's, Standard and Poor's, and Fitch. The ratings these companies provide reduce adverse selection in the bond market. Savers learn which bonds are safe and which are lemons, and interest rates adjust accordingly. Safe firms can issue bonds at low cost.

▶ Section 4.5 describes how rating agencies grade sovereign and corporate debt.

Bond ratings are available for free on the Web sites of rating agencies. To earn money, the agencies sell detailed reports on companies to financial institutions such as mutual funds. Most rated companies request the ratings and pay a fee to the rater. Companies know that ratings reduce adverse selection, making it easier to sell bonds for what they're worth. In addition to rating corporate and government bonds, rating agencies evaluate mortgage-backed securities (MBSs). This part of their business has generated controversy, as the following case study relates.

CASE STUDY

Rating Agencies and Subprime Mortgages

We discuss the subprime mortgage crisis that began in 2006 and its consequences throughout this book. Many economists and politicians place part of the blame on rating agencies. Before the crisis, the agencies gave top, triple-A ratings for safety to many securities backed by subprime mortgages. These ratings made it easier for the investment banks that created the securities to sell them. Clearly, the securities were far riskier than their ratings suggested. Financial institutions, such as pension funds, bought them in the belief they were safe and then suffered large losses when prices fell.

What went wrong? One factor was the novelty of these financially engineered securities. Rating agencies have long experience studying companies and estimating default risk for their bonds. In contrast, securities backed by subprime mortgages were invented only in the early 2000s. From then until 2006, default rates on subprime mortgages were low, so the scant historical evidence available suggested that the securities were safe. The rating agencies also failed to anticipate the fall in housing prices that caused defaults to increase. Like the investment banks that created mortgage-backed securities, rating agencies believed that national housing prices were likely to remain stable or rise, as they had for decades.

Critics of rating agencies suggest another reason that MBSs received high ratings: conflict of interest. Like corporations that issue bonds, issuers of mortgage-backed securities pay fees to be rated. Rating agencies charged high fees for rating subprime MBS, reflecting the difficulty of rating a new type of security. Issuers sometimes requested ratings from only one or two of the three agencies, so they were competing for business. Critics suggest that this competition created an incentive for easy grading. An agency was more likely to be hired by a security issuer if it readily handed out AAA ratings.

Rating agency critics include pension funds that lost money on MBS. In 2009, several funds, including those for state employees in California and Ohio, sued to recover their losses. These plaintiffs argue that the agencies misled them, citing incriminating e-mails. For example, one S&P executive cited the "threat of losing deals" to Moody's in arguing for favorable ratings. Another responded to suggestions for more rigorous standards with "Don't kill the Golden Goose."

In the past, rating agencies have successfully defended themselves against lawsuits on the grounds that their ratings are opinions protected under the First Amendment. Plaintiffs in the current cases maintain that the agencies went beyond expressing opinions to intentionally mislead MBS purchasers. At the beginning of 2011, cases were being argued before a number of courts.

Boards of Directors

A board of directors oversees every corporation that issues securities. Board members are elected by the corporation's shareholders at annual meetings. Part of the board's job is to reduce problems caused by asymmetric information—specifically, to reduce moral hazard. The board monitors managers and tries to prevent them from misusing shareholders' funds.

A board of directors has a lot of power. It hires the CEO of its firm and sets her salary. The CEO and other managers must report major decisions to the board and submit statements detailing the corporation's finances. The board can fire the CEO if she doesn't act in the best interests of shareholders.

Directors receive fees for their services. A large corporation might have around 15 directors, each of whom receives $50,000 a year for participating in five or ten meetings. These fees come out of the corporation's profits. In effect, each shareholder pays part of the fees, so no one can be a free rider.

Ⓐ Captive Boards Unfortunately, boards of directors don't always do their jobs. Critics suggest that boards can be "captured" by the managers they are supposed to monitor. The boards end up serving the interests of managers rather than the shareholders who pay them. They grant managers excessive salaries and bonuses and don't monitor them closely or penalize them for poor job performance.

One reason for this problem is that, at most corporations, some of the firm's managers are also members of the board of directors. The CEO is often the board's chair. Dennis Kozlowski, for example, was chairman of the Tyco board. He was responsible for monitoring his own behavior. Boards also include "outside" directors who are not managers of the firm. But these directors may have business dealings with the company. The Tyco board included two men whose companies leased planes to Tyco, and one who received large consulting fees. Directors with such involvements may be reluctant to question managers' actions, as they benefit from the status quo.

Ⓑ Elections In principle, a firm's shareholders can replace ineffective directors through elections. But this doesn't happen often. Elections take place at firms' annual meetings, which most shareholders don't attend. Typically, a firm's management mails a "proxy statement" to shareholders, asking for the right to vote on their behalf. Most shareholders agree, so managers end up controlling the election. They pick the directors who are supposed to supervise them.

If shareholders object, they can contest the election. Dissident shareholders send out their own proxy statements and collect votes. With enough votes, they can defeat management's candidates and elect other directors. However, this process is time-consuming and expensive. Dissidents must advertise for votes, like political candidates. In most elections, no shareholders are willing to pay the costs of a campaign.

Notice that the free-rider problem arises here. If directors are ineffective, all shareholders would benefit by replacing them. The total gains might exceed the costs of an election campaign. But no individual has enough incentive to launch the campaign and pay for it.

Ⓒ Shareholder Revolts Despite the difficulties, shareholders sometimes take control of boards of directors. They may oust directors through an election or use the threat of an election to force directors to discipline managers. These revolts are often led by large shareholders, who have enough money at stake to make the effort worthwhile.

A famous shareholder revolt occurred in 2007 at Home Depot. The firm's stock price had stagnated for several years, while the stock prices of other retailers rose. Many shareholders blamed questionable business decisions by Home Depot's CEO, Robert Nardelli. They also felt that Nardelli treated them disrespectfully. At the company's 2006 annual meeting, shareholders tried to question Nardelli about his performance, but he cut them off and ended the meeting after 30 minutes. The *New York Times* reported that Nardelli ran the meeting "like a lord over his fief." Yet Home Depot's board of directors supported Nardelli. From 2000 to 2006, his compensation averaged $40 million per year.

Among the shareholders critical of Nardelli was Relational Investors, a firm that buys stock on behalf of large pension funds. It owned about 1 percent of Home Depot's stock, worth $1 billion. The head of Relational Investors, Ralph Whitworth, argued that the stock would be worth much more if Home Depot were better managed. Whitworth announced that he would lead a revolt against Nardelli and Home Depot's board of directors at the 2007 annual meeting. Facing this threat, the board dropped its support for Nardelli. He resigned under pressure in January 2007.

 Recent Legislation The financial crisis of 2007–2009 led to increased criticism of corporate boards, especially at financial institutions. Many large firms, such as Bank of America and Morgan Stanley, suffered large losses during the crisis. Their stock prices fell by 50 percent or more, reducing the wealth of shareholders. At the same time, boards of directors at many of these institutions awarded large bonuses to top executives. Critics allege that boards overpaid executives, given the firms' poor performance.

Congress addressed this criticism in the Dodd-Frank Act, a broad reform of financial regulation passed in 2010. Formally known as the Wall Street Reform and Consumer Protection Act, this law requires publicly traded companies to hold a vote every three years in which shareholders say whether they approve of executive pay levels. The results are not binding, but the vote allows shareholders to put public pressure on boards of directors. Time will tell how effective this procedure will be in controlling executive pay.

We've discussed shareholders' conflicts with managers and boards of directors in the United States. The following case study discusses differences across countries in the shareholder–manager relationship.

Chapters 8–10 and 18 discuss the other major provisions of the Dodd-Frank Act.

Online Case Study
An Update on Shareholder Rights

CASE STUDY

International Differences in Shareholder Rights

Shareholders' ability to control managers depends on their rights under the laws governing corporations. These laws vary across countries. In several well-known studies, economists at Harvard and the University of Chicago have examined differences in shareholder rights and how these differences affect stock markets.

Shareholder rights vary in many ways. In some countries, it is even harder to replace directors than it is in the United States. In some cases, shareholders must appear in person to vote at annual meetings. They may have to deposit their shares with the company before the meeting, which is inconvenient.

Other countries have laws that strengthen shareholder rights. In some, companies are required to buy back stock from dissident shareholders. In others, shareholders can demand special meetings to vote out directors or can sue directors if they don't monitor managers effectively.

The Harvard and Chicago researchers found that countries fall into several groups in their treatment of shareholders. These groups have legal systems with different origins. For example, one set of countries, including the United States, has systems based on English common law. Shareholder rights are relatively strong in these countries. Another group has laws descended from France's Napoleonic Code; in these countries, shareholder rights are weak.

The researchers found large effects due to shareholder rights. In countries with stronger rights, firms issue more stock. In addition, a higher proportion of stock is bought by small savers. The researchers conclude that shareholder rights reduce moral hazard. Savers buy more stock if they are protected against misuse of their funds.

Figure 7.3 presents a sample of this research. It shows average data for countries with four types of legal systems: those with English, French, German, and Scandinavian roots. For each group of countries, the figure shows an index of overall shareholder rights. The researchers constructed this index by awarding points for various laws favoring shareholders. The figure also shows a measure of stock market activity based on the frequency of initial public offerings (IPOs). It shows a positive relationship between the two variables.

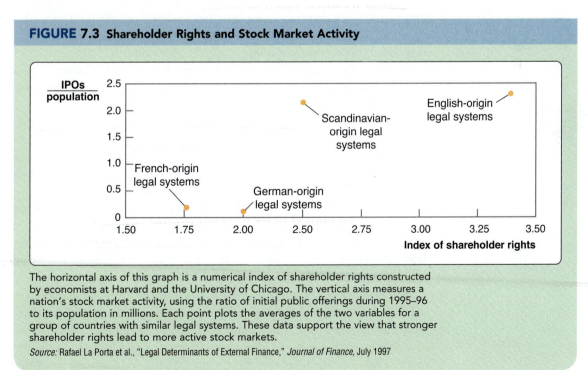

FIGURE 7.3 Shareholder Rights and Stock Market Activity

The horizontal axis of this graph is a numerical index of shareholder rights constructed by economists at Harvard and the University of Chicago. The vertical axis measures a nation's stock market activity, using the ratio of initial public offerings during 1995–96 to its population in millions. Each point plots the averages of the two variables for a group of countries with similar legal systems. These data support the view that stronger shareholder rights lead to more active stock markets.

Source: Rafael La Porta et al., "Legal Determinants of External Finance," *Journal of Finance*, July 1997

▶Section 1.5 discusses research on financial development and economic growth.

Research on economic growth in different countries finds that strong financial systems, including large stock markets, raise growth. Combining that evidence with the research discussed in this case study produces an argument for shareholder rights. Stronger rights lead to larger stock markets, which promote economic growth by channeling funds to investors.*

* The research discussed in this case study is presented in Rafael La Porta et al., "Legal Determinants of External Finance," *Journal of Finance* 52 (July 1997) 1131–1150; and Rafael La Porta et al., "Law and Finance," *Journal of Political Economy* 106 (December 1998) 1113–1155.

Private Equity Firms

We've discussed how information-gathering firms and boards of directors reduce problems in the financial system caused by asymmetric information. **Private equity firms** also perform this function. These institutions own large shares in private companies, that is, companies whose shares are not traded in stock markets.

Several types of private equity firms exist. The most important for reducing information problems are *takeover firms* and *venture capital firms*.

Private equity firm financial institution that owns large shares in private companies; includes takeover firms and venture capital firms

Takeover firm private equity firm that buys entire companies and tries to increase the companies' profits

Takeover Firms As their name implies, **takeover firms** buy entire companies. Some are already private, and some are public companies that the takeover firms "take private." A takeover firm buys a company if it thinks it can change the company's business practices and increase profits. Leading takeover firms include The Carlyle Group, The Blackstone Group, and Kohlberg, Kravis, Roberts (KKR).

When a takeover firm buys a company, it plans to run the company temporarily, improve profitability, and then resell it. Typically, the resale takes place 3 to 10 years after the takeover. The takeover firm may sell the company to another company seeking to acquire a new business. Or the takeover firm can take the company public again through an offering of stock. Either way, if the takeover firm has succeeded in raising profits, it can sell the company for more than it paid during the takeover.

A takeover firm can buy a public company in two ways. In a *friendly takeover*, it makes a deal with the company's managers and board of directors. Everyone agrees that stockholders will relinquish their shares in the company for a certain price. The company's managers usually keep their jobs, but now they are working for the takeover firm.

A *hostile takeover* is one opposed by a company's management. In this case, a takeover firm approaches the company's shareholders, offering a price for their stock. If a majority of shareholders agree to sell, the takeover firm gains control of the company. It can replace the managers and board of directors with people who agree to the takeover.

Hostile takeovers reduce the moral hazard problem involving shareholders and managers. If a company's managers are not doing their best to maximize profits, a takeover firm has an incentive to change things. The company will be worth more if the takeover firm buys it, fires the managers, and increases profits. Therefore, the takeover firm can offer a price for company stock that is *more* than the stock is currently worth but *less* than its value if management improves. Shareholders gain from selling stock at this price, and the takeover firm gains after it reforms the company and resells it.

Venture Capital Firms A **venture capital (VC) firm** buys ownership shares in new companies. The companies are typically small, private ones that plan to grow and need funds for investment. A venture capital firm doesn't buy a whole company, but it buys a substantial share. The company uses the payment from the VC firm to help finance its expansion.

> **Venture capital (VC) firm** private equity firm that buys shares in new companies that plan to grow

VC firms mainly finance companies that are developing new technologies, such as Internet applications or biotechnology products. For example, in 1999, shortly after it was founded, Google received $25 million from two VC firms, Sequoia Capital and Kleiner Perkins. The VC firms received a 10-percent share in Google, a share worth $2 billion when Google went public in 2004.

The adverse-selection problem makes it difficult for new, little-known companies to raise funds. VC firms reduce adverse selection by gathering information. They study companies to determine which are likely to succeed and fund those companies. VC firms employ experts in various industries to help them pick companies. For example, some VC firms hire doctors and scientists to evaluate biotech companies.

VC firms also face moral hazard problems. Often the managers of new companies have little experience running businesses (think of the graduate students who started Google). In the absence of track records, it's hard to judge whether the managers will do a good job or waste the funds they receive. To address this problem, a VC firm requires that companies it funds put officers of the firm on the companies' boards of directors. With seats on these boards, the VC firm can monitor companies' managers, reducing moral hazard.

7.4 REGULATION OF FINANCIAL MARKETS

Asymmetric information causes financial markets to malfunction. Because of the free-rider problem, individual savers do not have strong incentives to gather information. Institutions ranging from rating agencies to corporate boards of directors reduce information asymmetries, but they do not eliminate the problems entirely. This situation exemplifies the basic economic phenomenon of market failure.

Government policies can sometimes fix market failures. Because of the free-rider problem, nobody volunteers to pick up the trash in a dirty public park. The government can solve this problem by hiring park cleaners. Through taxes, it can force everyone to share in the costs. Similarly, failures in financial markets and the free-rider problem create a role for government regulation. Most economists agree on this basic principle. But regulation of financial markets can be controversial, and economists disagree about which regulations help the economy and which are counterproductive.

In the United States, financial markets are regulated primarily by the **Securities and Exchange Commission (SEC)**, which Congress

> **Securities and Exchange Commission (SEC)** U.S. government agency that regulates financial markets

established in 1934. The SEC creates rules designed to reduce information asymmetries, and it monitors compliance with the rules by firms and individuals. The SEC is often in the news as it modifies its regulations and responds to violations that it uncovers.

Many SEC regulations fall into two broad categories: requirements that firms disclose information to the savers that buy their securities, and restrictions on security trades by "insiders."

► The government regulations that we discuss here apply to firms in all industries. Financial institutions face many additional regulations, which we discuss in Chapters 10 and 18.

SEC powers

Information Disclosure

The SEC requires public companies to publish information about their businesses. The rationale is simple: the more savers know about companies, the smaller the information asymmetry between the buyers and sellers of securities. Savers are less fearful of buying lemons, so the adverse-selection problem is smaller.

Most required information is presented in firms' annual reports that summarize their operations over the past year. An annual report also includes detailed data on the firm's finances—its revenues, costs, assets, and debts. This information helps savers determine the value of the firm's securities.

To ensure that financial data are accurate, a firm must hire outside accountants to conduct an audit of its business. The annual report must include a statement from the auditors saying they have checked the firm's numbers. In 2002, Congress passed the **Sarbanes–Oxley Act**, which strengthened information-reporting requirements for public companies. The act responded to accounting scandals early in the 2000s, when the heads of several large companies were convicted of publishing false information.

Sarbanes-Oxley Act
federal legislation that strengthens the requirements for information disclosure by corporations

Executives at companies such as the huge energy company Enron and telecommunications giant WorldCom tried to hide losses suffered by the companies. Their motive: to prevent a drop in the companies' stock prices that would reduce the value of their stock and stock options. Eventually, mounting losses couldn't be hidden and forced the companies into bankruptcy. Employees of the companies that engaged in such financial deception lost their jobs. Many lost retirement savings held in company stock.

► The case study in Section 1.2 details what some Enron employees lost after the energy giant filed for bankruptcy.

The Sarbanes-Oxley Act includes a long list of provisions aimed at preventing false accounting. It requires corporations to establish audit committees to collect financial data and check its accuracy. The firm's CEO must review this work and certify the accounts. The act also requires greater scrutiny from a company's outside auditors: they must review the firm's procedures for accounting as well as checking the numbers in its accounts. Sarbanes-Oxley established a new agency, the Accounting Oversight Board, to monitor auditors' performance.

The act is controversial. To supporters, it has increased the confidence of savers in firms' financial statements, encouraging them to purchase stock. To critics, compliance requires too much time from company managers and too much expense for outside audits. They contend that the costs of Sarbanes-Oxley deter some private companies from going public, so fewer companies can finance investment through the stock market.

Insider Trading

Firms that issue securities know more than savers who buy securities. Disclosure requirements, which we've just discussed, reduce this asymmetry by increasing savers' information. The asymmetry can also be reduced by *decreasing* the information of firms' managers. Of course, regulators can't make people forget things. But they can require people to *act* as though they have less information than they do. That idea leads the SEC to prohibit **insider trading**, buying or selling securities based on information that is not public.

An "insider" is someone who knows more about a firm than the average saver. Insiders include the firms' employees and people who work with the firm, such as lawyers and accountants. These people often buy and sell the firm's securities. For example, executives receive company stock as part of their compensation and then sell some of it to diversify their assets. Generally, these trades are legal.

However, insiders must choose whether to trade based only on public information. They may *not* buy or sell securities because of something they have learned from their positions—something the average saver doesn't know. And insiders may not pass such information to someone else who will use it.

To understand why insider trading is prohibited, notice first that the temptations for insider trading are strong. Suppose you work for a company that is developing a new product. You learn that a test of the product has succeeded and that the company will announce this result the next day. When that happens, the company's stock is likely to rise as savers raise their estimates of future earnings. If you buy the stock today, when most people don't know the test result, you can make a large profit overnight.

The law forbids such behavior because it worsens adverse selection. If allowed, insiders will buy securities they know are valuable and sell lemons. This hurts uninformed savers on the other sides of the trades. If you, the insider, buy stock the day before the test announcement, your gain is a loss for the person who sells the stock. He loses the profits he would earn if he kept the stock.

If insider trading occurs frequently, then savers become wary of buying securities. They fear they will be ripped off by insiders. The end result is that firms find it harder to issue securities: insider trading impedes the flow of funds from savers to investors. But, as the next case study details, insider trading can prove hard to resist.

> **Insider trading** buying or selling securities based on information that is not public

CASE STUDY

Some Inside Traders

A classic case of insider trading involves ImClone Systems, a biotechnology firm. On December 27, 2001, the firm learned some bad news: the Food and Drug Administration had rejected its application for a cancer drug. This decision was announced publicly on December 28, causing the firm's stock to fall sharply.

On December 27, Sam Waksal, the chief executive of ImClone, sold $19 million of the company's stock. By selling that day, Waksal avoided a large loss on the next day. In 2003, he was convicted of insider trading and sentenced to 7 years in prison. The jury found that Waksal sold his stock because he knew about the FDA decision.

This case is well known because it involved a celebrity, Martha Stewart. Stewart and Waksal were close friends and used the same stockbroker, Peter Bacanovic of Merrill Lynch. Like Waksal, Stewart sold shares of ImClone on December 27. The government accused Stewart of selling because Bacanovic told her Waksal was selling—another type of inside information. In 2004, Stewart was convicted of lying about her actions to investigators and sent to prison for 5 months.

In November 2009, the SEC announced charges in an insider trading case that eventually included 13 defendants. The alleged profits exceeded $25 million, a record for known insider trading. At the center of the case was Raj Rajaratnam, billionaire manager of the Galleon hedge fund.

According to the SEC, Rajaratnam cultivated relationships with the other defendants, a group that included executives at major corporations such as Intel and IBM. Two were old friends from the Wharton Business School class of 1983. The executives gave Rajaratnam advance tips about earnings at their companies and information about other companies they did business with. Rajaratnam earned easy profits by purchasing companies' stock before they announced higher-than-expected earnings. He allegedly repaid co-conspirators with cash or by passing on inside information that he had received from others.

The defendants in the Galleon case also include prominent securities lawyers involved in arranging corporate takeovers. They told Rajaratnam about likely takeover bids before they were publicly announced. Rajaratnam bought the stock of takeover targets because a company's stock price usually rises when the public learns of a takeover bid.

As of November 2010, 12 defendants had pled guilty to charges in the Galleon case and Rajaratnam was scheduled for trial in January 2011. The evidence against him came largely from wiretaps—the first insider-trading prosecution in which investigators used wiretaps.

7.5 BANKS AND ASYMMETRIC INFORMATION

Asymmetric information makes it hard for investors to sell securities. Government regulators and information-gathering firms reduce this problem, but they cannot eliminate it. Many companies can't raise funds in securities markets because savers don't know enough about them. These companies are generally smaller and newer ones.

This is where banks come in. Banks specialize in reducing asymmetric information. As a result, firms and individuals can borrow from banks even

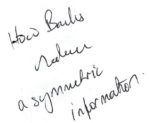
How Banks reduce asymmetric information.

if they are not well known to savers. They get funds from savers indirectly, because savers' deposits fund bank loans (see Figure 7.1 on p. 190).

Banks have several methods for reducing information asymmetries and the problems of adverse selection and moral hazard. Let's examine them.

Information Gathering: Screening Borrowers

Banks reduce adverse selection by gathering information about borrowers. When a firm applies for a bank loan, it must provide information about its finances: its assets, existing debts, profit history, and so on. The firm also submits a business plan detailing the project to be funded. Individuals seeking loans must provide information on their personal finances and plans.

Successful bankers are good at interpreting such information. They study past lending to learn what types of borrowers are likely to default. Loan officers are trained to screen borrowers and gain expertise by doing so repeatedly. As a result, banks can do better than the average saver at determining whom it's safe to lend to.

Recall the free-rider problem in securities markets: if many savers buy a company's securities, no individual has sufficient incentive to gather information. Banks reduce this problem, because a firm typically borrows from a single bank. The bank has an incentive to gather information because, as the sole lender, it gets all the benefits.

Banks enhance their information gathering by developing long-term relationships—by lending repeatedly to the same borrowers. Experience with a firm is often the best guide to its default risk. Banks encourage long-term relationships by offering **lines of credit**. These are commitments to lend up to a certain amount whenever the borrower asks. Lines of credit provide liquidity to borrowers: when needed, they can get funds quickly and easily. At the same time, banks benefit because credit lines create ongoing relationships.

> **Line of credit** a bank's commitment to lend up to a certain amount whenever a borrower asks

Reducing Default Risk: Collateral and Net Worth

In addition to gathering information, banks use provisions in loan contracts to reduce default risk. One type of provision concerns the borrowers' *collateral* and *net worth*.

Collateral **Collateral** is an asset of a borrower, such as a building or a firm's inventory, that it pledges to a bank when it takes out a loan. The bank can seize the asset if the borrower defaults.

> **Collateral** an asset of a borrower that a bank can seize if the borrower defaults

Collateral benefits a lender in two ways:

1. It reduces the loss when a borrower defaults. By seizing collateral and selling it, the bank can recover some or all the money it is owed.

2. It reduces the probability of default. Pledging collateral makes risky firms less eager to borrow, reducing adverse selection, and makes borrowers seek safety when choosing projects, reducing moral hazard. With no collateral at stake, borrowers have incentives to try risky projects: they

may win big, and they lose nothing if the project fails and they default. But default hurts borrowers if banks seize collateral.

A Final Numerical Example We can illustrate this point by varying our example of moral hazard from Section 7.2. Once again, a firm has two possible projects, one that produces $125 for sure and one that produces $150 with probability 2/3. A bank lends enough money for one project, and the firm promises to pay back $110. If there is no collateral, our earlier analysis applies again: the firm will choose the risky project, because it produces a higher expected profit.

But suppose the bank requires an asset as collateral—one worth $50. This changes the firm's calculations. If it chooses the safe project, it succeeds for sure, pays the bank, and keeps its collateral. It earns $125 − $110 = $15.

If the firm chooses the risky project, then with probability 2/3 it earns $150 and pays $110, for a profit of $40. With probability 1/3, it defaults. In this case, the firm loses its collateral, so its profit is −$50. The expected profit is (2/3) × ($40) + (1/3) × (−$50) = $10. This is less than the $15 guaranteed by the safe project.

So the story has a happy ending. The firm chooses the safe project and earns a profit, and the bank's loan is repaid for sure.

Net Worth A loan contract may also set a minimum for the borrower's **net worth**, also known as its **capital**. This is the difference between the borrower's total assets and its debts, or liabilities. A net-worth requirement restricts the borrower's actions; for example, it can't take out another loan if that would push net worth below the minimum.

Net-worth requirements serve the same purposes as collateral. They discourage borrowers from taking risks, because borrowers have something to lose if projects fail. They also protect lenders against default. If a borrower goes bankrupt, its assets are sold and lenders can claim some of the proceeds.

Covenants and Monitoring

Banks also address moral hazard by including **covenants** in loan contracts. Covenants are restrictions on the actions of borrowers that reduce default risk. A covenant may require that a loan be used for a specific purpose, such as buying equipment. A "negative" covenant may forbid certain risky activities on the part of the borrower. Some covenants protect the collateral for a loan. For example, if an individual uses his house as collateral, he must purchase fire insurance. Net-worth requirements, which we already discussed, are another type of covenant.

To enforce covenants, banks monitor firms. Under many loan agreements, the borrower must report periodically to the lender on its activities and financial situation. Financial data are audited by an independent accountant to keep the firm honest. If the firm violates a covenant, the bank has the right to demand immediate repayment of the loan.

A bank can improve its monitoring by requiring **compensating balances**. This means a borrower must maintain a checking account at the bank with

---

Net worth (or capital) difference between assets and liabilities

Covenant provision in a loan contract that restricts the actions of the borrower

Compensating balance minimum checking deposit that a borrower must maintain at the bank that has lent it money

a certain minimum balance. The bank learns a lot about the firm's activities by observing the funds flowing in and out of the account. Compensating balances are also collateral that the bank can seize easily.

Interest Rates and Credit Rationing

Banks try to minimize default risk through screening, collateral, and covenants. Most loans still carry some risk, however. Banks cope with this risk by adjusting interest rates. Riskier borrowers must pay higher rates to compensate for banks' losses from defaults.

Banks' safest borrowers, which pay the lowest interest rates, are usually large, well-established companies. Many small businesses pay interest rates 2 to 4 percentage points above their lender's best rate, depending on how risky they look. An upcoming case study discusses how banks evaluate business loans.

One might guess that banks will lend to any borrower if the interest rate is high enough. In fact, they won't. Some borrowers are offered loans at interest rates reflecting their risk, but those who look very risky can't borrow at all. A bank's refusal to lend at any interest rate is called **credit rationing**. Credit rationing occurs because high interest rates worsen adverse selection.

To see this, suppose a bank's highest interest rate is 10 percent. For some borrowers, default risk looks high enough that the bank will lose money if it lends at 10 percent. The bank could raise the rate to 20 percent to compensate for defaults, but this strategy might backfire. A 20 percent rate will drive away many loan applicants, leaving only the riskiest borrowers. The only way to earn a profit while paying 20 percent is to gamble on a project that could yield big returns. Raising the interest rate can increase default rates by enough to reduce the bank's profits. The bank does better by refusing to lend.

Credit rationing means that some people and firms who want to borrow can't get loans from banks. This fact creates a role for other types of lenders, such as finance companies. Credit rationing may also justify government policies that encourage bank lending.

> **Credit rationing** refusal of a bank to lend to a borrower at any interest rate

> ▶ Chapter 8 discusses nonbank institutions that make loans and surveys government programs that promote lending.

CASE STUDY

The Five Cs of Business Lending

Loan officers at banks decide whether to grant loans to applicants. They are trained to examine individuals and firms and judge their creditworthiness. For business loans, loan officers sometimes summarize their criteria as the "five Cs." These concepts are closely related to ideas that we have discussed.

- *Capacity* This means the financial capacity of the firm to repay the loan. Loan officers determine capacity by forecasting the firm's earnings. Typically, they take past earnings as a baseline and make adjustments for the impact of new projects. They make sure that forecasted earnings are high enough to support the payments promised under the loan.

> ▶ These five Cs come from the government's Small Business Administration. Other sources give slightly different lists of five or six Cs. Some mention "control" (meaning the ease of seizing capital) or "cash flow" (future earnings, which are included under "capacity" here).

- *Conditions* This refers to conditions outside the firm that affect its earnings and default risk. Is the firm's industry growing or shrinking? How strong are the firm's competitors? Will suppliers provide the firm's inputs at good prices? How healthy are the national and local economies?

- *Character* Firms are most likely to repay loans if their owners and managers are honest and responsible. So loan officers check the personal credit histories of applicants and look for criminal records. They check references and try to learn applicants' reputations in their industries. They often rely heavily on personal interviews.

- *Collateral* Loan officers estimate the value of collateral. For example, they get appraisals for buildings. They also consider the collateral's liquidity. If a bank seizes a firm's machinery, can it sell the machinery to anyone?

- *Capital* As we've discussed, this is another name for net worth, the difference between a borrower's assets and liabilities. Net worth gives borrowers something to lose if they take on risky projects. Loan officers are more likely to approve applicants with significant net worth.

CASE STUDY

Traditional Home Mortgages

For many people, the most important role of a bank is to provide money to buy a home. Home loans illustrate many of the ideas we have discussed. We'll focus here on traditional mortgage loans, which have fixed interest rates and are made to "prime" borrowers—that is, people with good credit histories.

A traditional mortgage loan covers $80-90$ percent of the price of a house. The borrower makes a constant monthly payment for 15 or 30 years. The bank calculates the payment based on the size of the loan and the interest rate. For example, a 30-year loan of $200,000 at a 6-percent interest rate requires monthly payments of $1184.

Screening Borrowers What are banks' criteria for approving mortgage loans? Applicants are asked lots of questions about their employment, earnings history, assets, and so on. However, loan approval depends primarily on two things:

1. *Debt–income ratios* These are ratios of monthly debt payments to the borrower's monthly income. Currently, for prime mortgages many banks require that mortgage payments be less than 28 percent of income. In addition, total debt payments—the mortgage plus credit cards, auto loans, and so on—must be less than 36 percent of income. Banks want to ensure that borrowers can afford their promised payments.

2. *Credit scores* Credit bureaus, such as Equifax and Experian, collect information on people's use of credit. Each person's history is summarized with a numerical rating called a **credit score**. A high score

▶Chapters 8 and 9 discuss the development of subprime mortgages and adjustable interest rates.

▶This calculation uses the techniques for measuring interest rates discussed in Section 3.6.

Credit score numerical rating capturing a person's likelihood to repay loans based on her credit history

means a person is likely to repay loans that she receives; a low score means a high risk of default.

A person's credit score changes over time, depending on how she uses credit. Borrowing money and repaying it on time raises the score. Points are lost for late payments; the more recent the delinquencies, the heavier the penalties. Of course, lots of points are lost if a borrower defaults permanently. Points are deducted for credit card balances near the card limit, because these suggest financial problems. Credit scores range from about 350 to the 800s. Banks set minimum scores, typically in the 600s, for prime mortgages.

Collateral and Down Payments The hallmark of a home loan is that the home serves as collateral. In addition, banks ensure that borrowers have significant net worth by requiring down payments. The bank lends less than 100 percent of the house price, so the borrower ends up owning a house worth more than his mortgage debt. For the best interest rates, banks usually require a down payment of 20 percent. Borrowers can put down less if they pay higher rates.

Covenants These focus on protecting the collateral. As mentioned before, borrowers must maintain homeowner's insurance. Often the bank monitors this by collecting monthly insurance payments along with the mortgage, then passing them on to the insurance company. Another common covenant requires the borrower to use the house as her primary residence. Lenders believe a house is more likely to be trashed if it is rented out. And an owner is more careful not to default if her home is at stake.

> The average U.S. house price fell 33% between 2006 and 2009 as the housing bubble deflated (see Section 3.4), and many people found that, despite down payments, they were *under water* on their mortgages: their homes were worth less than they owed. This unusual situation contributed to a wave of mortgage defaults during the financial crisis and in its aftermath, as we discuss in Chapters 8 and 18.

7.6 BANKS AND TRANSACTION COSTS

We have emphasized a central function of banks—reducing asymmetric information. Another function is also important—reducing **transaction costs**, the costs in time and money of exchanging goods, services, or assets. Banks reduce transaction costs for both savers and investors, creating another reason for indirect finance.

> **Transaction costs** costs in time and money of exchanging goods, services, or assets

Reducing Costs to Savers

Banks reduce transaction costs for savers in two ways: they reduce the costs of acquiring assets, and they provide liquidity.

Costs of Acquiring Assets It is costly for a saver to purchase securities. If she buys a stock or bond, she must contact a broker and pay a fee. If she buys many securities to diversify, she must pay many fees. It is easier and less expensive to set up a bank account and make deposits. Traditionally, this difference in transaction costs led most people to put their savings in banks. Only the wealthy bought securities.

Over the last several decades, the growth of mutual funds has eroded the transaction-cost advantage of banks. Mutual funds make it easy to hold a diversified set of securities, and many funds have low fees. For most people today, banks aren't the only way to save. However, most mutual funds have substantial minimum balances—often $2500—making them inaccessible to the smallest savers. In contrast, some bank accounts have minimum balances of $1.

▶ Section 2.4 introduces the concept of liquidity and compares the liquidity of various assets.

Liquidity An asset's liquidity is the ease of exchanging it for money. Bank deposits are highly liquid. Checking deposits *are* money, as they can be spent directly on goods and services; savings deposits can be exchanged for money in a few minutes at an ATM. In contrast, it usually takes a business day or more to sell securities or mutual fund shares and receive money.

The liquidity of bank deposits reduces transaction costs when people buy goods and services. If you see something appealing in a store, you can buy it easily with the funds in your bank account. Life would be less convenient if you had to sell mutual fund shares before making the purchase.

The benefit of liquidity reduces the interest that banks must pay to attract deposits. Often the interest rates on savings accounts are one or two percentage points below the rates on Treasury bills.

Reducing Costs to Investors

It is expensive for a firm to issue stocks or bonds. The firm usually hires an investment bank to underwrite the securities. It must also pay accountants to prepare financial statements and lawyers to draw up contracts, services that cost hundreds of thousands of dollars.

Many of these costs are "fixed"—they do not depend on the size of the security offering. When a large company issues $50 million of securities, the costs are moderate compared to the funds that are raised. But a restaurant seeking $50,000 for renovations can't afford to pay $200,000 to securities lawyers. Transaction costs are another reason, in addition to information problems, that small firms don't issue securities.

Transaction costs are lower when firms borrow from banks. This fact reflects *economies of scale:* a bank lends to many firms, reducing the cost of each loan. A bank's lawyers draw up one standard loan contract to use for many borrowers. The bank develops standard criteria for evaluating loan applicants, allowing it to process loans quickly.

Transaction costs are especially low when firms establish lines of credit with banks. These arrangements allow a firm to get funds quickly without submitting a new loan application. This benefit of credit lines complements their role in reducing information problems (see Section 7.5).

Summary

- The primary function of banks is to reduce the problems of adverse selection and moral hazard caused by asymmetric information in the financial system.

7.1 Adverse Selection

- Adverse selection arises in many markets, including financial markets. Issuers of securities know the securities' quality, but buyers do not. Markets can break down because only low-quality securities are offered for sale. This "lemons problem" is severe for unknown firms, so they can't issue securities.

- Adverse selection is exacerbated by the fact that risky projects may have high returns if they succeed. Risky firms would like to sell bonds to finance gambles.

7.2 Moral Hazard

- Moral hazard arises in many contexts, including financial markets. Savers can't observe what firms do with their funds, so firms may take actions that harm savers. Such actions include excessive risk taking and using funds for the personal benefit of managers.

7.3 Reducing Information Asymmetries

- Savers can reduce adverse selection and moral hazard by gathering information about firms. However, the free-rider problem reduces information gathering.

- Several types of financial firms, including investment banks and rating agencies, gather information on companies, reducing moral hazard and adverse selection. Rating agencies have been criticized, however, for giving high grades to risky mortgage-backed securities.

- A company's board of directors monitors managers to reduce moral hazard. However, a board may not do its job if it is captured by managers. Shareholders can replace directors through elections, but this is difficult.

- Shareholder rights vary across countries. Researchers have found that greater rights produce larger stock markets and more stockholding by small savers.

- Private equity firms include takeover firms and venture capital firms. Takeover firms reduce moral hazard by purchasing underperforming companies and replacing the management. Venture capital firms provide funds to new companies. They gather information on the companies, reducing adverse selection, and they help manage the companies, reducing moral hazard.

7.4 Regulation of Financial Markets

- U.S. financial markets are regulated by the Securities and Exchange Commission (SEC).

- The SEC requires companies to disclose information about their finances, with checks by outside accountants. These requirements were strengthened by the Sarbanes-Oxley Act of 2002.

- Other SEC regulations forbid insider trading, yet criminal prosecution for insider trading is common.

7.5 Banks and Asymmetric Information

- Because banks reduce the problem of asymmetric information, they can provide funds to borrowers who cannot issue securities.

- Banks address asymmetric information by screening and monitoring borrowers, establishing long-term relationships, requiring collateral or net worth, specifying loan covenants, adjusting interest rates for risk, and rationing credit.

- In evaluating applicants for business loans, banks consider the five Cs: capacity, conditions, character, collateral, and capital.

- When banks make traditional home mortgages, they evaluate borrowers based on debt–income ratios and credit scores. A home serves as collateral for a loan. Banks require down payments and impose covenants to protect the collateral.

7.6 Banks and Transaction Costs

- Banks reduce the costs to savers of acquiring assets, and they provide liquidity. Banks also allow investors to avoid the costs of issuing securities.

Key Terms

Questions and Problems

1. Would each of the following events increase or decrease the volume of bank loans? Explain.

   a. New regulations make it easier for shareholders to replace company directors.

   b. A new law makes it a felony to default on a bank loan.

   c. All the economy's small firms are bought by large firms.

   d. Mutual funds reduce their minimum balances for shareholders.

2. a. Suppose you are hiring a worker for your firm. You advertise a position for $50,000, but an applicant offers to work for $40,000. Should you jump at this offer?

   b. Suppose you have $1000 to lend and offer it for 10-percent interest. Someone promises to pay 20 percent if you lend to him. Should you jump at this offer?

3. In what ways is an asset price bubble (described Section 3.4) similar to a Ponzi scheme? In what ways is a bubble different?

4. Some U.S. companies have 1-year terms for directors. The entire corporate board must run for election at each annual meeting. Other companies have 3-year terms; only a third of directors face votes at each meeting. A 2004 study found that the companies with 3-year terms have lower stock prices, controlling for other factors. What might explain this finding?

5. Why do people commit each of the following crimes? Who is hurt by the crimes? Discuss who is hurt directly and also the broader effects on the financial system. (As an analogy, shoplifting hurts store owners directly; its broader effects include higher prices for goods.)

   a. False accounting

   b. Insider trading

6. Edward C. Johnson, III, was the CEO of Fidelity mutual funds and also the chair of the Fidelity board. In 2004, the SEC issued a regulation requiring chairs at mutual funds to be independent of management, forcing Johnson to resign as chair. Johnson opposed the SEC action. Here are two arguments he made:

   a. "Mandating an independent chairperson is akin to requiring that every ship have two captains. . . . If a ship I was sailing on were headed for an iceberg, I'd want one—and only one—captain giving orders. I'd like to know that he'd spent some time at sea and knew what he was doing."

   b. "If a wrong-doer is tempted to try some abuse against fund shareholders, which board chairman would they rather try sneaking it past—an industry veteran with a direct and personal interest in the fund—or a chairman with 40 years experience making carbonated beverages, and who has just flown in for a two-day board meeting?"

   Summarize Johnson's arguments against independent chairs in your own words. Also suggest responses that might be made by a supporter of the SEC regulation.

7. Consider the example in Figure 7.2. Assume that neither firm knows whether its project is safe or risky. For each firm, there is a 1/2 chance that the project is safe, producing $125 for sure. There is a 1/2 chance the project is risky, producing $150 with probability 2/3 and 0 with probability 1/3. This means that, overall, each firm has a 1/2 chance of earning $125, a 1/3 chance of earning $150, and a 1/6 chance of earning zero. Otherwise, make the same assumptions as before. Will the firms be able to sell bonds? Show your reasoning.

8. Consider the example in Figure 7.2 with asymmetric information: the two firms know which one is risky and which is safe, but savers do not. Keep the example the same as

in the figure, except for the earnings of the risky firm. For the following cases, say whether the safe firm can sell a bond, and whether the risky firm can sell a bond.

a. The risky firm's project earns $150 with probability 3/4 and 0 with probability 1/4.

b. The risky firm's project earns $150 with probability 4/5 and 0 with probability 1/5.

9. Consider the example of collateral in Section 7.5. The example assumes that collateral is $50. Determine the smallest level of collateral that causes the firm to choose the safe project. Assume the firm maximizes its expected profit.

10. Suppose you take out a 30-year mortgage of $100,000 with a fixed interest rate of 5 percent. You must make 360 equal monthly payments. Write an equation that defines what the payment is. (*Hint:* Use the approach to measuring interest rates in Section 3.6. The equation is hard to solve without a computer.)

▶ Online and Data Questions
www.worthpublishers.com/ball

11. Figure 7.3 presents data on IPOs and shareholder rights. The figure gives averages for four groups of countries. On the text Web site, get data for the 49 individual countries in the groups. Make a version of the figure that shows the data for each country. How strong is the relation between IPOs and shareholder rights? Are there exceptions to the usual relation? What might explain these exceptions?

12. Do some Internet research to find out what it means for a company to create a "poison pill." Why might a company do that? Some economists think poison pills should be illegal. What is their rationale?

The Banking Industry

AP Photo/Mark Lennihan; © Rab Harling/Alamy

Two places to get a loan.

Figure **8.1** on p. 222 shows the number of U.S. commercial banks operating in each year from 1960 through 2009. The number grew slowly over the first part of this period, peaking at about 15,000 in 1984. Then a sharp decline began, caused mainly by mergers of two or more banks into one larger bank. By 2010, there were fewer than 7000 commercial banks, and the number was still falling. Yet by worldwide standards, the United States still has a large number of banks. The United Kingdom and Japan each has about 200 commercial banks, and Canada has fewer than 100.

This chapter examines why the United States has so many banks and why the number is declining. We also discuss the diverse types of banks and the functions they serve. The banking industry includes giants such as Citigroup and JPMorgan Chase, which operate around the globe, and small banks that operate in a single town.

Another key trend in the banking industry is a rise in **securitization**. In this process, a financial institution buys a large number of loans from banks and then issues securities entitling the holders to shares of payments on the loans. Securitization is especially common for home

> **Securitization** process in which a financial institution buys a large number of bank loans, then issues securities entitling the holders to shares of payments on the loans

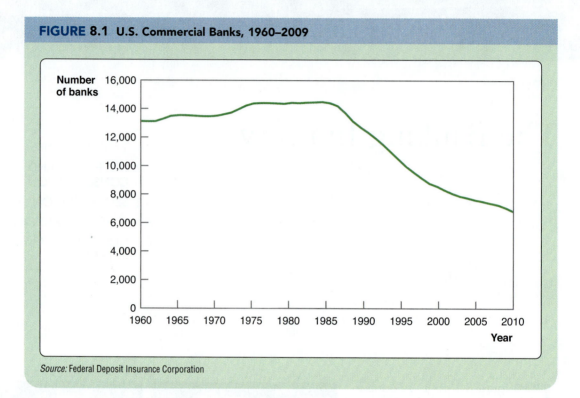

FIGURE 8.1 U.S. Commercial Banks, 1960–2009

Source: Federal Deposit Insurance Corporation

mortgages. We examine the reasons for securitization and its effects on banks, their borrowers, and buyers of the securities.

This chapter also examines a fringe of the banking industry called **subprime lenders**. These companies make loans to people with weak credit histories, who can't borrow from mainstream banks. Subprime lenders include a variety of institutions, ranging from finance companies to pawn-brokers. They have gained notoriety in recent years, largely because of defaults on subprime mortgage loans.

Finally, we discuss governments' involvement in bank lending. In many countries, the government owns the banks, so it determines who gets loans. In the United States, banks are private, but the government encourages lending to certain groups. We discuss policies that promote lending to home buyers, small businesses, students, and people who live in low-income areas.

Subprime lenders companies that lend to people with weak credit histories

8.1 TYPES OF BANKS

A bank is a financial institution that accepts deposits and makes private loans. This definition covers the several types of *commercial banks* and *thrift institutions* listed in **Table 8.1**.

Commercial Banks

Commercial banks are the largest part of the banking system. In 2010, U.S. commercial banks had about $8 trillion in deposits, including checking and savings deposits, and $6 trillion in outstanding loans to large corporations,

Commercial bank institution that accepts checking and savings deposits and lends to individuals and firms

small businesses, and individuals. Two million people worked for commercial banks.

Commercial banks are split into three groups based partly on size. A bank's size is measured by its total assets, which include outstanding loans and other assets, such as securities.

Money-Center Banks Five or six of the largest banks comprise this category. Two features define a **money-center bank**. First, its headquarters are located in a major financial center (New York, Chicago, or San Francisco). Second, it finances its lending primarily by borrowing from other banks or by issuing bonds. A money-center bank accepts deposits, but deposits are *not* its main source of funds. The money-center category includes two of the three largest banks in the United States: JPMorgan Chase, which had assets of $1.7 trillion in 2010, and Citibank, which had $1.2 trillion.

Money-center banks make many types of loans, including business loans and mortgages. They lend to consumers through the credit cards that they issue. Their largest loans go to private equity firms that take over other companies and to foreign governments.

Money-center banks also engage in many businesses beyond lending. They trade currencies and derivative securities, for example. In the late 1990s, money-center banks began to provide investment-banking services, such as underwriting securities. Investment banking continues to be a growing source of profits for money-center banks today.

Regional and Superregional Banks This category includes all non–money-center banks with assets of more than $1 billion. In 2010, they numbered about 400. A **regional bank** operates in a broad geographic area, such as the mid-Atlantic region. A **superregional bank** operates across most of the country.

These banks make many types of loans to firms and consumers, but their businesses are narrower than those of money-center banks. Regional and superregional banks concentrate on the core functions of deposit taking and lending. They raise relatively few funds by borrowing from other banks or issuing bonds, and they usually don't trade currencies or underwrite securities.

The largest superregional bank is Bank of America (BoA), with headquarters in Charlotte, North Carolina. In 2010, BoA had roughly 6000 branches and a presence in every U.S. state. Its $1.5 trillion in assets made it the nation's second largest bank, just behind JPMorgan Chase. Unlike most regional and superregional banks, BoA has expanded into investment banking, in part by purchasing Merrill Lynch in 2008.

I have a checking account at M&T Bank, a regional bank based in Buffalo, New York. In 2010, M&T had 650 branches in an area ranging

TABLE 8.1 Types of Banks

Commercial Banks
- Money-center banks
- Regional and superregional banks
- Community banks

Thrift Institutions
- Savings institutions
- Credit unions

Finance Companies*

*Finance companies perform only one of the two functions that define a bank. They make loans but do not accept deposits.

Money-center bank commercial bank located in a major financial center that raises funds primarily by borrowing from other banks or by issuing bonds

Regional bank commercial bank with assets above $1 billion that operates in one geographic region

Superregional bank commercial bank with assets above $1 billion that operates across most of the United States

from New York to Virginia, including one next to the Baltimore campus of Johns Hopkins University. M&T's assets were $68 billion, making it the twenty-fifth largest U.S. bank. The Baltimore Ravens play football in M&T Bank Stadium.

Community banks A **community bank** has less than $1 billion in assets. It operates in a small geographic area, raising funds from local depositors and lending them to consumers and small businesses. An example is Harford Bank, based in Aberdeen, Maryland, 40 miles north of Baltimore. In 2010, Harford Bank had $250 million in assets and seven branches in Aberdeen and neighboring towns.

> **Community bank**
> commercial bank with less than $1 billion in assets that operates in a small geographic area

Of the nearly 7000 commercial banks in the United States, more than 90 percent are community banks. However, the total assets of these banks barely top $1 trillion. JPMorgan Chase and Bank of America each is larger than all the community banks combined.

Thrift Institutions

The core functions of **thrift institutions (thrifts)**, like those of commercial banks, are deposit taking and lending. The two types of thrifts are *savings institutions* and *credit unions*.

> **Thrift institutions (thrifts)**
> savings institutions and credit unions

Savings Institutions These thrifts are also known as *savings banks* or *savings and loan associations* (S&Ls). The original purpose of **savings institutions** was to serve households by accepting savings deposits and by lending for home mortgages. Savings institutions were created in the nineteenth century, when commercial banks focused on business lending. Most savings institutions were established as *mutual banks,* meaning they were owned by their depositors and did not issue stock.

> **Savings institution** type of bank created to accept savings deposits and make loans for home mortgages; also known as savings banks or savings and loan associations (S&Ls)

Over time, most savings institutions issued stock and ceased being mutual banks. They also expanded their businesses; today, savings institutions offer checking as well as savings accounts and make many types of loans. These changes have blurred the distinction between savings institutions and commercial banks, although the former still focus more on mortgages.

> ▶ Savings banks and S&Ls are slightly different institutions, with minor differences in the regulations that govern them. These differences are not important for our purposes.

In 2010, the United States had about 1200 savings institutions with $1.3 trillion in assets. The largest is Sovereign Bank, with $800 million in assets and 750 branches located from Maryland to Maine. Since 2009, Sovereign has been a subsidiary of the Spanish bank Santandar.

Credit Unions A **credit union** is a not-for-profit bank. Like a mutual bank, it is owned by its depositors, who are called *members*. Only members can borrow from the credit union. Credit unions make several types of loans, including home mortgages, auto loans, and small personal loans.

> **Credit union** not-for-profit bank owned by its depositor members, who are drawn from a group of people with something in common

Membership in a credit union is restricted to a group of people who all have something in common. They might be employees of a company, members of a labor union, or veterans of a military service. Restricted membership reduces the problem of asymmetric information in lending. The fact that a borrower qualifies for membership provides information about his default risk. So does the history of his account at the credit union. This information helps loan officers screen out risky borrowers.

Sizable credit unions include those serving the U.S. Navy and the employees of various state governments. Most credit unions are small, however, with assets of less than $100 million. There are roughly 8000 credit unions in the United States—more than the number of commercial banks—but their assets only total $900 billion.

Finance Companies

The types of banks listed in Table 8.1 on p. 223 include **finance companies**, but with an asterisk. Like banks, finance companies make loans; for example, they compete with banks in issuing mortgages and auto loans. However, finance companies do *not* accept deposits, so they meet only half the definition of a bank. Finance companies raise funds exclusively by issuing bonds and borrowing from banks.

> **Finance company** non-bank financial institution that makes loans but does not accept deposits

Many finance companies specialize in a certain kind of loan. For example, some lend to businesses for new equipment. Others are owned by manufacturing companies and lend to their customers. This group includes General Motors Acceptance Corporation (GMAC) and Ford Motor Credit Company, which make auto loans. Another market niche that finance companies operate in is subprime lending, as we discuss in Section 8.4.

8.2 DISPERSION AND CONSOLIDATION

So far we've described the banking industry as it exists today. This description is just a snapshot of an industry that is changing rapidly. In recent years, mergers and bank failures have combined to reduce the number of banks and increase their average size. At the same time, banks have expanded into new businesses. Let's discuss this process and where the industry might be heading.

Why So Many Banks?

Let's start with a fact we discussed earlier: despite the mergers and failures of recent years, the United States has far more banks than other countries. The large number of banks reflects the history of government regulation. In 1927, Congress passed the McFadden Act, which forbade banks to operate in more than one state. This law meant that each state had a separate banking industry. In addition, states limited the number of branches a bank could operate. Many states mandated unit banking: each bank was allowed only one branch. Because of these policies, a bank served only a small geographic area, and many banks were needed to cover a whole state.

> ▶ A Case Study in Section 1.5 examines unit banking and its effects on the economy.

Over time, these restrictions on banks were relaxed. Most states removed their limits on branches in the 1970s and 1980s. In 1994, Congress passed the Riegle-Neal Act, which repealed the McFadden Act's ban on interstate banking. Today, banks can expand around the country.

Yet past regulations still influence the banking industry. Many banks from the old days have disappeared through mergers, but thousands are still around. Other countries have fewer banks because they never restricted branching or the geographic areas that banks could serve.

What motivated the restrictions on U.S. banks? The answers lie in the country's history. Bank regulations have evolved through a series of political battles, which we discuss in the next case study.

CASE STUDY

The Politics of Banking in U.S. History

Throughout U.S. history, debates over banking have been tied to broader political battles. One recurring theme is efforts by "populists" to limit the power of corporations and the wealthy. The targets of populists have often included banks. Another theme is the struggle for power between the federal government and the states. In banking, the two levels of government have competed to set regulations and to issue **bank charters** allowing banks to open.

Bank charter government license to operate a bank

▶ For more on Alexander Hamilton's monetary policies, see Section 2.2.

The First and Second Banks Starting in George Washington's administration, America's leaders split into Federalists, led by Alexander Hamilton, and Democratic-Republicans, led by Thomas Jefferson. Federalists wanted more power for the national government, and Democratic-Republicans wanted less.

Initially, banks were chartered by the states. Hamilton, as Washington's secretary of the treasury, proposed that the federal government create the First Bank of the United States. A charter was granted in 1791. The First Bank was a privately owned commercial bank, but it also served some functions of a central bank. It issued a national currency, lent money to the government, and served as lender of last resort.

Democratic-Republicans opposed the creation of the First Bank, starting a struggle that lasted several decades. The bank's 20-year charter expired in 1811, and Congress refused to renew it. In 1816, however, Congress chartered a replacement, the Second Bank of the United States, for another 20 years. The Second Bank, located in Philadelphia, is pictured on the cover of this book.

Andrew Jackson was elected president in 1828. He was a believer in states' rights, a champion of the common man, and an opponent of "moneyed interests" such as bankers. One of his primary goals was to eliminate the Second Bank of the United States.

Jackson criticized the profits earned by the bank's stockholders, a small group of wealthy people. He was also angered by a case of embezzlement at the bank's Baltimore branch. Jackson argued that the bank's profits "must come directly or indirectly out of the earnings of the American people." The establishment of the bank, he declared, was "a prostitution of our government to the advancement of the few at the expense of the many."

In 1832, Congress passed legislation to renew the Second Bank's charter, but Jackson vetoed it. The bank went out of business in 1836, leaving only state-chartered banks.

The National Bank Act Abraham Lincoln believed in a strong federal government, one that worked to build the national economy. Early in his political career, he was a strong supporter of the Second Bank.

As president, Lincoln proposed the National Bank Act, which Congress passed in 1863. The act established a federal agency, the Comptroller of the Currency, to charter banks. Since then, **national banks** chartered by the comptroller and **state banks** chartered by state agencies have coexisted in the United States.

Lincoln was motivated partly by episodes of fraud at state banks. In addition, like Alexander Hamilton, he hoped to unify the nation's currency. Each national bank was required to accept currency issued by the others. Finally, national banks helped finance Union spending on the Civil War, because they were required to purchase Treasury bonds.

National bank bank chartered by the federal government

State bank bank chartered by a state government

Battles Over Branching The late nineteenth century saw the rise of large corporations, such as Standard Oil and U.S. Steel. Populists vilified the leaders of these companies as "robber barons" who exploited workers and consumers. In 1890, Congress passed the Sherman Antitrust Act, which sought to curb firms' power to set monopoly prices.

In banking, the battle between big business and the populists focused on branching restrictions. Most banks were too small to provide the loans needed by large corporations. Banks wanted to merge, but branching restrictions prevented mergers in most states. Bankers proposed legislation to relax these restrictions, and the issue was debated from the 1890s to the 1920s.

Some states did relax branching restrictions, but many refused, especially in the Midwest. The populist movement was strong there, and banks were unpopular because they sometimes seized farms. In addition, although some bankers supported branching, others opposed it. Many unit banks were happy with the status quo, which gave them local monopolies. The American Bankers Association lobbied against branching.

Initially, branching restrictions applied only to state banks. Starting in 1927, however, the McFadden Act required national banks to obey the branching laws of the states where they operated. The McFadden Act also forbade branching across state lines, as noted earlier.

The Glass-Steagall Act Many banks failed in the 1930s, helping to cause the Great Depression. Populists blamed these events on risky and unethical behavior by bankers. Banks speculated in the stock market and lost money in the 1929 crash. They were also accused of making unsound loans to companies whose stocks they owned. Today, historians don't think such practices were a major cause of bank failures, but at the time there was a movement to discipline banks.

The result was the Glass-Steagall Act of 1933, which restricted the scope of banks' activities. Commercial banks were forbidden to engage in the businesses of securities firms. They couldn't own stocks, and they couldn't serve as underwriters. The goal was to keep banks out of risky businesses that could lead to failures.

The Decline of Restrictions After World War II, the tide turned toward deregulation of banks. Improved communications increased the incentives for geographic expansion. Populist fears of large banks waned, and experience showed that bank regulation, especially unit banking, could be a drag on the economy.

As noted earlier, most states eliminated branching restrictions in the 1970s and 1980s. Some interstate banking arose through "reciprocity" agreements, in which states agreed to let in branches of one another's banks. Finally, in 1994 the Riegle-Neal Act allowed branching throughout the country.

The Glass-Steagall restrictions on banks' activities were also eroded over time. Starting in the 1960s, court rulings allowed commercial banks to underwrite safe securities, such as commercial paper. In 1987, the Federal Reserve allowed commercial banks to provide investment-banking services as long as this work produced less than 5 percent of total revenue. This limit was later raised to 10 percent and then 25 percent. Finally, in 1999 Congress passed the Gramm-Leach-Bliley Act, which fully repealed the separation of commercial banks and securities firms.

Chapter 18 describes the aid offered to financial institutions by the government and Federal Reserve during the financial crisis.

The Financial Crisis The trend toward banking deregulation was arrested by the financial crisis of 2007–2009. Citizens and political leaders blamed the crisis and subsequent recession on excessive risk taking by bankers. Many were angered that the government used taxpayers' money to rescue large banks from failure. In 2008, Senator Bernard Sanders, an independent from Vermont, summed up the feelings of many:

> Those brilliant Wall Street insiders who have made more money than the average American can even dream of have brought our financial system to the brink of collapse. Now, as the American and world financial systems teeter on the edge of a meltdown, these multimillionaires are demanding that the middle class pick up the pieces that they broke.[*]

Andrew Jackson would likely have agreed with Senator Sanders's critique of bank rescues.

The financial crisis led to the Dodd-Frank Act, formally known as the Wall Street Reform and Consumer Protection Act, which President Obama signed into law in July 2010. The act created new regulations aimed at restricting risk-taking by banks. It also took small steps back toward Glass-Steagall's separation of commercial banks and securities firms. For example, the act limits banks' ability to sponsor hedge funds. We detail the Dodd-Frank Act further in several upcoming chapters.

[*] "Sanders' Speech on the Wall Street Bailout Plan," October 1, 2008, available at http://sanders.senate.gov/newsroom/news.

Consolidation in Commercial Banking

We've seen in Figure 8.1 that the number of U.S. commercial banks fell from 15,000 in 1984 to fewer than 7000 in 2010. Over the same period, the number of savings institutions fell from 3400 to 1200. As the banking industry has become more concentrated, assets have shifted from small banks to larger ones. Community banks held 22 percent of all commercial-bank assets in 1990, but only 10 percent in 2009. At the other end of the scale, the ten largest banks held 17 percent of total assets in 1990 and 58 percent in 2009. The primary factor behind this trend is mergers of healthy banks, but bank failures also played a significant role in 2008 and 2009.

The Role of Mergers In a merger, two banks agree to combine their businesses, or one bank buys the other. The end of branching restrictions allowed mergers between banks in the same state, and the Riegle-Neal Act prompted a surge of interstate mergers. Many of today's banks were created by a series of mergers. For example, Chemical Bank bought Manufacturers Hanover in 1991. Then, in 1996, Chase Manhattan Bank bought Chemical. In 2000, Chase Manhattan merged with JPMorgan to form JPMorgan Chase. Meanwhile, Banc One bought First Chicago Bank in 1998; JPMorgan Chase purchased Banc One in 2004.

Serial mergers such as these were not forced by distress at any of the institutions involved. Economists and bankers have suggested several motives for mergers:

- *Economies of Scale* Banks reduce transaction costs through economies of scale. When banks become larger, scale economies increase: banks can reduce the costs of making a loan or managing a customer's account. If two banks merge, for example, they can reduce costs by combining their computer systems.

- *Diversification* The benefits of diversifying—not putting all your eggs in one basket—apply to banks as well as to individuals. Banks can diversify by expanding geographically. If a bank operates in a small area, a slowdown in the local economy can cause many loan defaults. Mergers widen the bank's operating area, reducing its sensitivity to local problems.

- *Empire Building* Bank managers may also have personal motives for expansion. In banking, as in most industries, executives receive higher salaries at larger institutions. Managers may also enjoy the power and prestige of running a large bank. Consequently, they may push for mergers even if the deals don't increase profits.

The Role of Bank Failures The most recent financial crisis accelerated the consolidation of the banking industry. The impetus for some mergers was fear that a bank could not survive on its own. In September 2008, the country's fourth-largest bank, Wells Fargo, purchased the fifth largest, Wachovia. Wachovia agreed to the deal after it had suffered large losses on mortgages and government regulators threatened to shut it down. The acquisition pushed Wells Fargo's assets above $1 trillion.

In some cases, a bank actually failed before its business was taken over by another. The biggest failure was that of Washington Mutual (WaMu), a savings institution with $300 billion in assets. In September 2008, shortly before

▶ Section 10.7 describes the government's closure process for failed banks and details the closure of WaMu.

the Wells Fargo–Wachovia merger, the government took over WaMu and sold its assets and deposits to JPMorgan Chase. This deal helped JPMorgan surpass Bank of America as the largest U.S. bank.

Too Big to Fail? We've seen potential benefits, such as economies of scale, from banking consolidation. Many economists believe, however, that consolidation also poses dangers to the broader economy. Their reasoning centers on the linkages among banks and other financial institutions. Commercial banks often maintain deposits at other banks, and they borrow money from one another. Financial institutions such as investment banks buy commercial paper (short-term bonds) from banks and trade derivatives with them. Because of these interlinks, trouble at one bank can spread to others. If a bank fails, it defaults on its debts to other banks, and those banks suffer losses.

This problem is especially severe for large banks, which have more links to other financial institutions than do small banks. They are likely to borrow heavily and to hold deposits from smaller banks. Thus, the failure of a large bank can damage many institutions, triggering additional failures and possibly disrupting the entire financial system and the economy. Because of this risk, many economists believe that large financial institutions facing failure must be rescued to protect the financial system; in other words, some banks are **too big to fail (TBTF)**. The bank mergers of recent years have helped to create institutions that are TBTF.

Too big to fail (TBTF) doctrine that large financial institutions facing failure must be rescued to protect the financial system

During the most recent financial crisis, when many large banks were in peril, policy makers decided they *were* too big to fail. The Federal Reserve and the U.S. Treasury Department committed hundreds of billions of dollars to rescuing such financial institutions, angering people who agreed with Senator Sanders in opposing such uses of taxpayer funds.

 Chapter 18 addresses the too-big-to-fail problem in detail and recounts the history behind the term: how and why TBTF was coined.

Some economists advocate limits on the size of banks that would keep them from becoming TBTF. The only current limit is a restriction on deposits that dates to the 1994 Riegle-Neal Act. If a bank holds more than 10 percent of all commercial-bank deposits, it may not expand by merging with other banks. As of 2010, Bank of America was the only institution that had reached the 10-percent limit. The limit could be reduced to 5 percent or 2 percent, forcing big banks to shrink, but no such change appears imminent.

The Continuing Role of Community Banks Despite the consolidation of the banking industry, thousands of community banks still exist around the country. Economists think this situation will persist: despite the economies of scale that benefit large banks, community banks are not an endangered institution. The primary reason is that community banks have a niche in small-business lending.

Recall that lending requires information gathering. By focusing on a small area, community bankers come to know local businesses and the people who run them. As a result, they are better at screening borrowers than are bankers operating from long distances.

International Banking

The expansion of U.S. banks has not stopped at the nation's borders. About 100 banks have established overseas operations, some by opening branches in foreign countries and others by purchasing foreign banks.

U.S. banks' foreign operations started growing in the 1960s. It was legal for banks to open foreign branches even when they couldn't have branches in more than one state. Initially, foreign expansion was spurred by international trade: U.S. firms operating abroad wanted to deal with U.S. banks. Over time, U.S. banks started lending to foreign businesses and consumers. They also started underwriting securities, because the Glass-Steagall Act didn't apply outside the United States.

Today, many U.S. banks have branches in London, the financial center of Europe. They also maintain a large presence in Latin America and in East Asia, reflecting trade with these regions. U.S. banks in recent years have expanded in Eastern Europe and India, where governments have relaxed restrictions on foreign banks.

Eurodollars Foreign branches of U.S. banks accept two kinds of deposits: deposits in the local currency and deposits in U.S. dollars. Foreigners hold dollars because many international transactions require payments in dollars.

Many foreign banks also accept deposits of dollars. All dollar deposits outside the United States, whether in foreign banks or in foreign branches of U.S. banks, are called **Eurodollars**. Despite the name, the deposits can be located anywhere outside the United States, not just in Europe.

> **Eurodollars** deposits of dollars outside the United States

Foreign Banks in the United States Just as U.S. banks have expanded abroad, hundreds of foreign banks have opened U.S. subsidiaries or bought U.S. banks. The largest foreign-owned bank is HSBC USA, a subsidiary of Britain's HSBC Group. Its $200 billion in assets makes it the eighth-largest commercial bank in the United States. Its parent has worldwide assets of more than $1 trillion, putting it in the same league as the largest U.S. banks.

Consolidation Across Businesses

Commercial banks have expanded not only to larger geographic areas but also into new types of businesses. Large banks have moved beyond lending and now provide the services of securities firms, such as underwriting and brokerage. Some banks also sell insurance. Once again, deregulation made expansion possible.

The Rise of Financial Holding Companies The Gramm-Leach-Bliley Act of 1999, which repealed Glass-Steagall, allows for the creation of **financial holding companies (FHCs),** conglomerates that own groups of financial institutions. A financial holding company can own both commercial banks and securities firms, turning them into a single business.

> **Financial holding company (FHC)** conglomerate that owns a group of financial institutions

A number of commercial banks responded quickly to the Gramm-Leach-Bliley Act. Some turned themselves into FHCs by creating subsidiaries that offer the services of securities firms. Others merged with existing securities firms and insurance companies. In 2010, there were about 500 FHCs. Often their names are similar to those of the commercial banks they own. Citigroup, for example, is an FHC that owns Citibank and other financial institutions. JPMorgan Chase and Co. is an FHC whose holdings include JPMorgan Chase Bank.

The reasons for consolidation across businesses are similar to those for geographic expansion. Empire building is a possible motive. So is diversification: with a mix of businesses, FHCs don't lose too much if one business does badly.

Economies of scope cost reductions from combining different activities

A financial holding company also benefits from **economies of scope**: it reduces costs by combining different activities. For example, a commercial bank must gather information about a firm to lend it money, and an investment bank must gather information to sell the firm's securities. If one institution provides both services, it gathers the information only once. Similarly, an FHC can combine the marketing of several products. The company can offer a customer bank accounts, mutual funds, and insurance at the same time.

Limits on Financial Holding Companies? The most recent financial crisis has influenced thinking about the consolidation of financial institutions. Some economists believe the existence of financial holding companies magnified the crisis, because problems in one unit of an FHC hurt other units.

At Citigroup, for example, the investment-banking unit lost billions of dollars on mortgage-backed securities, leaving the entire FHC short of funds. As a result, Citigroup's commercial-banking units, including Citibank and the Student Loan Corporation (SLC), reduced lending. The SLC, for example, stopped lending to students at two-year colleges. If the Glass–Steagall Act had still existed, Citigroup's investment-banking and commercial-banking divisions would have been separate firms: mistakes by investment bankers would not have led to reduced funding for student loans.

The Dodd–Frank Act includes modest limits on the activities of financial holding companies, such as their involvement with hedge funds. The act also gives regulators the authority to break up an FHC if its existence poses a "grave threat" to the financial system. It remains to be seen how regulators will use this authority.

CASE STUDY

The History of Citigroup

Citigroup (often shortened to "Citi" in its marketing) is a huge financial holding company. In June 2010, its assets totaled about $2.0 trillion, $1.2 trillion held by Citibank and the rest by other units of the FHC. Citigroup has about 200 million customer accounts in 150 countries. It provides most of the services of securities firms, commercial banks, and finance companies, and it sells insurance.

Creation and Growth Citigroup was built through a series of mergers. Most were the work of one man, Sanford Weill, who had a vision of melding disparate businesses into a "financial supermarket." One biography of Weill is called *Tearing Down the Walls.*

In 1986, Weill became CEO of Commercial Credit, a failing finance company in Baltimore. He turned the company around and started buying other companies. In 1988, Commercial Credit bought the brokerage firm Smith Barney. In 1993, it bought Shearson, another brokerage, and Travelers Insurance, and the conglomerate took the Travelers name. In 1997, Travelers bought Salomon Brothers, one of the largest investment banks.

At that point, Weill wanted to acquire a commercial bank. After unsuccessful talks with JPMorgan, he struck a deal to merge Travelers with Citicorp, a holding company that owned Citibank. The new conglomerate, established in 1998, was named Citigroup. At the time, the deal was the largest corporate merger in history. Initially, Weill and John Reed, the head of Citicorp, agreed to run Citigroup together. In 2000, however, the board of directors forced Reed out and made Weill the sole chairman and CEO.

The Travelers–Citicorp merger was surprising because it appeared to violate the Glass-Steagall Act. Lawyers for Travelers found a loophole: the act allowed the companies to merge as long as they separated again within a few years. Weill

April 6, 1998: Sanford Weill, CEO of Travelers Group, on his way to the press conference announcing the merger of his firm with Citicorp—the deal that created Citigroup. In 2000, Weill became Citigroup's chairman and CEO.

© James Leynse/Corbis

and Reed knew that Congress was considering proposals to repeal Glass-Steagall. They agreed on a temporary merger, gambling that the law would change so they could make the merger permanent. This strategy succeeded when Congress passed the Gramm-Leach-Bliley Act in 1999.

In the early 2000s, Citigroup grew through a series of acquisitions. One large purchase, Associates First Capital, a finance company that specialized in subprime lending, became CitiFinancial. Citigroup also bought commercial banks in California, Mexico, and Poland.

Why was Citigroup created? In explaining his business strategy, Weill emphasized economies of scope. Citigroup is designed for "cross-selling," a practice in which agents in one division sell the services of other divisions. Stockbrokers offer insurance policies to their customers, and insurance agents offer mutual funds.

When Sanford Weill's biographers discuss the creation of Citigroup, they emphasize his personal ambition. Weill's roots were modest—he was the son of immigrants in Brooklyn, New York—and he is proud of his rise to become *King of Capital* (another biography title). Weill earned more than $1 billion from 1993 to 2006, but reportedly money wasn't his main motivation: "It's just a way of keeping score," said one associate. Weill's drive to be number one was exemplified by his efforts to oust John Reed from Citigroup.*

Recent Troubles Weill retired as CEO of Citigroup in 2003 and as chairman in 2006. He was replaced in both jobs by Charles Prince, who shifted the firm's business strategy. Prince believed that Citigroup had pushed as far as possible in broadening its scope and should focus on expanding its core banking operations.

Under Prince, Citigroup opened hundreds of new Citibank and CitiFinancial branches in U.S. cities such as Boston, where Citi hadn't operated previously, and in foreign countries, including Brazil, India, Russia, and Korea. At the same time, Citigroup shed some of its nonbanking units, including its asset-management business (sold to Legg Mason in 2005) and its insurance business (sold to Met Life in the same year). (Citigroup still markets the insurance policies of other companies but does not issue policies.)

Citi's new strategy did not prove successful: the FHC often reported disappointing profits, and its stock price hovered around $50 in the middle of the 2000s, a period of rising stock prices at most banks. Analysts blamed Citigroup's problems on high costs, including the costs of building new branches around the world. They suggested that Citigroup's expansion was overly aggressive, as its operations in many countries were too small to benefit from economies of scale.

Worse was to come during the subprime mortgage crisis. As we've discussed, Citigroup's investment-banking division suffered large losses on mortgage-backed securities. The firm's stock price fell below $30 in 2007, and CEO Prince was replaced by Vikram Pandit. As the subprime crisis intensified, fears grew that Citi would fail, and its stock price plummeted. On March 5, 2009, the stock reached a low of $1.02.

Citigroup survived the crisis partly by selling new stock. Large buyers included Warren Buffet's Berkshire Hathaway, the U.S. government, and funds run by the governments of Singapore and Kuwait. By late 2009, Citi's stock price had recovered to about $4, where it remained over the next year. In the end, the crisis was disastrous for those who owned Citigroup stock when the price was $50 but highly profitable for those who bought it at $1.02.

The text Web site links to Citigroup's annual reports, which provide updates on the firm's strategy.

*For more on Sanford Weill and the building of Citigroup, see *Tearing Down the Walls,* by Monica Langley, Free Press, 2003; *King of Capital,* by Amey Stone and Mike Brewster, Wiley, 2004; and Weill's autobiography, Sanford Weill and Judah S. Kraushaar, *The Real Deal: My Life in Business and Philanthropy,* Warner Books, 2006.

8.3 SECURITIZATION

Traditionally, when a bank makes loans, the loans become assets of the bank. The flow of interest on the loans is the bank's primary source of revenue. Over the last generation, however, this basic feature of banking has changed.

Today, banks sell many of the loans they make rather than holding them as assets. The loans are transformed into securities that are traded in financial markets. Loan securitization has had benefits for banks and for the economy, but it also played a role in the financial crisis of 2007–2009.

The Securitization Process

Figure 8.2 illustrates the securitization process. Banks and finance companies make loans and then sell them to a large financial institution, the *securitizer*. This institution gathers a pool of loans with similar characteristics. For example, a pool might be $100 million worth of mortgage loans to people with credit scores within a certain range. The securitizer issues securities that entitle an owner to a share of the payments on the loan pool. The securities are bought by financial institutions, including commercial and investment banks, pension funds, and mutual funds. The initial buyers often resell the securities in secondary markets.

Fannie Mae and Freddie Mac

Home mortgages are the type of loan most often securitized. The two largest issuers of these **mortgage-backed securities (MBSs)** are the Federal National Mortgage Association, commonly known as Fannie Mae, and the Federal Home Loan Corporation, or Freddie Mac. The government created Fannie Mae in 1938 as part of President Franklin Roosevelt's New Deal, and it created Freddie Mac in 1970. The purpose was to increase

Mortgage-backed securities (MBSs) securities that entitle an owner to a share of payments on a pool of mortgage loans

---

FIGURE 8.2 The Securitization Process

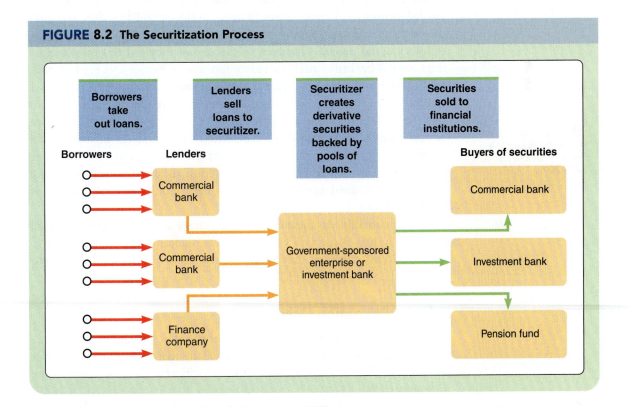

the supply of mortgage loans and thereby help more people achieve the "American dream" of home ownership.

Fannie and Freddie represent an unusual kind of institution called a **government–sponsored enterprise (GSE)**. They are private corporations owned by their shareholders but also linked to the government, which established them. The president appoints some of Fannie's and Freddie's directors, and both GSEs have a long-standing right to borrow money from the U.S. Treasury.

Fannie and Freddie raise funds by issuing bonds and then use the funds to purchase mortgages. Before the most recent financial crisis, they were highly profitable institutions, largely because of their links to the government. In theory, Fannie or Freddie could go bankrupt, but people have long believed the government would save them if they got in trouble, as indeed happened in 2008. The belief that the government stood behind Fannie and Freddie meant their bonds were considered safe. As a result, the bonds paid low interest rates, and Fannie and Freddie could raise funds more cheaply than other financial institutions.

Initially, Fannie and Freddie held onto all the mortgages they bought with the funds they raised. In the 1970s, however, they started issuing mortgage-backed securities, which they sold to other financial institutions. This business grew rapidly, and today more than half of U.S. mortgage debt is securitized by Fannie or Freddie.

From the 1970s to the early 2000s, Fannie and Freddie purchased only prime mortgages, those that appear to have low default risk based on borrowers' incomes and credit scores. Starting in the early 2000s, they also purchased subprime mortgages in an effort to increase the supply of mortgages to low-income people. However, the securities they sell to other institutions are still backed entirely by prime mortgages. Fannie and Freddie have held onto the subprime mortgages they purchased.

Like many financial institutions, Fannie and Freddie suffered losses in 2007 and 2008 as defaults on subprime mortgages rose. It appeared that one or both of the companies might go bankrupt, worsening the financial crisis. To prevent this outcome, the government put Fannie and Freddie under *conservatorship* in September 2008. This action meant that technically the companies remained private, but government regulators took control of their operations.

Conservatorship was meant to be a temporary arrangement, and as of fall 2010 the future of the two companies was unclear. They might return to their pre-crisis status, or they might change from private companies into traditional government agencies.

Why Securitization Occurs

Securitization occurs because banks want to sell loans and because securities backed by bank loans are attractive to many institutions. In this section, we discuss the incentives for securitization, focusing on home mortgages.

Government-sponsored enterprise (GSE) private corporation with links to the government

Chapter 18 expands on the role of Fannie Mae and Freddie Mac in the financial crisis of 2007–2009.

Benefits for Banks Banks sell mortgages because the possibility of default makes it risky to hold them. In addition, the loans made by a particular bank may be poorly diversified, increasing risk. If the bank lends in one geographic area, for example, a downturn in the local economy can cause a large number of defaults. By selling loans, the bank shifts default risk to the ultimate holders of the loans.

From one point of view, selling loans might seem an odd practice. Why should a bank lend money in the first place if it plans to get rid of the loan? The answer is that the bank still performs its basic function of reducing asymmetric information. It uses its expertise to screen borrowers, design loan covenants, and set collateral. Because it does this work, a bank can sell a loan for more than the original amount it gave the borrower. In effect, the institution buying the loan pays the bank for reducing asymmetric information problems. The bank earns a profit from the sale and avoids the default risk it would face if it held onto the loan.

Many banks both sell mortgage loans and buy mortgage-backed securities. In effect, they trade the relatively few loans they make for small pieces of many loans. They gain diversification, reducing risk. They also gain liquidity, because MBSs can be sold more quickly than individual mortgages.

Demand for Mortgage-Backed Securities Many financial institutions buy the securities issued by Fannie Mae and Freddie Mac. Large purchasers include mutual funds and pension funds as well as banks. For these institutions, Fannie and Freddie's securities are attractive alternatives to bonds. The MBSs are highly liquid and are considered safe because they are backed by prime mortgages and because of Fannie and Freddie's links to the government. At the same time, the securities pay a bit more interest than other safe assets, such as Treasury bonds.

Securities backed by subprime mortgages are a different matter. Before the financial crisis, the leading purchasers of subprime MBSs were risk-taking institutions such as hedge funds and investment banks. The results were sufficiently disastrous that no new securities backed by subprime mortgages were being issued in 2010.

The Spread of Securitization

Before the 1990s, there was little securitization of loans beyond the prime mortgage-backed securities created by Fannie Mae and Freddie Mac. Since then, investment banks have extended securitization in two directions: subprime mortgages and nonmortgage loans. The first proved a mistake; the second has been more successful. Today, financial institutions trade securities backed by auto loans, credit card debt, and student loans. At the end of 2009, 35 percent of all outstanding bank loans were securitized, compared to only 6 percent 30 years earlier.

Securitization is sometimes called *shadow banking*, a term that sounds vaguely ominous. We've seen the benefits of securitization: it reduces risk and increases liquidity for banks, and it raises the supply of loans. Yet securitization has gained a bad name because it played a role in the most recent financial crisis. An upcoming case study explains how securitization contributed to the crisis of 2007–2009.

8.4 SUBPRIME LENDERS

Banks lend to millions of firms and individuals. Yet not everyone can borrow from a bank. Banks ration credit: they deny loans to people whose default risk appears high. This group includes people with low incomes or poor credit histories.

Government regulators encourage banks to ration credit. They don't want banks to make risky loans that could lead to large losses. One reason is that the government insures bank deposits, so it stands to lose money if a bank fails.

People who can't borrow from banks often turn to subprime lenders, companies that specialize in high-risk loans. Subprime lenders include some finance companies, payday lenders, pawnshops, and illegal loan sharks. Each type of lender has methods for coping with default risk, which are summarized in **Table 8.2**.

TABLE 8.2 Subprime Lenders

Type of Lender	How Lender Copes with Default Risk
Finance company	Credit scoring; high interest rates
Payday lender	Postdated checks; very high interest rates
Pawnshop	Very high collateral
Illegal loan shark	Very high interest rates; threats to defaulters

Subprime Finance Companies

▶ We analyze bank regulation and deposit insurance in Chapter 10.

The government regulates finance companies less heavily than banks. One reason is that finance companies do not accept deposits, so the government doesn't owe insurance payments if a company fails. Light regulation allows finance companies to make loans that bank regulators might deem too risky. As a result, some finance companies specialize in subprime lending.

Finance companies make subprime mortgage loans, auto loans, and personal loans. Examples of subprime lenders are Household Finance Corporation (HFC), Countrywide Financial, and CitiFinancial. Many of these companies are subsidiaries of financial holding companies that also own commercial banks. CitiFinancial, for example, is part of Citigroup, and HFC is part of the HSBC Group.

Subprime lending grew rapidly in the 1990s and early 2000s, a trend that reflected the development of credit scoring. Asymmetric information is the reason that people with weak credit histories have trouble borrowing. Lenders fear high default risk, and they can't compensate by raising interest rates, because that would worsen the problem of adverse selection.

▶ Section 7.5 discusses the factors that determine a borrower's credit score.

Credit scoring supplies information that reduces adverse selection. During the subprime boom, finance companies gained confidence that credit scores were accurate measures of default risk. Knowing the risk, they could offset expected losses from defaults by charging sufficiently high interest rates. Less credit rationing was needed.

Before the financial crisis, home mortgages were the largest part of sub-prime lending. These mortgages typically carried interest rates two to five percentage points above the best mortgage rates. Often, lenders added to their profits by charging fees when a loan was made. As the next case study relates, default rates on subprime mortgages started rising in 2007, causing new lending for subprime mortgages to dry up. However, other kinds of subprime lending, such as subprime credit cards, have continued to grow.

CASE STUDY

The Subprime Mortgage Fiasco

The crisis that gripped the financial system from 2007 to 2009 had its roots in a wave of mortgage defaults. This disaster stemmed from the interplay of a housing bubble, the rise of subprime lending, securitization, and gaps in government regulation.

> Chapter 18 analyzes the role of the subprime meltdown within the broader financial and economic crisis.

The Housing Bubble From 2002 to 2006, U.S. house prices rose 71 percent on average. As we detail in Section 3.4, many people believed that prices would continue to rise. In reality, the rapid price increases were an unsustainable bubble that deflated as house prices fell by 33 percent from 2006 to 2009.

Risky Lending Eager to increase business as house prices soared, finance companies made mortgage loans to people who were likely to have trouble paying them back. Believing that credit scores were good measures of default risk, these lenders neglected traditional safeguards against default. For example, traditional mortgages require substantial down payments: a prospective home owner must put down 20 percent of the house price to borrow the other 80 percent. During the subprime boom, lenders reduced down payments and even offered mortgages with "zero down."

> ▶ A case study in Section 7.5 explains how traditional mortgage loans work.

Subprime lenders also loosened rules about borrowers' incomes. For a traditional mortgage, monthly payments cannot exceed a certain percentage of income, typically around 28 percent. Formally, subprime lenders kept this rule, but often with a "no documentation" policy: borrowers stated their incomes but weren't asked for proof such as pay stubs or past income tax forms. Some people obtained mortgages by exaggerating their incomes.

Finally, lenders tempted borrowers with low introductory interest rates, or *teaser rates*. In many of these mortgage contracts, the interest rate was 4 percent or less for the first two years but then jumped sharply. People took out loans they could afford initially but got in trouble when their payments rose.

Finance companies could engage in risky lending because the government did not regulate them strictly. In 2008, the Federal Reserve banned no-documentation loans, but this was like closing the barn door after the horse is gone.

The Boom Period Risky mortgage lending didn't produce a crisis immediately. Subprime lending was profitable for a number of years because

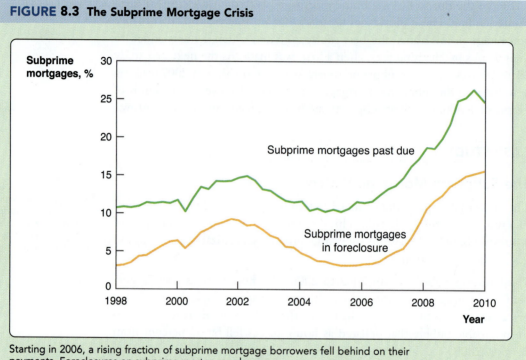

FIGURE 8.3 The Subprime Mortgage Crisis

Starting in 2006, a rising fraction of subprime mortgage borrowers fell behind on their payments. Foreclosures on subprime mortgages also rose.

Source: Mortgage Bankers Association

default rates were moderate. As shown in **Figure 8.3**, the percentage of subprime borrowers who were behind on their mortgage payments was about 10 percent in 2000. The delinquency rate rose during the recession of 2001 but moved back down to 10 percent in 2004. In 2005, only 3 percent of subprime mortgages were in foreclosure, meaning lenders had given up on repayment and moved to seize borrowers' houses. This was well above the 0.4 percent foreclosure rate for prime mortgages, but subprime interest rates were high enough to compensate.

The housing bubble was a key factor behind the subprime boom. Rising house prices made it easier for home owners to cope with high mortgage payments. Someone short on cash could take out a second mortgage; the higher value of her home gave her more collateral to borrow against. Or she could sell the house for more than she paid for it, pay off the mortgage, and earn a capital gain.

The subprime boom Fed on itself. Investment bankers saw the profits being made on subprime mortgages and wanted to get in on the action. They securitized these mortgages and held onto a large share of the MBS. Securitization provided more funds for subprime loans. In turn, more subprime lending increased the demand for housing and fueled the rise in house prices. As a result, subprime mortgages grew from almost zero in the early 1990s to 14 percent of outstanding mortgages in 2007.

During the boom period, few people—whether investment bankers, regulators, or economists—saw the risks of subprime lending that now seem obvious. The underlying reason is that few anticipated the sharp decline in house prices that started in 2006. A bursting bubble in Japan had cut that country's house prices by nearly half in the 1990s and early 2000s, but most Americans ignored this warning signal.

House prices had also fallen in some U.S. regions when their economies weakened in the 1980s and 1990s. Yet most observers agreed with Fed Chairman Alan Greenspan when, in 2005, he said, "Overall, while local economies may experience significant speculative price imbalances, a national severe price distortion [that is, a national housing bubble] seems most unlikely in the United States, given its size and diversity." Because many policy makers considered a housing bubble "most unlikely," they did not worry about the potential consequences of a bursting bubble.

The Crash When house prices started falling in 2006, home owners across the country found themselves with mortgage payments they couldn't afford and no way out. They couldn't borrow more, and they couldn't sell their houses for enough to pay off their mortgages. The delinquency rate on subprime mortgages, charted in Figure 8.3, started to rise. Late in 2009, subprime mortgages past due topped 25 percent. The foreclosure rate was 16 percent, about five times the level of four years earlier. Eventually, the effects of falling house prices spread to prime mortgages, where the foreclosure rate rose from 0.4 percent to 1.4 percent.

Online Case Study
An Update on the
Mortgage Crisis

The mortgage crisis was a disaster for the millions of people who lost their homes, and it also hurt financial institutions. The first to feel the effects were subprime finance companies: two large companies, Ameriquest and New Century Financial, went bankrupt in 2007. As we saw in Chapter 5, investment banks faced a crisis in 2008. Eventually the subprime crisis affected all parts of the financial system, including stock and bond markets, and it pushed the economy into a deep recession.

Payday Lenders

Payday lenders are companies that make small loans to people who need cash urgently. A typical loan is a few hundred dollars for a few weeks. Payday lenders range from small companies with a single office to national chains such as Advance America and ACE Cash Express.

Payday lender company that provides cash in return for a postdated check

To borrow from a payday lender, a customer writes a check with some future date on it—often the next payday. The check covers the amount of the loan plus a fee. The lender gets repaid by cashing the check on the designated day, unless the borrower repays the loan with cash or pays another fee to extend the loan.

Unlike banks, payday lenders gather little information about borrowers. They lend to anyone with a checking account and a pay stub to prove employment. Instead of screening borrowers, payday lenders rely on the postdated checks to reduce defaults. A check is written for a day when funds are likely to be available. In addition, bounced-check fees at a borrower's bank encourage him to make sure the check clears.

Payday lenders also compensate for default risk with *very* high interest rates. A common fee is 15 percent of the loan amount: for $200 in cash, you write a check for $230. For a 4-week loan, this fee is equivalent to an annual interest rate of 515 percent! Surveys suggest that the average annual rate on payday loans is around 400 percent.

Usury law legal limit on interest rates

Most states have **usury laws** that set legal limits on interest rates, often around 40 percent per year. In the 1990s, however, payday lenders lobbied state legislatures to exempt them from usury laws, and they succeeded in many states. These legal changes led to rapid growth in the industry. By 2010, payday lenders had more than 20,000 offices in the United States, most located in low-income areas. Studies estimate that 15 percent of U.S. households have borrowed from payday lenders.

CASE STUDY

Is Payday Lending Predatory?

Payday lenders say their industry benefits consumers. Although expensive, payday loans can stave off disaster when people are short of cash. They can be used, for example, to pay rent and avoid eviction. The Community Financial Services Association, an organization of payday lenders, says their loans are a "convenient and practical short-term credit option." On its Web site, Advance America says, "When your wallet's coming up short, we're here for you."

Predatory lending unfair lending practices aimed at poor and uninformed borrowers

Yet payday lenders are criticized by advocates for consumers and the poor, and they frequently receive negative attention in the media. Critics allege that payday lenders practice **predatory lending**: they take unfair advantage of borrowers who are poor and uninformed about financial matters. According to this view, default rates are not high enough to justify triple-digit interest rates on payday loans. And people who take out the loans often get into financial trouble.

Payday loans are dangerous because a borrower may still be short on cash when his loan is due. In this situation, some people make an interest payment but take out a new loan to cover their initial borrowing. Others take out a larger loan to "roll over" both the initial loan and the interest. Sometimes a loan is rolled over again and again. With high interest rates, the borrower quickly runs up a large debt.

A classic example involves Jason Withrow, a Navy petty officer in Georgia.[*] In July 2003, at age 25, Withrow was struck by a car while on sentry duty. His back injured, he had to quit a part-time job unloading beer kegs at the base liquor store. He ran short of cash to support his wife, a nursing student, and their daughter.

Withrow turned to a payday lender near his base that lent him $300 for a $90 fee. Two weeks later, he rolled over the loan. Over time, Withrow paid back part of his debt but kept borrowing to cover the rest. By February 2004, he had borrowed from four payday lenders and paid about

$5000 in interest—and still owed $1800. At that point he found help at a charity, the Navy-Marine Relief Society, which gave him an interest-free loan to settle his accounts.

In addition to high interest rates, critics of payday lending complain about aggressive debt-collection techniques. Some lenders have threatened defaulters with criminal prosecution for writing bad checks. In one egregious case in Tacoma, Washington, in the early 2000s, debt collectors posing as agents of a fictitious law-enforcement agency delivered this message. They also called borrowers' children, telling them, "Your Mommy and Daddy are going to jail."

Stories such as these have led some states to reconsider their lending laws. In 1997, North Carolina allowed payday lending for four years, but the legislature rejected an extension in 2001. In 2004, Georgia limited annual interest rates to 60 percent, driving payday lenders out of the state. Payday lending is also absent from 12 states, mostly in the Northeast, that never created exceptions to usury laws.

The U.S. Congress has also addressed payday lending—specifically, lending to military personnel. In the past, many customers of payday lenders were young service members like Petty Officer Withrow, people with modest incomes and limited financial experience. The Defense Department complained that debts distracted soldiers and sailors from their duties and jeopardized security clearances. In 2006, Congress responded with a 36-percent interest rate cap on loans to service members. President Bush signed this legislation, ending payday lending to the military.

Not everyone thinks payday lending should be banned. Economists at the Federal Reserve Bank of New York studied Georgia's ban and found harmful consequences for people in financial difficulty.[†] After the ban took effect, the state saw a 9-percent increase in personal bankruptcies, a 13-percent increase in bounced check fees, and a 64-percent increase in complaints against debt collectors.

In 2009, payday lenders in California expanded their business: they now lend to people with proof of government unemployment benefits. Business was brisk in 2010 as California's unemployment rate rose above 12 percent.

Loans to the unemployed have intensified the bitter debate over payday lending. A spokesperson for the Center for Responsible Lending, a consumer group, says that lenders give the unemployed "the illusion of assistance. But instead of throwing them a life jacket, they're throwing them a cinder block." A spokesperson for payday lenders retorts, "Who are they to decide? These people need money. We issue billions of dollars of credit. [Critics] issue platitudes and pats on the back. They tell them to go to their relatives. These people have bills to pay. These people need to go to job interviews. They need credit."[‡]

For more on the debate over predatory lending, link through the text web site to the sites of the Center for Responsible Lending and the Community Financial Services Association (the lender's organization).

[*]"JP Morgan, Banks Back Lenders Luring Poor with 780 Percent Rates," November 23, 2004, www.bloomberg.com.

[†]Donald P. Morgan and Michael R. Strain, "Payday Holiday: How Households Fare After Payday Credit Bans," *Federal Reserve Bank of New York Staff Report* #309, November 2007.

[‡]Robert Faturechi, "Payday lenders giving advances on unemployment checks," March 1, 2010, www.latimes.com.

Pawnshops

Pawnshop small lender that holds an item of value as collateral

Like a payday lender, a **pawnshop** is a source of small, short-term loans. It protects against default with very high collateral. A borrower deposits an item he owns and receives a loan for 30–50 percent of the resale value. The pawnshop has the right to sell the collateral if the loan is not repaid.

Roughly 13,000 pawnshops operate in the United States. A pawnshop's typical loan is $75–$100 for 60 or 90 days. Common collateral includes jewelry, televisions, and—in some states—guns. About 80 percent of borrowers repay their loans and get back the collateral.

Pawnshops appeared in Europe in the fifteenth century, and they have existed in the United States since colonial times. The industry grew rapidly from the 1970s to the 1990s. Since then business has leveled off because of competition with payday lenders.

A variation on pawnshop lending is an *auto title loan*. A borrower pledges her car as collateral and turns over the title. She can keep using the car as long as she makes her loan payments. However, she must give the lender a car key so the collateral can be seized if she defaults.

Illegal Loan Sharks

Loan shark lender that violates usury laws and collects debts through illegal means

Another source of subprime loans is illegal **loan sharks**. These lenders charge interest rates that violate usury laws. Loan-sharking is a traditional business of organized crime.

Loan sharks' disregard for the law helps them cope with default risk. They can encourage repayment with threats of violence. They can seize defaulters' property without the trouble of getting a court judgment.

Yet loan-sharking is a declining industry. Many customers have switched to legal payday lenders or pawnshops. Today loan sharks operate mainly in immigrant communities. They sometimes require immigration papers as collateral for loans.

The last organized-crime figure convicted of loan-sharking was Nicodemo Scarfo, Jr., of Philadelphia. In 2002, he was sentenced to 33 months in prison for charging an interest rate of 152 percent. Scarfo's defenders point out that he charged less than most payday lenders.

8.5 GOVERNMENT'S ROLE IN LENDING

Throughout this book, we've seen that asymmetric information impedes lending. People and firms may have productive uses for funds but be unable to borrow because lenders lack information about them. Banks reduce this problem by screening and monitoring borrowers, and subprime lenders address the problem in a variety of ways. Yet no lender has a perfect solution to the asymmetric-information problem. The financial system may fail to channel funds to good borrowers.

This market failure may justify government intervention. Governments intervene in banking to help people and firms who might have trouble getting loans. In the United States, policies focus on several kinds of borrowers: home buyers, small businesses, students, and residents of low-income neighborhoods. We'll discuss the main U.S. policies and then examine those of other countries. Many foreign governments own banks and therefore can dictate who receives loans.

Support for Housing

Many Americans believe that home ownership benefits both the owners and their neighbors, because having a stake in a community makes people better citizens. The government encourages home ownership through the work of government-sponsored enterprises, by guaranteeing mortgages, and through tax incentives.

Mortgage Agencies We've already discussed Fannie Mae and Freddie Mac, the government-sponsored enterprises that buy mortgages. By issuing bonds and mortgage-backed securities, the GSEs raise funds that increase the supply of mortgages. Despite Fannie's and Freddie's losses during the subprime crisis, their role in mortgage lending actually increased. After the government took over the agencies in September 2008, it encouraged them to purchase more mortgages to offset a fall in lending by troubled banks.

Loan Guarantees When the government makes a **loan guarantee**, it agrees to pay off a bank loan if the borrower defaults. Essentially, the government provides insurance to the bank, making it more willing to lend. Several government agencies guarantee mortgage loans. The two most important are the Veteran's Administration (VA), which guarantees mortgages for military veterans, and the Federal Home Administration (FHA), which guarantees mortgages for low-income people.

The FHA's role has increased dramatically since 2007, when finance companies began to cut subprime mortgage lending. People who previously would have borrowed from subprime lenders have turned to the FHA. With FHA guarantees, they can get mortgages from banks. The share of new mortgages guaranteed by the FHA has risen from 2 percent to more than 30 percent.

The FHA charges fees to borrowers whose loans it guarantees. Since the FHA was founded in 1934, its programs have been self-financing: fees have covered the costs of paying off banks when borrowers default. However, the rise in defaults during the financial crisis has created fears that the FHA may run out of money and, like Fannie Mae and Freddie Mac, require support from the government. In an effort to reduce defaults, in 2010 the FHA began requiring larger down payments on the mortgages it guarantees.

Tax Incentives The government also promotes mortgage lending through the tax system. A home owner's interest payments on her mortgage are deductible from her taxable income, so taking out a mortgage reduces taxes. Rent payments for housing are not tax deductible, so people have an incentive to buy homes.

▶ The U.S. government intervenes in the financial system in other ways, by regulating securities markets to reduce asymmetric information between the issuers and buyers of securities (see Section 7.4) and banks to protect consumers and to reduce the risk of bank failures (see Chapters 9 and 10).

Loan guarantee
government promise to pay off a loan if the borrower defaults

Small-Business Loans

The Small Business Administration (SBA), an agency within the Commerce Department, promotes business lending. Like the FHA and VA, it guarantees loans. A company qualifies for a loan guarantee if it is "small," which the SBA defines for each industry. For example, a furniture manufacturer qualifies if it has fewer than 500 employees. Banks pay fees for the guarantees, typically 1/2 to 1 percent of the loan, but the program costs the government money because the SBA pays out more than it receives in fees.

The rationale for the SBA loan program rests on the problem of asymmetric information. This problem is more severe for small firms than for large firms, which are better known to lenders. Without loan guarantees, banks might shy away from small-business lending because they can't judge default risk.

Some economists criticize the SBA. They point out that banks reduce the asymmetric-information problem through screening and monitoring. In their view, banks do well enough that promising businesses can get loans without government help. According to the American Enterprise Institute, a conservative think tank, spending by the SBA is simply a "wasteful, politically motivated subsidy."

Student Loans

Most college students must borrow to finance their education. Borrowing can be difficult, as students typically have low incomes and short credit histories. The federal Department of Education addresses this problem with tuition loans. It makes *Stafford Loans* to undergraduate and graduate students and *PLUS Loans* to the parents of undergraduates. At the start of 2010, more than $600 billion of these loans were outstanding.

In the past, the government guaranteed student loans made by banks and finance companies such as the Student Loan Marketing Association (Sallie Mae). In 2010, however, Congress passed legislation that abolished loan guarantees in favor of direct loans from the government to students. Supporters of this change argue that it will reduce the government's costs, because private lenders, who previously profited from guaranteed loans, are cut out of the process. Private lenders still make student loans that are *not* guaranteed by the government and carry relatively high interest rates to compensate for default risk.

▶ These figures apply to students who are dependents of their parents. Financially independent students can borrow larger amounts.

As of the 2010–2011 academic year, most college freshmen could borrow up to $5500 under the Stafford Loan program. Sophomores could borrow $6500, and juniors and seniors $7500. Repayment of a loan is usually spread over 10 years, starting 6 months after the borrower leaves school.

A student who demonstrates financial need receives "subsidized" Stafford Loans, which means he is not charged interest until his loan payments begin. Students who do not demonstrate need are charged interest starting when they receive a loan. Interest for the prepayment period is added to the students' debt. The interest rate on unsubsidized loans is 6.8 percent.

The rate on subsidized loans is lower, but it will rise to 6.8 percent for the 2012–2013 academic year.

Recent legislation reduces the burden of repaying student loans. Under a 2007 law, no one is required to pay more than 15 percent of her after-tax income for Stafford Loans. Under a 2010 amendment, the limit will be 10 percent starting in 2014. When payments are reduced under this rule, the unpaid amount will be added to the loan balance—but any balance remaining after 20 years will be forgiven.

The Community Reinvestment Act

People in low-income areas can have trouble getting bank loans. Until the 1970s, some banks practiced *redlining:* they marked areas on a map (usually outlined in red ink) where they wouldn't lend. People in these areas were denied credit regardless of their individual characteristics.

The reasons for redlining are debatable. It might be rational to think that loans in low-income areas are risky. On the other hand, lenders could be unfairly prejudiced against certain neighborhoods. Many redlined areas were predominantly African American, so racial discrimination could be a factor.

Either way, a scarcity of bank loans held back some communities' economic development. In 1977, Congress addressed this problem with the **Community Reinvestment Act (CRA)**, which requires banks to lend in poor areas. The CRA encourages loans for mortgages, small businesses, and "community development" projects such as job training and health care.

Community Reinvestment Act (CRA) law from 1977 that requires banks to lend in low-income areas

The government monitors banks to enforce the CRA. Each bank is examined every 3–5 years. Regulators determine the broad geographic area where a bank should lend, based on branch locations and where depositors live. Then they examine lending in the low-income parts of the area.

A standard CRA exam is a big project. The bank must write a report on its efforts to comply with the act. It must show that its advertising and loan screening don't favor one neighborhood over another. The bank must also submit data on individual loans, showing borrowers' incomes and residences. Examiners then visit the bank to interview the staff and study records. They also seek comments on the bank from local governments and community organizations. At the end of this process, the bank receives a grade on its CRA lending. Grades range from "outstanding" to "substantially not in compliance." A low grade creates bad publicity. In addition, regulators may forbid the bank to open new branches or merge with another bank.

Opinions vary on the CRA's effects. In recent years, more than 95 percent of banks have received grades of "outstanding" or "satisfactory." Banks say they are meeting the goals of the act. But some community groups allege grade inflation. They say banks still don't do enough lending in low-income areas.

Banks complain that CRA exams take too much of their managers' time. In 2005, the government responded by making community banks (those with assets below $1 billion) eligible for "streamlined" exams with less paperwork. Banks welcomed this change, but critics say it weakens enforcement of the CRA.

Government-Owned Banks

▶ The financial crisis of 2007–2009 caused a temporary departure from private ownership for some large U.S. banks. To prevent them from failing, the government bought their stock under the Troubled Asset Relief Program (TARP). The banks repurchased the stock from the government as the crisis eased. Chapter 18 discusses the TARP in detail.

In the United States, banks are private, profit-making corporations. In many other countries, the government owns banks. Government officials decide who gets loans and what interest rates they pay. In most European countries, the government owns some banks, but the majority are private. In many developing countries, most or all banks are government owned. Examples include China, India, Brazil, and most African countries.

Most economists oppose government ownership of banks. They believe that private banks are best at channeling funds to productive uses. Government bankers make wasteful loans to people with political connections. Sometimes they take bribes.

▶ These findings come largely from studies at the World Bank. See Section 1.5 for more on World Bank research on banking and economic growth.

Several studies have compared countries with different levels of government bank ownership. They find that government ownership reduces lending to the most productive firms. The quality of investment suffers, leading to lower economic growth.

China exemplifies the problems with government-owned banks. Four such institutions dominate Chinese banking. These banks report high default rates on loans, which suggest that their lending is imprudent. And critics allege that the banks underreport defaults, meaning the true problem is worse. Since 2000, China's banks have also suffered a series of corruption scandals, with numerous officials jailed for embezzlement or bribery. China's economic growth has been high since the 1990s, but its banking problems could threaten future growth.

Summary

8.1 Types of Banks

- Commercial banks take deposits and make loans. U.S. commercial banks include a handful of money-center banks, hundreds of regional and superregional banks, and thousands of community banks that operate in small geographic areas.

- Thrift institutions also take deposits and make loans. Thrifts include savings institutions that lend largely for home mortgages and credit unions—not-for-profit banks owned by their depositors.

- Finance companies make loans but do *not* take deposits. They raise funds by issuing bonds and borrowing from banks.

8.2 Dispersion and Consolidation

- The United States has far more banks than other countries, a legacy of political battles in the nineteenth

and early twentieth centuries, when populist opposition to large banks produced branching restrictions and a ban on interstate banking.

- States eliminated branching restrictions in the 1970s and 1980s, and Congress allowed interstate banking in 1994. These changes produced a merger wave that more than halved the number of commercial banks between 1984 and 2009. Possible motives for mergers include economies of scale, diversification, and empire building.

- U.S. banks have expanded their operations to countries around the world. Foreign branches of U.S. banks accept both deposits of local currency and deposits of dollars.

- The Glass-Steagall Act of 1933 forbade commercial banks to merge with other kinds of financial institutions. Glass-Steagall was repealed in 1999, allowing the creation of financial holding companies that combine banks, securities firms, and insurance companies. The largest FHC is Citigroup, built by Sanford Weill through a series of mergers.

■ The financial crisis of 2007–2009 stemmed the trend toward banking deregulation. Policy makers debated whether banks had grown too big to fail. In 2010, President Obama signed the Dodd-Frank Act, which restricts risk taking by financial holding companies, among other reforms.

8.3 Securitization

■ Many bank loans, from mortgages to car loans to credit card debt, are securitized. A financial institution buys loans, pools them together, and issues securities entitling owners to shares of the payments on the loan pool.

■ Securitization is most common for home mortgages. The largest issuers of mortgage-backed securities are Fannie Mae and Freddie Mac, which together securitize more than half of U.S. mortgage debt.

■ The U.S. government created Fannie and Freddie to increase the supply of mortgage loans. Before 2008, they were government-sponsored enterprises, private firms with links to the government. But as defaults on subprime mortgages ballooned, the government took over Fannie and Freddie to save them from bankruptcy.

■ Securitization allows banks to eliminate default risk on their loans, makes their assets more liquid, and raises the supply of loans. Yet securitization's role in the most recent financial crisis earned it the epithet "shadow banking."

8.4 Subprime Lenders

■ People with low incomes or poor credit histories have trouble getting bank loans. They must borrow from subprime lenders of various types.

■ Many finance companies specialize in subprime lending. They use credit scores to measure borrowers' default risk and adjust interest rates to offset this risk.

■ In the 1990s and early 2000s, subprime lenders loosened their standards for approving mortgages. The immediate result was a surge in lending; the ultimate result was a surge in mortgage defaults beginning in 2006. Many people lost their homes, finance companies went bankrupt, and holders of subprime MBSs suffered large losses.

■ Payday lenders make small, short-term loans at very high interest rates. Advocates for consumers and the poor accuse these companies of predatory lending, arguing that customers get into financial trouble through repeated borrowing.

■ Pawnshops also make small, short-term loans. They address default risk by requiring an item of value, such as jewelry, as collateral.

■ Loan sharks charge very high interest rates and use illegal means, such as threats of violence, to ensure repayment. Loan sharking has declined since the 1990s because of competition from legal payday lenders.

8.5 Government's Role in Lending

■ The U.S. government encourages lending to certain types of borrowers, including prospective home owners, small businesses, students, and people who live in low-income areas.

■ The government encourages home ownership through the work of government-sponsored enterprises, by guaranteeing mortgages, and through tax incentives.

■ The Small Business Administration guarantees loans that banks make to qualified small businesses.

■ The government makes Stafford Loans to college students and PLUS loans to their parents. Recent legislation limits the percentage of income that a person must devote to repaying a student loan.

■ The Community Reinvestment Act requires banks to lend in low-income neighborhoods.

■ In many countries, the government owns some or all banks. Most economists think that government-owned banks do a poor job of allocating funds, thus harming economic growth.

Key Terms

bank charter, p. 226

commercial bank, p. 222

community bank, p. 224

Community Reinvestment Act (CRA), p. 247

credit union, p. 224

economies of scope, p. 232

Questions and Problems

1. HSBC has more than $1 trillion in assets and operates in about 100 countries. It calls itself "the world's local bank." What business strategies does this phrase suggest? Why might these strategies be successful?

2. Suppose that Melvin's Bank purchases Gertrude's Bank, making Gertrude a subsidiary of Melvin. Does this acquisition benefit the stockholders of Melvin's Bank? Does the answer depend on the motives for the purchase? Explain. (*Hint:* Review the motives for bank consolidation discussed in Section 8.2.)

3. Securitization has spread from mortgages to student loans and credit card debt. However, few loans to businesses have been securitized. Explain why.

4. Suppose that loan sharks propose legislation to promote their industry. They want a legal right to break the kneecaps of loan defaulters.

   a. Suppose you were hired as a lobbyist for the loan sharks. What arguments could you make to support their proposal?

   b. How would you respond to these arguments if you oppose kneecap breaking?

5. Consider the example in Chapter 7 of two firms that want to issue bonds (see Figure 7.2). Assume as before that a firm makes the promised payment on a bond only if its project succeeds.

   a. Suppose the government guarantees the firms' bonds: it makes the promised payment if either firm defaults. Can both firms sell bonds? What payments must they promise?

   b. What is the average cost to the government of guaranteeing a bond, assuming it does so for each firm?

   c. What is the average profit on an investment project, assuming both firms finance their projects with government-guaranteed bonds?

   d. Which is higher—the average cost of a bond guarantee [part (b)] or the average profit on a project [part (c)]? In light of this comparison, do the guarantees promote economic efficiency? Explain why or why not. (*Hint:* How do the guarantees affect the adverse-selection problem?)

6. Discuss several reasons why the government guarantees student loans but not auto loans.

▶ Online and Data Questions

www.worthpublishers.com/ball

7. The text Web site provides data on 82 countries from a 2002 study on government bank ownership. For each country, the data include (a) the percentage of bank assets at government-owned banks in 1970, (b) the average growth rate of bank loans as a percentage of GDP from 1960 to 1995, and (c) the average growth rate of real GDP per person from 1960 to 1995.

   a. Make a graph with variable (a) on the horizontal axis and variable (b) on the vertical axis and plot each country. What might explain the relationship between these variables?

   b. Make a graph with (a) on the horizontal axis and (c) on the vertical axis. What might explain the relationship between these variables?

8. Many states allow payday lending but impose restrictions on the practice. For example, a state may limit the amount someone can borrow or the number of times a loan can be rolled over. Find out whether payday lending is legal in your state and, if so, what restrictions exist. How stringent are these restrictions compared to those in other states?

9. The Web site of the Community Financial Services Association, the payday lenders' organization, has a page on "Myths and Realities" about payday lending. Do you agree with the CFSA about what's a myth and what's reality? Do some research to answer this question, starting with the CFSA site and that of the Center for Responsible Lending (both linked to the text Web site).

10. What are the current interest rates on 1-year certificates of deposit at a commercial bank and a credit union located near you? Is one institution's rate higher than the other's? What might explain the difference?

The Business of Banking

NNECAPA/Flickr

Perhaps one day you will be president of a commercial bank. You probably have some idea what this job will be like. You'll dress well and have a nice office. Your salary will be high. But what exactly will you do to earn this salary?

Like the head of any business, you will try to make profits. As a banker, you earn profits by accepting deposits and lending them out at higher interest rates than you pay. You can add to these profits through other activities, such as currency dealing or speculating on derivatives.

Whether the bank you run is large or small, your job will be challenging, because banking is a risky business. If things go wrong, your bank will lose money. Losses can arise for many reasons, including defaults on loans, large withdrawals by depositors, changes in interest rates, and slowdowns in the general economy. Your bank might lose so much that it is forced out of business, costing you your job.

This chapter discusses the business of banking. It analyzes banks' strategies for raising funds and using them to make profits. We also discuss banks' efforts to contain risk, efforts that sometimes succeed and sometimes fail.

With just 5000 customer accounts, the First National Bank of Orwell, Vermont, is one of the country's smallest banks and the oldest bank in New England with a national charter. The bank's owners live in the attached house at left.

Banking is a rapidly changing business. In recent decades, banks have lost some traditional sources of profits while gaining new opportunities. These changes have arisen from new technologies, changes in government regulations, and the growth of financial markets. We will see how banks have responded to these developments and the state of the business today.

9.1 BANKS' BALANCE SHEETS

Remember the definition of a bank: it is a financial institution that accepts deposits and makes loans. Loans are assets of the bank and one of the uses it makes of its funds. They produce a flow of income in the form of interest payments. Deposits are **liabilities** of the bank—amounts the bank owes to others—and one source of its funds. If you have $100 in a checking account, the bank owes you $100.

Liabilities amounts of money owed to others

Balance sheet financial statement that summarizes an entity's assets, liabilities, and net worth at a given date

Net worth (equity or capital) difference between assets and liabilities

Banks have other assets besides loans, and other liabilities besides deposits. A bank's assets and liabilities are summarized in a statement called a **balance sheet**, which captures the bank's financial condition at a given date. The balance sheet lists the bank's assets on the left side and its liabilities on the right.

The right side of the balance sheet also includes the bank's **net worth**, defined as

$$\text{net worth} = \text{assets} - \text{liabilities}$$

A bank's net worth is also called **equity** or **capital**. It is the level of assets the bank would have if it paid off all its liabilities.

Each individual bank maintains a balance sheet. The combined assets and liabilities for a group of banks can be shown in a consolidated balance sheet. **Table 9.1** is a consolidated balance sheet for all U.S. commercial

TABLE 9.1 Consolidated Balance Sheet, U.S. Commercial Banks

On June 30, 2010
(Billions of Dollars)

Assets		Liabilities and Net Worth	
Cash Items	$1195.1	Checking Deposits	$989.5
Reserves (Vault Cash +		Nontransaction Deposits	6704.4
Deposits at Fed)		Savings Deposits	
Deposits at Other Banks		Small Time Deposits	
In Process of Collection		Large Time Deposits	
Securities	2286.9	Borrowings	1999.8
Loans	6789.7	Other Liabilities[†]	722.8
Other Assets*	1549.9	Net worth	1405.1
Total	$11821.6	Total	$11821.6

* Category includes miscellaneous items such as collateral seized from loan defaulters and the value of banks' buildings and equipment.

[†] Category includes miscellaneous items such as taxes due to the government and dividends due to stockholders.

banks on June 30, 2010. The total assets of these banks were $11.8 trillion, and total liabilities were $10.4 trillion. Net worth was $1.4 trillion (= $11.8 trillion − $10.4 trillion).

The balance sheet splits banks' assets and liabilities into several categories. A central part of bankers' jobs is determining the levels of these different items.

Liabilities and Net Worth

We begin with the liabilities side of the balance sheet (the right side of Table 9.1). When banks raise funds, they incur liabilities of several types to the people or firms that provide the funds. The major items are checking deposits, nontransaction deposits, and borrowings.

Checking Deposits This category covers deposits that customers use to purchase goods and services. People spend these deposits by writing checks, swiping debit cards, and authorizing electronic payments. Checking deposits are part of the narrow measure of the money supply, M1.

▶ Section 2.3 explains how the Federal Reserve measures the U.S. money supply.

Some checking accounts pay no interest. Others, called NOW accounts, pay low interest rates. (NOW stands for *negotiable order of withdrawal*.) NOW accounts usually have higher fees or minimum balances than zero-interest accounts.

In June 2010, checking deposits comprised only 9 percent of total bank liabilities. Because of low interest rates, few people hold large amounts of wealth in checking accounts.

Nontransaction Deposits These deposits cannot be spent directly with checks or debit cards. However, they pay higher interest rates than checking deposits. Nontransaction deposits include both savings deposits, which can be withdrawn from a bank at any time, and time deposits, which are committed for a fixed period of time. Time deposits are commonly called CDs, for *certificates of deposit*.

▶ Section 2.4 introduces savings deposits and time deposits.

Small CDs, those less than $100,000, are held mainly by individual savers. Most large CDs, those over $100,000, are held by corporations and financial institutions. After large CDs are issued by banks, their holders can resell them in secondary financial markets. This fact makes large CDs highly liquid: they can easily be traded for cash.

Together, savings and time deposits made up 64 percent of commercial-bank liabilities as of June 2010. They are the major sources of funds for commercial banks.

Borrowings A bank may want more funds than it raises from deposits. This can occur, for example, if the bank wants to increase its lending. In this case, the bank borrows money. In 2010, borrowings were 19 percent of commercial-bank liabilities. A bank can borrow in several ways:

- *Federal funds* First, a bank can borrow from another bank, one that has more funds than it needs for other purposes. Loans from one bank to another are called **federal funds**. They are usually *overnight loans*, meaning they have a term of one day.

Federal funds loans from one bank to another, usually for one day

Repurchase agreement (repo) sale of a security with a promise to buy it back at a higher price on a future date

We discuss how Fed lending supports its normal monetary policy in Chapter 11 and, in Chapter 18, how the Fed expanded its lending during the financial crisis.

Discount loan loan from the Federal Reserve to a bank

- *Repos* A bank can also borrow from a corporation or financial institution that has spare cash. This borrowing occurs through a **repurchase agreement**, or **repo**. To see how repos work, suppose a bank makes a repo agreement with a pension fund. The bank sells the pension fund a security, such as a Treasury bill, and agrees to buy it back later at a higher price. This deal is equivalent to a loan, because the bank receives cash temporarily. The security is collateral for the loan, and the increase in the security's price is interest.

- *Bonds* Bonds are another means of borrowing. Technically, it is not legal for commercial banks to issue bonds. But financial holding companies issue bonds, and they pass on the funds they raise to banks that they own. Bonds are an important source of funds for large banks.

- *Loans from the Fed* Banks also can borrow from the Federal Reserve. A loan from the Fed to a bank is called a **discount loan**. During the most recent financial crisis, the Fed supplemented discount loans with a variety of emergency programs that lent to banks and other financial institutions.

Net Worth The final item on the right side of the balance sheet is net worth, or capital. Recall that this variable, defined as assets minus liabilities, ensures that the balance sheet balances—that the two sides add up to the same amount. In June 2010, U.S. commercial banks had net worth equal to 13 percent of their liabilities, or 12 percent of assets.

A bank acquires capital by issuing stock. Savers buy the stock, providing funds to the bank in return for ownership shares. A bank's capital is available to buy assets, along with the funds from deposits and borrowing. The bank's profits are added to its capital. Losses reduce capital. Capital also falls when a bank pays dividends to its stockholders.

Assets

We now turn to the asset side of the balance sheet, which shows how banks use the funds they raise. Banks hold several types of assets, which are listed on the left side of Table 9.1. The major categories are cash items, securities, and loans.

Vault cash currency in banks' branches and ATMs

Reserves vault cash plus banks' deposits at the Federal Reserve

Cash Items This category includes several components, which together comprised 10 percent of bank assets in 2010. One component is **vault cash**, the currency sitting in banks' branches and ATMs. Another is deposits in banks' accounts at the Federal Reserve. The sum of these two components is called **reserves**.

Reserves are a bank's most liquid asset. Banks need reserves so they can provide money when depositors want it. If a depositor wants cash, she gets it from a bank branch or ATM. When she buys something with a check or debit card, the funds come from her bank's account at the Fed.

Reserves produce little income. A bank earns nothing on its vault cash. In October 2008, banks started receiving interest on their deposits at the

▶ Section 2.3 describes how banks process payments using their accounts at the Fed.

Fed, but the interest rates are low. As a result, banks hold only a small part of total assets as reserves. In the past, Fed regulations required banks to hold more reserves, but these regulations have become ineffective.

In addition to reserves, a bank's cash items include deposits at other banks. Often a small bank holds deposits at a larger bank that provides it with services. For example, large banks trade foreign currencies on behalf of small banks.

A final component of cash assets is *cash items in process of collection*. These are checks that have been deposited in a bank but have not yet cleared. The bank is waiting for the funds promised by the check.

Securities Securities are 19 percent of bank assets listed in Table 9.1. By law, banks are restricted to securities with low risk. These include Treasury bonds, municipal bonds, and corporate bonds or mortgage-backed securities (MBSs) that receive high grades from rating agencies. Banks are not allowed to hold stocks or junk bonds.

▶ In the period leading up to the financial crisis, banks were allowed to hold sub-prime MBSs that carried AAA ratings but were riskier than their ratings indicated. Section 9.6 describes banks' losses on MBSs.

Securities pay interest. The interest rates are lower than rates on bank loans, but banks hold securities because they pay more than reserves while also providing liquidity. If depositors make large withdrawals, a bank may run low on reserves, but it can easily get more by selling securities. For this reason, securities held by banks are often called *secondary reserves*.

Loans Loans are banks' most important asset class, accounting for 56 percent of total assets in Table 9.1. Banks make loans to several types of borrowers: consumers, businesses, governments, and other banks. We detail these different types of loans in Section 9.3.

Loans are less liquid than securities: it is hard to turn them into cash quickly. In addition, borrowers sometimes default on loans. Nonetheless, loans can be profitable because they pay higher interest rates than safe securities.

9.2 OFF-BALANCE-SHEET ACTIVITIES

Banks earn income from the loans and securities listed on their balance sheets. They also receive income from **off-balance-sheet (OBS) activities** that are not revealed on bank balance sheets, because they don't affect the current levels of the assets and liabilities reported there. OBS activities are a growing part of the banking business. Of the many kinds of activities, we discuss five important examples. You will recognize several from earlier chapters.

Off-balance-sheet (OBS) activities bank activities that produce income but are not reflected in the assets and liabilities reported on the balance sheet

Lines of Credit

A line of credit (also called a *loan commitment*) gives an individual or firm the right to borrow a certain amount of money at any time. Banks grant lines of credit to build long-term relationships with borrowers. Lines of credit also produce income for banks, because firms pay fees to keep them open. Firms are willing to pay for the guarantee of a quick loan when it is needed. A line of credit does not affect a bank's balance sheet until an actual loan is made, at which point the loan category of assets rises by the amount of money lent out and cash assets fall by the same amount.

Letters of Credit

When a bank issues a **letter of credit**, it guarantees some payment promised by a firm. In return for a fee, the bank agrees to make the payment if the firm does not. In effect, the bank sells insurance against default. There are two kinds of letters of credit:

- A *commercial letter of credit* guarantees a payment for goods or services. To see its purpose, suppose an importer has ordered goods from a foreign company, promising to pay when the goods arrive. The foreign company may be wary of shipping the goods, because the importer might not pay the bill. The importer solves this problem by purchasing a letter of credit from a bank. The foreign company is willing to ship because payment is guaranteed.

- A *standby letter of credit* guarantees payments on a security. A company might buy a standby letter when it issues commercial paper. The bank that provides the letter agrees to pay off the paper if the company defaults. As a result of this guarantee, the commercial paper gets higher grades from bond-rating agencies. Higher ratings reduce the interest rate that the company must pay on the paper.

Asset Management

In addition to holding their own assets, banks manage assets for others. A small pension fund, for example, might want to buy securities but lack the expertise to choose the right mix. The pension fund entrusts its money to a bank that purchases securities on its behalf and pays fees to the bank for this service. Wealthy individuals also hire banks to manage assets, an activity called *private banking*.

Derivatives

Large banks trade derivative securities such as futures contracts and options on stocks, bonds, and currencies. Derivatives do not appear on bank balance sheets, because they are not currently assets or liabilities. Rather, they are agreements about future transactions.

▶ Sections 5.6 and 6.6 discuss the uses of derivatives for hedging and speculation. We introduce the Dodd-Frank Act, formally known as the Wall Street Reform and Consumer Protection Act, in Section 7.3.

Banks use derivatives to hedge against risks they face, such as changes in interest rates. Some banks also seek income by speculating with derivatives. Some economists view this activity as exploiting a loophole in bank regulation. Commercial banks are forbidden to own stocks because they are too risky, but they *can* trade derivatives tied to stock prices, which are equally or more risky. The Dodd-Frank Act of 2010 requires regulators to develop rules limiting banks' derivative trading, but it is not clear how stringent these new regulations will be.

Investment Banking

Some commercial banks provide investment-banking services, such as under-writing securities and advising on mergers and acquisitions. Commercial banks were allowed to enter these businesses in 1999, when the Glass–Steagall Act was repealed. Investment-banking activities are important sources of income for the largest banks.

▶ Section 8.2 discusses the Glass-Steagall Act and its repeal.

9.3 HOW BANKS MAKE PROFITS

So far we've outlined commercial banks' main business activities, both on and off the balance sheet. Let's now discuss how banks combine these activities to earn profits. We start with a fictional example that introduces some key ideas.

Melvin Opens a Bank

One day a man named Melvin opens a bank in Baltimore and calls it Melvin's Bank. Melvin raises $20 by selling shares of the bank's stock to his friends. This $20 is the bank's initial capital, or net worth.

At first, Melvin's Bank deposits part of its $20 at the Federal Reserve Bank of Richmond and holds the rest as vault cash. The entire $20 counts as reserves. These reserves are the bank's only asset, and it has no liabilities. So the bank's balance sheet has only two items:

Assets		Liabilities and Net Worth	
Reserves	20	Net Worth	20

To raise more funds, Melvin seeks deposits. He puts a sign outside his bank saying. "Deposit Your Money Here!" Britt, the star pitcher, passes by the bank and notices the sign. He has just been traded to the Orioles and needs a bank in Baltimore. He deposits $50 in cash in a Melvin's checking account. He also deposits $50 in a savings account so he can earn interest.

▶ You met Britt the saver and Harriet the investor in Chapter 1.

Britt's two deposits change Melvin's balance sheet. They add $100 to the bank's reserves, and they also create liabilities. Now the balance sheet looks like this:

Assets		Liabilities and Net Worth	
Reserves	120	Checking Deposits	50
		Nontransaction Deposits	50
		Net Worth	20
TOTALS	120		120

This situation does not last long. The bank does not want to keep reserves as its only asset, because they pay little interest. Out of $120, Melvin's Bank keeps $10 in reserves, in case Britt wants to make a withdrawal. It buys $30 in Treasury bills to provide secondary reserves. This leaves $80, which it lends to Harriet for her iSmells business.

Let's say that all these transactions occur in the year 2020. Reflecting this activity, the balance sheet at the end of the year is:

MELVIN'S BANK BALANCE SHEET
December 31, 2020

Assets		Liabilities and Net Worth	
Reserves	10	Checking Deposits	50
Securities	30	Nontransaction Deposits	50
Loans	80	Net Worth	20
TOTALS	120		120

At this point, Melvin's banking business is in full swing. The bank has raised funds and used them to acquire assets. If the income from assets exceeds the interest paid on deposits, the bank can make a profit.

As this example illustrates, actions by a bank and its customers shift the bank's balance sheet. Sometimes assets and liabilities change together, as when Melvin's Bank gains $100 in deposits and $100 in reserves. Other times, only one side of the balance sheet changes, as when the bank shifts assets from reserves to loans and securities. Whatever happens, total assets always equal total liabilities plus net worth.

In addition to holding assets, Melvin's Bank engages in off-balance-sheet activities. For example, it issues letters of credit to Harriet's company when Harriet orders computers from other companies. Fees for letters of credit add to the bank's income.

The Income Statement

How profitable is Melvin's Bank? We can address this question by analyzing the bank's **income statement**, the financial statement that summarizes its income and expenses. Let's construct Melvin's income statement for the year 2021.

Income statement financial statement summarizing income, expenses, and profits over some time period

This exercise requires several assumptions. First, for simplicity, let's say that Melvin's balance sheet does not change during 2021. Throughout the year, Melvin maintains the balance sheet for December 31, 2020 that we examined above.

We also assume the interest rate on loans is 8 percent and the rates on both Treasury bills and savings deposits are 4 percent. In this example, checking accounts pay no interest, and the bank earns no interest on reserves. (We ignore the small amounts of interest on checking deposits and reserves that exist in reality.) During 2021, Melvin's Bank earns $5 from OBS activities, such as letters of credit. Finally, the bank has $6 in costs, such as salaries for its employees.

Based on these assumptions, **Table 9.2** presents Melvin's income statement. The statement divides Melvin's revenue into two parts: interest income and noninterest income. As interest income, the bank earns 4 percent on its $30 in securities, yielding 4% ($30) = $1.20. It also earns 8 percent on $80 in loans, yielding 8% ($80) = $6.40. Adding these numbers, total interest income

TABLE 9.2 Income Statement for Melvin's Bank

For the year ended December 31, 2021

Interest Income		
Securities	4% ($30) = $1.20	
Loans	8% ($80) = $6.40	
Total		$7.60
Noninterest Income		$5.00
(letters of credit)		
TOTAL INCOME		$12.60
Interest Expense	4% ($50) = $2.00	
(savings accounts)		
Noninterest Expense		$6.00
(salaries, etc.)		
TOTAL EXPENSE		$8.00
PROFITS (Income − Expense)		$4.60

$$\text{ROA} = \frac{\text{profits}}{\text{assets}} = \frac{\$4.60}{\$120} = 3.8\%$$

$$\text{ROE} = \frac{\text{profits}}{\text{capital}} = \frac{\$4.60}{\$20} = 23\%$$

is $7.60. Noninterest income is $5.00, the bank's earnings from OBS activities. Total income is $12.60, the sum of interest and noninterest income.

The income statement also divides the bank's expenses into interest and noninterest components. The bank pays 4 percent interest on $50 in savings accounts: 4% ($50) = $2.00. This is the only interest expense, because checking accounts don't pay interest. The bank's noninterest expenses are $6.00 in salaries and other costs. Total expenses are $8.00.

Finally, Melvin's profits are total income minus total expenses. Profits are $12.60 − $8.00 = $4.60.

Profit Rates

Is $4.60 a high level of profits? Banks evaluate their profitability with two variables. One is the **return on assets (ROA)**. This is the ratio of a bank's profits to its assets:

$$\text{ROA} = \frac{\text{profits}}{\text{assets}}$$

Recall that Melvin's Bank has $120 in assets. Its ROA is $4.60/$120 = 3.8%.

The second measure of profitability is more important. The **return on equity (ROE)** is the ratio of a bank's profits to its capital:

$$\text{ROE} = \frac{\text{profits}}{\text{capital}}$$

The ROE for Melvin's bank is $4.60/$20 = 23%.

Return on assets (ROA) ratio of a bank's profits to its assets; ROA = profits/assets

Return on equity (ROE) ratio of a bank's profits to its capital; ROE = profits/capital

The ROE shows how much the bank earns for each dollar its stock-holders put in the business. Bank managers try to produce high ROEs, just as managers in other businesses try to produce high returns for stockholders.

9.4 THE EVOLVING PURSUIT OF PROFITS

Let's now turn from Melvin's Bank to the real world. Like Melvin, real banks make profits if their income exceeds their expenses. So they try to raise funds cheaply and find good sources of income.

How can banks achieve these goals? The answers to this question change over time. Over the last several decades, banks have transformed both their balance sheets and their OBS activities. The evolution of banking has been complex, but many changes have occurred for three basic reasons: competition from securities markets, deregulation, and financial innovation. **Table 9.3** summarizes the effects of these three forces on banks' assets, liabilities, and OBS activities. Some traditional sources of bank profits have disappeared, and new opportunities have arisen. Banks have had to adapt rapidly to remain profitable.

Before detailing the evolving banking environment, let's examine the bottom line. Despite challenges, in recent decades banks in the United States have *usually* produced healthy profits. **Figure 9.1** shows the average return on equity for commercial banks in each year from 1960 through 2009. Over most of this period, ROE ranged from 10 to 15 percent. The two exceptions, during the late 1980s and 2008–2009, mark major banking crises that depressed returns on equity. We return to these episodes at the end of the chapter.

Sources of Funds

From the liability side of the balance sheet, we see that banks raise funds in a variety of ways. Some liabilities are more costly than others because of differences in interest rates. Banks try to maximize their funding from low-cost sources.

TABLE 9.3 Changes in Commercial Banking: Causes and Effects

Competition from Securities Markets
Growth of mutual funds → banks lose deposits
Development of junk bonds and commercial paper → fewer C&I loans

Deregulation
Elimination of interest rate caps → banks compete with mutual funds, retain savings and time deposits
Repeal of Glass-Steagall → banks offer investment banking services

Financial Innovation
Credit scoring and securitization → more real estate loans
Development of derivatives → opportunities for speculation

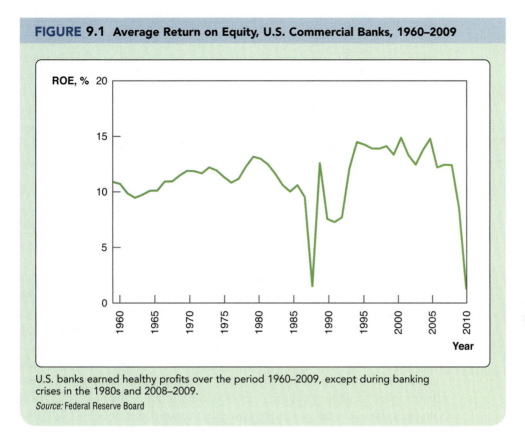

FIGURE 9.1 Average Return on Equity, U.S. Commercial Banks, 1960–2009

U.S. banks earned healthy profits over the period 1960–2009, except during banking crises in the 1980s and 2008–2009.

Source: Federal Reserve Board

Cheap and Expensive Funds The cheapest source of funds is checking deposits, which pay little or no interest. These deposits create noninterest expenses for processing checks and debit payments, but they are still inexpensive overall. Other low-cost funds include savings deposits and small time deposits. These deposits, held by small savers, typically pay interest rates 1 or 2 percent lower than Treasury securities with the same maturity. Savers accept low interest rates because they value the liquidity of bank deposits. In addition, some people simply don't know that higher interest rates are available from securities.

Banks' other funds come from large time deposits and borrowings, such as federal funds and repurchase agreements. These funds are relatively expensive, because they are provided by large, sophisticated institutions that shop for the highest interest rate. To borrow from these institutions, banks must offer interest rates close to Treasury rates.

Bankers call their inexpensive sources of funds **core deposits**. Core deposits are the sum of checking deposits, savings deposits, and small time deposits. Borrowings and large time deposits are called **purchased funds**.

A Two-Step Process Because of the varying costs, many banks raise funds in two steps. First, they try to maximize core deposits. They attract these deposits by establishing convenient branches, providing good service, and

Core deposits banks' inexpensive sources of funds (checking deposits, savings deposits, and small time deposits)

Purchased funds banks' expensive sources of funds (borrowings and large time deposits)

advertising. Second, banks choose their levels of purchased funds. Most of the time, they can choose these levels, because the supply of purchased funds is essentially unlimited. Except during a severe financial crisis, many institutions are happy to buy large CDs or lend to banks if the interest rates match Treasury rates.

Banks' choices of purchased funds depend on their opportunities for using these funds. For example, a bank might have a large number of attractive loan applications but lack enough core deposits to make all the loans. In this situation, the bank uses purchased funds to increase its lending.

Some History Banks' sources of funds have changed over time. **Figure 9.2** splits commercial-bank liabilities into three categories: checking deposits; other core deposits, meaning savings deposits and small CDs; and purchased funds, meaning large CDs and borrowings. The figure shows the share of each category in total liabilities for the period 1973–2009.

In 1973, checking deposits and other core deposits were banks' primary sources of funds. Purchased funds were only 25 percent of liabilities. Core deposits were plentiful, because small savers had few alternatives to putting their money in banks. High brokerage fees prevented them from buying securities.

This situation changed with the growth of mutual funds, especially money-market funds that hold Treasury bills and commercial paper. These funds are safe, and they paid high interest rates in the 1970s and 1980s. Bank deposits started to fall as money flowed into mutual funds.

FIGURE 9.2 U.S. Commercial Bank Liabilities, 1973–2009

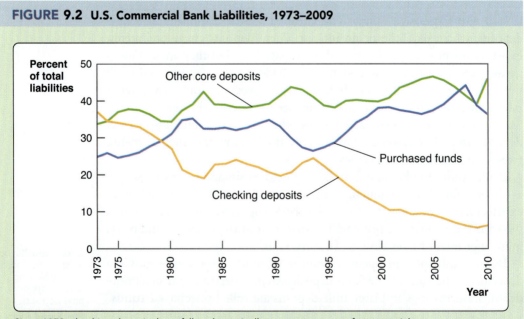

Since 1973, checking deposits have fallen dramatically as a percentage of commercial bank liabilities. They have been replaced by other core deposits (savings deposits and small time deposits) and by purchased funds (large time deposits and borrowings).

Source: Federal Reserve Board

Banks responded by raising interest rates on savings and time deposits. This response was made possible by deregulation: the Federal Reserve had set caps on deposit rates but eliminated most of them during the 1980s. Since then, interest rates for the "other core deposits" category have been high enough to attract small savers.

However, money has continued to flow out of checking accounts, which still pay little or no interest. Checking deposits fell from 37 percent of liabilities in 1973 to 6 percent in 2009. These losses have been partly replaced by other core deposits, but banks have also turned increasingly to purchased funds. Although purchased funds fell during the financial crisis as banks worried about one another's creditworthiness—from 42 percent of liabilities in 2007 to 36 in 2009—the decline is probably temporary.

To summarize, banks have seen a fall in their least expensive source of funds (checking deposits) and a rise in their most expensive source (purchased funds). So interest expenses have risen. To offset this trend, banks have sought higher income from loans and off-balance-sheet activities.

Seeking Income

Just as different liabilities have different costs, different assets produce different levels of income. The search for profits has led banks to shift their asset holdings over time. They have also expanded their off-balance-sheet activities.

Banks' primary assets are loans. For commercial banks, loans have been a steady 60–70 percent of assets since the 1960s. But banks have shifted their funds among different types of loans. For the period 1973–2009, **Figure 9.3** shows how three major types of lending—commercial, real estate, and consumer—have changed as percentages of total loans. Let's examine each category.

Commercial and Industrial (C&I) Loans Before the 1980s, the largest component of bank lending was *commercial and industrial loans*. These are loans to firms: long-term loans for investment and short-term loans for working capital. Figure 9.3 shows that C&I loans have declined in importance, falling from a peak of 40 percent of total loans in 1982 to 18 percent in 2009.

A major reason is the growth of bond markets. The junk-bond market, created in the late 1970s, allows more firms to bypass banks in raising funds. Commercial paper has also become common, allowing firms short-term as well as long-term borrowing in securities markets.

The C&I lending that remains has become relatively unprofitable for banks. Interest rates have been driven down by competition, both among banks and with securities markets. Companies that receive C&I loans are good at shopping around for low rates. For some banks, the motive for C&I lending may be to establish relationships with firms that will lead to more lucrative business, such as underwriting securities. According to the *Wall Street Journal*, banks act "like a bar that puts out free chips and then charges $8 a beer."[1] C&I loans are the chips, and underwriting is the beer.

---

[1] See Jathon Sapsford and Paul Beckett, "Loss Leader: Linking of Loans to Other Businesses Has Peril for Banks," *Wall Street Journal*, September 19, 2002, p. A1.

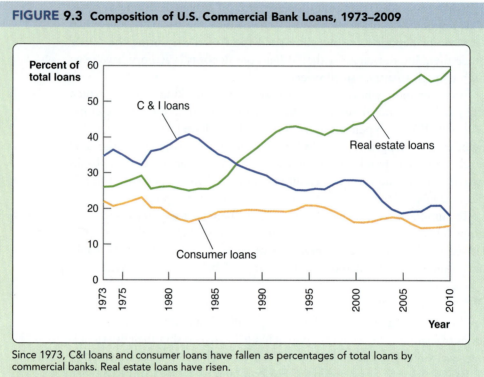

FIGURE 9.3 Composition of U.S. Commercial Bank Loans, 1973–2009

Since 1973, C&I loans and consumer loans have fallen as percentages of total loans by commercial banks. Real estate loans have risen.

Source: Federal Reserve Board

Real Estate Loans This category includes both home mortgages and commercial real estate loans for the construction of offices, factories, and stores. Real estate grew from 26 percent of total loans in 1973 to 59 percent in 2009 and dipped only slightly in 2007–2008 during the financial crisis.

Real estate loans are risky. In the 1980s, banks suffered large losses when commercial real estate developers failed and defaulted on loans. In the most recent financial crisis, defaults on home mortgages were costly. Yet banks have continued to expand their real estate lending because they need to replace dwindling C&I lending. Real estate loans are also attractive because they carry higher interest rates than C&I loans, and banks need higher interest income to offset rising interest expenses.

Real estate lending has also been spurred by financial innovations that reduce banks' risk. One tool is securitization, which shifts risk from banks to the holders of mortgage-backed securities. Another is credit scoring, which helps banks screen out the riskiest mortgage applicants. Because of this credit rationing, losses on real estate loans during the financial crisis were lower for banks than for finance companies that lent to subprime borrowers.

▶ Section 8.3 explains securitization and Section 8.4 discusses subprime lending.

Consumer Loans Overall, consumer lending fell from 22 percent of loans in 1973 to 15 percent in 2009. Within this category, traditional personal loans declined rapidly, but credit card lending rose. You take out a bank loan any time you carry a balance on a credit card issued by a bank.

Banks earn high profits from issuing credit cards. The cards produce high interest income plus fees from both cardholders and merchants who accept the cards. The profitability of credit cards leads banks to market them aggressively. In 2009, Americans received 2 billion credit card offers in the mail despite a high default rate on credit card debt during the financial crisis.

Off-Balance-Sheet Activities OBS activities are a growing part of the banking business, producing higher noninterest income. Once again, as summarized in Table 9.3, the sources of change include deregulation and financial innovation. The repeal of the Glass-Steagall Act allowed commercial banks to offer investment-banking services. Growing markets for derivatives have created opportunities for banks to speculate on these securities.

Like most businesses, banks search constantly for new ways to earn profits. The next case study discusses recent strategies that have generated controversy.

CASE STUDY

Fees

We've seen that noninterest income is a rising share of bank profits. This trend is partly the result of OBS activities such as underwriting. But it also reflects a new twist on the traditional activities of deposit taking and lending. Banks have boosted their income by raising a variety of fees charged to depositors and borrowers. Examples include fees for using ATMs, monthly service fees on checking accounts, and fees for stopping payment on a check. Two types of fees have produced especially large revenues: overdraft fees and credit card fees. Each has generated complaints about unfair practices and new legislation to restrict banks' behavior.

Overdraft Programs In the late 1990s, many banks started granting "courtesy overdrafts." Under this policy, a bank honors a customer's check or an electronic withdrawal such as a loan payment even if his account has insufficient funds. The account balance is allowed to become negative and the bank charges a fee, which averaged $34 per overdraft in 2009. Then the customer has a grace period, typically a week or two, to bring his balance above zero. If he doesn't, the bank adds more fees.

Around 2004, many banks extended courtesy overdrafts to debit card purchases and ATM withdrawals. Before 2004, someone who swiped her card at a store had her purchase denied if her account balance didn't cover it. With a courtesy overdraft, the purchase may be approved, with the bank charging the same overdraft fee as for a check.

Banks say overdrafts save depositors from the costs and embarrassment of bouncing checks or being turned down for debit purchases. Yet consumer groups argue that courtesy overdrafts amount to short-term loans with exorbitant interest rates, because the amounts overdrawn are often small compared to fees. A 2007 study by the Center for Responsible Lending (CRL) estimated that the average person paid $0.86 in fees for

▶ We met the CRL when we discussed payday lending in Section 8.3.

every dollar overdrawn with a check and $2.17 for every dollar overdrawn with a debit card.

The CRL reports a horror story about a college student identified only as G.C. On March 30, 2007, G.C. had $3.49 in his bank account and used his debit card for a $4.58 purchase. The bank covered the difference of $1.09 but charged a $35 fee. Over the next two days, G.C. used his card six more times to buy coffee and school supplies. These purchases ranged from $1.70 to $3.01, and the bank charged $35 each time. Overall, between March 30 and April 2, G.C. spent $13.06 with his debit card and ran up $245 in fees.

In 2009, banks earned $24 billion in overdrafts fees. These earnings are endangered, however, by a Federal Reserve regulation promulgated in 2010. In the past, many banks enrolled customers in overdraft programs automatically when they established accounts. Under the new regulation, banks must ask customers' permission to allow overdrafts and charge fees on ATM and debit card transactions. Bank of America and Citibank responded to the regulation by creating new versions of overdraft programs with lower fees. The new regulation does not apply to overdrafts on checks and automatic electronic payments, so fees for these overdrafts may remain high.

Credit Card Fees Since the 1990s, banks have steadily raised several types of credit card fees. The average fee for a late payment or for exceeding a credit limit rose from $13 in 1994 to $39 in 2009. Fees have also risen for cash advances, balance transfers, overseas purchases, and inactive accounts. In addition to flat fees, late payments and high balances can trigger interest rate increases. At some banks, interest rates can rise to *penalty rates* of 30 percent or more.

Like overdraft programs, credit card fees have received bad publicity. In 2007, a U.S. Senate hearing on card fees featured testimony from Wesley Wannemacher, an Ohio man who used a Chase credit card for $3200 in purchases (most related to his wedding) in 2001 and 2002. These purchases exceeded Wannemacher's credit limit of $3000, so Chase raised his interest rate to 32 percent. It also charged him 47 overlimit fees between 2002 and 2007. During that period, Wannemacher made card payments totaling $6300, almost twice his original debt, but was still left with a $4400 balance.

▶ The Credit CARD Act includes another provision that may be relevant to you. If you are under 21, you can get a credit card only if you provide evidence of your ability to make payments or if someone over 21 cosigns your account agreement.

In 2009, Congress enacted the Credit Card Accountability, Responsibility, and Disclosure (or Credit CARD) Act, which imposes a long list of restrictions on card issuers. Overlimit and late fees are limited to $25 in most instances. Customers must agree to accept overlimit fees, and card issuers must give them at least 21 days to pay their bills before charging late fees (the previous standard was 14 days). If lateness triggers a penalty rate, the interest rate must return to its previous level if a customer's payments are on time for the next six months.

Critics of credit card issuers say the 2009 act does not go far enough, because it does not restrict the level of penalty interest rates. What's more,

banks have recently increased fees not covered by the act; for example, the typical fee for transferring a balance from another credit card has risen from 3 percent to 4 percent.[*]

The Dodd-Frank Act of 2010 created a Consumer Financial Protection Bureau within the Federal Reserve. This new agency will monitor credit card fees and interest rates and has the authority to impose new restrictions. We will surely see debates about credit card regulation in the coming years.

[*]For more on the Credit CARD Act, see The Pew Health Group, "Two Steps Forward: After the Credit CARD Act," July 2010, available at www.pewtrusts.org/creditcards

9.5 MANAGING RISK

Banking is a risky business. Banks' loans and OBS activities usually produce profits, but they can produce large losses if things go wrong. A key task for bankers is to identify risks and take steps to reduce them. This job is complicated, because banks face many kinds of risk. Major categories include liquidity risk, credit risk, interest rate risk, market risk, and economic risk. Let's discuss each category and how banks address it.

Liquidity Risk

Banks hold reserves to be ready for withdrawals. They also hold liquid securities that they can turn quickly into reserves. However, a bank's liquid assets usually total to much less than deposits in the bank. If depositors want to withdraw large amounts, the bank may not have enough reserves and securities to meet this demand. This is **liquidity risk**.

If withdrawals exceed a bank's liquid assets, it can fall back on illiquid assets—its loans. It can sell loans to other financial institutions, giving up future payments on the loans in return for reserves. These extra reserves allow the bank to satisfy its customers' demand for withdrawals.

However, by definition an illiquid asset is hard to sell quickly. We've seen that banks sometimes sell loans profitably; for example, they sell mortgages to Fannie Mae and Freddie Mac. However, many types of loans are difficult to sell. To find buyers quickly, a bank may have to accept low prices—less than the loans are really worth. The bank loses money on the deals. Bankers say the loans are sold at *fire-sale prices*.

The illiquidity of loans reflects the basic problem of asymmetric information. A bank gathers information about its borrowers, so it has a good idea of the default risk for its loans. Other banks, which have not screened the borrowers, may be uncertain of this risk. Because of this uncertainty, they will not pay much for the loans. The seller must accept fire-sale prices, even if it knows that default risk is low.

An Example To illustrate liquidity risk, let's return to Melvin's Bank. We assume the bank starts with the balance sheet shown in **Table 9.4A**. Notice that total deposits are $100 and liquid assets (reserves plus securities) are only $40.

> **Liquidity risk** the risk that withdrawals from a bank will exceed its liquid assets

▶ The metaphor behind the term *fire sale* is a company whose warehouse has burned down: it must quickly unload any salable goods that remain for whatever prices it can get.

TABLE 9.4 Liquidity Risk at Melvin's Bank

(A) Initial Balance Sheet				(B) Balance Sheet After $50 Withdrawal			
Assets		**Liabilities and Net Worth**		**Assets**		**Liabilities and Net Worth**	
Reserves	10	Checking Deposits	50	Reserves	0	Checking Deposits	50
Securities	30	Nontransaction Deposits	50	Securities	0	Nontransaction Deposits	0
Loans	80	Net Worth	20	Loans	60	Net Worth	10
TOTAL	120	TOTAL	120	TOTAL	60	TOTAL	60

Suppose that Britt, the bank's depositor, decides to get married. He withdraws the entire $50 in his savings account to buy a ring. This withdrawal causes a crisis. The bank uses its $40 in liquid assets to pay Britt, but it is still $10 short. To raise this amount, it must sell loans. A competitor, Gertrude's Bank, agrees to buy loans, but only at a fire-sale price: Gertrude will pay 50 cents for each dollar of loans. So Melvin's Bank must sell $20 of loans to raise $10.

Table 9.4B shows Melvin's balance sheet after these transactions. Liabilities fall by $50, the amount of Britt's withdrawal. On the asset side, liquid assets fall by $40 and loans fall by $20, the amount sold to Gertrude. So total assets fall by $60. The bank's capital—assets minus liabilities—falls from $20 to $10. Because of its liquidity crisis, Melvin's Bank has lost half the money that its stockholders put in.

The Liquidity–Profit Trade-Off There is a simple way to reduce liquidity risk: hold more liquid assets. The more a bank holds, the less likely it will be to run out when depositors make withdrawals.

Table 9.5 illustrates this point. In this example, Melvin's Bank starts with a high level of liquidity. On its initial balance sheet, shown in Table 9.5A, the bank holds $20 more in securities than in Table 9.4A and $20 less in loans. Once again Britt withdraws $50, but this time the bank has enough liquid assets to cover the withdrawal. Let's say it uses $45 of securities and $5 of reserves, producing the balance sheet in Table 9.5B. The bank avoids a fire sale of loans, so its capital does not fall.

We've previously seen a disadvantage to liquid assets: they pay less interest than loans. Therefore, if high liquidity is not needed, it reduces profits.

TABLE 9.5 The Benefit of Liquidity

(A) Melvin's Initial Balance Sheet				(B) Melvin's Balance Sheet After $50 Withdrawal			
Assets		**Liabilities and Net Worth**		**Assets**		**Liabilities and Net Worth**	
Reserves	10	Checking Deposits	50	Reserves	5	Checking Deposits	50
Securities	50	Nontransaction Deposits	50	Securities	5	Nontransaction Deposits	0
Loans	60	Net Worth	20	Loans	60	Net Worth	20
TOTAL	120	TOTAL	120	TOTAL	70	TOTAL	70

This happens if depositors do not make large withdrawals. In our example, Melvin's Bank increases liquidity by replacing $20 in loans with securities. This shift reduces the bank's income by $20 times the difference in interest rates. If loans pay 8 percent and securities pay 4 percent, then the bank loses $20 \times (8\% - 4\%) = \$0.80$.

So a bank faces a balancing act when it chooses its level of liquidity. It wants to hold enough liquid assets to avoid running out, but it doesn't want to hold too many, because profits would suffer.

Short-Term Borrowing Banks try to ease the trade-off we've discussed. They want to minimize liquid assets but still avoid running out. One tool for reconciling these goals is borrowing. When a bank needs funds to meet withdrawals, it can borrow rather than sell loans at fire-sale prices. As we've discussed, banks can borrow from a variety of sources, including corporations and the Federal Reserve, but most short-term borrowing is from other banks. If one bank is low on liquidity, it borrows federal funds from another bank with more liquidity than it needs.

▶ *Federal funds* are loans from one bank to another, not loans from the Federal Reserve. In the past, banks often borrowed federal funds to satisfy reserve requirements set by the Fed, hence the terminology.

This process is quick and easy. Two banks agree on a loan, and the lender contacts its district Federal Reserve Bank electronically. It tells the Fed to debit its account there and move the funds to the borrower's account. Some loans are made for a single day: the transfer of funds is reversed the next day, with a small amount of interest added on. Other loans are "continuing," meaning the borrower bank keeps the funds until it or the lender bank chooses to end the loan.

Table 9.6 shows how Melvin's Bank can use the federal funds market. The bank starts with a low level of liquidity in Table 9.6A: it has only $40 in reserves and securities. Once again Britt withdraws $50, and a liquidity crisis looms.

Fortunately, Gertrude's Bank has just received a large deposit, raising its reserves. This bank has more reserves than it needs, so it is happy to lend some out and earn interest. Melvin borrows $50 of federal funds from Gertrude and uses the money to pay Britt. On Melvin's balance sheet, deposits fall by $50 and borrowings rise by $50 in Table 9.6B. The bank replaces one liability with another. Its assets and capital don't change.

TABLE 9.6 Using the Federal Funds Market

(A) Melvin's Initial Balance Sheet				(B) Melvin's Balance Sheet After $50 Withdrawal			
Assets		**Liabilities and Net Worth**		**Assets**		**Liabilities and Net Worth**	
Reserves	10	Checking Deposits	50	Reserves	10	Checking Deposits	50
Securities	30	Nontransaction Deposits	50	Securities	30	Nontransaction Deposits	0
Loans	80	Net Worth	20	Loans	80	Borrowings	50
						Net Worth	20
TOTAL	120	TOTAL	120	TOTAL	120	TOTAL	120

Because of the federal funds market, banks can usually get liquidity when they need it. The system is not foolproof, however. It can break down if the economy experiences a banking panic, with withdrawals from many banks at once. We discuss this scenario in Chapter 10.

Credit Risk

Credit risk is another name for *default risk*, the risk that borrowers won't repay their loans. Banks reduce this risk by screening borrowers, demanding collateral, and putting covenants in loan contracts. Nonetheless, borrowers sometimes default.

If a borrower defaults on a bank loan, the loan ceases to be an asset for the bank. A loan is worthless if it is not going to produce payments. The bank must *write off* the loan: it removes the loan from its balance sheet. This action reduces the bank's total assets, so its net worth falls. The bank's stockholders have lost money.

Table 9.7 gives an example. Initially, Melvin's Bank has $80 in loans (Table 9.7A), but one of its borrowers defaults on a loan of $5. The bank writes off this loan, reducing its loans to $75. As shown in Table 9.7B, total assets on the bank's balance sheet fall by $5. Liabilities don't change, so the $5 fall in assets causes a $5 fall in net worth.

Banks seek to reduce their credit risk. One way is to shift this risk to other institutions through loan sales. When a bank sells a loan, the loan is removed from its balance sheet. If the borrower defaults, the loss falls on the buyer of the loan.

If a bank must sell loans quickly, it may have to accept fire-sale prices. However, in nonemergency situations, banks can get attractive prices for some kinds of loans. This happens when loan buyers are relatively well informed about default risk. For example, banks can sell mortgages because borrowers' incomes and credit scores provide information about default risk. Banks earn profits by making mortgage loans and selling them, and they avoid credit risk.

One version of a loan sale is *syndication*. Before making a loan, a bank agrees to sell parts of the loan to a group of other financial institutions called a *syndicate*. These institutions may include pension funds and investment banks as well as other commercial banks. The original lender keeps

TABLE 9.7 **Credit Risk at Melvin's Bank**

(A) Initial Balance Sheet				(B) Balance Sheet After Loan Defaults			
Assets		**Liabilities and Net Worth**		**Assets**		**Liabilities and Net Worth**	
Reserves	10	Checking Deposits	50	Reserves	10	Checking Deposits	50
Securities	30	Nontransaction Deposits	50	Securities	30	Nontransaction Deposits	50
Loans	80	Net Worth	20	Loans	75	Net Worth	15
TOTAL	120	TOTAL	120	TOTAL	115	TOTAL	115

only a fraction of the loan on its balance sheet. Syndication is common for very large loans, because no single bank wants to take on all the credit risk. For example, companies often use syndicated loans to finance acquisitions of other companies.

Interest Rate Risk

Banks' profits are affected by short-term interest rates in financial markets, such as the Treasury bill rate. Increases in interest rates tend to reduce profits, and decreases raise profits. The resulting instability in profits is called **interest rate risk**.

The explanation for interest rate risk involves the maturities of banks' assets and liabilities. Most liabilities have short maturities, meaning funds are not committed to the bank for long. Checking and savings deposits have zero maturities: they can be withdrawn at any moment. Time deposits typically mature after a year or two. Most borrowing by banks is short-term; for example, federal funds are usually borrowed for one day at a time.

Because of these short maturities, interest rates on bank liabilities must compete with rates on securities. Suppose the Treasury bill rate rises. Rates on banks' purchased funds (borrowings and large CDs) adjust immediately. Rates on core deposits move more slowly, but they must rise before long or depositors will take their money elsewhere. Bankers say their liabilities are *rate sensitive*.

In contrast, bank assets typically have long maturities. Many business loans have terms of 10 years. Traditional home mortgages have 30-year terms. If the T-bill rate rises, banks can charge higher rates on future loans. But the loans they hold currently have lower rates locked in for long periods. These loans are *not* rate sensitive.

To summarize, higher short-term interest rates raise the rates that banks pay on liabilities and have less effect on rates received on assets. So interest expense rises by more than interest income, and bank profits fall.

An Example Table 9.8 illustrates interest rate risk at Melvin's Bank. The column headed "Initial Statement" repeats Table 9.2 on page 261, which assumes interest rates of 4 percent on T-bills, 4 percent on savings deposits, and 8 percent on loans. These interest rates imply profits of $4.60 and a return on equity of 23 percent.

The right-hand column shows how the income statement changes if the T-bill rate rises to 7 percent. We assume that savings deposits are rate sensitive: their rate also rises to 7 percent. In contrast, the interest rate on loans stays at its previous level of 8 percent.

To see how profits change, notice first that the bank owns $30 in T-bills. With a 4-percent interest rate, total earnings on T-bills were 4% ($30) = $1.20. With an interest rate of 7 percent, these earnings are 7% ($30) = $2.10. The bank's earnings on loans do not change. Total interest income rises by the increase in earnings on T-bills: $2.10 − $1.20 = $0.90.

The bank has $50 in savings deposits, with interest rates that also rise from 4 percent to 7 percent. At 4 percent, total payments on savings

Interest rate risk instability in bank profits caused by fluctuations in short-term interest rates

TABLE 9.8 Interest Rate Risk

Income Statement for Melvin's Bank
For the year ended December 31, 2021

	Initial Statement	Statement After a Rise in Short-Term Interest Rate
Interest Income		
Securities	4% ($30) = $1.20	7% ($30) = $2.10
Loans	8% ($80) = $6.40	8% ($80) = $6.40
Total	$7.60	$8.50
Noninterest Income (letters of credit)	$5.00	$5.00
TOTAL INCOME	$12.60	$13.50
Interest Expense (savings accounts)	4% ($50) = $2.00	7% ($50) = $3.50
Noninterest Expense (salaries, etc.)	$6.00	$6.00
TOTAL EXPENSE	$8.00	$9.50
PROFITS (Income − Expense)	$4.60	$4.00
$\text{ROA} = \dfrac{\text{profits}}{\text{assets}}$	$\dfrac{\$4.60}{\$120} = 3.8\%$	$\dfrac{\$4.00}{\$120} = 3.3\%$
$\text{ROE} = \dfrac{\text{profits}}{\text{capital}}$	$\dfrac{\$4.60}{\$20} = 23\%$	$\dfrac{\$4.00}{\$20} = 20\%$

Note: Highlighted items are affected by the rise in short-term interest rates.

deposits were 4% ($50) = $2.00; at 7 percent, these payments are 7% ($50) = $3.50. The bank's interest expense rises by $3.50 − $2.00 = $1.50.

To summarize, the bank's interest income rises by $0.90 but its interest expense rises by $1.50, for a net loss of $0.60. The bank's total profits fall from $4.60 to $4.00 and its ROE falls from 23 percent to 20 percent.

Measuring Interest Rate Risk Banks want stable profits, so they try to contain interest rate risk. The first step is to measure this risk. One measure is the **rate–sensitivity gap**, which captures the mismatch between a bank's assets and liabilities:

Rate-sensitivity gap
difference between rate-sensitive assets and rate-sensitive liabilities

> rate–sensitivity gap = rate–sensitive assets − rate–sensitive liabilities

The rate-sensitivity gap is usually negative. In Table 9.8, rate-sensitive assets (T-bills) are $30 and rate-sensitive liabilities (savings deposits) are $50. The rate-sensitivity gap is −$20.

When interest rates change, the effect on a bank's profits is proportional to its rate-sensitivity gap. The more negative the gap, the more the bank loses if rates rise. Specifically,

$$\text{change in profits} = (\text{change in short–term interest rate}) \times (\text{rate–sensitivity gap}) \tag{9.1}$$

In our example, the short-term interest rate rises from 4 percent to 7 percent, so the change in the rate is 3 percent. With a rate-sensitivity gap of −$20, the change in profits is 3% (−$20) = −$0.60. This calculation confirms Table 9.8, which shows the same decrease in profits, from $4.60 to $4.00.

Reducing Risk Banks use several techniques to reduce interest rate risk: loan sales, floating interest rates, and derivatives.

Loan Sales We saw earlier that loan sales reduce credit risk. They can also reduce interest rate risk. If a bank sells long-term loans, it has fewer assets with fixed interest rates, so it can acquire more rate-sensitive assets. The rate-sensitivity gap moves closer to zero, making profits more stable.

Floating Rates A bank can also use **floating interest rates** for its long-term loans. A floating rate is tied to a short-term interest rate. For example, the rate on a 10-year business loan might be the T-bill rate plus 2 percent. If T-bills pay 4 percent, the bank receives 6 percent on the loan. If the T-bill rate rises to 7 percent, the loan rate rises to 9 percent.

> **Floating interest rate** interest rate on a long-term loan that is tied to a short-term rate

Floating rates turn long-term loans into interest-sensitive assets. The loans themselves are committed for long periods, but the interest rates respond to short-term rates. Like loan sales, floating rates push a bank's rate-sensitivity gap toward zero.

Today, most C&I loans in the United States have floating rates. At times, many mortgages have had floating rates, as we discuss in the next case study.

Derivatives Finally, banks can hedge interest rate risk with derivatives. For example, a bank can sell futures contracts for Treasury bonds, a transaction that yields profits if bond prices fall. Bond prices fall when interest rates rise, so higher rates produce profits for the bank. These profits offset the loss arising from the rate-sensitivity gap.

CASE STUDY

The Rise and Decline of Adjustable-Rate Mortgages

Interest rates on traditional home mortgages are fixed for the term of the loan, typically 30 years. These fixed-rate assets contribute to banks' rate-sensitivity gaps and overall interest rate risk. Since the 1970s, banks have reduced this risk by offering mortgages with floating rates, known as *ARMs* (for *adjustable-rate mortgages*). A basic ARM, like other floating-rate loans, has an interest rate tied to a short-term rate. Banks also offer "hybrid" mortgages with rates that are fixed for an initial period of 3 or 5 years and then float.

ARMs have enjoyed widespread popularity among borrowers. The initial interest rate usually is less than the rate on a traditional mortgage. That makes it easier for people to get mortgages because approval depends on the ratio of initial mortgage payments to a borrower's income. In addition, the chances that the rate on an ARM will stay low are good. Over their history, ARMs have been less expensive than fixed-rate mortgages in most years.

ARMs *are* risky for borrowers: a rise in short-term interest rates pushes the interest rates and payment on ARMs above those on traditional mortgages. Yet the benefits of ARMs have led many borrowers to accept the risks. Between 1987 and 2007, the percentage of new prime mortgages with adjustable rates fluctuated between 11 percent and 62 percent. ARMs were most popular at times when short-term interest rates, and hence initial ARM rates, were especially low compared with long-term rates.

During the financial crisis of 2007–2009, ARMs plummeted in popularity. Short-term interest rates had risen rapidly over 2004–2006, raising payments on ARMs. When house prices started falling in 2006, mortgage defaults rose and were concentrated in ARMs. In 2007, 3 percent of prime borrowers with ARMs were behind on their payments, compared to 1 percent of prime borrowers with fixed rates.

To compensate for greater default risk, banks raised interest rates on ARMs. In 2009, initial rates were about the same as fixed mortgage rates, eliminating much of the ARMs' appeal to borrowers. In addition, the mortgage crisis made borrowers more cautious and less willing to take on the risk of ARMs. In 2009, only 3 percent of new prime mortgages were ARMs.

Market and Economic Risk

Market risk risk arising from fluctuations in asset prices

Banks face two more categories of risk: *market risk* and *economic risk*. **Market risk** arises from fluctuations in asset prices. Price decreases can create large losses on bank assets, such as the losses on mortgage-backed securities during the financial crisis. Large banks also face risk because they use derivatives to bet on the prices of stocks, bonds, and currencies. This speculation can produce either large profits or large losses.

Economic risk risk arising from fluctuations in the economy's aggregate output

Economic risk arises from fluctuations in the economy's aggregate output. A temporary fall in output—a recession—reduces banks' profits for various reasons. For example, if firms cut investment, they borrow less. This reduces banks' opportunities for profitable loans. A recession also hurts banks' off-balance-sheet activities. The number of transactions among companies decreases, so banks sell fewer letters of credit. Fewer companies issue securities, reducing large banks' income from underwriting.

Interactions Among Risks

Managing risk is a complex task. Banks face many risks, and different risks interact with one another. For example, a rise in interest rates is likely to reduce asset prices, so banks are hurt by interest rate risk and market risk at the same time. A recession can push down asset prices and increase loan defaults, causing losses from economic risk, market risk, and credit risk.

Complicating matters further, strategies for reducing one kind of risk may increase another kind. For example, we've seen that loan sales reduce interest rate risk and credit risk. But this practice also reduces interest income, forcing banks to rely more heavily on income from OBS activities. These activities carry market risk and economic risk.

The interactions among risks mean that banks need to manage all of them together. Analysts at a bank examine its entire business and look for excessive risk. They do so largely by examining scenarios for the economy, such as a recession or a rise in interest rates. The analysts judge the likelihood that these events will occur and estimate the bank's losses given its current balance sheet and OBS activities. If plausible scenarios produce large losses, the bank tries to adjust its business to reduce potential risk.

Risk management can never be perfect, because unanticipated events can occur. Before the most recent financial crisis, analysts at banks, like many others, made assumptions based on historical experience that a large, nationwide fall in house prices was highly unlikely. As a result, they did not guard themselves against such risk and suffered large losses when house prices did fall over 2006–2009.

9.6 INSOLVENCY

We've seen that banks face many risks, from loan defaults to rising interest rates, from recessions to full-blown financial crises. A bank loses money when events like these occur. If the losses are large enough, the bank can face **insolvency**: its total assets fall below its liabilities, and its net worth becomes negative.

An insolvent bank cannot stay in business. With negative net worth, it cannot pay off all its deposits and borrowings. Government regulators step in and force the bank to close.

Insolvency hurts a bank's stockholders, whose stock becomes worthless, because the bank will have no future earnings. Bank managers and employees also suffer because they lose their jobs, so managers seek to avoid insolvency.

Insolvency liabilities exceed assets, producing negative net worth

▶ Chapter 10 discusses the process of closing insolvent banks.

An Example

Insolvency can occur if a bank suffers large losses for any reason. Let's consider an example in which insolvency is caused by loan defaults.

In **Table 9.9A**, Melvin's Bank starts with net worth of $20. It has $80 in loans. Then disaster strikes: borrowers default on $30 of the loans (not just $5, as in our earlier example of credit risk). When the bank writes off the bad loans, its net worth falls to −$10, as shown in **Table 9.9B**, and it

TABLE 9.9 Insolvency

(A) Melvin's Initial Balance Sheet				(B) Balance Sheet After Loan Defaults			
Assets		**Liabilities and Net Worth**		**Assets**		**Liabilities and Net Worth**	
Reserves	10	Checking Deposits	50	Reserves	10	Checking Deposits	50
Securities	30	Nontransaction Deposits	50	Securities	30	Nontransaction Deposits	50
Loans	80	Net Worth	20	Loans	50	Net Worth	−10
TOTAL	120	TOTAL	120	TOTAL	90	TOTAL	90

becomes insolvent. It owes depositors $100, and it has only $90 in assets to pay them back. The story of Melvin's Bank ends sadly as the government shuts it down.

The Equity Ratio

Banks can reduce the risk of insolvency by holding more capital. Suppose Melvin's Bank had started with $50 in capital rather than $20. Then its capital would have stayed positive even after it lost $30 to bad loans. Higher capital means a deeper cushion against losses.

To be more precise, a bank's insolvency risk depends on its level of capital relative to its assets. This is measured by its **equity ratio (ER)**:

Equity ratio (ER) ratio of a bank's capital to its assets; ER = capital/assets

$$\text{equity ratio} = \frac{\text{capital}}{\text{assets}}$$

The equity ratio shows what percentage of assets a bank would have to lose to become insolvent. In Table 9.9, the initial equity ratio for Melvin's Bank is $20/$120 = 16.7%. The bank becomes insolvent because it loses 25 percent of its assets ($30/$120) but would have survived if its equity ratio were greater than 25 percent.

Holding capital constant, a higher level of assets reduces the equity ratio. The greater a bank's assets, the more it has to lose if things go wrong. It therefore faces greater insolvency risk. A bank can raise its equity ratio either by raising capital (the numerator) or by reducing assets (the denominator). The bank can raise capital by issuing new stock or by reducing dividends to stockholders. It can reduce assets by making fewer loans or purchasing fewer securities. Any of these actions reduces insolvency risk.

The Equity Ratio and the Return on Equity Raising the equity ratio also has a big disadvantage: it makes a bank less profitable. Recall that profitability is measured by the return on equity (ROE), which is the ratio of profits to capital. This variable falls when the equity ratio rises.

We can see this effect with a little algebra. We take the formula for ROE and divide both the numerator and denominator by assets:

$$\text{ROE} = \frac{\text{profits}}{\text{capital}} = \frac{\dfrac{\text{profits}}{\text{assets}}}{\dfrac{\text{capital}}{\text{assets}}}$$

In this formula, profits/assets is the return on assets (ROA). Capital/assets is the equity ratio. So we can simplify to

$$\text{ROE} = \frac{\text{ROA}}{\text{ER}} \tag{9.2}$$

The return on equity depends on the return on assets and the equity ratio. For a given ROA, raising the equity ratio reduces the ROE.

·To understand this effect, suppose a bank raises its equity ratio by issuing new stock and keeping its assets the same. With the same assets, the bank gets the same flow of profits—but now these profits are split among more stockholders. Each share of stock earns less.

To summarize, a bank faces a trade-off when it chooses its equity ratio. A higher ratio reduces insolvency risk but also reduces the return on equity. A bank would like a ratio that is high enough to make insolvency unlikely but low enough to produce good returns for its stockholders.

CASE STUDY

The Banking Crisis of the 1980s

Figure 9.4 shows the number of U.S. bank failures in each year from 1960 through 2009. In most of these years, fewer than 10 banks failed. The biggest exception is the 1980s, when failures grew rapidly, peaking at 534 in 1989. Some of the failed institutions were commercial banks, but the majority were savings and loan associations. The episode is often called the *S&L crisis*. Two of its causes were rising interest rates and loan defaults. Examining the episode yields a deeper understanding of interest rate risk and credit risk.

Rising Interest Rates Banks' rate-sensitivity gaps were highly negative in the 1980s, especially at S&Ls, where most liabilities were deposits with zero

FIGURE 9.4 Failures of U.S. Commercial Banks and Savings Institutions, 1960–2009

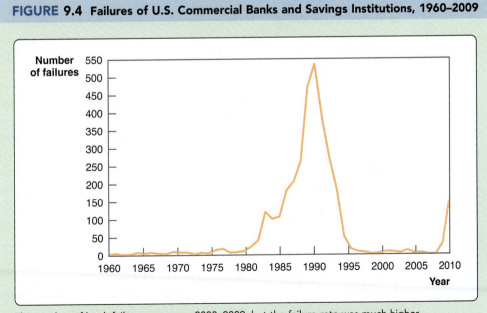

The number of bank failures rose over 2008–2009, but the failure rate was much higher during the S&L crisis of the 1980s.

Source: Federal Deposit Insurance Corporation

maturities and most assets were long-term, fixed-rate mortgages. Many of these loans had been made in the 1960s, when the level of interest rates was moderate. In 1965, the Treasury bill rate was about 4 percent and the 30-year mortgage rate was 6 percent.

Interest rates rose rapidly in the 1970s and early 1980s. Recall that the nominal interest rate is the sum of the real rate and inflation ($i = r + \pi$). For much of the 1970s, real rates were low, but inflation pushed up nominal rates. Then, at the end of the decade, the Fed raised real rates to fight inflation. It took time for inflation to respond, so both real rates *and* inflation were high in the early 80s. The nominal rate on T-bills peaked at 14 percent in 1981.

▶ Figure 3.5 shows nominal and real interest rates over time.

You can guess what happened from our earlier discussion of interest rate risk. Banks were forced to raise interest rates on deposits along with the T-bill rate. In the early 1980s, they paid higher rates on deposits than they received on many mortgages, so they suffered large losses.

The Commercial Real Estate Bust In the early 1980s, banks sharply raised their lending for commercial real estate projects, such as office buildings and shopping centers. This lending rose for several reasons:

- Real estate prices were high, spurring new construction. So there was a large demand for real estate loans.

- Banks were looking for new loan opportunities. They sought to replace the C&I loans they were losing as borrowers turned to bonds and commercial paper.

- Regulations changed. Traditionally, S&Ls specialized in home mortgages and were forbidden to lend for commercial real estate. Congress lifted this ban in 1980, so S&Ls joined commercial banks in lending to commercial real estate developers.

In retrospect, this lending was imprudent. Banks made the same basic mistake as subprime mortgage lenders two decades later: eager for business, they relaxed their loan standards. Banks approved loans for risky projects with low collateral. When the real estate industry experienced problems, many developers went bankrupt and defaulted on loans.

Several events triggered these defaults. Many occurred during the recession of 1981–82, which decreased the demand for real estate. More defaults occurred in 1986, when world oil prices fell, hurting the oil-producing economies of Texas and neighboring states. The final blow came at the end of the 1980s. Rapid building in the first part of the decade created an oversupply of commercial real estate. Developers had a hard time renting space, and property prices plummeted. Loan defaults mounted, pushing many banks into insolvency.

This analysis blames the S&L crisis on loan defaults and rising interest rates. Many economists cite a third cause: poor government regulation. We return to this point in Chapter 10, where we discuss bank regulation.

CASE STUDY

Banks' Profitability in the Financial Crisis of 2007–2009

Defaults on subprime mortgages triggered this financial crisis. Finance companies that specialized in subprime lending suffered huge losses, as did investment banks that held large quantities of securities backed by subprime mortgages. Largely because of government regulation, commercial banks and savings institutions had less exposure to these mortgages. They made few subprime loans and were not allowed to hold the riskiest mortgage-backed securities. These restrictions limited their losses from the bursting of the housing bubble and rising mortgage defaults.

Yet commercial banks and savings institutions hardly escaped unscathed. Figure 9.1 on p. 263 shows that commercial banks' return on equity plummeted in 2008–2009, and Figure 9.4 shows that bank failures rose. The financial crisis hurt commercial banks and savings institutions for a number of reasons:

- Rating agencies gave AAA ratings to some securities backed by subprime mortgages. Banks chose to hold these MBSs, and regulators let them, because the ratings implied safety. Losses ensued when the securities proved riskier than thought and their prices fell.

- Generally, banks are not allowed to hold corporate stock, but there was an exception: banks could hold stock in Fannie Mae and Freddie Mac, the government-sponsored mortgage agencies. When Fannie and Freddie almost failed in September 2008, a government rescue prevented them from defaulting on their bonds, but the value of their stock plummeted, and banks took their share of the losses.

- The wave of mortgage defaults eventually spread from subprime mortgages to the prime mortgages made by banks. Many borrowers found themselves "under water": the value of their houses fell below their mortgage debt. Eventually, some mortgage holders chose to escape the situation by walking away from their houses, even if they had sufficient income to make their mortgage payments.

- The fall in house prices caused a sharp drop in construction of new housing. Construction companies and land developers lost money, increasing defaults on bank loans to those companies.

- The recession caused financial problems for companies and individuals throughout the economy, raising defaults on C&I loans and consumer loans as well as real estate loans.

▶ A case study in Section 7.3 discusses the overrating of mortgage-backed securities. Section 8.3 discusses the rescues of Fannie Mae and Freddie Mac.

By summer 2010, the worst of the financial crisis was past, house prices appeared to be stabilizing, and extremely low short-term interest rates made it inexpensive for banks to raise funds. But the prospects for banks remained unclear as the economy remained weak and defaults rose on commercial real estate loans.

Online Case Study
An Update on Bank Profits and Bank Failures

Summary

9.1 Banks' Balance Sheets

- A bank's balance sheet shows its assets on the left side and its liabilities and net worth (equity or capital) on the right.

- The major liabilities (sources of funds) of commercial banks are checking deposits, nontransaction deposits, and borrowings. The major assets (uses of funds) are cash items (including reserves), securities, and loans.

9.2 Off-Balance-Sheet Activities

- In addition to holding assets and liabilities, banks engage in off-balance-sheet activities. OBS activities include lines of credit, letters of credit, asset management, derivatives trading, and investment banking services.

9.3 How Banks Make Profits

- A bank starts with capital from its owners and raises additional funds from deposits and borrowings. It uses these funds to acquire assets that produce interest income. It also earns noninterest income from OBS activities.

- A bank's income statement shows its interest and noninterest income, its interest and noninterest expenses, and its profits over some period, such as a year.

- Banks' profitability is measured by the return on assets (profits/assets) and the return on equity (profits/capital).

9.4 The Evolving Pursuit of Profits

- Core deposits include checking deposits, savings deposits, and small time deposits, all relatively inexpensive sources of funds. Purchased funds, which include large time deposits and borrowings, are more expensive.

- Banks seek to maximize core deposits through advertising and customer service. They choose their levels of purchased funds based on loan opportunities.

- Over time, banks' sources of funds have shifted away from checking deposits and toward purchased funds. These trends have raised banks' interest expenses.

- Commercial and industrial loans have fallen over time, while real estate loans and credit card loans have risen.

- Banks' off-balance-sheet activities have grown over time, raising the importance of noninterest income to profitability.

- Fees are a rising share of bank income. Criticism of overdraft fees and fees on credit cards have led to new regulations that restrict their use.

9.5 Managing Risk

- Liquidity risk is the danger that withdrawals will exhaust a bank's liquid assets, forcing a fire sale of loans. In choosing assets, banks face a trade-off between liquidity risk and profits. The federal funds market reduces liquidity risk.

- Banks reduce credit risk—the risk of loan defaults—through loan sales.

- interest rate risk arises from the maturity mismatch between bank liabilities, which are mainly short-term, and assets, which are mainly long-term. A rise in interest rates reduces bank profits. Banks reduce interest rate risk through loan sales, floating interest rates, and trades of derivatives.

- Adjustable rate mortgages were common from the 1970s until 2007, but their popularity waned during the financial crisis of 2007–2009.

- Changes in asset prices create market risk for banks, and fluctuations in the economy's aggregate output create economic risk.

9.6 Insolvency

- If a bank suffers large losses, its capital can become negative. The bank is insolvent and must shut down.

- The risk of insolvency depends on the equity ratio (capital/assets). A higher ER reduces risk but also reduces the return on equity.

- The S&L crisis of the 1980s, triggered by rising interest rates and defaults on commercial real estate loans, drove many banks into insolvency. The financial crisis of 2007–2009 reduced the profits of commercial banks and savings institutions through a number of channels, even though these institutions made few subprime mortgage loans.

Key Terms

balance sheet, p. 254

core deposits, p. 263

credit risk, p. 272

discount loan, p. 256

economic risk, p. 276

equity ratio (ER), p. 278

federal funds, p. 255

floating interest rate, p. 275

income statement, p. 260

insolvency, p. 277

interest rate risk, p. 273

letter of credit, p. 258

liabilities, p. 254

liquidity risk, p. 269

market risk, p. 276

net worth, p. 254

off-balance-sheet (OBS) activities, p. 257

purchased funds, p. 263

rate-sensitivity gap, p. 274

repurchase agreements (repos), p. 256

reserves, p. 256

return on assets (ROA), p. 261

return on equity (ROE), p. 261

vault cash, p. 256

Questions and Problems

1. Suppose Melvin's Bank starts with the balance sheet in Table 9.4A and the income statement in Table 9.2. Show how the balance sheet and income statement change in each of the following scenarios. Also calculate the new ROA, ROE, and rate-sensitivity gap.
   a. The bank issues $20 of new stock and uses the proceeds to make loans.
   b. Britt moves $25 from his savings account to his checking account.
   c. The bank is hired to manage the assets of a wealthy person, for which it is paid $10 a year.
   d. The bank lends $5 of reserves to another bank in the federal funds market. (Assume the federal funds rate is the same as the Treasury bill rate.)
   e. The bank replaces $10 of its loans with floating-rate loans, which pay the Treasury bill rate plus 2 percent.

2. Suppose again that Melvin's Bank starts with the balance sheet in Table 9.4A. Then the bank sells $10 of loans for $10 of cash.
   a. What is the immediate effect on the balance sheet?
   b. After the loan sale, what additional transactions is the bank likely to make? What will the balance sheet look like after these transactions?

3. Suppose Ashley's Finance Company raises most of its funds by issuing long-term bonds. It uses these funds for floating-rate loans.
   a. How does the company's rate-sensitivity gap differ from those of most banks?
   b. What deal could Ashley and Melvin make to reduce risk for both of their institutions?

4. Canada does not have an institution like Fannie Mae that securitizes mortgages. How do you think this fact affects the types of

mortgages offered by Canadian banks? (*Hint:* Think about interest rate risk.)

5. Robert Shiller of Yale University has suggested a variation on ARMs in which mortgage interest rates are tied to inflation, not to short-term interest rates. Discuss the pros and cons of this idea for banks and for borrowers.

6. Suppose the Federal Reserve raises short-term interest rates, an action that is likely to reduce aggregate output temporarily. Describe the various effects on the profits of commercial banks.

7. How does each of the following developments affect banks' desired equity ratios? Explain.

   a. An increase in OBS activities

   b. A shift from C&I lending to real estate lending

   c. A shift from fixed-rate to floating-rate loans

   d. An increase in securitization

8. As noted in Section 9.4, the Credit CARD Act of 2009 has made it more difficult for people under 21 to obtain credit cards. Do you think this policy helps or hurts young adults? Explain your view.

▶ Online and Data Questions
www.worthpublishers.com/ball

9. Examine a recent annual report for the bank where you have a checking account. (The bank's Web site is likely to have a link to its annual report.) Also examine the updated Table 9.1 and Figure 9.1 at the text Web site.

   a. How does your bank's composition of assets and liabilities differ from averages for U.S. commercial banks? What explains these differences?

   b. In recent years, how has your bank's return on equity differed from the U.S. average? What factors might explain the above- or below-average performance?

10. Do some research on adjustable rate mortgages. One source is Freddie Mac's Annual ARM Survey (the text Web site links to Freddie Mac's site, which contains the surveys). Since 2009, when ARMs were 3 percent of prime mortgages, has this percentage remained low or risen? What explains the answer?

11. Do some research on the Consumer Financial Protection Bureau, established in 2010 (the text Web site links to the bureau's site). What regulations on credit cards has the bureau created? Is it considering additional regulations on credit cards? How do existing and proposed regulations affect the fees and interest you pay if you are late paying a credit card bill, transfer a balance between cards, or take a cash advance?

10

Bank Regulation

AP/Wide World Photos

September 17, 2007: Customers of Northern Rock Bank line up to withdraw money from a branch in York, England, during a run on the bank.

Bank run sudden, large withdrawals by depositors who lose confidence in a bank

Federal and state governments regulate the U.S. banking industry heavily. The preceding chapters touch on regulations that require lending in low-income areas and limit the fees banks charge customers. This chapter focuses on the core purpose of bank regulation: to prevent bank failures. Over history, failures have caused devastating losses to bank depositors, the government, and the overall economy.

Regulators try to reduce two problems at the root of bank failures. One is the phenomenon of a **bank run**, in which depositors lose confidence in a bank and make sudden, large withdrawals. The federal government addresses this problem by insuring bank deposits. The second source of failure is a problem of moral hazard: owners and managers of banks may misuse the funds they are given by depositors.

To address moral hazard, federal and state governments restrict banking in many ways. Regulators decide who can open a bank, limit the types of assets that banks can hold, and set minimum levels of capital that banks must maintain. Government examiners visit banks regularly to review their activities. If regulators disapprove of a bank's practices, they can order changes or even force the bank to close.

This chapter examines the rationale for bank regulation and surveys current regulations in the United States. Commercial banks and thrift institutions that take deposits and make loans are the most heavily regulated financial institutions and are our focus in this chapter. Chapter 18 discusses the regulation of other financial institutions, such as investment banks, and of financial holding companies (FHCs) that own both commercial banks and other institutions.

10.1 BANK RUNS

In any industry, a firm can fail. It can lose money, run out of funds, and be forced out of business. Often, economists think this outcome is efficient. If a firm is not profitable, its resources should be freed up for more productive uses.

When it comes to banks, however, economists have a less benign view of failure. One reason is the occurrence of bank runs. A run can push a healthy bank into insolvency, causing it to fail for no good reason. Both the bank's owners and its depositors suffer needless losses.

How Bank Runs Happen

The risk of a bank run is an extreme form of liquidity risk, the risk that a bank will have trouble meeting demands for withdrawals. As discussed in Section 9.5, banks manage this risk by holding reserves and secondary reserves, such as Treasury bills. If they are short on reserves, they borrow federal funds from other banks. Normally these methods are sufficient to contain liquidity risk.

However, things are different when a bank experiences a run. A sudden surge in withdrawals overwhelms the bank. It runs out of liquid assets and cannot borrow enough to cover all of the withdrawals. The bank is forced to sell its loans at fire-sale prices, reducing its capital. If the bank loses enough, capital falls below zero: the run causes insolvency.

What causes runs? Some occur because a bank is insolvent even before the run: the bank does not have enough assets to pay off its liabilities and will likely close. In this situation, depositors fear they will lose their money. These fears are compounded by the first-come, first-served nature of deposit withdrawals. The first people to withdraw get their money back, while those who act slowly may find that no funds are left. Depositors rush to withdraw before it's too late, and a run occurs.

A run can also occur at a bank that is initially solvent. This happens if depositors lose confidence in the bank, which can happen suddenly and without good reason. Suppose someone starts a rumor that a bank has lost money and become insolvent. This rumor is totally false. However, depositors hear the rumor and worry that it might be true. Some decide to play it safe and withdraw their funds.

Seeing these withdrawals, other depositors begin to fear that a run is starting. They decide to get their money out before everyone else does. Suddenly, there are lots of withdrawals: a run *does* occur. Ultimately, the bank is forced into a fire sale of assets, its capital is driven below zero, and the bank fails.

You may recognize the phenomenon of self-fulfilling expectations at work here. We know that expectations can influence asset prices. If people expect stock prices to fall, then they sell stocks, causing prices to fall. Bank runs are the same kind of event: if people expect a run, then a run occurs. This can happen even if nothing is wrong at the bank before the run.

▶ Sections 3.4 and 3.5 describe how self-fulfilling expectations can produce bubbles and crashes in asset prices.

A Run on Melvin's Bank

Suppose Melvin's Bank has the balance sheet shown in **Table 10.1A.** The bank has a positive level of capital, or net worth. It also has enough reserves and Treasury bills to meet normal demands for withdrawals. There is no good reason for Melvin's Bank to go out of business.

Then a negative rumor about the bank starts circulating. Worried depositors decide to withdraw their funds. We'll assume they want to withdraw all the money in savings and checking accounts, a total of $100.

To pay depositors, Melvin's Bank first uses its reserves and Treasury bills, a total of $40. Then, with its liquid assets exhausted, the bank must quickly sell its loans. We'll assume this fire sale produces only 50 cents per dollar of loans. The bank sells its $80 in loans, receives $40, and gives this money to depositors. At this point, the bank has paid off a total of $80 in deposits.

Melvin's new balance sheet is shown in **Table 10.1B.** The bank now has no assets. It still has $20 in liabilities, as it paid off only $80 out of the $100 in deposits. (The table assumes the remaining deposits are split evenly between checking and savings accounts.) The bank is insolvent. It cannot pay the last $20 demanded by depositors, so it goes out of business.

This example assumes that Melvin's Bank *cannot* borrow federal funds to pay depositors, which, in this case, is a plausible assumption. Other banks see the run on Melvin's Bank and recognize that it threatens Melvin's solvency. They won't lend federal funds because the loan won't be repaid if Melvin is forced to close.

The run on Melvin's Bank hurts two groups of people. The first are the owners of the bank: they lose the $20 in capital that they had before the run. The second are the holders of the last $20 in deposits. When the bank closes, these deposits become worthless.

TABLE 10.1 A Run on Melvin's Bank

(A) Initial Balance Sheet				(B) Balance Sheet After Run			
Assets		**Liabilities and Net Worth**		**Assets**		**Liabilities and Net Worth**	
Reserves	10	Checking deposits	50	Reserves	0	Checking deposits	10
Securities	30	Savings deposits	50	Securities	0	Savings deposits	10
Loans	80	Net worth	20	Loans	0	Net worth	−20
TOTAL	120	TOTAL	120	TOTAL	0	TOTAL	0

Suspension of Payments

Suspension of payments
refusal by a bank to allow
withdrawals by depositors

A bank run often leads to a **suspension of payments**. Overwhelmed by the demand for withdrawals, a bank announces that it will not allow them. A depositor who shows up at the bank finds the doors closed.

Sometimes suspension of payments is a prelude to permanent closure of a bank, but often it is meant to be temporary. The bank hopes that suspension will stop the run that threatens its solvency. If this happens, the bank can reopen. Depositors leave their money in the bank, and it carries on business as before.

Suspension of payments can end a run in two ways. First, it can help change the self-fulfilling psychology of the run. While the bank is closed, depositors have a chance to calm down. They can check that the bank is solvent and there's no good reason to withdraw their money. Second, suspension gives the bank a chance to increase its liquid assets. It may be able to borrow from other banks. With a little time, it may find buyers that will pay what its loans are worth instead of fire-sale prices. With a high level of liquid assets, the bank can meet demands for withdrawals when it reopens.

In the United States, suspensions of payments were common in the nineteenth and early twentieth centuries. Banks facing runs suspended payments for periods of a few days to a few months and then reopened. Often these actions were not strictly legal, because depositors had the right to immediate withdrawals. However, bank regulators granted exceptions or simply ignored suspensions because they wanted banks to survive.

CASE STUDY

Bank Runs in Fiction and in Fact

Bank runs have produced many colorful stories. Let's discuss three examples, one fictional and two real.

A Disney Bank Run A run occurs in the classic Walt Disney movie *Mary Poppins*. It is caused by a family argument. The story begins when Mr. Banks takes his young son Michael to the bank where he works to deposit Michael's savings of tuppence (two pence).

Outside the bank, a woman is selling birdseed for tuppence a bag. Seeing her, Michael decides he would rather feed the birds than deposit his money. Mr. Banks rejects this foolish idea and gives Michael's tuppence to Mr. Dawes, the head of the bank. Michael becomes angry and starts struggling with Mr. Dawes, shouting, "Give me back my money!"

Bank customers see the commotion and fear the bank has become insolvent. They rush to withdraw their money, and a run is underway. The bank runs out of liquid assets and is forced to suspend payments.

Hollywood gives us a happy ending. The bank clears up the misunderstanding about Michael's tantrum and convinces depositors it is solvent. It reopens, and depositors leave their money in their accounts. Mr. Banks is initially fired for his role in the run, but he is soon rehired and promoted.

Guta Bank In the real world, bank runs often end less happily than in the movies. One example comes from Russia in 2004. A financial crisis in the late 1990s had caused many bank failures, leaving depositors nervous. They became more nervous in May 2004, when the Central Bank of Russia closed a small bank for financing criminal activities.

In announcing this closure, an official mentioned that other banks were under investigation. This prompted rumors about which banks might be closed, with lists circulating on the Internet.

Many rumors involved Guta Bank, Russia's twentieth largest, with $1 billion in assets. In retrospect, there is no evidence that Guta did anything wrong, and it was solvent. But the rumors spooked depositors. They withdrew $345 million in June, and Guta ran out of liquid assets. On July 5, customers couldn't get cash from Guta's ATMs. On July 6, the bank closed its doors, posting a notice that payments were suspended.

Initially, Guta hoped to reopen, like the bank in *Mary Poppins*, but it wasn't able to regain depositors' confidence. On July 9, Guta's owners sold it to a government-owned bank, Vneshtorgbank, for the token sum of 1 million rubles ($34,000). At that point, Guta's branches reopened, but as branches of Vneshtorgbank.

It's not known who started the rumors about Guta Bank. Journalists have speculated that the culprits were rival banks or government officials. They suggest the Russian government wanted to help the banks it owned, including Vneshtorgbank, take business from private banks like Guta. One piece of evidence: the Central Bank refused a plea from Guta for an emergency loan but approved a loan to Vneshtorgbank after it took over Guta.

Northern Rock Before September 2007, the United Kingdom had not experienced a bank run for 140 years (if we don't count *Mary Poppins*). Then suddenly, on September 14, long lines of worried depositors formed at branches of Northern Rock Bank (see the photo on p. 285). Depositors also jammed the banks' phone lines and crashed its Web site. Between September 14 and September 17, depositors managed to withdraw 2 billion pounds (roughly $4 billion) from Northern Rock.

Northern Rock Bank is headquartered in Northern England (hence the name), and it lends primarily for home mortgages. Before the run, Northern Rock was the fifth-largest mortgage lender in the United Kingdom and growing rapidly. The bank's lending far exceeded its core deposits, so it used purchased funds to finance much of the lending. A major source of funds was short-term loans from other banks (the equivalent of federal funds in the United States).

▶ See Section 9.4 to review the concepts of core deposits and purchased funds.

Northern Rock's problems began across the Atlantic, with the subprime mortgage crisis in the United States. In the summer of 2007, people worried that the U.S. crisis might spread, threatening the solvency of other countries' financial institutions. With this idea in the air, banks became wary of lending to each other—and especially wary of lending to banks that specialized in mortgages. As a result, Northern Rock had trouble raising purchased funds. Other banks either refused to lend to Northern Rock or demanded high interest rates.

In a bind, Northern Rock turned to the United Kingdom's central bank, the Bank of England, asking it to perform its role as lender of last resort. The Bank of England approved a loan to Northern Rock and planned an announcement, but the news leaked out prematurely. On September 13, a well-known business reporter said on television that Northern Rock "has had to go cap in hand" to the Bank of England. Hearing that their bank had a problem, Northern Rock's depositors had the typical reaction: on September 14, they rushed to withdraw their funds.

Deposits flowed out of Northern Rock for three days, until the British government intervened. On September 17, the government announced it would guarantee the bank's deposits: if the bank failed, the government would compensate depositors. This action restored confidence enough to end the run.

Yet Northern Rock's problems were not over. The run damaged the bank's reputation, and it continued to have trouble raising funds. With fears growing about Northern Rock's solvency, the British government took over the bank in February 2008, with compensation for the bank's shareholders. As of 2010, the bank was still owned by the British government.

Bank Panics

Sometimes runs occur simultaneously at many individual banks. People lose confidence in the whole banking system, and depositors everywhere try to withdraw their money. This event is called a **bank panic**.

Bank panic simultaneous runs at many individual banks

Nationwide bank panics were once common in the United States. Between 1873 and 1933, the country experienced an average of three panics per decade. Bank panics occur because a loss of confidence is contagious. A run at one bank triggers runs at others, which trigger runs at others, and so on.

Suppose a run occurs at Melvin's Bank. Gertrude's Bank is next door to Melvin's, and Gertrude's depositors notice the run. It occurs to these depositors that the same thing might happen at their bank. To be safe, they withdraw their money, and Gertrude's experiences a run. Now runs have hit two banks. Seeing this, depositors at other banks get nervous. More runs occur, and the panic spreads through the economy.

In the United States, a typical bank panic started with runs on New York banks. These triggered runs in other parts of the East, and then the panic spread westward. The next case discusses the last and most severe bank panics in U.S. history.

CASE STUDY

Bank Panics in the 1930s

Figure 10.1 shows the percentage of all U.S. banks that failed in each year from 1876 to 1935. Before 1920, the failure rate was low despite periodic panics. Banks suspended payments, but most eventually reopened.

FIGURE **10.1** **U.S. Bank-Failure Rate, 1876–1935**

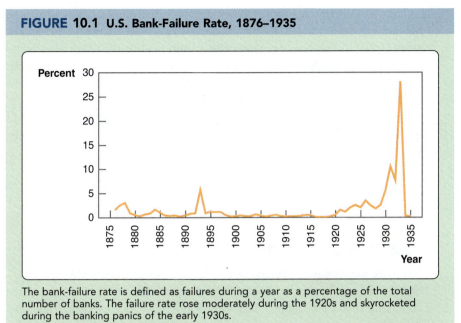

The bank-failure rate is defined as failures during a year as a percentage of the total number of banks. The failure rate rose moderately during the 1920s and skyrocketed during the banking panics of the early 1930s.

Source: Adapted from George J. Benston et al., *Perspectives on Safe and Sound Banking: Past, Present and Future,* Cambridge: MIT Press, 1986, pp. 54–57 (Table 2).

Bank failures rose moderately in the 1920s. Most failures occurred at small, rural banks that made loans to farmers. Falling agricultural prices during the 1920s led to defaults. These failures were isolated, however, and most banks appeared healthy.

Major trouble began in 1930. Failures rose at rural banks in the Midwest, and this made depositors nervous about other banks in the region. These worries were exacerbated by general unease about the economy, a result of the 1929 stock market crash. Bank runs started in the Midwest, and this time they spread eastward.

A psychological milestone was the failure of the New York–based Bank of the United States in December 1930. It was one of the country's largest banks, and the largest ever to fail. Although it was an ordinary commercial bank, its name suggested some link to the government, and its failure shook confidence in the whole banking system.

Other events eroded confidence further. Some well-known European banks failed in 1931. In the 1932 election campaign, Democrats publicized banking problems to criticize the Republican government. The stream of worrisome news produced a nationwide panic.

The bank panics of the 1930s were the most severe in U.S. history. One reason, say economic historians, was that banks were slow to suspend payments. Suspensions had helped end the panics of the late nineteenth and early twentieth centuries. In the 1930s, however, banks were influenced by the Federal Reserve, which was founded in 1913. The Fed discouraged suspensions, which in retrospect was a mistake.

Democrat Franklin Roosevelt became president on March 4, 1933, and he quickly took charge of the banking crisis. On March 6, Roosevelt announced a bank holiday: across the country, all banks were required to suspend payments. Starting on March 13, banks were allowed to reopen, but only if the Secretary of the Treasury certified they were solvent. A quarter of all U.S. banks failed in 1933, but Roosevelt's policies ended the panic.

President Roosevelt understood the psychology of panics. His famous statement that "we have nothing to fear but fear itself" referred partly to banking. It captures the fact that panics result from self-fulfilling expectations.[*]

*For more on the bank panics of the 1930s, see Chapter 7 of Milton Friedman and Anna Schwartz, *A Monetary History of the United States, 1867–1960,* Princeton University Press, 1963.

10.2 DEPOSIT INSURANCE

No bank panics have occurred in the United States since 1933. Even during the financial crisis of 2007–2009, depositors at most banks remained confident that their money was safe. Runs have occurred at individual banks but are rare, because the government has figured out how to solve the problem: **deposit insurance**.

How Deposit Insurance Works

Deposit insurance
government guarantee to compensate depositors for their losses when a bank fails

Deposit insurance is a government's promise to compensate depositors for their losses when a bank fails. In our example of Melvin's Bank, insurance would pay off the last $20 in deposits after Melvin runs out of assets in Table 10.1B. In addition to protecting depositors when bank failures occur, insurance makes failures less likely. This effect arises because insurance eliminates bank runs, a major cause of failures.

The reason is simple. A run occurs when depositors start worrying about the safety of their deposits and try to withdraw them. Deposit insurance eliminates the worry, because depositors know they will be paid back if their bank fails. They have no reason to start a run, even if they hear bad rumors about the bank. A solvent bank keeps its deposits and remains solvent.

Deposit Insurance in the United States

Federal Deposit Insurance Corporation (FDIC) government agency that insures deposits at U.S. commercial banks and savings institutions

Deposit insurance is provided primarily by the **Federal Deposit Insurance Corporation (FDIC)**, a U.S. government agency. Congress created the FDIC in 1933 in response to the bank panics of the early 1930s. Today, the FDIC insures all deposits at commercial banks and savings institutions. Credit unions have a separate insurance fund.

If a bank fails and depositors lose money, the FDIC compensates them up to a limit of $250,000. Anyone with a deposit below $250,000 is protected fully. The limit on insurance was previously $100,000, but Congress raised it in 2008 to bolster depositors' confidence during the financial crisis.

The FDIC makes payments from an insurance fund that holds U.S. government bonds. The fund is financed by premiums charged to banks;

currently, the FDIC charges about 1 percent of a bank's assets each year. Because of this financing, the costs of deposit insurance ultimately fall on the nation's banks—unless the FDIC runs out of money. The assets of the insurance fund are far less than total insured deposits, so widespread bank failures could exhaust the fund before it paid all claims. In this event, it is likely the government would step in and use taxpayers' money to make insurance payments to depositors.

During the 1980s, the S&L crisis exhausted the funds of the Federal Savings and Loan Insurance Company, which insured S&Ls at the time. In 1989, Congress abolished this agency, and the FDIC started insuring savings institutions as well as commercial banks. Meanwhile, the government paid off depositors at failed S&Ls at a cost to taxpayers of $150 billion (about 3 percent of GDP at the time). In contrast, the financial crisis of 2007–2009 did not cause enough bank failures to exhaust the FDIC fund.

Not all countries have deposit insurance. In Russia, insurance was created only in 2005—too late for Guta Bank. The United Kingdom had deposit insurance in 2007, but it paid only 90 percent of losses. Northern Rock's customers ran to the bank because they stood to lose 10 percent of their deposits if the bank failed (that is, until the fourth day of the run, when the government guaranteed deposits fully). Later we'll compare the use of deposit insurance in different parts of the world.

10.3 MORAL HAZARD AGAIN

Deposit insurance fixes the problem of bank runs. Unfortunately, it makes the problem of moral hazard worse: bankers have incentives to misuse insured deposits. Let's discuss moral hazard and how it interacts with deposit insurance.

Misuses of Deposits

One of banking's central functions is to reduce moral hazard in loan markets. Recall that moral hazard is also called the *principal–agent problem*. Borrowers (the agents) have incentives to misuse the funds they receive from savers (the principals). Banks reduce this problem through monitoring, loan covenants, and collateral.

▶ Section 7.5 describes how banks reduce moral hazard in loan markets.

Unfortunately, banking creates new moral hazard problems. Here, bankers are the agents and their depositors are the principals. Bankers have incentives to use deposits in ways that benefit themselves but hurt depositors. The misuse of deposits takes two basic forms: excessive risk taking and looting.

Excessive Risk Bankers can exploit depositors through risky activities. Suppose a bank lends to borrowers with risky projects who are willing to pay high interest rates. If the projects succeed, the interest income produces high profits for the bank's owners. If the projects fail, the borrowers default and the bank may become insolvent.

However, not all the losses from insolvency fall on the bank. Depositors also lose when the bank can't pay them back. Bankers have incentives to gamble because someone else pays part of the costs if their gambles fail.

Similarly, bankers have incentives for risky off-balance-sheet activities. Suppose a bank speculates with derivatives—it makes a bet on future interest rates or asset prices. The bank earns large profits if the gamble pays off, and depositors share the costs if it doesn't. The gamble is "heads I win, tails you lose."

Suppose a bank's net worth, or capital, is $20. The bank uses derivatives to make a gamble, one that has a 50-percent chance of earning $50 and a 50-percent chance of losing $50. If the bank wins this gamble, its net worth rises by $50, to $70. If it loses, its net worth falls to −$30, and the bank fails.

If the bank fails, its owners lose only $20, their initial capital. Depositors lose $30, because the insolvent bank can't pay off all its deposits. The gamble is a good deal for the bank, because it risks only $20 to gain $50. It is a bad deal for depositors, who gain nothing if the gamble succeeds but lose $30 if it fails.

Looting Bankers can also exploit depositors in a less subtle way: by stealing their money. The famous robber Willie Sutton was once asked why he chose to hold up banks. His response was, "That's where the money is."

The same reasoning applies to white-collar crime when a bank's management is unscrupulous. Large amounts of money flow in and out of banks, creating opportunities for fraud and embezzlement. History provides many examples of bank failures caused by dishonesty.

As usual, at the root of moral hazard is asymmetric information. If depositors could see what bankers do with their money, they could forbid gambling and stealing. But it isn't easy to observe what happens inside banks, as the following case study illustrates.

CASE STUDY |

The Keystone Scandal

The town of Keystone, West Virginia, has only about 400 residents. But it was the scene of one of the costliest bank failures in U.S. history, an episode that vividly illustrates the problem of moral hazard in banking.

The First National Bank of Keystone was a community bank founded in 1904. In 1977, when it had only $17 million in assets, the bank was bought by an ambitious entrepreneur, J. Knox McConnell, and started growing quickly. It expanded its business beyond the Keystone area, making mortgage loans throughout West Virginia and western Pennsylvania.

The bank's assets rose to $90 million in 1992. At that point, its managers started purchasing loans from banks around the country. They bought risky loans with high interest rates, including subprime loans for home improvements and debt consolidation loans (loans used to pay off other debt). In buying these loans, First National took on more risk than commercial banks usually tolerate. Managers securitized and sold some of the loans and kept others on the bank's balance sheet. First National's assets reached $1.1 billion in 1999.

The bank needed large deposits to fund its growing assets. It got these by offering interest rates on CDs that were two percentage points above the industry norm. It advertised these rates on the Internet, attracting deposits from around the country.

First National appeared very profitable. It earned high interest income on its risky assets, so it easily covered its interest expense. In 1995, it reported a return on equity of 81 percent. The newspaper *The American Banker* named First National Bank of Keystone the most successful small bank in the country.

But two related problems did Keystone Bank in. First, over the decade of the 1990s, defaults rose on the types of loans the bank purchased. The bank suffered losses on the loans it held on its balance sheet, and it started receiving lower prices for the securitized loans that it sold. In retrospect, Keystone's losses on risky loans look similar to the losses of subprime mortgage lenders a decade later.

Second, top bank managers embezzled tens of millions of dollars. They paid fees for phony work on their loan securitization business to themselves and to companies they owned. Some commentators suggest that Keystone's managers knew this business was unprofitable and pursued it only because it facilitated their theft.

For years, the managers of First National Bank of Keystone deceived government regulators about their behavior. They kept loans on the balance sheet after the loans were sold, inflating the bank's assets and net worth. They forged documents in which the bank's board of directors approved payments. When regulators investigated the bank, desperate executives buried two truckloads of documents on the ranch of Senior Vice President Terry Church.

Eventually, regulators found out the truth. In 1999, they determined that 70 percent of First National's assets were fictitious, which implied that its true net worth was deeply negative. They closed the bank, and federal prosecutors brought criminal charges against managers. Several were convicted and sentenced to prison; Vice President Church got 27 years. (J. Knox McConnell, founder and longtime bank president, had died in 1997 before the scandal broke.)

Many people were hurt by the Keystone fiasco. It cost the FDIC $70 million in insurance payments. About 500 people lost deposits that exceeded the FDIC limit. One was the retired owner of a hardware store in the town of Keystone, who saw his life savings fall from $220,000 to $100,000.

Innocent bank employees lost their jobs when the bank closed, and many also lost their wealth because they held stock in the bank. The town of Keystone lost the taxes paid by First National, which were two-thirds of its revenue. The town laid off seven of its fifteen employees, including two of four police officers.

The Problem with Deposit Insurance

We can now see a drawback of deposit insurance: it exacerbates the problem of moral hazard. Without insurance, depositors worry that banks may fail, giving them an incentive to monitor banks. Before depositing money, prudent people will investigate a bank's safety. For example, they might check balance sheets and income statements to be sure that insolvency risk is low. After making deposits, people will watch the bank and withdraw their money if signs of trouble emerge.

We saw that nervous depositors can cause bank runs. But they also have a positive effect: they discourage bankers from misusing deposits. If a bank takes excessive risks or money disappears mysteriously, depositors are likely to notice and withdraw their funds, and the bank will have trouble attracting new deposits. This threat gives bankers a reason to keep deposits safe.

Insurance eliminates depositors' incentives to monitor banks. Depositors know they will be compensated if banks fail, so they don't care much if bankers take risks or embezzle their money. They don't bother to check balance sheets for danger signs. This inattention gives bankers greater freedom to misuse deposits: they have no fear that bad behavior will be punished by withdrawals.

With deposit insurance, bank failures aren't costly for depositors, but they *are* costly for the insurance fund. If moral hazard produces a high rate of failures, the fund must charge higher insurance premiums, which are costly for banks—even those that take good care of deposits. A surge of failures can force the government to absorb part of the costs, as in the S&L crisis. Moral hazard and the absence of monitoring can end up hurting taxpayers.

Limits on Insurance

Governments recognize the problem with deposit insurance and have tried to reduce it by limiting the protection they provide. Recall that the FDIC limits its payments to $250,000 per account. Some deposits exceed this level, such as accounts of large corporations and state governments. Large depositors stand to lose from bank failures, so they have incentives to monitor banks and withdraw their funds if banks misuse them.

Many countries have stronger limits on deposit insurance than the United States does. Many European countries have limits of 50,000 or 100,000 euros (around $60,000 or $120,000). In the past, European countries also limited insurance payments to 90 percent of depositors' losses, but most raised this rate to 100 percent during the most recent financial crisis. About half the countries in the world, including most of the poorer ones, have no deposit insurance at all.

What's the best level of deposit insurance? The answer isn't clear. More insurance reduces bank runs but increases moral hazard. The first effect reduces the risk of bank failure, but the second increases it. Economists disagree about which effect is larger.

CASE STUDY

Deposit Insurance and Banking Crises

The debate over deposit insurance has stimulated much research. Economists have tried to measure the effects of insurance by comparing different countries and time periods. One well-known study was published in 2002 by economists at the World Bank and the International Monetary Fund (IMF).[*]

This study examined 61 countries over the period 1980–1997. Deposit insurance became more common over this period: 12 of the 61 countries had insurance in 1980, and 33 in 1997. Where insurance existed, its generosity varied widely. Limits on coverage ranged from the equivalent of $20,000 in Switzerland to $260,000 in Norway.

The study examined the effects of deposit insurance on national banking crises. A "crisis" was defined as a year with a high level of bank failures, as measured by several criteria. For example, the researchers counted a year as a crisis if at least 2 percent of GDP was lost through bank failures, or if the government declared a lengthy bank holiday. A total of 40 bank crises occurred in the countries and years covered by the study.

Overall, the World Bank–IMF study found that the negative effects of deposit insurance outweigh the positive effects. Banking crises occurred more often in countries with insurance than in countries without it. In addition, raising the limit on insurance coverage made crises more likely.

However, there is an important qualification: the effects of insurance depend on other bank regulations. Some of the countries in the study—generally the richer ones—enforced strict supervision of banks, monitoring them to prevent theft and excessive risk taking. Other countries, including most of the poorer ones, lacked effective supervision.

The study found that deposit insurance makes crises more likely in countries with weak supervision but less likely in countries with strong supervision. This finding makes sense. Supervision reduces moral hazard: with regulators watching, it is harder for banks to misuse deposits. Thus, supervision dampens the adverse effect of deposit insurance while preserving the beneficial effect of fewer bank runs.

[*]See Asli Demirguc-Kunt and Enrica Detragiache, "Does Deposit Insurance Increase Banking System Stability?" *Journal of Monetary Economics* 49 (October 2002): 1373–1406.

10.4 WHO CAN OPEN A BANK?

Governments are keenly aware of the moral hazard problem in banking. They can reduce it by eliminating deposit insurance, but that can lead to bank runs. For this reason, many governments maintain insurance and combat moral hazard through bank regulation. Regulators monitor banking activities and try to prevent bankers from misusing depositors' funds. Regulators do the job that depositors neglect when they are insured.

The rest of this chapter discusses the major facets of bank regulation. Regulators' involvement with a bank starts when it opens. Melvin cannot decide on his own when to open his bank. Instead, he needs a *bank charter*—a license from the government to operate a bank. Regulators grant a charter only if they think the new bank will keep its deposits safe.

Chartering Agencies

▶ A case study in Section 8.2 describes the political history behind the creation of state and national banks.

A commercial bank or savings institution may be chartered either by the federal government or by a state. Federal charters are granted by the Office of the Comptroller of the Currency (OCC), which is part of the Treasury Department. Each state government has its own chartering agency, such as Maryland's Office of Financial Regulation. Banks chartered by the OCC are called *national banks*, and banks chartered by states are called *state banks*. A credit union may also be chartered by a federal agency, the National Credit Union Administration, or by a state agency.

In the past, the regulations imposed on state and national banks have sometimes differed, leading banks to prefer national over state charters, or vice versa. Today, there isn't much difference in regulations, so state and national banks coexist. About three quarters of commercial banks are state banks, but they are generally smaller than national banks.

Obtaining a Charter

To obtain a charter, a prospective banker completes a lengthy application and submits it to the chartering agency. The application describes the bank's business plan, its expected earnings, its initial level of capital, and its top management. Regulators review the application and judge the soundness of the bank's plans. If the risk of failure appears too high, the application is denied. This process is analogous to a bank's evaluation of loan applications. Banks study applicants' business plans to screen out borrowers who will misuse loans; similarly, regulators try to screen out bankers who will misuse deposits.

Much of the chartering process concerns a review of key personnel. Regulators gather information on the proposed bank's owners and top managers to be sure they have the experience to run a bank. Most important, regulators try to weed out crooks and gamblers who might be attracted to banks because "that's where the money is." To that end, regulators examine applicants' careers and interview past employers. They check credit histories and tax records and send fingerprints to the FBI. If a proposed banker has a questionable past, regulators may demand that he be replaced before granting a charter.

In addition to chartering new banks, regulators must approve changes in ownership. They check the background of anyone buying a large share of a bank to prevent untrustworthy people from entering the business.

The Separation of Banking and Commerce

▶ Section 8.2 discusses the repeal of Glass-Steagall and its effects on the banking industry.

A perennial controversy is whether firms outside banking should be allowed to establish or merge with banks. The repeal of the Glass–Steagall Act in 1999 enabled commercial banks to merge with other types of financial institutions, such as investment banks and brokerage firms. However, a wall still exists between banks and nonfinancial firms. The Bank Holding Company Act of 1956 prohibits a nonfinancial company from owning a bank and vice versa. Citigroup can acquire other financial institutions, but it can't merge with General Motors or Microsoft. This restriction is called the *separation of banking and commerce*.

Supporters of this policy cite a number of dangers from mixing banking and commerce. One is the potential for conflicts of interest. Suppose, for example, that a bank and an auto firm are owned by the same conglomerate. The bank may feel pressure to lend to the auto firm, even for unsound investment projects. The bank may deny loans to competing auto companies with good projects. This bias in lending prevents funds from flowing to the most productive uses, thus reducing the efficiency of the economy. Unsound lending also increases a bank's default risk, potentially threatening its solvency.

Despite these arguments, some economists think the separation of banking and commerce should be relaxed. They argue that links between financial and nonfinancial firms can create economies of scope—cost reductions from combining different business activities. They also point out that European countries allow banks and nonfinancial firms to own one another, without disastrous consequences. In recent years, much of the debate about banking and commerce has revolved around a single company.

CASE STUDY

Walmart Bank?

The separation of banking and commerce has a loophole: **industrial loan companies (ILCs)**, a type of financial institution that exists in seven states, with the largest number in Utah. ILCs were first established in the early twentieth century to lend to industrial workers who couldn't get other credit; they were the subprime lenders of the day. However, ILCs have evolved over time and now engage in most activities of commercial banks.

> **Industrial loan company (ILC)** financial institution that performs many functions of a commercial bank; may be owned by a nonfinancial firm

ILCs are regulated by state banking authorities and the FDIC, agencies that also regulate some commercial banks. However, ILCs are not counted as banks when it comes to the separation of banking and commerce. A number of nonfinancial firms own ILCs, General Motors, General Electric, and Target among them.

ILCs occupy a small niche in the financial system and didn't attract much attention—until Walmart became interested in owning one. In 2002, Walmart tried to buy an ILC in California, but the state legislature passed a law to prevent it. In 2005, Walmart applied for an ILC charter in Utah, but the application was criticized by groups as diverse as labor unions and bankers. Several members of Congress proposed legislation to block Walmart's plan.

Some groups opposed Walmart for reasons unrelated to banking, such as the company's policies on employee benefits. But the strongest opposition came from community banks, small banks that serve a single locality. These

At a 2006 rally in Washington, D.C., members of the National Community Reinvestment Coalition protest Walmart's plan to establish an industrial loan company.

Mark Wilson/Getty Images

banks feared that Walmart's ability to cut costs could drive them out of business. Ronald Ence, vice president of Independent Community Bankers of America, said of Walmart, "There's no doubt in my mind they'll be able to do to community banks what they've done to the local grocery store and the local hardware store and the local clothing store."

In its application for an ILC charter, Walmart denied that it would compete with community banks. It proposed to use its ILC for a narrow purpose: to process credit and debit card payments at its stores. Walmart pays outside banks to process these transactions, and the company estimated it would save $5 million a year by doing the work internally. Walmart officials promised repeatedly that its ILC would not accept deposits from consumers or make loans. Critics, however, were skeptical. The president of a North Dakota bank said, "I cannot believe they are doing all of this to save $5 million a year" ($5 million may sound like a lot, but for Walmart it represents less than 10 minutes of sales).

Facing hostility, and uncertain whether Utah regulators would approve its ILC charter, Walmart backed off. In 2007, it withdrew its charter application. Yet the story of Walmart bank is not over. Walmart has edged toward the banking business with "money centers" that cash checks and sell stored-value cards, activities that have always been legal for nonfinancial firms. Walmart also has a partnership with Sun Trust Bank, which operates branches within Walmart stores. Some bankers suggest that Walmart is considering a new ILC application; the company denies it.

In any case, Walmart has clearly entered the banking business to the north and south of the United States: Mexico and Canada have no laws separating banking and commerce, and regulators granted charters to Mexico's Banco Walmart in 2007 and Walmart Bank Canada in 2010. At a Mexican Walmart, a customer can deposit money or talk to a loan officer after buying a pair of socks. In Canada, Walmart Bank has introduced a credit card and says it will expand into other areas of banking.

In contrast to its U.S. experience, Walmart encountered little opposition to opening banks in Canada and Mexico. Both countries have banking industries dominated by a few large institutions; they lack the large number of community banks that opposed Walmart in the United States. In addition, consumer groups in both countries supported Walmart in the hope that its entry into banking would drive down interest rates on loans.

10.5 RESTRICTIONS ON BANK BALANCE SHEETS

After a U.S. bank receives a charter, regulators restrict its activities in many ways. One set of regulations governs the assets that banks are allowed to hold on their balance sheets. Other regulations mandate minimum levels of capital that banks must hold. All these rules are meant to reduce moral hazard and the risk of insolvency.

The United States has a complex system in which different agencies regulate different groups of banks. Before describing regulations in detail, let's discuss who the regulators are.

Who Sets Banking Regulations?

The agency that regulates a commercial bank is determined by two factors: (1) whether the bank is a national or state bank, and (2) whether it's a member of the Federal Reserve System. All national banks are required to join the Fed system, but membership is optional for state banks.

Table 10.2 lists the regulators of commercial banks. All national banks are regulated by the OCC, the agency that chartered them. A state bank that belongs to the Fed system has two regulators: the state agency that chartered it and the Federal Reserve Bank for its region. A state bank that does *not* belong to the Fed system is regulated by a state agency and the FDIC. The FDIC not only regulates this group of banks but also provides deposit insurance for all commercial banks and savings institutions.

For example, M&T Bank is a state bank chartered in New York and a member of the Federal Reserve System, so it is regulated by the State of New York Banking Department and by the Federal Reserve Bank of New York. These regulators oversee all of M&T's operations, which stretch from New York to Virginia.

TABLE 10.2 Who Regulates Commercial Banks?

National Banks	Office of the Comptroller of the Currency (OCC)
State Banks	
Members of Federal Reserve System	Federal Reserve and state agencies
Non-members of Federal Reserve System	FDIC and state agencies

► As we discuss in Chapter 18, financial holding companies, conglomerates that own banks and other financial institutions, face regulation by the Federal Reserve at the holding company level as well as regulation of the individual banks they own. In addition, the Dodd-Frank Act created the Financial Services Oversight Council, with authority to impose additional regulations on the largest FHCs.

Savings institutions and credit unions are also regulated by a mix of federal and state agencies. Before 2010, the Office of Thrift Supervision regulated federally chartered savings institutions, but the office was abolished under the Dodd-Frank Act, and its responsibilities were transferred to the OCC. Credit unions are still regulated by a separate federal agency, the National Credit Union Administration.

This complex system is based not on any logical design but rather reflects the historical development of the banking system, including political battles over the regulatory powers of states and the federal government. Periodically, policymakers have considered proposals to streamline bank regulation. In 1993, for example, the Clinton Administration proposed the creation of a federal banking commission as the primary regulator of all banks. Such proposals have not been enacted, in part because the Federal Reserve has not wanted to relinquish its regulatory role. However, the abolition of the Office of Thrift Supervision is a small step toward simpler regulation.

In any case, the different agencies that regulate banks set broadly similar rules. Therefore, we will discuss most regulations without distinguishing among different regulators or groups of banks.

Restrictions on Banks' Assets

Banks can choose among a variety of assets, including safe assets with relatively low returns and riskier assets with high returns. As we've discussed, moral hazard distorts this choice. Banks have incentives to take on too much risk, because the costs that might result are paid partly by depositors or the deposit insurance fund.

To address this problem, regulators restrict banks' menu of assets. U.S. regulators impose strict limits on securities holdings: banks can hold only the safest securities, such as government bonds and highly rated corporate bonds and mortgage-backed securities (MBSs). They can't hold junk bonds or corporate stock.

In some countries, regulators are less restrictive. For example, banks in Germany and Japan can own stocks as well as bonds. In Japan's case, this policy proved costly when stock prices crashed during the 1990s. Losses on stocks helped push many banks there into insolvency.

U.S. regulators also restrict the loans that banks make. Again, the goal is to reduce the risk of large losses. To this end, lending must be diversified: no single loan can be too large. At national banks, loans to one borrower cannot exceed 15 percent of a bank's capital. Loan limits at state banks vary by state.

After the S&L crisis of the 1980s, regulators introduced special limits on real estate loans. For example, a loan for commercial real estate cannot exceed 80 percent of the property's value. In the wake of the most recent financial crisis, the Dodd-Frank Act established restrictions on home mortgage lending. The focus is on ensuring that people can afford their mortgages, for example, by requiring that banks demand proper documentation of borrowers' income. A borrower who defaults on a mortgage can block foreclosure in the courts if he shows that the bank did not adequately verify his ability to pay.

Capital Requirements

When a bank chooses its level of capital, it faces a trade-off. Lower capital raises the return on equity, but it also raises the bank's insolvency risk. This trade-off creates moral hazard. Bank owners benefit from the higher return on equity, but, as we've stressed throughout this chapter, they don't bear the full cost of insolvency. As a result, banks have incentives to choose low levels of capital, creating excessive risk.

▶ Section 9.6 analyzes banks' decisions about how much capital to hold.

Regulators address this problem by imposing **capital requirements**. These rules mandate minimum levels of capital that banks must hold. The goal is to keep capital high enough to keep insolvency risk low.

Capital requirements regulations setting minimum levels of capital that banks must hold

The Basel Accord Most bank regulations—like most laws of all types—are set separately for each country by national governments. Capital requirements are an exception. These rules are determined largely by international agreements.

Specifically, current capital requirements are based on the **Basel Accord**, an agreement signed by bank regulators from around the world in 1988 in the Swiss city of Basel. The accord is a set of recommendations, not a binding treaty, but more than 100 countries have adopted its provisions.

Basel Accord 1988 agreement that sets international standards for bank capital requirements

The accord was motivated by the internationalization of banking. Regulators believe that when banks compete internationally, those based in countries with low capital requirements have an advantage over those facing stricter requirements. Consequently, each country has an unhealthy incentive to weaken capital requirements to help its banks. The goal of the Basel Accord is to maintain a level playing field with strong requirements everywhere.

Current U.S. Requirements In the United States, capital requirements have two parts. The first is a simple rule that predates the Basel Accord. This rule sets a minimum equity ratio, or ratio of capital to assets. Currently, the minimum is 5 percent: a bank's capital must equal at least 5 percent of its assets.

The second requirement is part of the Basel Accord. This rule accounts for the riskiness of different kinds of assets. Among the assets that banks hold, some are very safe and others are relatively risky. The riskier a bank's assets, the more capital it is required to hold. Higher capital protects banks from insolvency if risky assets lose value.

Specifically, the Basel Accord requires banks to hold capital of at least 8 percent of *risk-adjusted assets*. This variable is a weighted sum of different groups of assets, with higher weights for higher risk. The safest assets, such as reserves and Treasury bonds, have weights of zero. Loans to other banks have weights of 20 percent. A number of assets have 50 percent weights, including municipal bonds and home mortgages (which were considered fairly safe when the Basel Accord was signed). The weights on most other loans are 100 percent.

An Example of Minimum Capital Levels To understand these rules, let's return to our favorite financial institution, Melvin's Bank. **Table 10.3A** shows the asset side of Melvin's balance sheet, with the usual asset classes (reserves, securities, and loans) broken into subcategories. **Table 10.3B** calculates Melvin's required level of capital based on the two rules that he faces, the minimum equity ratio and the risk-based Basel requirement.

Recall that the minimum equity ratio is 5 percent. Melvin's total assets in this example are $150, so his capital must be at least 5 percent of $150, or $7.50.

To calculate the Basel requirement, we apply the appropriate weights to different assets in Table 10.3A. For example, Melvin's Bank owns $10 in municipal bonds. The Basel rules give municipal bonds a weight of 0.5, so this item contributes $5 to the weighted sum of assets. The bank has $90 in commercial and industrial loans; with a weight of 1.0, this item contributes the full $90 to the weighted sum. Adding up the weighted assets, we get a total of $107. Melvin's capital must be at least 8 percent of $107, which is $8.56.

To conclude, the minimum equity ratio requires Melvin's Bank to hold at least $7.50 in capital, and the Basel rule requires at least $8.56. In this example, the second requirement is the more stringent one. This is not always the case, however; which requirement is stricter depends on the bank's mix of assets. (Problem 7 explores this point.)

▶ This example ignores off-balance-sheet activities, which are addressed in a 1996 amendment to the Basel Accord. A bank must hold extra capital, beyond 8 percent of risk-weighted assets, if it engages in risky OBS activities such as speculating with derivatives. The OBS activities of Melvin's Bank could push its required capital above $8.56.

TABLE 10.3 Capital Requirements for Melvin's Bank

(A) Computing Weighted Assets

	Assets	Weights	Weighted Assets
Reserves	10	0.0	0
Securities			
Treasury bonds	10	0.0	0
Municipal bonds	10	0.5	5
Loans			
Interbank	10	0.2	2
Home mortgages	20	0.5	10
C&I	90	1.0	90
TOTAL	150		107

(B) Minimum Levels of Capital

Based on minimum equity ratio:

Minimum capital = (0.05)(total assets)
= (0.05)($150)
= $7.50

Based on Basel requirement:

Minimum capital = (0.08)(weighted assets)
= (0.08)($107)
= $8.56

The Future Capital requirements are in a state of flux. Banks have long complained that they are too restrictive. In 2004, the committee of regulators that wrote the original Basel Accord proposed a new, more flexible set of rules called *Basel 2*. Basel 2 allows large banks to develop their own methods for determining how much capital they must hold, subject to regulators' approval. Many European countries adopted the Basel 2 rules, but U.S. regulators hesitated. They worried that capital could fall to dangerously low levels.

In 2008, just as it appeared that the United States was on the verge of implementing Basel 2, the financial crisis hit critical mass. Bank failures rose sharply over 2008–2009, revealing that many banks held insufficient capital to survive a major shock. In the wake of the crisis, sentiment for more flexible capital requirements shifted to favoring stricter ones.

In 2010, international regulators were debating proposals for a "Basel 3" with stricter rules. In the United States, the Dodd-Frank Act required bank regulators to establish new capital requirements. The act does not specify the new rules but stipulates that they must be at least as strict as current rules. For their part, bankers expected significant increases in required capital.

In many areas of government regulation, businesses have incentives to find loopholes that weaken the regulations' effectiveness. In the case of capital requirements, banks have looked for ways to minimize the amount of capital they must hold. The following case study discusses an approach that banks used successfully for almost two decades—until the financial crisis of 2007–2009.

Online Case Study
An Update on Capital Requirements

CASE STUDY

Skirting Capital Requirements with SIVs

A **structured investment vehicle (SIV)** is a company created by a financial institution, usually a commercial bank, as a means of holding assets off its balance sheet, thus allowing it to circumvent capital requirements. The SIV raises funds by issuing commercial paper and uses the funds to purchase securities backed by bank loans. It is a "shell" company without offices or employees. Citibank created the first SIV in 1988. Financial institutions such as JPMorgan Chase and Bank of America followed suit. However, over 2007 and 2008, SIVs abruptly disappeared.

Theoretically, an SIV was an independent business, but it had strong links to the bank that created it. Typically, the bank sold some stock in the SIV to outsiders but kept a large share for itself. It also earned fees for managing the SIV. In some cases, banks agreed to aid SIVs if they were in danger of insolvency, either by lending money or by purchasing some of the SIVs' assets.

Because of their links to banks, SIVs were considered safe. Their commercial paper received high ratings, so it paid low interest rates. The assets owned by the SIVs paid higher rates, so SIVs produced a steady stream of profits for their sponsoring banks.

Structured investment vehicle (SIV) company created by a bank as a means of holding assets off its balance sheet, thus allowing it to circumvent capital requirements

If banks had simply purchased the securities owned by SIVs, their balance-sheet assets would have risen, and they would have needed more capital to achieve required equity ratios. Because SIVs were considered independent companies, however, their assets were not counted on banks' balance sheets. Banks profited from the securities held by SIVs without increasing their capital, which meant a higher return on equity.

Like many parts of the financial system, SIVs ran into trouble in 2007 and 2008. They owned large quantities of mortgage-backed securities, and falling prices for these securities created doubts about the solvency of SIVs. Other institutions became leery of buying their commercial paper, making it difficult to roll over this debt as it matured. At that point, the banks that sponsored SIVs stepped in to prevent them from defaulting. The banks dissolved the SIVs and took their assets and liabilities onto their own balance sheets. In some cases, this action was required by prior agreement; in others, the banks could have allowed the SIVs to go bankrupt but feared the effects on their reputations.

Banks suffered substantial losses on the MBSs they took from SIVs—the same losses they would have suffered if they, rather than the SIVs, had bought the MBSs in the first place. In retrospect, it is clear that banks took on risk that capital requirements were meant to forbid. Losses related to SIVs helped push large banks to the brink of insolvency, necessitating capital injections by the government under the Troubled Asset Relief Program (TARP).

▶ See Chapter 18 for more on the TARP.

10.6 BANK SUPERVISION

Another element of government regulation is **bank supervision**, or monitoring of banks' activities. The agency that regulates a bank checks that the bank is meeting capital requirements and obeying restrictions on asset holdings. Regulators also make more subjective assessments of the bank's insolvency risk. If they perceive too much risk, they demand changes in the bank's operations.

Supervision is a big job, as regulators must keep abreast of what's happening at thousands of banks. Let's discuss the main parts of the supervision process: information gathering, bank ratings, and enforcement actions.

Information Gathering

A bank's supervisors gather information in two ways. First, they require the bank to report on its activities. Most important are **call reports**, which a bank must submit every quarter. A call report contains detailed information on the bank's finances, including a balance sheet and income statement. Regulators examine call reports for signs of trouble, such as declining capital, increases in risky assets, or rising loan delinquencies.

Second, regulators gather information through **bank examinations**, in which a team of regulators visits a bank's headquarters. Every bank is visited

Bank supervision monitoring of banks' activities by government regulators

Call report quarterly financial statement, including a balance sheet and income statement, that banks must submit to regulators as part of bank supervision

Bank examination visit by regulators to a bank's headquarters to gather information on the bank's activities; part of bank supervision

at least once a year, more often if regulators suspect problems based on call reports or past exams. Examiners sometimes arrive without warning, making it harder for banks to hide questionable activities.

Examiners review a bank's detailed financial records. They study internal memos and minutes of meetings to better understand the bank's business. They interview managers about various policies, such as the criteria for approving loans. Examiners also check outside sources to verify information provided by the bank. For example, they contact some of the bank's loan customers to ensure that the loans really exist and that borrowers have the collateral reported by the bank.

CAMELS Ratings

After examiners visit, banks have an experience familiar to college students: they get grades. The grades are evaluations of risks to solvency. Regulators give each bank a rating for six different kinds of risk, plus an overall rating. The ratings range from 1 to 5, with 1 the best. A rating of 1 means a bank is "fundamentally sound"; a 5 means "imminent risk of failure."

These scores are called **CAMELS ratings**. CAMELS is an acronym, with each letter standing for a risk that regulators evaluate: **c**apital, **a**sset quality, **m**anagement, **e**arnings, **l**iquidity, and **s**ensitivity.

- *Capital* A bank's examiners check that it is meeting the capital requirements outlined in Section 10.5. They also make a more subjective assessment of whether the bank has enough capital given the risks it faces. They look for signs that the bank will lose capital in the future. A bank's rating can fall, for example, if it is paying large dividends to shareholders, because these deplete capital.

- *Asset quality* Examiners gauge the riskiness of a bank's assets, especially default risk on loans. They select a sample of loans and gather information on the borrowers, such as their credit histories and current financial situation, to judge the likelihood of default. Examiners also check whether any borrowers have already stopped making payments, so loans should be written off; banks may be slow to write off bad loans because this reduces their capital. In addition to reviewing specific loans, examiners consider a bank's general policies for loan approval. They evaluate whether these policies are effective at screening out risky borrowers. They also check whether the bank follows its stated policies or makes exceptions.

- *Management* Examiners try to evaluate the competence and honesty of bank managers. This is important because many bank failures result from flawed management, as you'll recall from the Keystone case. Examiners also check whether a bank's board of directors is monitoring managers effectively. And they check how well managers control lower-level employees. For example, they look for safeguards against rogue traders who gamble the bank's money, as Nick Leeson did at Barings Bank.

CAMELS ratings evaluations by regulators of a bank's insolvency risk based on its **c**apital, **a**sset quality, **m**anagement, **e**arnings, **l**iquidity, and **s**ensitivity

▶ Section 5.6 recounts how Leeson bankrupted Barings by speculating with derivatives.

- *Earnings* Examiners look at a bank's current earnings and try to project future earnings. High earnings raise the bank's capital over time, reducing insolvency risk.

- *Liquidity* Examiners evaluate a bank's liquidity risk—the risk that it will have difficulty meeting demands for withdrawals. Liquidity risk depends on the bank's level of reserves (vault cash plus deposits at the Fed) and on its holdings of liquid securities, or secondary reserves.

- *Sensitivity* This means sensitivity to interest rates and asset prices—in other words, interest rate risk and market risk. Examiners look for activities that could produce large losses if asset prices move in an unexpected direction. One example is excessive speculation with derivatives.

Enforcement Actions

If a bank's overall CAMELS rating is 1 or 2, regulators leave it alone until its next examination. If the rating is 3 or worse, regulators require the bank to take action to reduce risk and improve its score. Regulators can either negotiate an agreement with the bank or issue a unilateral order.

Banks are required to fix whatever problems are creating excessive risk. This could mean tightening the loan-approval process. It could mean slowing the growth of assets or cutting dividends to shareholders or firing bad managers.

Regulators also have the power to impose fines on banks. They do so when a bank's problems are severe or the bank is slow to fix them. If regulators find evidence of criminal activity, such as embezzlement, they turn the case over to the FBI.

10.7 CLOSING INSOLVENT BANKS

Regulators try to prevent banks from becoming insolvent, but sometimes it happens. Consequently, another task of regulators is to deal with banks that are insolvent or on the brink of insolvency. During the financial crisis, the Treasury Department helped ensure the solvency of systemically important banks by injecting capital under the TARP. In normal circumstances—and for smaller banks even during the crisis—troubled banks are the responsibility of the FDIC. The FDIC forces insolvent banks to close quickly.

The Need for Government Action

In most industries, an unprofitable firm cannot survive for long. If it loses enough money, it becomes insolvent: its debts to banks and bondholders exceed its assets. In this situation, the firm has trouble making debt payments, and lenders won't provide additional funds. The firm is forced into bankruptcy.

However, this process may not occur for an insolvent bank because the bulk of bank liabilities are insured deposits. As discussed in Section 10.3, insurance makes depositors indifferent to their banks' fates. An insolvent bank is likely to fail eventually, but depositors don't suffer. So the bank may be able to attract deposits and stay in business for a long time.

This situation is dangerous for two reasons. First, the bank may continue practices that led it to insolvency, such as lax procedures for approving loans. This behavior is likely to produce further losses, so the bank's net worth becomes more and more negative. Eventually, the bank collapses at a high cost to the insurance fund.

Second, the bank may do risky things that it *didn't* do in the past. The reason is that the moral hazard problem, which exists for all banks, is particularly severe for insolvent ones. When a bank has a positive level of capital, its owners have something to lose if they take excessive risks. By contrast, if the owners' capital has already fallen below zero, *all* the losses from failed gambles fall on others.

At the same time, risk taking can have large benefits for owners of an insolvent bank. If their gambles succeed, the bank may earn enough to push its capital above zero. The owners gain wealth, and the bank is in a good position to continue in business. So insolvent banks are likely to take big risks. This behavior is called *gambling for resurrection*.

Because of these problems, most economists think regulators should force an insolvent bank to shut down. And it's important to act quickly, before the bank has a chance to incur further losses.

Forbearance

Despite the dangers posed by insolvent banks, regulators have sometimes chosen *not* to shut them down. Banks have continued to operate with negative capital. A regulator's decision not to close an insolvent bank is called **forbearance**.

Forbearance occurs because bank closures are painful. Bank owners lose any chance for future profits, managers lose their jobs, and depositors lose their uninsured funds. Closures are costly for the FDIC, which must compensate insured depositors. Closures can also be embarrassing for regulators, because they suggest that bank supervision has been inadequate. For all these reasons, regulators are tempted to let insolvent banks stay open.

Forbearance is a gamble on the part of regulators. As we've discussed, an insolvent bank may start earning profits and become solvent. If that happens, everyone avoids the pain of closure. On the other hand, if the bank continues to lose money, closure is more costly when it finally occurs.

Forbearance exacerbated the savings and loan crisis of the 1980s. Many S&Ls were insolvent early in the decade, when interest rates peaked. In retrospect, regulators should have closed these banks promptly, but they did not. Instead, the Federal Home Loan Bank Board, which regulated S&Ls at the time, loosened regulations to help banks stay open. It reduced capital requirements in 1980 and 1982. It also changed accounting rules to allow S&Ls to report higher levels of assets, and hence higher capital. For example, it allowed banks to write off bad loans over a 10-year period rather than all at once.

Forbearance regulator's decision to allow an insolvent bank to remain open

A case study in Section 9.6 analyzes the economic conditions that brought about the savings and loan crisis.

This policy was unsuccessful: bank failures surged in the late 1980s, ultimately exhausting the funds available to cover insured deposits. As noted in Section 10.2, the government ended up using taxpayer funds to compensate depositors at failed banks. This episode motivated Congress to pass the FDIC Improvement Act of 1991, which established stringent rules for closing banks. These rules govern bank closures today.

Deciding on Closure

Regulators monitor banks' capital as part of the supervision process. Under the rules established in 1991, regulators can close a bank immediately if its capital falls below 2 percent of its assets. Note that closure can occur while the bank is still barely solvent—capital can be low but positive. Regulators try to act before capital becomes negative, which would create severe moral hazard.

Regulators have a second option when capital falls below 2 percent of assets: they can give the bank a final chance to increase its capital. The bank can try to add capital by issuing new stock, which people will buy if they think the bank will be profitable in the future. Usually the bank is given 3 months to increase capital substantially. If it can't, then it must close.

The Closure Process

The decision to close a bank is made by the agency that granted the bank a charter (either the OCC or a state agency). This agency calls in the FDIC, which becomes a *receiver* for the bank. This means the FDIC takes over the bank's assets and liabilities. It then disposes of these items using one of two methods:

1. Under the *payoff method*, the FDIC pays insured depositors what they are owed by the closed bank. Then the FDIC sells the bank's assets for as much as it can get. The proceeds offset part of the cost of paying depositors. The bank ceases to exist, and depositors must find a new place to put their funds.

2. Under the *purchase and assumption method*, the FDIC sells most of the assets and liabilities of the closed bank to another, healthier bank. This new bank takes over the business of the closed bank. Often the FDIC must accept a negative price for the closed bank—it pays the bank that acquires it—because the liabilities that are sold exceed the assets. Under the purchase and assumption method, depositors keep their deposits and bank branches stay open under new ownership.

In every bank closure, the FDIC is required to choose the method that is least expensive to the insurance fund. Usually, this is the purchase and assumption method. When a healthy bank takes over a closed bank, it gains relationships with new customers that produce deposits and loan opportunities. The value of customer relationships reduces the amount the FDIC must pay to sell the closed bank.

When the FDIC uses the purchase and assumption method, it seeks to keep the business of the failed bank running smoothly. It negotiates the sale of the bank's assets and liabilities in advance but keeps the deal secret. Usually FDIC officials arrive at the failed bank on a Friday afternoon and announce that its charter has been revoked. Over the weekend, they work with the staffs of both the failed bank and the acquiring bank on practical aspects of the takeover, such as integrating the two banks' computer systems. Generally, bank branches reopen for business on Monday morning. Employees of the failed bank do not lose their jobs immediately, but eventually the acquiring bank may eliminate jobs to cut costs.

The largest bank failure in U.S. history occurred in September 2008 at the height of the financial crisis. Washington Mutual (WaMu), the country's largest savings institution and sixth-largest bank overall, fell victim to the subprime mortgage crisis. The FDIC took over WaMu and sold its assets and deposits to JPMorgan Chase for $1.9 billion, a tiny price considering that WaMu had amassed $300 billion in assets in 2007. Neither the FDIC nor JPMorgan took responsibility for WaMu's borrowings; institutions that had lent the failed bank money received only a share of the $1.9 billion purchase price. WaMu's stockholders were wiped out completely.

Atypically, the FDIC closed WaMu on a Thursday. Rumors that the bank was in trouble were causing a rapid volume of withdrawals, and the FDIC feared that WaMu would run out of liquid assets if it were not shut down immediately. JPMorgan Chase managed to reopen the former WaMu branches on Friday morning.

Summary

- U.S. banks are heavily regulated by the government. Most regulations are intended to reduce the risk of bank failure.

10.1 Bank Runs

- A bank run occurs when depositors lose confidence in a bank and make sudden, large withdrawals. A run can drain a bank's liquid assets, force a fire sale of loans, and cause the bank to fail.

- A run can result from self-fulfilling expectations: people withdraw money because they expect withdrawals by others.

- Sometimes a bank facing a run can suspend payments temporarily and then reopen. Suspension gives the bank time to reassure depositors and increase its liquid assets.

- A bank panic is a wave of runs at many banks. The United States experienced severe bank panics in the early 1930s.

10.2 Deposit Insurance

- Deposit insurance is a promise by the government to compensate depositors if a bank fails. In the United States, deposits are insured up to $250,000 per account by the Federal Deposit Insurance Corporation (FDIC).

- Deposit insurance prevents bank runs because it makes depositors confident that their money is safe.

10.3 Moral Hazard Again

- Banking creates a problem of moral hazard: bankers have incentives to misuse deposits. Bankers may take excessive risks, or they may simply steal money, as happened at the First National Bank of Keystone.

- Deposit insurance exacerbates moral hazard because it reduces depositors' incentives to monitor banks. Because of this effect, governments limit the coverage of deposit insurance.

- Some research suggests that deposit insurance makes banking crises more likely, at least in countries with weak bank supervision.

10.4 Who Can Open a Bank?

- A new bank must obtain a charter from either a federal or state agency. The prospective bank must convince officials that its risk of failure is low.

- U.S. law requires the separation of banking and commerce. Banks can't own commercial firms, and vice versa.

- Walmart has tried to establish an industrial loan company that could perform some banking functions, but it has been stymied by political opposition in the United States. Walmart has established banks in Canada and Mexico.

10.5 Restrictions on Bank Balance Sheets

- In the United States, banks are regulated by a variety of federal and state agencies. However, the different regulators usually set similar rules.

- Regulators restrict the riskiness of banks' assets. For example, banks can hold only safe securities, and their loans must be diversified.

- U.S. banks must hold capital equal to at least 5 percent of total assets. Under the Basel Accord, they must also satisfy capital requirements based on risk-adjusted assets. Some banks have used SIVs to circumvent capital requirements. Regulators are likely to tighten capital requirements in the wake of the most recent financial crisis.

10.6 Bank Supervision

- One part of bank regulation is supervision, or monitoring of banks' activities. Banks must submit quarterly call reports on their finances. In addition, regulators perform on-site examinations of every bank at least once a year.

- After an examination, a bank is given a set of CAMELS ratings that summarize various types of insolvency risk. If a bank's CAMELS ratings are poor, regulators require changes in the bank's practices to reduce risk.

10.7 Closing Insolvent Banks

- Insolvent banks may stay in business because insured depositors continue to provide them with funds. Regulators must close these banks quickly to prevent them from losing more money.

- Regulators sometimes allow insolvent banks to stay open, hoping to avoid the pain of closure. Such forbearance can ultimately lead to expensive, taxpayer-funded bailouts, as occurred during the S&L crisis of the 1980s.

- Under current law, regulators can close a bank when its capital falls below 2 percent of its assets. The FDIC either closes the bank and compensates depositors (the payoff method) or arranges a takeover by a healthier bank (the purchase and assumption method).

Key Terms

bank examination, p. 306

bank panic, p. 290

bank run, p. 285

bank supervision, p. 306

Basel Accord, p. 303

call report, p. 306

CAMELS ratings, p. 307

capital requirements, p. 303

deposit insurance, p. 292

Federal Deposit Insurance Corporation (FDIC), p. 292

forbearance, p. 309

industrial loan company (ILC), p. 299

structured investment vehicle (SIV), p. 305

suspension of payments, p. 288

Questions and Problems

1. Suppose you are a depositor at Melvin's Bank, which has the balance sheet shown in Table 10.1A. Deposit insurance does not exist. You originally deposited your money in Melvin's Bank because its branch locations are more convenient than those of other banks.

   a. Suppose you know that Melvin's other depositors plan to keep their money there. Should you do the same or withdraw your money and deposit it elsewhere?

   b. Suppose you know that other depositors plan to make large withdrawals from Melvin's Bank. What should you do?

   c. What do your answers to parts (a) and (b) tell you about the likelihood and causes of bank runs?

2. Suppose an economy has a high level of loans from one bank to another. How might this fact affect the likelihood of a bank panic?

3. Some economists suggest that banks should be charged premiums for deposit insurance based on their levels of capital. Premiums should be higher if capital is lower. What is the rationale for this proposal? Are there any drawbacks to the idea?

4. Suppose Walmart is allowed to open a bank that accepts deposits and makes loans at its U.S. stores.

   a. How might this affect existing banks, especially community banks? (See Section 8.2 for a review of community banks.)

   b. In general, who might gain and who might lose if Walmart opens a bank?

5. Consider an analogy (the type on the SATs): "A bank regulator is to a bank as a bank is to a borrower." In what ways is this analogy true? (See Section 7.5 for a review of the bank–borrower relationship.)

6. Suppose Melvin's Bank can make a bet on derivatives that has a two-thirds probability of earning $20 and a one-third probability of losing $40.

   a. Assume Melvin has $20 in capital. What are the possible costs and benefits of the bet for Melvin and the deposit insurance fund? Is Melvin likely to make the bet?

   b. How are the answers in part (a) different if Melvin's Bank has $50 in capital? What if it has $0 in capital?

   c. In light of these examples, discuss the benefits of (i) capital requirements (ii) bank supervision, and (iii) quick closure of insolvent banks.

7. Let's change the example of capital requirements in Table 10.3. Assume that Melvin's Bank holds $40 in Treasury bonds (rather than $10) and $30 in loans to other banks (rather than $10). Otherwise, Melvin's assets are the same as in the table.

   a. Calculate the level of capital that Melvin must hold to satisfy (i) the minimum equity ratio and (ii) the risk-based Basel requirement.

   b. Which of the two requirements is more stringent in this case? Is the answer different than it was for the original Table 10.3? If so, why?

8. Consider two possibilities: (i) a bank is forced to close even though there is no good reason for it to close; (ii) a bank remains open even though there *are* good reasons for it to close.

   a. Explain why (i) and (ii) are possible and what regulations affect the likelihood of these outcomes.

   b. Can some combination of regulations make both (i) and (ii) unlikely?

▶ Online and Data Questions

www.worthpublishers.com/ball

9. Through the text Web site, connect to the site of the Office of the Comptroller of the Currency and look up "Enforcement Actions." Find an example of a specific enforcement action against a bank. Explain what the OCC did and what problem it was trying to rectify.

10. The text Web site has a link to a paper by Christine Blair, an economist at the FDIC, called "The Mixing of Banking and Commerce." Read this paper and briefly summarize the arguments for and against the "mixing" in the title. Which side do you agree with?

chapter eleven

The Money Supply and Interest Rates

Reuters/Joe Pavel/Landov

March 17, 2009: a meeting of the Federal Open Market Committee, which sets monetary policy, in Washington, DC.

Early in his tenure as chairman of the Federal Reserve, on a Saturday night in April 2006, Ben Bernanke attended the annual White House Correspondents Dinner, where he chatted with CNBC anchor Maria Bartiromo. The next Monday, Bartiromo reported that she asked Bernanke whether he was sure the Fed would keep interest rates constant in the near future. According to Bartiromo, Bernanke's answer was "no." This news caused stock prices to drop sharply over the next hour. Bernanke later called his loose talk "a lapse in judgment" and promised to keep quiet at future dinners.

The media's interest in Ben Bernanke reflects the Fed's influence on the national economy. The Fed's power arises primarily from its control of monetary policy. Earlier chapters have sketched how monetary policy works. The Fed adjusts the money supply, which affects interest rates, which in turn affect the levels of output, unemployment, and inflation.

Part IV of this book, Chapters 11 through 14, fleshes out the story of how the Fed affects the economy. In this chapter, we begin by describing the Federal Reserve System and how it determines the money supply. Previously we've simply assumed that the Fed picks a level for the money supply. Here we'll study the process through which money is created, one that involves commercial banks and the public as well as the Fed. We'll examine the Fed's tools for pushing the money supply to the level it chooses.

This chapter also examines the relation between the money supply and interest rates. We'll see that the Fed sets targets for one particular interest rate, the rate on federal funds, and adjusts the money supply to hit these targets.

11.1 THE FEDERAL RESERVE SYSTEM

▶The case study in Section 8.2 discusses Andrew Jackson and the Second Bank, and Section 10.1 discusses bank panics in U.S. history.

The United States had a central bank for brief periods in the early 1800s—the First Bank of the United States and then the Second Bank. Andrew Jackson put the Second Bank out of business in 1836, because he and fellow populists feared the bank's power. However, bank panics in the late nineteenth and early twentieth centuries strengthened support for a central bank. Political leaders became convinced that the country needed a central bank to serve as lender of last resort during panics. In 1913, Congress passed the Federal Reserve Act, which established the Fed system.

Under the Federal Reserve Act, the United States is divided into 12 Federal Reserve Districts, each with a Federal Reserve Bank. For example, the first district includes most of New England and is served by the Federal Reserve Bank of Boston; the twelfth district covers Western states and is served by the Federal Reserve Bank of San Francisco. The board of Governors, located in Washington, D.C., oversees the system. The board has seven members, including the chair (currently Ben Bernanke) and vice chair (currently Janet Yellen).

 Visit the text Web site to view a map showing the 12 Federal Reserve Districts and the locations of their banks.

Formally, a Federal Reserve Bank is not part of the government. It is owned by commercial banks in its district, which buy shares in the bank and receive dividends of 6 percent per year. Each Federal Reserve Bank has a board of directors with nine members, six elected by the commercial banks and three appointed by the board of governors in Washington. The directors appoint a president to run the bank, with the approval of the board of governors. Under this system, commercial banks and the board in Washington share control over Federal Reserve Banks.

Members of the board of governors are appointed by the president of the United States and confirmed by Congress. Once appointed, governors are independent of elected officials and often serve for a long time. A governor's term lasts 14 years and cannot be ended involuntarily (although many governors leave early for high-paying jobs in the private sector). The term of the Fed chair is only 4 years, but some chairs have been reappointed many times. Ben Bernanke was appointed by President Bush in 2005 and reappointed by President Obama in 2009. Before Bernanke took office, Alan Greenspan was chair for more than 18 years.

▶Chapter 16 discusses the rationale for the Fed's independence from elected officials.

11.2 THE FED AND THE MONETARY BASE

M = Money supply [handwritten]

How does the Fed control the money supply? In answering this question, we focus on the primary definition of the money supply, M1. This aggregate is the sum of currency in circulation, checking deposits, and traveler's checks. We ignore traveler's checks here, because this component is small and shrinking. We use M to stand for the money supply, C for currency in circulation, and D for checking deposits, giving us

$$M = C + D$$

▶ Section 2.3 details how the Federal Reserve measures the money supply.

The Federal Reserve does *not* directly create the money supply. The Fed issues currency, but checking deposits are created by banks and their customers. What the Fed *does* create is the monetary base.

The Monetary Base

Base = Currency + Reserves. [handwritten]

The **monetary base**, B, is the sum of two quantities: currency in circulation, C, and bank reserves, R. Currency in circulation is also part of the money supply. Bank reserves are vault cash plus banks' deposits at the Fed. In symbols,

$$B = C + R$$

Monetary base (B) sum of currency in circulation and bank reserves ($B = C + R$); the Federal Reserve's liabilities to the private sector of the economy

A fine distinction: All currency created by the Fed is included in the monetary base, but it is split between the C and R components. Currency outside banks—cash held by people and nonbank firms—counts as currency in circulation. Currency does *not* fall in this category if it is sitting in a bank or ATM. In this case, it counts as vault cash, which is part of bank reserves.

What is the meaning of the monetary base? Economists interpret it as the liabilities of the Federal Reserve to the private sector of the economy. Currency in circulation is a liability of the Fed to the people and firms that hold the currency. Formally, if you own a $20 bill, that means the Fed owes you $20.

Reserves are a liability of the Fed to banks. If a bank holds $100 of vault cash, the Fed owes it $100. The same is true if the bank has $100 of deposits in its account at the Fed.

Creating the Base

Suppose that a central bank is established and wants to create a monetary base of $100, or that an existing central bank wants to raise or lower the base by $100. Central banks have two methods for changing the base: open-market operations and loans.

Open-Market Operations Purchases or sales of securities by a central bank are **open-market operations**. Most open-market operations by the Federal Reserve are trades of U.S. Treasury bonds; during the most recent financial crisis, the Fed also purchased bonds and prime mortgage-backed securities issued by Fannie Mae and Freddie Mac. A central bank purchase of any type of securities (an *expansionary open-market operation*) raises the monetary base. A sale of securities (a *contractionary open-market operation*) reduces the base.

Open-market operations purchases or sales of securities by a central bank

To see how this works, consider an expansionary open-market operation: the Fed purchases $100 of bonds. It buys them from a bond dealer, paying the dealer either by giving it $100 in cash or (more realistically) by depositing $100 in a bank account held by the dealer. In either case, the monetary base rises:

- If the Fed gives the dealer cash, then currency in circulation (C) rises by $100. Currency in circulation is part of the monetary base, so the base rises by $100.

- If the Fed deposits $100 in the dealer's bank account, it changes the balance sheet of the dealer's bank. On the liability side, deposits rise by $100; on the asset side, the bank gains $100 in reserves ($R$). Reserves are part of the monetary base, so the base rises by $100.

To summarize, no matter how the Fed pays the bond dealer,

$$\$100 \text{ purchase of bonds by Fed} \rightarrow B \uparrow \$100$$

A contractionary open-market operation reverses this process. Say the Fed sells $100 of bonds to a dealer. To pay for the bonds, the dealer either hands over cash, reducing currency in circulation, or withdraws funds from a bank, reducing reserves. Either way the base falls by $100:

$$\$100 \text{ purchase of bonds by Fed} \rightarrow B \downarrow \$100$$

Loans The Fed can also change the monetary base by lending money to a financial institution, primarily through a **discount loan** to a bank. A bank can approach the Fed at any time and request such a loan. The Fed sets an interest rate on discount loans called the **discount rate**.

During the most recent financial crisis, the Fed broadened its lending. For example, from December 2007 to March 2010, it held auctions in which it allocated loans to banks that submitted the highest interest rate bids. The Fed also lent to financial institutions, such as investment banks and insurance companies, that are not usually eligible for discount loans. We discuss this emergency lending later in the chapter.

Regardless of how the Fed makes a loan and what institution receives it, the loan increases the monetary base. This happens in slightly different ways, depending on whether the borrower is a bank that holds deposits at the Fed or another type of financial institution:

If the Fed lends $100 to a bank, it simply adds $100 to the bank's account at the Fed. The bank's deposits are part of the monetary base, so the base rises by $100.

If the Fed lends $100 to an institution without an account at the Fed, such as an investment bank, it transfers the funds to the borrower's account at some bank (just as it transfers funds to a bond dealer's bank account in an open-market operation). Reserves rise by $100 at the borrower's bank, so the base rises by $100.

To summarize,

$$\$100 \text{ loan from Fed to financial institution} \rightarrow B \uparrow \$100$$

Discount loan loan from the Federal Reserve to a bank made at the bank's request

Discount rate interest rate on discount loans

A financial institution that receives a loan from the Fed usually repays the loan. When that happens, the repayment drains reserves from some bank. Therefore,

$$\text{Repayment of \$100 loan from Fed} \rightarrow B \downarrow \$100$$

The Fed's Balance Sheet

In Chapter 9, we summarized the operations of commercial banks by examining their balance sheets. We can do the same for the Federal Reserve. We've already discussed the key items on the Fed's balance sheet; pulling them together, we get

Know.

THE FED'S BALANCE SHEET

Assets	Liabilities
Securities	Currency in circulation
Loans to financial institutions	Bank reserves

▶ The Fed's balance sheet also includes items that we ignore here:

■ Liabilities include deposits by the U.S. Treasury. (These are liabilities of the Fed to the government, not to the private sector, and so are not part of the monetary base).

■ Assets include reserves of foreign currency, which the Fed uses to intervene in foreign exchange markets.

■ Capital is provided by commercial banks, the formal owners of the Federal Reserve Banks.

The Fed's assets are the securities it has purchased through open-market operations and the loans it has made to financial institutions. Its liabilities are the two components of the monetary base: currency and reserves.

When the Fed adjusts the monetary base, its actions are reflected on its balance sheet. Suppose the Fed purchases $100 of Treasury bonds (an expansionary open-market operation). It sends $100 to the bank account of a security dealer, raising the bank's reserves. The Fed's balance sheet shows a $100 rise in a liability, reserves, and a $100 rise in an asset, securities.

Now suppose the Fed lends $100 to a bank, adding to the bank's reserves. The Fed's balance sheet shows a $100 rise in a liability, reserves, and a $100 rise in an asset, loans to financial institutions.

The Fed's balance sheet is also influenced by a factor beyond its control: the public's decisions about how much currency to hold. Suppose you take $100 from your bank's ATM and put it in your wallet. Your action reduces your bank's vault cash, which is part of reserves. So, on the liability side of the Fed's balance sheet, reserves fall by $100. The other liability, currency in circulation, rises by $100.

Notice that your action does *not* affect the monetary base, which is the sum of currency in circulation and reserves. One component of the base falls by $100 and the other rises by $100, leaving the base unchanged.

▶ Problem 11.7 asks you to explore how the Fed's actions in response to the most recent financial crisis affected its balance sheet.

11.3 COMMERCIAL BANKS AND THE MONEY SUPPLY

So far we've focused on the monetary base (B), which is currency plus reserves ($C + R$). Our goal is to understand the money supply (M), or currency plus checking deposits ($C + D$). The base, which the Fed controls, is one factor that affects the money supply. However, the money supply also depends on the behavior of banks and their customers, which the Fed does not control.

$M = C + D$

Usually the money supply is larger than the base, because banks' checking deposits (*D*) exceed their reserves (*R*). We focus here on an example with this feature. During the most recent financial crisis, a huge increase in reserves pushed the base above the money supply; a case study in Section 11.4 examines this abnormal episode.

An Economy Without Banks

To understand the role of banks in determining the money supply, first imagine an economy where banks don't exist. There are no bank reserves and no checking deposits. Cash is used for all transactions.

In this economy, the monetary base and the money supply are the same thing. Each equals currency in circulation. In algebraic terms, $C + R$ (the base) and $C + D$ (money) are the same thing if R and D are zero. Suppose currency in circulation is \$1000. Then the components of the base and the money supply are

C	1000
R	0
D	0
$B = C + R$	1000
$M = C + D$	1000

A Bank Creates Money. . .

One day in the bankless economy we've just described, an enterprising person opens a commercial bank called The Friendly Bank. Let's examine how this bank can influence the money supply. We use the bank's balance sheet to summarize its actions.

Let's keep the example simple to focus on key ideas. Assume The Friendly Bank raises funds entirely through checking deposits. It holds some of these funds as reserves and uses the rest for loans. We'll ignore the other items on the balance sheets of real-world banks, such as securities, savings deposits, and net worth.

▶ Problem 11.3 examines how the money-creation process changes when we include more items on The Friendly Bank's balance sheet.

The Bank Takes Deposits When The Friendly Bank opens, people have a place to deposit their money. Recall that the people in this economy initially have \$1000 in cash. For our example, assume that \$800 is deposited in checking accounts at The Friendly Bank, leaving \$200 in cash. This implies that the ratio of currency in circulation (*C*) to checking deposits (*D*) is 200/800, or 0.25. This term is called the **currency–deposit ratio**.

Currency–deposit ratio (C/D) ratio of currency in circulation to checking deposits

These deposits occur on a Monday. Initially, The Friendly Bank either holds the \$800 as vault cash or deposits it at the central bank. Either way, the \$800 counts as reserves. So the bank's balance sheet is

THE FRIENDLY BANK'S BALANCE SHEET AS OF MONDAY

Assets		Liabilities	
R	800	D	800

Remember, we're interested in the monetary base and the money supply. Let's tally up these aggregates:

MONDAY

C	200
R	800
D	800
B = C + R	1000
M = C + D	1000

The base is still $1000, its level in the bankless economy. At this point, the money supply is also stuck at $1000. Money has shifted from currency to deposits, but the total of the two is unchanged.

The Bank Makes Loans The Friendly Bank doesn't want to keep reserves as its only asset; it wants to make loans that pay more interest. Of its $800 in checking deposits, assume the bank lends $600 and keeps $200 as reserves. This implies that the bank's **reserve–deposit ratio** is 200/800 = 0.25.

The bank makes its loans (L) on Tuesday. On its balance sheet, assets shift from reserves to loans:

R/D

Reserve–deposit ratio (R/D) ratio of bank reserves to checking deposits

THE FRIENDLY BANK'S BALANCE SHEET AS OF TUESDAY

Assets		Liabilities	
R	200	D	800
L	600		

Assume the loans are made in cash. When people receive the loans, currency in circulation rises by $600. Now the monetary aggregates are

TUESDAY

C	800
R	200
D	800
B = C + R	1000
M = C + D	1600

At this point, the base is still $1000. But the money supply is $1600, higher than its level before The Friendly Bank opened.

This example shows how a bank can create money. The bank gives people deposits in return for currency then lends out part of the currency. The sum of currency in circulation and deposits—the money supply—ends up higher than it started.

. . . and More Money

The loans made by The Friendly Bank on Tuesday trigger further transactions that further increase the money supply. Let's watch these next steps.

More Deposits In the last transaction, borrowers received $600 in cash loans from The Friendly Bank. They may spend some or all of this money, so other people receive it. Regardless, whoever ends up with the $600 doesn't want to keep all of it in cash. Let's assume again that people choose a currency–deposit ratio of 0.25. Out of $600, they keep $120 in cash and deposit $480, because 120/480 = 0.25.

The deposits occur on Wednesday, raising The Friendly Bank's total deposits and reserves. The bank's balance sheet becomes

THE FRIENDLY BANK'S BALANCE SHEET AS OF WEDNESDAY

Assets		Liabilities	
R	680	D	1280
L	600		

The monetary aggregates are

WEDNESDAY

C	320
R	680
D	1280
$B = C + R$	1000
$M = C + D$	1600

More Loans You can probably guess the next step: after Wednesday's increase in reserves, the bank makes more loans. Assume the bank still chooses a reserve–deposit ratio of 0.25. Because total deposits are $1280, the bank wants reserves of $(0.25)(\$1280) = \$320$. To reduce reserves to this level, the bank lends $360.

These loans occur on Thursday. The bank's balance sheet becomes

THE FRIENDLY BANK'S BALANCE SHEET AS OF THURSDAY

Assets		Liabilities	
R	320	D	1280
L	960		

The monetary aggregates are

THURSDAY

C	680
R	320
D	1280
$B = C + R$	1000
$M = C + D$	1960

At this point, the money supply has risen again, as the new loans add to currency in circulation. The monetary base is still $1000, its level before the bank opened.

And So On. . . We can continue this story indefinitely. Of the $360 lent out on Thursday, people keep $72 in cash and deposit $288 on Friday (because $72/288 = 0.25$, the currency–deposit ratio in this example). The bank's reserves rise. The bank closes for the weekend, but the following Monday it makes new loans to push its reserve–deposit ratio back to 0.25. The loans on Monday lead to new deposits on Tuesday, which produce new loans on Wednesday, and on it goes.

None of these transactions affects the monetary base. In each one, currency and reserves change by offsetting amounts. In contrast, the money supply rises over time. Money is created each time the bank makes new loans.

Limits to Money Creation

Let's step back from our calculations and see where we're heading. Although The Friendly Bank creates more and more money, the money supply does not become infinite. In the process we've examined, the increases in money get smaller at each stage. Eventually, the increases die out and the money supply settles at a stable level.

Figure 11.1 summarizes the process of money creation. Of $1000 in cash, $800 is deposited in The Friendly Bank when it opens; $600 of the deposits are lent out, increasing the money supply by that amount; $480 is redeposited; and $360 is lent out again. This process continues, but each deposit or loan is less than the one before.

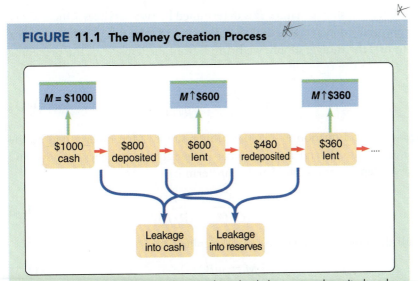

FIGURE 11.1 The Money Creation Process

$M = \$1000$

$M \uparrow \$600$

$M \uparrow \$360$

| $1000 cash | $800 deposited | $600 lent | $480 redeposited | $360 lent | .... |

Leakage into cash

Leakage into reserves

Banks create money. Money is deposited in a bank, lent out, redeposited, and lent out again, causing the money supply to rise repeatedly. The increases in money die out eventually because of leakages into currency and bank reserves. (Here, the currency–deposit ratio is 0.25, and the reserve–deposit ratio is 0.25.)

Money creation dies out because of "leakage" from the deposit–loan process. Two types of leakage occur. First, not all of the bank's loans are redeposited: the public holds some as cash. Second, not all deposits are lent out again, because the bank keeps some as reserves.

What is the final level of the money supply? We will answer this question by deriving a general formula for the money supply that we can then apply to our example.

11.4 A FORMULA FOR THE MONEY SUPPLY

We've seen that the money supply depends on the monetary base, which the Fed creates, and the behavior of banks and their depositors. A little algebra will show us the exact relationship between the money supply and the base.

Deriving the Formula

The money supply, M, is $C + D$, and the base, B, is $C + R$. The ratio of these two variables, M/B, is

$$\frac{M}{B} = \frac{C + D}{C + R}$$

On the right side of this equation, divide both the numerator and the denominator by D:

$$\frac{M}{B} = \frac{(C/D) + 1}{(C/D) + (R/D)}$$

This equation shows that M/B is determined by two variables. One is C/D, the currency–deposit ratio, and the other is R/D, the reserve–deposit ratio.

To find the money supply, we bring B from the left side of the preceding equation to the right side:

$$M = \frac{(C/D) + 1}{(C/D) + (R/D)} B \qquad (11.1)$$

According to Equation (11.1), the money supply, M, is determined by the monetary base, B, and another term involving the currency–deposit and reserve–deposit ratios. We denote this term by m:

$$m = \frac{(C/D) + 1}{(C/D) + (R/D)} \qquad (11.2)$$

With this notation, Equation (11.1) simplifies to

$$M = mB \qquad (11.3)$$

Money multiplier (m)
ratio of the money supply to the monetary base; $M = mB$

The term m is greater than 1 if R/D is less than 1, meaning banks' reserves are less than their deposits. This condition usually holds. Because m is usually greater than 1, it is called the **money multiplier**. Equation (11.3) says *the money supply equals the money multiplier times the monetary base.*

Let's apply our formula for the money supply to the example of The Friendly Bank. We assume again that the currency–deposit ratio (C/D) is 0.25 and the reserve–deposit ratio (R/D) is also 0.25. Plugging these numbers into the expression for the money multiplier, Equation (11.2), we get

$$m = \frac{0.25 + 1}{0.25 + 0.25} = 2.5$$

In the example, the monetary base, B, is always $1000. The money supply, mB, is (2.5) × ($1000) = $2500. We saw how the Friendly Bank's loans raised the money supply from $1000 to $1600, and then to $1960. If we continued our calculations, we would find that the money supply eventually reaches $2500.

Changes in the Money Supply

We can use our formula to see why the money supply might change. First, the money supply rises if the base rises:

m > 1

$$\uparrow B \rightarrow \uparrow M$$

As long as the multiplier m exceeds 1, a rise in B has a more than one-for-one effect on M. If the multiplier is 2.5, then a $100 rise in the base (say, from $1000 to $1100) raises the money supply by $250 (from $2500 to $2750).

The money supply also changes if the money multiplier changes. This occurs if either the currency–deposit ratio or the reserve–deposit ratio changes. Specifically, a rise in either ratio reduces the multiplier, and hence the money supply:

$$\uparrow C/D \rightarrow \downarrow m \rightarrow \downarrow M$$
$$\uparrow R/D \rightarrow \downarrow m \rightarrow \downarrow M$$

Very Important.

For example, if C/D rises from 0.25 to 0.50 and R/D stays at 0.25, then m falls from 2.5 to 2.0. If the monetary base is $1000, the money supply falls from $2500 to $2000. You can check that a rise in R/D has a similar effect.

These effects should make sense to you. Recall that the money supply is limited by leakages from the process of depositing and lending. A higher currency–deposit ratio means more leakage into cash: banks receive fewer deposits. A higher reserve–deposit ratio means more leakage into reserves: banks lend less. In each case, greater leakage means less money is created from a given monetary base.

leakge ratio more leakge

Let's return now to two events we have discussed before—the Great Depression of the 1930s and the financial crisis of 2007–2009. Examining the monetary base and money multiplier in the following case studies helps us understand what happened to the money supply and the economy during each crisis.

FIGURE 11.2 The Money Multiplier and the Great Depression

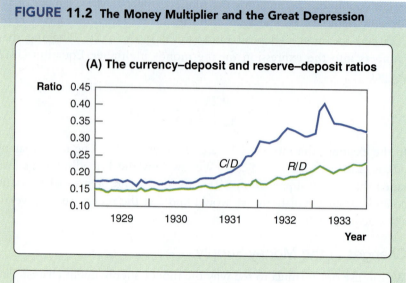

(A) The currency–deposit and reserve–deposit ratios

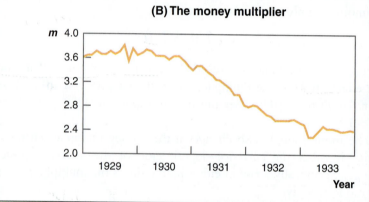

(B) The money multiplier

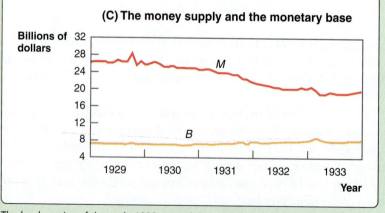

(C) The money supply and the monetary base

The bank panics of the early 1930s raised the currency–deposit ratio and the reserve–deposit ratio (A), reducing the money multiplier (B). The fall in the multiplier reduced the money supply despite a rise in the monetary base (C).

Source: Milton Friedman and Anna Jacobson Schwartz, *A Monetary History of the United States, 1867–1960*, Princeton University Press, 1963, pp. 703–748

CASE STUDY

The Money Multiplier and the Great Depression

Changes in the money supply have strong effects on the economy. Nothing demonstrates this fact more clearly than the Great Depression of the 1930s. Between 1929 and 1933, the money supply fell by 33 percent. Over the same period, real GDP fell by 31 percent, and the unemployment rate rose from 3 percent to 25 percent.

What caused the money supply to fall? The story begins with the bank panics of the early 1930s that produced widespread bank failures and large losses to depositors. Fearing additional failures, people started taking money out of banks and keeping it in cash. This behavior raised the currency–deposit ratio, C/D. As shown in **Figure 11.2A**, C/D rose from 0.17 in 1929 to a peak of 0.41 in March 1933.

The panics also changed the behavior of the banks that remained open. They, too, feared that new panics might occur, prompting large withdrawals. To guard against liquidity crises, banks started holding more reserves. In Figure 11.2A, the reserve–deposit ratio, R/D, rose from 0.14 to 0.23.

The rises in C/D and R/D both reduced the money multiplier, m. As shown in **Figure 11.2B,** the multiplier fell from 3.8 in 1929 to 2.4 in 1933. The monetary base rose, as graphed in **Figure 11.2C**, but not enough to offset the fall in the multiplier. The money supply fell, helping to precipitate the depression.

The fall in the money supply resulted from the behavior of banks and their customers, not from any deliberate policy of the Federal Reserve. Nonetheless, economic historians fault the Fed for allowing the money supply to fall. In retrospect, the Fed should have increased the monetary base more quickly. Such action could have prevented the fall in the money supply and dampened the economic downturn. At the time, however, Fed officials remained passive and blamed the deteriorating economy on forces beyond its control.[*]

[*]The classic account of this episode is in Milton Friedman and Anna Jacobson Schwartz, *A Monetary History of the United States, 1867–1960*, Princeton University Press, 1963, Chapter 7.

CASE STUDY

The Monetary Base and Money Multiplier, 2007–2010

The most recent financial crisis had dramatic effects, both on the monetary base and on the money multiplier. As shown in **Figure 11.3**, over 2007 and the first half of 2008, the base was stable at around $850 billion (Figure 11.3C) and the multiplier at 1.6 (Figure 11.3B). Then, over the brief period from August 2008 to January 2009, the base roughly doubled to $1.7 trillion and the multiplier fell to 0.9, just above half its previous level. At less than 1.0, the "multiplier" became a "divider." After January 2009, the base continued to rise while the multiplier stayed below 1.0.

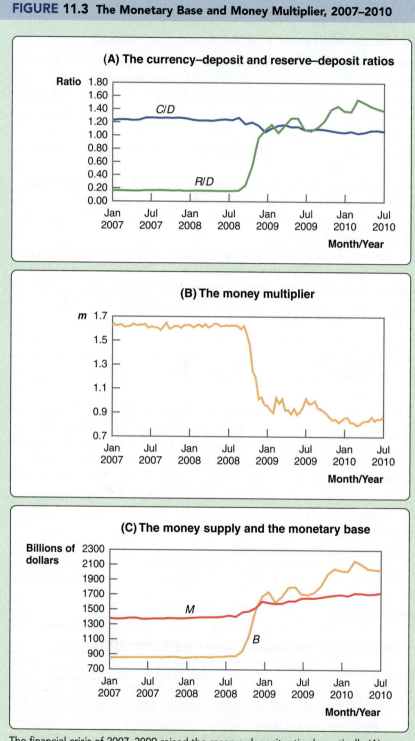

FIGURE 11.3 The Monetary Base and Money Multiplier, 2007–2010

(A) The currency–deposit and reserve–deposit ratios

(B) The money multiplier

(C) The money supply and the monetary base

The financial crisis of 2007–2009 raised the reserve-deposit ratio dramatically (A), pushing the money multiplier below one (B). Yet the money supply rose because of a huge rise in the monetary base, a result of emergency Fed policies (C).

Source: Federal Reserve Bank of St. Louis

The increase in the base reflected the Fed's emergency policies during the financial crisis. After Lehman Brothers failed in September 2008, many other institutions appeared to be on the brink of failure. The Fed responded with emergency lending programs such as the Term Auction Facility (TAF), which auctioned loans to commercial banks, and the Primary Dealer Credit Facility (PDCF), which lent to large investment banks. The Fed also negotiated special loans to the insurance conglomerate American International Group and the financial holding company Citigroup. All this lending by the Fed caused bank reserves and hence the monetary base to rise rapidly.

As the threat of failure waned during 2009, many borrowers paid back the Fed's emergency loans. In isolation, repayment of loans reduced the monetary base. Yet bank reserves and the base continued to grow overall because of expansionary open-market operations.

Specifically, the Fed purchased huge quantities of long-term Treasury bonds and prime mortgage-backed securities (MBS) issued by Fannie Mae and Freddie Mac; its holdings of MBS rose from zero at the start of 2009 to more than $1 trillion a year later. The Fed's goal was to drive up the prices of long-term bonds and prime MBS and thereby to reduce interest rates (yields to maturity) on these securities. Policymakers hoped that lower interest rates would stimulate spending, especially on housing, which would help to dampen the recession caused by the financial crisis.

The sharp fall in the money multiplier was caused by an increase in the reserve–deposit ratio (Figure 11.3A). In December 2008, this ratio passed 1.0, implying that the base exceeded the money supply (Figure 11.3C). Once again, the explanation lies in the abnormal condition of the financial system.

When banks receive reserves, they usually lend out most of them, as in the example of The Friendly Bank in Section 11.3. During the financial crisis, however, banks were reluctant to increase their lending, because the weak economy raised default risk and because defaults could drive the banks into insolvency. Thus, when banks received reserves as a result of the Fed's lending and open-market operations, they simply held onto them, and the reserve–deposit ratio rose.

The increase in the monetary base (B) and decrease in the multiplier (m) had opposite effects on the money supply (mB). The increase in the base was somewhat larger, so the money supply rose 23 percent from August 2008 to June 2010. As predicted by the liquidity preference theory, the increase in the money supply reduced interest rates: short-term rates fell almost to zero. The Fed welcomed the fall in interest rates because it stimulated spending.

As 2011 began, the money multiplier was still below 1.0 and the base was over $2 trillion. This situation is temporary, however. Eventually, economic recovery will lead banks to lend out more reserves, and the reserve–deposit ratio will fall to a more normal level. The Fed also plans to shrink its holdings of securities to precrisis levels, reducing the monetary base. The Fed will face the challenge of managing this process without too great an increase in the money supply, which could lead to inflation, or too great a decrease, which could slow economic growth.

▶ Chapter 18 discusses Fed policy during the financial crisis in more detail.

Online Case Study:
Unwinding the Expansion of the Monetary Base

11.5 THE FED'S MONETARY TOOLS

Now that we've seen how the money supply is determined, let's examine how the Federal Reserve can control it. Money creation involves choices on levels of reserves by banks and on cash holdings by individuals and firms. Yet the Fed ultimately controls the process: it can choose a level for the money supply and push it there.

The Fed has four main tools for controlling the money supply. Two tools, open-market operations and the discount rate, affect the monetary base. The other two, reserve requirements and interest on reserves, influence the money multiplier.

Open-Market Operations

Of all its monetary tools, the Fed uses open-market operations the most heavily. The Fed buys and sells billions of dollars of securities every day. We've seen that purchases and sales of securities by the Fed change the monetary base. For example, a $100 purchase of securities (an expansionary open-market operation) raises the base by $100.

We can now see that open-market operations affect the money supply as well as the base. The effect on the money supply depends on the money multiplier. A $100 purchase of bonds raises the base by $100 and the money supply by $100($m$). If the multiplier is 1.5, for example, the money supply rises by $150.

The Fed can use open-market operations to change the money supply when it wants to. It can also use this tool for a different purpose: to *prevent* the money supply from changing when the multiplier changes. If m falls, for example, the Fed can use open-market operations to raise the base, B. The correct increase leaves mB, the money supply, unchanged. Such a reaction is called a *defensive open-market operation*.

The Discount Rate

The Fed affects the monetary base through lending as well as through open-market operations. Outside of financial crises, the Fed's primary type of lending is discount loans to banks. Discount loans are initiated by the borrowers, so the Fed does not directly control their level. However, the Fed can influence banks' borrowing by changing the interest rate it charges, the discount rate.

For example, suppose the Fed raises the discount rate. This action discourages banks from borrowing. Discount loans fall, reducing the monetary base and hence the money supply:

$$\uparrow \text{discount rate} \rightarrow \downarrow \text{discount loans} \rightarrow \downarrow B \rightarrow \downarrow M$$

A decrease in the discount rate has the opposite effects: it encourages banks to borrow, raising the base and the money supply.

In practice, however, the Fed rarely uses the discount rate to manipulate the money supply. In recent years, it has kept the rate high enough so the level of discount loans is usually low. When the Fed wants to raise the monetary base, it uses open-market operations rather than trying to increase discount loans.

Specifically, the Fed sets the discount rate above the federal funds rate—the rate at which banks lend reserves to one another. In 2010, the discount rate was about one-half a percentage point above the federal funds rate. When banks want reserves, they can get them more cheaply from another bank than from the Fed, so they usually don't seek discount loans. Most Fed lending occurs during financial crises and other emergencies when banks have trouble borrowing from their usual sources.

▶ The Case Study in Section 2.5 discusses the terrorist attacks of September 11, 2001, when lending among banks was disrupted and discount loans from the Fed rose sharply.

Reserve Requirements

The Fed's third monetary tool is **reserve requirements**, regulations that set a minimum level for banks' reserve–deposit ratios. This minimum is called the *required reserve ratio*. If the required reserve ratio is 0.1, for example, each bank's reserves must equal at least 10 percent of its checking deposits. If deposits are $1000, minimum reserves are $100.

Reserve requirements regulations that set a minimum level for banks' reserve–deposit ratios

The Fed can influence the money supply by changing the required reserve ratio. Suppose the required ratio is initially 0.1. Banks must choose a reserve–deposit ratio, R/D, that is 0.1 or higher. Let's assume that banks choose a ratio between 0.1 and 0.2.

Then the Fed raises the required reserve ratio to 0.2. To meet the new requirement, banks must raise their reserve–deposit ratios to at least 0.2. This higher reserve–deposit ratio reduces the money multiplier, which in turn reduces the money supply:

$$\uparrow \text{required reserve ratio} \to \uparrow (R/D) \to \downarrow m \to \downarrow M$$

The Banking Act of 1933 gave the Fed the power to set reserve requirements. The original purpose was to prevent liquidity crises by keeping bank reserves high. In the years that followed, the Fed sometimes used reserve requirements to influence the money supply, as we see in an upcoming case study.

In the 2000s, however, reserve requirements have fallen into disuse as a policy tool, because required reserves for most banks are significantly less than the reserves that banks voluntarily choose to hold; that is, banks hold high levels of *excess reserves*. This was true even before the big rise in reserves in 2008. With reserves well above required levels, reserve requirements are irrelevant: if a bank chooses to hold $100 in reserves, it doesn't matter if the Fed tells it to hold at least $75. In economists' language, reserve requirements are not "binding."

One reason that reserve requirements are not binding is sweep programs, in which banks move funds out of checking accounts temporarily. As discussed in Section 2.4, the invention of sweep programs in 1994 has reduced banks' required reserves. At the same time, the reserves banks *want* to hold have risen because of the widespread use of ATMs, which must be stocked with cash. The cash in ATMs is counted as vault cash, which is part of reserves.

How Reserve Requirements Prolonged the Great Depression

As we saw in an earlier case study, U.S. output and employment fell calamitously from 1929 through 1932. In 1933, however, a strong recovery began. Real GDP grew an average of 10 percent per year from 1934 through 1937, and the unemployment rate fell from 25 percent to 14 percent.

It appeared that unemployment was headed down farther, but then something went wrong. A sharp recession occurred, with real GDP falling 5 percent in 1938 and unemployment rising back to 19 percent. Unemployment was still 15 percent in 1940, on the eve of World War II.

As in the early 1930s, a major cause of the downturn was the behavior of the money supply, which grew by 14 percent per year during 1934–1936 but fell during 1937–1938. Once again, historians blame a mistake by the Federal Reserve, this time involving reserve requirements.

The story starts with the high reserve–deposit ratios of the 1930s. Banks chose high levels of reserves to guard against bank runs, as discussed in the earlier case study on the Great Depression. At many banks, reserves greatly exceeded the minimum established by reserve requirements—they had substantial levels of excess reserves.

The Fed worried that this situation weakened its control of the money supply. Banks might decide at some point that their excess reserves were unnecessary and lend them out. If that happened, the reserve–deposit ratio would fall, raising the money multiplier and the money supply. A sharp rise in the money supply could cause inflation.

To address this risk, the Fed raised reserve requirements at three points in 1936 and 1937. Overall, the required reserve ratio for major banks rose from 0.14 to 0.25. The goal was *not* to change the current level of reserves or the money supply. Instead, the Fed wanted to turn excess reserves into required reserves. Without excess reserves, bank lending could not suddenly reduce the reserve–deposit ratio.

The Fed's actions backfired. Banks wanted to hold excess reserves: they wanted a cushion so they would still meet reserve requirements if large withdrawals occurred. When the Fed raised required reserves, banks raised their actual reserves to maintain a gap between the two. The result was a sharp rise in the reserve–deposit ratio. This increase reduced the money multiplier, which in turn reduced the money supply and prolonged the depression.

This episode has an echo in recent history. In 2010, bank reserves were again unusually high, and some economists worried about an increase in the money supply if banks started lending out the reserves. The Fed was hoping to deal with this problem better than it did in 1937, as we discuss in this chapter's online case study.

Interest on Reserves

The Fed's final and newest tool for controlling the money supply is the interest rate on banks' deposits at the Fed. These deposits are part of reserves. If the Fed raises the interest rate it pays, then banks are likely to desire more reserves, increasing the reserve–deposit ratio. Once again, a rise in the R/D ratio reduces the money multiplier and the money supply:

$$\uparrow \text{ interest rate on reserves} \rightarrow \uparrow (R/D) \rightarrow \downarrow m \rightarrow \downarrow M$$

The Fed started paying interest on banks' deposits in the fall of 2008, when the financial crisis intensified following the failure of Lehman Brothers. The monetary base and money multiplier were both changing rapidly (see Figure 11.3). Amidst this volatility, the Fed sought a new means of controlling the money supply.

At the beginning of 2011, the interest rate on reserves was close to zero, in line with other short-term rates. It is likely, however, that the Fed will raise the rate in the future to help control the money supply as the base and money multiplier return to normal levels.

11.6 MONEY TARGETS VERSUS INTEREST RATE TARGETS

Now that we've seen how the Fed controls the money supply, let's remember why the money supply is important. According to the liquidity preference theory, the nominal interest rate, i, is determined by money supply and money demand. The Fed can raise the interest rate by cutting the money supply or reduce it by raising the money supply. In turn, changes in the nominal interest rate affect the real interest rate, aggregate output, and inflation.

▶ You can review the liquidity preference theory in Section 4.3. Chapter 12 details the effects of changes in i on the economy.

This brings us to a point that sometimes confuses people. Economics textbooks (including this one) say the Fed affects the economy by changing the money supply. However, when news media discuss Fed policies, they rarely mention the money supply; instead, they focus on interest rates. A typical headline is "Fed Raises Interest Rate by 1/4 Percent," not "Fed Reduces Money Supply by $10 Billion." So what is it the Fed really sets—the money supply, the interest rate, or both?

Two Approaches to Monetary Policy

This issue arises because the Fed can run monetary policy in two ways: money targeting and interest rate targeting. We can understand these two approaches using the liquidity preference theory of interest rates.

A Money Target **Figure 11.4** illustrates **money targeting**. Under this approach, the Fed chooses a level for the money supply, labeled $\overline{M}$. It uses the tools discussed in this chapter, primarily open-market operations, to move the money supply to $\overline{M}$. According to the liquidity preference theory, $\overline{M}$ and the money-demand curve determine the equilibrium nominal interest rate.

Money targeting approach to monetary policy in which the central bank chooses a level for the money supply and adjusts it when economic conditions change

FIGURE 11.4 **Money Targeting**

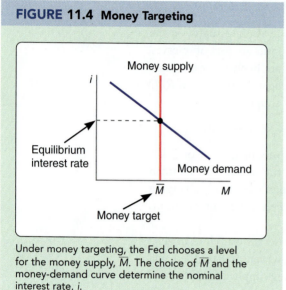

Under money targeting, the Fed chooses a level for the money supply, $\overline{M}$. The choice of $\overline{M}$ and the money-demand curve determine the nominal interest rate, i.

FIGURE 11.5 **Interest Rate Targeting**

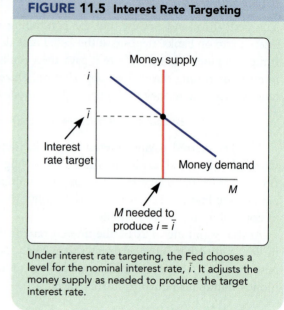

Under interest rate targeting, the Fed chooses a level for the nominal interest rate, $\overline{i}$. It adjusts the money supply as needed to produce the target interest rate.

The Fed adjusts $\overline{M}$ periodically as conditions change. If the economy is in a slump, for example, the Fed may increase $\overline{M}$. This action reduces the interest rate, which stimulates economic activity.

An Interest Rate Target **Figure 11.5** illustrates **interest rate targeting**. In this approach, the Fed chooses a nominal interest rate, labeled $\overline{i}$. Using its monetary tools, the Fed adjusts the money supply to whatever level produces the target interest rate. As shown in the figure, this level is the one that intersects the money demand curve at $\overline{i}$.

When conditions change, the Fed adjusts $\overline{i}$. In a slump, it might reduce $\overline{i}$ to stimulate the economy. To implement this policy, the Fed adjusts the money supply so supply and demand intersect at the new $\overline{i}$.

Interest rate targeting approach to monetary policy in which the central bank chooses a level for the nominal interest rate and adjusts it when economic conditions change. The central bank sets the money supply at the level needed to hit the interest rate target

Does the Choice Matter?

Does it matter which variable the Fed targets? In some cases it doesn't: an interest rate target and a money target can be different ways of describing the same policy. But the distinction does matter in some circumstances, namely, when the money-demand curve shifts.

Equivalent Policies To see this point, let's examine a specific money-demand curve—one with numbers attached. **Figure 11.6** presents such a curve. One policy the Fed might choose is a money target of $10 billion. For the assumed money-demand curve, the figure shows that this policy produces a nominal interest rate of 4 percent.

An alternative policy is an interest rate target of 4 percent. However, this policy is not really different from the money target. To hit a 4-percent interest rate, the Fed must set a money supply of $10 billion. The money supply and interest rate end up the same with either one targeted.

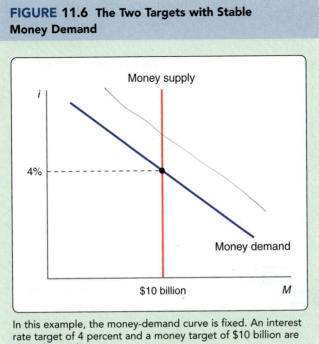

FIGURE 11.6 The Two Targets with Stable Money Demand

i

Money supply

4%

Money demand

$10 billion   *M*

In this example, the money-demand curve is fixed. An interest rate target of 4 percent and a money target of $10 billion are equivalent policies.

Shifting Money Demand So far, we've assumed the money–demand curve is fixed in one position. In reality, money demand can shift because of changes in aggregate spending or in transaction technologies.

▶ Section 4.3 discusses the factors that determine money demand.

When money demand shifts, the Fed's response depends on its target. **Figure 11.7** illustrates this point. Initially the money-demand curve is the same as shown in Figure 11.6, so a money target of $10 billion and an interest rate target of 4 percent are equivalent. Then the demand curve shifts to the right: the quantity of money demanded rises at every interest rate.

Figure 11.7A shows what happens if the Fed has a money target of $10 billion. The Fed keeps the money supply at this level when money demand shifts. The equilibrium interest rate rises from 4 percent to 5 percent.

Figure 11.7B shows what happens with a 4-percent interest rate target. Under this policy, the Fed adjusts the money supply to the level needed to keep the interest rate at the target. That money-supply level is $10 billion before the money-demand shift but $11 billion after the shift. So the Fed raises the money supply to $11 billion.

To summarize, the Fed's choice of target determines what changes when money demand shifts. With a money target, the money supply stays fixed and the interest rate adjusts. With an interest rate target, the interest rate stays fixed and the money supply adjusts.

The Fed's Choice

In practice, the Fed targets the interest rate. Fed officials meet periodically to choose a level for the interest rate and then announce their choice. The Fed adjusts the money supply constantly to hit the interest rate target, but

FIGURE 11.7 The Two Targets with Shifting Money Demand

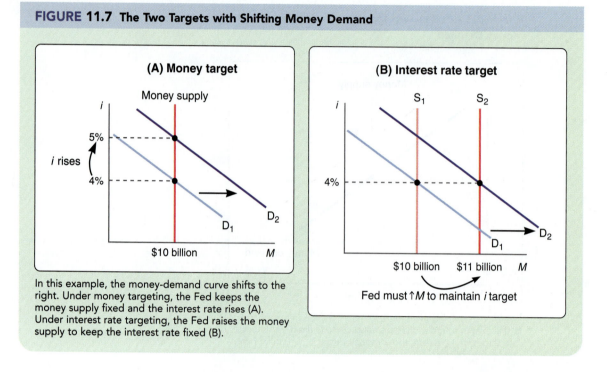

In this example, the money-demand curve shifts to the right. Under money targeting, the Fed keeps the money supply fixed and the interest rate rises (A). Under interest rate targeting, the Fed raises the money supply to keep the interest rate fixed (B).

that occurs in the background. This approach explains why headlines say "Fed Raises Interest Rate" rather than "Fed Reduces Money Supply."

Why has the Fed chosen interest rate targeting? Economists believe the money-demand curve shifts frequently because of changes in transaction technologies. Changes occur in the number of ATM machines, the use of credit cards, and other factors that affect money demand. Under money targeting, these shifts would cause interest rates to fluctuate over time. Most economists think these fluctuations would be undesirable. Changes in interest rates cause changes in aggregate output: economic growth fluctuates. Interest rate targeting keeps rates stable when money demand shifts, which in turn stabilizes output. The Fed prefers stability.

The Fed has tried money targeting in the past, most recently from 1979 to 1982. Most economists think money targeting was a failure. The 1979–1982 experience is a major reason the Fed uses interest rate targeting today. The following case study discusses this episode.

CASE STUDY

The Monetarist Experiment

▶Chapter 16 discusses the monetarists and their views on economic policy.

The *monetarist* school of economics, led by Milton Friedman, advocated money targeting during the 1960s and 1970s. Monetarists said the Fed should increase the money supply at a slow, steady rate, arguing that this policy would stabilize the economy. They pointed to periods such as the 1930s when shifts in the money supply caused problems such as those described in the earlier case studies on the Great Depression.

For many years the Fed ignored the monetarists' advice and targeted interest rates. In October 1979, however, Fed Chairman Paul Volcker announced a new policy, a form of money targeting. The Fed would set a target range for the growth of M1 and seek to keep actual M1 growth within this range. It would allow interest rates to fluctuate in response to money-demand shifts. Volcker's announcement began the Fed's "monetarist experiment."

Most economists think the experiment failed. Money demand fluctuated during this period, reflecting financial innovations such as money-market mutual funds and NOW accounts (checking accounts that pay interest). As one would expect with money targets, interest rates were unstable. During 1980, the 3-month Treasury bill rate rose to 15 percent, then fell to 7 percent, then rose to 15 percent again. The T-bill rate continued to fluctuate over 1981–1982.

Instability in interest rates caused instability in economic growth. A recession occurred in 1980, then the economy recovered briefly, then another recession occurred in 1981–82—at the time, the deepest one since the 1930s, with unemployment more than 10 percent.

This experience did not convince everyone that money targets are unwise. According to monetarists, the Fed under Volcker did not give their policy a fair chance. As shown in **Figure 11.8**, the growth of M1 was *not* stable after 1979, when Volcker began his experiment. Money growth bounced above and below the target ranges. Critics say the Fed didn't really try to meet its targets.

FIGURE 11.8 The Monetarist Experiment

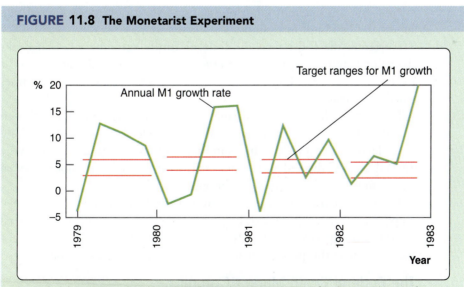

From October 1979 to October 1982, the Fed set target ranges for the growth rate of M1. Opponents of money targeting view this policy as a failure, citing the volatility of interest rates. Others argue that money targeting wasn't given a fair chance, as the Fed didn't keep M1 growth within the announced ranges.

Source: Brian Snowden and Howard R. Vane, *A Macroeconomics Reader*, Routledge, 1997.

Why would the Fed announce targets it didn't intend to meet? Economic historians give a political explanation. Volcker wanted to reduce inflation, which was more than 10 percent per year in the late 1970s. Reducing inflation requires that the Fed raise interest rates and cause a recession, which is unpopular. Volcker feared criticism and perhaps efforts in Congress to reduce the Fed's independence.

With interest rate targets, raising rates means announcing higher targets. Volcker preferred to announce a reduction in money growth, which sounds less objectionable. Lowering money growth raises interest rates, but the public doesn't fully understand this effect. It is less obvious that the Fed is intentionally raising rates and slowing the economy.

So perhaps the 1979 policy was a just a political gimmick. Nonetheless, the post-1979 experience damaged the reputation of money targets. In October 1982, Volcker announced that the Fed was switching back to interest rate targets, and it has stuck with that policy ever since.

Visit the text Web site to read a 1984 debate on the monetarist experiment between Milton Friedman and Benjamin Friedman (an antimonetarist and no relation to Milton).

11.7 INTEREST RATE POLICY

Now that we've explored the concept of interest rate targeting, we can describe some practical aspects of monetary policy. We'll discuss how the Fed chooses interest rate targets and how it uses its policy tools to hit the targets.

The Federal Funds Rate

"The" interest rate exists only in theory. In real economies, there are many interest rates on different kinds of loans and securities. To set interest rate targets, the Fed must first choose *which* rate to target.

Currently, the Fed targets the **federal funds rate**, the rate that banks charge one another for loans of reserves. The loans are made for one day at a time, so the federal funds rate is a very short-term rate. It is sometimes called the *overnight interest rate*.

Federal funds rate
interest rate that banks charge one another for one-day loans of reserves, or federal funds; also *overnight interest rate*

Remember that, despite its name, the federal funds rate is *not* chosen directly by the Fed. It is determined in the federal funds market, where banks lend to one another. (In contrast, the discount rate *is* set directly by the Fed, because the Fed is the lender.) So what the Fed sets is not the actual federal funds rate but a *target* for this rate.

In our theoretical analysis, we assumed the Fed can adjust the money supply to hit its target exactly. In practice, the Fed's control of the federal funds rate is imperfect, so the actual rate deviates somewhat from the target. We'll return to this point after we discuss how the target is chosen.

The Federal Open Market Committee

Federal Open Market Committee (FOMC) body that sets the Fed's targets for the federal funds rate

Within the Federal Reserve System, monetary policy is set by the **Federal Open Market Committee**, or **FOMC**. This committee chooses the target for the federal funds rate. It gets its name from the open-market operations that the Fed uses to implement the committee's decisions.

As we described in Section 11.1, the Federal Reserve System includes 12 Federal Reserve Banks and a board of governors. The FOMC has 12 members: the seven governors and the presidents of five of the banks. The 12 presidents take turns serving on the FOMC, except for the president of the New York Fed, who is a permanent member. The chair of the board of governors (currently Ben Bernanke) is also chair of the FOMC.

The FOMC meets every six weeks at the board headquarters in Washington, D.C. The committee members discuss the state of the economy and choose a target for the federal funds rate. The target is announced at the end of the meeting, and the news is reported immediately. That's when you see headlines like "Fed Reduces Rates by 1/4 Percent."

Once a target is set, it usually stays in place for six weeks, until the next scheduled meeting of the FOMC. However, if conditions change rapidly between meetings, the chair can arrange a videoconference among committee members to consider an immediate response. For example, facing a weakening economy, Chairman Bernanke convened a videoconference on January 22, 2008. On that occasion, the committee cut its federal funds rate target by 3/4 of a percent, from 4.25 percent to 3.5 percent.

Figure 11.9 shows the FOMC's target for the federal funds rate from January 2000 through September 2010. We can see that the target moves around a lot. It fell rapidly in 2001–2002, rose over 2004–2006, and started falling again late in 2007. In December 2008, the target fell almost to zero. At that point, the FOMC departed from its usual practice by announcing

---

FIGURE 11.9 The Federal Funds Rate Target

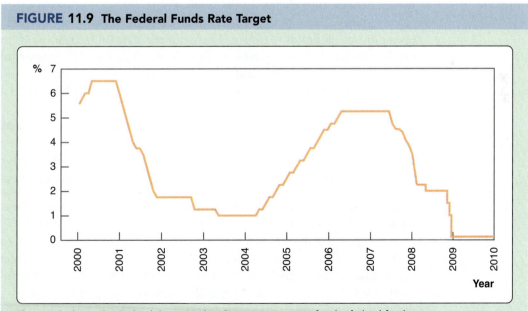

This graph shows the Federal Open Market Committee's target for the federal funds rate from January 2000 through September 2010. For the period starting in December 2008, when the FOMC set a target range of 0 to 0.25 percent, the graph shows the midpoint of the range, 0.125 percent.

Source: Federal Reserve Board

a target *range* for the federal funds rate, from 0 to 0.25 percent, rather than a single number. The Fed's target was still 0 to 0.25 percent as 2010 ended. *A central goal in the rest of this book is to understand why the Fed adjusts its federal funds rate target.*

Implementing the Targets

After the FOMC has chosen a target for the federal funds rate, the job of hitting the target, or coming as close as possible, falls to the Federal Reserve Bank of New York. A group of bond traders at the bank's "trading desk" uses open-market operations to push the federal funds rate to the target level. Let's discuss this process.

Effects of Open-Market Operations

Open-market operations change the money supply, which affects the overall level of interest rates. Rates on many types of bonds and loans respond to open-market operations. However, some rates are affected more quickly and directly than others. The federal funds rate is especially responsive to open-market operations, which is one reason the Fed targets this rate.

Banks use the federal funds market to manage liquidity. At any point in time, some banks have more reserves than they need to meet customers' demands for withdrawals, while other banks are short on reserves. Banks with extra reserves lend to banks that need reserves. The interest rate on these loans, the federal funds rate, is determined by supply and demand. Open-market operations affect supply and demand in the federal funds market because they change banks' levels of reserves.

For example, suppose the Fed carries out a contractionary open-market operation: it sells bonds to dealers. These dealers draw on bank accounts to pay for the bonds, draining reserves from banks. Some banks run short of reserves, increasing the demand for federal funds. Other banks that had extra reserves see these reserves disappear, reducing the supply of federal funds. Higher demand and lower supply push up the federal funds rate.

The federal funds market is active throughout the business day. Banks lend to each other continuously as their reserves fluctuate with deposits and withdrawals. When the Fed performs open-market operations, the market reacts quickly. The federal funds rate usually adjusts within a few minutes.

Choosing Daily Operations

Traders at the New York Fed perform open-market operations in an effort to keep the federal funds rate at the FOMC's target—or, during the recent financial crisis, within the target range of 0 to 0.25 percent. During normal times, when the FOMC sets a precise target rather than a range, the Fed's traders perform open-market operations every day. On most days, the target is the same as it was the day before, so the traders are trying to keep the federal funds rate constant. Their basic approach is to adjust bank reserves so the supply of overnight loans equals the demand. An imbalance between supply and demand would push the funds rate away from the target.

The central problem is to determine the right level of reserves. New York Fed economists spend the first part of each morning researching this issue. They examine the current level of reserves and the behavior of the funds rate in the day's early trading. They phone federal funds traders to get their views on what might happen in the coming hours. They also examine various factors that affect day-to-day fluctuations in reserves.

One such factor is currency holdings. When people withdraw cash from their bank accounts, reserves fall. So Fed economists must forecast the day's demand for cash. Another factor is receipts and payments by the U.S. Treasury. If Social Security checks have just been mailed, for example, bank reserves are likely to rise as the checks are deposited. The increase in reserves will lower the federal funds rate unless the Fed offsets it with open-market operations.

After the morning analysis of reserves is complete, the manager of open-market operations has a conference call with officials at the Fed Board of Governors and one of the Fed Bank presidents outside New York. This group approves a plan for the day's open-market operations. They choose the quantity of bonds to buy or sell and details such as the choice of maturities.

Making the Trades The Fed trades bonds with about 20 financial institutions known as *primary dealers*. These dealers are major commercial and investment banks, such as JPMorgan Chase and Goldman Sachs. When the Fed wants to make a trade, it notifies all primary dealers electronically, giving them 10 or 15 minutes to respond with bids. For example, the Fed might say it wants to sell Treasury bonds with a certain maturity, and primary dealers say what prices they are willing to pay. The Fed accepts the most favorable bids.

The Fed performs two kinds of trades. In an *outright open-market operation*, it simply buys or sells bonds. This transaction permanently changes bank reserves and the monetary base. In a *temporary open-market operation*, the Fed makes a repurchase agreement, or *repo*, with a bond dealer, which means that it buys or sells bonds with an agreement to reverse the transaction in a certain number of days. This action temporarily changes bank reserves. The Fed uses this approach to offset temporary shifts in the supply and demand for federal funds.

▶ Section 9.1 discusses how banks use repos to borrow in financial markets.

The Results The Fed's bond traders try to keep the federal funds rate at the FOMC's target. The system doesn't work perfectly, because open-market operations are based on forecasts in the early morning. Events later in the day can change the supply and demand for federal funds, pushing the funds rate away from the target.

However, the system works pretty well. Usually, the Fed judges the market accurately enough to keep the funds rate close to the target. **Figure 11.10** compares the actual federal funds rate to the target for each day during the first three months of 2008. On most days, the difference between the two variables is small.

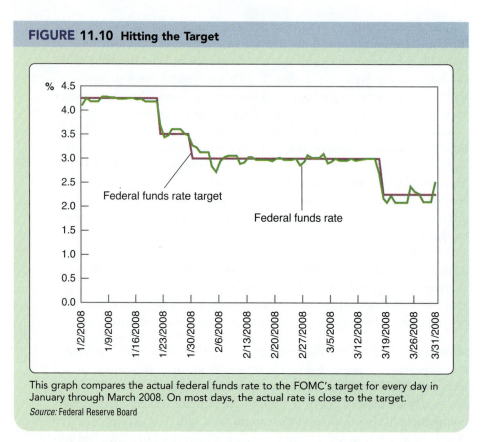

FIGURE 11.10 Hitting the Target

This graph compares the actual federal funds rate to the FOMC's target for every day in January through March 2008. On most days, the actual rate is close to the target.

Source: Federal Reserve Board

Summary

11.1 The Federal Reserve System

■ The Federal Reserve System includes 12 regional Federal Reserve Banks and a board of governors in Washington, D.C. A Federal Reserve Bank is formally owned by the commercial banks in its region. Members of the board of governors are appointed by the president and confirmed by Congress. Once in office, they are independent of elected officials.

11.2 The Fed and the Monetary Base

■ The Federal Reserve controls the monetary base: the sum of currency in circulation and bank reserves $(B = C + R)$. The base is the total liabilities of the Fed to the private sector.

■ The Fed can change the monetary base by conducting open-market operations (purchases and sales of securities) or by lending to financial institutions. Its primary type of lending is discount loans requested by banks.

■ The Fed's assets include the bonds purchased in open-market operations and the loans it has made. Its liabilities include currency in circulation and bank reserves, the two components of the monetary base.

11.3 Commercial Banks and the Money Supply

■ Ignoring traveler's checks, the money supply is currency in circulation plus checking deposits: $M = C + D$. The money supply is influenced by the behavior of commercial banks and the public as well as by the Fed.

■ Money is created through a process in which funds are deposited in banks, banks lend out the deposits, the loans are redeposited, and so on. Money creation is limited by leakages from the deposit–loan process into cash and into bank reserves.

11.4 A Formula for the Money Supply

■ The money supply is the money multiplier times the monetary base: $M = mB$. The multiplier depends on the currency–deposit ratio and the reserve–deposit ratio: $m = [(C/D) + 1]/[(C/D) + (R/D)]$.

■ A rise in the monetary base raises the money supply. A rise in the currency–deposit ratio reduces the money multiplier and the money supply. A rise in the reserve–deposit ratio also reduces the multiplier and the money supply.

■ The bank panics of the early 1930s led to increases in the currency–deposit ratio and the reserve–deposit ratio, which reduced the money multiplier. The fall in the multiplier reduced the money supply, helping to cause the Great Depression.

■ In 2008 and 2009, the monetary base roughly doubled as the Fed made emergency loans to financial institutions and purchased mortgage-backed securities. The money multiplier fell below 1.0 because of a large rise in the reserve-deposit ratio. The rise in the base was somewhat larger than the fall in the multiplier, so the money supply rose by a moderate amount.

11.5 The Fed's Monetary Tools

■ Although money creation involves commercial banks and the public, the Federal Reserve ultimately controls the level of the money supply.

■ Open-market operations are the Fed's main tool for controlling the money supply. A $100 purchase of bonds raises the money supply by $100 times the money multiplier.

■ The Fed can also influence the money supply by changing the discount rate, the reserve requirements imposed on banks, or the interest rate on bank reserves.

11.6 Money Targets Versus Interest Rate Targets

■ A central bank can practice money targeting, in which it chooses a level for the money supply. Alternatively, it can practice interest rate targeting, in which it chooses a level for the interest rate and adjusts the money supply to hit this target.

■ Under money targeting, shifts in money demand cause the interest rate to change. Under interest rate targeting, shifts in money demand do not affect the interest rate. Because of this difference, the Fed targets interest rates rather than money.

■ The Fed tried money targeting from 1979 to 1982. Many economists think this policy caused instability in interest rates and the economy.

11.7 Interest Rate Policy

■ The Fed targets a specific interest rate: the federal funds rate. This is the interest rate on overnight loans between banks. Starting in December 2008, the Fed targeted a range for the federal funds rate (0 to 0.25 percent) rather than a single rate.

■ Targets for the federal funds rate are chosen by the Federal Open Market Committee, which includes the seven Fed governors and five of the Federal Reserve Bank presidents. The FOMC meets every six weeks to choose a target.

■ The Fed uses open-market operations to control the federal funds rate. Open-market operations change the level of bank reserves, which affects the supply and demand for overnight loans.

■ Bond traders at the Federal Reserve Bank of New York conduct open-market operations every day. On most days, these actions keep the federal funds rate close to the FOMC's target or within its target range.

Key Terms

currency–deposit ratio (C/D), p. 320

discount loan, p. 318

discount rate, p. 318

federal funds rate, p. 338

Federal Open Market Committee (FOMC), p. 338

interest rate targeting, p. 334

monetary base (B), p. 317

money multiplier (m), p. 324

money targeting, p. 333

open-market operations, p. 317

reserve requirements, p. 331

reserve–deposit ratio (R/D), p. 321

Questions and Problems

1. Continue the story of The Friendly Bank (Section 11.3) for a few more days. Show the bank's balance sheet, the monetary base, and the money supply for Friday and the following Monday, Tuesday, and Wednesday. Continue to assume the currency–deposit ratio and reserve–deposit ratio are 0.25.

2. Start with the Wednesday balance sheet for The Friendly Bank on page 322. Suppose that, at the end of Wednesday, the Fed buys $100 in government bonds from a dealer with an account at the bank. Otherwise, everyone behaves the same way as in the text. Show the bank's balance sheet, the monetary base, and the money supply for Thursday and Friday.

3. Let's change the story of The Friendly Bank by introducing savings deposits. Assume that when people put money in the bank, half of it goes to checking deposits (D) and half to savings deposits (S). The ratio of currency to total deposits, $C/(D + S)$, is 0.25. The ratio of reserves to checking deposits, R/D, is 0.25.

   a. Notice that reserves are a fraction of checking deposits and don't depend on savings deposits. Why might this be a reasonable assumption?

   b. Redo the story of The Friendly Bank, showing the bank's balance sheet and the monetary aggregates for the first four days the bank is in business.

   c. Compare your answer for part (b) to the corresponding calculations on pages 320–322, where we ignore savings deposits. In which case is the most money created? What explains this result?

4. Suppose someone keeps $100 in cash under her pillow. One day, she takes it out and deposits it in a checking account.

   a. Does this action directly affect the monetary base or the money supply? Explain why or why not.

   b. Does the action eventually lead to a change in the monetary base or the money supply? Explain why or why not.

5. Suppose that foreigners start holding more U.S. currency. For a given interest rate, Americans don't change their holdings of either currency or checking deposits. Assume the Fed keeps the monetary base constant. Describe what happens to (a) the money supply, (b) the money-demand curve, and (c) the equilibrium interest rate. Explain your answers.

6. Redo Question 5, but do *not* assume the monetary base is constant. Instead, answer each part of the question assuming the Fed targets the money supply. Then answer each part assuming the Fed targets the interest rate. What happens to the monetary base in each of these cases?

7. How did the Federal Reserve's actions over 2008–2009 in response to the financial crisis (see the case study in Section 11.4) affect its balance sheet, diagrammed in Section 11.2?

8. Suppose the discount rate is below the federal funds rate and banks can borrow as much as they want from the Fed. How could a bank earn easy profits? Would the federal funds rate stay above the discount rate? Explain.

9. Milton Friedman believed the Fed should control the money supply precisely. In the 1960s, he proposed that the required reserve ratio be raised to 100 percent. How would this policy improve control of the money supply? What are the drawbacks to the policy?

10. In the text, we ignored traveler's checks in deriving the money multiplier. Suppose we are more careful and include traveler's checks in the money supply. Let T be the level of traveler's checks, so T/D is the ratio of traveler's checks to checking deposits. Derive the money multiplier in terms of C/D, R/D, and T/D.

11. Suppose the Fed wants to reduce the money supply by $100. Should it buy or sell government bonds? How much should it buy or sell?

12. Assume the monetary base is $100, the currency–deposit ratio is 0.5, and the reserve–deposit ratio is 0.1.

    a. Calculate the money multiplier and the money supply.

    b. Suppose the currency–deposit ratio rises to 1.0. If the Fed holds the monetary base constant, what happens to the money multiplier and the money supply?

    c. Suppose the Fed wants to keep the money supply constant at the level found in part (a). How must it adjust the monetary base when the currency–deposit ratio rises?

13. The Fed bought an unusually large quantity of Treasury bonds at the end of December 1999. What explains this behavior? (*Hint*: Search online for "Y2K.")

14. Which is more stable from day to day—the discount rate or the federal funds rate? Explain.

Short-Run Economic Fluctuations

Courtesy Cecilia Varas

The economy is always an issue at election time.

Figure 12.1 on page 348 shows the rates of U.S. unemployment and inflation from 1960 through 2009. These variables fluctuate a lot. Since 1960, the inflation rate has been less than 2 percent in some years and more than 10 percent in others. Unemployment has been below 4 percent and close to 10 percent.

People care greatly about these short-run economic fluctuations. One way to see this is by examining presidential elections. When an incumbent is running, many voters are influenced by unemployment and inflation rates. As Figure 12.1 shows, both variables were fairly low in the 1960s and early 1970s, which helped Lyndon Johnson win the presidency in 1964 and Richard Nixon win reelection in 1972. Unemployment and inflation both rose after that, to the misfortune of Gerald Ford in 1976 and Jimmy Carter in 1980.

By 1984, inflation was low again and unemployment was falling; Ronald Reagan declared "morning in America" and won reelection in a landslide. George H. W. Bush ran for reelection in 1992 while

FIGURE 12.1 The Economy and Presidential Elections

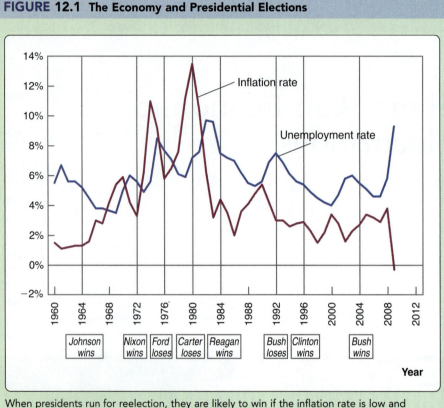

When presidents run for reelection, they are likely to win if the inflation rate is low and unemployment is low or at least falling. In the opposite circumstances, incumbents are likely to lose.

Source: Bureau of Labor Statistics

unemployment was rising and lost. Both 1996 and 2004 were years of low inflation and falling unemployment, helping Bill Clinton and George W. Bush to reelection.[1]

This chapter discusses short-run economic fluctuations. We start by describing the **business cycle**, the year-to-year movements in an economy's output and unemployment. The business cycle causes the unemployment movements we see in Figure 12.1, because firms adjust their workforces as their output changes.

We then develop a model to explain the business cycle. In this model, output is determined by total spending on goods and services by people, firms, and governments. Spending and output shift over time for many reasons, but monetary policy is a major factor. The central bank can raise output in the short run by reducing interest rates or lower output by raising rates.

Business cycle short-run (year-to-year) fluctuations in an economy's output and unemployment

---

[1] For more on the economy and presidential elections, see Ray Fair, *Predicting Presidential Elections and Other Things*, Stanford University Press, 2002.

The model we develop also explains short-run fluctuations in the inflation rate. High output and low unemployment cause inflation to rise; low output and high unemployment cause inflation to fall. Inflation also responds to events that affect firms' production costs, such as changes in oil prices.

12.1 THE BUSINESS CYCLE

An economy's output and unemployment rate fluctuate over the business cycle. *Output* means the level of real gross domestic product (real GDP). The **unemployment rate (U)** is the percentage of the labor force without jobs. For example, if 100 people are available for work but 6 don't have jobs, the unemployment rate is 6 percent.

The business cycle is made up of *short-run* movements in output and unemployment. From year to year, these variables fluctuate around their normal or average levels. Before discussing the cycle, we need to discuss these normal levels.

Long-Run Output and Unemployment

The normal level of output is called *potential output*, and the normal unemployment rate is the *natural rate*. These variables are also called the *long-run* levels of output and unemployment. If we take the average of output over a long time period—say, 10 or 20 years—it is close to potential output. Similarly, average unemployment is close to the natural rate.

Output **Potential output (Y^*)** is the normal level of output that an economy is able to produce. It depends on the levels of resources, such as the number of workers and the amount of physical capital (factories and machines). Potential output also depends on the technologies available for turning resources into goods and services.

Potential output is not the *maximum* amount the economy can produce. Instead, it is the amount produced when resources are used with a normal intensity. This means that people work their usual number of hours and factories produce at their usual rates. Output can rise above potential if people work overtime and factories go on double shifts.

In most countries, potential output rises slowly over time. The economy becomes more productive as its labor force grows, capital accumulates, and new technologies are invented. This process is long-term economic growth.

In the United States, the growth of potential output has varied over time. Potential output grew 1–2 percent per year in the 1970s and 1980s, then started growing around 3 percent per year in the mid-1990s. Economists attribute this speedup to the spread of computers and related technologies. The growth of potential output stayed around 3 percent at least until 2007; amid the economic turmoil since then, economists have been uncertain of the path of potential output.

Unemployment The **natural rate of unemployment (U^*)** is the normal or average level of unemployment. It is the unemployment rate when the

Unemployment rate (U) percentage of the labor force without jobs

▶ To review the concept of real GDP, see the Chapter 1 Appendix.

Potential output (Y*) the normal or average level of output, as determined by resources and technology

Natural rate of unemployment (U*) normal or average level of unemployment

economy's resources, including its labor force, are used with a normal intensity. Unemployment is at the natural rate when output equals potential output.

All economies have unemployment. Some workers lose their jobs and take time to find new ones. Others are unemployed indefinitely because they lack skills or don't live where the jobs are. The extent of such problems determines the natural rate of unemployment.

The natural rate varies across countries and time periods. The following case study examines the natural rate in the United States since 1960 and the factors that have influenced it.

CASE STUDY

The Natural Rate in the United States

We do not observe the natural rate directly, but economists estimate it. One approach is to draw a trend line through the unemployment data—a line that follows long-term movements but smooths out yearly fluctuations. **Figure 12.2** uses this technique to estimate the U.S. natural rate from 1960 through 2009. According to these estimates, the natural rate rose from 1960 to 1983, fell from 1983 to 2002, and then began to rise again. Let's discuss movements during each period.

1960–1983: Baby Boomers and the Productivity Slowdown In explaining the rise in the natural rate over these years, many economists cite two factors.

FIGURE 12.2 The U.S. Natural Rate of Unemployment, 1960–2009

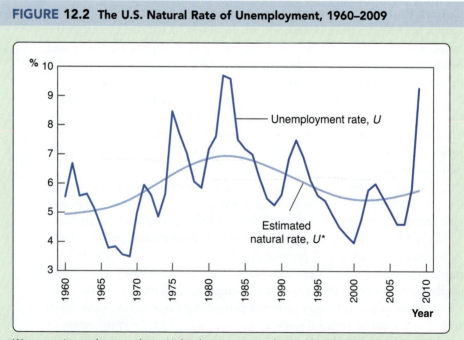

We can estimate the natural rate U^* by drawing a smooth trend line through unemployment data.

Sources: Bureau of Labor Statistics and author's estimates of U^*

One is a decrease in the average age of workers: when a larger fraction of the workforce is young, the overall unemployment rate rises. The so-called baby boom generation born after World War II entered the labor force as young workers in the 1960s and 1970s. As a result, the share of workers younger than 25 rose from 17 percent in 1960 to 24 percent in 1978. On average, young workers have less training and job security than older workers, so they are unemployed more often.

The other factor behind the rising natural rate during this period was productivity growth. The rate of productivity growth was high after World War II but fell in the 1970s, reducing the growth of potential output. With slower productivity growth, firms could not afford to raise wages as quickly as before, but workers resisted a slowdown in wage growth. With wage demands too high relative to productivity, firms hired fewer workers.

1983–2002: Aging Boomers and Productivity Acceleration The factors that explain the rise in the natural rate before 1983 also help explain its subsequent fall. In the 1980s, the baby boomers grew into older, experienced workers. The share of workers younger than 25 fell to 16 percent in 2000. Starting in the 1990s, the computer and Internet revolutions caused productivity growth to accelerate and outstrip workers' wage demands. An older workforce and rapid productivity growth reduced the natural rate, just as a young workforce and slow productivity growth had increased it during the preceding decades.[*]

2002–2009: A Shift in the Natural Rate? In Figure 12.2, the entire path of the natural rate is an estimate, but the accuracy of the estimate after 2002 is especially uncertain. The trend line through the unemployment data turns up to capture the fact that actual unemployment, U, rose rapidly over 2008–2009. It is not yet clear how to interpret the increase: it could reflect an increased average level of unemployment, U^*, or it could be a temporary deviation. Figure 12.2 reflects a case in which the rise in U is partly a rise in U^* and partly a deviation from it, with the natural rate headed higher.

If the natural rate *has* risen, what is the cause? One possible answer is that movements in actual unemployment affect the natural rate. In this theory, called *hysteresis*, the deep recession that began in 2007 left scars on the labor force that will keep unemployment high for a long time. In Section 12.5, we examine this controversial idea in more detail.

*For more on these issues, see Laurence Ball and N. Gregory Mankiw, "The NAIRU in Theory and Practice," *Journal of Economic Perspectives*, vol. 16, Fall 2002, pp. 115–136.

Booms and Recessions

Potential output grows smoothly over time. It rises gradually as resources increase and technology improves, but it does not jump sharply from year to year. Similarly, the natural rate of unemployment can vary over time but changes gradually.

In contrast, the growth of *actual* output—of real GDP—fluctuates erratically. Sometimes actual output rises above potential, and sometimes it

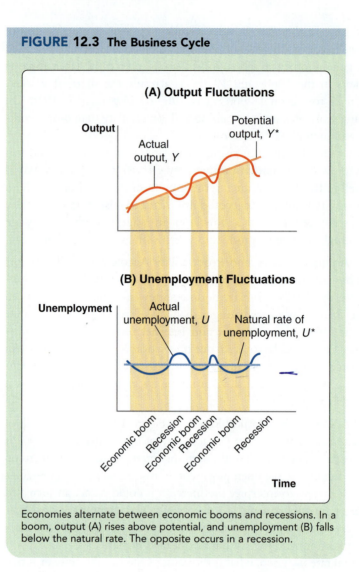

FIGURE 12.3 The Business Cycle

Economies alternate between economic booms and recessions. In a boom, output (A) rises above potential, and unemployment (B) falls below the natural rate. The opposite occurs in a recession.

falls below. Unemployment also fluctuates from year to year, as we saw in Figure 12.2. These short-run fluctuations define the business cycle.

Output Fluctuations **Figure 12.3A** illustrates the behavior of output. In this graph, Y^* is potential output, which grows smoothly, and Y is actual output. Y follows the trend in Y^*, but it is volatile.

Periods when actual output exceeds potential output are called **economic booms**. In these periods, the economy produces more than usual given its resources. Periods with output below potential are called **recessions**.

Economists measure the size of booms and recessions with the **output gap** ($\tilde{Y}$). This variable is the percentage difference between actual and potential output. Mathematically,

$$\tilde{Y} = \frac{Y - Y^*}{Y^*}$$

Economic boom period when actual output exceeds potential output

Recession period when actual output falls below potential output

Output gap ($\tilde{Y}$) percentage difference between actual and potential output; $(Y - Y^*)/Y^*$

The output gap is positive in booms and negative in recessions. For example, a gap of −5 percent means a recession, with actual output 5 percent below potential.

Unemployment Fluctuations **Figure 12.3B** shows the behavior of unemployment over the business cycle. In this graph, U is actual unemployment and U^* is the natural rate. Unemployment is above the natural rate in recessions and below it in booms.

Notice the close relationship between unemployment and output. Unemployment is low when output is high (in booms) and high when output is low (in recessions). This should make sense. When output rises, firms hire more workers to produce the output. This hiring reduces unemployment. When output falls, firms lay off workers, raising unemployment.

Okun's Law We can be more precise about this relationship between output and unemployment. In the 1960s, economist Arthur Okun noted a statistical fact that we now call **Okun's law**:

$$\frac{Y - Y^*}{Y^*} = -2(U - U^*) \tag{12.1}$$

Okun's law captures the relative sizes of output and unemployment fluctuations over the business cycle. The equation says that the output gap falls by 2 percentage points when unemployment rises 1 point above the natural rate.

Suppose the natural rate, U^*, is 6 percent. If actual unemployment is also 6 percent, then Okun's law says the output gap is zero. With unemployment at the natural rate, output equals potential output.

Now suppose the unemployment rate rises to 8 percent. If the natural rate is still 6 percent, the output gap is

$$\frac{Y - Y^*}{Y^*} = -2(U - U^*)$$
$$= -2(8\% - 6\%)$$
$$= -4\%$$

The negative output gap indicates a recession: output is 4 percent below potential.

If unemployment falls to 4 percent, the output gap becomes

$$\frac{Y - Y^*}{Y^*} = -2(U - U^*)$$
$$= -2(4\% - 6\%)$$
$$= +4\%$$

The positive gap indicates a boom: output is 4 percent above potential.

Figure 12.4 shows the evidence for Okun's law. For each year from 1960 through 2009, it plots estimates of the output gap against the deviation of unemployment from the natural rate. We see the close relationship predicted by Okun's law. The line drawn through the data has a slope of −2.0,

Okun's law relation between output and unemployment over the business cycle: the output gap falls by 2 percentage points when unemployment rises 1 point above the natural rate; $(Y - Y^*)/Y^* = -2(U - U^*)$

FIGURE 12.4 Okun's Law, 1960–2009

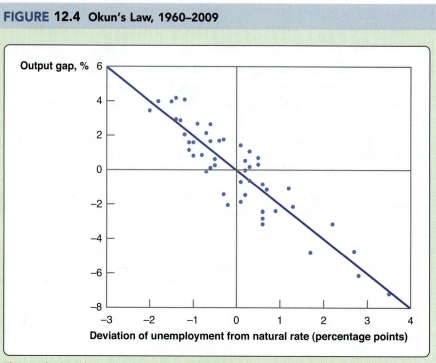

This graph plots the U.S. output gap and the deviation of unemployment from the natural rate. Each dot represents a year. The line through the data has a slope of −2.0, confirming Okun's law: the output gap falls by 2 percentage points when unemployment rises by one point relative to the natural rate.

Sources: Department of Commerce; Bureau of Labor Statistics; and author's estimates of U^* and Y^*

confirming that the output gap falls by two percentage points when unemployment rises by 1 point.

We have defined a recession as a period when output is below potential and unemployment is above the natural rate. While common, this definition is not the only one used by economists. You may see the term *recession* used in a somewhat different way, as the next case study explains.

CASE STUDY

What Is a Recession?

▶The best measure of an economy's output is real GDP, which is measured on a quarterly basis. Because NBER wants to determine the months in which recessions begin and end, the committee examines monthly indicators, such as retail sales and manufacturing output.

Suppose you see a headline that says the United States entered a recession in a certain month. This report is probably based on an announcement from the National Bureau of Economic Research. NBER is a private organization, not a government agency, but its judgments about recessions are widely viewed as "official."

A group of NBER economists, the Business Cycle Dating Committee, decides when recessions begin and end. The committee bases its decisions on the behavior of output. It does *not* seek to determine whether output is above or below potential. Instead, it simply asks whether output is rising or falling—whether the growth rate of output is positive or negative.

For the NBER, a "recession" is a period when output falls by a substantial amount. A period when output rises is an "expansion" (NBER does not use the term *boom*). Because output growth over time is positive on average, the economy spends more time in expansions than in recessions.

NBER identified seven recessions between 1960 and 2006, with an average length of 11 months. The last of these recessions occurred from March to November 2001. The most recent recession, triggered by the financial crisis, began in December 2007 and ended in July 2009. At 18 months, it was the longest recession since the 1930s.

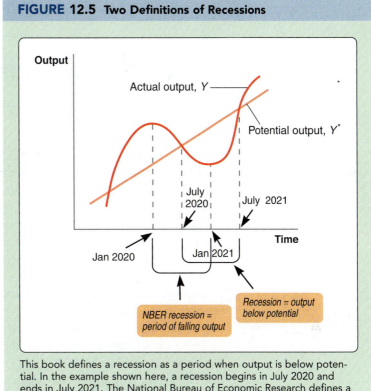

FIGURE 12.5 Two Definitions of Recessions

This book defines a recession as a period when output is below potential. In the example shown here, a recession begins in July 2020 and ends in July 2021. The National Bureau of Economic Research defines a recession as a period of falling output. By that definition, a recession begins in January 2020 and ends in January 2021.

Figure 12.5 illustrates the difference between NBER's definition of a recession and the primary definition we use in this book. In this example, output starts falling in January 2020. An NBER recession starts then, even though output is still above potential. The recession ends in January 2021, when output starts rising. Using our primary definition, the recession starts later and ends later. It runs from July 2020 to July 2021, the period when output is below potential.

The actual period from mid-2009 to mid-2010 is similar to the hypothetical period from January 2021 to July 2021 in Figure 12.5. Output reached a trough in July 2009 and started growing, so the NBER recession ended and an expansion began. Yet output remained significantly below potential during late 2009 and 2010, and unemployment exceeded the natural rate. The economy was still in recession in the sense that its productive capacity was underutilized.

Aggregate Expenditure

What causes booms and recessions? Why do firms sometimes reduce their output and lay off workers? Why do they sometimes hire extra workers and produce more than usual?

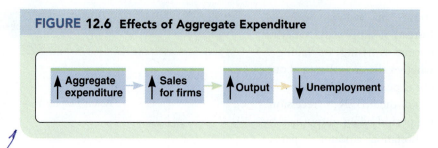

FIGURE **12.6** Effects of Aggregate Expenditure

Aggregate expenditure (AE) total spending on an economy's goods and services by people, firms, and governments

[handwritten: ↑ Spending   ↑Y]
[handwritten: ↑ Revenue   ↓U]
[handwritten: ↑ Production]

The short answer is that these fluctuations are caused by changes in **aggregate expenditure (AE)**. This variable is total spending on an economy's goods and services by people, firms, and governments. Total spending varies over time, causing the business cycle.

Figure 12.6 outlines the effects of aggregate expenditure. A rise in spending means higher sales for the firms that produce goods and services. When firms sell more, they respond by increasing their production. So higher expenditure leads to higher output. As we've discussed, higher output means firms need more workers, so unemployment falls. A decrease in aggregate expenditure has the opposite effects. It reduces firms' sales, leading to lower output and higher unemployment.

These ideas were developed by the British economist John Maynard Keynes in his 1936 book *The General Theory of Employment, Interest, and Money.* Before Keynes, economists who studied output movements focused on the economy's productive capacity. In our terminology, they assumed that actual output always equals potential output. They attributed the business cycle to shifts in resources and technologies that change potential output.

Keynes wrote during the Great Depression, when output fell by more than 30 percent in both the United States and Britain. It was obvious to Keynes that potential output had *not* fallen sharply. Workers and factories hadn't disappeared, and firms hadn't forgotten their production methods. Instead, something had pushed actual output below potential. Keynes argued that this factor was a fall in aggregate expenditure, and today most economists agree.

12.2 WHAT DETERMINES AGGREGATE EXPENDITURE?

If the business cycle is caused by shifts in aggregate expenditure, then the next question is, What causes expenditure to shift?

The Components of Expenditure

[handwritten: Components of GDP determine AE.]

To understand shifts in aggregate expenditure, the first step is to review the different types of spending in an economy. AE can be broken into four components that you may recall from your principles of economics course:

- *Consumption (C)* covers purchases of goods and services by individuals—everything from loaves of bread to cars to haircuts.

- *Investment (I)* means purchases of physical capital, such as new factories, machines, and houses.

■ *Government purchases (G)* includes roads, military jets, and the salaries of government workers (which economists interpret as purchases of the workers' services).

■ *Net exports (NX)* is exports minus imports. It measures net purchases of a country's goods and services by foreigners.

These four components sum to aggregate expenditure. We assume that output, Y, equals AE:

$$Y = AE = C + I + G + NX \qquad (12.2)$$

GDP

Anything that affects one of the spending components affects aggregate expenditure, and therefore affects output.

▶ Section 1.2 discusses the concept of investment, and Section 6.4 discusses net exports.

The Role of the Interest Rate

Many factors affect AE, but one is central: the interest rate. More precisely, what matters is the ex ante real interest rate, $r^{\text{ex ante}}$, which is the nominal interest rate minus expected inflation: $r^{\text{ex ante}} = i - \pi^e$. Throughout this chapter, we'll denote this variable simply as r.

r ex ante

▶ Section 3.7 introduces the ex ante real interest rate.

Changes in the interest rate have complex effects, but they can be summarized simply: *A rise in the real interest rate reduces aggregate expenditure. Conversely, a fall in the interest rate raises AE.* Let's discuss why.

↑r ↓AE
↓↑AE

Effects on Spending The real interest rate affects three of the four components of spending, all but government purchases. We've seen these effects in earlier chapters:

■ *Consumption* A higher real interest rate encourages people to save. Higher saving means lower spending on consumption. Spending on durable goods, such as cars and appliances, is especially sensitive to the interest rate. Many consumers borrow to buy these goods, so higher rates make the goods more expensive.

■ *Investment* A higher real interest rate makes it more expensive for firms to finance investment projects. Thus, investment spending falls.

■ *Net exports* An increase in the real interest rate reduces a country's net capital outflows, which in turn raises the real exchange rate. The higher exchange rate makes the country's goods more expensive relative to foreign goods, reducing net exports.

▶ Section 4.1 describes the effects of the real interest rate on saving and investment, and Section 6.5 describes the effects on the exchange rate and net exports.

The Consumption Multiplier The effects of a higher interest rate on aggregate expenditure are magnified by the **consumption multiplier**. A fall in spending reduces people's incomes, which in turn reduces their consumption. If firms reduce investment in new factories, for example, construction companies do less business. Construction workers are laid off, losing their pay, and company owners lose profits. With less income, people reduce their spending on goods and services.

Consumption multiplier effect of income on consumption that magnifies changes in aggregate expenditure

This decrease in consumption affects firms that might not have been affected directly by the rise in interest rates. Sales fall, for example, at the stores where

FIGURE 12.7 The Aggregate Expenditure Curve

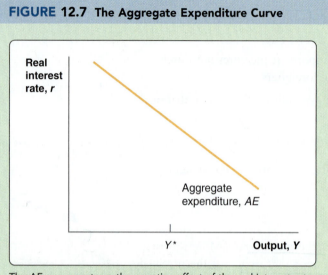

The AE curve captures the negative effect of the real interest rate on aggregate expenditure, which determines output in the short run.

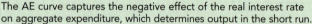

Aggregate expenditure (AE) curve the negative short-run relationship between the real interest rate and output

▶Many macroeconomics textbooks present the AE curve under another name, the IS curve (for *investment and saving*; both influence aggregate expenditure).

construction workers shop. This fall in spending reduces incomes for store owners and employees, which causes another decrease in consumption. In the end, lower spending spreads through the economy.

These effects, while complex, are really only the beginning of the story. Higher interest rates also reduce spending for reasons involving the stock market, the banking system, and other parts of the economy. We discuss these other channels in Chapter 13.

The Aggregate Expenditure Curve

Figure 12.7 summarizes our discussion with a graph of the **aggregate expenditure curve**. The **AE curve** shows how the real interest rate affects aggregate expenditure and hence output. The AE curve slopes downward, capturing the negative effects we've discussed. Output can be either higher or lower than potential output (Y^*), depending on the interest rate.

Monetary Policy and Equilibrium Output

If the real interest rate determines aggregate expenditure, what determines the real interest rate? In the short run, the answer is the central bank—in the United States, the Federal Reserve.

Monetary Policy and the Real Rate Chapter 11 discusses how the central bank controls the interest rate by choosing an interest rate target then adjusting the money supply so that it intersects money demand at the target (review Figure 11.4). The central bank sets a target for the *nominal* interest rate, i. However, *in the short run, the central bank's control of the nominal interest rate allows it to control the real rate as well.*

Again, the real rate is the nominal rate minus expected inflation: $r = i - \pi^e$. Economists disagree about what determines expected inflation, but most believe this variable does *not* shift abruptly when the central bank changes its interest rate target. Therefore, we'll assume the central bank can take expected inflation as given when it chooses the target.

For a given level of expected inflation, the central bank can set a nominal interest rate that produces the real rate it desires. Say policymakers want a real rate of 3 percent. If expected inflation is 2 percent, they set a nominal interest rate of 5 percent. The real rate is 5% − 2% = 3%.

Suppose expected inflation rises to 4 percent. If the central bank wants to maintain a real interest rate of 3 percent, it can raise the nominal rate. A nominal rate of 7 percent produces a real rate of 7% − 4% = 3%.

[Handwritten note: CB chooses i which affects r.]

FIGURE 12.8 Equilibrium Output

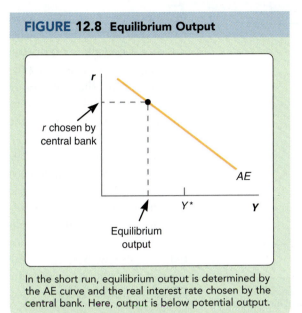

In the short run, equilibrium output is determined by the AE curve and the real interest rate chosen by the central bank. Here, output is below potential output.

FIGURE 12.9 A Shift in Monetary Policy

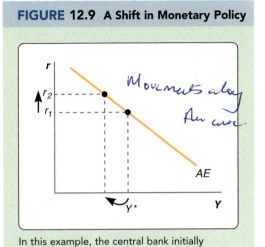

[Handwritten note: Movements along the curve.]

In this example, the central bank initially chooses a real interest rate of r_1, which makes output equal potential output. Then the central bank raises the interest rate to r_2, pushing output below potential.

Equilibrium Output We can now see how the equilibrium level of output is determined in the short run. As shown in **Figure 12.8**, output depends on the AE curve and the central bank's choice of the real interest rate. In effect, the central bank picks a point on the AE curve. The figure shows an example in which equilibrium output is below potential output. Output could be at or above potential if the central bank chose a lower interest rate.

Shifts in Monetary Policy At this point, we can understand one reason that output fluctuates over the business cycle: shifts in monetary policy. Output rises or falls when the central bank changes the real interest rate.

[Handwritten note: 1) Y shifts is MP. MP → Δ u C.]

Figure 12.9 gives an example. Initially, the central bank chooses a real interest rate of r_1, which implies that output equals potential output. Then the central bank raises the interest rate to r_2, and output falls below potential. The central bank has caused a recession.

You may wonder why a central bank would ever behave this way. If output is at potential, why reduce it? The short answer is that a recession may be necessary to control inflation. We discuss this point later in the chapter.

Expenditure Shocks

[Handwritten note: ⇒ Shifts due to changes in components of AE]

The AE curve captures the effects of the real interest rate on expenditure. Now we turn to other factors. Any event that changes aggregate expenditure for a given interest rate is called an **expenditure shock**. An expenditure shock causes the AE curve to shift.

An Example One kind of expenditure shock is a change in government spending. For example, the government might increase military spending during a war. This action raises the government purchases component (G)

Expenditure shock event that changes aggregate expenditure for a given interest rate, shifting the AE curve

+vc ES causes AE to shift Right
−vc ES causes AE to Shift Left

FIGURE 12.10 An Expenditure Shock

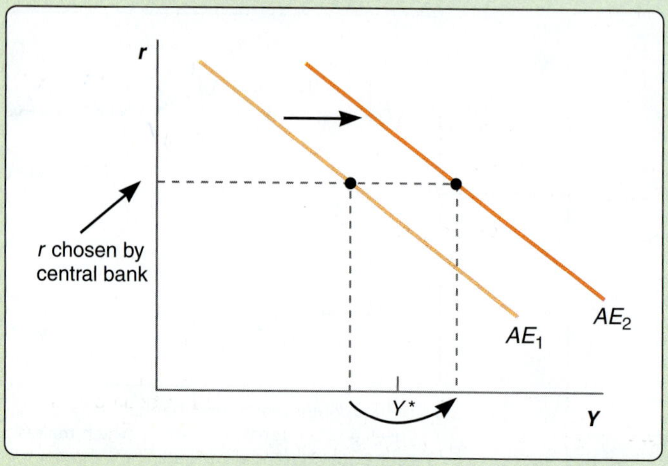

holding real i constant.

A positive expenditure shock, such as a rise in military spending, shifts the AE curve to the right. If the central bank holds the real interest rate constant, equilibrium output rises. In this example, output rises from a level below potential to a level above potential.

of aggregate expenditure. **Figure 12.10** shows the effects of this shock. For any given interest rate, higher government purchases mean that aggregate expenditure is higher. Therefore, the AE curve shifts to the right, from AE_1 to AE_2.

Assume for now that the central bank keeps the real interest rate constant. In this case, the shift in the AE curve raises equilibrium output. In our example, output rises from below potential to above potential: the expenditure shock moves the economy from a recession to a boom.

Types of Expenditure Shocks

Each of the four components of spending can shift for various reasons, so there are many kinds of expenditure shocks. Shocks can raise spending, shifting the AE curve to the right, or reduce spending, shifting it to the left. In each case, output changes if the central bank keeps the interest rate constant, as in Figure 12.10. Let's examine some types of expenditure shocks that have occurred in the United States and elsewhere.

↑G ↑Y = Boom

- *Government spending* We already mentioned the effect of higher military spending. In U.S. history, an important example is the Vietnam War. In the late 1960s, rising spending on the war shifted the AE curve to the right, contributing to an economic boom. (As a percentage of GDP, spending on the Iraq War was lower than spending on Vietnam, so the impact on AE was smaller.)

↑t ↓Y

- *Taxes* A tax increase means consumers have less income left to spend. Consumption falls, shifting the AE curve to the left. The reverse happens if taxes are reduced. The most recent recession led to two pieces of legislation that cut taxes: the Economic Stimulus Act, signed by President Bush in 2008, and the Economic Recovery Act, signed by President Obama in 2009. The goal of these tax cuts was to shift AE to the right and raise output. (The Economic Recovery Act also increased government spending for the purpose of raising output.)

↓ Private
↓ Savings
tax

- *Consumer confidence* Consumption depends partly on public confidence in the economy. If consumers fear trouble, they save more for a rainy day when their incomes might fall. An unusually large drop in confidence occurred in August 1990, when Iraqi forces under Saddam Hussein invaded Kuwait. Oil supplies were interrupted, and people feared the onset of a major oil crisis like those of the 1970s. Consumption fell sharply, shifting the AE curve to the left. This shock helped cause a recession in 1990–91.

■ *New technologies* Investment spending depends partly on whether firms see good investment opportunities. In the late 1990s, many firms believed that computers and related technologies would boost productivity. Investment in computers soared, shifting the AE curve to the right and raising output. The euphoria about new technologies died down around 2000, and firms reduced investment. This shock helped cause a recession in 2001–2002.

■ *Changes in bank lending* Many firms depend on banks to finance investment. Sometimes banks reduce their lending sharply, an event called a **credit crunch**, and firms are forced to cut investment. For example, widespread loan defaults during the savings and loan crisis of the 1980s made banks wary of all but the safest borrowers. They cut back on lending, helping to cause the recession of 1990–1991. Over 2007–2009, banks' losses on mortgages and a breakdown in loan securitization caused a severe credit crunch, a major factor behind the deep recession of the period and its aftermath.

Credit crunch a sharp reduction in bank lending

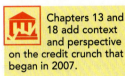 Chapters 13 and 18 add context and perspective on the credit crunch that began in 2007.

■ *Foreign business cycles* Booms and recessions are contagious: a change in one country's output affects the output of its trading partners. Canada, for example, exports a large fraction of its GDP to the United States. A U.S. recession reduces spending by U.S. consumers, including their spending on Canadian goods. For Canada, net exports fall, shifting that country's AE curve to the left and reducing output. Because of this effect, the most recent U.S. recession spread quickly to Canada.

Countercyclical Monetary Policy

In analyzing expenditure shocks, we've assumed the central bank holds the real interest rate constant. In this case, a shock causes output to change. In reality, the central bank may want to keep output constant. If so, it adjusts the interest rate to offset the effect of the expenditure shock. This practice is called **countercyclical monetary policy**. **Figure 12.11** gives an example. Initially the real interest rate is r_1, and output is at potential. Then there is an expenditure shock—let's say a change in consumer confidence.

In Figure 12.11A, we assume confidence falls, so the AE curve shifts to the left. Output would fall if the interest rate stayed at r_1. But the central bank reduces the interest rate to r_2, keeping output at potential. The lower interest rate raises expenditure, offsetting the effect of lower confidence. In Figure 12.11B, confidence rises and the AE curve shifts to the right. Here the central bank keeps output constant by *raising* the interest rate to r_2.

In Figure 12.11, we assume the central bank can raise or lower the interest rate by enough to stabilize output. This assumption is usually reasonable, but it was not accurate during the most recent U.S. recession. As the economy deteriorated, the Federal Open Market Committee cut its target for

Countercyclical monetary policy adjustments of the real interest rate by the central bank to offset expenditure shocks and thereby stabilize output

FIGURE 12.11 Countercyclical Monetary Policy

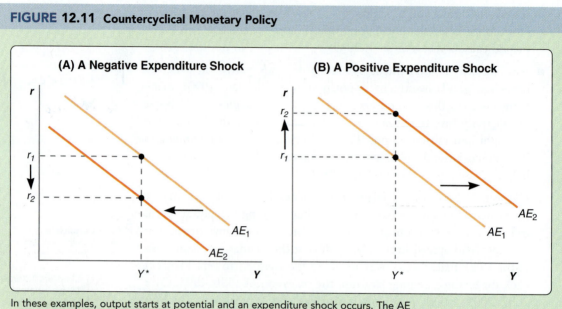

In these examples, output starts at potential and an expenditure shock occurs. The AE curve shifts, but the central bank adjusts the real interest rate to keep output constant. It lowers the real interest rate to offset a negative expenditure shock (A), and it raises the interest rate to offset a positive shock (B).

Zero Bound

i cannot be less
than 0.

the federal funds rate 8 times, moving it from 5.25 percent in August 2007 almost to zero in December 2008 in an attempt to spur output.

The Fed's actions were not enough to return output to potential. Further rate cuts were impossible, because nominal interest rates cannot fall below zero. We ignore this *zero bound problem* in this chapter's analysis of the AE/PC model but return to flesh it out in Chapter 14.

12.3 FLUCTUATIONS IN THE INFLATION RATE

We now turn to the short-run behavior of the inflation rate, the average percentage change in the prices of goods and services from year to year. For example, the inflation rate for the year 2020 is an average of price changes from 2019 to 2020. These price changes are made by the firms that sell goods and services. Therefore, to understand inflation movements, we must discuss the factors behind firms' pricing decisions.

Suppose you are the manager of a firm. It is the end of 2019, and you are pricing your products for 2020. How much will you raise prices over those of the previous year? We discuss three major factors in your decision: expected inflation, output, and supply shocks.

Expected Inflation

When you price a product for 2020, one consideration is what other firms will do. Say you expect other firms to raise prices by an average of 5 percent. In other words, you expect a 5-percent inflation rate. As part of this inflation, the costs of your inputs are likely to rise 5 percent. Your workers will want 5-percent raises to keep up with inflation.

Everything else equal, you want to keep your price in line with other prices. If you expect your costs and your competitors' prices to rise by 5 percent, you will raise your price by the same amount. In economic language, you raise your *nominal* price (your price in dollars) to maintain the same *relative* price (your price compared to other prices).

Now suppose that every firm is in the situation we've described: everyone expects 5-percent inflation in 2020. Every firm raises its prices 5 percent to keep up. These price increases mean that the inflation rate turns out to be 5 percent.

This reasoning applies for any level of expected inflation. The inflation rate that firms expect becomes the rate that actually occurs. In symbols,

$$\pi = \pi^e$$

where π is actual inflation and π^e is expected inflation.

What Determines Expected Inflation?

If expected inflation affects actual inflation, then what determines expectations? In 2019, what determines the inflation rate that firm managers expect in 2020?

Earlier chapters of this book introduce two theories about expectations: rational expectations and adaptive expectations. Economists disagree about which theory is better for understanding inflation behavior. Let's review the two theories and then discuss the debate.

▶ We introduce rational expectations in Section 3.2 and adaptive expectations in Section 4.2.

Rational Expectations The classical theory of asset prices assumes rational expectations about firms' earnings. This means that expectations are the best possible forecasts based on all available information. Many economists also assume rational expectations about inflation.

Under this assumption, any news about inflation affects expectations. For example, because monetary policy affects inflation, expectations depend on the actions and statements of the central bank. If the Fed chair announces a plan to fight inflation, and people believe he will carry it out, then expected inflation falls.

Adaptive Expectations This theory is also known as *backward-looking expectations*. It says that expectations are *not* based on all available information. Instead, expected inflation is determined by just one thing: past inflation. People expect inflation to continue at the rate they've seen recently.

We'll focus here on a specific version of adaptive expectations—expected inflation equals inflation over the previous year:

$$\pi^e = \pi(-1) \tag{12.3}$$

where (-1) indicates the previous year. Under this assumption, expected inflation for 2020 is actual inflation over 2019. Problem 12.9 examines adaptive expectations based on past inflation over longer time periods.

Is adaptive expectations a reasonable assumption? Supporters make two points:

1. For the firm managers who set prices, adaptive expectations is a convenient way to forecast inflation. Rational expectations means that price setters study all information relevant to inflation, such as the statements of central bank officials. Busy firm managers may not have time for this analysis. Forecasting that inflation will equal past inflation is an easy shortcut.

2. Firms don't lose much by relying on this shortcut. Although adaptive expectations are not the best possible forecasts, they are fairly good ones. In recent U.S. history, the inflation rate has moved slowly: in most years, the change in inflation is no more than one or two percentage points. As a result, adaptive forecasts of inflation have not been far off.

Past is better based on info.

Inflation rate moves slowly.

Choosing an Assumption To analyze the economy, we must choose an assumption about expectations. For most of this chapter, we assume adaptive expectations as in Equation (12.3). This assumption helps keep our analysis simple. In addition, it appears fairly realistic. Research that measures expectations with surveys suggests that inflation expectations in the United States are similar to adaptive expectations.

One such survey is run by the Federal Reserve Bank of Philadelphia. Every 6 months, the bank asks U.S. business economists what inflation rate they expect over the next year. **Figure 12.12** presents data from surveys

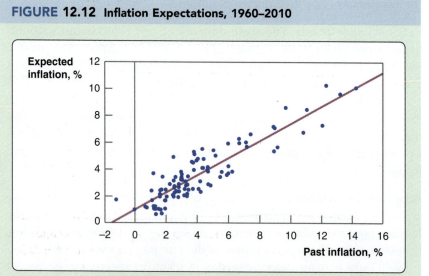

FIGURE 12.12 Inflation Expectations, 1960–2010

Each point on this graph represents the results of a survey of business economists performed every 6 months. The vertical axis is the average of the inflation rates that survey respondents expect over the next year. The horizontal axis is the actual inflation rate over the previous year. The strong relationship between expected inflation and past inflation suggests that adaptive expectations is a reasonable assumption.

Sources: Federal Reserve Bank of Philadelphia; Bureau of Labor Statistics

over the period from 1960 to mid-2010. For each survey, the figure plots the average of reported inflation expectations against the actual inflation rate over the previous year. We see a strong positive relationship, as predicted by adaptive expectations. This assumption does not fit the data perfectly, but it is a reasonable approximation.

Nonetheless, not all economists accept the assumption of adaptive expectations. So while we make this assumption for now, we return to the debate over expectations in Chapter 16.

The Effect of Output

Whatever determines expected inflation, it is one variable that affects actual inflation rates. We now turn to another factor: the level of output.

Why Output Matters To understand the role of output, suppose an economy enters a boom. In this situation, a typical firm produces more than usual. High production increases the firm's *marginal cost*—the cost of producing an extra unit of output. Marginal cost rises because firms are straining their productive capacity. In addition, unemployment falls in a boom, making workers more aggressive in pushing for wage increases. Large wage increases further raise marginal costs.

A basic economic principle is that firms adjust prices in line with marginal costs. Therefore, when a boom raises marginal costs, firms raise prices faster than usual. The reverse happens in a recession. Firms reduce production, so they have unused capacity. Facing high unemployment, workers are less aggressive in pushing for raises. These factors reduce marginal costs, so firms raise prices by less than usual.

The Phillips Curve Remember our earlier assumption that inflation equals expected inflation. We now modify this assumption to account for the effect of output. We assume that inflation equals expected inflation *when output is at potential*. With normal levels of production, firms raise prices at the expected inflation rate to keep relative prices stable.

Movements in output change inflation relative to this baseline. When output exceeds potential, the rise in marginal costs gives firms extra incentives to raise prices. As a result, inflation rises above expected inflation. When output is below potential, lower marginal costs push inflation below expected inflation.

Figure 12.13A captures these ideas in a graph called the **Phillips curve (PC)**. This curve shows the short-run relationship between output and inflation. It captures our assumptions that inflation equals expected inflation when output is at potential, and that higher output raises inflation.

The Phillips curve can also be presented in another way as shown in **Figure 12.13B**. This version of the curve involves unemployment rather than output, and it reveals a negative relationship. Inflation equals expected inflation if unemployment equals its natural rate, U^*. Inflation rises if unemployment falls below the natural rate, and it falls if unemployment rises.

> **Phillips curve (PC)** the positive short-run relationship between output and inflation; also, the negative short-run relationship between unemployment and inflation

[handwritten: Rational vs Adaptive]

FIGURE 12.13 The Phillips Curve *[handwritten: (The Two.]*

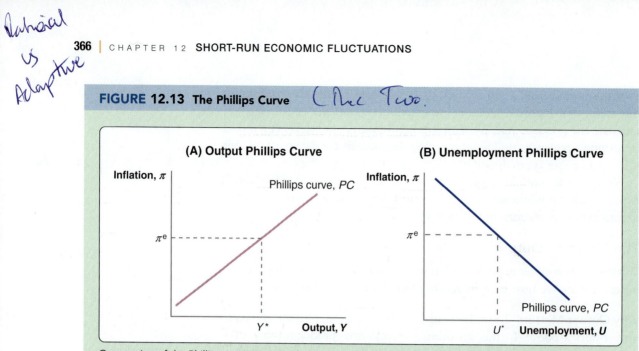

One version of the Phillips curve captures the short-run relationship between inflation and output: inflation equals expected inflation if output is at potential, and higher output raises inflation (A). The Phillips curve can also be expressed as a relationship between inflation and unemployment: inflation equals expected inflation if unemployment is at the natural rate, and higher unemployment reduces inflation (B).

[handwritten: $\frac{Y - Y^*}{Y} = -2(u - u^*)$ Because of Okun's law.]

▶ The Phillips curve is named after A. W. ("Bill") Phillips, an economist from New Zealand. In a famous 1958 paper using British data, Phillips noted a negative relationship between unemployment and inflation (as in Figure 12.13B).

Why can we draw the Phillips curve in two different ways? The answer is Okun's law [Equation (12.1)], which tells us that output and unemployment move in opposite directions over the business cycle. Low unemployment accompanies high output in an economic boom; a recession means low output and high unemployment. The key idea behind the Phillips curve is that *an economic boom raises inflation and a recession reduces it*. Figure 12.13A captures this idea with a positive effect of output on inflation, and Figure 12.13B captures it with a negative effect of unemployment.

In analyzing the economy, it is sometimes convenient to use the output version of the Phillips curve (Figure 12.13A) and sometimes the unemployment version (Figure 12.13B). Always remember that both curves express the same basic idea.

Equations for the Phillips Curve We can also express the Phillips curve mathematically. Just as there are two versions of the Phillips curve graph, there are two equations for the Phillips curve. The first relates inflation to output:

[handwritten: Inflation by Output (Equation)]

OUTPUT PHILLIPS CURVE

$$\pi = \pi^e + \alpha \frac{(Y - Y^*)}{Y^*} \qquad (\alpha > 0) \qquad (12.4)$$

[handwritten: $\pi = \pi^e + \alpha \tilde{Y}$]

Recall that the term $(Y - Y^*)/Y^*$, which we also denote by $\tilde{Y}$, is the output gap—the percentage deviation of output from potential. Like Figure 12.13A, Equation (12.4) says that inflation equals expected inflation if output is at potential. When output deviates from potential, inflation moves in the same direction.

[handwritten: α = 0.5 coefficient]

The coefficient α is a positive constant that measures how strongly output affects inflation. If $\alpha = 0.5$, for example, then an output gap of 1 percent (meaning output is 1 percent above potential) raises the inflation rate by half a percentage point.

[handwritten margin: × unemployment.]

We derive the second Phillips curve equation by combining Equation (12.4) with Equation (12.1), which expresses Okun's law. Equation (12.1) is $(Y - Y^*)/Y^* = -2(U - U^*)$: the output gap equals –2 times the deviation of unemployment from the natural rate. In Equation (12.4), substituting $-2(U - U^*)$ for $(Y - Y^*)/Y^*$ gives us

[handwritten margin: Derived from Okun's Law & Equation 12.4.]

UNEMPLOYMENT PHILLIPS CURVE *[handwritten: eq π.]*

$$\pi = \pi^e + \alpha\,[-2(U - U^*)]$$
$$\pi = \pi^e - 2\alpha(U - U^*) \tag{12.5}$$

Like Figure 12.13B, Equation (12.5) says that inflation equals expected inflation if unemployment is at the natural rate and that movements in unemployment push inflation in the opposite direction.

Notice that the coefficient on unemployment in Equation (12.5) is -2 times the output coefficient in Equation (12.4). If $\alpha = 0.5$, for example, the coefficient on unemployment is -1.0. A 1-percentage point rise in the unemployment rate reduces the inflation rate by 1 percentage point.

The Phillips Curve with Adaptive Expectations Remember our assumption of adaptive expectations: $\pi^e = \pi(-1)$. With this assumption, we can write the Phillips curve in a different way. In the output Phillips curve, Equation (12.4), substituting $\pi(-1)$ for π^e gives us

[handwritten: Since $\pi^e = \pi(-1)$ sub into]

$$\pi = \pi(-1) + \alpha\frac{(Y - Y^*)}{Y^*}$$

Moving $\pi(-1)$ to the left side yields

OUTPUT PHILLIPS CURVE WITH ADAPTIVE EXPECTATIONS *[handwritten: with adaptive expectations]*

$$\pi - \pi(-1) = \alpha\frac{(Y - Y^*)}{Y^*} \tag{12.6}$$

In this equation, the left side is current inflation minus last year's inflation—in other words, the *change* in the inflation rate. So the output gap determines the change in inflation. When output exceeds potential, the change in inflation is positive: inflation rises. When output is below potential, inflation falls.

Once again, Okun's law lets us replace the output gap with $-2(U - U^*)$. Making this substitution in Equation (12.6) gives us

UNEMPLOYMENT PHILLIPS CURVE WITH ADAPTIVE EXPECTATIONS

$$\pi - \pi(-1) = -2\alpha(U - U^*) \tag{12.7}$$

When unemployment equals the natural rate, the change in inflation is zero: the inflation rate is constant. For this reason, the natural rate is sometimes

NAIRU acronym for *nonaccelerating inflation rate of unemployment,* the unemployment rate that produces a constant inflation rate; another name for the natural rate of unemployment, *U**

▶If you have taken statistics: We obtain a coefficient of −0.99 when we run a regression of the change in inflation on *U* − *U** without a constant term. The line in Figure 12.14 is the regression line.

called the *nonaccelerating inflation rate of unemployment,* or **NAIRU**. Inflation falls when unemployment exceeds the natural rate, and it rises when unemployment is below the natural rate.

Some Data Does the Phillips curve describe reality? Let's examine the version that relates the change in inflation to unemployment, Equation (12.7). **Figure 12.14** plots the change in U.S. inflation against $(U - U^*)$, the deviation of unemployment from the natural rate, for each year from 1960 through 2009. $(U - U^*)$ is calculated using the estimates of U^* in Figure 12.2 (p. 350).

Figure 12.14 shows a negative relation between unemployment and the change in inflation, as predicted by the Phillips curve. The line that best fits this relation has a slope of approximately −1.0. This means the inflation rate falls by 1 percentage point when unemployment is 1 point above the natural rate.

The Phillips curve relation is far from perfect, however. In Figure 12.14, inflation sometimes moves in ways our theory does not predict. In 1974, for example, inflation rose almost 5 points even though unemployment was near the natural rate. In 1980, inflation rose 2 points when unemployment was *above* the natural rate. To understand such episodes, we turn to the final factor that affects inflation.

FIGURE 12.14 Evidence for the Phillips Curve, 1960–2009

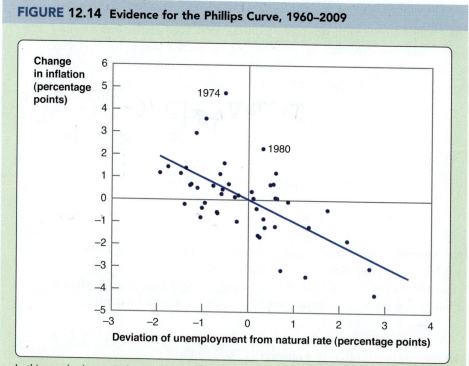

In this graph, the vertical axis is the change in the U.S. inflation rate from the previous year, $\pi - \pi(-1)$. The horizontal axis is the difference between unemployment and the natural rate, $U - U^*$. Each dot represents a year. On average, a one percentage point rise in unemployment reduces the inflation rate by about one point. This negative relationship is predicted by the Phillips curve with adaptive expectations.

Sources: Bureau of Labor Statistics and author's calculations of U^*.

Supply Shocks

So far we've seen that the inflation rate depends on expected inflation and on output or the unemployment rate. The final factor is *supply shocks*.

What Are They? A **supply shock**, ν (the Greek letter nu), is an event that causes a major change in firms' production costs. An *adverse supply shock* raises costs, and a *beneficial supply shock* reduces costs. In the short run, these shocks cause changes in the inflation rate.

One kind of supply shock is a change in oil prices. Many firms use oil in their production processes. If oil prices rise (an adverse shock), then costs rise for oil users, leading them to increase the prices of their goods by more than usual. The inflation rate rises. A fall in oil prices (a beneficial shock) has the opposite effect, reducing firms' costs and pushing inflation down.

A shock can stem from a change in the prices of raw materials, such as oil. It can be a jump in wages when firms negotiate new labor contracts. It can be a change in the exchange rate, which affects the costs of importers. There are many kinds of supply shocks.

Supply Shocks and the Phillips Curve We can capture the effects of supply shocks in our graph of the output Phillips curve. An adverse supply shock raises inflation for any given levels of expected inflation and output. As shown in **Figure 12.15**, the Phillips curve shifts up, from PC_1 to PC_2. A beneficial supply shock has the opposite effect, shifting the Phillips curve down.

Supply shock, ν event that causes a major change in firms' production costs, which in turn causes a short-run change in the inflation rate

FIGURE 12.15 An Adverse Supply Shock

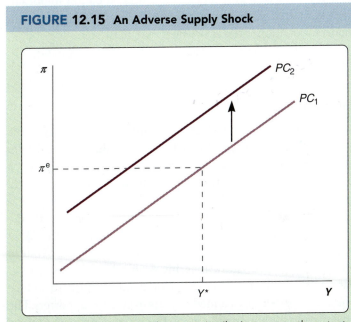

An adverse supply shock, such as a rise in oil prices, causes the output Phillips curve to shift up.

In the equation for the Phillips curve, we add the term ν, which captures supply shocks:

THE OUTPUT PHILLIPS CURVE WITH SUPPLY SHOCKS

$$\pi = \pi^e + \alpha \frac{(Y - Y^*)}{Y^*} + \nu \qquad (12.8)$$

If no supply shock occurs, then $\nu = 0$. A positive ν is an adverse shock, and a negative ν is a beneficial shock. For example, $\nu = 2\%$ means a shock that raises inflation by 2 percent.

Let's again rewrite the Phillips curve using adaptive expectations, $\pi^e = \pi(-1)$. This assumption leads to

THE OUTPUT PHILLIPS CURVE WITH ADAPTIVE EXPECTATIONS
AND SUPPLY SHOCKS

$$\pi - \pi(-1) = \alpha \frac{(Y - Y^*)}{Y^*} + \nu \qquad (12.9)$$

Once again, $\pi - \pi(-1)$ is the change in inflation from the previous year.

Equation (12.9) offers a compact summary of inflation behavior. If output is at potential ($Y = Y^*$) and no supply shock occurs ($\nu = 0$), then the change in inflation is zero. In other words, inflation stays at its previous level. Inflation can rise above its previous level for two reasons: a positive output gap ($Y > Y^*$) or an adverse supply shock ($\nu > 0$). Similarly, inflation can fall because of a negative output gap or a beneficial supply shock.

Among the many kinds of supply shocks, historically the most important type is the one we started with: changes in oil prices. Oil prices explain many movements in inflation rates, as the next case illustrates.

CASE STUDY

Oil Prices and Inflation

Look at Figure 12.1 (p. 348), which shows U.S. inflation rates since 1960. You can see that inflation rose rapidly at two points during the 1970s, peaking at 11 percent in 1974 and 13.5 percent in 1980. In each case, a major factor behind the inflation run-up was an increase in world oil prices.

The oil price increases reflected political and military events in the Middle East. The first followed the Yom Kippur War of October 1973, in which Egypt and Syria attacked Israel. The United States and Western European countries supported Israel, angering Arab oil producers. OPEC (the Organization of Petroleum Exporting Countries) decided to reduce oil production, and it temporarily banned exports to Israel's supporters. The supply of oil fell sharply, pushing up the price. The price more than doubled in December 1973, from about $4 per barrel to $10, spurring inflation throughout the world.

Before the second price increase, in early 1979, oil prices were stable at about $15 per barrel. Then a revolution broke out in Iran, a major oil producer. Ultimately, Iran's monarch, the Shah, was overthrown and replaced by a fundamentalist Islamic government. In the interim, the revolution disrupted Iran's oil production, reducing world supply. The price of oil climbed to $40 per barrel in 1980, and inflation rose again.

Oil prices also explain some of the smaller inflation movements in Figure 12.1. Dissension within OPEC caused a fall in oil prices in 1986, which in turn caused a dip in U.S. inflation. Oil prices rose in 1990, when Iraq invaded Kuwait, and U.S. inflation rose.

More recently, oil prices have been a less important factor in U.S. inflation. The reason is *not* that oil prices have been stable. To the contrary, prices have fluctuated dramatically in recent years, climbing from $20 per barrel in 2002 to more than $100 in 2008 and then falling below $50 in 2009. These fluctuations have caused large movements in the gas prices paid by U.S. consumers, but the effects on overall inflation have been modest. During the big rise in oil prices, for example, the inflation rate edged up from about 2 percent to 4 percent, hardly a return to 1970s levels. Evidently, oil prices don't affect inflation the way they used to.

What explains this change? One factor is that oil has become less important to the U.S. economy. The manufacturing sector has shrunk while the service sector, which uses less energy, has grown. Since the 1970s, the amount of oil used per unit of aggregate output has fallen by almost half.

Economists speculate about other factors. One theory involves a change in the behavior of inflation expectations. In the 1970s, people expected oil price hikes to raise inflation, and these expectations were self-fulfilling. To match expected inflation, firms throughout the economy raised their prices when they saw oil prices rise, and workers demanded larger wage increases. This behavior magnified the direct effects of oil prices on inflation.

According to this theory, expectations behave differently now: changes in oil prices no longer produce self-fulfilling expectations of large changes in inflation. The ultimate reason for this change is the behavior of the Federal Reserve. The Fed has shown a commitment to keeping the inflation rate low and stable, so firms and workers believe that any inflationary blip caused by oil prices will soon be reversed.

12.4 THE COMPLETE ECONOMY

We have used the aggregate expenditure curve to explain output movements and the Phillips curve to explain movements in the inflation rate. We now put the two curves together to get a complete view of short-run economic fluctuations: the **aggregate expenditure/Phillips curve model**. The **AE/PC model** assumes a negative relationship between the interest rate and output (the AE curve) and a positive relationship between output and inflation (the Phillips curve).

Aggregate expenditure/ Phillips curve (AE/PC) model theory of short-run economic fluctuations that assumes a negative relationship between the interest rate and output (the AE curve) and a positive relationship between output and inflation (the Phillips curve)

Combining the Two Curves

Figure 12.16 shows how both output and the inflation rate are determined in the AE/PC model. The central bank chooses the real interest rate. In Figure 12.16A, the real interest rate and the AE curve determine equilibrium output. Then output and the Phillips curve determine inflation in Figure 12.16B. The figure shows a case in which output is below potential and inflation is less than expected inflation.

We can use the AE and Phillips curves to see how various events affect the economy. Let's consider three examples. In each one, we assume initially that output is at potential and inflation equals expected inflation. Then something happens, and we trace out the effects.

A Rise in the Real Interest Rate In **Figure 12.17A**, the central bank raises the real interest rate from r_1 to r_2. This action moves the economy along

You may be familiar with the aggregate demand/aggregate supply (AD/AS) model of short-run economic fluctuations. The AE/PC and AD/AS models make similar predictions about the economy's behavior, but the AE/PC model is especially convenient for analyzing the effects of interest rate changes by the central bank. The Online Appendix to Chapter 12 compares these models in detail.

FIGURE 12.16 The Complete Economy

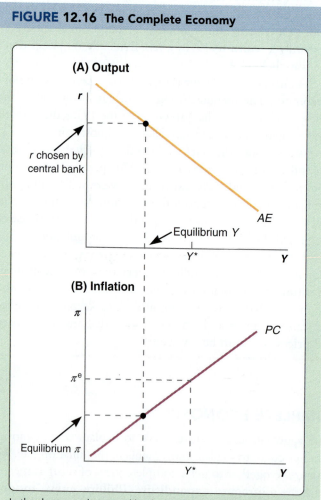

In the short run, the central bank chooses the real interest rate. The real rate and the AE curve determine output (A). Output and the Phillips curve determine inflation (B). Here, output is below potential and inflation is below expected inflation.

the AE curve, pushing output below potential. In **Figure 12.17B,** lower output moves the economy along the Phillips curve, reducing inflation below expected inflation.

This example illustrates a basic trade-off facing central banks. *Policymakers can reduce inflation by raising the real interest rate, but at the cost of reducing output in the short run.*

An Expenditure Shock **Figure 12.18** shows the effects of a positive shock, such as a tax cut or a rise in consumer confidence, which raises aggregate expenditure. The shock shifts the AE curve to the right in Figure 12.18A. Assuming the central bank keeps the real interest rate constant, output rises above potential. Higher output moves the economy along the Phillips curve to a higher inflation rate in Figure 12.18B.

A Supply Shock Finally, we examine the effects of an adverse supply shock, such as a rise in oil prices. Depending on the central bank's reaction to this shock, two possible outcomes can occur.

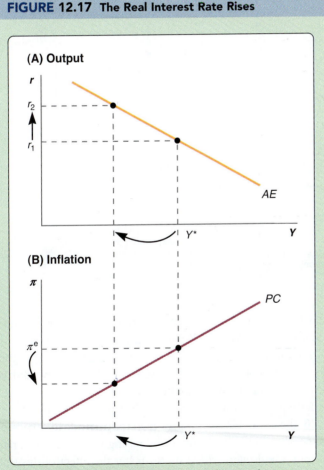

FIGURE 12.17 The Real Interest Rate Rises

(A) Output

(B) Inflation

In this example, the real interest rate is initially r_1, and output is at potential. Then the central bank raises the interest rate to r_2, which pushes output below potential (A). The fall in output pushes inflation below expected inflation (B).

[Handwritten margin notes:]

+ve Exp. Expenditure shock shifts AE to right with constant r.

However

$Y^* \lessgtr Y \Rightarrow \pi > \pi^*$

movement up curve.

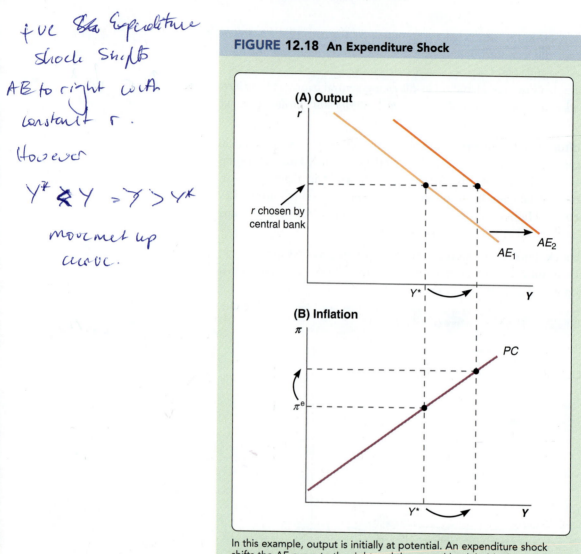

FIGURE 12.18 An Expenditure Shock

(A) Output

r chosen by central bank

AE_2

AE_1

Y*   Y

(B) Inflation

PC

π^e

Y*   Y

In this example, output is initially at potential. An expenditure shock shifts the AE curve to the right and the central bank holds the real interest rate constant, so output rises above potential (A). The rise in output pushes inflation above expected inflation (B).

In **Figure 12.19**, the central bank keeps the real interest rate constant. Because the shock does not affect the AE curve, output stays at potential. The adverse supply shock causes the Phillips curve to shift up, leading to higher inflation. The central bank's behavior in this case is called **accommodative monetary policy**. The central bank responds passively to (accommodates) the supply shock, letting inflation go where the adverse shock pushes it.

In **Figure 12.20**, the central bank chooses **nonaccommodative monetary policy**. It acts to keep inflation constant by raising the real interest rate, which reduces output. The Phillips curve shifts up, but the effect of this shift on inflation is offset by the effect of lower output, and inflation stays at π^e.

This example shows that *an adverse supply shock creates a dilemma* for the central bank. Nonaccommodative policy prevents the shock from raising

Accommodative monetary policy decision by the central bank to keep the real interest rate constant when a supply shock occurs, allowing inflation to change

Nonaccommodative monetary policy decision by the central bank to adjust the interest rate to offset a supply shock and keep inflation constant

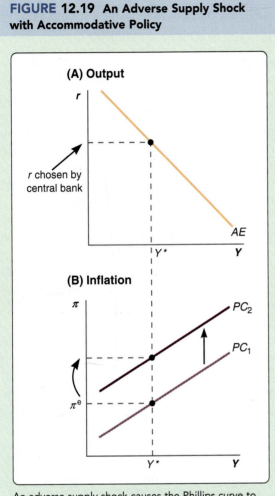

FIGURE 12.19 An Adverse Supply Shock with Accommodative Policy

An adverse supply shock causes the Phillips curve to shift up. Here, the central bank does not change the real interest rate, so output remains constant (A). With constant output, the Phillips curve shift raises inflation above expected inflation (B).

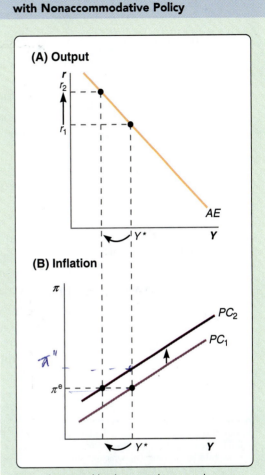

FIGURE 12.20 An Adverse Supply Shock with Nonaccommodative Policy

Here, the central bank responds to an adverse supply shock by raising the real interest rate. This action reduces output (A). Lower output offsets the shift in the Phillips curve, keeping inflation at its expected level (B).

inflation, but at the cost of lower output. Sometimes central banks are unwilling to accept this cost to the economy, so they accommodate the shock by holding the interest rate steady and allowing the inflation rate to rise.

The Economy Over Time

We've seen how various events affect the economy at a point in time. This is not the end of the story, because these events also affect the future. Here we examine how the economy evolves over time.

The link from the present to the future occurs through the Phillips curve. With our assumption of adaptive expectations, the Phillips curve says that the current inflation rate depends on last year's inflation. So anything

Disinflation [handwritten margin note]

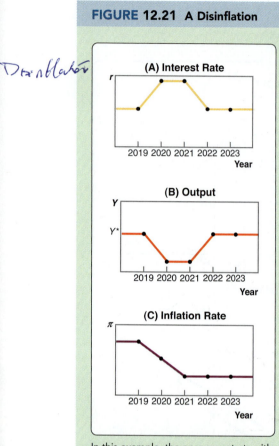

FIGURE 12.21 **A Disinflation**

(A) Interest Rate

2019 2020 2021 2022 2023
Year

(B) Output

2019 2020 2021 2022 2023
Year

(C) Inflation Rate

2019 2020 2021 2022 2023
Year

In this example, the economy starts with output at potential and stable inflation. In 2020, the central bank raises the real interest rate temporarily (A), which pushes output below potential (B). The inflation rate falls while output is below potential and then levels off (C).

Disinflation monetary policy of reducing inflation by temporarily raising the real interest rate

that affected inflation last year also affects inflation this year. Similarly, anything that affects inflation this year will affect inflation next year. Let's consider two examples of how the economy might behave over time.

A Rise in the Real Interest Rate Assume the economy starts out with output at potential and no supply shocks. In this situation, the Phillips curve implies that inflation is constant over time. Then the central bank raises the real interest rate. Specifically, assume the central bank raises the interest rate in 2020. It keeps the interest rate high in 2021, and then returns it to the initial level in 2022. **Figure 12.21A** shows the movements in the interest rate over this period.

Figure 12.21B shows the behavior of output. As we've seen before, a higher interest rate moves the economy along the AE curve, reducing output. In 2020 and 2021, when the interest rate is higher, output is below potential. When the interest rate returns to its initial level in 2022, output returns to potential.

Figure 12.21C shows the behavior of inflation over these years. With adaptive expectations, the Phillips curve says that output affects the *change* in inflation [see Equation (12.6)]. With output below potential, the change in inflation is negative in 2020 and 2021, which means the *level* of inflation falls. When output returns to potential in 2022, the change in inflation is zero: inflation stays constant at the level it reached in 2021.

This scenario exemplifies the monetary policy of **disinflation**, a temporary rise in the real interest rate that reduces inflation. A central bank adopts such a policy if it thinks the inflation rate is too high. The cost of disinflation is lower output. The good news is that *a temporary fall in output reduces inflation permanently*. Once inflation reaches an acceptable level, the central bank can reverse its interest rate increase (Figure 12.21A). At that point, output returns to potential (Figure 12.21B) and inflation stays low (Figure 12.21C).

An Adverse Supply Shock Assume again that the economy starts with output at potential and steady inflation. In 2020, a supply shock occurs: oil prices jump up. If we denote supply shocks with ν, then $\nu > 0$ in 2020 and $\nu = 0$ in all other years.

As we've seen before, the effects of supply shocks depend on the central bank's response. **Figure 12.22** shows an accommodative policy. The central bank keeps the interest rate constant despite the shock, so output stays constant. Inflation jumps up in 2020 because the Phillips curve shifts, as in Figure 12.19 on page 375.

Notice that inflation stays high after 2020. With output at potential and no further shocks, the change in inflation is zero. Inflation stays where it was pushed by the shock in 2020. *An accommodative monetary policy allows a supply shock to raise inflation permanently.*

Figure 12.23 shows the effects of a supply shock when policy is nonaccommodative. The central bank raises the real interest rate in 2020 and output

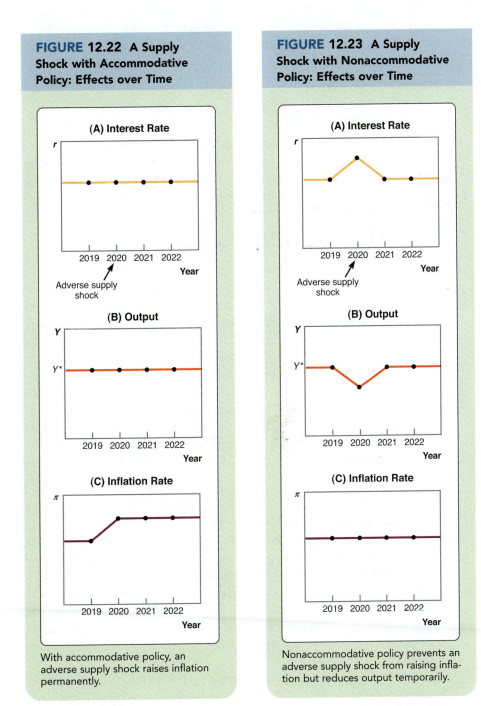

FIGURE 12.22 A Supply Shock with Accommodative Policy: Effects over Time

(A) Interest Rate

Adverse supply shock

(B) Output

(C) Inflation Rate

With accommodative policy, an adverse supply shock raises inflation permanently.

FIGURE 12.23 A Supply Shock with Nonaccommodative Policy: Effects over Time

(A) Interest Rate

Adverse supply shock

(B) Output

(C) Inflation Rate

Nonaccommodative policy prevents an adverse supply shock from raising inflation but reduces output temporarily.

falls. Inflation stays constant in 2020, as the effect of lower output offsets the Phillips curve shift, as in Figure 12.20 on page 375. In 2021, the central bank reduces the interest rate and output returns to potential. As with accommodative policy, inflation stays constant after 2020—but here it is constant at its original level. Nonaccommodative policy prevents inflation from ratcheting up.

We've worked hard to develop a theory of economic fluctuations based on the AE and Phillips curves. The payoff is that the AE/PC model helps explain fluctuations in real economies, as the next case study shows.

JUMBO CASE STUDY

The U.S. Economy, 1960–2010

We began this chapter with Figure 12.1 (page 348), which shows fluctuations in U.S. unemployment and inflation since 1960. We've touched on parts of this history over the course of the chapter. Here we pull everything together to tell the story of the economy over the past half-century—a story of expenditure shocks, supply shocks, and shifts in monetary policy.

The 1960s This decade began with a mild recession, which you can see in Figure 12.1. Unemployment peaked at 7.1 percent in May 1961. The Fed reduced the real interest rate and the economy recovered.

In the mid-1960s, two shocks shifted the AE curve outward. One was the "Kennedy tax cuts" of 1964. President Kennedy proposed these tax cuts during the early 1960s recession, but they took effect after the economy had recovered and Kennedy had died. The second shock was an increase in government spending. The Johnson administration spent heavily on both its "Great Society" domestic programs and the Vietnam War.

Initially, the Fed did not act to offset the AE shift, so output rose above potential (as in Figure 12.10). As predicted by Okun's law, unemployment fell below the natural rate, reaching 3.4 percent in September 1968. As predicted by the Phillips curve, the economic boom raised inflation from 1.3 percent in 1964 to 5.9 percent in 1970. The Fed finally responded with a sharp interest rate hike in 1969.

The 1970s This was a volatile period for the U.S. economy. It started with a mild recession caused by the 1969 interest rate increase. Inflation fell slowly, but the Nixon administration became impatient and adopted a radical policy: price controls. In August 1971, prices were frozen for 90 days; after that, large firms needed permission from a government agency to raise prices.

▶ Chapter 16 discusses the relationship between President Nixon and Fed Chairman Burns.

At the same time, the Fed lowered interest rates, creating an economic boom. (Some historians think that Arthur Burns, the Fed chairman, was trying to help President Nixon get reelected.) Normally, the boom would have pushed the inflation rate up, but the price controls held inflation down artificially.

In 1973, things started to fall apart. The price controls were relaxed, allowing inflation to pick up. An oil price shock occurred around the same time. So did another adverse supply shock: a sharp increase in food prices caused by bad weather.

Initially, the Fed accommodated these shocks, not wanting to raise unemployment. Inflation rose to 11.0 percent in 1974. At that point, the Fed became alarmed and raised interest rates sharply. This action produced a disinflation like the one in Figure 12.21. High interest rates caused a recession: output fell and the unemployment rate rose to 9.0 percent in mid-1975. The recession pushed inflation down to 5.8 percent in 1976.

With unemployment rising, the Fed switched gears again and lowered interest rates. Arthur Okun described the Fed's behavior as "stop–go monetary policy." In retrospect, it appears the Fed reduced rates too much. Low rates pushed output above potential, raising inflation over 1977–78. Then in 1979, disaster struck again: the second oil shock of the decade. Inflation was 11.2 percent in 1979 and 13.5 percent in 1980.

Many historians criticize the Fed for allowing inflation to get out of control in the 1970s. They deride the passivity of William Miller, who was Fed chairman in 1978–79. In August 1979, however, Miller was replaced by Paul Volcker, a man determined to beat inflation. This appointment led to dramatic events.

The 1980s Volcker's Fed raised interest rates sharply in late 1979 and early 1980. Around the same time, the Carter administration temporarily imposed "credit controls"—regulations that discouraged the use of credit cards and other consumer borrowing. This action decreased consumption spending, shifting the AE curve to the left; along with higher interest rates, it pushed output down and unemployment up.

▶ To review Paul Volcker's tactics for fighting inflation, see the case study in Section 11.5.

The Fed briefly reduced rates in mid-1980, but then, determined to beat inflation, raised them to very high levels. In mid-1981, the nominal federal funds rate exceeded 17 percent, and the real rate was almost 8 percent.

The spike in interest rates caused a deep recession: in late 1982, the unemployment rate reached 10.8 percent, its highest level since the Great Depression (a record that still stood in 2010). With unemployment high, inflation fell quickly, leveling off around 4 percent in 1983–84. At that point, the Fed lowered interest rates, and unemployment slowly headed back toward 6 percent over the next few years. This episode is a classic example of a disinflation: a temporary rise in interest rates reduced inflation permanently, at the cost of a recession.

The rest of the 1980s was fairly tranquil. Inflation stayed around 4 percent, and unemployment drifted down. The only significant supply shock was a beneficial one—an oil price decrease in 1986. At the end of the decade, strong spending on consumption and investment shifted the AE curve out, pushing output a bit above potential and reducing unemployment to 5.3 percent. Inflation crept toward 5 percent, and the Fed responded by raising interest rates in 1989.

The 1990s A recession started in 1990, caused partly by the 1989 interest rate increase. Two other factors were negative expenditure shocks that we've mentioned before: the fall in consumer confidence when Iraq invaded Kuwait, and the credit crunch that followed the S&L crisis.

The recession was fairly mild, with unemployment peaking at 7.8 percent in June 1992. Inflation fell to 3.0 percent in 1992 and 1993. At the same time, the Fed reduced the nominal federal funds rate to 3 percent and the real rate to around zero. The economy recovered and seemed headed toward a stable regime of low inflation and unemployment around 6 percent.

Starting in the mid-1990s, the economy exceeded expectations. Unemployment fell below 6 percent in 1994 and kept falling. It reached 3.8 percent in April 2000. Economists believed that a boom was occurring, with unemployment below the natural rate. They warned that inflation would rise—but inflation fell slightly instead.

In retrospect, it appears that the natural rate of unemployment fell because of high productivity growth (see the case study in Section 12.1). A lower natural rate allowed actual unemployment to fall without spurring inflation. Productivity improvements also produced fast growth in output and wages. Many observers raved about the "New Economy" and the "Roaring '90s."

The 2000s The economy slowed in the early 2000s, dampening the euphoria about the New Economy. A recession started in 2001. One cause was a fall in investment when companies scaled back their computer spending. Consumption also fell because the stock market fell, reducing people's wealth. Unemployment peaked at 6.4 percent in June 2003. This rate was low compared to previous recessions, but it was significantly above the natural rate.

Inflation was low entering the 2000s, and the recession pushed it lower. Inflation fell to 1 percent in 2003. Economists started fretting about the possibility of zero or negative inflation—*deflation*. We discuss the dangers of deflation in Chapter 14.

Responding to the recession, the Fed reduced interest rates steadily. The federal funds rate fell from 6.5 percent in 2000 to 1.0 percent in late 2003. Low interest rates stimulated spending; car sales, for example, were boosted by "zero-percent financing." Tax cuts proposed by the new Bush administration, which were enacted in 2001 and 2002, also stimulated spending.

By the end of 2003, unemployment was falling. As the economy recovered, fears of deflation waned and the Fed raised interest rates. In 2005–2006, the economy seemed to settle into an equilibrium, with unemployment around 5 percent and inflation around 3 percent. The federal funds rate reached 5.25 percent in June 2006 and stayed there until August 2007.

 Then the subprime mortgage crisis hit the economy, threatening the survival of large financial institutions. The effects of the crisis included a credit crunch, plummeting prices of stocks and of housing, and a sharp fall in consumer confidence, all of which reduced aggregate expenditure. The Fed responded by reducing interest rates almost to zero, and the Bush and Obama administrations cut taxes and raised government spending, but these actions did not fully offset the factors that were reducing AE. The economy entered a long, deep recession, with unemployment peaking at 10.1 percent in October 2009.

A year later, economists were debating how long unemployment would stay high and whether policymakers had any means of reducing it. The recession had pushed the inflation rate down—it was running at about 1 percent after dipping briefly below zero in 2009—and fears of a sustained deflation reemerged. We return to this recent history throughout the rest of this book.

Online Case Study: An Update on the U.S. Economy

12.5 LONG-RUN MONETARY NEUTRALITY

We have seen that monetary policy has powerful effects on the economy. By changing the nominal interest rate, the Fed can change the real interest rate, which in turn affects output, unemployment, and inflation. However, *most of these effects are temporary.* They occur in the short run but not in the long run. Practically speaking, most effects of monetary policy disappear within a few years.

Specifically, in the long run, monetary policy usually does not affect *real variables*, those that are adjusted for inflation, such as real GDP and real interest rates. In the long run, policy affects only variables that are *not* adjusted for inflation, such as nominal GDP, nominal interest rates, and inflation itself. This is the principle of **long-run monetary neutrality**.

The analysis in Section 12.4 illustrates long-run neutrality. For example, recall what happens during a disinflation (see Figure 12.21). The central bank raises the real interest rate and output falls, but these effects are temporary. Only inflation changes in the long run. Here, we go beyond examples to discuss the basic forces behind long-run neutrality.

Long-run monetary neutrality principle that monetary policy cannot permanently affect real variables (variables adjusted for inflation)

Long-Run Output and Unemployment

Let's first consider the behavior of output. Look again at Figure 12.3A on page 352, which shows how output changes over time. The long-run path of output, Y, is determined by potential output, Y^*. Output deviates from potential during booms and recessions, but it returns to potential in the long run.

Potential output is the normal level of output the economy produces and depends on such factors as the labor force, the capital stock, and technology. Potential output is *not* influenced by monetary policy. When the central bank changes the interest rate, it affects aggregate expenditure but not the economy's productive capacity. Therefore, the central bank's action affects Y but not Y^*. Because Y^* determines output in the long run, monetary policy does not affect output in the long run.

The unemployment rate is also independent of monetary policy in the long run. Okun's law [Equation (12.1)] implies that if output is at potential, then unemployment is at its natural rate. Because output equals potential output in the long run, unemployment equals the natural rate in the long run. And economists generally believe that the natural rate depends on features of the labor market that monetary policy does not influence. We discuss possible exceptions later in this section.

A Permanent Boom?

We can explain long-run monetary neutrality in a different way. Suppose a central bank ignores this principle and tries to change output permanently. Let's say it lowers the real interest rate, pushing output above potential. It keeps the real rate low indefinitely, so output stays high indefinitely. What happens to the economy?

The answer comes from the Phillips curve. When output exceeds potential, the inflation rate rises above its previous level. As long as output stays high, inflation continues to rise. The inflation rate reaches higher and higher levels and eventually becomes astronomical.

A central bank is not likely to let this happen. At some point, inflation will rise high enough that policymakers won't tolerate further increases. They will do what's necessary to stabilize inflation: raise the real interest rate and return output to potential. Accelerating inflation forces the central bank to abandon the goal of raising output permanently.

The Neutral Real Interest Rate

Like output and unemployment, the real interest rate is independent of monetary policy in the long run. **Figure 12.24** shows why. Given the AE curve, a unique real interest rate makes output equal potential output, Y^*. This interest rate is called the **neutral real interest rate (r^n)**, because it implies neither a boom nor a recession.

In the long run, the central bank must move output to potential; to do so, it must move the real interest rate to the neutral rate. As shown in the

▶ This reasoning is not absolute. Occasionally, inflation reaches astronomical levels, yet the central bank doesn't act to stabilize it. In Zimbabwe, where the inflation rate rose above 1 million percent in 2008, the normal workings of the economy broke down. The central bank certainly did not succeed in keeping output high. We return to the topic of hyperinflation, and to Zimbabwe, in Chapter 14.

Neutral real interest rate (r^n) the real interest rate that makes output equal potential output, given the aggregate expenditure curve

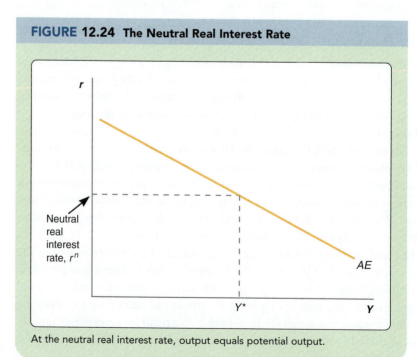

FIGURE 12.24 The Neutral Real Interest Rate

At the neutral real interest rate, output equals potential output.

figure, the neutral rate is determined by potential output and the position of the AE curve, factors that the central bank doesn't control.

How does this theory of the neutral real interest rate square with the loanable funds theory, which states that the supply and demand for loans determines the long-run behavior of the real rate? It may seem that we have two different theories of long-run interest rates, but in reality, the factors that raise or lower the real interest rate in the loanable funds theory have the same effects on the neutral rate in the AE/PC model. The appendix on p. 387 develops this point.

▶ Section 4.2 explains the long-run behavior of the real interest rate with the loanable funds theory.

An Exception to the Rule?

The principle of long-run monetary neutrality is a central tenet of economic theory, and we assume it throughout most of this book. Yet long-run neutrality may not be absolutely true. Some economists think that monetary policy *can* have long-run effects on an important real variable: unemployment.

Economists who hold this view argue that a tightening of monetary policy can cause a deep recession, and that unemployment during the recession leaves scars on the labor force—scars that raise the natural rate of unemployment. Because the natural rate rises, unemployment remains high even after the recession is over.

The scarring effects of prolonged unemployment can take many forms. People who lose their jobs can lose skills and fail to keep up with new technologies and other developments in their industries. Young people who try to enter the labor force and can't find jobs lose a chance to gain experience that would help them find future jobs. Unemployed workers may become discouraged as a recession drags on and dial back the intensity of their job searches. For all these reasons, a recession can make the workforce less employable, raising the natural rate of unemployment.

Economists summarize these ideas about persistent high unemployment rates by proposing that unemployment exhibits **hysteresis**. The term, which comes from physics, means that the short-run path of a variable—unemployment in this case—influences its long-run level—here, the natural rate. Economists first applied ideas about hysteresis to unemployment in an effort to explain the experience of Europeans in the 1980s and 1990s.

Hysteresis theory that the short-run path of a variable, such as unemployment, affects its long-run level, such as the natural rate of unemployment

In the early 1980s, many central banks in Europe tightened monetary policy to reduce inflation, as did the Fed in the United States, and unemployment rose as a result. In some countries, unemployment stayed high; in France, for example, unemployment rose from 4 percent in 1976 to 10 percent in 1984, then stayed between 9 and 12 percent through 2000. One interpretation is that the tight monetary policy of the 1980s had long-run effects on European unemployment. Because of hysteresis, long-run neutrality did not hold.

In 2010, some economists saw hysteresis at work in the United States. As we note in the Case Study in Section 12.1, some estimates show the natural rate of unemployment rising after 2007. Those who see hysteresis at work attribute this rise to the harm inflicted on workers during the deep recession that arose from the financial crisis. This view is controversial, and the behavior of U.S. unemployment in the coming years will shed light on whether hysteresis is a relevant factor.

Summary

- This chapter analyzes short-run economic fluctuations using the aggregate expenditure/Phillips curve (AE/PC) model.

12.1 The Business Cycle

- The long-run level of output is potential output, Y^*, which is determined by the economy's resources and technology. The long-run unemployment rate is the natural rate, U^*, which is determined by problems in the labor market.

- In the short run, output fluctuates around potential output and unemployment fluctuates around the natural rate. Over this business cycle, output and unemployment move in opposite directions (Okun's law). In an economic boom, output exceeds potential and unemployment is below the natural rate; the opposite occurs in a recession.

- The business cycle is caused by fluctuations in aggregate expenditure—total spending on the economy's goods and services. When AE rises, firms sell more, leading them to increase their output. To produce more they hire more workers, reducing unemployment. The opposite effects occur when aggregate expenditure falls.

12.2 What Determines Aggregate Expenditure?

- Aggregate expenditure is the sum of consumption, investment, government purchases, and net exports. A rise in the real interest rate reduces three of these components (C, I, and NX) and therefore reduces aggregate expenditure and output. The AE curve summarizes the negative relationship between the interest rate and output.

- In the short run, the central bank's control of the nominal interest rate allows it to control the ex ante real interest rate as well. Equilibrium output is determined by the AE curve and the real interest rate chosen by the central bank.

- An expenditure shock is an event that changes aggregate expenditure for a given real interest rate.

Expenditure shocks include changes in government spending or taxes, shifts in consumer confidence, new technologies that spur investment, changes in bank lending, and foreign booms and recessions. An expenditure shock shifts the AE curve, and output changes if the central bank holds the real interest rate constant.

- Countercyclical monetary policy can offset expenditure shocks, keeping output stable. Policymakers offset negative shocks by reducing the real interest rate and positive shocks by raising the interest rate.

12.3 Fluctuations in the Inflation Rate

- Firms increase their prices to keep up with the inflation rate they expect in the future, so expected inflation is one determinant of actual inflation.

- Economists debate whether expectations of inflation are rational or adaptive. Adaptive expectations are roughly consistent with evidence from surveys.

- An economic boom raises inflation above expected inflation, and a recession reduces inflation below expected inflation. This relationship is summarized by the Phillips curve, which can be expressed *either* as a positive relationship between output and inflation *or* as a negative relationship between unemployment and inflation.

- If inflation expectations are adaptive, the Phillips curve implies a positive relationship between output and the *change* in inflation, and a negative relationship between unemployment and the change in inflation.

- A supply shock is an event that causes a major change in firms' production costs. It causes the Phillips curve to shift, changing the level of inflation for given levels of output and expected inflation.

- Historically, the most important type of supply shock has been a change in oil prices. Increases in oil prices caused jumps in U.S. inflation in the 1970s. However, the effects of oil prices on inflation have diminished over time.

12.4 The Complete Economy

■ In the AE/PC model, the central bank chooses the real interest rate; the interest rate and the AE curve determine output; and output and the Phillips curve determine inflation. Economic fluctuations arise from expenditure shocks, supply shocks, and shifts in monetary policy.

■ In a disinflation, the central bank raises the real interest rate temporarily. This action causes a temporary fall in output (a recession) and a permanent fall in inflation.

■ When an adverse supply shock occurs, accommodative monetary policy allows inflation to rise permanently. Nonaccommodative policy prevents inflation from rising but reduces output temporarily.

■ The AE/PC model captures U.S. economic fluctuations since the 1960s—fluctuations resulting from a variety of expenditure shocks, supply shocks, and shifts in monetary policy.

12.5 Long-Run Monetary Neutrality

■ Although monetary policy influences the business cycle, it does not affect real variables, such as output or unemployment, in the long run.

■ The long-run real interest rate is the neutral rate, r^n, the rate that makes output equal potential output. Monetary policy does not affect the neutral interest rate.

■ Proponents of hysteresis theory contend that an exception to long-run monetary neutrality exists: the effects of a deep recession on the workforce cause the natural rate of unemployment to rise.

Key Terms

accommodative monetary policy, p. 374

aggregate expenditure (AE), p. 356

aggregate expenditure (AE) curve, p. 358

aggregate expenditure/Phillips curve (AE/PC) model, p. 371

business cycle, p. 348

consumption multiplier, p. 357

countercyclical monetary policy, p. 361

credit crunch, p. 361

disinflation, p. 376

economic boom, p. 352

expenditure shock, p. 359

hysteresis, p. 383

long-run monetary neutrality, p. 381

NAIRU, p. 368

natural rate of unemployment, U^*, p. 349

neutral real interest rate, r^n, p. 382

nonaccommodative monetary policy, p. 374

Okun's law, p. 353

output gap, p. 352

Phillips curve, PC, p. 365

potential output, Y^*, p. 349

recession, p. 352

supply shock, ν, p. 369

unemployment rate, U, p. 349

Questions and Problems

1. Suppose potential output grows 2 percent per year and the natural rate of unemployment is constant at 6 percent. In 2020, the unemployment rate is 7 percent.

   a. Assuming Okun's law, what is the output gap in 2020?

   b. If output grows 5 percent from 2020 to 2021, what is the unemployment rate in 2021?

2. Suppose the growth rate of potential output rises. The behavior of the output gap (the fluctuations of output around potential) does

not change. Do NBER recessions become more or less common? Explain.

3. Suppose a country bans trade with other countries, so net exports are always zero. How would this affect the slope of the AE curve? Explain.

4. Suppose the Fed raises the real interest rate and consumer confidence falls around the same time (as occurred in 1990). Show with a graph what happens to the AE curve and to output.

5. Suppose the economy starts with output at potential. Then a supply shock occurs: oil prices rise sharply. The Fed is *partly* accommodative: it raises the real interest rate, but not by enough to keep inflation from rising. Show with graphs what happens to the AE and Phillips curves, and to output and inflation.

6. Suppose oil prices jump up and the Fed is completely accommodative: it keeps the real interest rate constant. How must the Fed adjust the nominal interest rate? How must it adjust the money supply? Explain.

7. Suppose again that oil prices increase. This has two effects: (a) firms' costs jump up and (b) because more of consumers' income goes to pay for oil imports, there is less to spend on U.S. goods. [We emphasized (a) but ignored (b) in the chapter.] Assume the Fed holds the real interest rate constant. Show what happens to the AE and Phillips curves and to output and inflation.

8. Suppose the economy starts with output at potential and constant inflation. In 2020, oil prices jump up. Initially, the Fed is accommodative. In 2023, a new Fed chair is appointed and resolves to return inflation to the level before 2020. Show with graphs what happens over time to the real interest rate, output, and inflation.

9. Suppose that expected inflation is the average of inflation over the two previous years:

$$\pi^e = \left(\frac{1}{2}\right)[\pi(-1) + \pi(-2)]$$

a. Write the equation for the Phillips curve in this case.

b. Redo the disinflation example in Figure 12.21. Assume the path of the real interest rate is the same as before. Is the path of output different with the new Phillips curve? The path of inflation? Explain.

10. The United States was on a gold standard from 1879 to 1914. During that period, the average inflation rate was about zero. Inflation was sometimes positive and sometimes negative, and there was no relation between inflation in one year and the next. Each year, inflation was equally likely to be positive or negative, regardless of past inflation.

a. For the gold-standard era, is the assumption of adaptive expectations a good one? If not, what assumption about inflation expectations would be more reasonable?

b. Write the Phillips curve for the alternative assumption about expectations.

c. Suppose the real interest rate rises temporarily, as in Figure 12.21. Compare the effects on inflation under adaptive expectations and under the alternative assumption in parts (a) and (b).

11. The data in Figure 12.14 suggest an unemployment coefficient of approximately -1.0 in the Phillips curve; that is, the Phillips curve is

$$\pi - \pi(-1) = -(1.0)(U - U^*)$$

Assume the natural rate, U^*, is 5 percent. Actual unemployment is 5 percent in 2020, 7 percent in 2021, 6 percent in 2022, and 5 percent in 2023. Inflation is 5 percent in 2020. What is inflation in 2023? (Assume there are no supply shocks.)

▶ **Online and Data Questions**
www.worthpublishers.com/ball

12. The text Web site has U.S. data on output, unemployment, and inflation from 1960 through 2010, along with estimates of potential

output and the natural rate of unemployment. Focus on the data for the year 2010.

 a. Do the data for 2010 fit Okun's law? (The relationship is graphed in Figure 12.4.)

 b. Do the data for 2010 fit the unemployment Phillips curve? (The relationship is graphed in Figure 12.14.)

 c. If you find deviations from Okun's law or the Phillips curve in 2010, what might explain the deviations?

13. From the text Web site, follow the link to the site of the Federal Reserve Bank of St. Louis; also, see the "Guide to St. Louis Fed Data." Get annual data on the inflation rate, the interest rate on 3-month Treasury bills, and the unemployment rate.

 a. According to the AE curve and Okun's law, what is the relationship between the real interest rate and unemployment?

 b. Using data from 1960 to the present, plot the unemployment rate against the real interest rate, defined as the nominal T-bill rate minus inflation. In other words, make a graph with the unemployment rate on one axis, the real interest rate on the other, and a point for each year. What relationship, if any, do you see?

 c. Are the relationships in parts (a) and (b) similar or different? If they are different, try to explain why. Do the results in (b) show that our theory about the AE curve is wrong?

A Small Research Project

14. Interview a few people who are not economists but who are old enough to remember the 1970s. Ask them what caused the high inflation of the 1970s and the deep recession of the early 1980s. Also ask about the 1990s: Why was there a recession at the start of the decade and a roaring economy at the end? Do their answers agree with this chapter? If not, whom do you believe?

APPENDIX: THE LOANABLE FUNDS THEORY AND THE NEUTRAL REAL INTEREST RATE

In the AE/PC model, the long-run real interest rate equals the neutral rate. In Section 4.2, we explain the long-run behavior of the real interest rate with the loanable funds theory, which states that the supply and demand for loans determine the real rate. These two theories prove to be similar: factors that affect the long-run real interest rate in the loanable funds theory also affect the neutral rate in the AE/PC model.

In the loanable funds theory, the supply and demand for loans depend on three factors: investment, saving, and net capital inflows (NCI). Higher investment at a given interest rate raises the demand for loans and the equilibrium interest rate. Higher saving or net capital inflows at a given interest rate raise the supply of loans and reduce the equilibrium interest rate. To summarize, the loanable funds theory says

$$\uparrow \text{investment} \rightarrow \uparrow r$$
$$\uparrow \text{saving} \rightarrow \downarrow r$$
$$\uparrow \text{NCI} \rightarrow \downarrow r$$

Figure 12A.1 examines how investment, saving, and net capital inflows affect the neutral real interest rate, as determined by the AE curve and

FIGURE 12A.1 Determinants of the Neutral Real Interest Rate

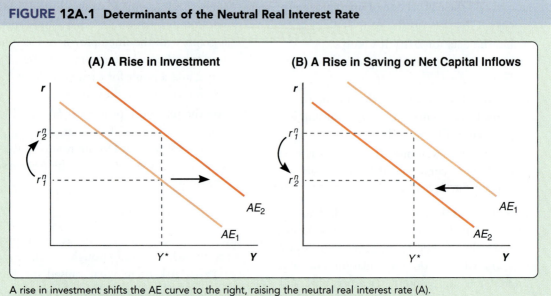

A rise in investment shifts the AE curve to the right, raising the neutral real interest rate (A). A rise in saving or in net capital inflows shifts the AE curve to the left, reducing the neutral rate (B). The effects of investment, saving, and capital flows match their effects on the real interest rate in the loanable funds theory.

potential output. Figure 12A.1A shows the effect of investment. As discussed in Section 12.2, a rise in investment for a given interest rate shifts the AE curve to the right. This AE shift raises the neutral real interest rate.

Figure 12A.1B shows the effects of saving and net capital inflows. Consider saving first. Saving rises for a given interest rate if consumers reduce their spending, or if the government reduces its spending or raises taxes. Any of these events shifts the AE curve to the left, reducing the neutral interest rate.

To see the effect of net capital inflows, we must remember a point from Chapter 6: a rise in net capital inflows (or equivalently, a fall in net capital outflows) raises the real exchange rate. The relevance here is that a higher real exchange rate reduces net exports, one of the components of aggregate expenditure. Lower net exports shift the AE curve to the left, reducing the neutral interest rate.

The general lesson from Figure 12A.1 is that investment, saving, and net capital inflows affect the neutral real interest rate in the same ways they affect the interest rate in the loanable funds theory.

chapter thirteen

Economic Fluctuations, Monetary Policy, and the Financial System

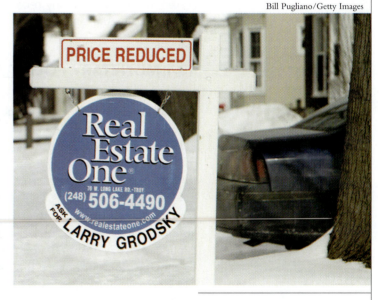

Bill Pugliano/Getty Images

The U.S. economy entered a recession in 2001. The causes included a fall in investment, especially spending on computers, and a stock market slump that reduced consumption. Shocks like these cause aggregate expenditure to fall.

In the aggregate expenditure/ Phillips curve (AE/PC) model we developed in Chapter 12, expenditure shocks need not cause recessions. If an adverse shock shifts the AE curve to the left in the model, the Fed can offset the shock by reducing the real interest rate. With the appropriate rate cut, aggregate output remains constant.

Reality is more complicated. In 2001, the Fed quickly recognized the adverse expenditure shocks that were occurring. It started cutting the federal funds rate in January and kept cutting it: over the year, the funds rate fell from 6.5 percent to 1.75 percent. Nonetheless, the economy slumped. An NBER recession occurred from March to November. The unemployment rate rose from 3.9 percent in December 2000 to 5.7 percent a year later.

Changes in asset prices, including house prices, help to cause economic booms and recessions.

In time, the Fed's actions did produce an economic recovery. In 2002, low interest rates spurred rapid growth in auto sales and housing construction. Other components of spending followed, and real GDP grew 3.7 percent over 2003. Unemployment peaked at 6.3 percent in June 2003 and then drifted down, falling below 5 percent in 2005.

Monetary transmission mechanism process through which monetary policy affects output

The AE curve says simply that a higher interest rate reduces aggregate output and a lower rate increases it. This chapter delves more deeply into the actual process through which monetary policy affects output—what economists call the **monetary transmission mechanism**. The process involves both major parts of the financial system: financial markets and banks.

The steps in the monetary transmission mechanism take time to unfold. As a result, significant lags occur between central banks' policy actions and the actions' ultimate effects on output and inflation. These time lags make it harder for central banks to stabilize the economy.

In this chapter, we also look closely at some of the expenditure shocks that buffet economies. Specifically, we examine shocks that arise within the financial system, such as decreases in asset prices and failures of financial institutions. Previous chapters have discussed the causes of these events and the costs to savers and the government. This chapter emphasizes the effects on aggregate expenditure. Problems in the financial system have caused many recessions, including the deep U.S. recession that began in 2007 as the financial crisis unfolded.

13.1 MONETARY POLICY AND THE TERM STRUCTURE

We first examine the effects of monetary policy on interest rates. The AE/PC model assumes the economy has just one interest rate. The Fed influences aggregate expenditure by adjusting this rate. In reality, there are many interest rates that can move in different directions.

The rates that affect aggregate expenditure are mainly intermediate and long-term rates. For example, most cars are bought with 5-year loans, so the rate on these loans affects car sales. Ten-year rates affect firms' investment, which is often financed with 10-year corporate bonds. In contrast, the Fed controls a very-short-term interest rate: the federal funds rate. This rate applies to 1-day loans. It does not directly affect firms and consumers, because they do not finance their spending with 1-day loans.

Does this mean the Fed is irrelevant to the economy? No, because changes in the federal funds rate affect longer-term rates. Because longer rates affect spending, the Fed affects spending indirectly. Let's see how this works.

The Term Structure Again

Section 4.4 discusses the relationships among short-term and long-term interest rates, known as the *term structure*. We analyzed these relationships using the *expectations theory of the term structure*. Returning to this theory will help us understand how Fed policy affects interest rates.

The expectations theory is summarized by an equation that gives the interest rate on an n-period bond in period t, denoted $i_n(t)$:

A = # of terms.

$$i_n(t) = \frac{1}{n}\left[i_1(t) + Ei_1(t+1) + \cdots + Ei_1(t+n-1)\right] + \tau_n$$

where ⒜ $i_1(t)$ is the current one-period rate, ⒝ $E_1(t+1)$ is the one-period rate expected at $t+1$, and so on. The variable τ_n is a *term premium*, the extra return that compensates for the risk from holding long-term bonds. The equation says the n-period rate equals the average of one-period rates expected over the next n periods, plus the term premium.

▶ Equation (4.3) expresses the pure expectations theory of the term structure, and Equation (4.4) introduces the term premium.

As a specific case, let's examine the relation between the 1-year interest rate and the federal funds rate. Because the federal funds rate is a 1-day rate, let's say a "period" is a day. Then $i_1(t)$ is the current federal funds rate. The 1-year rate is a 365-period rate. Applying the preceding equation, the 1-year rate is

$$i_{365}(t) = \frac{1}{365}\left[i_1(t) + Ei_1(t+1) + \cdots + Ei_1(t+364)\right] + \tau_{365}$$

The 1-year rate is the average of expected federal funds rates over the next year, plus the term premium for 1-year bonds.

1 year = 365 days.

A Policy Surprise

To see how the Fed affects interest rates, suppose the federal funds rate is initially 3 percent. Bond traders expect the rate to stay at 3 percent for the next year. However, at a meeting on April 1, the Federal Open Market Committee surprises everyone: it raises the federal funds rate by half a percentage point to 3.5 percent. What happens to longer-term rates?

r = 3%
but
r_n = 3.5%.

The One-Year Rate The 1-year rate on April 1 is the average of that day's federal funds rate and expected rates from April 2 through March 31 of the next year, plus the term premium. The funds rate on April 1 has a weight of only 1/365 in the average. When the Fed raises this rate by 0.5 percent, the *direct* effect on the 1-year rate is small: it rises by only $(1/365)(0.5\%)$, or 0.001%.

But the 1-year rate is likely to rise much more than this. The reason is that the current federal funds rate affects expected future rates. Remember that the funds rate usually stays constant between FOMC meetings, which occur every 42 days (6 weeks). If the funds rate rises to 3.5 percent on April 1, it is likely to stay there until the next FOMC meeting on May 13. Before the Fed's surprise, expected funds rates from April 2 to May 13 were 3 percent, but afterward they are 3.5 percent. Thus the Fed's action raises the first 42 terms in the formula for the 1-year rate.

In addition, when the FOMC meets on May 13, it is unlikely to change the funds rate back to 3.0 percent. The Fed rarely reverses course quickly after an interest rate change. Indeed, an increase in the funds rate is often followed by further increases as the Fed slowly tightens policy.

▶ Figure 11.9 on p. 339 shows changes over time in the FOMC's target for the federal funds rate.

Therefore, when the Fed raises the funds rate on April 1, its action is likely to raise the expected rate over the entire next year. The action increases all 365 terms in the formula for the 1-year interest rate, not just the first term or the

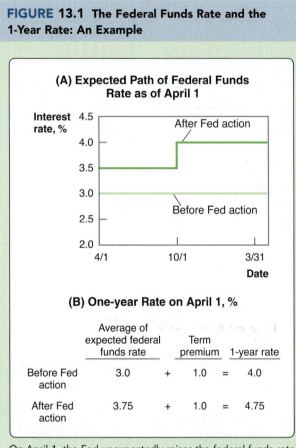

FIGURE 13.1 The Federal Funds Rate and the 1-Year Rate: An Example

On April 1, the Fed unexpectedly raises the federal funds rate from 3.0 percent to 3.5 percent. This action raises bond traders' expectations of the funds rate over the next year, causing the 1-year interest rate to rise.

first 42 terms. With all the terms rising, the 1-year rate jumps up substantially.

Figure 13.1 gives an example of how the 1-year rate might react when the FOMC raises the federal funds rate. Figure 13.1A shows the expected path of the funds rate before and after the Fed's action. Before the action, bond traders expect the funds rate to be 3.0 percent over the next year. But when they see the rate rise to 3.5 percent on April 1, they decide that the Fed is tightening policy. Now they expect the funds rate to stay at 3.5 percent for six months, until October 1, and then rise to 4.0 percent for the following six months.

Figure 13.1B calculates the 1-year interest rate. For this example, we assume that the term premium τ is 1.0 percent. Before the Fed acts, the average expected funds rate over the next year is 3.0 percent; adding the term premium, the 1-year rate is 3.0% + 1.0% = 4.0%. After the Fed acts, the average expected funds rate is $(1/2)(3.5\% + 4.0\%) = 3.75\%$; with the term premium, the 1-year rate is 4.75 percent. In this example, the 0.5-percentage-point rise in the federal funds rate has caused the 1-year rate to rise by 0.75 percentage points.

Longer-Term Rates A surprise change in the federal funds rate also affects rates at maturities beyond a year. It may be several years before the policy change is reversed. The Fed's action can strongly affect the 5-year interest rate, for example, because it changes the expected funds rate over much or all of the next 5 years.

Fed actions have less effect on very-long-term interest rates. The 30-year rate, for example, depends on expected funds rates over the next 30 years. Any policy the Fed is pursuing today is likely to end much sooner than 30 years from now. Thus current actions have little effect on most of the expected rates that determine the 30-year rate.

A Historical Example An episode that illustrates these ideas occurred in January 2008. At that time, the Fed was cutting interest rates in response to the financial crisis and weakening economy. The FOMC had reduced its target for the federal funds rate from 5.25 percent in August 2007 to 4.25 percent in December.

FIGURE 13.2 Effect of a Cut in the Federal Funds Rate on the Yield Curve

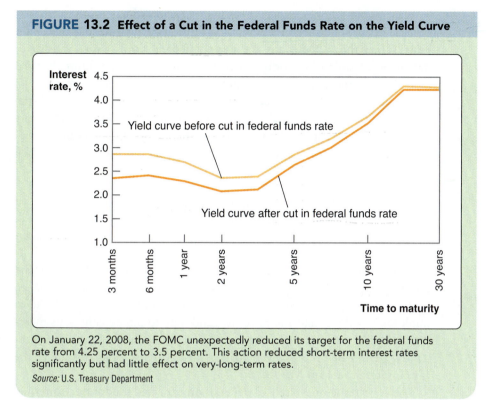

On January 22, 2008, the FOMC unexpectedly reduced its target for the federal funds rate from 4.25 percent to 3.5 percent. This action reduced short-term interest rates significantly but had little effect on very-long-term rates.

Source: U.S. Treasury Department

However, policymakers started worrying that interest rates were not falling quickly enough to stimulate spending. The next FOMC meeting was not scheduled until January 29, but on January 21 Chairman Bernanke convened a videoconference. The FOMC decided to reduce the Fed funds rate immediately by 0.75 percentage points to 3.5 percent.

Figure 13.2 shows what happened to interest rates on Treasury securities of various maturities, that is, to the yield curve. On January 22, bond traders realized that the funds rate was falling faster than they had expected. They lowered their expectations of future rates, causing short- and intermediate-term rates to fall. The 3-month rate fell by 0.51 percentage points and the 2-year rate fell by 0.28 points. However, as our analysis predicts, there was little effect on 20- and 30-year interest rates.

Expected Policy Changes

We have seen that a change in the federal funds rate can trigger changes in rates for longer maturities. This does not always happen, however. For other rates to jump when the funds rate changes, the change must be a surprise. If everyone expects in March that the FOMC will raise the funds rate on April 1, then bond traders learn nothing new when the increase occurs. They have no reason to change their expectations about the future, and it is those expectations that determine longer-term rates.

Why might people expect a change in the federal funds rate? Fed officials never announce precisely what future rates will be, but they offer hints. When the FOMC sets the current federal funds target, it issues a statement discussing its action and what it might do in the future. FOMC members also make speeches that provide clues about their plans.

In addition, bond traders can sometimes infer what the Fed will do from the state of the economy. If a recession is beginning, for example, it is likely that the Fed will respond by reducing the funds rate. If bond traders correctly predict the Fed's actions, then longer-term rates do not jump when the funds rate changes.

The Effects of Changing Expectations This does *not* mean that expected changes in the funds rate are irrelevant to longer-term rates. The Fed's actions still matter if they are expected, but their effects occur *before* the actions themselves.

To see this point, suppose it is March 15. The funds rate is 3 percent, and everyone expects it to stay at 3 percent. Then the Fed chair makes a speech suggesting that policy needs to tighten. Based on this speech, bond traders think the FOMC is likely to raise the funds rate to 3.5 percent at its meeting on April 1. As usual, they expect the rate to stay at this level for a substantial period of time or even to rise further. How does this affect the 1-year interest rate on March 15?

The 1-year rate on March 15 depends on expected funds rates from then until March 14 of the next year. The Fed chair's speech does not affect expected rates for the first 17 days, before the FOMC meeting. However, it raises expected rates from April 1 to next March 14.

Thus the March 15 speech raises 348 of the 365 expected 1-day interest rates that determine the current 1-year rate. The 1-year rate jumps up substantially on March 15. If the Fed raises the funds rate as expected on April 1, the 1-year rate does *not* jump on that day: it has responded in advance.

A Historical Example The 1-year interest rate moved before Fed actions in 2004. **Figure 13.3** shows the federal funds target and the 1-year rate for the first 9 months of 2004. At the start of the year, the funds target was 1 percent. It had reached this level as the Fed eased policy in response to the slow growth over 2001–2003 described in the introduction to this chapter. The 1-year rate was about 1.25 percent.

For three months, the 1-year rate stayed near 1.25 percent. Then good economic news started arriving. In April, May, and June, the government released statistics showing that employment was growing more quickly than before. Bond traders began to expect that signs of recovery would lead the Fed to tighten policy.

The FOMC encouraged this view. In a May 4 statement, it noted the news of stronger growth and stated that "at this juncture, policy accommodation [i.e., low rates] can be removed at a pace that is likely to be measured." Expectations of future funds rates rose, pushing the 1-year rate above 2 percent in June.

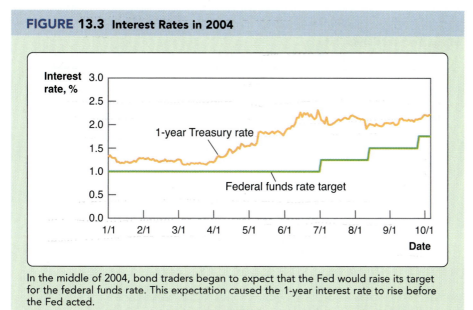

FIGURE 13.3 Interest Rates in 2004

In the middle of 2004, bond traders began to expect that the Fed would raise its target for the federal funds rate. This expectation caused the 1-year interest rate to rise before the Fed acted.

Sources: Federal Reserve Board; U.S. Treasury Department

In July, the FOMC started raising the funds rate as expected. By the end of September, the funds rate had climbed to 1.75 percent in three steps. Over this period, the 1-year rate was fairly stable. It did not jump on days when the funds rate rose, because the FOMC's actions were not surprises.

So far, we have used historical examples to illustrate the effects of Fed actions on interest rates. A number of economists have conducted broader statistical studies on this topic. They examine whether interest rates respond to the federal funds rate in the ways predicted by the expectations theory of the term structure. The next case study describes some of this research.

CASE STUDY

Measuring the Effects of Monetary Policy on the Term Structure

Kenneth Kuttner of Oberlin College studied the effects of FOMC actions in a paper published in 2001.[*] Kuttner examined all changes in the federal funds target that occurred between 1989 and 2000—a total of 42 changes. He measured the average responses of the yield curve on days when the target changed.

▶ In Section 3.3, we discuss Kuttner's research with Ben Bernanke on the effects of FOMC actions on stock prices.

Only *unexpected* changes in the funds rate should affect longer-term rates. So a key part of Kuttner's study was determining the rates that bond traders expected. He measured expected rates with data from the federal funds futures market. The interest rate in a futures contract is a good measure of the rate expected on the day the contract will be executed.

▶ To review futures contracts, see Section 5.6.

[*] See Kenneth Kuttner, "Monetary Policy Surprises and Interest Rates: Evidence from the Fed Funds Futures Market," *Journal of Monetary Economics*, vol. 47, June 2001, pp 523–544.

FIGURE 13.4 Typical Effects on the Yield Curve of an Unexpected Rise in the Federal Funds Rate

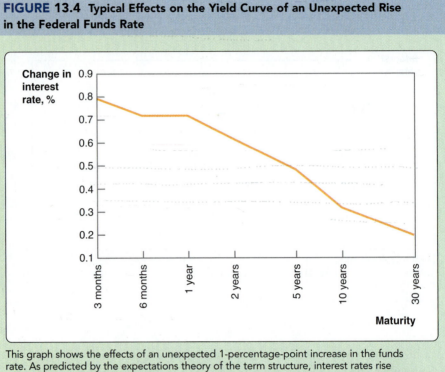

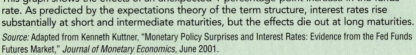

This graph shows the effects of an unexpected 1-percentage-point increase in the funds rate. As predicted by the expectations theory of the term structure, interest rates rise substantially at short and intermediate maturities, but the effects die out at long maturities.

Source: Adapted from Kenneth Kuttner, "Monetary Policy Surprises and Interest Rates: Evidence from the Fed Funds Futures Market," *Journal of Monetary Economics*, June 2001.

For each day the funds rate changed, Kuttner subtracted the change predicted by a futures rate from the actual change. The difference is the unexpected change in the funds rate. If the Fed raises the funds rate by 0.5 percentage points when the expected change is 0.25 points, the unexpected change is $0.50 - 0.25 = 0.25$ percentage points.

Kuttner then used the statistical technique of linear regression to measure the average effects of unexpected funds-rate changes on longer-term rates. He found, for example, that the 1-year rate rises by 0.72 times the unexpected change in the funds rate. If the funds rate unexpectedly rises by 0.25 percentage points, the 1-year rate rises by $(0.72) \times (0.25) = 0.18$ percentage points.

Figure 13.4 summarizes Kuttner's results. It shows the effects of a surprise change in the funds rate on the yield curve. As predicted by the expectations theory of the term structure, changes in the funds rate cause substantial changes in short and intermediate rates.

As the theory also predicts, the effects die out for long maturities. The change in the 3-month rate is 0.79 times as large as the change in the funds rate, but the change in the 30-year rate is only 0.19 times as large. Research such as Kuttner's has increased economists' confidence in the expectations theory of the term structure.

13.2 THE FINANCIAL SYSTEM AND AGGREGATE EXPENDITURE

Section 1.5 discusses the role of the financial system in long-run economic growth. Financial factors are also important in short-run fluctuations, because the components of the system, financial markets and banks, influence aggregate expenditure. These influences are important for two reasons.

1. Events in the financial system are one initial cause of output fluctuations. Asset-price declines and banking crises have caused many recessions in the United States and elsewhere, for example.

2. The financial system is part of the monetary transmission mechanism. Actions by the central bank affect not only interest rates but also asset prices and bank lending. These effects magnify the response of output to policy actions.

Changes in Asset Prices

The prices of many assets change greatly over time. For example, stock prices fluctuate due to changes in companies' expected earnings and to the growth and collapse of bubbles. House prices also experience steep rises and falls.

▶ Sections 3.3–3.5 survey the causes of asset-price fluctuations, bubbles, and crashes.

Generally, an increase in asset prices raises aggregate expenditure. In graphic terms, the AE curve shifts to the right: output is higher for any given real interest rate. Conversely, a fall in asset prices shifts the AE curve to the left. Asset prices affect expenditure in several ways related to consumption and investment.

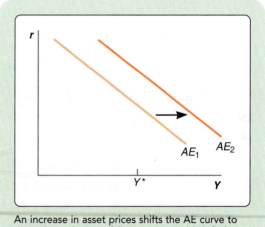

An increase in asset prices shifts the AE curve to the right, as here. A fall in prices would shift the curve to the left.

Wealth and Consumption Changes in asset prices affect people's wealth. If stock prices rise 20 percent, for example, the values of people's stock holdings rise 20 percent. Greater wealth leads people to spend more on goods and services. Thus, a rise in asset prices raises consumption, one of the four components of aggregate spending.

Economists have studied data on consumption to measure this effect. According to current estimates, a $1 rise in wealth raises consumption by about $0.04 (four cents). Given the large swings in asset prices, this effect can be important.

For example, the value of U.S. stocks held by individuals and mutual funds was 58 percent of a year's GDP in 1994. This value was 131 percent of GDP in 1999, so it rose by 73 percent of GDP. Multiplying this increase by 0.04 yields 2.9 percent of GDP, which for 1999 is $270 billion. This gives us an idea of how much rising stock prices raised consumption in the late 1990s. The rise in consumption explains much of the economic boom during this period.

Online Case Study:
An Update on Asset Prices and Consumption

Stock Prices and Investment Changes in asset prices also affect the investment component of aggregate expenditure. One reason is that firms can finance investment by issuing new stock. If a firm's stock price rises, it receives more for each share that it sells. It can raise a given amount of money from fewer shares, so the current owners give up a smaller fraction of their stakes in the firm. In effect, raising funds through stock issues becomes cheaper. With cheaper financing, firms are more likely to undertake new investment projects.

▶ Section 7.5 describes the role of collateral and borrowers' net worth in bank lending.

Effects on Net Worth and Collateral Changes in asset prices also affect spending by changing the availability of bank loans. Banks require borrowers to post collateral or maintain certain levels of net worth. These requirements help overcome the problems of adverse selection and moral hazard: borrowers are less likely to undertake risky projects if their own assets are at stake. In addition, banks reduce their losses from defaults by seizing borrowers' assets.

A rise in asset prices raises collateral and net worth. A firm's net worth is the total value of its stock, so net worth rises when stock prices rise. Likewise, higher real estate prices raise the value of buildings that firms use as collateral. As a result, banks become more willing to lend: fewer firms are credit rationed, and interest rates are lower. Greater lending leads to higher investment. Conversely, a fall in asset prices reduces collateral and net worth, so lending and investment fall.

Higher real estate prices also increase lending to individuals. If a person's house rises in value, she can obtain a *home-equity loan* that uses the house as collateral. People use home-equity loans for spending, such as vacations and home improvements, further increasing aggregate expenditure. When house prices fall, people lose access to home-equity loans, dampening expenditure.

Changes in Bank Lending Policies

Bank lending shifts when asset prices change. Lending also shifts as a result of events within the banking system. Banks may become more willing to lend, increasing investment, or less willing, reducing investment. A sharp fall in lending—a credit crunch—can significantly reduce aggregate expenditure.

Why might banks change their lending policies? There are three main reasons:

1. *Risk Perception* Banks refuse to lend to borrowers who appear too risky. Sometimes events cause banks to change their assessment of risk. This happens, for example, when they experience a large number of defaults. If many real estate loans go bad, banks are likely to decide that these loans are riskier than they thought and reduce lending to home-buyers and real estate developers.

2. *Regulation* Bank regulators usually discourage lending with too much risk, but regulations change over time, becoming more or less stringent.

When regulators become more tolerant of risky loans, lending is likely to rise.

3. *Capital* Capital requirements set a minimum for a bank's equity ratio, the ratio of capital to assets. Capital falls if banks suffer losses for any reason, such as a rise in loan defaults. When this happens, banks must reduce their assets, including loans, to maintain the required equity ratio. A fall in capital that forces banks to reduce lending is called a **capital crunch**. A capital crunch is one possible cause of a credit crunch.

▶ Section 10.5 describes capital requirements for banks.

Capital crunch a fall in capital that forces banks to reduce lending

Recent Recessions

Expenditure shocks that began in the financial system have contributed to the last three U.S. recessions. The savings and loan crisis of the 1980s produced a credit crunch as banks' capital fell and regulators tightened their restrictions on lending. This credit crunch was one cause of the 1990–91 recession. In the early 2000s, U.S. stock prices declined sharply, an episode that many interpret as the bursting of an asset-price bubble. Falling stock prices contributed to the recession that began in 2001.

Most recently, over 2007–2009, the United States was struck by its worst financial crisis since the Great Depression of the 1930s. The crisis included large declines in stock and housing prices and the failure or near failure of such financial institutions as Lehman Brothers, AIG, and Fannie Mae. Banks' losses on subprime mortgages led to a credit crunch that was worsened by a breakdown in loan securitization. All these problems contributed to the deep recession that started in 2007.

We return to the details of the 2007–2009 crisis in Chapter 18. Here we illustrate the effects of financial crises with an example from a different time and place: Japan in the 1990s. The episode is important in its own right, and it also helps us understand the recent U.S. experience. Japan's crisis produced a "lost decade" of economic stagnation from 1992 to 2002, and economists debate whether the U.S. crisis will have equally long-lasting effects.

CASE STUDY

Asset Prices, Banking, and Japan's Lost Decade

Figure 13.5A shows the growth rate of output in Japan from 1981 through 2002. During the first half of this period, from 1981 through 1991, output growth averaged 4.0 percent per year. Then the economy stagnated, with average growth of 0.9 percent from 1992 through 2002. Slow growth produced rising unemployment, political discontent, and a higher suicide rate, among other problems.

What caused the prolonged Japanese slump? The story starts in the 1980s, when the economy was booming, but banks encountered problems. As in other countries, deregulation and competition from securities markets

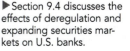

▶ Section 9.4 discusses the effects of deregulation and expanding securities markets on U.S. banks.

FIGURE 13.5 Japan's Financial Crisis and Economic Stagnation

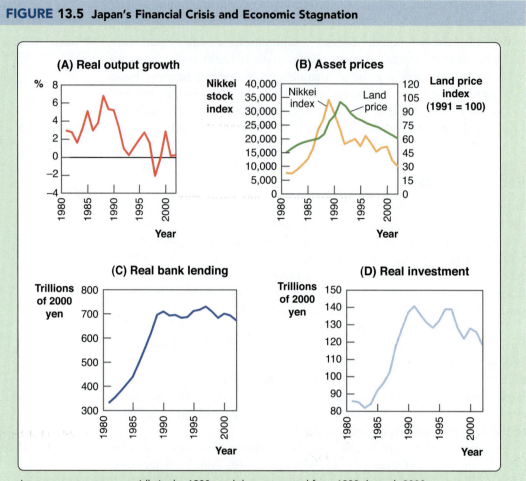

Japanese output grew rapidly in the 1980s and then stagnated from 1992 through 2002 (A). The output slump reflected a collapse in asset prices (B) and stagnation in bank lending (C), which curtailed investment (D).

Sources: International Monetary Fund; Bank of Japan; OECD

▶ Asset prices continued to decrease after 2002 despite a modest economic recovery. The Nikkei bottomed out in 2003 at 73 percent below its peak level, and land prices in 2006 were 52 percent below their peak.

cut into traditional sources of bank profits. For example, loans to large firms fell when Japan's commercial-paper market was created in 1988.

Government regulations prevented Japanese banks from moving into new lines of business, such as derivatives and investment banking, which banks in other countries used to boost profits. Low profits during the 1980s prevented Japan's banks from building up capital. In addition, banks replaced the lending business they lost by increasing real estate loans.

Optimism about the Japanese economy in the 1980s fueled rapid growth in asset prices. In retrospect, the asset-price boom appears to have been an irrational bubble, and eventually, it burst. The Japanese stock index, the Nikkei, peaked in 1989 and fell by 70 percent between then and 2002 (**Figure 13.5B**). Japanese land prices peaked in 1991 and then fell by

41 percent through 2002. These price collapses are large even compared to the recent U.S. crisis, in which the Dow Jones stock index fell by 55 percent and housing prices fell by 33 percent.

The collapse in Japan's asset prices had severe effects on the country's banks. Capital levels, which were already low at the end of the 1980s, were reduced further by defaults on real estate loans. Borrowers' collateral and net worth fell sharply, leading to greater credit rationing. After growing rapidly in the 1980s, bank lending stagnated after 1990 (**Figure 13.5C**).

Japanese firms rely mainly on banks rather than securities markets to raise funds for investment, so the stagnation in lending produced stagnation in investment (**Figure 13.5D**). Investment and consumption were also reduced directly by the crash in asset prices, and Japan entered its long slump.

Once the slump began, the Japanese economy fell into a vicious spiral. Banking problems weakened it. At the same time, the weak economy reduced firms' earnings, leading to more defaults on bank loans. These defaults further weakened the banks.

In the late 1990s, Japanese savers started to fear that their banks were becoming insolvent and moved their money to cash and government savings accounts. Foreign banks started charging default premiums on loans to Japanese banks. Finding it harder to raise funds, Japanese banks cut back further on loans, and investment fell again.

Many economists believe that Japanese regulators should have declared some banks insolvent and closed them. However, regulators chose a policy of forbearance, much as U.S. regulators did during the savings and loan crisis of the 1980s. Japanese regulators allowed banks to keep bad loans on their balance sheets rather than writing them off. Forbearance helped banks maintain the appearance of solvency.

▶ Section 10.7 discusses regulatory forbearance during the S&L crisis in the United States.

Critics suggest that this policy caused a misallocation of loans. Unprofitable firms that should have been cut off from credit continued to receive funds, leaving less for firms with good investment projects. In particular, too much lending was directed to construction firms while the manufacturing industry was starved for loans. This misallocation made Japan's economy less productive.

Eventually, regulators became stricter, forcing banks to write off bad loans. This shift in policy contributed to a modest economic recovery from 2003 through 2007, with average output growth of 2.1 percent. The recovery was also spurred by a rise in Japanese exports, the result of a weak yen and high demand from trading partners such as China. The recovery was short-circuited in 2008, however, as the U.S. financial crisis spread around the world. Japan's exports plummeted, and its economy fell back into a deep slump.*

▶ Chapter 18 discusses how the financial crisis of 2007–2009 spread from the United States to other countries.

* For more on Japan's experience, see Kenneth Kuttner and Adam Posen, "The Great Recession: Lessons for Macroeconomic Policy from Japan," *Brookings Papers on Economic Activity*, 2001:2, pp. 93–160; and Takeo Hoshi and Anil Kashyap, "Japan's Financial Crisis and Economic Stagnation," *Journal of Economic Perspectives*, vol. 18, Winter 2004, pp. 3–26.

The Investment Multiplier

We have seen that events in the financial system cause shifts in aggregate spending. The financial system also contributes to economic fluctuations in another way. It creates a multiplier that magnifies the effects of expenditure shocks, even when the shocks themselves are unrelated to the financial system.

This multiplier involves the behavior of investment. In general, a firm can finance investment either with profits it has earned or by borrowing. We have seen, however, that asymmetric information makes borrowing difficult. Some firms are credit rationed because lenders think they are too risky. Even if a firm can borrow, it pays an interest rate that includes a premium to compensate for default risk.

These problems disappear if the firm has sufficiently high earnings. It can use these earnings to pay for investment projects. Because the firm does not need an outside lender, there is no risk of credit rationing and no need to pay the interest rate premium arising from asymmetric information. In sum, high earnings make it easier and cheaper to finance investment.

We can now understand the **investment multiplier**, illustrated in **Figure 13.6**, and its role in economic fluctuations. Suppose aggregate expenditure rises for any reason—say, an increase in government spending or consumer confidence. This event causes an economic boom. In a boom, firms sell more and their earnings rise, allowing them to finance investment more cheaply. As a result, they increase investment spending, magnifying the economic boom. Firms' earnings rise even more, they undertake even more investment, and so on.

The investment multiplier also works in reverse. If aggregate expenditure falls for any reason, firms' earnings fall, reducing investment. Thus, the feedback between earnings and investment magnifies both booms and recessions.

Investment multiplier effect of firms' earnings on investment, which magnifies fluctuations in aggregate expenditure

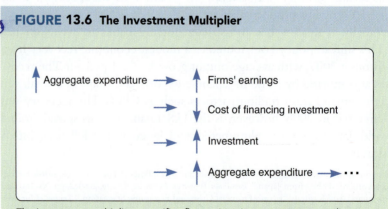

FIGURE 13.6 The Investment Multiplier

The investment multiplier magnifies fluctuations in aggregate expenditure.

13.3 THE MONETARY TRANSMISSION MECHANISM

We now have the background needed to understand how the monetary transmission mechanism works. This process, through which monetary policy affects output, includes the effects of asset prices and bank lending on expenditure that we've just described.

Figure 13.7 summarizes the monetary transmission mechanism by charting how the Fed affects the economy when it changes its target for the federal funds rate. We have already discussed most of the individual steps in this process; the chart shows how they all fit together.

When the Fed raises the federal funds rate target, as shown at the left, it is tightening policy. This action triggers a series of events that lead to lower output, shown at the right in the figure. Bear in mind that everything works in reverse if the Fed lowers its federal funds rate target, an easing of policy that leads to higher output.

Effects in Financial Markets   *Know.*

When the federal funds rate rises, several effects occur in financial markets, as summarized in Figure 13.7:

- The rise in the funds rate causes longer-term interest rates to increase. As we discuss in Section 13.1, this occurs either at the time of the Fed's action or earlier, depending on whether or not the action is expected.

+ Know.

FIGURE 13.7 The Monetary Transmission Mechanism When Policy Tightens

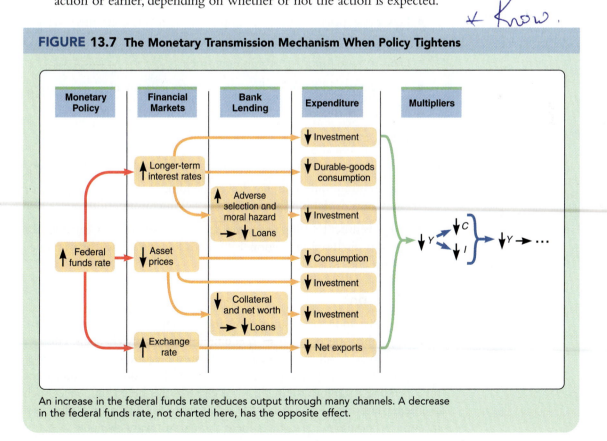

An increase in the federal funds rate reduces output through many channels. A decrease in the federal funds rate, not charted here, has the opposite effect.

▶We discuss the effects of interest rates on asset prices in Chapter 3 and on exchange rates in Chapter 6.

- Increases in interest rates reduce the present value of future earnings from assets. Thus they reduce asset prices, such as stock prices.

- Higher interest rates attract capital inflows from abroad and reduce capital outflows. As a result, the exchange rate appreciates.

Effects on Bank Lending

When the Fed tightens, the effects in financial markets lead to further effects, summarized in the column headed "Bank Lending" in Figure 13.7:

▶Chapter 7 discusses the effects of interest rates on adverse selection and moral hazard.

- A rise in interest rates worsens the problems of adverse selection and moral hazard in loan markets. With higher rates, a larger proportion of loan applicants becomes risky. Banks respond by reducing their lending.

- The fall in asset prices also reduces lending, because it reduces borrowers' collateral and net worth.

Effects on Expenditure

The effects of policy on financial markets and banks influence aggregate expenditure in many ways:

- Higher interest rates discourage firms and consumers from borrowing, so they spend less on investment, including housing, and on durable goods.

- Lower asset prices reduce consumption by reducing consumers' wealth.

- Lower asset prices reduce investment by making it more expensive for firms to raise funds by issuing new stock.

- The decrease in bank lending also reduces investment.

- The appreciation of the exchange rate reduces net exports.

Multiplier Effects

Finally, the decrease in aggregate spending is magnified by two multipliers:

▶Section 12.2 explains the consumption multiplier.

- The consumption multiplier: lower spending means lower income for consumers, which produces a further fall in consumption.

- The investment multiplier: lower spending means lower earnings for firms, as discussed in Section 13.2. With lower earnings, firms reduce investment.

Some Lessons

Examining the monetary transmission mechanism yields two lessons. First, monetary policy affects aggregate spending through many channels. This fact helps explain why policy has broad effects on the economy. Second, policy has especially strong effects on certain sectors of the economy. In these sectors, spending is sensitive to the financial variables that policy influences, such as interest rates and bank loans. For example, policy has strong effects on investment because it affects investment through so many channels.

The next case study discusses another way in which monetary policy affects some parts of the economy more than others.

CASE STUDY

Monetary Policy, Inventories, and Small Firms

A tightening of monetary policy reduces aggregate spending partly by reducing bank loans. Lending falls because higher interest rates and lower asset prices exacerbate asymmetric information problems between borrowers and lenders. Mark Gertler of New York University and Simon Gilchrist of Boston University helped convince economists of this effect in a well-known 1994 paper.[*]

Gertler and Gilchrist started with the idea that asymmetric information is a bigger problem for small firms than for large firms. General Electric is sufficiently well known that it can always issue bonds or borrow from banks; Joe's Hardware Store can't issue bonds, and banks are wary because they don't know Joe. Joe's Store may get a loan in normal times. But if monetary policy tightens, worsening moral hazard and adverse selection, the bank may deny Joe credit. Monetary policy thus has bigger effects on lending and investment for smaller firms.

Gertler and Gilchrist tested this idea by examining a particular kind of investment: inventories. To operate, many firms must accumulate inventories of materials or of the goods they sell. Joe's Hardware, for example, must buy hammers and nails to stock its shelves. Like other investment, inventories are often financed by borrowing. Large firms usually issue commercial paper, and small firms get short-term bank loans.

Gertler and Gilchrist measured the response of this borrowing and of inventories to monetary tightenings. Specifically, they examined seven dates from the 1940s through the 1980s when the Fed raised interest rates to fight inflation. They compared the effects on small and large firms, as defined by their levels of assets (above or below $200 million in 1986). For each group of firms, Gertler and Gilchrist traced the average paths of short-term borrowing and inventories in the three years after a tightening.

Figure 13.8 shows the results. A monetary tightening has little effect on inventory investment by large firms. Borrowing by these firms rises temporarily (Figure 13.8A). Borrowing rises because the Fed's tightening slows the economy. Firms' revenues fall, leading them to borrow more to cover inventories and other costs. Large firms can increase their borrowing because they are well known to lenders.

A monetary tightening has very different effects on small firms (Figure 13.8B). They may want to borrow more, but they can't: their borrowing falls as lenders ration credit. Inventories fall because small firms are unable to finance them. Gertler and Gilchrist also show that lower inventories lead to lower sales.

[*] See Mark Gertler and Simon Gilchrist, "Monetary Policy, Business Cycles, and the Behavior of Small Manufacturing Firms," *Quarterly Journal of Economics*, vol. 109, May 1994, pp. 309–340.

FIGURE 13.8 Effects of a Monetary Tightening on Large and Small Firms

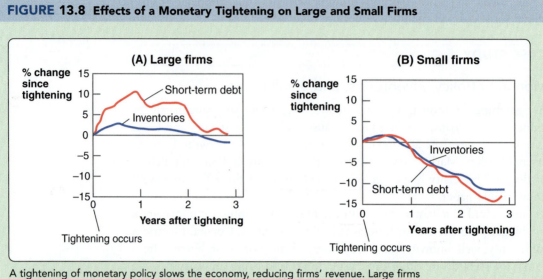

A tightening of monetary policy slows the economy, reducing firms' revenue. Large firms compensate with greater short-term borrowing and their inventory investment does not change significantly (A). By contrast, small firms face increased credit rationing. Their borrowing falls and they are forced to cut inventories (B).

Source: Adapted from Mark Gertler and Simon Gilchrist, "Monetary Policy, Business Cycles, and the Behavior of Small Manufacturing Firms," *Quarterly Journal of Economics*, May 1994.

This research demonstrates the importance of asymmetric information in loan markets. If this problem didn't exist, small firms would be more like large firms. Monetary policy would have little effect on their short-term borrowing or inventories. Policy would probably have less effect on other investment as well.

13.4 TIME LAGS

If the Fed tightens or loosens policy, how long does it take for the economy to respond? The AE/PC model assumes that an increase in the real interest rate (r) moves the economy along the aggregate expenditure curve. Output (Y) falls immediately. And when output falls, the Phillips curve says that inflation (π) falls immediately as well. Thus, in the model, the Fed controls the current levels of output and inflation by adjusting the interest rate.

In reality, monetary policy affects the economy through processes that take time. It takes time for the interest rate to affect output, and for output to affect inflation. These time lags reduce the Fed's ability to control the economy.

Lags in the AE Curve

Figure 13.7 on page 403 shows the process behind the AE curve. A change in the federal funds rate affects financial variables, such as interest rates, asset prices, and exchange rates. Then these variables affect spending through various channels.

The first parts of this process—the effects in financial markets—are quick. Interest rates and asset prices react on the day of a Fed action, or even earlier if the action is expected. However, the rest of the process is slower, so it takes time for the Fed's action to affect spending.

To understand this slow adjustment, recall that many effects of monetary policy involve investment. Investment projects take time to plan and implement. If the Fed reduces interest rates, firms do not start building new factories and houses on the same day. Instead, low rates affect planning about what projects to undertake in the coming months and years. Similarly, it takes time to adjust investment plans when stock prices rise or banks increase their lending.

Other types of spending also take time to adjust to financial variables. For example, if a firm imports materials from abroad, a depreciation of the currency makes the materials more expensive. The firm might switch to a domestic supplier, reducing the economy's imports and raising net exports. But it takes time for the firm to find the new supplier; it does not stop importing the day the exchange rate rises.

The multiplier effects in Figure 13.7 also take time to unfold. For example, when people see their incomes rise, it takes time for them to adjust their consumption patterns. Because of all these lags, it can be a year or more before a change in monetary policy has its main effects on output.

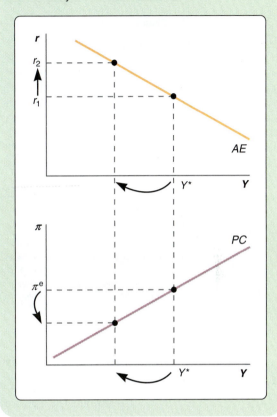

In the basic AE/PC model, an increase in the real interest rate reduces output and inflation immediately.

Lags in the Phillips Curve

The Phillips curve shows that the level of output affects the inflation rate. High output causes firms to raise prices more quickly, and low output does the reverse. However, this process also takes time. As a result, monetary policy affects inflation with a long lag. It can take a year for policy to affect output and then *another* year for output to affect inflation.

This additional lag arises because firms' price setting adjusts slowly. Many firms review their pricing decisions only once or twice a year. If output changes, it takes time for firms to recognize the situation and start raising prices more quickly or slowly.

In addition, changes in inflation are slowed by the interactions among different firms. If the economy is booming, for example, firms would like to raise prices quickly. However, each firm fears it will lose sales if its price rises too far above its competitors' prices. No firm wants to go first in making a big adjustment. Inflation edges up slowly as some firms make small adjustments and others copy them.

FIGURE 13.9 Effects of a Monetary Tightening

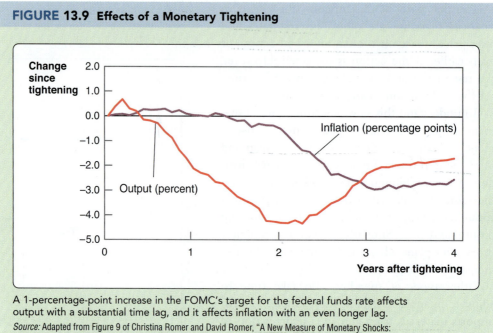

A 1-percentage-point increase in the FOMC's target for the federal funds rate affects output with a substantial time lag, and it affects inflation with an even longer lag.

Source: Adapted from Figure 9 of Christina Romer and David Romer, "A New Measure of Monetary Shocks: Derivation and Implications," *American Economic Review*, vol. 94, September 2004, pp. 1055–1084.

Evidence for Time Lags

Economic history reveals the time lags in the effects of monetary policy. For example, the Fed's easing during the 2001 recession described at the start of this chapter affected spending mainly in 2002 and 2003. Another example is the tightening that Fed Chairman Paul Volcker used to halt rising inflation in the 1970s. Volcker started raising interest rates late in 1979. The biggest effects on output occurred in the recession of 1981–1982. Inflation fell mainly in 1982–1983.

Economists also use statistical techniques to measure time lags in policy effects. This research includes a 2004 paper by Christina Romer and David Romer of the University of California, Berkeley.[1] Romer and Romer examine changes in the FOMC's federal funds target from 1969 through 1996. They first isolate changes in the target that were policy surprises given the state of the economy. Then they trace the paths of output and inflation after each target change and average them to find the typical effects of policy.

Figure 13.9 shows Romer and Romer's results. They find that a monetary tightening causes output to fall gradually. The maximum impact is felt

[1] See Christina Romer and David Romer, "A New Measure of Monetary Shocks: Derivation and Implications," *American Economic Review*, 94 (September 2004): 1055–1084.

between 22 and 27 months after the Fed's action, and then output starts recovering slowly. As we should expect, it takes longer for the tightening to affect inflation. There is almost no impact for the first 18 months; then inflation falls slowly and levels off after 36 months.

13.5 TIME LAGS AND THE EFFECTS OF MONETARY POLICY

The time lags we've discussed make it harder for central banks to stabilize the economy. To see how, let's add time lags to the AE and Phillips curves and see how they change the effects of monetary policy.

In the AE curve (**Figure 13.10A**), output is still determined by the real interest rate—but here it is the rate a year ago rather than the current rate. The real rate one year ago is denoted $r(-1)$. This change means that it takes monetary policy a year to affect output, roughly capturing the lag we see in reality.

Similarly, in the Phillips curve (**Figure 13.10B**), inflation depends on output in the previous year, $Y(-1)$, rather than on current output. As before, inflation also depends on expected inflation. We assume throughout this discussion that expected inflation equals the previous year's inflation rate, $\pi(-1)$.

With these modifications, we will analyze two policies that we discuss in Chapter 12: a disinflation and a countercyclical response to an expenditure shock.

$$\pi^e = \pi(-1)$$

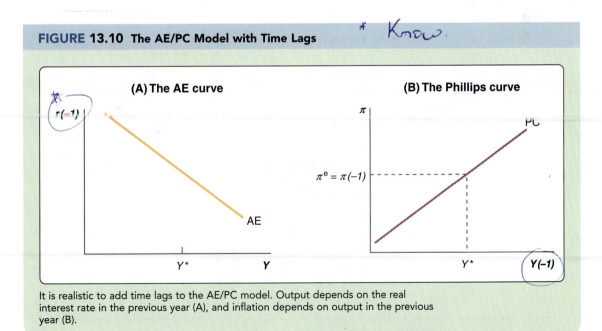

FIGURE 13.10 The AE/PC Model with Time Lags

Know.

(A) The AE curve

$r(-1)$

AE

Y^* Y

(B) The Phillips curve

π

PC

$\pi^e = \pi(-1)$

Y^* $Y(-1)$

It is realistic to add time lags to the AE/PC model. Output depends on the real interest rate in the previous year (A), and inflation depends on output in the previous year (B).

A Disinflation

A disinflation is a temporary rise in the real interest rate that reduces inflation. Here we investigate how time lags in the AE and Phillips curves affect the disinflation process. We assume the economy starts with output at potential and constant inflation.

▶ Figure 13.11 expands on Figure 12.21, which shows the effects of disinflation without time lags. The interest rate path shown in Figure 13.11A is the same as in Figure 12.21A.

As shown in **Figure 13.11A**, the central bank raises the real interest rate in 2020, keeps it high in 2021, and returns it to the initial level in 2022. **Figure 13.11B** shows the behavior of output under our assumption of time lags. For comparison, the figure also shows the output path without lags in the AE and Phillips curves.

The difference between the two cases is clear. With no time lags, output is low in the years when the interest rate is high: 2020 and 2021. But when the AE curve has a lag, output depends on the previous year's interest rate, not the current rate. Therefore, the high rate in 2020 reduces output in 2021, and the high rate in 2021 reduces output in 2022. Output returns to potential in 2023, the year after the interest rate returns to its initial level.

FIGURE 13.11 A Disinflation with Time Lags

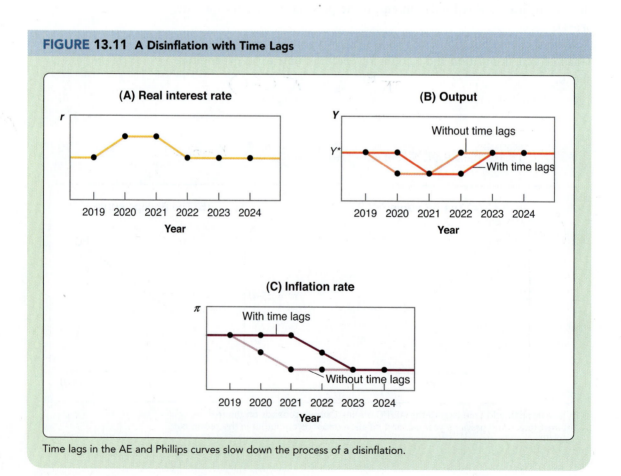

Time lags in the AE and Phillips curves slow down the process of a disinflation.

Figure 13.11C shows the behavior of inflation. With no time lags, inflation falls in the years when output is below potential. But when the Phillips curve has a lag, low output reduces inflation a year later. Because output is low in 2021 and 2022, inflation falls in 2022 and 2023.

Together, the lags in the AE and Phillips curves slow the disinflation by two years. Without lags, inflation reaches its final level in 2021; with lags, this occurs in 2023.

Countercyclical Policy

An expenditure shock, such as a change in consumer confidence or in government spending, affects output and inflation if the central bank does not react. However, in the AE/PC model with no time lags, policymakers can eliminate these effects completely. If an expansionary shock occurs, for example, a sufficient rise in the real interest rate keeps output constant. With no movement in output, inflation is constant as well. With time lags, such countercyclical policy is a messier process. An expenditure shock causes fluctuations in output and inflation, even if the central bank responds immediately.

Suppose again that the economy starts with output at potential and constant inflation. In 2020, an expenditure shock shifts the AE curve to the right (for example, government spending rises to finance a war). This shock is temporary: in 2021, the AE curve shifts back to its initial position. Policymakers know in 2020 that the shock is temporary.

Assume the central bank follows the countercyclical policy shown in **Figure 13.12A**. In 2020, when the expenditure shock occurs, the central bank raises the real interest rate. In 2021, when the shock disappears, policymakers return the interest rate to its initial level. Let's examine the effects of these actions, once again comparing the AE/PC model with and without time lags.

Figure 13.12B shows the behavior of output. In the no-lag case, we assume the interest rate increase in 2020 is the right size to offset the AE shift. As a result, output stays at potential. Output also remains constant in 2021, when the shock disappears and the AE curve returns to its initial position.

To understand the behavior of output with time lags, it's helpful to examine the AE curve. In 2020, the curve shifts out, as shown in **Figure 13.13A**. The high interest rate in 2020 doesn't affect spending in that year: what matters is $r(-1)$, the interest rate in 2019. For that interest rate, the AE shift raises output above potential.

In 2021, when the AE curve shifts back in (**Figure 13.13B**), $r(-1)$ is the interest rate in 2020, which was high. The high $r(-1)$ and the inward AE shift combine to push output *below* potential. So the economic boom in 2020 is followed by a recession in 2021. Figure 13.12B shows this output path. Output returns to potential in 2022, the year after the interest rate returns to its initial level.

Figure 13.12C shows the behavior of inflation. In the no-lag case, the inflation rate never changes, because output stays at potential. With time

FIGURE 13.12 Countercyclical Policy with Time Lags

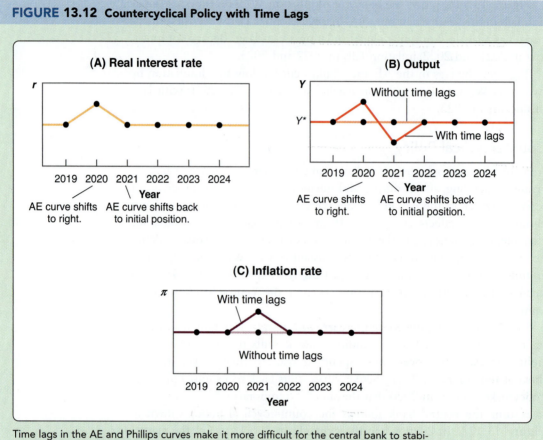

Time lags in the AE and Phillips curves make it more difficult for the central bank to stabilize the economy. Despite countercyclical policy, an expenditure shock causes short-run movements in output and inflation.

FIGURE 13.13 Determining the Output Path in Figure 13.12B

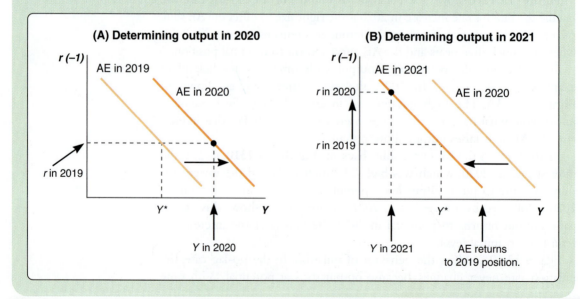

lags, the movements in output affect inflation a year later. The boom in 2020 causes inflation to rise in 2021; the recession in 2021 pushes inflation back down in 2022. The expenditure shock has no long-run effect on inflation, but it causes short-run volatility.

In the time-lag case, one might ask why the central bank raises the interest rate in 2020. This action doesn't affect the economy in that year, and it causes a recession in 2021. If policymakers can't offset the expenditure shock when it occurs, why not keep the interest rate constant? The answer is that passive policy would allow a permanent rise in inflation, which the central bank might find unacceptable. Problem 13.6 explores this point.

CASE STUDY

Fiscal Versus Monetary Policy

When it comes to stabilizing the economy, policymakers have two tools that you probably learned about in an introductory economics course. One tool is monetary policy, which is controlled by the Federal Reserve. The other is **fiscal policy**, the choice of taxes and government spending. Fiscal policy is controlled by Congress and the president.

If we ignore time lags, either monetary or fiscal policy can offset an expenditure shock. **Figure 13.14** shows a negative shock to spending that shifts the AE curve to the left, from AE_1 to AE_2. In response to this shock, the Fed can reduce the real interest rate (**Figure 13.14A**). Alternatively,

Fiscal policy the government's choice of taxes and spending

FIGURE 13.14 Two Types of Countercyclical Policy

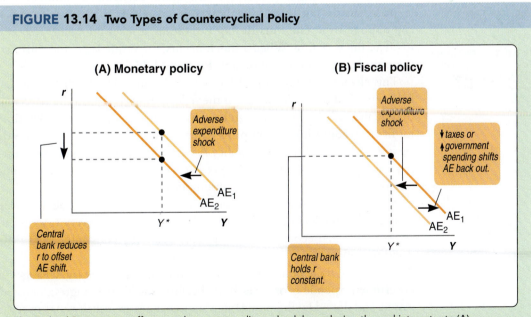

The Federal Reserve can offset an adverse expenditure shock by reducing the real interest rate (A). Alternatively, Congress and the president can offset the shock by enacting legislation that raises government spending or cuts taxes (B).

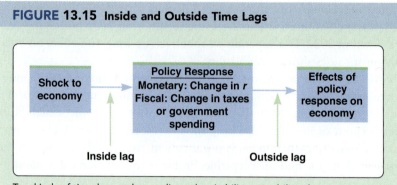

FIGURE 13.15 Inside and Outside Time Lags

Two kinds of time lags reduce policymakers' ability to stabilize the economy.

the Fed can do nothing while the president and Congress adjust fiscal policy. An expansionary policy—either a tax cut or a rise in government spending—shifts the AE curve back to the right (**Figure 13.14B**). Either type of policy keeps output constant.

In practice, monetary policy is used more often than fiscal policy to stabilize the economy. When an expenditure shock occurs, it's likely that the Fed responds, not the president and Congress. The reasons involve time lags. We've seen that lags reduce the effectiveness of monetary policy as a stabilization tool. Most economists believe, however, that the problem is worse for fiscal policy.

To discuss this issue, we must first distinguish between two kinds of time lags. The **inside lag** is the time it takes policymakers to recognize a shock and respond to it. The **outside lag** is the time it takes the policy response to affect the economy. When a shock occurs, the inside lag comes first and the outside lag second, as shown in **Figure 13.15**.

This chapter has emphasized the outside lag in monetary policy: the lag between a Fed action (a change in the federal funds rate) and the effects on output and inflation. This lag can be substantial, partly because it takes time for firms to adjust investment plans when interest rates change. The outside lag is generally *shorter* for fiscal policy. A rise in government spending directly raises aggregate expenditure. A tax cut raises people's after-tax incomes, leading fairly quickly to higher consumption.

The story about inside lags is very different. For monetary policy, this lag is short. As discussed in Section 13.1, the FOMC meets every 6 weeks to adjust policy. Fed economists monitor the economy constantly, so FOMC decisions reflect the most recent developments.

In contrast, fiscal policy moves slowly through the inside lag. Changes in government spending or taxes must be introduced in Congress, debated, passed, and signed by the president. Major changes are usually controversial, and it can take years to build political support. Consequently, fiscal policy is not used commonly to offset expenditure shocks.

Inside lag time between a shock and the policy response

Outside lag time between the policy response and its effects on the economy

Fiscal policy *was* used as a stabilization tool during the most recent recession. In February 2008, President Bush signed legislation granting tax cuts of $152 billion, or about 1 percent of GDP. In February 2009, President Obama signed a fiscal stimulus act that included a mix of tax cuts, spending on infrastructure, and aid to state governments. The total cost was about $800 billion, or 5 percent of GDP. Controversy abounds on the effectiveness of the Obama stimulus, but one nonpartisan source, the Congressional Budget Office, estimates that without it the unemployment rate in 2010 would have been between 0.7 and 1.8 percentage points higher.

A major reason for these fiscal expansions is that monetary policy has a limit. As the economy slumped, the Federal Reserve lowered its target for the federal funds rate from 5.25 percent in summer 2007 to below 0.25 percent—for practical purposes, to zero—in December 2008. The target remained below 0.25 percent through 2009 and 2010.

In contrast to previous recessions, however, the Fed's interest rate decreases were not sufficient either to boost output back to potential or to reduce the unemployment rate significantly. And further decreases were impossible, because nominal interest rates cannot fall below zero. Many economists believe that fiscal policy is a cumbersome stabilization tool, but one that it is needed when the primary tool of interest rate cuts is unavailable.

> Chapters 14 and 18 analyze the options for stabilization policy when the federal funds rate is at its lower bound.

Summary

- The monetary transmission mechanism is the process through which monetary policy affects output. It involves both financial markets and banks, the major parts of the financial system.

13.1 Monetary Policy and the Term Structure

- The Federal Reserve controls a 1-day interest rate—the federal funds rate. The rates that influence spending are longer-term rates. However, the Fed does affect spending indirectly, because the federal funds rate affects longer-term interest rates.

- According to the expectations theory of the term structure, longer-term rates depend on the current federal funds rate and on expectations of future rates. The direct effect of the current rate is small. But a change in the current funds rate can change longer-term rates substantially by changing expectations of future interest rates. This occurs because the Fed does not reverse changes in the funds rate quickly.

- A change in the funds rate must be unexpected to cause longer-term rates to change substantially at the same time. An expected change causes longer-term

Finar

funds

stater.

- Kenn
  increa
  es lor
  perce
  0.19

13.2 Tl
    Ex

- Event
  short-
  shock
  tribut

- A rise in asset prices raises aggregate expenditure, because higher wealth stimulates consumption, higher stock prices encourage investment, and higher net worth and collateral produce greater lending by banks.

- Events in the banking industry cause shifts in bank lending that influence aggregate spending. These events include changes in risk perception, in regulation, and in bank capital.

- Japan experienced a deep economic slump—a lost decade from 1992 to 2002—caused by, among other things, banking problems and crashes in asset prices.

- The investment multiplier magnifies economic fluctuations. A rise in aggregate spending raises firms' earnings, which provides cheap funds for investment, which raises investment, which further increases aggregate spending.

13.3 The Monetary Transmission Mechanism

- Monetary policy affects aggregate spending through a complex process. In this monetary transmission mechanism, a change in the federal funds rate affects longer-term interest rates, asset prices, and exchange rates. These financial variables affect various components of spending, both directly and through effects on bank lending. Eventually, changes in spending are magnified by the consumption multiplier and the investment multiplier.

- Gertler and Gilchrist find that monetary policy has larger effects on small firms than on large firms. This finding confirms the importance of bank lending in the monetary transmission mechanism.

13.4 Time Lags

- It takes around a year for a shift in monetary policy to exert its main effects on output. It then takes about another year for a change in output to exert its main effects on inflation.

13.5 Time Lags and the Effects of Monetary Policy

- Time lags make monetary policy less effective in stabilizing the economy. They slow down the process of disinflation, and they make it harder to offset the effects of expenditure shocks.

- In theory, either fiscal or monetary policy can be used to stabilize the economy. In practice, the job usually falls to monetary policy, because the political process makes it hard to adjust fiscal policy quickly.

- Fiscal policy played an atypically large role in responding to the most recent U.S. recession, because the economy remained in a slump even after the Fed reduced interest rates almost to zero.

Key Terms

capital crunch, p. 399

fiscal policy, p. 413

inside lag, p. 414

investment multiplier, p. 402

monetary transmission mechanism, p. 390

outside lag, p. 414

estions and Problems

ose the federal funds rate is 3 percent.
ders expect it to remain at that level
hs and then rise to 3.5 percent for
wever, the FOMC raises the
ent immediately. After this
t the funds rate to stay at
ear. How does the

FOMC's action affect the 3-month interest rate, the 6-month rate, and the 1-year rate?

2. Suppose that bond traders expect an increase in the federal funds rate, but the FOMC surprises them by keeping it constant. What happens to longer-term rates? Explain.

3. Describe all the ways that a rise in stock prices affects aggregate expenditure. Do the same for a rise in housing prices. Do stock prices have some effects that housing prices don't or vice versa?

4. The riskiness of banks' assets fluctuates over time. For example, default risk on loans rises and falls.

   a. How are banks likely to adjust their equity ratios (their ratios of capital to assets) when the riskiness of assets changes? Explain. (*Hint*: See Section 9.6.)

   b. How do the adjustments in part (a) affect the sizes of booms and recessions? Explain.

5. Economists have found that recent earnings have larger effects on investment for small firms than for large firms. What might explain this fact?

6. Figure 13.12 shows what happens if the AE curve shifts out temporarily and the central bank raises the real interest rate. Now suppose the same shock occurs but the central bank keeps the interest rate constant. Assuming lags in the AE and Phillips curves, show what happens to output and inflation over time. Discuss the pros and cons of raising the interest rate in response to the shock.

7. Consider the expenditure shock in Figure 13.12: the AE curve shifts to the right in 2020 and returns to its initial position in 2021. Suppose the central bank anticipates the shock: in 2019, it knows what will happen in the following two years. Assuming lags in the AE and Phillips curves, can the central bank keep output and inflation constant? If it can, explain how; if it can't, explain why not.

8. Consider the AE/PC model with time lags. Suppose the economy starts in 2019 with output at potential and constant inflation. In 2020, an adverse supply shock occurs, shifting the Phillips curve up.

   a. Show the paths of output and inflation over time if the central bank keeps the real interest rate constant.

   b. Can the central bank prevent inflation from rising temporarily as a result of the supply shock? Can it prevent inflation from rising permanently? Explain.

   c. Suppose policymakers want to return inflation to its 2019 level as quickly as possible and then keep inflation constant. What path should policymakers choose for the real interest rate? What are the resulting paths of output and inflation?

▶ **Online and Data Questions**
www.worthpublishers.com/ball

9. From the text Web site, get Bernanke and Kuttner's data on expected and unexpected changes in the federal funds rate by the FOMC. (You may have used these data to solve Problem 3.12.) Choose one day when the expected change in the funds rate was large and the unexpected change was small, and one day when the opposite was true. Then link to the site of the Federal Reserve Bank of St. Louis, which has daily data on the interest rate on 1-year Treasury bonds. For each of the days you selected from the Bernanke–Kuttner data, compute the change in the 1-year interest rate from the day *before* the FOMC's action to the day *after* the action. If you can, explain why the change in the 1-year rate was larger in one case than in the other.

10. Link from the text Web site to the online Economic Report of the President and get annual data on real GDP and real investment. Calculate the growth rates of the two variables for each year since 1960. (A variable's growth rate in a given year is the percentage change from the previous year.) Which is more volatile—GDP or investment? What might explain the difference in volatility?

Inflation and Deflation

14.1 MONEY AND INFLATION IN THE LONG RUN

14.2 WHAT DETERMINES MONEY GROWTH?

14.3 THE COSTS OF INFLATION

14.4 DEFLATION AND THE LIQUIDITY TRAP

U.S. inflation caused great concern in the 1970s, when the rate rose above 10 percent. In 1974, President Gerald Ford called inflation "public enemy number one." Voters' unhappiness with inflation contributed to Ford's loss to Jimmy Carter in the 1976 presidential election and then to Carter's loss to Ronald Reagan in 1980.

By worldwide standards, however, U.S. inflation in the 1970s was hardly extreme. **Table 14.1** on page 420 illustrates the spectacular variation in inflation rates across countries and time periods. Inflation can be negative, as it was in Japan from 1999 through 2005. A sustained period of negative inflation is called **deflation**. When inflation is positive, it can average less than 3 percent per year (as in the United States in the 2000s), more than 500 percent (as in Argentina in the late 1980s), or any level in between.

For briefer periods, economies can experience **hyperinflation**—inflation above 50 percent per *month*, or about 13,000 percent per year.[1] In the infamous hyperinflation of post–World War I Germany, annual inflation reached 855 million percent in 1923. More recently in Zimbabwe, the government reported an inflation rate of 231 million percent in 2008, and some economists believe the true rate was much higher.

Three Lions/Getty Images

Germany, 1923: Hyperinflation provided children with new toys.

Deflation sustained period of negative inflation

Hyperinflation inflation of more than 50 percent per month (or roughly 13,000 percent per year)

---

[1] This definition of hyperinflation was proposed by Phillip Cagan of Columbia University in "The Monetary Dynamics of Hyperinflation," in Friedman (ed.), *Studies in the Quantity Theory of Money*, University of Chicago Press, 1956.

TABLE 14.1 Some Inflation Rates

Country	Period	Average Annual Inflation Rate (%)
United States	1870s	−1.8
Japan	1999–2005	−0.5
United States	2000–2007	2.7
United States	1970s	7.8
Italy	1970s	13.9
Turkey	1990s	76.1
Russia	1992–2000	121.3
Argentina	1985–1990	559.1
Zimbabwe	2008	231 million
Germany	1923	855 million

Sources: International Monetary Fund; Milton Friedman and Anna Schwartz, *Monetary Trends in the United States and the United Kingdom: Their Relation to Income, Prices, and Interest Rates 1867–1975*, University of Chicago Press, 1982; Thomas J. Sargent, "The Ends of Four Big Inflations," in Hall (ed.), *Inflation*, University of Chicago Press, 1983.

▶ Mathematical note: If the monthly inflation rate in decimal form is π^{month}, then the annual rate is $(1 + \pi^{month})^{12} - 1$. A monthly rate of 50 percent means $\pi^{month} = 0.5$. This implies an annual rate of $(1 + 0.5)^{12} - 1 = 128.75$ in decimal form, or 12,875 percent.

These astronomical inflation rates make money virtually worthless—at least for purchasing goods and services. In hyperinflations, people find other uses for money. In the German episode, children used blocks of currency as toys, and families saved on firewood by burning money in their stoves.

What determines the level of inflation? Why is it sometimes low or even negative and sometimes ridiculously high? This chapter addresses these issues. We start with one basic principle: *in the long run, inflation is determined by the growth rate of the money supply.* If a country experiences high inflation for a sustained period, its central bank is expanding the money supply rapidly.

This idea leads to further questions. What determines the growth rate of the money supply? Why do some central banks increase the money supply quickly if that produces high inflation? What levels of inflation harm the economy? How does deflation occur, and how do its effects compare to those of positive inflation rates?

14.1 MONEY AND INFLATION IN THE LONG RUN

Monetary policy affects both real variables, such as output, and nominal variables, such as the inflation rate. The effects on real variables, however, are transitory. Monetary policy influences output in the short run, but it is neutral in the long run.

▶ Section 12.5 introduces the principle of long-run monetary neutrality.

In contrast, monetary policy has its strongest effects on inflation in the long run. Various expenditure and supply shocks cause year-to-year movements in the inflation rate. But *average* inflation over a decade or more is tied closely to the growth of the money supply. Let's see why.

Velocity and the Quantity Equation

Remember the basic purpose of money: it is a medium of exchange. People spend money to acquire goods and services. The reason that the money supply affects inflation is that it affects the level of spending in the economy.

To see this point, we need to introduce a new concept: the **velocity of money**. This variable is the ratio of total spending in the economy to the money supply:

Velocity of money ratio of nominal GDP to the money supply ($V = PY/M$); shows how quickly money moves through the economy

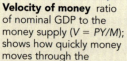

$$V = \frac{\text{total spending}}{M}$$

PV => Spaelin

If spending is \$500 and the money supply is \$100, then velocity is 500/100 = 5.

An economy's total spending is measured by nominal GDP. This variable equals the price level (P) times real output (Y). Therefore, velocity is

▶See the Chapter 1 appendix to review nominal GDP.

$$V = \frac{PY}{M}$$

Price × Y.

Velocity measures how quickly money circulates through the economy. Specifically, velocity is the number of times a typical dollar is spent over a year. If $V = 5$, then a dollar is spent five times. Someone spends the dollar in a store, the store owner spends it somewhere else, and it changes hands three times after that.

Economists often rearrange the definition of velocity, bringing M to the left side:

QUANTITY EQUATION OF MONEY

$$MV = PY \tag{14.1}$$

This **quantity equation of money** says that total spending in the economy (PY) equals the money supply (M) times the number of times each dollar is spent (V). If M is \$100 and V is 5, then total spending is \$500.

The concept of velocity is closely related to the concept of money demand—the amount of money that individuals and firms choose to hold. When the market for money is in equilibrium, the money supply, M, equals money demand, M^d. We can rewrite the definition of velocity as

> **Quantity equation of money** relationship among the money supply, velocity, and nominal GDP: $MV = PY$

$$V = \frac{PY}{M^d}$$

Inverse relationship between V & Md

This equation says that, for a given level of nominal GDP, an inverse relationship exists between velocity and money demand. Factors that raise money demand also reduce velocity.

For example, suppose ATMs become more common. People start carrying less cash, because they can get it easily when needed. This change reduces money demand for a given level of nominal GDP, so velocity rises. Say money holdings fall from \$100 to \$80. If GDP is still \$500, then velocity rises from 5 to 6.25 because 500/80 = 6.25.

▶Section 4.3 explores money demand.

↑V ↓Md
↑Md ↓V.

Deriving the Inflation Rate

The inflation rate is defined as the growth rate of the price level—the percentage change from one year to the next. With a little algebra, we can derive an equation for inflation from Equation (14.1), the quantity equation of money. Because the quantity equation always holds, the percentage change in the left side, MV, must equal the percentage change in the right side, PY:

$$\% \text{ change in } (MV) = \% \text{ change in } (PY)$$

Mathematically, the percentage change in MV is the sum of the percentage changes in M and V; the percentage change in PY can be decomposed in the same way. Therefore,

> ▶ Mathematical note: Formally, Equation (14.2) is a first-order Taylor approximation. It is accurate if the various percentage changes are not too large.

$$(\% \text{ change in } M) + (\% \text{ change in } V) = (\% \text{ change in } P) + (\% \text{ change in } Y) \quad \textbf{(14.2)}$$

In Equation (14.2), notice that the first term on the right, percentage change in P, is the inflation rate. As usual, we denote inflation by π. Rearranging terms yields a formula for π:

$$\pi = (\% \text{ change in } M) + (\% \text{ change in } V) - (\% \text{ change in } Y) \quad \textbf{(14.3)}$$

Equation (14.3) says that inflation is determined by the percentage changes, or growth rates, of three variables: the money supply, velocity, and real output.

In the long run, two of the growth rates in Equation (14.3) are outside the control of the central bank:

- Output growth depends on factors that affect the economy's productivity, such as new technologies. Long-run neutrality means that monetary policy is irrelevant.

> ▶ For the calculation of velocity growth, the money supply is defined as M1 adjusted for sweep accounts (see Section 2.4).

- Long-run changes in velocity are driven primarily by changes in transaction technologies—the methods people use to acquire and spend money. As discussed earlier, velocity moves in the opposite direction from money demand. In the United States, innovations such as ATMs have slowly reduced money demand, so velocity has risen. The growth rate of velocity averaged about 2 percent from 1960 to 2010. This long-run growth rate, like long-run output growth, is independent of monetary policy.

In contrast, the central bank chooses the growth rate of the money supply. For given levels of output growth and velocity growth, there is a one-for-one effect of money growth on inflation. In the long run, the central bank can raise or lower the inflation rate by changing money growth.

The Data

We've seen that central banks influence inflation through their choices of money growth. These choices vary widely across countries and time periods. Money growth rates are sometimes negative, sometimes close to zero, and sometimes hundreds or thousands of percent. This variation causes big differences in inflation.

This point is obvious when we examine some data. **Figure 14.1** presents data for 52 countries during the period 1980–1990. For each country, the figure shows the average growth rate of the money supply (the M1 measure) and average inflation. We see a close relation: the countries with high inflation rates are those with high money growth.

The relationship in Figure 14.1 is not perfect: the data points do not fall exactly on a straight line. The reason is that inflation is influenced by the growth rates of output and velocity [see Equation (14.3)]. However, these growth rates vary much less across countries than does money growth. As a result, money growth explains most differences in inflation.

Figure 14.2 illustrates our point another way. It shows money growth and inflation in one country, the United States, in different decades. We again see a strong relation between the two variables. Decades of high money growth, such as the 1910s and 1970s, are decades of high inflation. Low money growth in the 1930s produced deflation during the Great Depression.

As we have discussed, the relation between money growth and inflation holds *in the long run*—practically speaking, over periods of a decade or more. It may not hold for shorter periods. To illustrate this point, **Figure 14.3** presents U.S. data for individual years rather than decades. Specifically, it shows inflation and money growth for each year between 1990 and 2009. There is little relation between year-to-year fluctuations in the two variables. This reflects the short-run influence of expenditure and supply shocks on inflation.

The great economist Milton Friedman said that "inflation is always and everywhere a monetary phenomenon." The data show that Friedman is right—as long as we add "in the long run" to the end of his statement.

The Phillips Curve Again

In Section 12.4, we explain the behavior of inflation with a Phillips curve: inflation depends on past inflation, output, and supply shocks. Here we say that average inflation is determined by money growth. Superficially, these two theories sound different, and people sometimes interpret them as contradictory. In fact, they fit together nicely.

Specifically, the Phillips curve is part of the mechanism by which money growth produces inflation. Using the quantity equation of money, $MV = PY$, we've shown algebraically that these two variables are linked. In economic terms, however, the link is not direct. If the central bank increases the rate of money

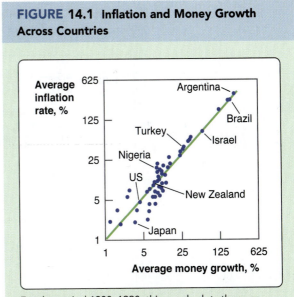

FIGURE 14.1 Inflation and Money Growth Across Countries

For the period 1980–1990, this graph plots the average growth rate of the money supply (as measured by M1) and the average inflation rate in 52 countries. Differences in money growth explain most cross-country differences in inflation.
Source: International Monetary Fund

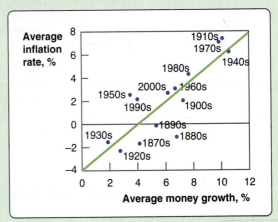

FIGURE 14.2 U.S. Inflation and Money Growth Across Decades

This graph plots the average growth rate of the money supply and the average inflation rate for each decade from the 1870s to the 2000s. The money supply is measured by M2 because M1 data are not available so far back in time. Differences in money growth explain most differences in inflation across decades.

Sources: Milton Friedman and Anna Schwartz, *Monetary Trends in the United States and the United Kingdom: Their Relation to Income, Prices, and Interest Rates 1867–1975*, University of Chicago Press, 1982; and Federal Reserve Board.

FIGURE 14.3 U.S. Inflation and Money Growth Across Individual Years

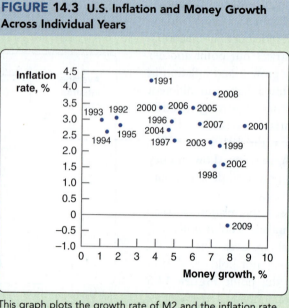

This graph plots the growth rate of M2 and the inflation rate in each year from 1991 through 2009. Differences in money growth do not explain differences in inflation across individual years.

Source: Federal Reserve Board

growth, it is *not* the case that firms observe this action and respond directly by raising prices faster. Instead, higher money growth sets off a chain of events that involves the Phillips curve.

Figure 14.4 outlines these events. In the money market, higher money growth pushes down the nominal interest rate, which reduces the real rate for a given level of expected inflation. The lower real interest rate moves the economy along the aggregate expenditure curve, raising output. Finally, higher output moves the economy along the Phillips curve, raising the inflation rate. In the end, we confirm this chapter's central idea: higher money growth leads to higher inflation.

FIGURE 14.4 From Money Growth to Inflation

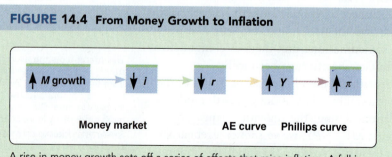

A rise in money growth sets off a series of effects that raise inflation. A fall in money growth has the opposite effects, reducing inflation.

The AE/PC model presented in Chapter 12 captures some of the steps in Figure 14.4: the links from interest rates to output to inflation. But the model leaves out the first step, from money growth to interest rates, because it assumes a policy of interest rate targeting. Under this policy, however, money growth is always adjusting in the background. A long-run rise in inflation requires an increase in money growth.

$$\uparrow M \quad \uparrow \pi_{LR}$$

For details on the behavior of money growth under interest rate targeting, see the Chapter 14 Online Appendix at the text Web site.

14.2 WHAT DETERMINES MONEY GROWTH?

At one level, the question "What determines inflation in the long run?" has a simple answer: the growth rate of the money supply. However, this answer raises another question: What determines money growth? Why is it sometimes slow and sometimes fast, producing the different inflation rates that we see?

The answer to this question is more complex. Different factors determine money growth in different circumstances. **Table 14.2** summarizes the main cases that we will discuss. As shown in the table, one key issue is whether an economy uses commodity money or fiat money.

TABLE 14.2 Determinants of Money Growth and Inflation

Commodity Money	Fiat Money
Production of the commodity (e.g., U.S. gold standard, 1879–1913)	Choice of the central bank ■ Often central banks keep inflation low (e.g., United States, 2000s) ■ Desire for high output → high inflation (e.g., United States, 1970s) ■ Government budget deficits → very high inflation (e.g., Zimbabwe, 2000s)

Commodity Money

Commodity money, such as gold coins or paper money exchangeable for gold, has intrinsic value. With commodity money, the money supply is determined by how much of the commodity is produced.

One example of a commodity money system is the classical gold standard, which existed in the United States from 1879 to 1913. During that period, money was mainly gold certificates. If you turned in gold to the government, you received gold certificates at a rate of $20.67 per ounce. If you held gold certificates, you could trade them back to the government for gold.

Under this system, the government did not try to control the money supply. Instead, money growth was determined by how much gold people exchanged for gold certificates. This was the amount of gold produced minus the amount people kept for "nonmonetary" uses, such as making jewelry.

Ultimately, the main factor determining money growth was developments in the mining industry. In the first half of the gold-standard period, mines produced new gold at a slow rate. As a result, money growth was low for most of the period from 1879 to 1897.

At the end of the nineteenth century, gold was discovered in Colorado, Alaska, and South Africa. In addition, new mining techniques made it easier to extract gold from ore. Gold production boomed, causing rapid money growth from 1897 to 1913.

▶ Section 2.2 compares commodity money to fiat money and discusses the uses of each over the course of U.S. history.

The slow money growth of the early gold-standard period led to deflation: the inflation rate averaged −1 percent from 1879 to 1897. From 1897 to 1913, higher money growth produced average inflation of +2 percent.

These inflation developments had important effects on the economy, which in turn produced political conflict. The next case study discusses politics in the 1890s.

CASE STUDY

The Free Silver Movement

▶ The case study in Section 8.2 chronicles the politics of banking in U.S. history.

Issues in money and banking have sparked political controversy throughout U.S. history. Supporters of large banks, centered traditionally in Eastern cities, have battled antibank populists in farming regions. The episodes in this saga include the fight over the Second Bank of the United States in the 1830s and the fight over bank branching in the early 1900s.

One of the biggest battles occurred during the gold-standard era. The underlying cause was the deflation from 1879 to 1897. This deflation was unforeseen: people did not expect inflation to be negative. In other words, actual inflation (π) over the period was lower than expected inflation (π^e).

▶ Section 3.7 compares the ex ante and ex post real interest rates.

This divergence meant that the ex post real interest rate, $i - \pi$, was higher than the ex ante real rate, $i - \pi^e$. In real terms, debtors paid more interest on their loans than they had expected when the loans were made.

Farmers in the western United States had large debts to banks. The 1880s and 1890s were tough times for this group because of poor agricultural conditions, including drought and insect infestations. Rising debt burdens caused by deflation pushed many farmers into bankruptcy.

Farmers and their political allies wanted to raise the inflation rate, which would reduce real interest rates. They understood that inflation required faster money growth and that the gold standard was keeping money growth low.

Bimetallism monetary system in which money is backed by both gold and silver

Consequently, supporters of higher inflation pushed for a monetary system called **bimetallism** (literally, two metals). In this system, the government would issue money backed by silver as well as by gold. Specifically, a dollar could be issued for *either* 0.0484 ounces of gold *or* 0.774 ounces of silver (making silver worth 1/16 as much as gold). Silver mining was booming during this period, so bimetallism would have caused a large increase in the money supply.

The debate over bimetallism came to a head in the presidential campaign of 1896. The Republicans nominated William McKinley, who supported the gold standard. The Democrats nominated William Jennings Bryan, known as "the Great Commoner" for his populist views. Bryan's primary campaign issue was "Free Silver," meaning bimetallism.

At the Democratic convention in Chicago, Bryan made one of the most famous speeches in American political history, expressing his views on monetary policy with a dramatic Biblical metaphor. Referring to his opponents, the Eastern bankers, Bryan said, "We will answer their demand for a gold standard by saying to them: You shall not press down upon the brow of labor this crown of thorns, you shall not crucify mankind upon a cross of gold."

In the 1896 election, Bryan carried the South and West and lost badly in the East. The election turned on Midwestern states such as Ohio and Michigan, whose economies were shifting from agriculture to industry. McKinley carried these states, giving him the presidency. The gold standard was secure.

Ironically, Bryan's supporters ultimately got what they wanted: inflation. Deflation ended because gold production fortuitously rose after 1896. With this development, the fervor for bimetallism waned (although Bryan was twice more the Democratic presidential candidate, in 1900 and 1908).

Fiat Money and Inflation

Today, economies use fiat money—pieces of paper that are not exchangeable for any commodity. The supply of fiat money is controlled by an economy's central bank, not its mining industry. The central bank has tools, such as open-market operations, which allow it to increase the money supply at whatever rate it chooses.

OPEN MKT OPS

← ↓ π

As noted in Table 14.2, central banks often choose low levels of money growth. The reason is obvious: to keep inflation low. For example, the Federal Reserve kept money growth low in the 1990s and early 2000s, producing an average inflation rate below 3 percent.

In other cases, central banks choose higher money growth. We've seen that the Fed allowed money to grow rapidly in the 1970s, producing average inflation of 8 percent. Central banks in some countries have produced hyperinflation.

Such experiences may appear puzzling. Central bank officials dislike high inflation. Most understand the link between inflation and money growth. So why don't they always choose low money growth and low inflation? One answer is that rapid money growth can raise output temporarily.

The Output–Inflation Trade-Off

One step on the path from money growth to inflation is a rise in output, which raises inflation through the Phillips curve (see Figure 14.4). This output boom increases people's incomes and reduces unemployment. This prospect tempts central banks to follow inflationary policies.

A central bank also allows inflation to rise if it accommodates an adverse supply shock, such as a rise in oil prices. Here the aim of policymakers is not to raise output but merely to keep it from falling below potential. With an adverse supply shock, however, stable output requires an increase in money growth and inflation.

Finally, once money growth and inflation are high, central banks may keep them high. We've seen that a policy of reducing inflation—a disinflation—causes a temporary output loss. In a disinflation, the process in Figure 14.4 works in reverse: along the path from lower money growth to lower inflation,

Section 12.4 uses the Phillips curve to show how accommodative policy leads to higher inflation. The Chapter 14 Online Appendix shows how money growth rises during this process.

▶ A disinflation: ↓ M growth → ↑ i → ↑ r → ↓ Y → ↓ π

← ↗

interest rates rise and output falls. If policymakers are unwilling to pay this cost, they keep money growth high and live with inflation.

The factors we've outlined help explain U.S. inflation in the 1970s. Large supply shocks occurred in 1973 and 1979—the two OPEC oil-price increases. The Fed accommodated these shocks, allowing money growth and inflation to rise. Then, under Chairmen Burns and Miller, the Fed was unwilling to reduce output to disinflate. Inflation fell only after Paul Volcker was appointed chairman in 1979; Volcker decided enough was enough, reduced money growth, and accepted a deep recession.

The output–inflation trade-off helps explain many episodes of inflation. However, it is *not* the main reason for very high inflation. Policymakers may allow 10-percent inflation to keep output high, but this motive doesn't explain 500-percent inflation in Argentina or hyperinflation in Zimbabwe. Something else is going on in these cases.

Seigniorage and Very High Inflation

What explains inflation in the hundreds or thousands of percent? The short answer is government budget deficits. Governments frequently spend more than they raise in taxes, creating deficits. Most often, governments cover deficits by issuing bonds—in other words, by borrowing. This borrowing pushes up interest rates, which reduces investment and hurts economic growth. However, deficits financed by bonds do *not* necessarily cause inflation. For example, the U.S. government has run large deficits in the 2000s, but inflation has stayed low.

Sometimes, however, governments with deficits have trouble selling bonds. This occurs when savers fear the government will default on its debt. This fear arises when debt reaches a high level, especially if the government or those of similar countries have defaulted in the past.

When private savers refuse to buy government bonds, the government turns to another buyer: the central bank. Some central banks are legally required to buy the bonds; others do so voluntarily to keep the government functioning. Purchases of bonds by the central bank cause an increase in the monetary base, which in turn raises the money supply. When the government runs large deficits, the money supply rises rapidly, fueling inflation.

Formally, the government is borrowing money when it sells bonds to the central bank. However, the central bank is set up by the government, and it gives back the interest it earns from government bonds. So when the government sells bonds to the central bank, it does not really create a debt to an outside entity. In effect, the central bank just creates money and gives it to the government. Financing deficits this way is known as **printing money**. The money that the government receives is called **seigniorage revenue** (after the *seigneurs*, or feudal lords, who created money in the Middle Ages).

Budget deficits have caused high inflation in much of the world. Some examples:

- In the 1980s, populist governments in Latin America spent large amounts on programs for the poor yet raised little revenue because of

▶The jumbo case study in Section 12.4 includes the story of inflation in the 1970s.

▶Section 4.2 explores the effects of government deficits financed by borrowing.

▶Section 11.2 describes the links between central bank purchases of bonds, the monetary base, and the money supply.

Printing money financing government budget deficits by selling bonds to the central bank

Seigniorage revenue revenue the government receives from printing money

[Handwritten margin notes: "Bonds do to interest rates?" and "CB + Gov't Bonds?"]

tax evasion. At first they financed budget deficits by borrowing; they had trouble selling bonds, but they received loans from U.S. banks. These loans were cut off after Mexico defaulted on its debt in 1982. At that point, countries such as Argentina and Brazil turned to seigniorage revenue, producing inflation rates of hundreds and thousands of percent per year.

■ In the 1990s, three- and four-digit inflation plagued Russia and other countries that had recently abandoned communism. Budget deficits were caused partly by subsidies to unprofitable firms left over from the old regime. Savers were wary of lending to countries with uncertain futures, so seigniorage revenue was needed. In 1993, the inflation rate was 256 percent in Romania, 875 percent in Russia, and 4735 percent in Ukraine.

Beyond inflation of "only" a few thousand percent lies hyperinflation. Most hyperinflations have occurred during or after wars, especially World Wars I and II. Wars destroy economies and create political turmoil, leading to huge budget deficits. Money growth explodes, producing inflation rates that sound like science fiction.

Two hyperinflations have occurred since 1990:

■ In the early 1990s, Serbia set the all-time record for hyperinflation. In this episode, the war in Bosnia fueled high government spending. At the same time, output fell sharply, because trade was interrupted by the breakup of Yugoslavia and by embargoes imposed as punishment for the war. Falling output reduced tax revenue, and the deficit rose to one-third of GDP. Serbia's government financed its deficit by printing money, producing a staggering inflation rate of 116 trillion percent in 1993 (that's 116,000,000,000,000%).

■ The first hyperinflation of the 2000s occurred in Zimbabwe. The country's output collapsed as a result of the disastrous policies of President Robert Mugabe, including a chaotic land redistribution, protectionist trade policies, controls on exchange rates, and political repression that destabilized the country. Tax revenue plummeted and, as in Serbia, the government budget deficit reached a third of GDP. The inflation rate was around 100 percent in 2001, climbed to 1000 percent in 2006, and then exploded. Inflation exceeded 100,000

A 10-million-dollar note issued by the Reserve Bank of Zimbabwe. When it was printed in January 2008, it could buy six loaves of bread; a few months later, it was nearly worthless.

AP PHOTO/Tsvangirayi Mukwazhi

▶ Section 2.2 discusses various alternatives to a national currency, including dollarization, currency boards, and currency unions.

percent in 2007 and reached hundreds of millions of percent the next year. The hyperinflation ended only when the government *dollarized* in January 2009: it abolished the Zimbabwe dollar and adopted the U.S. dollar as its currency.

The next case study examines history's most famous hyperinflation.

CASE STUDY

The German Hyperinflation

After World War I, the German government spent heavily to rebuild its country. Under the Treaty of Versailles, it also paid large reparations—about 6 percent of its GDP—to the victors of the war. All this spending produced large budget deficits that were financed by printing money. The result was inflation of 167 percent in 1921 and 4130 percent in 1922.

Berlin, Germany, 1923: A woman lights her stove with millions of deutsche marks, the German currency.

© Bettmann/CORBIS

In 1923, things fell apart. Germany fell behind on its reparations payments, leading France to occupy the industrial Ruhr Valley. German output fell sharply, reducing tax revenue. Workers in the Ruhr went on strike to protest the occupation, and the German government paid their wages.

Tax receipts covered only 11 percent of government spending, so huge levels of seigniorage were needed. Money growth and inflation erupted. Monthly inflation was about 100 percent in January 1923 and rose to 30,000 percent in October. This inflation rate meant that prices doubled every four days. For all of 1923, inflation was 855 million percent.

This period produced amazing stories. Bar patrons ordered two beers at a time, because the price of the second was likely to rise before they finished the first. Cash lost so much of its value that people used it to make toys, as shown at the beginning of this chapter, or to heat their homes, as shown in the accompanying photo.

Huge amounts of money were needed to buy goods. One man went to buy a loaf of bread, pushing his cash in a wheelbarrow. He carelessly left it outside when he entered the store.

When he came out, he found that someone had dumped out the cash and stolen the wheelbarrow.

Just as budget deficits caused the hyperinflation, it ended when deficits were eliminated. At the end of 1923, the German government fired a third of its workers and raised taxes. Around the same time, the Allies agreed to reduce reparations and leave the Ruhr. In 1924, the German government ran a budget surplus. Inflation in 1924 was 4 percent.

History is full of dramatic episodes of high inflation. However, as the next case discusses, such episodes are becoming more rare.

CASE STUDY

The Worldwide Decline in Inflation

Figure 14.5 shows the behavior of inflation in several groups of countries in recent decades. Each group's inflation rate is an average of inflation in individual countries, weighted by the country's real GDP. The figure shows that inflation has fallen throughout the world.

In the most advanced economies (Figure 14.5A), average inflation was 9 percent in the early 1980s. It fell to 2 percent in the late 1990s and has remained near 2 percent in the 2000s. In developing economies (Figure 14.5B), inflation was high in the 1990s but has fallen since then. For example, inflation in Latin America and the Caribbean averaged 240 percent over 1990–1994 and 5 percent over 2005–2009.

Why have inflation rates fallen? Recall that different factors explain different levels of inflation. The stories behind the inflation decreases in advanced economies and in countries with higher initial inflation differ.

In advanced economies such as the United States, inflation has fallen largely because policymakers have changed their views about the economy. There have been two related developments.

First, policymakers have become convinced of the long-run neutrality of monetary policy. In the 1960s, many believed that expansionary policy would raise both inflation and output permanently. Policymakers were willing to accept some inflation to keep output high.

In a famous 1968 address, Milton Friedman argued that the effects on output are transitory—the idea of long-run neutrality. It took awhile for Friedman to persuade policymakers, but most were convinced by the early 1980s. Long-run neutrality makes disinflation more attractive: it requires only a temporary sacrifice of output, not a permanent one. A growing belief in this idea prompted central banks in the United States and Europe to disinflate in the 1980s.

The second development is that experience with inflation has made policymakers in advanced economies dislike it more. Policymakers of the 1960s and 1970s had lived through the Great Depression of the 1930s. Because of this experience, they put a priority on keeping unemployment low. When adverse supply shocks occurred in the 1970s—the OPEC oil-price

▶ As we've noted, Zimbabwe is an exception to the trend toward low inflation. Another exception, though less extreme, is Venezuela. In 1999, Venezuela elected a populist president, Hugo Chavez, who raised government spending. Venezuela's inflation rate was about 30 percent per year in 2010.

FIGURE 14.5 The Worldwide Fall in Inflation

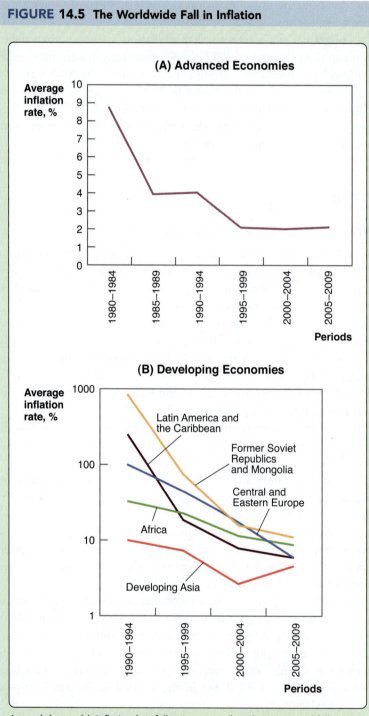

Around the world, inflation has fallen in recent decades. It started falling in advanced economies in the 1980s (A) and in developing economies in the 1990s (B). Both graphs chart average inflation rates in groups of countries over five-year periods.

Source: International Monetary Fund

hikes—central banks accommodated them. This policy avoided recessions but allowed inflation to rise.

Eventually, high inflation created a backlash against overly expansionary policy. From the 1980s through the early 2000s, the inflationary 1970s replaced the Depression as the "bad old days" that policymakers were determined not to repeat. Central bankers in developed countries were more willing to endure recessions to reduce inflation and keep it low. Perhaps the deep world recession of 2007–2009 will lead to another shift in attitude, but in 2010, policymakers such as Ben Bernanke maintained that they were still determined to keep inflation low.

In developing countries as well, experience with inflation—often very high inflation—has made policymakers determined to reduce it. Remember, though, that the underlying cause of very high inflation is budget deficits. To reduce inflation, governments have had to reduce deficits.

In many countries, populist governments have been replaced by more conservative ones that reduced spending. In Latin America, for example, average deficits fell from 4.6 percent of GDP over 1970–1989 to 2.7 percent over 1990–2002. In addition, economic reforms have convinced foreigners to lend more to developing countries, reducing the need for seigniorage to finance the deficits that remain.

Peru is one country that reduced inflation dramatically. A left-wing president, Alan Garcia, was elected in 1985. He raised food subsidies and wages for government workers, and the budget deficit reached 9 percent of GDP. Inflation rose to 40 percent per month—almost hyperinflation.

In 1990, a new president, Alberto Fujimori, shifted course. He eliminated subsidies and fired government workers. He cracked down on tax evasion, raising tax revenues from less than 5 percent of GDP in 1990 to 12.5 percent in 1999. Additional revenues came from sales of state-owned firms. These policies produced a budget surplus, and inflation fell to 2 percent per year in 2000. Inflation remained low under Fujimori's successor as president, Alejandro Toledo.

In 2006, Alan Garcia was again elected president. Many people feared that his policies would produce high inflation as they had two decades before. But Garcia had learned his lesson. "Do you think," he asked, "I want my tombstone to read 'He was so stupid that he made the same mistakes twice?'" The second Garcia administration has limited government spending and kept the inflation rate close to 2 percent.

14.3 THE COSTS OF INFLATION

So far we have discussed the causes of inflation. We now turn to its effects. Does inflation harm the economy, and if so how? What levels of inflation are acceptable and what levels are dangerous?

Central bankers believe that inflation is very harmful. Jean-Claude Trichet, president of the European Central Bank from 2003 to 2011, called inflation "a betrayal of the people." However, policymakers are often vague in describing *why* inflation is so bad. This reflects the fact that no one fully understands its effects.

Nobody knows, for example, whether annual inflation rates of 5 or 10 percent are truly harmful. Economists have researched this issue, but we have not made much progress. As economist Paul Krugman of Princeton University has put it, "one of the dirty little secrets of economic analysis is that even though inflation is universally regarded as a terrible scourge, efforts to measure its costs come up with embarrassingly small numbers."[2]

The Inflation Fallacy

You may find the last paragraph puzzling. Many people consider it obvious why inflation is harmful. Inflation means that prices of goods and services rise—things become more expensive. People cannot afford to buy as much as before, so their standard of living suffers. In a 1996 survey, 77 percent of the U.S. public agreed with the statement that inflation "hurts my real buying power, making me poorer."

Economists have a different view. When surveyors presented the same statement to economics professors, only 12 percent agreed. Harvard's Gregory Mankiw has called this statement "the inflation fallacy." Economists don't see a necessary connection between inflation and changes in living standards.[3]

The reason is that inflation increases *all* the economy's prices—including wages and salaries. Workers demand wage increases to compensate for inflation, and firms can afford to raise wages because prices are higher. If inflation rises by 1 percent, wage growth normally rises by 1 percent as well. Wages keep pace with inflation, so people can afford the same things as before.

To put it differently, a worker's standard of living depends on her *real* wage—the ratio of her wage to the aggregate price level. Inflation raises the numerator and denominator of this ratio by the same amount, so the real wage is unchanged. The real wage is determined by other factors, such as the worker's productivity.

History supports this reasoning. When U.S. inflation fell from 10 percent to 4 percent in the early 1980s, wage growth slowed as well. Both before and after disinflation, real wages grew about 1 percent per year, reflecting growth in productivity. Lower inflation had no obvious benefit for living standards.

Very High Inflation

This does *not* mean that economists consider inflation harmless. Although inflation does not directly reduce living standards, it can hurt the economy in subtler ways. As you might expect, inflation costs are easiest to identify when inflation is very high—in the hundreds of percent or more. Among the adverse effects of high inflation that economists have identified are "shoe leather costs," distracted firms, relative-price variability, and income inequality.

---

[2] See Paul Krugman, *The Age of Diminished Expectations,* MIT Press, 1997.
[3] The survey on attitudes toward inflation is presented in Robert J. Shiller, "Why Do People Dislike Inflation?," in Romer and Romer (eds.), *Reducing Inflation: Motivation and Strategy*, University of Chicago Press, 1997.

Shoe Leather Costs With high inflation, money loses its value quickly. Anyone who holds a significant amount of money sees his wealth eroded. As a consequence, people try to minimize their money holdings. Lower money holdings mean that transactions become harder, making life less convenient.

This effect is important at high inflation rates. To avoid holding cash, people visit their banks frequently, causing long lines. If people lack bank accounts, as is common in developing countries, they rush to buy goods as soon as they receive their pay. They buy things they don't really want just to get rid of cash. These effects of inflation are called **shoe leather costs**—a metaphor referring to the shoe leather worn out on frequent trips to the bank.

Distracted Firms High inflation causes headaches for the managers of firms. They must push their customers to pay bills promptly, before inflation erodes the value of payments. At the same time, they can reduce costs by delaying payments to other firms. Like people, firms try to minimize money holdings; they constantly move cash into bank accounts with interest that compensates for inflation.

These activities consume managers' time and attention. Coping with inflation leaves less time for normal business activities, such as developing new products or improving productivity. It is difficult to quantify this effect, but some economists think it hurts economic growth.

Relative-Price Variability When inflation is high, all firms raise their prices by large amounts. But they do so at different times. At any moment, some prices are abnormally high compared to others, just because they have adjusted more recently. In other words, inflation causes dispersion in relative prices.

Research has confirmed this effect. For example, an Argentine study found that high inflation increases the variation in prices across different grocery stores. Price differences distort consumers' purchases and firms' sales, harming economic efficiency. And consumers must spend more time comparing prices to get a good deal.[4]

Income Inequality High inflation hurts the overall economy, but the biggest problem may be the unevenness of its effects. Studies from Latin America show that inflation increases the inequality between rich and poor.

One reason is that the poor have relatively large money holdings. They receive their wages in cash and have no bank accounts, so inflation is costly. By contrast, the rich have access to bank accounts with high nominal interest rates that compensate for inflation.

There are also differences in wage adjustment. The salaries of professional workers are often indexed to inflation, meaning they change automatically to preserve their real value. The wages of unskilled workers are slower to adjust when inflation accelerates.

During the 1980s, Brazil experienced many of the effects of high inflation that we have discussed.

Shoe leather costs
inconveniences that result from holding less money when inflation is high

---

[4] See Mariano Tommasi, "Inflation and Relative Prices: Evidence from Argentina," in Sheshinski and Weiss (eds.), *Optimal Pricing, Inflation, and Costs of Price Adjustment*, MIT Press, 1993.

CASE STUDY

Life in Inflationary Brazil

In the 1960s and 1970s, annual inflation in Brazil fluctuated between 28 percent and 77 percent. Then, in the 1980s, inflation rose steadily, reaching 273 percent in 1985 and 3467 percent in 1990.

High inflation produced efforts to minimize money holdings. Middle-class Brazilians had "overnight" bank accounts with interest rates adjusted daily to keep up with inflation. However, they could not write checks on these accounts. A typical person visited her bank twice a week and waited in long lines to shift funds to her checking account. People tried to carry the minimum amount of cash to finance daily spending—but frequent price changes made it hard to know how much was needed. Bus fares, for example, often rose from one day to the next.

Many people were paid at the beginning of the month. They rushed to grocery stores to buy a month's food before prices rose. Early in the month, the wait in the grocery checkout line was an hour. People bought extra refrigerators to store their food purchases.

Relative prices varied erratically. Brazilian economist Eliana Cardoso has given some colorful examples: "In the last week of December, 1989, a Chevette cost the same as 42 standard-size brassieres, and a refrigerator the same as a linen shirt. The same bottle of wine cost 50 cruzados in one supermarket and 15 cruzados in another." On the bright side, confusion about prices benefited producers of electronic calculators, whose sales doubled from 1988 to 1989.*

As we have discussed, the costs of high inflation are greatest for the poor. In Brazil, the salaries of professional workers were adjusted every month to keep up with inflation. The poor were not protected as well.

Figure 14.6 shows the real minimum wage in Brazil over the 1980s. This wage was reduced by inflation and periodically increased through an increase in the nominal wage. In the early 1980s, the nominal wage was increased twice a year. Workers lost purchasing power between wage adjustments, but it was

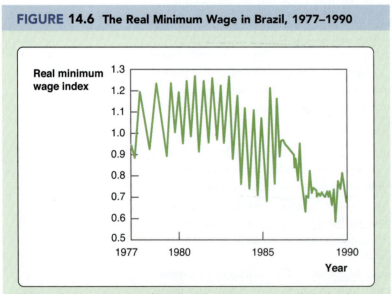

FIGURE 14.6 The Real Minimum Wage in Brazil, 1977–1990

This graph shows an index of Brazil's real minimum wage, with the level in January 1978 defined as 1.0. In the early 1980s, the real wage fluctuated as inflation pushed it down and increases in the nominal wage pushed it back up. In the late 1980s, inflation accelerated and nominal wage adjustments did not keep pace, so the real wage fell.

Source: Adapted from Rudiger Dornbusch et al., "Extreme Inflation: Dynamics and Stabilization," *Brookings Papers on Economic Activity*, 1990: 2, 1–64.

eventually restored. In the late 1980s, however, inflation accelerated and wage adjustments did not keep pace. By 1989, the real minimum wage fell to around 60 percent of its 1980 level.

*The anecdotes in this case study come from Eliana Cardoso, "Brazil: From Inertia to Megainflation," Chapter 5 in Michael Bruno and Stanley Fischer (eds.), *Lessons of Economic Stabilization and Its Aftermath*, MIT Press, 1991; and from personal communication with Cristina Terra, another Brazilian economist.

Moderate Inflation

Inflation causes concern even when it is far below the levels Brazilians experienced. We saw that President Ford declared U.S. inflation "public enemy number one" when it reached 11 percent in 1974. Polls from the 1970s show that the public also viewed inflation as the country's worst problem.

However, most costs we have discussed so far do not appear important for moderate inflation rates—say 10 percent or below. For example, cash loses its value only slowly, so people do not go to much trouble to hold less of it. And U.S. studies find that moderate rises in inflation do *not* raise income inequality.

Some economists conclude that 10-percent inflation is not much of a problem. In this view, public distaste for inflation simply reflects the inflation fallacy. Other economists disagree, suggesting ways that even moderate inflation is harmful. Two costs stand out as possibly most important: increased uncertainty and distortions of the tax system.

Inflation Uncertainty One view is that 10-percent inflation would *not* be a problem if it were steady—if prices rose exactly 10 percent year after year. In practice, however, the inflation rate bounces around. And studies have found that the variability of inflation is higher when its average level is high. In other words, as inflation rises, it becomes less stable. It is harder to predict future inflation.

Uncertainty about inflation creates risk in loan markets. When inflation changes unpredictably, the ex post real interest rate differs from the ex ante rate, as described in the case study on the free silver movement in Section 14.2. Wealth is redistributed between borrowers and lenders.

This redistribution can harm the economy. One cause of the savings and loan crisis of the 1980s was the unexpected rise in inflation in the 1970s, which reduced ex post real interest rates on the mortgages the S&Ls held. Banks' losses in this episode drove many into insolvency, requiring a costly government bailout.

In addition, uncertainty about inflation discourages both borrowers and lenders from entering the loan market. Each group is deterred by the risk of redistributions. The financial system becomes less effective at channeling funds to investors, hurting economic growth.

Inflation and Taxes The final inflation cost we'll discuss involves taxation. When inflation rises, people pay higher taxes on the income they earn from savings.

For example, consider the interest you earn on a bank account. Suppose inflation rises and the nominal interest rate rises by the same amount. Before taxes, the real interest rate is the same as before. (This is the Fisher effect from Section 4.2.) In most countries, however, you pay taxes based on your nominal interest income. This income has risen, so you pay higher taxes on the same real income.

As another example, suppose you purchase a share of stock and sell it for a higher price 5 years later. You pay a capital gains tax on your profit—the difference between the prices when you buy and sell. When inflation occurs, it causes the price of the stock to increase over time, raising the capital gain in nominal terms. Once again, taxes are based on nominal quantities, so you pay more.

Some economists think that taxes on interest and capital gains discourage saving. When inflation raises these taxes, saving falls. The result is lower investment and lower economic growth.

CASE STUDY

The After-Tax Real Interest Rate

Previously, we've measured the return on saving with the real interest rate, defined as the nominal rate minus inflation. This concept ignores taxes. When interest income is taxed, the return on saving is the **after-tax real interest rate**, $\hat{r}$. This variable adjusts for the losses from both inflation and taxes. Examining it will help us understand the effects of inflation on saving.

As usual, let i be the nominal interest rate and π be inflation. The real interest rate ignoring taxes is $r = i - \pi$. Finally, let μ (the Greek letter mu) be the tax rate. Savers pay a fraction μ of their nominal interest income in taxes.

> **After-tax real interest rate ($\hat{r}$)** the interest rate adjusted for both taxes and inflation: $\hat{r} = (1 - \mu)\, r - \mu\pi$

After taxes, savers receive a nominal interest rate of $(1 - \mu)i$. For example, if the pretax nominal rate is 10 percent and μ is 0.3, the after-tax nominal rate is $(0.7)(10\%) = 7\%$. Someone with \$100 in the bank receives nominal interest of \$10, pays \$3 in taxes, and is left with \$7.

To get the after-tax real interest rate, we subtract inflation from the after-tax nominal rate:

$$\hat{r} = (1 - \mu)i - \pi$$

Because $i = r + \pi$, we can rewrite the equation for $\hat{r}$ as

$$\hat{r} = (1 - \mu)(r + \pi) - \pi$$

Then a little algebra gives us

$$\hat{r} = (1 - \mu)r + (1 - \mu)\pi - \pi$$
$$= (1 - \mu)r - \mu\pi \qquad (14.4)$$

Equation (14.4) shows how inflation affects the return on savings. Assume that the Fisher effect holds, so inflation has no effect on r, the pretax real interest rate. With this assumption, a one-point rise in π reduces the after-tax real rate by μ.

This effect can be large. Suppose that r is 4 percent and μ is 0.3. If inflation is zero, then Equation (14.4) implies

$$\hat{r} = (1 - 0.3)(4\%) - (0.3)(0)$$
$$= 2.8\%$$

For the same r and μ, if inflation is 10 percent, then

$$\hat{r} = (1 - 0.3)(4\%) - (0.3)(10\%)$$
$$= -0.2\%$$

In this example, inflation wipes out the real return on savings: the negative $\hat{r}$ means that savers lose slightly more from taxes and inflation than they receive in interest. Inflation substantially reduces the incentive to save.

14.4 DEFLATION AND THE LIQUIDITY TRAP

In the 2000s, inflation has been low in most of the world (see Figure 14.5). In some places, inflation has been so low that economists worry about the opposite problem: deflation.

Japan experienced deflation from 1999 to 2005. Inflation then turned positive for a few years until deflation returned in 2008. The United States flirted with deflation in 2003, when the inflation rate fell to about 1 percent, and again in 2009, when it dipped below zero briefly. As 2011 began, U.S. inflation was running at about 1 percent, but some economists feared that a sustained deflation could be on the horizon.

Why do economists worry about deflation? Why might it occur, and what problems might it cause? Once again, in answering these questions we must distinguish among different times and places.

Money Growth Again

The central point of this chapter is that money growth determines inflation. Historically, this principle has explained negative as well as positive inflation. Deflation arises when money growth is low.

In the United States, low money growth under the gold standard caused deflation—the deflation that spurred the free silver movement of the 1890s. Deflation also occurred from 1930 to 1933, when the money supply fell sharply and inflation averaged −7 percent. The money supply fell because bank panics reduced the money multiplier.

▶ Section 11.3 discusses the behavior of the money supply during the 1930s.

Notice that these examples are not recent. Today, there is little risk of deflation caused by low money growth. Central banks have tools to control the money supply, and they don't want deflation. They are unlikely to let the money supply fall as it did in the 1890s or 1930s. Yet a scenario that can produce deflation still exists.

The Liquidity Trap

Deflation can occur if the economy falls into a **liquidity trap**, a situation in which output is below potential at a nominal interest rate of zero. This *zero-bound problem* eliminates the central bank's usual ability to raise output and inflation. Let's discuss how a liquidity trap might happen.

Liquidity trap situation in which output is below potential at a nominal interest rate of zero (a real interest rate of $-\pi$), eliminating the central bank's usual ability to raise output and inflation; also, *zero-bound problem*

[Handwritten margin notes:]
Central bank sets i which sets r.

The bond pays back less than initial worth

Since i = 0 then r = -π and that is lowest it can go.

Lower Bounds on Interest Rates In the AE/PC model, the central bank influences economic fluctuations by setting a target for the nominal interest rate, which helps determine the real interest rate. The real rate affects output through the AE curve, and output affects inflation through the Phillips curve.

In discussing this mechanism, we have assumed that the central bank can set interest rates at whatever levels it chooses. In fact, there is a limit on the central bank's options: it must set a nominal rate of zero or higher. A negative nominal interest rate is impossible.

It is easy to see why. A negative nominal rate means someone pays $100 for a bond that pays back *less* than $100 in the future. A saver would never buy such a bond, because she can do better holding cash. If she puts a $100 bill in a safe deposit box, it is still worth $100 in the future.

This **zero bound** on the nominal interest rate implies a lower bound on the real rate as well, one that depends on inflation. The real interest rate r is $i - \pi$. Because i cannot fall below zero, the real rate cannot fall below $-\pi$. For example, if π is 2 percent, the real rate can't be less than -2 percent. If π is 3 percent, the real rate can't be less than -3 percent.

This constraint doesn't matter if the central bank wants a real interest rate above the lower bound. This is usually the case. But a problem can arise if an adverse expenditure shock occurs, causing a recession. To end the recession, the central bank must reduce the real interest rate, and the lower bound may get in the way.

> **Zero bound** limit on the nominal interest rate; a central bank cannot reduce i below zero, which limits its ability to stimulate the economy

Figure 14.7 illustrates this point. The economy starts with output at potential, but then a shock pushes the AE curve to the left. To keep output from falling, the central bank would have to reduce the real interest rate to the level labeled $r^{\#}$. But $r^{\#}$ is less than $-\pi$, the lower bound on the real interest rate. The best that policymakers can do is to reduce the real rate to $-\pi$. With that interest rate, output falls to the level labeled Y', which is below potential.

This situation is a liquidity trap. The term was coined by John Maynard Keynes, who first warned of the problem. Keynes argued that the risk of a liquidity trap makes monetary policy an unreliable tool for combating recessions.

FIGURE 14.7 A Liquidity Trap

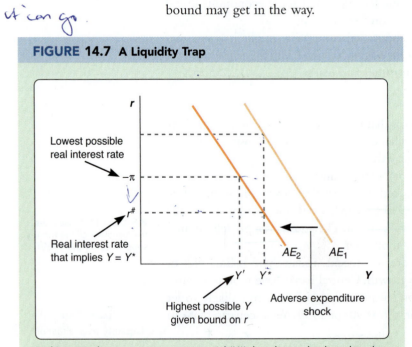

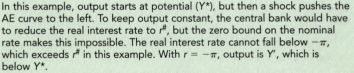

In this example, output starts at potential (Y^*), but then a shock pushes the AE curve to the left. To keep output constant, the central bank would have to reduce the real interest rate to $r^{\#}$, but the zero bound on the nominal rate makes this impossible. The real interest rate cannot fall below $-\pi$, which exceeds $r^{\#}$ in this example. With $r = -\pi$, output is Y', which is below Y^*.

The Role of Deflation We can now see the danger of deflation. The lower bound on the real interest rate is $-\pi$. This bound is negative if $\pi > 0$, but it is positive under deflation. If inflation is -2 percent, for example, the lower bound on the real interest rate is $+2$ percent. A positive bound makes it more likely that the central bank won't be able to push the real rate low enough to end a recession.

Although deflation raises the risk of a liquidity trap, danger also exists if the inflation rate is positive but low. Inflation of $+1$ percent, for example, means the lower bound on the real interest rate is -1 percent. That level is usually low enough to boost output to potential, but it may not be during an unusually deep recession.

If an economy enters a liquidity trap, it can be hard to escape. Indeed, the economy can fall into a vicious circle in which the liquidity trap and deflation reinforce one another. **Figure 14.8** outlines this scenario. In a liquidity trap, a high real interest rate keeps the economy in a recession. The recession reduces inflation through the Phillips curve; even if inflation is positive initially, it may fall below zero. With the nominal interest rate stuck at zero and inflation falling, the real interest rate rises. The higher real interest rate worsens the recession, which pushes inflation down further, and so on. Output and inflation can spiral downward.

The Irrelevance of Money Growth We've seen how an economy can get stuck in deflation. However, this idea may seem inconsistent with the emphasis we placed on the long-run link between inflation and money growth early in this chapter. If inflation is negative, why can't the central bank push it above zero by raising money growth?

The answer is that the normal money growth–inflation relation breaks down in a liquidity trap. Remember Figure 14.4, which shows how money

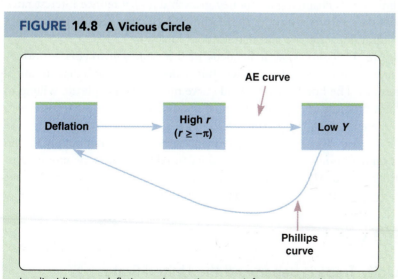

FIGURE 14.8 A Vicious Circle

In a liquidity trap, deflation and recession can reinforce one another. Deflation raises the lower bound on the real interest rate, $-\pi$; a high real interest rate reduces output; and low output causes further deflation.

Know #

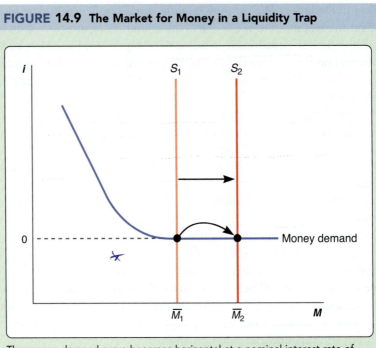

FIGURE 14.9 The Market for Money in a Liquidity Trap

The money demand curve becomes horizontal at a nominal interest rate of zero. In a liquidity trap, money-market equilibrium occurs on the horizontal part of money demand, and an increase in the money supply does not change the interest rate.

↑Md ↓r ↑Y

(↑π

) In liquidity trap.

↑Md ≠ ↓r
(lower bounds)

Hence ↓Y and

↓π

Md/Ms ✗

growth affects the economy. Higher money growth pushes down interest rates, which raises output, which raises inflation. A liquidity trap breaks the first link in this chain: higher money growth does *not* reduce interest rates, because they are already at their lower bounds. Because interest rates do not fall, output does not rise and neither does inflation.

Figure 14.9 shows what happens in the money market. The money demand curve usually slopes down, but it becomes flat at a zero nominal interest rate. The horizontal demand curve means that people are willing to hold any amount of money. The usual reason for holding other assets—to earn interest—disappears if the interest rate is zero.

On the flat part of the money demand curve, the money supply has no effect on the nominal interest rate. If the central bank raises the money supply from $\overline{M}_1$ to $\overline{M}_2$, the equilibrium interest rate remains at zero. We see again that the usual effects of monetary policy disappear.

CASE STUDY

Liquidity Traps in Japan and the United States

Keynes wrote about the liquidity trap in the 1930s, but the idea didn't get much attention for next half-century. Throughout the world, inflation rates were high enough that, through the Fisher effect, nominal interest rates were well above zero. It seemed unlikely that interest rates would ever hit their lower bounds.

Things changed in the 1990s, when inflation reached very low levels in many countries. Nominal interest rates fell far enough that the zero bound became relevant. Japan fell into a liquidity trap in the wake of its financial crisis in the 1990s: the Bank of Japan's interest rate target was near zero from 1999 to 2006. Then the United States fell into a liquidity trap during *its* financial crisis, in 2008, and side effects from the U.S. crisis pushed Japan back into a liquidity trap. Let's discuss the experiences of the two countries.

Japan Hits the Zero Bound As we discuss in Section 13.2, Japan experienced disastrous declines in stock and housing prices in the early 1990s, leading to a credit crunch and a "lost decade" for economic growth. **Figure 14.10A** captures this slump by comparing Japan's output to estimates of its potential output. The estimates are based on the assumptions that actual and potential output were equal in 1990 and that potential has grown 2 percent per year since then.* The difference between the two variables—Japan's output gap—reached 14 percent in 2003.

As predicted by the Phillips curve, Japan's output slump reduced inflation. As shown in **Figure 14.10B**, the inflation rate fell below zero in 1999 and remained negative through 2005: Japan experienced deflation.

For much of this period, the Bank of Japan (BoJ) tried to raise output through countercyclical policy. As shown in **Figure 14.10C**, the BoJ started reducing the interest rate that it targets, the call-money rate, in 1992. However, lower rates did not stimulate spending enough to offset the adverse shocks to the economy. In 1999, the nominal interest rate fell below 1/10 of a percent: for practical purposes, it was zero. At that point, Japan was stuck in a liquidity trap. Output was below potential, but further interest rate cuts were impossible.

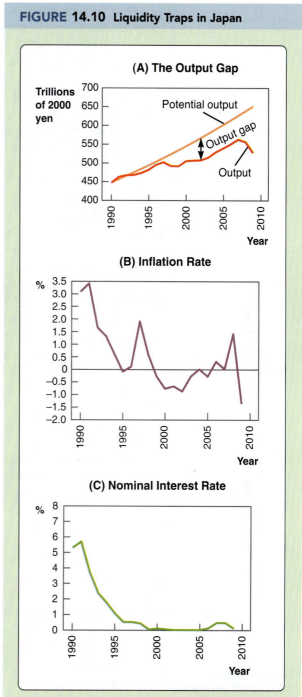

FIGURE 14.10 Liquidity Traps in Japan

(A) The Output Gap

(B) Inflation Rate

(C) Nominal Interest Rate

Japan experienced a deep recession in the 1990s (A), leading to deflation over 1999–2005 (B). The Bank of Japan lowered its interest rate target in response to the recession, but the target rate hit the zero bound in 1999: the economy entered a liquidity trap (C). Signs of recovery prompted the BoJ to raise the interest rate in 2006, but the spreading effects of the U.S. financial crisis pushed Japan back into a liquidity trap in 2009.

Source: International Monetary Fund

With the interest rate at zero, the Bank of Japan performed large, expansionary open-market operations. As a result, M1 in Japan grew by 14 percent in 2001 and by 24 percent in 2002. However, as predicted by our analysis of liquidity traps, rapid money growth did not raise output or inflation.

In 2003, Japan's output gap narrowed somewhat and inflation rose slightly above zero. The Bank of Japan decided the worst was over and raised its interest rate target from 0 to 0.25 percent in 2006, and to 0.50 percent in 2007. With the BoJ choosing positive interest rates, it appeared that the zero bound was becoming irrelevant once again.

The United States Hits the Zero Bound The U.S. financial crisis of 2007–2009 was in many ways a repeat of the Japanese crisis, with falling stock and house prices, losses by financial institutions, and a severe credit crunch. As in Japan, the crisis caused a deep recession: output fell and the unemployment rate more than doubled. The U.S. economy flirted with deflation as the inflation rate dipped to −0.3 percent in 2009 before rising to around 1.0 percent in 2010.

▶ See Figure 12.1 for data on U.S. inflation and unemployment and Figure 11.9 for the path of the Fed's interest rate target.

The parallel between Japan and the United States carries over to monetary policy. The Federal Reserve reduced its target for the federal funds rate from 5.25 percent in August 2007 to a range between 0 and 0.25 percent in December 2008, and the target remained in that range at the start of 2011. Yet, as in Japan, a nominal interest rate near zero was not enough to boost the economy out of its slump.

As 2011 began, great uncertainty about the U.S. economy persisted. Some economists suggested that, with very low interest rates and the financial crisis in the past, the economy would recover before long. Others predicted that, like Japan, the United States would be stuck in a liquidity trap and recession for many years. The most pessimistic worried that the economy could fall into the vicious circle of deflation and falling output depicted in Figure 14.8.

Japan Returns to the Zero Bound The U.S. financial crisis reverberated around the world. One hard-hit country was Japan: as shown in Figure 14.10, its output fell sharply in 2008–2009, widening the output gap, and inflation fell to −1.6 percent in 2009. The reasons included a 47-percent fall in the Nikkei stock index and output declines in industries, such as autos and electronics, that export to the United States.

As Japan's economy faltered again, the Bank of Japan quickly reversed the interest rate increases of 2006–2007. In January 2009, the BoJ reduced the call-money rate to 0.1 percent—once again, zero for practical purposes. Like the United States, Japan entered 2011 in the throes of a liquidity trap and facing an uncertain economic future.

Online Case Study:
An Update on Liquidity Traps in Japan and the United States

---

*A number of economists have argued that these assumptions are reasonable. See, for example, Takeo Hoshi and Anil Kashyap, "Japan's Financial Crisis and Economic Stagnation," *Journal of Economic Perspectives*, 18 (Winter 2004): 3–26.

Any Escaping a Liquidity Trap?

Recent history suggests that an economy in a liquidity trap can remain stuck there for a long time. Is there any way to escape? Some economists think that central banks can stimulate the economy by reducing long-term interest rates or by raising expected inflation. Others think that central banks can do little but that fiscal policy can boost the economy out of a liquidity trap. Let's discuss this controversy.

Reducing Long-Term Interest Rates As we discuss in Section 13.1, a central bank sets a target for a short-term interest rate, but long-term rates have larger effects on aggregate expenditure. In a liquidity trap, the short-term rate is near zero, but longer term rates are often significantly higher. In the United States, for example, the 10-year Treasury bond rate ranged between 2 and 4 percent over the period from December 2008 to September 2010, when the federal funds rate was near zero. With positive long-term rates, policymakers can potentially stimulate the economy by pushing these rates down.

How can policymakers reduce long-term rates? We address this question with the expectations theory of the term structure of interest rates, which is summarized by

▶ See Sections 4.4 and 13.1 for background on the term structure of interest rates.

$$i_n(t) = \frac{1}{n}[i_1(t) + Ei_1(t + 1) + \ldots + Ei_1(t + n - 1)] + \tau_n$$

where $i_n(t)$ is the interest rate on an n-period bond in period t. This equation states that the interest rate on an n-period bond is determined by two factors: the expected (E) path of one-period rates in the future and the term premium τ_n. The central bank can reduce long-term rates by reducing either expected short rates or term premiums. Over 2008–2010, the Federal Reserve tried to do both:

- The Fed sought to influence expected interest rates through announcements. During 2009 and 2010, as the Federal Open Market Committee maintained a target range of 0 to 0.25 percent for the federal funds rate, it repeatedly signaled an intention to keep its target low. A typical announcement occurred on August 10, 2010, when the FOMC said that economic conditions "are likely to warrant exceptionally low levels of the federal funds rate for an extended period." The "extended period" language was meant to drive down expected future interest rates in the equation for long-term rates.

- The Fed sought to influence term premiums by shifting the composition of its open-market operations: it increased its purchases of long-term bonds and bought relatively few short-term bonds. Over the period from March to October 2009, the Fed purchased $300 billion of long-term Treasury bonds. By raising the demand for long-term bonds, the Fed hoped to raise their prices relative to those of short-term bonds and thereby reduce their yields to maturity. If successful, such an action reduces long-term interest rates for a given path of short-term rates; in other words, it reduces term premiums.

Some economists think the Fed's policies helped to reduce long-term interest rates, but the sizes of the effects are unclear. In any case, the Fed's efforts to influence long-term rates were far from enough to end the economy's slump.

Raising Expected Inflation Some economists suggest that a central bank facing a liquidity trap should announce that it plans to increase inflation in the future. These economists have advocated an inflation goal for the Federal Reserve in the neighborhood of 4 percent, significantly above the 2 percent level that prevailed before the financial crisis. If the public believes that the central bank eventually will raise inflation, then expected inflation rises. Even if nominal interest rates are stuck near zero, higher expected inflation reduces the ex ante real interest rate, $i - \pi^e$, which raises aggregate expenditure.

The efficacy of this tactic is unclear, partly because the Federal Reserve has *not* tried it. Chairman Bernanke has argued that seeking to increase the level of inflation would raise uncertainty about inflation, which is costly to the economy (see Section 14.3). In August 2010, Bernanke said that announcing a goal of higher inflation would harm the economy by "undermining confidence and the ability of firms and households to make longer-term plans."

Using Fiscal Policy Keynes, who pointed out the problem of the liquidity trap, also suggested a solution: expansionary fiscal policy. An increase in government spending or a tax cut shifts out the AE curve, raising output at the current real interest rate. If an inward shift of the curve has produced a liquidity trap, as in Figure 14.7, a fiscal expansion can reverse this shift. In addition, if deflation is occurring, fiscal policy can cause an output boom that pushes inflation above zero.

▶The case study in Section 13.4 discusses U.S. fiscal policy during the most recent recession.

A disadvantage of fiscal expansion, however, is that it increases the level of government debt. Because of concerns about debt, Japan's government has resisted calls for a fiscal expansion to boost its economy. In the United States, President Obama and Congress approved a fiscal stimulus package in 2009, but since then concern over debt has stood in the way of another major stimulus.

Summary

- Inflation varies tremendously across countries and time periods. It ranges from negative levels (deflation) to hyperinflation (monthly inflation above 50 percent).

14.1 Money and Inflation in the Long Run

- The velocity of money is the ratio of nominal GDP to the money supply. It measures how quickly money circulates through the economy. Factors that raise money demand also reduce velocity.

- The quantity equation of money is $MV = PY$: the money supply times velocity equals nominal GDP.

- Long-run inflation is determined by the growth rates of the money supply, velocity, and real output. The central bank can raise or lower inflation by changing money growth.

- Empirically, there is a close relation between money growth and inflation across countries and across decades within a country. However, this relation does not explain short-run, year-to-year inflation movements.

- Money growth influences inflation through a chain of effects: higher money growth reduces interest rates, which raises output, which raises inflation.

14.2 What Determines Money Growth?

- When money is backed by a commodity, money growth and inflation are determined by how much of the commodity is produced.

- Under the gold standard in the United States, low gold production led to deflation in the late nineteenth century. The adverse effects on debtors spurred a campaign for bimetallism, a system in which money is backed by gold and silver. Bimetallism was not adopted, but increased gold production eventually ended deflation.

- With fiat money, central banks choose the growth rate of the money supply. Often they choose low money growth to keep inflation low.

- Sometimes central banks allow money growth and inflation to rise to avoid a fall in output. For example, U.S. inflation rose in the 1970s because the Fed accommodated adverse supply shocks, and it stayed high because the Fed was unwilling to pay the costs of disinflation.

- The underlying cause of very high inflation is government budget deficits. If governments cannot borrow, they finance deficits with seigniorage revenue—by printing money. The money supply rises rapidly, fueling inflation. The most famous example is the German hyperinflation of 1923. Zimbabwe's is the first hyperinflation of the 2000s.

- Today, inflation is low in most of the world. It fell in developed countries in the 1980s as policymakers decided to pay the output costs of disinflation. It fell in developing countries in the 1990s as conservative governments cut budget deficits.

14.3 The Costs of Inflation

- Many people believe that inflation erodes living standards, but this view is fallacious. A rise in inflation causes a parallel rise in nominal wage growth, so real wages are not affected.

- Very high inflation causes inconvenience as people hold less money (shoe leather costs), distracts firms from their business, causes variability in relative prices, and worsens income inequality.

- The costs of moderate inflation are unclear. Possible costs include effects of inflation uncertainty and distortions of the tax system. Inflation reduces the after-tax real interest rate, which may discourage saving.

14.4 Deflation and the Liquidity Trap

- In the past, deflations have been caused by low money growth, as in the United States in the 1890s and 1930s.

- A liquidity trap means that output is below potential when the nominal interest rate is at its zero bound. The central bank loses its usual ability to end a recession, because a rise in money growth doesn't affect interest rates.

- Deflation increases the risk of a liquidity trap. An economy can fall into a vicious circle of recession, deflation, and high real interest rates.

- Japan experienced a liquidity trap in the early 2000s. During its most recent financial crisis, the United States fell into a liquidity trap late in 2008. Spreading effects of the U.S. crisis then tipped the Japanese economy back into a liquidity trap.

- Economists disagree on what strategies—if any—the central bank can use to escape a liquidity trap. They debate policies aimed at reducing long-term interest rates and raising expected inflation. Expansionary fiscal policy can boost an economy out of a liquidity trap but has the drawback of increasing government debt.

Key Terms

Questions and Problems

1. Suppose that country A and country B have the same rate of money growth and velocity is constant in both. Output growth is higher in country A. Which country has higher inflation? Explain.

2. In Figure 14.1, the relation between money growth and inflation is less perfect among countries with inflation below 10 percent than it is among countries with higher inflation. What might explain this difference?

3. Should the United States return to the gold standard? What might be the advantages and disadvantages?

4. [Advanced] Assume that a central bank's nominal seigniorage revenue equals the change in the money supply, denoted ΔM. Real seigniorage revenue is $\Delta M/P$. Assume the inflation rate equals the growth rate of the money supply, which is $\Delta M/M$.

   a. What is the rationale for these assumptions? Are they realistic?

   b. Write real seigniorage revenue in terms of the inflation rate and the real money supply, M/P.

   c. When inflation rises, what happens to the real money supply and to seigniorage revenue? (*Hint*: In equilibrium, money supply must equal money demand.)

   d. Sometimes a small increase in the government budget deficit produces a large increase in inflation. Explain this fact using the answer to part (c).

5. Suppose all firms in an economy adjust prices once per year. Half the firms adjust prices in January, and the other half adjusts in July. Suppose inflation rises from zero to 10 percent per year. What is the likely effect on the variability of relative prices? Explain.

6. Consider the market for loanable funds, which determines the real interest rate in the long run (see Section 4.1).

   a. As usual, draw the supply and demand for loans as functions of the *pretax* real interest rate, r.

   b. Suppose savers are taxed on their nominal interest income. If inflation rises, what happens to the supply and demand curves in part (a)?

   c. What happens to the equilibrium levels of the pretax real interest rate, loans, and investment?

7. Suppose the pretax real interest rate (r) is 2 percent, the tax rate (μ) is 0.4, and the inflation rate (π) is 8 percent. Calculate the after-tax real interest rate ($\hat{r}$).

8. What inflation rate would make the after-tax real interest rate equal the pretax real rate (that is, what inflation rate implies $\hat{r} = r$)? Explain.

9. Explain the difference between deflation and disinflation.

10. "Inflation is always and everywhere a monetary phenomenon, but deflation is not." Comment.

11. How does each of the following events affect the risk of a liquidity trap?

    a. The central bank decides to push long-run inflation to zero.

    b. The neutral real interest rate rises (see Section 12.5 for a review of the neutral rate).

    c. The government introduces a tax on people's holdings of currency. Other assets are not taxed.

▶ Online and Data Questions

www.worthpublishers.com/ball

12. From the text Web site, connect to the St. Louis Fed site for data on (1) nominal GDP and (2) interest rates on 3-month Treasury bills. Link to sweepmeasures.com for data on

M1 adjusted for sweep accounts (use the series labeled M1RS).

a. Using these data, compute the velocity of money for each year from 1980 to the present. Make a graph showing velocity and the T-bill rate over time.

b. Does velocity fluctuate from year to year? What might explain these movements?

c. What is the long-run trend in velocity? What might explain this trend?

13. Link from the text Web site to the site of the International Labour Organization, whose LABORSTA database reports consumer price indexes for most of the world's countries. For a recent year, identify the country with the highest inflation rate (that is, the largest percentage change in its price index). Do some research and explain why inflation is high in that country.

14. [Advanced] From the St. Louis Fed Web site, get annual data on U.S. inflation from 1960 to the present.

a. For each decade from the 1960s through the 2000s, calculate the mean and variance of inflation over the decade. For example, calculate the mean and variance for the 10 years from 1960 through 1969.

b. Make a graph that plots the mean of inflation against the variance, with a point for each decade. What is the relation between the two variables?

c. What might explain the relation found in part (b)?

Policies for Economic Stability

Martin Sundberg/Gettty Images

These sailors are leaning against the wind. We'll see the relevance to monetary policy in Section 15.3.

Suppose you do very well in your money and banking course. You embark on a brilliant career as an economist or banker. Eventually, you are appointed chair of the board of governors of the Federal Reserve System. In this job, you run the monetary policy of the United States. What should you do?

The U.S. Congress has provided some guidance. Congress created the Federal Reserve in 1913. It prescribed goals for the Fed in the Employment Act of 1946 and the Humphrey-Hawkins Act of 1978. On its Web site, the Fed summarizes these goals as "maximum sustainable output growth," "maximum employment," "stable prices," and "moderate long-term interest rates."[1]

Unfortunately, these goals are vague. As the new Fed chair, you may have some questions. What exactly do the goals mean—for example, what is the "maximum" level of employment? Can the Fed really achieve all the goals? How? What if one goal conflicts with another?

[1]See *The Federal Reserve System: Purposes and Functions*, Chapter 2, www.federalreserve.gov.

Part V of this book—the last four chapters—surveys current thinking about monetary policy. We discuss the goals of the Fed and other central banks, their strategies for pursuing these goals, and the challenges they face.

This chapter discusses two basic tasks of a central bank. The first is to choose the long-run level of inflation. The central bank controls this variable because it controls the money supply. We discuss the question of what long-run inflation rate is best.

The central bank's second task is to stabilize the economy. Expenditure and supply shocks cause output and inflation to fluctuate around their long-run levels. Central banks can dampen these movements with the right policies—or exacerbate them with policy mistakes. We discuss the pros and cons of alternative stabilization policies.

We've seen that most central banks target a short-term interest rate. In this regime, stabilization policy takes the form of interest rate adjustments. We discuss theories of how central banks should move their targets in response to economic developments. We also discuss practical aspects of U.S. policy—how people at the Fed analyze the economy and choose targets for the federal funds rate. One lesson is that interest rate policy during a financial crisis differs from policy during normal economic times.

▶ Section 14.1 explains how the growth rate of the money supply determines the long-run inflation rate. Sections 12.2–12.4 describe how expenditure and supply shocks cause economic fluctuations.

15.1 CHOOSING THE LONG-RUN INFLATION RATE

Economic shocks cause short-run movements in the inflation rate that central banks cannot eliminate. But central banks control long-run inflation—the average level around which inflation fluctuates. What long-run inflation rate should policymakers choose?

Congress has told the Federal Reserve to seek "stable prices." In response, the Fed has kept inflation low in recent decades, as have central banks in most other countries. The Fed's mandate also includes "moderate long-term interest rates," which means nominal rates that are not too high. However, this goal is not really separate from the goal of stable prices.

▶ Section 4.1 introduces the Fisher equation.

The Fisher equation says that the nominal interest rate is the real rate plus expected inflation: $i = r + \pi^e$. The Fed doesn't influence the real rate in the long run, but it does influence expected inflation. If it consistently keeps actual inflation low, then expected inflation will also be low, holding down the nominal interest rate. If the Fed produces "stable prices," it produces moderate interest rates as well.

The precise meaning of "stable prices" is debatable. Some economists define this term as the complete absence of inflation. They argue that the long-run inflation rate should be zero. Others believe that a low but positive rate—say, 2 percent—also constitutes price stability or is close enough to be acceptable. Indeed, they believe that a modest amount of inflation is good for the economy. Let's discuss these two points of view.

The Case for Zero Inflation

The case for zero inflation is simple. Inflation has harmful effects on the economy. For example, it causes variability in relative prices, and its interaction with the tax system discourages saving. The lower the inflation rate, the smaller these distortions. They are minimized if inflation is pushed all the way to zero.

▶ Section 14.3 surveys the costs of inflation.

Some studies support this argument. A well-known example is a 1997 paper by Martin Feldstein, a Harvard professor and longtime president of the National Bureau of Economic Research (NBER). Feldstein argued that the Fed should reduce inflation from 2 percent, its level in 1997, to zero. He reasoned that this action would reduce tax distortions, leading to higher saving and economic growth. Specifically, Feldstein estimated that reducing inflation to zero would permanently increase output by 1 percent, a substantial benefit.[2]

▶ As we discuss in the case study in Section 12.1, NBER's activities include deciding when recessions officially begin and end.

The Case for Positive Inflation

Why might a positive inflation rate be better than zero? Economists have suggested several reasons. We'll focus on two influential arguments involving the costs of disinflation and the risk of liquidity traps.

Costs of Disinflation The first argument favoring positive inflation rests on the transitional costs of reducing it. If the inflation rate is currently positive, pushing it to zero requires a tightening of monetary policy. The central bank must push up the real interest rate temporarily, reducing output and raising unemployment.

▶ Section 12.4 examines the costs of reducing inflation in the AE/PC model and gives examples from U.S. history.

If inflation is high, most economists think it's worth paying the price to reduce it. But once inflation reaches a low level—say, 2 or 3 percent—then it may cause only small economic distortions. Unlike Martin Feldstein, many economists think that a small amount of inflation is a nuisance, not a major economic problem. In this view, the central bank should live with a little inflation indefinitely rather than slow the economy to eliminate it.

Avoiding Liquidity Traps Section 14.4 discusses the liquidity trap, in which the nominal interest rate hits its lower bound of zero. In this situation, the central bank loses its usual ability to stimulate the economy. Another argument for positive inflation is that it reduces the risk of a liquidity trap.

Gives room for r to fall

This point follows from our earlier discussion of the liquidity trap. The real interest rate is the nominal rate minus inflation: $r = i - \pi$. Because i cannot fall below zero, r cannot fall below $-\pi$. The bound on r is zero if inflation is zero, but it is negative if inflation is positive. If $\pi = 2\%$, for example, then r can fall as low as -2%.

---

[2]See Martin Feldstein, "The Costs and Benefits of Going from Low Inflation to Price Stability," Chapter 3 in C. Romer and D. Romer (Eds.), *Reducing Inflation: Motivation and Strategy*, University of Chicago Press, 1997.

Because of this effect, a positive inflation rate increases the central bank's leeway for stabilizing the economy. If necessary, the central bank can push the real interest rate below zero to stimulate spending. Inflation reduces the risk that a desired policy will be impossible.

How much inflation is necessary to avoid liquidity traps? In the early 2000s, Federal Reserve economists analyzed this issue and concluded that, based on the shocks that typically hit the U.S. economy, an inflation rate of 2 percent was high enough to make a liquidity trap unlikely. Recent history has cast doubt on that conclusion: U.S. inflation was about 2 percent over 2006–2008, yet the economy fell into a liquidity trap during the financial crisis, when the federal funds rate approached zero in December 2008.

This experience has led some economists to advocate higher inflation to guard against future liquidity traps. In February 2010, for example, Olivier Blanchard, chief economist of the International Monetary Fund, suggested that central banks might aim for an inflation rate of 4 percent.[3]

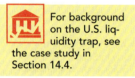 For background on the U.S. liquidity trap, see the case study in Section 14.4.

Current Practice

It is hard to know what long-run inflation rate is best. Nonetheless, central banks must make a choice. What do they do?

Explicit inflation target a rate or range that a central bank announces as its long-run goal for inflation

Many central banks state an **explicit inflation target**. They publicly announce that they aim for a specific inflation rate or range. The Bank of England, for example, has an inflation target of 2 percent. The Bank of Canada targets a range from 1 to 3 percent. The European Central Bank has a somewhat vaguer target of "below, but close to, 2 [percent]." **Table 15.1** gives examples of some central banks' inflation targets as of 2010.

As the table illustrates, most central banks have chosen positive inflation rates, with many targets near 2 percent. There appears to be an international consensus that inflation should be around this level. Nobody has scientifically derived the ideal inflation rate, but 2 percent is the best guess among today's central bankers. They evidently reject the argument that inflation should be zero but also the argument that it should be as high as 4 percent to avoid liquidity traps.

TABLE 15.1 Inflation Targets (as of 2010)

Country	Target (%)
Australia	2.0–3.0
Canada	1.0–3.0
Euro Area	"Below, but close to, 2%"
New Zealand	1.0–3.0
Norway	2.5
Sweden	2.0
Switzerland	"Less than 2%"
United Kingdom	2.0
United States	1.0–2.0 (?)

Implicit inflation target an inflation level that policymakers seek without a formal announcement

The Federal Reserve has not announced an explicit inflation target. However, many observers believe the Fed has an **implicit inflation target** of about 1–2 percent (noted by the entry with a question mark in Table 15.1). Policymakers aim for inflation in this range even though they have not announced this goal formally.

---

[3]Federal Reserve research on the danger of liquidity traps includes John Williams and David Reischneider, "Three Lessons for Monetary Policy in a Low-Inflation Era," *Journal of Money, Credit, and Banking* 32 (2000), pp. 936–966. Olivier Blanchard's comments appear in "Rethinking Macroeconomic Policy," *IMF Staff Position Note*, SPN 10/03, February 2010.

Evidence for this implicit target includes statements by individual Fed officials and by the Federal Open Market Committee (FOMC). Ben Bernanke gave several speeches between 2003 and 2005—when he was a member of the board of governors but not yet chair—in which he said his personal "comfort zone" for inflation was 1–2 percent. When inflation dropped below 1 percent in 2003, the FOMC said the fall was "unwelcome" and eased policy to raise inflation. On the other hand, Fed officials have declared that the 4-percent inflation rate suggested by Olivier Blanchard is too high.

15.2 INFLATION AND OUTPUT STABILITY

As Fed chair, you have chosen an inflation target, whether explicit or implicit. Let's say the target is 2 percent. If inflation has risen higher than 2 percent, then you have temporarily raised the real interest rate to disinflate. Now the economy is in long-run equilibrium with 2-percent inflation. Output is at potential, and the real interest rate is at its neutral level.

Unfortunately, your work is far from done. The economy will not stay tranquilly in long-run equilibrium. It will be buffeted by expenditure and supply shocks—changes in fiscal policy, consumer confidence, oil prices, and so on—causing short-run fluctuations in output and inflation. As Fed chair, you can't eliminate these fluctuations completely. But part of your job is to dampen them as much as possible, keeping output and inflation close to their long-run levels.

The rest of this chapter discusses central banks' methods for stabilizing output and inflation. Let's first look more closely at why economic stability is desirable.

Inflation Stability

Inflation has numerous different costs. Some depend on the long-run level of inflation, but others depend on inflation variability. When the long-run inflation rate is 2 percent, for example, the resulting distortions are minimized if inflation stays close to that level in the short run. The economy suffers more if inflation bounces much above and below 2 percent from year to year.

Why is unstable inflation costly? One reason, discussed in Section 14.3, is the effect on loan markets. Variability in inflation causes variability in ex post real interest rates, which increases risk for both borrowers and lenders. Greater risk reduces the level of lending, depressing investment and economic growth.

Unstable inflation also exacerbates the problem of relative price variability. If inflation is steady, firms adjust prices periodically to keep up with it, and different prices tend to stay in line with one another. If inflation is unpredictable, by contrast, firms are likely to make different guesses about appropriate price adjustments. Some firms raise prices more quickly than others, causing inefficient movements in relative prices.

▶Central bankers use the term *target* in different ways. Most target a short-term interest rate in the sense that this variable is their policy *instrument*: they control it and adjust it to influence the economy. An inflation target, by contrast, is a long-run *goal* of policy. Many central banks are both interest rate targeters (an interest rate is their policy instrument) and inflation targeters (they seek a specific inflation rate in the long run). See Chapter 16.

▶We can express these ideas with terms you may know from statistics. The long-run level of inflation is the *mean* of the inflation rate. Fluctuations around the long-run level determine the *variance* of the inflation rate. Some costs of inflation depend on the mean and some on the variance.

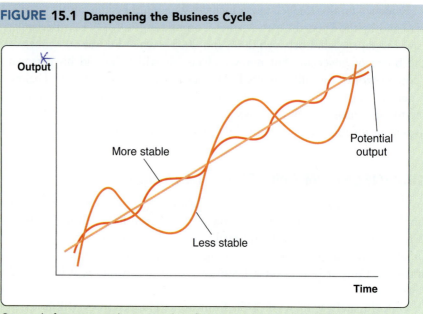

One goal of monetary policy is to reduce fluctuations in aggregate output, keeping it close to potential output.

[Handwritten note in left margin: "In the long run MP doesn't affect Y_g + U"]

Output Stability

Congress tells the Fed to seek "maximum sustainable output growth" and "maximum employment." The Fed's ability to influence output and employment is limited: according to the principle of long-run neutrality, monetary policy does not affect these variables in the long run. Policy *does*, however, affect short-run movements in output and employment. Central banks try to minimize the year-to-year fluctuations of these variables around their long-run levels. In other words, central banks try to dampen the business cycle.

Figure 15.1 illustrates this idea. It shows the path of an economy's output when the central bank does and does not succeed in stabilizing output. Note that potential output, which determines output in the long run, follows the same path in both cases. Potential output is not affected by monetary policy. The difference between the two scenarios is that successful policy keeps output closer to potential.

▶ Section 12.5 discusses the principle of long-run monetary neutrality.

Central banks want to stabilize unemployment as well as output. But recall Okun's law: output and unemployment move together closely over the business cycle. Reducing fluctuations in output automatically reduces fluctuations in unemployment. So the two goals are really the same, just as the goals of price stability and moderate interest rates are the same.

[Handwritten note in left margin: "Okun's law affect 1)Y 2)U move closely together"]

Balancing the Goals

Central banks want to stabilize both output and inflation. Sometimes the right policies can achieve both goals, but sometimes the goals conflict. As we'll see, a policy that stabilizes output can destabilize inflation and vice versa. In such situations, the central bank must decide which type of stability is more important.

This is another unresolved question. Economists don't understand the effects of inflation very well, so we don't know how important it is to stabilize inflation. The benefits of output stability are also unclear, as the next case study relates.

How Costly Is the Business Cycle?

Stabilizing output means reducing the size of the business cycle. Is this desirable? At first glance, the answer might seem obvious. The business cycle includes recessions when output falls and unemployment rises. Recessions create hardships for people who find themselves with lower incomes or even without jobs. Clearly, it is desirable to reduce the size of recessions.

However, the business cycle includes economic booms as well as recessions. Both are dampened if the business cycle is reduced. This is shown in Figure 15.1: with greater stability, output falls less in recessions and rises less in booms. By Okun's law, unemployment rises less in recessions and falls less in booms. It is not clear that there are large overall benefits from output stability.

In 1987, Robert Lucas of the University of Chicago—winner of the 1995 Nobel Prize in Economics and, since the death of Milton Friedman in 2007, arguably the most influential living macroeconomist—published a provocative paper arguing that the business cycle is *not* costly. Lucas pointed out that aggregate output and consumption fall by only a few percentage points in a typical recession, with offsetting increases during booms. Based on microeconomic theories of consumption, he argued that people do not suffer significantly from these fluctuations.

Lucas estimated that eliminating the business cycle completely—making actual output equal potential output at all times—would raise economic welfare by the same amount as permanently increasing output by 0.05 percent. This benefit is very small: compare it to Feldstein's estimate that a modest disinflation would raise output by a full 1.00 percent. Since Lucas wrote, many economists have disputed his conclusion, making two broad arguments.

Lucas's critics point out, first, that he examined fluctuations in *aggregate* variables over the business cycle. These fluctuations are modest, but the cycle has much larger effects on some *individuals*. If a person becomes unemployed, for example, his income and consumption can fall sharply. Accounting for this fact produces higher estimates of the cost of business cycles.

The other criticism of Lucas's calculation is that it assumes business cycles are symmetric: losses in output and employment during recessions are balanced by gains during booms. Some economists believe that the losses exceed the gains. This asymmetry implies that, on average, the business cycle reduces output and employment, which has substantial costs.

The asymmetry argument has been bolstered by the recession that started in 2007, which raised the unemployment rate by about 5 percentage points, from 5 percent to 10 percent. No economic boom could reduce unemployment from 5 percent to 0 percent, because the turnover of workers always causes some unemployment.

The costs of business cycles remain controversial. Economists do not have precise measures of how cycles affect individuals or of their asymmetries. In the end, the costs of business cycles are like the costs of inflation: many economists think they are large, but they are difficult to quantify.[*]

[*] For an in-depth discussion of the costs of business cycles, see Chapter 10 of David Romer, *Advanced Macroeconomics* (4th ed.), McGraw Hill, 2011.

15.3 THE TAYLOR RULE

Now that we've discussed the policy goals of output and inflation stability, let's see how central banks try to achieve them. Most central banks use a short-term interest rate as their policy instrument. As a result, stabilization policy takes the form of interest rate adjustments. Central banks must decide when to raise or lower interest rates and by how much.

Martin's Metaphor

When shocks push output and inflation away from their long-run levels, the central bank seeks to push them back by adjusting the real interest rate. In a recession, for example, the central bank cuts the interest rate to increase output. If inflation rises, the central bank raises the interest rate to slow the economy and push inflation down.

This is an old idea. In the 1950s, Federal Reserve Chair William McChesney Martin expressed it with a metaphor based on sailing. He said the Fed's job is to "lean against the wind"—where "wind" means movements in inflation and output.

Martin's metaphor captures the basic idea of stabilization policy, but it does not yield very precise instructions for central banks. When exactly should they lean against the wind, and how hard should they lean? In other words, what interest rate should they set in various circumstances? Economists have long debated these questions.

Taylor's Formula

A breakthrough in analyzing stabilization policy came in a 1993 paper by John Taylor of Stanford University. Much current thinking about stabilization is based on the **Taylor rule** proposed in that paper. Taylor's insight was to express the idea of leaning against the wind in a simple equation. The equation gives a precise rule, or formula, for setting the interest rate:[4]

Taylor rule formula for adjusting the interest rate to stabilize the economy: $r = r^n + a_y \tilde{Y} + a_\pi(\pi - \pi^T)$

THE TAYLOR RULE

$$r = r^n + a_y \tilde{Y} + a_\pi(\pi - \pi^T) \tag{15.1}$$

[4] See John Taylor, "Policy Rules in Practice," *Carnegie-Rochester Conference Series on Public Policy,* December 1993.

[handwritten at top: r = ex ante interest rate. r^n = neutral. $\tilde{Y}$ = output gap = $(Y - {}^*Y)/y^*$. π^T = long run inflation target.]

In this equation, r is the ex ante real interest rate, $i - \pi^e$. In the short run, the central bank's control of the nominal interest rate allows it to control this real rate as well. Under the Taylor rule, the central bank sets r based on the following factors. *[handwritten: r^n]*

- The neutral real interest rate, r^n: this term is the interest rate that makes output (Y) equal potential output (Y^*).

- The output gap, $\tilde{Y}$: this variable is the percentage deviation of output from potential, $\tilde{Y} = (Y - Y^*)/Y^*$.

- The *inflation gap*, $\pi - \pi^T$: the term π^T is the central bank's long-run inflation target—either explicit or implicit. The inflation gap is the current deviation of inflation from the target. *[handwritten: π]*

- The coefficients a_y and a_π: these terms are positive constants that measure how strongly the interest rate responds to the output and inflation gaps, respectively. If $a_y = 0.5$, for example, then a one-percentage point rise in the output gap raises the interest rate by one-half a percentage point.

[handwritten right margin: a_y , a_π]

To understand the Taylor rule, suppose first that the economy is in long-run equilibrium. The output gap is zero and inflation is at its target: $\pi = \pi^T$. In this situation, the last two terms in the rule are zero, so the rule says $r = r^n$. The central bank sets the interest rate to the neutral level to maintain the status quo.

Now suppose that output changes. If the output gap rises above zero—there is an economic boom—the Taylor rule says to raise the interest rate above r^n. If the output gap is negative, then the rule says to reduce the interest rate. In each case, the central bank leans against the wind.

The Taylor rule also prescribes interest rate adjustments when the inflation rate departs from its long-run level. Once again, the central bank leans against the wind, raising the real interest rate when inflation rises and reducing it when inflation falls.

[handwritten right margin: rate, ① $\tilde{Y} > 0 \Rightarrow$ Boom. $\therefore r > r^n$. ② $\tilde{Y} < 0 \Rightarrow$ Recession. $\therefore r < r^n$.]

[handwritten: with the wind ① / against the wind ②.]

Applying the Rule

To use the Taylor rule, we must assign numbers to some of its terms. Let's assume the central bank's inflation target, π^T, is 2.0 percent. The neutral real interest rate, r^n, is 1.8 percent. These numbers are reasonable estimates for the United States in recent years.

For the coefficients in the Taylor rule, assume $a_y = 1.0$ and $a_\pi = 0.5$. We will see that these numbers fit the behavior of the Fed before the financial crisis of 2007–2009. With our assumptions, the Taylor rule [Equation (15.1)] becomes

$$r = 1.8 + 1.0\tilde{Y} + 0.5(\pi - 2.0) \qquad (15.2)$$

Equation (15.2) prescribes a real interest rate for any state of the economy. For example, suppose the output gap is 1.0 percent and the inflation rate is 3.0 percent. Then the equation says

$$r = 1.8 + 1.0(1.0) + 0.5(3.0 - 2.0) = 3.3$$

▶ We can also define the Taylor rule with a formula for the nominal interest rate. Substituting the definition of r, $i - \pi^e$, into Equation (15.1) leads to $i = \pi^e + r^n + a_y\tilde{Y} + a_\pi(\pi - \pi^T)$. This new equation and (15.1) are two ways of expressing the same policy.

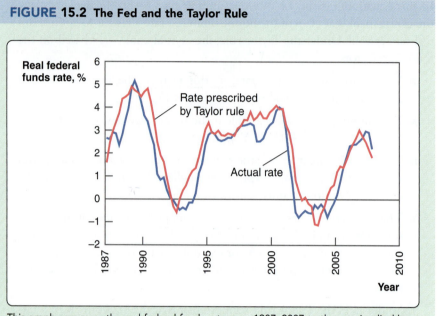

FIGURE 15.2 The Fed and the Taylor Rule

This graph compares the real federal funds rate over 1987–2007 to the rate implied by the Taylor rule in Equation (15.2). The Taylor rule approximates how the Fed sets interest rates fairly well.

Sources: Federal Reserve Bank of St. Louis and author's calculations

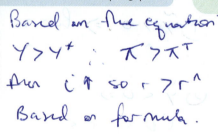

Visit the text Web site for details on the measurement of the real interest rate, inflation, and the output gap.

Based on the equation $Y > Y^*$: $\pi > \pi^T$ then $i \uparrow$ so $r > r^\wedge$ Based on formula.

In this example, output is above potential and inflation is above its target. To slow the economy, the central bank chooses a real interest rate of 3.3 percent, which is higher than the neutral rate.

The Rule in Action

The Taylor rule is not just a theoretical idea about monetary policy. It has become famous because it appears to capture the actual behavior of the Federal Reserve over a long period. From 1987, when Alan Greenspan became Fed chair, to the middle of 2007, the interest rates chosen by the Fed were usually close to the rates prescribed by the Taylor rule.

Figure 15.2 demonstrates this point. For 1987 to mid-2007, the figure shows the real interest rates implied by the Taylor rule. The calculations assume the specific version of the rule in Equation (15.2), with coefficients of $a_y = 1.0$ and $a_\pi = 0.5$. The figure also shows the actual path of the real federal funds rate chosen by the FOMC. The two series move together fairly closely, suggesting that the Taylor rule is a good summary of Fed policy.

As we discuss in Section 15.7, however, the Fed deviated from the Taylor rule starting in the fall of 2007, first as it cut interest rates in response to the financial crisis and then when it hit the zero bound on nominal rates during the recession that followed. Many economists expect that the Taylor rule will capture policy again when the effects of the latest crisis recede and the economy returns to normal.

To be clear, the FOMC has never consciously followed the Taylor rule. It does not use any simple formula to choose interest rates. Instead, as we discuss in Section 15.6, policymaking is a complicated process in which Fed economists analyze hundreds of variables. Nonetheless, this process often produces interest rates that are close to those implied by the Taylor rule. The rule seems to capture important factors behind policy choices.

Since Taylor's article, economists have applied his idea to many countries. Some version of the Taylor rule fits the behavior of many central banks for roughly the same two-decade period as for the Fed. However, the coefficients in the rule, a_y and a_π, differ across countries.

15.4 THE TAYLOR RULE IN THE AE/PC MODEL

We've seen that the Taylor rule captures much of the behavior of monetary policy in the United States and elsewhere. We've also discussed the basic rationale for the rule: by leaning against the wind, monetary policy stabilizes output and inflation. We can explore the Taylor rule in more depth using the AE/PC model of economic fluctuations. The model shows how the Taylor rule stabilizes the economy when expenditure and supply shocks occur. It also shows how the choices of a_y and a_π, the coefficients in the rule, affect the economy.

The online appendix to this chapter analyzes the Taylor rule in the AE/PC model. This analysis uses a version of the model with time lags, which captures the fact that central banks can't shift output or inflation immediately. Here we summarize some results of the analysis.

> If you are interested in the precise assumptions and math behind the results of the Taylor rule–AE/PC analysis, consult the Chapter 15 online appendix at the text Web site.

An Example

Initially we examine one specific version of the Taylor rule, labeled TR-I in **Table 15.2**. We assume that the neutral real interest rate is 2.5 percent and the inflation target is 2.0 percent. The coefficients on output and inflation, a_y and a_π, are both 1.0.

To illustrate the workings of TR-I, **Figure 15.3** shows how monetary policy and the economy respond to a supply shock. Suppose that in 2019 the economy is in long-run equilibrium: the output gap is zero (Figure 15.3A) and the inflation rate equals the target of 2 percent (Figure 15.3B). In 2020, an adverse supply shock occurs. This shock causes inflation to jump from 2 percent to 4 percent.

Because the inflation rate rises in 2020, the Taylor rule prescribes an increase in the real interest rate. In TR-I, the coefficient a_π is 1.0, so the two-point rise in inflation implies an interest rate increase of two points. The central bank raises the interest rate from 2.5 percent, the neutral level, to 4.5 percent (Figure 15.3C).

Because of time lags, the interest rate increase in 2020 does not affect output or inflation in that year. However, through the AE curve, the high interest rate in 2020 reduces output in 2021. Through the Phillips curve, low

$$r = r^\wedge + a_y(\tilde{y}) + a_\pi(\bar{\pi} - \bar{\pi}^*)$$

TABLE 15.2 Two Possible Taylor Rules

TR I (more aggressive)
$r = 2.5 + 1.0\tilde{Y} + 1.0\,(\pi - 2.0)$
TR II (less aggressive)
$r = 2.5 + 0.5\tilde{Y} + 0.5\,(\pi - 2.0)$

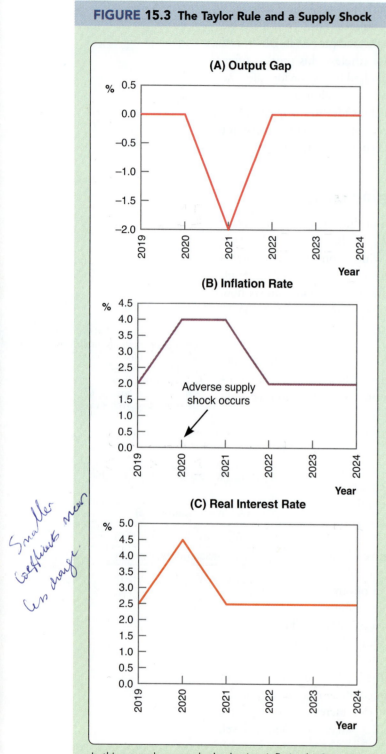

FIGURE 15.3 The Taylor Rule and a Supply Shock

(A) Output Gap

(B) Inflation Rate

Adverse supply
shock occurs

(C) Real Interest Rate

In this example, a supply shock raises inflation by 2 percentage points in 2020. The central bank follows Taylor rule TR-I in Table 15.2, which guides the economy back to long-run equilibrium in 2022.

output reduces inflation in 2022. At that point, inflation is back to the 2-percent target and the output gap is zero. This example illustrates a general point: *when a shock pushes the economy away from long-run equilibrium, the Taylor rule guides it back.*

In this example, the interest rate increase lasts for only one year: r rises in 2020 but returns to r^n in 2021. To understand why, notice that output is below potential in 2021, which reduces r in the Taylor rule. But inflation is still above target in 2021, which increases r. The two effects cancel, implying $r = r^n$. In 2022, r stays at r^n because the economy is back in long-run equilibrium.

Choosing the Coefficients

The effects of the Taylor rule depend on the coefficients a_y and a_π—on how strongly policy leans against the wind. Economists debate which coefficients are best. To see some of the issues involved, let's compare the two Taylor rules in Table 15.2. We assumed TR–I in our previous example. The other rule, TR–II, has smaller coefficients: both a_y and a_π are 0.5 rather than 1.0. Smaller coefficients mean that r changes by less for given movements in output and inflation. The central bank responds less aggressively to economic fluctuations with TR–II than with TR–I.

In comparing the two rules, we examine the same shock as before: in 2020, an adverse supply shock raises inflation from 2 percent to 4 percent. **Figure 15.4** shows the economy's path with TR–II and compares it to the path with TR–I, which we saw previously in Figure 15.3.

Like TR–I, TR–II returns the economy to long-run equilibrium, but the process is more gradual. When inflation rises in 2020, the smaller a_π in TR–II implies a smaller rise in r. Output doesn't fall as sharply, and in 2022 inflation is still above

Since with smaller coefficient r small rise
Y doesn't fall as sharply,
r > rⁿ for longer.

15.5 Uncertainty and Policy Mistakes | **463**

target. Because inflation falls more slowly with TR-II, r must stay above r^n longer.

Which version of the Taylor rule is better? The answer is ambiguous. The more aggressive rule, TR-I, does a better job of stabilizing inflation. When a supply shock pushes inflation above the 2-percent target, the rule pushes it back quickly. With TR-II, inflation stays above target longer.

On the other hand, the more aggressive TR-I is worse for stabilizing output. Policy tightens sharply when the supply shock occurs, causing a deep recession in 2021. Output follows a smoother path with the less aggressive TR-II.

This example illustrates a general principle: *central banks face a trade-off between output stability and inflation stability.* The Taylor rule that is best for achieving one of these goals is not best for achieving the other. As we've discussed, economists are unsure about the relative importance of the two goals, so it's hard to know which rule is best overall.

15.5 UNCERTAINTY AND POLICY MISTAKES

The AE/PC model captures some of the trade-offs that central banks face in trying to stabilize the economy. Yet the model is a simplification of reality. Running monetary policy in a real economy is much harder than analyzing policy with the model.

A major reason is uncertainty about the economy's behavior. When we examine policy options, we usually assume that we know the precise AE and Phillips curves that determine output and inflation. In reality, policymakers do not have textbooks in which they can look up these curves. Central bank economists try to estimate the behavior of the economy, but their estimates may be wrong.

These misestimates can lead to policy mistakes. Actions that stabilize the economy under certain assumptions may

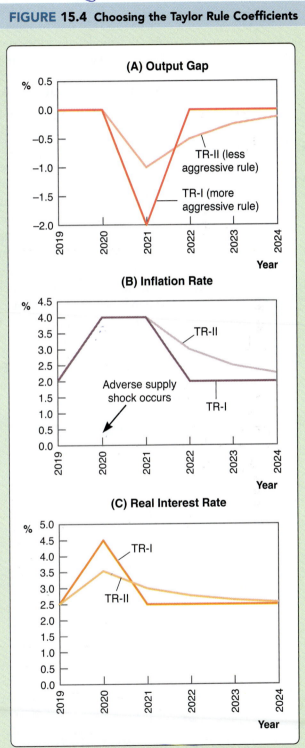

FIGURE 15.4 Choosing the Taylor Rule Coefficients

This figure compares the effects of an adverse supply shock under two Taylor rules, TR-I and TR-II. TR-I is more aggressive: it prescribes larger interest rate adjustments for given movements in output and inflation. This rule is better for stabilizing inflation, but the less aggressive rule is better for stabilizing output.

destabilize it if the assumptions are incorrect, so well-intentioned policies can backfire. As we discuss some examples of this problem, we assume that the AE/PC model describes the economy accurately, and that policymakers know this. However, they are mistaken about important details of the model.

A Mistake About the AE Curve

One type of misestimate involves the slopes of the AE and PC curves—how flat or steep they are. The slope of the AE curve shows how much a rise in the real interest rate reduces output, and the slope of the Phillips curve shows how much a rise in output raises inflation. These slopes determine how strongly the economy responds to policy actions.

Let's focus on the AE curve. Economists try to measure its slope by observing how much output changes when interest rates change. This is tricky, however, because output is also influenced by expenditure shocks, such as shifts in fiscal policy or consumer confidence. When output changes, it is difficult to disentangle the effects of interest rates from other factors.

In addition, the AE coefficient may change over time. Interest rates affect expenditure through complex channels that may change as the financial system evolves. Estimates of interest rate effects based on past experience may not be reliable.

An Example of a Mistake **Figure 15.5** illustrates this problem. For simplicity, we examine an AE curve without a time lag: expenditure depends

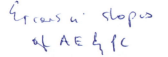

▶Figure 13.7 summarizes the channels in the monetary transmission mechanism through which policy affects aggregate expenditure.

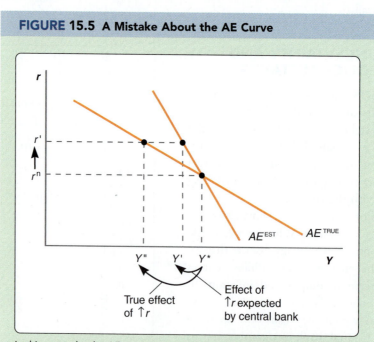

FIGURE 15.5 A Mistake About the AE Curve

In this example, the AE curve estimated by the central bank is steeper than the true AE curve. This means the central bank underestimates the effect of changing the interest rate r. It thinks an increase from r^n to r' will reduce output to Y'; in fact, output falls to Y''.

on the current real interest rate. The figure shows two versions of the curve. One is the *true* AE curve that describes how the economy works (AE^{TRUE}). The other, an AE curve *estimated* by central bank economists (AE^{EST}), differs from the true curve.

In this example, the curve AE^{EST} is steeper than AE^{TRUE}. This means that the central bank underestimates the effect of the real interest rate on output. Suppose the interest rate rises from the neutral level, r^n, to a higher level, r'. The central bank, believing in its estimated AE curve, thinks the higher interest rate will reduce output from potential, Y^*, to Y'. AE^{TRUE} shows that output actually falls by more, to Y''.

The Response to a Shock Suppose the economy starts with r at r^n and output at potential. Then a positive expenditure shock occurs, say an increase in government spending. The shock raises output by an amount Δ (Greek letter delta) for any given interest rate. Assume the central bank measures this shock correctly.

The central bank doesn't want output to rise, because that would lead to higher inflation through the Phillips curve. So policymakers decide to offset the expenditure shock by raising the real interest rate. Unfortunately, their mistake about the slope of the AE curve leads them astray.

Figure 15.6 shows what happens. The central bank knows a shock has raised spending by Δ, meaning the AE curve has shifted right by that

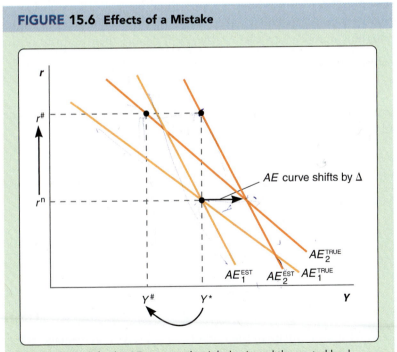

FIGURE 15.6 Effects of a Mistake

Here a shock shifts the AE curve to the right by Δ, and the central bank raises the interest rate from r^n to $r^\#$. Based on their estimated AE curve, policymakers think their action will keep output at potential. The true effect is to reduce output to $Y^\#$.

amount. Policymakers *think* the curve that has shifted is the steep one, AE^{EST}. Given that belief, an interest rate of $r^{\#}$ will keep output at potential. So the central bank raises r to $r^{\#}$.

What's really happened is that the flat curve, AE^{TRUE}, has shifted by Δ. When the interest rate rises to $r^{\#}$, output does *not* stay at potential. Instead, it falls below potential, to $Y^{\#}$. The central bank's reaction to the positive expenditure shock has actually caused a recession. The lesson: *When the central bank makes a mistake, an effort to stabilize the economy can actually destabilize it.*

Mismeasurement of the Output Gap

Another kind of mistake involves measurement of the output gap, $\tilde{Y}$, the percentage difference between actual and potential output. We've assumed that policy responds to this variable. In reality, central banks don't know the output gap, because they don't observe potential output. They try to estimate it, but once again their estimates may be wrong.

A common way to estimate the output gap is to use Okun's law, the relation between output and unemployment over the business cycle:

$$\tilde{Y} = -2(U - U^*)$$

where U is unemployment and U^* is the natural rate. With this approach, estimates of the output gap depend on estimates of U^*. Economists are often unsure of the current natural rate, leading to mismeasurement of the gap.

An Example of a Mistake Suppose the central bank uses Okun's law to estimate the output gap. Policymakers think the natural rate is 5 percent, so they plug this number into Okun's law. We'll denote their estimate of the gap with the symbol $\hat{\tilde{Y}}$:

$$\hat{\tilde{Y}} = -2(U - 5.0)$$

Unfortunately, the central bank is wrong about the natural rate. The true natural rate is 6 percent, so the true output gap is

$$\tilde{Y} = -2(U - 6.0)$$

To understand this mistake, combine the expressions for $\hat{\tilde{Y}}$ and $\tilde{Y}$:

$$\hat{\tilde{Y}} - \tilde{Y} = [-2(U - 5.0)] - [-2(U - 6.0)]$$

This equation reduces to

$$\hat{\tilde{Y}} - \tilde{Y} = -2.0$$

or

$$\hat{\tilde{Y}} = \tilde{Y} - 2.0 \tag{15.3}$$

The central bank's estimate of the output gap is always 2 percentage points below the true gap.

For example, suppose in some year the unemployment rate U is 6 percent. This is the true natural rate, so $U - U^*$ is zero and the true output gap is zero. In this situation, the central bank thinks the gap is -2 percent, which signals a recession. Policymakers believe output is below potential because unemployment exceeds 5 percent, their estimate of the natural rate.

The Effect on Policy To see the effects of this mistake, assume the central bank follows a Taylor rule, specifically TR-II in Table 15.2. However, in applying the rule, policymakers use their misestimate of the output gap, $\hat{Y}$. They can't respond to the true gap, $\tilde{Y}$, because they don't observe this variable. With this change, TR-II becomes

$$r = 2.5 + (0.5)\hat{\tilde{Y}} + (0.5)(\pi - 2.0)$$

(15.4)

Recall that $\hat{\tilde{Y}}$ is always 2 percentage points less than the true output gap, $\tilde{Y}$. Because the coefficient on the output gap is 0.5, underestimating it by 2 points reduces the real interest rate by 1 point. Mismeasurement makes monetary policy more expansionary.

Effects on the Economy Suppose in 2020 the economy is in long-run equilibrium. Output is at potential—the true output gap is zero—and inflation is at the target of 2 percent. In this example, no expenditure or supply shocks hit the economy. If the central bank measured the output gap correctly, it would set the interest rate at the neutral level, keeping output and inflation constant.

Mismeasurement of the output gap produces a different outcome, which is shown in **Figure 15.7**. The figure shows the paths of the interest rate, inflation, and two versions of the output gap—the true gap, $\tilde{Y}$, and the central bank's estimate, $\hat{\tilde{Y}}$. The figure is derived using equations for the AE and Phillips curves in the online appendix to this chapter.

In 2020, the true output gap is zero, but the central bank perceives a gap of −2 percent. Following its Taylor rule, Equation (15.4), the central bank sets a real interest rate of 1.5 percent, 1 point below

FIGURE 15.7 Mismeasurement of the Output Gap

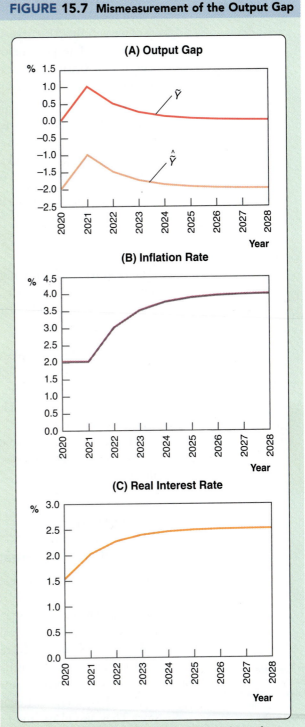

Here the central bank underestimates the natural rate of unemployment. As a result, its estimates of the output gap ($\hat{\tilde{Y}}$) are less than the true gap ($\tilde{Y}$). Policymakers perceive a negative output gap when the true gap is zero or positive, leading to overexpansionary policy. The central bank's inflation target is 2 percent, but its mistake pushes inflation to 4 percent.

the neutral rate. Policymakers think they are setting a low interest rate to end a recession.

Through the AE curve, the low interest rate pushes the true output gap above zero. The positive output gap raises inflation through the Phillips curve. This situation persists for a number of years. Even as the economy experiences an inflationary boom, the central bank *thinks* a recession is occurring: after 2020, $\tilde{Y}$ is positive but $\hat{\tilde{Y}}$ is negative. The central bank keeps r below r^n and the boom continues.

This process finally ends when inflation rises to 4 percent. At that point, the central bank *still* thinks the output gap is negative, which reduces the interest rate in the Taylor rule. But inflation exceeds the 2-percent target, which raises the interest rate. Specifically, $\hat{\tilde{Y}} = -2.0\%$ and $\pi = 4.0\%$, so Equation (15.4) implies

$$r = 2.5 + (0.5)(-2.0) + (0.5)(4.0 - 2.0) = 2.5$$

The negative $\hat{\tilde{Y}}$ and the high inflation rate offset one another, implying an interest rate of 2.5 percent, the neutral rate. With $r = 2.5$ percent, the true output gap is zero and inflation stabilizes—but at 4 percent, not the central bank's 2-percent target.

Summary In this example, the central bank's basic mistake is that it thinks the natural rate of unemployment is lower than it really is. By Okun's law, this mistake underestimates the output gap, which leads to overly expansionary monetary policy. The ultimate effect is to push inflation above the central bank's target.

Mismeasurement of the output gap is not just a theoretical idea. It helps explain important episodes in economic history, as the next case study illustrates.

CASE STUDY

The Fed and the Great Inflation

Since World War II, the U.S. inflation rate has usually been low. The big exception is the 1970s. In the "Great Inflation" of 1973–1980, inflation averaged 9 percent per year. The memory of this episode is still fresh for many Fed officials. One reason for the Fed's current commitment to low inflation is a desire not to repeat the 1970s.

What caused the Great Inflation? One factor was supply shocks: jumps in food and energy prices caused inflation to spike upward in 1973–1974 and in 1979. However, most economists don't think these shocks are the whole story. They also blame the Fed for overly expansionary monetary policy.

▶ The case studies in Sections 12.3 and 12.4 discuss the effects of food and energy prices on inflation in the 1970s.

We can see why by examining history. Inflation started its rise in the late 1960s, well before the oil- and food-price shocks. In addition, inflation accelerated from 1976 through 1978, when no shocks occurred. In both these periods, inflation was pushed up by output booms, which in turn were fueled by low real interest rates. The real federal funds rate was negative during much of the 1970s.

Why was policy so expansionary? Economic historians agree that the Fed did not raise inflation on purpose. It tried to keep inflation low, but it made mistakes. In particular, its behavior can be captured by a version of the Taylor rule, but one with an inflationary flaw.

Although there is consensus that the Fed erred in the 1970s, there is disagreement about the nature of its mistakes. Economists have proposed two different stories about what went wrong.

Perverse Inflation Responses? John Taylor has proposed one of the stories. He suggests that Fed policy followed his rule in the 1970s but with inappropriate coefficients. In particular, a_π, the response to inflation, was negative. This meant that a rise in inflation caused the Fed to *reduce* the real interest rate. The Fed was leaning with the wind rather than against it.

The Fed behaved this way because it was confused about nominal and real interest rates. The rate set directly by the Fed is a nominal rate. When inflation rose, the Fed increased this rate. Specifically, Taylor finds that each 1-point rise in inflation caused the nominal federal funds rate to rise by 0.8 points. The Fed thought it was tightening policy.

But what really matters is the real interest rate, the nominal rate minus expected inflation: $r = i + \pi^e$. During the 1970s, the rise in actual inflation caused a parallel rise in expected inflation, as suggested by the assumption of adaptive expectations. When π rose 1 point, π^e rose roughly 1 point as well. With i rising 0.8 points in response, r fell by 0.2 points. So a_π, the effect of inflation on the real interest rate, was -0.2.

In Taylor's story, the negative a_π created an inflationary spiral. Initially, economic shocks raised inflation a little bit. With $a_\pi < 0$, higher inflation caused the Fed to lower the real interest rate. The lower real rate caused an output boom, raising inflation further. The more inflation rose, the more the real rate fell and vice versa. This process continued until Paul Volcker was appointed Fed chair in 1979. Volcker responded aggressively to inflation—he raised a_π above zero—and this brought inflation under control.

Mismeasurement of the Output Gap? Another explanation for the Great Inflation was proposed by Athanasios Orphanides, a former Fed economist and now governor of the Central Bank of Cyprus. In this story, the Fed made a mistake that we have recently discussed: it mismeasured the output gap. As in our theoretical example, this occurred because the Fed's estimate of the natural rate of unemployment was too low. This mistake led to overexpansionary policy, which pushed inflation above the Fed's target, as in Figure 15.7.

The natural rate was 5 percent or less in the 1960s but rose to about 6 percent in the 1970s as the majority of baby boomers entered the labor force and productivity growth slowed. In Orphanides's story, the Fed didn't recognize this change. This is not surprising: economists had not yet developed methods for estimating the natural rate. Orphanides points to statements by Fed officials suggesting that they still believed in a 5-percent natural rate in the 1970s.

▶ The case study in Section 12.1 discusses the history behind the natural rate of unemployment in the United States over the past half-century.

Orphanides has reexamined John Taylor's work on the Taylor rule for the 1970s. When Taylor determined which rule fits the Fed's behavior, he used the most recent estimates of output gaps in the 1970s, which were probably close to the true gaps. Orphanides, by contrast, uses "real-time" output gaps—the flawed estimates that the Fed used when it made its decisions. These estimates come from internal Fed documents from the 1970s. In our notation, Orphanides examines the Fed's reaction to $\hat{Y}$, not $\tilde{Y}$.

With this approach, Orphanides finds that the a_π coefficient in the Taylor rule was positive in the 1970s. Thus, he argues, the Fed did *not* make the mistake of reducing the real interest rate when inflation rose. Its mistake was in how it measured economic conditions, not in how it responded to the conditions that it perceived.[*]

[*] See John Taylor, "An Historical Analysis of Monetary Policy Rules," Chapter 7 of Taylor (ed.), *Monetary Policy Rules*, University of Chicago Press, 1999; and Athanasios Orphanides, "Historical Monetary Policy Analysis and the Taylor Rule," *Journal of Monetary Economics*, 50 (July 2003): 983–1022.

Coping with Uncertainty

We've seen that uncertainty about the economy can lead central banks into costly mistakes. What can be done about this problem? Let's discuss some possible answers.

Learning About the Economy The best way to deal with uncertainty is to reduce it. Central banks are less likely to make mistakes if they gain a better understanding of the economy. To this end, economists at central banks do extensive research. The Federal Reserve System employs about 500 economists, half at the board of governors and half at the 12 Fed banks. The Fed also hires university professors as part-time consultants.

As part of this work, economists at the board of governors have developed a model of the U.S. economy. This model is a system of equations that describe the determinants of output, inflation, and other aggregate variables. It is called the FRB/US model, where FRB stands for Federal Reserve Board. The term is commonly pronounced "Furbus."

The FRB/US model is similar in spirit to the AE/PC model but much more complicated. There are hundreds of equations rather than just two. For example, rather than one equation for aggregate expenditure, FRB/US has separate equations for different kinds of consumption, such as durables and nondurables; different kinds of investment, such as housing and inventories; and so on. All these equations must be combined to determine total spending.

Fed economists constantly refine the FRB/US model based on economic theory and new data. They use statistics to get the best possible estimates of the model's coefficients, such as coefficients capturing the effects of interest rates on spending.

Cautious Interest Rate Movements Research reduces uncertainty but cannot eliminate it. Central bankers will never know the exact equations describing their economies. How should this fact influence policy?

A common answer is that central banks should move interest rates cautiously. When doubtful about the right response to a shock, they should choose a small adjustment. Alan Blinder, a former vice chair of the Fed, summarized this idea by saying, "the Fed should decide what policy is best and then do less."

The reason for caution is to avoid changing interest rates too much. We saw the danger of overadjustment in one of our examples of policy mistakes—the one in which the central bank misestimates the slope of the AE curve. This mistake led policymakers to raise the interest rate too much in response to an expenditure shock, causing a recession (Figure 15.6). Such an outcome is less likely if the central bank "does less."

Caution means a central bank may not offset a shock fully when it occurs, but policymakers can make another adjustment later if more action is needed. The delay slows the economy's return to long-run equilibrium. However, many economists think it's worth paying this price to guard against overadjustment.

Policymakers seem to take these ideas to heart. When shocks occur, central bankers usually do not respond with large, immediate changes in interest rates. Instead, they practice **interest rate smoothing**. They change rates by a small amount at a time, making a series of adjustments if they eventually want a large change.

Aside from periods of financial crisis, the Fed usually changes its target for the federal funds rate by 1/4 of a percentage point at a time. For example, as the economy recovered from the recession of the early 2000s, the Fed raised its target by 1/4 point on 17 occasions. Overall, the target rose from 1.00 percent in 2004 to 5.25 percent in 2006.

Interest rate smoothing
central banks' practice of moving interest rates through a series of small changes

Smaller Responses to Output Gaps? We've seen that mismeasurement of the output gap can lead to costly mistakes in monetary policy. It is difficult to measure the gap, because central bankers don't observe potential output or the natural rate of unemployment. They measure the inflation rate much more accurately.

Some economists conclude that policy should not respond much to output gaps. In the Taylor rule, the inflation coefficient a_π should be large, but the output coefficient a_y should be small. Athanasios Orphanides argues that a small a_y would prevent the kind of mistake the Fed made in the 1970s. At the same time, a large a_π would keep the economy reasonably stable.

Other economists disagree. They think that a low coefficient on the output gap would allow recessions to drag on for a long time. It is better to measure the gap imperfectly than to ignore it. Policymakers should be cautious in the sense of smoothing interest rates, these economists argue, but eventually they should respond strongly to estimated output gaps.

Most central banks have *not* been convinced to deemphasize output gaps. The Fed, for example, reduced interest rates significantly in response to the negative gaps of the early 2000s (see Figure 15.2). The Taylor rule that fits the Fed's behavior has a sizable coefficient on the gap.

15.6 MAKING INTEREST RATE POLICY

Much of this chapter has focused on the Taylor rule, but this rule only approximates how central banks behave. Policymakers choose interest rates through a process that is far more complex than applying a formula. Sometimes this process produces significant deviations from the Taylor rule.

The broad approach is similar at many central banks. A committee of top officials meets periodically to set policy. In the United States, the Federal Open Market Committee meets every 6 weeks. The European Central Bank's Governing Council meets once a month. At these meetings, policy-makers discuss the state of the economy and then choose an interest rate target. The policy committee is supported by a staff of economists that continuously monitors the economy, makes forecasts, and analyzes policy options. The staff reports on this work to policymakers before each of their meetings.

At the Federal Reserve, much of the staff's analysis is summarized in a document with the formal name of *Report to the FOMC on Economic Conditions and Monetary Policy*. It is better known as the "Teal Book" because of the color of its cover. We will discuss what's in the Teal book and how this content is assembled.

Monitoring the Economy

The first job of Fed economists is to monitor the state of the economy. Much of this task consists of estimating the current level of output. We've already discussed the fact that the Fed doesn't observe potential output, Y^*. At any point in time, it also doesn't know actual output, Y. The reason is that data on the main measure of output, real GDP, are produced with a substantial time lag.

Specifically, GDP is calculated quarterly, but the final number for a quarter is not published until the end of the following quarter. For example, GDP for the first quarter of the year, January through March, is not reported until the end of June. So economists never know the current level of GDP.

Outside the Fed, economists wait for complete data before analyzing events. For example, the NBER announces the starts and ends of recessions many months after they occur. But the Fed can't afford to wait before assessing the state of the economy and responding to it. Monetary policy offsets the effects of shocks with a lag, and the lag is worsened if actions are delayed.

So Fed economists try their best to estimate current output. To do so, they examine data series that are calculated monthly and with relatively short lags. These series include retail sales, employment, and industrial production. These variables tend to move in the same direction as GDP, so they provide hints about GDP before that variable is calculated.

On most Mondays, economists on the staff of the Fed Board in Washington brief the governors about data released during the previous week. They also interpret the data. For example, if retail sales have fallen, they discuss what that means. Does it suggest the economy is slowing? Or does it just reflect the big storm that curtailed shopping last month?

The analysis of the board's economists is summarized every 6 weeks in the Teal Book. This document includes estimates of the current level of GDP based on all available data. The Teal Book is distributed to the FOMC the week before it meets.

While economists at the board are preparing the Teal Book, economists at the Fed banks are briefing their presidents. At each bank, the staff studies the economy of its Federal Reserve district as well as the national economy. At the FOMC meeting, the bank president may report on his or her district.

Each Federal Reserve Bank also contributes to the Beige Book. This document is a collection of anecdotes about various industries that are doing well or badly in different parts of the country. Sometimes changes in the economy show up in these stories before they are reflected in national data.

Forecasting the Economy

In addition to analyzing the current economy, the Fed staff forecasts its future. Each Teal Book presents forecasts of output and inflation over the next 2 years. Forecasts are important, because policymakers would like to respond preemptively to shifts in the economy. If they can predict movements in output and inflation, they can adjust interest rates in advance. This reduces the problems caused by lags in the effects of policy, allowing the Fed to stabilize the economy more effectively.

One tool for forecasting is the FRB/US model of the economy. In this model, most variables depend on past values of other variables—as in the AE/PC model with time lags. For example, current investment depends on past investment, GDP, and interest rates. Because of these linkages, an analyst can plug current data into the equations to get forecasts.

Forecasts from the FRB/US model do not go directly into the Teal Book. The Teal Book forecasts are "judgmental": they are chosen by people rather than by equations in a computer. Within the Fed staff, different economists forecast different variables, such as consumption and investment. These people take account of the forecasts from FRB/US, but they also examine other information that they think is relevant.

This information can include many factors. For example, the consumption forecaster may examine surveys of consumer confidence, which some economists think are good predictors of consumption. The forecaster may use various statistical techniques to forecast consumption, supplementing the forecasts from the FRB/US model. She may consider anecdotal evidence, such as retailers' predictions about holiday sales.

The preceding paragraph is somewhat speculative. The Fed publishes the equations used in the FRB/US model, but it doesn't say how judgmental forecasts are made. Fed economists are not allowed to reveal this information. Outsiders must rely on bits of gossip to get a rough picture of the forecasting process. This reflects the imperfect transparency of Fed policymaking, which we discuss in Chapter 16.

A "forecast coordinator" oversees the many economists working on forecasts, with the goal of ensuring that different forecasts fit together. Conflicts can develop: one economist might forecast that net exports will fall because of rising imports of consumer goods, while another forecasts a big fall in consumption, for example. The various forecasters meet to work out these differences. When the coordinator is satisfied with the forecasts, they go into the Teal Book.

Evaluating Policy Options

The Teal Book also helps prepare the FOMC for its upcoming meeting by outlining policy options. Usually, the Teal Book presents three possible interest rate decisions that appear reasonable in current circumstances. These options might be a 1/4-percent cut in the federal funds rate, no change, and a 1/4-percent increase. If it seems clear that the FOMC is leaning toward tightening, the options might be no change or a 1/4- or 1/2-percent increase.

The Teal Book lays out the pros and cons of each choice. In analyzing a rate increase, for example, it might discuss evidence that the economy is growing too quickly and contrast that with evidence that growth is slowing. The Teal Book also proposes language for the FOMC statement that will accompany the interest rate announcement.

The FOMC Meeting

▶An FOMC meeting is pictured on page 315.

The policy process culminates every 6 weeks with a meeting of the Federal Open Market Committee. The committee gathers at board headquarters in Washington, D.C., typically on a Tuesday. The committee consists of the seven Fed governors and 5 of the 12 Fed bank presidents. The other presidents attend the meeting and participate in the discussion, but they can't vote on the interest rate decision. Top members of the Fed staff are also present.

The meetings have a formal structure that determines who speaks when. In the first part of the meeting, participants review the state of the economy without explicitly discussing policy options. The director of the board's Division of Research and Statistics summarizes the economic forecasts in the Teal Book and takes questions. Then the bank presidents take turns giving their views on the economy, both nationally and in their regions. Finally, there are remarks by each of the governors, with the chair speaking last.

Then the meeting turns to policy. The director of the board's Division of Monetary Affairs summarizes the three proposals in the Teal Book and their rationales. Once again, each president and governor takes a turn making comments. The chair summarizes the discussion and makes a final proposal for an interest rate target. He also proposes language for a brief statement in which the committee will explain its decision. The statement might say, for example, that the Fed is raising interest rates because it sees a risk of higher inflation.

After hearing the chair's proposal, the 12 FOMC members vote to accept or reject it. For practical purposes, however, the outcome is decided before the vote. A chair's proposal has never been defeated, and it is rare to record more than one or two dissents. Committee members usually defer to the chair unless they have strong objections. Also, the chair gauges the opinions of others during the discussion and makes a proposal that he knows will pass.

After the interest rate vote, the committee sometimes discusses longer-term issues. In 2006 and 2007, it held several discussions on the pros and cons of adopting an explicit inflation target. More recently, the committee has discussed possible ways to boost aggregate expenditure when the nominal interest rate is at its zero bound. The meeting ends by 2:15, when the board's press office announces the new interest rate target. The news flashes across computer screens around the world, often causing immediate changes in asset prices and interest rates.

Online Case Study:
An FOMC Meeting

15.7 DEVIATIONS FROM THE TAYLOR RULE

This chapter has reviewed central banks' efforts to stabilize output and inflation. We've seen that policymakers adjust interest rates based on current estimates of these variables and forecasts of their future paths. Often, policy actions are close to those prescribed by the Taylor rule.

Sometimes, however, interest rates deviate significantly from the prescriptions of the Taylor rule. One reason is the zero bound on nominal rates. As we've discussed, this bound implies that the real rate cannot fall below $-\pi$. In a deep recession, the Taylor rule may prescribe an interest rate below this level, but it is impossible for the central bank to follow the rule.

In other situations, a central bank chooses to deviate from the Taylor rule. Since the 1980s, the primary reason has been developments in the financial system. Adverse events, such as asset-price declines or failures of financial institutions, have led central banks to reduce interest rates. Some economists think policymakers should also *raise* interest rates when asset-price bubbles occur, but this idea is controversial.

Responses to Financial Crises

Policymakers sometimes face a *financial crisis*, with plummeting asset prices and failures of financial institutions, or fear that a crisis is on the way. In such situations, the central bank is likely to lower interest rates—and to lower them by more than the Taylor rule prescribes.

In the United States, such an episode occurred in the summer of 1998, when Russia defaulted on its sovereign debt and a huge hedge fund, Long-Term Capital Management, nearly failed. The Fed feared that these events might trigger a financial crisis that would damage the economy. It responded by cutting the federal funds rate by 3/4 of a point over 1998–1999.

If you look closely at Figure 15.2 on p. 460, you can see that this action caused the real federal funds rate to fall below the level prescribed by the Taylor rule. In this episode, a broad financial crisis did not materialize, so the Fed raised interest rates back to the Taylor-rule level in 2000.

Why do central banks respond aggressively when they fear a financial crisis? There are two related reasons:

1. A financial crisis is likely to reduce output in the near future. Among other reasons, a crisis shakes consumer confidence, reduces bank lending, and causes asset prices to fall. These events lead to lower consumption and investment. The process takes time to unfold. Given the lags in policy effects, the central bank wants to act preemptively. It lowers rates when it sees a financial crisis developing rather than waiting for output to fall.

2. During a financial crisis, the risk that the crisis will suddenly worsen always looms. The failure of one financial institution, for example, can trigger a loss of confidence that causes other failures. Because of such risk, a central bank is likely to respond more strongly than is justified by the current situation. Policymakers provide extra stimulus to the economy as insurance against worst-case scenarios. Recent history vividly illustrates this rationale, as we discuss in the following case study.

CASE STUDY

Deviating from the Taylor Rule, 2007–2010

We've seen that the Fed's choices of interest rates were close to the Taylor rule for two decades, from 1987 to 2007 (recall Figure 15.2). As shown in **Figure 15.8**, this correspondence broke down in 2007 and 2008 as the Fed pushed the real interest rate *below* the level prescribed by the Taylor rule. After that, the real interest rate leveled off, and starting in late 2008 it was far *above* the Taylor rule level.

Specifically, from June 2007 to April 2008, the interest rate prescribed by the Taylor rule dropped by only 0.7 percentage points (from 2.3 percent to 1.6 percent). Yet the *actual* real rate fell by 3.1 percentage points (from 3.1 percent to 0.0 percent). This sharp easing of monetary policy reflected the onset of the most recent financial crisis. As in 1998, the Fed saw signs of trouble—in this case, a decrease in lending among banks in the federal funds market. It starting cutting interest rates as insurance in case the situation deteriorated. In contrast to 1998, things *did* get worse, so the Fed's early response to the crisis is fortunate. The most recent recession would probably have been even deeper if the Fed had held interest rates at Taylor-rule levels through 2007 and 2008.

Interest rates after Fall 2008 reflect the zero bound on nominal rates. As the recession deepened, the real interest rate prescribed by the Taylor rule fell rapidly, reaching −4.5 percent in May 2009. The actual real rate could not follow the Taylor rule down once the nominal rate hit the zero bound in December 2008. In fact, the real rate rose a bit over 2009–2010 because inflation fell. The forced deviation from the Taylor rule is another way to see that the zero bound prevented the Fed from pursuing countercyclical policy.

▶ Section 18.3 describes the unfolding of the financial crisis and the policy responses in detail.

FIGURE 15.8 Deviating from the Taylor Rule, 2007–2010

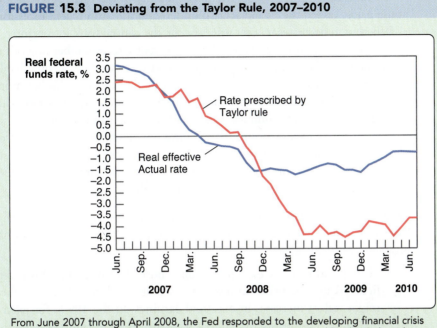

From June 2007 through April 2008, the Fed responded to the developing financial crisis by reducing the real federal funds rate more quickly than prescribed by the Taylor rule. The real funds rate leveled off when the nominal rate hit the zero bound, and it was far above the Taylor rule level in 2009 and 2010.

Source: Federal Reserve Bank of St. Louis

Responses to Bubbles

Clearly, central banks respond to problems in financial markets, including large falls in asset prices. Some economists argue that this policy should have a complement: the central bank should react to unusually large *increases* in asset prices. In particular, it should raise interest rates if a bubble pushes asset prices above the assets' true values.

To understand this issue, we must make a distinction. Asset prices affect output through various channels, including the effect of wealth on consumption and the effect of stock prices on investment. Because central banks respond to output movements, they respond indirectly to asset prices. The controversial question is whether they should also respond *directly*. For a given level of output, should a central bank raise interest rates by more than normal if it perceives an asset-price bubble? Let's examine both sides of this issue.

Why Respond to Asset Prices? The affirmative argument is based on the link between asset-price bubbles and subsequent declines in asset prices. A bubble is driven by self-fulfilling expectations of rising prices. At some point, expectations shift and prices fall, sometimes rapidly. Just as high asset prices raise output, falling prices can cause a recession. After U.S. stock prices rose rapidly in the 1990s, a fall in prices contributed to the U.S.

recession of 2001. After house prices rose rapidly in the early 2000s, falling house prices fueled the financial crisis underlying the most recent recession.

When such decreases in asset prices occur, the central bank lowers interest rates. But this response may be too late to prevent a recession because of the lags in policy effects. Rather than react to asset price declines, central banks would do better to prevent them from occurring. They can do this by dampening the bubbles that eventually burst. If asset prices don't rise to irrationally high levels, they won't plummet when markets come to their senses.

Central banks have a tool for dampening bubbles: interest rate increases. Higher rates reduce asset prices by reducing the present value of future asset income. So when central banks see a bubble developing, this argument goes, they should lean against it with tighter policy.

Why Not Respond to Asset Prices? Many economists are skeptical that monetary policy should respond to asset prices. They point out several problems with this idea.

- To respond to bubbles, central banks must identify them. This is difficult. Rapid increases in asset prices might reflect bubbles, or they might reflect increases in expected earnings. In the 1990s, for example, some economists argued that stock prices were rising because the productivity acceleration raised firms' expected profits. Economists can be sure of a bubble only when they see it end—and then it's too late to prevent the bubble.

- The effects of interest rates on bubbles are unpredictable. Depending on market sentiment, an increase in rates might have little effect on asset prices. Or it might shake confidence and cause a big decline. In the worst case, an attempt to contain a bubble might cause the kind of crash that the central bank wants to prevent.

- A policy tightening aimed at asset prices has adverse side effects. It reduces aggregate expenditure and raises unemployment. It is unwise to accept this cost when the benefits of the policy are uncertain.

Fed Policy Fed officials have weighed the arguments about responding to bubbles and, in the past, found the negative case more persuasive. Under Chairman Alan Greenspan, the Fed ignored advice to lean against the stock market boom of the 1990s. In the 2000s, Greenspan and then Ben Bernanke kept interest rates low as house prices rose rapidly.

Bernanke's behavior is not surprising, because he has long argued that monetary policy should not respond to bubbles. In 2001, when Bernanke was still a professor, he and Mark Gertler wrote that responding to bubbles would have "dangerously unpredictable effects" and "no significant benefits."[5]

In the view of many economists, recent history casts doubt on the wisdom of Fed policy. They argue that the last two recessions show the damage

---

[5] Ben Bernanke and Mark Gertler, "Monetary Policy and Asset Price Volatility," in *New Challenges for Monetary Policy*, Federal Reserve Bank of Kansas City, 1999.

that can occur if policymakers ignore a bubble until it bursts. In 2007, as the decline in housing prices began, Stephen Roach, of investment bank Morgan Stanley, criticized the Fed along with other central banks: "For the second time in seven years, the bursting of a major asset bubble has inflicted great damage on world financial markets. In both cases—the equity bubble of 2000 and the credit bubble of 2007—central banks were asleep at the switch."[6]

This line of criticism intensified in 2008 and 2009 as the financial crisis and recession deepened. Whether this viewpoint will influence Fed policy during future bubbles remains to be seen.

---

[6] Stephen Roach, "The Failure of Central Banking," CNN Money Crisis Counsel, August 2007, money.cnn.com.

Summary

- A central bank's tasks include choosing a long-run level for the inflation rate and dampening short-run fluctuations in inflation and output.

15.1 Choosing the Long-Run Inflation Rate

- Some economists believe that zero is the ideal level for long-run inflation. Others advocate a low but positive inflation rate to avoid the costs of disinflation and reduce the risk of a liquidity trap.

- In practice, many central banks target inflation rates around 2 percent, either explicitly or implicitly. Fed Chairman Ben Bernanke's stated "comfort zone" for inflation is 1–2 percent.

15.2 Inflation and Output Stability

- Central banks seek to stabilize the inflation rate at its long-run level. They also seek to stabilize output—to dampen the business cycle. However, these goals sometimes conflict, and economists are unsure of their relative importance.

15.3 The Taylor Rule

- Central banks have long followed the principle of "leaning against the wind": they adjust interest rates to offset movements in output and inflation.

- The Taylor rule, invented in 1993, captures the idea of leaning against the wind in a formula. The rule prescribes a real interest rate based on the neutral real rate, the output gap, and the deviation of inflation from target.

- In the two decades 1987 to 2007, the interest rates set by the Fed usually were close to those prescribed by the Taylor rule.

15.4 The Taylor Rule in the AE/PC Model

- In the AE/PC model with time lags, the Taylor rule guides the economy back to long-run equilibrium after a shock occurs.

- The behavior of the economy depends on the Taylor rule's coefficients on output, a_y, and inflation, a_π. Different coefficients are best for stabilizing output and for stabilizing inflation, so it's not clear which are best overall.

15.5 Uncertainty and Policy Mistakes

- Because of uncertainty about the economy, central banks may adjust the interest rate too much in response to a shock, destabilizing output and inflation.

- If the central bank underestimates the output gap, its policy is overly expansionary, and inflation rises above target. Such a mistake may help to explain the high inflation of the 1970s.

- Central banks try to minimize their mistakes through research on the economy. They also practice interest rate smoothing to avoid overreacting to shocks.

15.6 Making Interest Rate Policy

- The Federal Open Market Committee meets every 6 weeks to review the state of the economy and choose a target for the federal funds rate. To accomplish these and its other policy goals, the Federal Reserve employs hundreds of economists who monitor the economy and forecast its future.

- This analysis is summarized in the Teal Book prepared for the FOMC. Fed economists also prepare the Beige Book, which discusses conditions in various industries around the country.

15.7 Deviations from the Taylor Rule

■ Financial crises lead the Fed to reduce interest rates. Rates typically fall by more than the Taylor rule prescribes. However, the zero bound on nominal interest rates can keep real rates *above* the Taylor rule level. Both of these deviations from the Taylor rule occurred between 2007 and 2010.

■ Some economists argue that central banks should raise interest rates to dampen asset-price bubbles. Yet this idea is controversial, and the Fed has not adopted it.

Key Terms

Explicit inflation target, p. 454

Implicit inflation target, p. 454

Interest rate smoothing, p. 471

Taylor rule, p. 458

Questions and Problems

1. Suppose the neutral real interest rate is 3 percent in country A and 1 percent in country B.
   a. What might explain this difference? (*Hint*: See the appendix at the end of Chapter 12.)
   b. If the central banks of the two countries choose the same inflation target, which country is at greater risk of a liquidity trap? Explain.
   c. Should the two countries choose the same inflation target? Explain.

2. Suppose an economist has a bright idea: a central bank should lean against the wind when output falls but *not* when it rises. In other words, policymakers should lower the interest rate below the neutral level when a recession occurs but not raise it in a boom.
   a. Why might this plan appear attractive?
   b. Would it be wise for a central bank to adopt the plan? (*Hint*: Think about the Phillips curve.)

3. We have assumed that the coefficients in the Taylor rule, a_y and a_π, are both positive. Under this assumption, the rule guides the economy back to long-run equilibrium after a shock. The output gap $\tilde{Y}$ eventually returns to zero, and inflation returns to its long-run level π^T.
   a. Suppose the inflation coefficient a_π is positive but the output coefficient a_y is zero. Does the economy still return to equilibrium with $\tilde{Y} = 0$ and $\pi - \pi^T$ after a shock? Explain.
   b. How is the answer to the previous question different if a_y is positive and a_π is zero? Explain.

4. Suppose the central bank measures the output gap accurately but mismeasures the neutral real interest rate. It believes the neutral rate is 1 percent, but the true neutral rate is 3 percent. If the central bank follows the Taylor rule, how does its mistake affect the interest rates it sets and the behavior of output and inflation? Explain.

5. In Figure 15.6, the central bank responds to an expenditure shock. Suppose policymakers know the true slope of the AE curve but mismeasure the shock: they think the curve shifts to the right by 2Δ, twice the actual shift. How will the central bank adjust the interest rate if it wants to keep output at potential? What will really happen to output? Explain.

6. Consider a variation on the Taylor rule:

$$r = (0.25)r^{\text{TAYLOR}} + (0.75)r(-1)$$

where r is the real interest rate in a quarter, r^{TAYLOR} is the interest rate implied by the Taylor rule, and $r(-1)$ is the interest rate in the previous quarter. Call this rule TR-S.

a. Compare the behavior of the interest rate under TR-S to its behavior under the basic Taylor rule. (*Hint:* What might "S" stand for?)

b. Is TR-S a realistic description of central banks' behavior? Why might they follow such a rule rather than the basic Taylor rule?

7. Suppose the Fed had a policy of responding to asset-price bubbles. Under this policy, it would have set higher interest rates than it actually did during the stock market boom of the late 1990s and the housing bubble of the 2000s.

a. For the period 1990–2007, draw a graph showing roughly what interest rates the Fed would have chosen under the antibubble policy. Compare this hypothetical interest rate path to the actual path of rates (see Figure 15.2).

b. How would the antibubble policy have changed the behavior of output and inflation? Draw rough graphs comparing the likely paths of these variables to the paths they actually followed. (See pp. 379–380 for a summary of the actual paths.) In this part of the question, assume the antibubble policy was unsuccessful: stock and house prices rose rapidly despite higher interest rates.

c. Now suppose the hypothetical policy succeeded: it dampened the stock market and housing bubbles. How does this change the answer to part (b)?

▶ **Online and Data Questions**
www.worthpublishers.com/ball

8. [Advanced] Suppose the economy is in long-run equilibrium in 2019. In 2020, an adverse expenditure shock reduces output by 2 percent.

a. Assume the central bank uses TR-I in Table 15.2. Using the equations for the AE and Phillips curves in the online appendix, derive the paths of output, inflation, and the interest rate from 2020 until the economy is back in long-run equilibrium.

b. Redo the calculations in part (a) assuming TR-II. Which of the two rules is better for stabilizing output? For stabilizing inflation? Explain.

9. From the text Web site, connect to the site of the Federal Reserve Board, which includes minutes from FOMC meetings. Choose any meeting at which the committee changed its federal funds rate target.

a. Based on the minutes, briefly summarize the rationale for the target change.

b. Does the FOMC's action appear consistent with the Taylor rule? Explain.

c. Did any members dissent from the committee's decision? If so, why did they dissent?

Monetary Institutions and Strategies

We are in the midst of studying central banks' efforts to control inflation and stabilize the economy. The preceding chapter focused on an issue that central bank officials face continuously: the choice of an interest rate target. In this chapter, we step back from immediate decisions about interest rates to analyze longer-term monetary-policy issues. Some are strategic decisions that the Fed and other central banks must make. Others are policy issues facing the governments that establish central banks and determine their powers.

One such issue is central bank independence. In most of the world, governments have given central banks great freedom to run monetary policy. Elected political leaders have little control over interest rate adjustments or other policy actions. Some people think this is undemocratic, but most economists support central bank independence. We discuss why.

We also discuss limits on central banks' authority. Independence gives these institutions enormous power over the economy. Some economists think this power should be constrained by a policy rule—a rule that tells the central bank what to do in various circumstances. We survey the debate over what rule, if any, should govern monetary policy. Currently, much of this debate focuses on explicit inflation targeting, a policy adopted by many countries over the last two decades.

A final issue we consider is communication by central banks. Traditionally, central banks have been secretive about their decision making, but recent years have seen a trend toward openness. Today,

Scott J. Ferrell/Congressional Quarterly/Getty Images

December 16, 2009: At a news conference in Washington, D.C., Senator Bernard Sanders (I–Vermont) opposes Ben Bernanke's reappointment as Fed chairman.

policymakers provide the public with lots of information about what they are doing and why. We discuss the reasons for this change and debates over what information central banks should release.

To address all these issues, we begin by explaining some economic theories that have greatly influenced the behavior of central banks in recent decades. Theoretical research on monetary policy underlies developments around the world in central bank independence, policy rules, and communication.

16.1 TIME CONSISTENCY AND INFLATION

Economics professors develop abstract theories and publish them in scholarly journals. Sometimes the only people who pay attention are other economics professors. But other times, academic theories actually prompt real-world policymakers to change their behavior. The use of time-consistency theories in monetary policy is a prime example.

Time-consistency theories follow from an idea introduced in Section 12.3—that people have rational expectations about inflation. We need to review theories of inflation expectations before defining the *time-consistency problem*.

Rational Expectations and the Phillips Curve

The behavior of inflation depends on expectations, an idea captured by the Phillips curve:

$$\pi = \pi^e + \alpha \tilde{Y}$$

▶ In mathematical terms, $\tilde{Y} = (Y - Y^*)/Y^*$, where Y is output and Y^* is potential output.

where π is inflation, π^e is expected inflation, $\tilde{Y}$ is the output gap (the percentage deviation of output from potential), and α is a coefficient showing how strongly output affects inflation. Expected inflation enters this equation because firms raise prices to match the price increases they expect from other firms.

▶ To keep the analysis here as simple as possible, we use a version of the Phillips curve without supply shocks and ignore the time lag in the effect of output on inflation (see Section 13.4).

There are two leading theories of inflation expectations. One theory is **adaptive expectations**, or *backward-looking expectations*, which says that expectations of the inflation rate are determined by past inflation. Much of this book uses a simple version of this theory in which expected inflation equals inflation over the previous year: $\pi^e = \pi(-1)$.

The other theory, **rational expectations**, says that people make the best possible forecasts of future inflation based on all available information. The behavior of the central bank is a key part of this information. If the central bank tightens policy, for example, then expected inflation is likely to fall.

Adaptive expectations theory that people's expectations of a variable are based on past levels of the variable; also, *backward-looking expectations*

Rational expectations theory that people's expectations of future variables are the best possible forecasts based on all available information

The concept of rational expectations was introduced in a 1961 paper by John Muth of Carnegie-Mellon University. At first the idea had little impact, but that changed in the 1970s, when the "rational-expectations revolution" swept macroeconomics. This movement was led by Robert Lucas of the University of Chicago, who won a Nobel Prize for his work in 1995.

In Lucas's view, rational expectations follows from the basic economic principle that firms maximize profits. Remember why expectations matter: firms base their price increases on the increases they expect from other firms. If expectations are mistaken, firms set the wrong relative prices, and this reduces profits. So when firms choose prices, they have incentives to forecast inflation as well as possible—to form expectations rationally.

Not all economists accept this argument. Some believe that adaptive expectations is a more realistic assumption than rational expectations. Nonetheless, there is no doubt that rational-expectations theories have been hugely influential, in part by providing foundations for time-consistency theories.

The Time-Consistency Problem

A **time–consistency problem** can arise in many contexts. It occurs when someone has incentives to make a promise but then to renege on the promise later. Other people understand this inconsistency, so they don't believe the promise when it's made. Ultimately, we will use time-consistency theories to explain the behavior of inflation.

> **Time-consistency problem** situation in which someone has incentives to make a promise but later to renege on it; because of these incentives, others don't believe the promise

But first, to illustrate the basic idea, let's put aside the topic of monetary policy and consider family life. Suppose a family is preparing for a holiday visit to Grandpa and Grandma's house, where the kids will receive lavish presents. Dad wants the kids to clean their rooms before the trip. To get them to comply, he makes a threat: if the rooms aren't cleaned, the family will stay home. If the kids believe the threat, they will promptly clean up. They don't like cleaning, but they won't do anything to jeopardize their presents.

Unfortunately for Dad, his threat is not time-consistent. If the kids refuse to clean their rooms, he will relent and take them to their grandparents anyway. Otherwise, Grandpa and Grandma will be left with dinner on the table and get angry at Dad, which he can't stand. The kids, of course, understand this. They realize that Dad is bluffing, so they ignore him and play video games until it's time to leave. Their rooms stay messy.

Time-consistency problems arise in economic policy as well as in families. Suppose a government wants firms to build factories, making the economy more productive. The government might encourage this investment by promising not to tax firms' profits from the factories. But this promise is not time-consistent. Once the factories are built, the government will be tempted to enact taxes to raise revenue. Knowing this, firms may not build the factories.

for Economy.

How the Time-Consistency Problem Increases Inflation

How is time consistency relevant to monetary policy? This question was answered in a 1977 paper by Finn Kydland of Carnegie-Mellon University and Edward Prescott, then of the University of Minnesota (now at Arizona State University). According to Kydland and Prescott, the time-consistency problem explains why central banks sometimes produce high inflation, and solving the problem is the key to controlling inflation. Kydland and Prescott won the Nobel Prize in 2004.

▶ Section 14.2 discusses why central banks sometimes increase the money supply rapidly, producing high inflation.

The Puzzle of High Inflation To understand the Kydland–Prescott argument, recall why central banks create inflation. A traditional explanation is that disinflation is costly. If inflation is high, the central bank can reduce it by tightening policy, but this action reduces output in the short run. Sometimes policymakers are unwilling to pay this price.

This reasoning rests on the assumption of adaptive expectations. With that assumption, we can write the Phillips curve equation as $\pi = \pi(-1) + \alpha \tilde{Y}$. Inflation equals past inflation if the output gap is zero; to reduce inflation, the central bank must push output below potential.

The assumption of rational expectations undermines the traditional explanation for inflation, because it implies that disinflation can be costless. If the central bank plans to reduce inflation, it can first announce its intention to the public. If people believe the announcement, then expected inflation falls. From the Phillips curve, a fall in expected inflation reduces actual inflation, even if the output gap is zero. Because disinflation doesn't require an output loss, the central bank has no reason to produce high inflation.

Figure 16.1 illustrates this point. We assume that expected inflation starts at a high level, implying an initial Phillips curve of PC_1. The central bank wants to reduce inflation to the level it considers best, π^{ideal}. You might think of π^{ideal} as 2 percent, the inflation rate that many central banks target. Policymakers announce that inflation will fall to π^{ideal}, causing expected inflation to fall and shifting the Phillips curve down to PC_2. With this Phillips curve, the central bank can produce inflation of π^{ideal} while keeping output at potential.

When Kydland and Prescott published their article in the late 1970s, the rational-expectations revolution was at its height. Ironically, it was also a period when the U.S. inflation rate reached double digits and policymakers seemed unable to reduce it. Economic theory was saying that inflation is easy to eliminate, but real-world inflation was stubbornly high. Kydland and Prescott sought to resolve this paradox—to explain how high inflation can occur despite rational expectations.

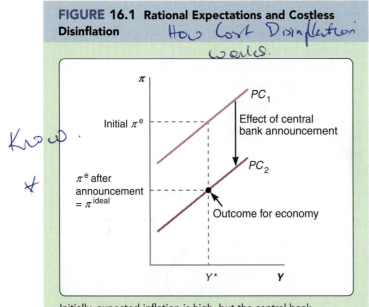

FIGURE 16.1 Rational Expectations and Costless Disinflation

Initially, expected inflation is high, but the central bank announces it will reduce inflation to π^{ideal}. Expectations are rational and the public believes the announcement, so expected inflation falls. The Phillips curve shifts down, allowing the central bank to reduce inflation without reducing output.

Answering the Puzzle In the Kydland–Prescott theory, the central bank would like to follow the anti-inflation policy shown in Figure 16.1. It would like to promise low inflation so that expected inflation falls. Unfortunately, this policy is not time consistent. The central bank has an incentive to renege on its promise, just like a dad issuing threats to his kids.

This incentive arises from the Phillips curve. Once expected inflation is set, there is a trade-off between output and inflation. If expected inflation is low, the central bank has an incentive for expansionary policy—a decrease in interest rates. This policy causes an output boom but also raises inflation above the expected level.

Figure 16.2 illustrates this point. We assume for the moment that the central bank has promised an inflation rate of π^{ideal}, and the public believes this promise. So π^e in the Phillips curve is π^{ideal}. In this situation, the central bank has two options. One is to keep output at potential, producing the inflation rate that's expected. In this case, the economy ends up at outcome A in Figure 16.2. The other option is to raise output above potential, which the central bank can do by lowering interest rates. Raising output moves the economy along the Phillips curve to outcome B, with an inflation rate somewhat above π^{ideal}. In this case, the public's inflation expectations turn out to be wrong.

Will the central bank choose point A or point B on the Phillips curve? We will call this choice the *inflation-surprise decision*. According to Kydland and Prescott, policymakers are likely to choose point B, where output exceeds potential and inflation is higher than the public expects. An increase in output has large benefits: people's incomes rise and unemployment falls. Policymakers don't like the higher inflation, but they may decide it is an acceptable cost of producing an economic boom.

You may see what's coming. The public understands the central bank's incentives. If policymakers promise inflation of π^{ideal}, people realize the

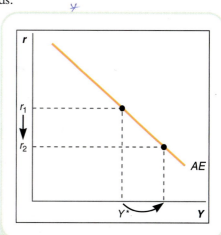

In the short run, the central bank can raise output above potential by reducing the real interest rate.

FIGURE 16.2 The Inflation-Surprise Decision

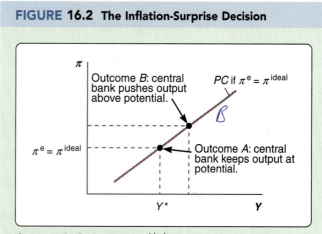

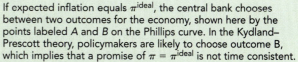

If expected inflation equals π^{ideal}, the central bank chooses between two outcomes for the economy, shown here by the points labeled A and B on the Phillips curve. In the Kydland–Prescott theory, policymakers are likely to choose outcome B, which implies that a promise of $\pi = \pi^{\text{ideal}}$ is not time consistent.

policymakers are likely to renege, so everyone ignores the promise. The situation in Figure 16.2, with $\pi^e = \pi^{\text{ideal}}$, never arises. Instead, as shown in **Figure 16.3**, expected inflation is high. Through the Phillips curve, high expected inflation produces high actual inflation. We call this outcome the *high-inflation trap*.

In Figure 16.3, we assume the central bank keeps output at potential. Notice that policymakers still have the option of raising output and moving along the Phillips curve. But this option is less appealing than it was in Figure 16.2. In the high-inflation trap, expected inflation is high. This

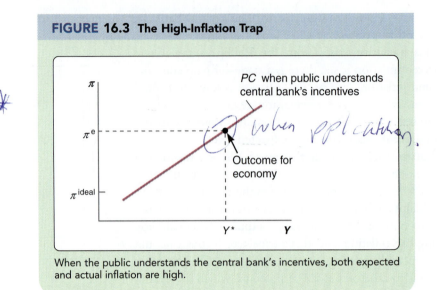

FIGURE 16.3 The High-Inflation Trap

When the public understands the central bank's incentives, both expected and actual inflation are high.

means inflation is a serious problem even if policymakers keep it at the expected level. Pushing inflation even higher would have large costs, so policymakers don't do it.

Solving the Time-Consistency Problem

In the Kydland–Prescott theory, the time-consistency problem dooms the economy to high inflation. But is the situation really hopeless? Is there any way for central banks to solve the time-consistency problem? These questions have stimulated much analysis. Economists have suggested several methods for reducing the problem.

Conservative Policymakers One idea was suggested in 1983 by Kenneth Rogoff, a young economist at the Federal Reserve Board (now an older Harvard professor). His idea is based on the fact that governments appoint the policymakers who run central banks. The U.S. president, for example, appoints the chair of the Federal Reserve. Rogoff suggests that governments can solve the time-consistency problem via their choices of policymakers.

The criterion for choosing policymakers is their views about inflation. Economists have not reached a consensus about how inflation affects the economy. Some believe it does severe damage, while others think the costs are modest. Rogoff uses the term *conservative* for those who strongly dislike inflation. These people think it is more important to keep inflation low than to stimulate output. Rogoff argues that governments should appoint **conservative policymakers** to run central banks.

To see how this strategy solves the time-consistency problem, look again at the surprise-inflation decision in Figure 16.2. In this scenario, the public expects inflation of π^{ideal}. Kydland and Prescott say the central bank will create an output boom that raises inflation above π^{ideal}. But that won't happen if policymakers are conservative. Conservatives won't raise output,

▶ Section 14.2 surveys economists' thinking on the costs of inflation.

Conservative policymaker central bank official who believes it is more important to keep inflation low than to stimulate output because they believe the benefits of doing so are outweighed by the costs of higher inflation. If the public expects inflation of π^{ideal}, that's what it gets.

Therefore, if policymakers are conservative, the time-consistency problem disappears. The central bank can promise inflation of π^{ideal} and people will believe it. Then policymakers produce the promised inflation rate by keeping output at potential. They achieve the low-inflation outcome in Figure 16.1, which eludes less conservative policymakers.

Remember this in case you become president of the United States. If Rogoff's analysis is correct, then you should choose conservatives to run the Fed. Note that you, the president, should appoint conservatives even if you are *not* conservative yourself. You might care more about output than inflation, but it would be foolish to appoint a Fed chair who shares your concern. Such an appointment would lead to the high-inflation trap in Figure 16.3. A conservative will produce lower inflation without reducing output.

Reputation Conservative policymakers are one hope for escaping high inflation. Another is central bankers' concern for their reputations. Regardless of whether policymakers are conservative in Rogoff's sense of the term, they would like people to *believe* they are conservative. This concern can solve the time-consistency problem.

To see this point, suppose a new Fed chair is appointed. Initially, the public doesn't know this person's views about inflation—policymakers don't wear labels saying they are or are not conservative. The public judges the chair based on her performance in office. If the chair produces low inflation, then she gains a reputation as a conservative, and the public expects low inflation in the future. Conversely, a record of high inflation produces high expected inflation.

High expected inflation is bad for the economy. It shifts the Phillips curve up, raising actual inflation for any given output gap. This shift worsens the trade-off facing policymakers. So any Fed chair would like to gain a conservative reputation that keeps expected inflation low.

This desire influences the surprise-inflation decision in Figure 16.2. As before, expansionary policy has the benefit of raising output and the cost of raising inflation. But now it has an additional cost: it damages the chair's reputation as an inflation fighter, hurting the economy in the future. Even if the Fed chair is *not* conservative, this additional cost may tip her decision away from expansionary policy. Like a true conservative, she keeps inflation at π^{ideal} if that's what the public expects. This eliminates the time-consistency problem, making low inflation feasible.

In this theory, it is desirable for policymakers to care a lot about their reputations. This happens if policymakers have long time horizons—if they put a large weight on how their actions today affect the future. Then the costs of raising expected inflation are a strong deterrent to inflation.

One way to encourage long horizons is to give central bank officials long terms in office. If policymakers come and go, each may decide to do what's best for the economy while he's in charge, and that leads to the high-inflation trap. If a policymaker will be around for a long time, he cares more about his reputation.

► Although people use the word *conservative* to describe viewpoints on many issues, from tax policy to Supreme Court decisions, Rogoff's definition has caught on in monetary-policy discussions.

A Policy Rule The last solution to the time-consistency problem is the simplest. The government imposes a rule requiring the central bank to produce low inflation. Kydland and Prescott advocated such a rule in their 1977 article.

Suppose again you are the U.S. president. Don't worry about whom you appoint as Fed chair or the length of the chair's term. Instead, ask Congress to pass a law requiring the Fed to produce an inflation rate of π^{ideal}. The law might say that any Fed chair who produces inflation significantly above π^{ideal} is fired. Or, to be really safe, the punishment could include a prison term.

This law quickly eliminates the time-consistency problem. To avoid punishment, Fed chairs will try hard to keep inflation at π^{ideal}, even if they think higher inflation would benefit the economy. In other words, the rule forces policymakers to act conservative even if they are not. Understanding this, the public will expect inflation of π^{ideal}.

16.2 CENTRAL BANK INDEPENDENCE

The United States is a representative democracy. Most decisions about economic policy are made by elected officials. For example, fiscal policy— taxation and government spending—is determined by Congress and the president. If the majority of citizens don't like these leaders' policies, they can vote them out of office.

Monetary policy is a critical part of economic policy, with strong effects on people's jobs and incomes. But unlike taxes and spending, monetary policy is not determined by elected government officials. It is run by the independent Federal Reserve System, most of whose leaders have never won an election.

Politicians and economists have long debated whether central banks should be independent of governments. Today, a consensus holds that independence is good. We will see that this belief reflects the Kydland–Prescott theory of time consistency and inflation.

The Independent Federal Reserve

▶ Section 11.1 explains the structure of the Federal Reserve System.

The U.S. Constitution gives Congress the power to create money, but Congress has delegated this job to the Federal Reserve, which it established in 1913. The government has little control over Fed officials. Governors of the Fed system are chosen by the U.S. president initially, but they serve 14-year terms and can't be fired. Presidents of Federal Reserve Banks are chosen by the member banks' boards of directors without any input from elected officials.

In addition, the U.S. government has an informal tradition of treating the Fed as independent and nonpolitical. Fed governors are likely to be chosen for technical expertise in monetary policy rather than political connections. Ben Bernanke's 2005 appointment as Fed chair is a clear example. Bernanke had served briefly as a Bush administration economist, but he spent most of his career as a professor at Stanford and Princeton universities. He made his name by publishing papers in academic journals, and he was not active in politics.

Another tradition is that Fed chairs serve for a long time. The U.S. president has the right to replace the chair every 4 years but often forgoes this

▶ At least, Bernanke was not active in national politics. While at Princeton, he was twice elected to the school board of Montgomery Township, New Jersey.

opportunity—even if the president and the Fed chair belong to different political parties. Bernanke was appointed by Republican George W. Bush and reappointed by Democrat Barack Obama. Bernanke's predecessor, Alan Greenspan, was chair from 1987 to 2006, when he retired at age 79. He was appointed by Republican Ronald Reagan and reappointed by Democrat Bill Clinton, as well as both Republican Bushes. Before that, Paul Volcker was appointed by Democrat Jimmy Carter and reappointed by Reagan.

Recent administrations have helped strengthen the Fed's independence by resisting the temptation to give it advice or to criticize its actions publicly. In 1999, President Clinton said, "I've made a real practice of trying not to comment on interest rate changes and trying to let Chairman Greenspan and the Fed do their work and I would do mine." Presidents Bush and Obama have followed the same policy. Reporters ask administration officials about their views on Fed policy, but generally they don't get an answer.

Another factor behind the Fed's independence is its income. Most government agencies depend on funding from Congress, so members of Congress can use the threat of budget cuts to influence agencies' policies. The Fed, however, does not need congressional appropriations. In creating the monetary base, it trades money for bonds that produce billions of dollars in interest income each year. It uses part of this income to fund its operations and returns the rest to the U.S. Treasury. Like an independently wealthy person, the Fed is free to do what it chooses without fear that someone will punish it financially.

▶ Section 11.2 describes how the Fed acquires bonds in creating the monetary base.

Congress does monitor what the Fed does. Congressional acts require the Fed chair to testify twice a year before the Senate Banking Committee and the House Committee on Financial Services. The chair is asked to explain the Fed's policies, and committee members sometimes criticize the chair or ask sharp questions. But this is just talk—under current law, Congress can't force the Fed to change its policies.

Independence Around the World

Before the 1990s, most central banks were less independent than the Federal Reserve. The Bank of England was an extreme example, because it had no authority to set interest rates. Rates were chosen instead by a government official, the chancellor of the exchequer (the British equivalent of the U.S. secretary of the treasury). The central bank had only a technical job: it performed open-market operations to produce the interest rates chosen by the chancellor.

Other central banks were more independent than the Bank of England but less independent than the Fed. In Japan, interest rates were chosen by the Policy Board of the Bank of Japan. However, the board was not entirely independent: it included one official from the government's ministry of finance and another from its economic-planning agency. In addition, the Japanese government had the authority to fire the governor of the bank.

In continental Europe, countries such as Germany and Switzerland had highly independent central banks. But in countries such as France and Italy, governments had the right to veto central-bank decisions.

This landscape has changed drastically over the last two decades. Around the world, governments have enacted legislation to make their central banks more independent. This movement started in New Zealand, where a 1989 law changed the central bank from one of the least independent in the world to one of the most independent. In 1997, the United Kingdom shifted interest rate decisions from the chancellor of the exchequer to the Bank of England. In 1998, Japan eliminated most of the government's influence over the Bank of Japan. Many Latin American countries also granted independence to their central banks during the 1990s. Today, U.S.-style independence is the worldwide norm.

The European Central Bank (ECB) is highly independent. The creation of the ECB in 1999 was authorized by the Maastricht Treaty of 1992. Under the treaty, European governments agreed to give up authority over monetary policy when they adopted the euro as their currency. The ECB's independence has unusually strong foundations because it does not depend on legislation in any one country. The Maastricht Treaty can be changed only by agreement of all the countries that signed it.

Yet not *all* central banks are independent. For example, the People's Bank of China must receive approval for major decisions from the State Council, part of the Chinese government. Officials at the People's Bank have argued for greater independence, as have outside economists and the International Monetary Fund, but so far the government has not relaxed its control.

What explains the trend toward central bank independence? Why do economists urge China to follow this trend? Policymakers have debated the pros and cons of independence for many years. In the 1990s, many countries decided that the pro-independence side had the stronger arguments. Let's survey both sides of this debate.

Opposition to Independence

Many people have criticized the independence of the Fed. Their central argument is a political one: in a democracy, elected officials should control economic policy. At a minimum, Congress should have greater influence over the Fed.

One person with this view is Congressman Barney Frank (D-Massachusetts), the ranking minority member of the House committee that oversees the Fed. In a 2007 speech, then-chairman Frank criticized the idea that "the Fed somehow should be above democracy." He asserted a role for Congress in monetary policy, saying sarcastically, "God forbid anybody in elected office should talk about whether or not we need a 25-basis-point increase in interest rates. Somehow that's sacrosanct. No, it isn't. It's public policy."

For many critics of Fed independence, a desire for democracy is mixed with another concern. They fear that the priorities of central banks are those of financial interests, not ordinary citizens. These critics follow in a long tradition of populists, such as Andrew Jackson, who have distrusted central banks. Today's populists argue that the Fed is too concerned with fighting inflation, which Wall Street dislikes, and does not care enough about promoting employment. At a 2007 hearing, Barney Frank reminded Ben Bernanke that Congress has set "maximum employment" as one of the Fed's goals. Frank said, "I am concerned there are people at the Fed who don't really accept that."

Periodically, members of Congress propose legislation that would reduce the Fed's independence. In 1991, Lee Hamilton of Indiana proposed that Fed bank presidents be removed from the Federal Open Market Committee (FOMC), leaving only the Fed governors. In his view, the power of bank presidents is particularly undemocratic, because they are not appointed by elected officials. Hamilton also proposed that the secretary of the treasury be *added* to the FOMC. In 1996, Senators Dorgan of North Dakota and Reid of Nevada proposed that Congress assume authority over the Fed's budget.

The financial crisis of 2007–2009 spawned criticism of the Fed across the political spectrum. Republicans blamed the housing bubble that preceded the crisis on the low interest rates set by the Fed in the early 2000s. Democrats criticized the Fed for inadequate regulation of financial institutions. Congress members from both parties supported a proposal by Congressman Ron Paul (R-Texas) for the Government Accountability Office (GAO) to audit the Fed regularly. Under this plan, the GAO would report to Congress on the Fed's performance and make recommendations for monetary policy.

The Fed vigorously opposed Congressman Paul's proposal, arguing that it would subject its decision making to harmful political influence. The House of Representatives passed the proposal as part of the financial reform legislation of 2010, but the Senate did not. The act that President Obama signed includes a watered-down version of Paul's proposal. It authorizes a one-time GAO audit of the Fed's emergency lending during the crisis but not of monetary policy in general.

▶ In January 2011, Ron Paul became chairman of the House committee that oversees the Fed.

Anger at the Fed also produced opposition to Ben Bernanke's reappointment as Fed Chair in 2009. For a time it appeared that Bernanke might not be reconfirmed by the Senate. After lobbying by President Obama, the Senate confirmed Bernanke by a vote of 70–30 in January 2010. The 30 no votes totaled the most opposition ever to a Fed chair's appointment.

Some observers think the battles over GAO oversight and Bernanke's reconfirmation have weakened the Fed. In the future, Fed officials may hesitate to undertake policies that will cause political trouble. The *Wall Street Journal* suggested during the confirmation debate that Bernanke "won't speak with the same authority, and the Fed will have a harder time casting itself as above partisan politics."[1]

The Traditional Case for Independence

What are the arguments for central bank independence? At a philosophical level, supporters argue that Fed independence is not really undemocratic. Congress still has ultimate authority over monetary policy. Congressional

---

[1] Jon Hilsenrath, WSJ online edition, Jan. 25, 2010.

acts prescribe the goals of policy, and it was Congress's choice to assign the pursuit of these goals to the Fed.

Most important, proponents of independence believe that it leads to better monetary policy. The arguments about why have evolved over time. A long-standing argument is that independence protects the Fed from political pressures for unwise policies—in particular, policies that produce high inflation.

To understand this traditional argument, assume the following Phillips curve: $\pi = \pi(-1) + \alpha \tilde{Y}(-1)$. This version of the Phillips curve is based on the assumption of adaptive expectations, where inflation depends on past inflation. The equation also assumes that inflation depends on output one year in the past, a realistic time lag that will be important here.

▶ Section 13.4 examines time lags in the Phillips curve.

Economic events affect politics as well. Presidential elections are influenced heavily by the state of the economy in election years. Suppose you are the U.S. president and want to be reelected. Suppose also that the Fed is *not* independent: you can tell it what to do. You can help yourself by ordering a monetary expansion, one that causes an economic boom during the election year. The boom will cause inflation to rise, but with a lag; if you time it right, inflation will rise *after* the election. On election day, voters will see a booming economy and stable inflation and reward you with another term.

Unfortunately, this shortsighted strategy is bad for the economy in the long run. Inflation rises after the election. And with the Phillips curve we have assumed, the increase is permanent. Future policymakers must either live with high inflation indefinitely or cause a recession to disinflate. Either way, your reelection has a high cost.

This scenario is less likely if the central bank is independent. Fed policymakers don't have to run for reelection. They are free to concentrate on the long-run health of the economy, not its performance in any particular year. They won't expand policy if the future inflationary costs exceed the short-run benefits.

Independence and Time Consistency

The arguments we have discussed have been around for many decades. In the 1980s and 1990s, supporters of central bank independence added new arguments. These do *not* involve elections; instead, they are based on Kydland and Prescott's time-consistency problem. Economists argue that central bank independence reduces this problem for two reasons.

Conservative Central Bankers Ironically, the first argument is closely related to an argument *against* central bank independence. Populists complain that Fed officials are out of step with the public in caring too much about inflation and not enough about output and employment. In Rogoff's terminology, Fed officials are too conservative. Elected leaders are more likely to share the public's concerns, so they should control monetary policy.

In the Kydland–Prescott theory, however, conservatism is a virtue. It helps central banks to escape the time-consistency problem. Turning monetary policy over to less-conservative politicians would worsen this problem, leading to higher inflation without any gain in output. So everyone, even populist members of Congress, should want conservative central bankers to run policy.

Long Horizons The time-consistency problem can be solved if policymakers establish reputations for hating inflation. As we have discussed, this is more likely to happen if policymakers have long time horizons. Economists argue that central bankers have longer horizons than politicians, giving them a better chance of escaping the time-consistency trap.

Long horizons partly reflect long periods in office. We've seen that Fed governors have 14-year terms and that Alan Greenspan was chair for nearly 19 years. If Fed officials acquire reputations for producing high inflation, they know this will raise inflation expectations for a long time. So policymakers have strong incentives to keep inflation low.

In addition, central banks can acquire reputations that are not tied to individual people. This occurs because policy is made by groups of people whose terms in office overlap. In particular, most economists agree that the Fed has a reputation for low inflation after nearly three decades of producing it. As an institution, a central bank has a very long horizon, because its authority lasts indefinitely. So policymakers care a lot about preserving an anti-inflation reputation.

Evidence on Independence and Inflation

The different arguments for central bank independence have a point in common: they imply that independence reduces inflation. Inflation falls because policymakers don't need to get reelected or because the time-consistency problem is reduced. In the 1980s and 1990s, economic researchers tested these theories by comparing central banks in different countries. Most concluded that independence really does reduce inflation.

The first step in this research was to measure the independence of central banks. Economists created numerical ratings of independence based on various factors. For example, a central bank received points if its top policymakers served long terms and could not be fired. It lost points if monetary-policy boards included government officials, or if the government had veto power over central bank decisions.

Once researchers measured central bank independence in various countries, they compared it to inflation. **Figure 16.4** shows one set of results from a 1993 study by Harvard's Alberto Alesina and Lawrence Summers. The figure plots an index of independence against average inflation for the period 1955–1983, revealing a strong negative relation. For the period before 1983, the countries with the most independent central banks, Germany and Switzerland, had the lowest inflation. The least independent banks, in New Zealand and Spain, produced the highest inflation.

Some economists question these results, pointing out that a correlation between two variables does not prove that one causes the other. It could be that some third factor determines both independence and inflation. In particular, some countries may simply dislike inflation more than others.

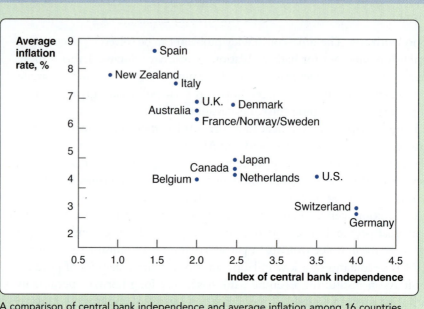

FIGURE 16.4 Central Bank Independence and Inflation, 1955–1988

A comparison of central bank independence and average inflation among 16 countries reveals that countries with more independent central banks have lower inflation.

Source: Adapted from Alberto Alesina and Lawrence H. Summers, "Central Bank Independence and Macroeconomic Performance: Some Comparative Evidence," *Journal of Money, Credit, and Banking*, May 1993, vol. 25, pp. 151–162.

One commonly cited example is Germany. Polls in that country find that people consider inflation very harmful, an attitude that may reflect the scarring experience of the 1920s' hyperinflation. Because Germans hate inflation, their central bank kept inflation low. The government supported this policy by making the central bank independent, but this was not the underlying cause of low inflation. Granting the same independence to Spain's central bank would not have reduced inflation to German levels, because Spaniards don't hate inflation as much as Germans do.

Despite this argument, governments in most countries have become convinced that central bank independence does reduce inflation. They interpret the relationship in Figure 16.4 as causal. Evidence like this is a major reason for the trend toward independence since 1989.

16.3 MONETARY-POLICY RULES

Independent central banks wield great power over the economy. How freely should they exercise this power? Should central banks be able to adjust policy in any way they like, or should their actions be constrained? This is a classic controversy in economic policy. In economists' language, the question is whether central banks should use discretionary policy or follow a monetary-policy rule.

FOMC example.

Two Approaches to Policy

Discretionary policy means the central bank acts at each point in time based on its judgment of what's good for the economy. This is how the Fed currently operates. The FOMC meets every 6 weeks to set the federal funds rate. At each meeting, committee members examine whatever information they think is relevant and decide what interest rate is best in the current situation.

A **monetary-policy rule**, by contrast, is a simple rule or formula that tells the central bank what to do. When such a rule is in place, the job of policymakers is to follow the rule, not to use their judgment about what actions are best.

One policy rule was proposed by the great economist Milton Friedman. Under this rule, the central bank increases the money supply by a fixed percentage every year. A different rule might dictate that money growth varies over time according to some formula. If the central bank uses an interest rate as its policy instrument, a rule could say how the interest rate is set.

Where does a policy rule come from? It could be imposed on the central bank by legislation or even a constitutional amendment. But a central bank can also adopt a rule on its own. Policymakers can announce the rule and commit themselves to follow it rather than to use discretionary policy.

The traditional distinction between rules and discretion has been somewhat muddied by the work of John Taylor. Fed policies for most of the period since 1987 can be captured approximately by a "Taylor rule" in which the interest rate adjusts to output and inflation. But the Fed has *not* followed a rule in the sense of the rules-versus-discretion debate. Policymakers don't consciously use Taylor's formula, and sometimes they deviate from it significantly.

Which is better—a policy rule or discretion? It might seem obvious that discretion is preferable. Under this approach, the central bank always chooses the policy that appears best in current circumstances. A rule may force the central bank *not* to choose the policy that appears best. How can that be a good idea?

Like the case for central bank independence, the case for rules comes in older and newer styles. And once again, the newer arguments are based on Kydland and Prescott's time-consistency problem.

Traditional Arguments for Rules

The classic case for policy rules was developed in the 1960s by Milton Friedman and his followers, a group called **monetarists**. Monetarists believe that monetary policy has strong effects on output and inflation. In theory, this means that policy can be an effective tool for stabilizing the economy. But in practice, monetarists believe, central banks misuse this tool. Their discretionary policies do more harm than good, so they should be constrained by rules.

Monetarists point out two problems with discretionary policy, both related to ideas we've discussed before. Policymakers can make well-intentioned mistakes, and they can succumb to political pressure.

Discretionary policy monetary policy that is adjusted at each point in time based on the judgment of the central bank

Monetary-policy rule a simple rule or formula that tells the central bank how to run policy

▶ To review the Taylor rule, see Chapter 15.

Monetarists school of economists who believe that monetary policy has strong effects on the economy and that policy should be set by a rule

Mistakes for
Discretionary
Policy and

▶ Section 15.5 discusses central bankers' uncertainty about the economy.

Well-Intentioned Mistakes Central bankers are uncertain about the economy. They may misjudge parameters such as the natural rate of unemployment or the effects of interest rates on spending. Because of these mistakes, efforts to stabilize the economy can backfire and destabilize it. It would be better, monetarists conclude, if a rule prevented the central bank from attempting stabilization.

Milton Friedman expressed these ideas with a metaphor. In 1960, he wrote:

> *What we need is not a skilled monetary driver of the economic vehicle continuously turning the steering wheel to adjust to the unexpected irregularities of the route, but some means of keeping the monetary passenger who is in the back seat as ballast from occasionally leaning over and giving the steering wheel a jerk that threatens to send the car off the road.*[2]

A monetary rule is a way of keeping the Fed's hands off the steering wheel.

Support for these ideas grew during the 1970s. During that period, the Fed appeared to jerk the steering wheel: it overreacted to movements in output and inflation. It allowed inflation to rise in the early 1970s, perhaps because it underestimated the natural rate of unemployment. It then became alarmed by inflation and tightened sharply, causing a deep recession in 1974–75, at which point it loosened again, causing another rise in inflation. The decade ended with another sharp tightening, the start of the Volcker disinflation. These policy shifts were meant to stabilize the economy, but critics think they did the opposite.

Political Influence The other traditional argument against discretion is that it allows politics to influence monetary policy. As we have discussed, politicians would like monetary expansions before elections, even if these actions hurt the economy in the long run. They may pressure the central bank for overly expansionary policies.

Central bank independence is meant to solve this problem, but this solution has not always worked. Recent presidents have respected the Fed's independence, but some of their predecessors have not. Some historians argue that presidents have been able to influence the Fed to an unhealthy extent. This could not happen if the Fed's hands were tied by a policy rule. The next case study discusses a famous episode of presidential pressure on the Fed.

CASE STUDY

Nixon and Burns

Richard Nixon understood the effects of monetary policy on elections. In his book *Six Crises*, he complained that a Fed tightening had slowed the economy before the 1960 presidential election. Voters blamed the Eisenhower administration, in which Nixon was vice president. Nixon thought this contributed to his narrow loss to John Kennedy.

---

[2] Milton Friedman, *A Program for Monetary Stability*, New York: Fordham University Press, 1960.

Once Nixon became president in 1968, he didn't want monetary policy to interfere with his reelection. William McChesney Martin's term as Fed chair expired in 1970, and Nixon replaced him with Arthur Burns. Burns was a highly respected economist and long-time Nixon advisor. At the time of his Fed appointment, Burns was part of Nixon's White House staff. Some historians suggest that Nixon chose a Fed chair whom he thought would follow his wishes.

Richard Nixon (center) consults with his economic advisors during the 1968 presidential campaign. The group includes Arthur Burns (second from right) and Milton Friedman (second from left).

Clearly, Nixon tried to influence Burns's policies. At the ceremony to announce Burns's appointment, Nixon said, half-jokingly, "I respect his independence. However, I hope that independently he will conclude that my views are the ones that should be followed." When his audience applauded, Nixon said, "You see, Dr. Burns, that is a standing vote for lower interest rates and more money."

In private, Nixon gave Burns blunt advice. A biographer of Burns quotes Nixon as telling him, "You see to it: no recession." In a letter to Burns, Nixon acknowledged why this was so important: "I must register with you, as strongly as I can, my concern that what really determines the result of an election is not interest rates, but unemployment statistics around election time." White House aides sometimes called on Burns to reiterate the president's desire for expansionary policy.

According to William Safire, a Nixon speechwriter, the administration used the press to pressure Burns. When Burns resisted Nixon's policy suggestions, the White House planted a false and unflattering story that Burns was seeking a pay raise. Administration officials also suggested they were considering legislation to increase the number of Fed governors, which would have diluted Burns's power.

Was this pressure effective? In retrospect, monetary policy was clearly too loose before the 1972 election. The economy grew too rapidly, helping to fuel the high inflation of the mid-1970s. Some historians think the Fed made an honest mistake because it mismeasured the natural rate of unemployment. But others think Burns was overly eager to help Nixon. They point out that Burns resisted proposals by other Fed governors to tighten policy.[*]

▶ Section 15.5 discusses alternative explanations for the Fed's policy mistakes during the 1970s.

* For more on this episode, see Burton A. Abrams, "How Richard Nixon Pressured Arthur Burns: Evidence from the Nixon Tapes," *Journal of Economic Perspectives*, 20 (Fall 2006): 177–188.

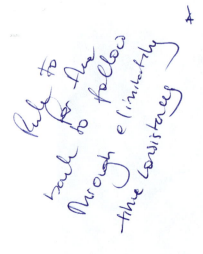

Time Consistency Again

The case for monetary-policy rules was bolstered by Kydland and Prescott's analysis of the time-consistency problem. This problem arises under discretionary policy, which gives the central bank power to loosen policy whenever it wants. As we have discussed, a policy rule is a simple solution to the problem. A rule can force the central bank to produce low inflation. The time-consistency problem disappears.

Notice that this argument is quite different from the traditional arguments for rules. Suppose that central banks pay no attention to politicians. And suppose they don't make mistakes—they understand exactly how their policies affect the economy. The time-consistency problem still causes central banks with discretion to produce too much inflation.

Money Targets

Suppose you are convinced that central banks should follow a policy rule. What rule is best? Thinking on this topic has changed over time. From the 1960s to the 1980s, the leading proposal was Milton Friedman's rule of fixed money growth.

▶ Section 11.5 discusses interest rate targeting and the rationale for this policy.

Currently, most central banks use an interest rate as their policy instrument. They set targets for the interest rate and adjust the money supply to hit the targets. Friedman and the monetarists argued that central banks should instead target the money supply and let markets determine interest rates.

Further, they proposed a simple rule for money targets: the targets should grow over time at a low, constant rate, such as 3 percent per year. Each year, the central bank should raise the money supply 3 percent above its level in the previous year. Money growth determines inflation in the long run, so low money growth would keep average inflation low. In addition, the monetarists argued, the constancy of money growth would promote stability in output and inflation.

Crucially, the monetarist rule implies that central banks do *not* "lean against the wind" of output and inflation movements. In a recession, a central bank with discretion is likely to raise money growth to stimulate aggregate spending; in a boom, it slows money growth. The monetarist rule forbids these variations in money growth, because they are likely to backfire and destabilize the economy.

Today, few economists advocate a fixed growth rate for the money supply—or any policy based on money targets. Most economists believe that money demand is unstable, which implies that money targets destabilize output. In the United States, money targeting was discredited by the experience of 1979–1982, when the Fed tried this policy and output fluctuated sharply.

Most other central banks have also dismissed the idea of money targets. But there is a major exception: the European Central Bank. The ECB announces targets for money growth, although it doesn't try to hit them precisely. We discuss the ECB's approach in an upcoming case study.

16.4 INFLATION TARGETS

During the 1980s, many central bankers were unsure of the best approach to monetary policy. They were convinced of the dangers of discretion. But they didn't like the monetarist rule of fixed money growth, both because of instability in money demand and because they were reluctant to give up entirely on leaning against the wind. So central bankers searched for new policy ideas.

Today, many central bankers think they have found a good way to run policy: explicit inflation targeting. Policymakers announce that they want to keep inflation near a certain level, such as 2 percent, or in a certain range, such as 1–3 percent. They also declare that achieving this goal is the primary focus of policy.

Explicit inflation targets were first introduced by New Zealand in 1989, Chile in 1990, and Canada in 1991. Since then, inflation targeting has spread around the world, and many economists advocate it for the United States. Let's discuss how inflation targeting works and the arguments for and against this policy.

How Inflation Targeting Works

Inflation targeting is a different type of policy from money or interest rate targeting. "Targeting" in those cases refers to the choice of a policy instrument, a variable the central bank controls precisely.

An inflation target, by contrast, is a goal for the economy that the central bank can't achieve perfectly. Inflation is influenced by economic shocks, which policy can offset only with a lag. So inflation inevitably fluctuates somewhat around the target. This imprecision is one reason why countries sometimes announce a target range rather than a single number.

⟹ fluctuations around the target.

A related feature of inflation targeting is that it is forward looking. The lags in policy effects mean that central banks can't raise or lower current inflation if it is off-target. Instead, they try to push future inflation toward the target.

Adjusting Interest Rates Most central banks use an interest rate as their policy instrument, including most central banks with inflation targets. Thus, in common terminology, many central banks are both interest rate targeters *and* inflation targeters. They use their interest rate instrument to pursue their goal for inflation.

Because of time lags, a major part of inflation targeting involves forecasting inflation. Central bank economists forecast inflation using various economic models and statistical methods. They try to predict how inflation would respond to different interest rates. Policymakers choose interest rates that imply forecasts of inflation heading toward the target.

Figure 16.5 graphs an example of inflation targeting in the Republic of Laurencia. The Central Bank of Laurencia has an inflation target of 2 percent, but in 2020 a rise in world oil prices has pushed inflation to 3.5 percent. If the bank keeps interest rates constant, its economists forecast that inflation will follow path A, staying well above 2 percent. So the bank needs to raise rates.

▶ Section 15.6 describes how the Federal Reserve forecasts inflation and other economic variables.

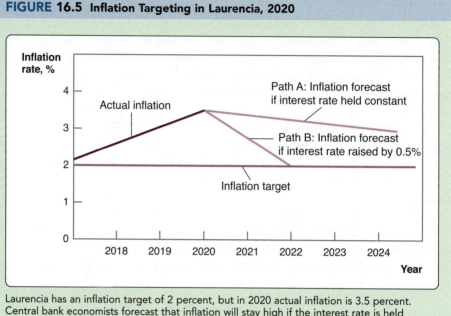

FIGURE 16.5 Inflation Targeting in Laurencia, 2020

Laurencia has an inflation target of 2 percent, but in 2020 actual inflation is 3.5 percent. Central bank economists forecast that inflation will stay high if the interest rate is held constant. Policymakers raise the interest rate, pushing inflation forecasts back to the target.

The bank's economists estimate that a half-point rise in interest rates will shift inflation to path B, which leads back to the target in 2022. So the bank raises rates by this amount. Depending on shocks after 2020, inflation in 2022 may end up higher or lower than forecasted, so the bank may continue to miss its target. But it will keep adjusting interest rates to push inflation in the right direction.

Flexible Targets Economists distinguish between two types of inflation targeting. *Strict targeting* means that hitting the inflation target is the central bank's only goal. If shocks push inflation away from the target, policy pushes it back as quickly as possible.

Flexible targeting means the central bank is not concerned *only* with inflation; it also pays attention to the goal of output stability. As a result, it may tolerate some deviations from the inflation target. If inflation is above target, for example, policymakers may reduce it slowly. They don't disinflate quickly, because that would require a sharp increase in interest rates and a sharp fall in output.

In practice, it appears that central banks choose flexible inflation targeting. No central bank ignores output stabilization entirely. The Bank of England has expressed a typically flexible attitude, saying that strict targeting would create "unnecessary uncertainty and volatility." The bank's goal is that "inflation can be brought back to target within a reasonable time period without creating undue instability in the economy."[3]

---

[3] "Monetary Policy Framework" at www.bankofengland.co.uk

An open question is, just how flexible should targeters be? How long is it acceptable for inflation to vary from the target? How much output volatility is acceptable to control inflation? Central banks have not given clear answers to these questions. The Bank of England, for example, does not define the "reasonable time period" in which inflation should return to target.

Because of this vagueness, inflation targeting is not as rigid as a traditional policy rule, such as money targeting. It allows more leeway for policymakers to use their judgment. Policy under inflation targeting is sometimes called *constrained discretion*, meaning it is a compromise between a monetary-policy rule and purely discretionary policy.

The Spread of Inflation Targeting

The 1990s were a momentous period for monetary policy. Many central banks became more independent during that decade, as we saw in Section 16.2. At the same time, many countries adopted explicit inflation targeting.

Figure 16.6 presents a time line showing when countries adopted inflation targeting. Starting with New Zealand, seven countries adopted the policy between 1989 and 1993. These pioneers inspired other countries, and inflation targeting spread around the world in the late 1990s and 2000s.

In some countries, the decision to adopt inflation targets was made by the central bank. At some point, central bank officials simply announced that they would start targeting a certain inflation rate. In other countries, the government has imposed inflation targeting on the central bank. One example is the

FIGURE 16.6 The Spread of Inflation Targeting

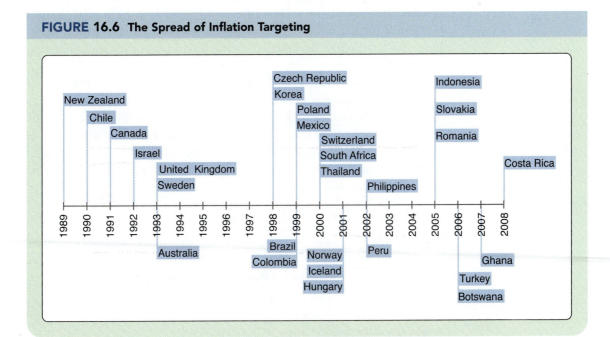

United Kingdom. The British government has granted independence to the Bank of England in the sense that the bank sets interest rates. But the chancellor of the exchequer still tells the bank what goal to pursue in adjusting rates. Currently, the bank is required to target 2-percent inflation.

Another variation is inflation targets chosen jointly by the government and the central bank. In Canada, for example, the government's finance minister and the central bank governor sign periodic agreements on targets. A 2006 agreement extended the target range of 1–3 percent through 2011.

Monitoring the Policy When inflation targeting is established, it is usually accompanied by another change: the central bank starts publishing more information about its policies. One purpose is to assure the government and the public that policymakers are doing their best to achieve the announced targets. Typically, the central bank publishes an inflation report every 3 months. These reports present forecasts of inflation and discuss what interest rates are needed to push inflation to its target. For example, the Bank of England publishes a detailed report that usually runs about 50 pages.

In some countries, the central bank must provide a formal explanation if inflation deviates significantly from target. If the Bank of England misses its 2 percent target by more than 1 percentage point, the governor must write an open letter to the chancellor of the exchequer discussing what happened and how the bank will rectify the situation. This requirement was triggered for the first time in April 2007, when inflation reached 3.1 percent.

Inflation Targeting in the United States? The Federal Reserve has not adopted explicit inflation targeting, but many economists think it should. Ben Bernanke's 2005 appointment as Fed chair increased speculation about this possibility, because Bernanke had advocated inflation targeting as an economics professor. Bernanke and Frederic Mishkin of Columbia University coined the term *constrained discretion* in a 1997 paper.[4] After Bernanke took office, he initiated several discussions of inflation targeting at FOMC meetings.

Yet it is not clear whether inflation targeting is in the Fed's future. Facing opposition from some governors, Bernanke did not push to adopt the policy immediately. Starting in 2007, the Fed was distracted from the issue by urgent problems arising from the financial crisis. It's likely that discussions of inflation targeting will heat up again when the economy is more tranquil.

Why do some people support inflation targeting and others oppose it? Let's turn to the pros and cons of this policy.

The Case for Inflation Targeting

In some ways, inflation targeting is not very different from policy in non-targeting countries, including the United States. The Fed appears to have an *implicit* inflation target of around 1–2 percent. It tightens policy when

---

[4] Ben Bernanke and Frederic Mishkin, "Inflation Targeting: A New Framework for Monetary Policy," *Journal of Economic Perspectives*, 11 (Spring 1997): 97–116.

inflation rises above this level and loosens when inflation falls, just as it would if the target were explicit. Some economists conclude that it doesn't matter whether central banks announce inflation targets. This action has little effect because it doesn't change policymakers' choices of interest rates.

Yet many economists believe that explicit inflation targets have marked benefits. Advocates of inflation targeting make two main arguments: targeting reduces the dangers of discretionary policy, and it anchors inflation expectations.

Locking in Good Policy We've seen that inflation targeting is less rigid than a traditional policy rule. Yet the central bank's behavior is "constrained" by the commitment to targets. Constraints reduce the dangers of discretionary policy.

In particular, explicit targets help to prevent high inflation. If inflation rates were consistently above target, it would be obvious that the central bank was not doing its job. This would prompt criticism and embarrass policymakers. It would probably endanger their reappointments. All this gives policymakers incentives to keep inflation low.

Another constraint is the requirement that policymakers explain their actions in inflation reports. This requirement reduces the risk of erratic policy or political influence. Under inflation targeting, it would have been hard for Arthur Burns to expand policy to help Richard Nixon. Burns would have been hard-pressed to justify his actions on economic grounds.

Anchored Expectations Supporters of inflation targeting argue that it changes the behavior of expectations in a way that stabilizes output and inflation. The argument starts from the premise that, in the absence of inflation targeting, expectations are likely to be adaptive. In other words, a shock that causes the inflation rate to change also changes expected inflation going forward. In contrast, if the central bank announces an inflation target, the public comes to understand that changes in inflation will be temporary—that policymakers will push inflation back to the target. Expectations become "anchored": the public expects inflation to equal the target even if recent inflation did not.

Anchored expectations benefit the economy if an adverse supply shock raises inflation. With adaptive expectations, a rise in inflation becomes permanent unless the central bank tightens policy and reduces output. With inflation targets and anchored expectations, by contrast, an inflationary shock does not affect expectations and therefore does not influence future inflation. After the initial shock disappears, inflation goes back to its target automatically, with no policy tightening or output loss required.

▶ Sections 12.4 and 15.4 analyze the effects of a supply shock under adaptive expectations, and Problem 16.7 considers the case of anchored expectations.

Anchored expectations are also beneficial when an economy is threatened by deflation—a relevant situation in the wake of the most recent financial crisis. A deep recession reduces inflation *below* the level desired by policymakers

▶ Section 14.4 discusses the risk of deflation when expectations are adaptive.

and possibly below zero. With adaptive expectations, a fall in inflation reduces expected inflation, which in turn causes actual inflation to fall further. If an inflation target anchors expectations, it arrests this process and helps to keep inflation positive.

These ideas are controversial. Many economists doubt that inflation targeting changes the basic behavior of people's expectations. Some argue that expectations remain adaptive even with targets. Others argue that anchoring can occur with or without targets if the central bank has a track record of keeping inflation stable. Debate on this issue is continuing as part of the larger debate about inflation expectations.

Opposition to Inflation Targeting

Why not adopt an inflation target? Many critics of this policy make a simple argument. Central banks such as the Fed should seek to stabilize both output and inflation. Under inflation targeting, policy focuses primarily on inflation, so output stability suffers. For example, if the economy enters a recession, the central bank may not act aggressively to raise output.

Supporters of inflation targeting respond with two counterarguments. First, in many circumstances inflation targeting naturally stabilizes output as well as inflation. This fact follows from the Phillips curve. When output rises above potential, it causes inflation to rise above its target. To contain inflation, the central bank must tighten policy and curtail the output boom. Conversely, a recession causes inflation to fall *below* its target, so the central bank will loosen policy to fight a recession.

Second, as we discussed earlier, inflation targeting is flexible. Policymakers allow temporary deviations from the target when necessary to stabilize output. An inflation-targeting central bank can stabilize output just as well as a nontargeting central bank.

But will it? Skeptics argue that, in practice, inflation targeting leads policymakers to deemphasize output stability. Remember that one argument *for* inflation targeting is that the policy is not *too* flexible. It "constrains" central banks, putting pressure on them to achieve targets or at least to explain why they don't. Policymakers may be judged as failures if they miss inflation targets too often or by large amounts.

In contrast, central banks do not announce numerical goals for output, and there are no clear criteria for judging the success of output stabilization. Policymakers feel less pressure to stabilize output than to hit inflation targets, and this asymmetry leads them to sacrifice output too readily. If inflation exceeds its target, for example, policymakers may push it down quickly even if this causes a recession.

Some economists think the U.S. experience during the financial crisis illustrates the benefits of not targeting inflation. As we saw in Section 15.7, financial-system problems prompted the Fed to lower interest rates rapidly starting in September 2007. These problems did not immediately reduce the Fed's forecasts of future inflation. If the Fed had been practicing inflation targeting, which makes inflation forecasts central to policy, it might not have eased policy as aggressively as it did. In retrospect, it is fortunate that the Fed eased, because lower interest rates probably dampened the recession that accompanied the financial crisis.

We conclude our discussion of inflation targeting with two case studies. The first discusses evidence on the effects of the policy, and the second discusses a variation on inflation targeting practiced by the European Central Bank.

Online Case Study:
Inflation Targeting and the Financial Crisis

CASE STUDY

Targeters and Nontargeters

A number of economists have tried to measure the effects of inflation targeting by examining countries that adopted it. One study was published in 2005 by this author and Niamh Sheridan of the International Monetary Fund.[*] We examined seven countries that adopted inflation targeting in the early 1990s, comparing their economic performance before and after targeting. We also compared these countries to 13 others that did *not* adopt inflation targets.

Ball and Sheridan found that performance usually improved after a country introduced inflation targeting. Average inflation fell, and both inflation and output became more stable. Inflation expectations, as measured by economists' forecasts of future inflation, also became more stable.

However, countries that *didn't* adopt inflation targets experienced similar improvements in their economies. This result suggests that the improvements were not caused by targeting. Instead, some positive development—perhaps better policy, perhaps fewer adverse shocks—was common to targeters and nontargeters.

Table 16.1 presents some of Ball and Sheridan's results. The table shows inflation rates for the 20 countries in the study. For each country, it presents average inflation for two periods: one from 1985 until the early 1990s, when inflation targeting started; and one from the early 1990s to about 2000 (the exact dates vary across countries).

The table shows that average inflation dropped from the first, pretargeting period to the second, posttargeting period in 19 of the 20 countries in the sample. (The Netherlands was the exception.) These decreases were part of a worldwide trend toward lower inflation. The key result is that the decreases were similar for targeters and nontargeters. In each group, inflation in most countries fell to between 1 and 3 percent in the posttargeting period.

One interpretation of Ball and Sheridan's results is that explicit inflation targeting doesn't have much effect on the economy. However, it is too early to draw strong conclusions, because targeting has only a two-decade history. Perhaps nontargeting central banks will perform less well in the future

TABLE 16.1 Inflation Targeting and Average Inflation

		Average Inflation over Pretargeting Period, %	Average Inflation over Posttargeting Period, %
Targeters	Australia	5.4	2.6
	Canada	4.4	1.6
	Finland	4.1	1.1
	New Zealand	10.2	1.9
	Spain	5.9	2.5
	Sweden	5.4	1.0
	United Kingdom	5.5	2.4
Nontargeters	Austria	2.7	1.8
	Belgium	2.5	1.7
	Denmark	3.2	2.2
	France	3.1	1.4
	Germany	2.2	1.7
	Ireland	3.1	2.1
	Italy	5.7	3.3
	Japan	1.6	0.1
	The Netherlands	1.6	2.2
	Norway	4.9	2.2
	Portugal	10.6	3.5
	Switzerland	3.3	0.8
	United States	3.7	2.5

Source: Laurence Ball and Niamh Sheridan, "Does Inflation Targeting Matter?" in Bernanke and Woodford (eds.), *The Inflation Targeting Debate,* University of Chicago Press, 2005, Table 3.

because of the dangers of discretionary policy. If so, future data may show clearer benefits of inflation targeting.

*See Laurence Ball and Niamh Sheridan, "Does Inflation Targeting Matter?", in Bernanke and Woodford (Eds.), *The Inflation Targeting Debate*, University of Chicago Press, 2005, pp. 249–276. For a skeptical evaluation of Ball and Sheridan's evidence, see Mark Gertler's Comment, pp. 277–282 in the same volume.

CASE STUDY

The ECB's Two Pillars

Most central banks can be identified clearly as inflation targeters or non-targeters. The European Central Bank, however, is an intermediate case. The ECB has an inflation target, but it's a fuzzy one: the ECB seeks inflation "below but close to 2 percent." Policymakers haven't said exactly what that means.

In addition, the ECB's approach to interest rate adjustment differs from pure inflation targeting. Inflation targeters set rates based on forecasts of inflation (see Figure 16.5). The ECB bases interest rate decisions *partly* on inflation forecasts but also on another variable: the growth rate of the money supply. According to the ECB, inflation forecasts and money growth are the "two pillars" of its policy.

Specifically, the ECB has announced a "reference value" of 4.5 percent for annual growth in M3, a broad measure of the money supply. The ECB's M3 aggregate is comparable to the Fed's M2. If the growth of M3 exceeds 4.5 percent, the ECB is more likely than otherwise to tighten policy; if M3 growth is below 4.5 percent, policy is more likely to loosen.

▶ Section 2.4 discusses the Fed's M2 aggregate.

Why respond to money growth? In explaining their policy, ECB officials cite the strong long-run relation between money growth and inflation. Rapid money growth is likely to produce high inflation at some point in the future. So it is prudent to tighten policy, even if short-run forecasts of inflation are low.

More generally, two pillars are better than one because of uncertainty about the economy. Flawed assumptions can lead to inaccurate forecasts of inflation, so it is risky to base policy entirely on these forecasts. Examining money growth is a method of "cross-checking" that reduces the risk of policy mistakes.

Outside the ECB, many economists question the two-pillar approach. One reason is instability in money demand, which has dissuaded other central banks from targeting money. Yet the ECB has resisted suggestions to modify its policy.

16.5 COMMUNICATION BY CENTRAL BANKS

Throughout this chapter, we've seen that expectations about monetary policy affect the economy. Policymakers influence expectations not only by their actions but also by what they say. A big issue for central banks is how best to communicate with the public.

We've already discussed one question about communication: whether central banks should announce explicit inflation targets. Here we address two other issues: how policymakers can establish anti-inflation reputations and how much information they should release about the policy process.

Reputation

In the Kydland–Prescott theory, policymakers should seek reputations as conservatives, people who hate inflation and are determined to keep it low. Such reputations help overcome the time-consistency problem that produces high inflation. Central bankers around the world have taken this idea to heart.

What determines their reputations? The largest factor is past performance: a central banker gains a reputation for low inflation by producing low inflation. However, public statements also matter. Policymakers try to say things that enhance their reputations as inflation fighters.

When he was Fed chair, Alan Greenspan had a strong anti-inflation reputation based on both performance and statements. When Ben Bernanke succeeded Greenspan, he hoped to inherit some of that reputation. Partly for that reason, Bernanke promoted the idea that his policies were similar to Greenspan's. In congressional testimony in 2006, Bernanke said, "My intention is to maintain continuity with the practices of the Federal Reserve in the Greenspan era."

Policymakers at the European Central Bank have tried hard to establish conservative reputations. The ECB was only created in 1999, so it doesn't have a long track record of fighting inflation. Perhaps for this reason, ECB officials have gone to great lengths to assure the public of their opposition to inflation.

▶ Section 14.3 surveys research on the costs of inflation.

One example is a 2000 speech by Ottmar Issing, then the ECB's chief economist, on the costs of inflation. Research has not clearly established that moderate inflation has large costs, but you wouldn't know that from Issing's speech. He mentions several economic costs, such as relative price variability. He then continues:

> [T]he case for price stability goes beyond the purely economic sphere. Price stability, the ability to rely on stable money, is the basis for trust in the interaction between economic agents, trust in property rights, trust in society, and trust in the future more generally. Trust in stable money is also the basis for a free society, the ability of people to take decisions and plan their future for themselves. . . . There is a saying that "peace is not everything, but without peace everything else comes to nothing." I am tempted to say the same thing for price stability. Inflation—like war, to which it is often closely associated—destroys the fruit of honest labour, it devalues savings and investment, it erodes the social fabric of society, and ultimately, puts the very foundations of democracy and freedom at risk.[5]

Statements like this help convince the public that the ECB will keep inflation low.

To illustrate the importance of anti-inflation reputations, the next case study shows what can happen if a policymaker doesn't have one.

CASE STUDY

Alan Blinder

In 1994, President Clinton appointed Alan Blinder as vice chair of the Fed. Blinder had strong qualifications: he was a long-time professor at Princeton University and an expert on monetary policy. (He had coauthored several papers with a younger Princeton colleague, Ben Bernanke.) When Blinder was appointed, journalists speculated that he might eventually succeed Alan Greenspan as Fed chair.

But some observers were critical of the appointment. They feared that Blinder was not strong enough in his opposition to inflation. In a 1987

---

[5] Ottmar Issing, "The Case for Price Stability," St. Edmund's College Millennium Year Lecture, Cambridge University, 2000. Available at www.ecb.int.

book, he had argued that the Fed sometimes overreacted to inflation. Using a medical analogy, he called inflation "a head cold"—annoying, but not a major disease. As a result, he lacked the anti-inflation reputation sought in many central bankers.

When Blinder was appointed, Chairman Greenspan asked David Mullins, the outgoing vice chair, to review Blinder's writings. Mullins was to report on whether Blinder's views were appropriate for a Fed official. Mullins told Greenspan, "It's not perfect." Then he said, "Don't worry, it's not like he's a Communist or anything. It's just in his early publications he's noticeably soft on inflation." Greenspan's response: "I would have preferred he were a Communist."

Once he took office, Blinder was careful not to compare inflation to a head cold. However, he soon ran into trouble at a Fed conference where he was asked to make concluding comments. The topic of the conference was "Reducing Unemployment," so Blinder talked about the effects of monetary policy on unemployment. A Fed publication summarized his remarks as follows:

> [Blinder] pointed out monetary policy could affect short-run cyclical fluctuations in unemployment. Moreover, he argued that central banks should attempt to guide the unemployment rate to the natural rate. He thus viewed the legislative mandate calling upon the Federal Reserve to pursue both maximum employment and stable prices as being an appropriate charge for central banks.[*]

These ideas are basic economic principles that we have discussed in this book. It is clear that the Fed tries to stabilize unemployment at the natural rate. (By Okun's law, this is equivalent to stabilizing output at potential.) Nonetheless, in stressing unemployment rather than the battle against inflation, Blinder's talk differed from many comments by central bankers. As a result, it strengthened impressions that Blinder was not sufficiently conservative in Rogoff's sense, making him a poor choice to run a central bank.

Journalists played up the idea that Blinder had unconventional views. A front-page story in *The New York Times* said Blinder "publicly broke ranks with most of his colleagues today, saying he believed that the nation's central bank should seek to hold down unemployment in setting interest rates." *Newsweek* columnist Robert Samuelson wrote that Blinder's comments showed he lacked "the moral or intellectual qualities needed to lead the Fed."

Chairman Greenspan chose not to comment on the controversy, which many interpreted as lack of support for Blinder. According to journalist Bob Woodward, the result was a "subtle but deadly sting." The controversy probably cost Blinder any chance of promotion to Fed chair. In 1996 he left the Fed for his old job at Princeton.

Blinder thinks he got a raw deal. In writing about his experience, he points out that the views in his speech were conventional, and that Congress has instructed the Fed to seek high employment as well as low inflation. As Blinder puts it ironically, "My endorsement of the Fed's dual mandate meant that the Vice Chairman of the Federal Reserve was publicly endorsing the Federal Reserve Act. Now there's news for you!"

On the other hand, critics suggest that Blinder's remarks were politically naive. They think the Fed's conservative reputation helps keep inflation low, and that policymakers should be careful not to endanger this reputation.[†]

* Bryon Higgins, "Reducing Unemployment: Current Issues and Policy Options—a Summary of the Bank's 1994 Symposium," Federal Reserve Bank of Kansas City *Economic Review*, Fourth Quarter 1994, pp. 45–48.

[†] For more on this episode, see Bob Woodward, *Maestro: Greenspan's Fed and the American Boom*, Simon and Schuster, 2000; and Alan Blinder, "Central Banking in a Democracy," *Federal Reserve Bank of Richmond Review*, 82 (1996): 1–14. The *New York Times* article is Keith Bradsher, "Fed Official Disapproves of Rate Policy," August 28, 1994, p. A6. The Samuelson column is "Economic Amnesia: Alan Blinder Forgets the Dangers of Inflation," *Newsweek*, September 12, 1994 (www.newsweek.com/1994).

Transparency

So far we have discussed policymakers' statements about their basic goals. Many central banks go beyond these broad statements to discuss the rationales for specific actions. They refer to this provision of information as **transparency**. For example, the Web site of the European Central Bank says, "Transparency means providing the public with all relevant information on the ECB's strategy, assessments, and policy decisions as well as on its procedures in an open, clear and timely manner."

> **Transparency** providing clear, detailed information about policymaking to the public

In the last two decades, many central banks have become more transparent, a trend that has accompanied movements toward central bank independence and inflation targeting. Like these other reforms, transparency is motivated partly by academic theories of inflation expectations.

Transparency can take many forms. Different central banks provide different types of information about their policies. However, several approaches have become common:

- Many central banks issue publications that give the rationale for recent decisions. These publications also discuss the likely course of future policy. In countries with inflation targets, this material is usually included in inflation reports. Other central banks have publications that serve the same purpose, such as the ECB's *Monthly Bulletin*.

- Some central banks publish the economic forecasts produced by their staffs. Typically they provide forecasts of inflation and output over the next 2 or 3 years.

- Some central banks publish minutes of the meetings at which interest rates are set. The Fed, for example, publishes minutes of FOMC meetings. This gives the public a picture of the debate behind policy decisions.

- At some central banks, officials hold press conferences to explain their actions and take questions. At the ECB, for example, the president and vice president hold a press conference after each announcement of an interest rate target.

Why Practice Transparency? Central bankers give several reasons for moving toward transparency:

- One reason is political. Many economists support central bank independence but feel uncomfortable with unelected officials making policy in secret. They believe central bankers should be accountable. Policymakers have a duty to explain their actions to the public, from whom their authority ultimately derives.

- Another motive for transparency is its effect on inflation expectations. As we've seen, policymakers want the public to believe that they will keep inflation stable. Broad statements about this intention only go so far. The public is more likely to be convinced if policymakers provide details about what they are doing to control inflation.

- Finally, transparency helps policymakers control long-term interest rates. Aggregate expenditure is influenced by these rates, which in turn depend on expectations of the short-term rates set by central banks (see Section 13.1). A transparent central bank can influence long-term rates by guiding expectations of short-term rates. For example, it can raise long rates by telling the public that short rates will rise in the future.

The Fed's Tradition of Secrecy Transparency hasn't always been popular. Before the 1990s, many central banks were opaque. Mystery surrounded policymaking in many countries, including the United States. A 1987 bestseller about the Fed was called *Secrets of the Temple*.

Before 1994, the FOMC did not release any information at the end of a meeting—not even its interest rate target. The committee ordered open-market operations to achieve the target, but outsiders had to figure out what the target was by observing actual interest rates. Only after 6 weeks, following the *next* FOMC meeting, did the committee release any information. At that point it issued a "Policy Record" giving a broad summary of the meeting.

It was difficult to get more information out of the Fed. The chair was required to testify before Congress, but he described policy only in generalities. Alan Greenspan, the chair from 1987 to 2006, was famous for the opacity of his statements—and proud of it. He once said, "Since I've become a central banker, I've learned to mumble with great coherence. If I seem unduly clear to you, you must have misunderstood what I said."[6]

Why this attitude? Probably the main reason was fear of political criticism. The Fed did *not* want to be overly accountable for its actions, so it was reluctant to talk about them.

Although undemocratic, this attitude is defensible. As we've discussed, the Fed sometimes needs to do unpopular things for the long-run good of the economy. In particular, it sometimes needs to tighten policy and reduce

---

[6] Alan Greenspan, testimony to the U.S. Congress, September 1987.

output to control inflation. If it's obvious what the Fed is doing, it will hear criticism from populist politicians and face threats to its independence. Obfuscation may be necessary for the Fed to do the right thing.

Chapter 11 discussed the example of disinflation in the early 1980s. Fed Chair Volcker knew that a severe tightening of policy was needed to reduce inflation and that this action would be unpopular. Therefore, some historians argue, Volcker tried to confuse people about what he was doing. They surmise that he shifted from interest rate targeting to money targeting to make it less obvious that the Fed was responsible for high interest rates.

Moving Toward Transparency Despite this history, the Fed has been influenced by the worldwide trend toward transparency and has become more transparent over time through a series of small steps, which are charted in **Figure 16.7**. Some of these steps involve the minutes of FOMC meetings. In 1993, the Fed started releasing minutes 6 weeks after each meeting. In 2004, this delay was reduced to 3 weeks.

The Fed has also expanded the information provided immediately after FOMC meetings. The committee started announcing its interest rate targets in 1994. Since then it has added brief statements discussing its decisions and what it might do in the future. It also announces dissents from committee decisions by individual members.

Since 1979, the FOMC has issued semiannual projections of future output, unemployment, and inflation. Initially, this practice was a response to congressional pressure for greater openness. In 2007, however, the Fed took the initiative to provide more information. It started releasing projections four times a year, increased the number of variables it projects, and extended the horizon for projections from 2 years to 3. It also started publishing explanations for the projections.

Following in the tradition of past Federal Reserve chairs, Alan Greenspan never granted press interviews during his tenure. Ben Bernanke broke with

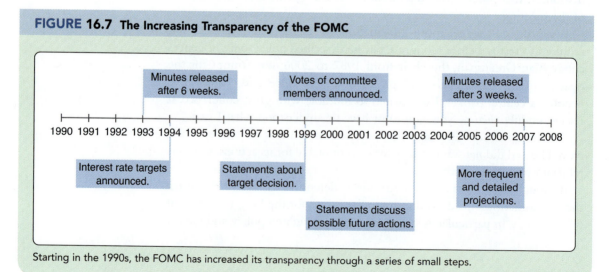

FIGURE 16.7 The Increasing Transparency of the FOMC

Starting in the 1990s, the FOMC has increased its transparency through a series of small steps.

tradition in an effort to increase transparency. In March 2009, he granted the first-ever interview of a sitting Fed chairman to Scott Pelley of CBS's *60 Minutes*. Topics ranged from Fed policy to Bernanke's personal background. In July 2009, he answered questions about Fed policy from citizens at a town hall–style meeting in Kansas City, moderated by Jim Lehrer of the PBS *NewsHour* and pictured on p. 25. One aim of Bernanke's accessibility is to build political support for the Fed, which is sorely needed after the controversy sparked by the financial crisis.

Despite recent changes, the Fed remains less transparent than many central banks. The Teal Book, which includes the detailed economic forecasts of the Fed's staff, is released only after 5 years, for the benefit of historians. The minutes of policy meetings are less detailed than in some countries, such as the United Kingdom, and Fed officials do not hold regular news conferences. The Fed still appears somewhat skittish about providing ammunition for its critics.

Summary

16.1 Time Consistency and Inflation

- Monetary institutions and strategies have been heavily influenced by theories of inflation expectations and by Kydland and Prescott's theory of the time-consistency problem facing central banks.

- A time-consistency problem arises when someone has incentives to make a promise but later to renege on it; because of these incentives, others don't believe the promise.

- The time-consistency problem can produce high inflation. If central bankers promise to keep inflation low, then they have incentives to renege with expansionary policies that raise inflation. Therefore, the public doesn't believe policymakers' promises, and the economy ends up in a high-inflation trap.

- Possible solutions to the time-consistency problem include the appointment of conservative central bankers (inflation haters), policymakers' concern for their reputations, and rules for monetary policy.

16.2 Central Bank Independence

- The Federal Reserve is independent of the government: elected officials can't control its policies. Throughout the world, central banks have become more independent over the last two decades.

- Populist politicians argue that central bank independence is undemocratic and that it leads policymakers to overemphasize the problem of inflation relative to unemployment.

- Supporters of independence argue that it protects policymakers from political pressure for unsound policies. It also reduces the time-consistency problem because central bankers tend to be conservative and to care about their reputations. Research has found that countries with more independent central banks have lower average inflation rates.

16.3 Monetary-Policy Rules

- A central bank can either use discretionary policy, adjusting it at each point in time based on policymakers' judgment, or follow a monetary-policy rule that tells the bank what to do.

- Milton Friedman and the monetarists argued that policy rules reduce the risks of unstable or politically motivated policies. Modern supporters also argue that rules reduce the time-consistency problem.

- The rule advocated by monetarists was a fixed growth rate for the money supply. Few economists advocate this rule today, largely because of the instability of money demand.

16.4 Inflation Targets

- In the last two decades, many countries have adopted an explicit inflation target. When inflation deviates from the target, the central bank adjusts interest rates to guide it back. Policymakers report regularly to the public on their efforts to control inflation.

- Many economists think the Federal Reserve should adopt an inflation target. Supporters interpret inflation targeting as "constrained discretion," a policy that combines flexibility with the benefits of a monetary rule. Inflation targeting also anchors inflation expectations.

- Other economists oppose inflation targeting, fearing that it causes policymakers to overemphasize inflation stability at the expense of output stability.

- The European Central Bank practices a variation on inflation targeting in which it adjusts policy based on the growth rate of the money supply.

16.5 Communication by Central Banks

- Central bankers try to establish reputations for hating inflation. A policymaker gets in trouble if people perceive him as soft on inflation, as illustrated by the case of Alan Blinder.

- The Fed and other central banks have become more transparent in recent decades. They publish information such as economic forecasts and minutes of policy meetings. Transparency makes central banks accountable to the public, and it improves policymakers' control of inflation expectations and long-term interest rates.

Key Terms

Adaptive expectations, p. 484

Conservative policymaker, p. 488

Discretionary policy, p. 497

Monetarists, p. 497

Monetary-policy rule, p. 497

Rational expectations, p. 484

Time-consistency problem, p. 485

Transparency, p. 512

Questions and Problems

1. Suppose a parent paid your college tuition this year. He or she wants you to get a summer job so you can contribute next year. You would prefer to spend your time with friends at the beach. Your parent says, "There's no way I'll pay for everything next year. If you don't get a job, you'll have to take a semester off."

   Are you likely to take this threat seriously and get a job? Explain why or why not. Answer this question under two different assumptions:

   a. You are an only child.

   b. You are the oldest of 10 children.

2. Suppose the Phillips curve becomes steeper: a given change in output has a larger effect on inflation. How does this affect the time-consistency problem facing the central bank and the likelihood of high inflation? (*Hint*: Think about the inflation-surprise decision in Figure 16.2.)

3. In the Kydland–Prescott theory, it is desirable for central bank officials to hate inflation passionately. Is it also desirable for them to hate unemployment passionately? Explain why or why not.

4. Governors of the Federal Reserve serve overlapping terms in office. When one governor is appointed, the others are at various points in their terms. Suppose a new law mandates that all governors be appointed at the same time for concurrent terms. Would this increase or decrease the risks of discretionary monetary policy? Explain.

5. Consider the relationship between inflation targeting and Taylor rules (Section 15.3).

   a. The adjustment of interest rates under inflation targeting is similar to a Taylor rule. Explain why.

   b. If a central bank shifts from flexible inflation targeting to strict targeting, does the equivalent Taylor rule become more or less aggressive? (A more aggressive rule responds more strongly to movements in output and inflation.)

6. In 2005, when President Bush announced Ben Bernanke's appointment as Fed chair, the Dow Jones stock index jumped by more than 1 percent in a few minutes.

   a. Why do you think that happened?

   b. If the United States adopted inflation targeting, how might that affect the reaction of the stock market to Fed appointments? Explain.

7. Figures 12.22 and 12.23 on p. 377 show the effects of an adverse supply shock in the AE/PC model. The figure assumes adaptive inflation expectations, $\pi^e = \pi(-1)$ and shows how the economy evolves if the central bank accommodates the supply shock and if it doesn't. Now suppose the central bank adopts an explicit inflation target, π^T. Inflation expectations become anchored at the target: $\pi^e = \pi^T$.

   a. For these anchored expectations, show how the economy responds to a supply shock under both an accommodative and a nonaccommodative policy.

   b. Does the anchoring of expectations make it more or less desirable to accommodate the shock? Explain.

8. Consider a policy of "output and inflation targeting": the central bank announces numerical targets for both inflation and real GDP. What are the pros and cons of such a policy? No central bank has seriously considered this approach; why not?

9. Suppose the growth rate of Europe's money supply exceeds the ECB's reference value, leading the ECB to raise its interest rate target. Will this action push money growth toward the reference value? Explain. (*Hint*: Review money and interest rate targeting in Section 11.6).

10. In 2006, Ben Bernanke said the goals of strong output growth and low inflation "are almost always consistent with each other." Alan Greenspan once called the trade-off between output and inflation "ephemeral."

    a. Are these statements accurate? Explain.

    b. Why do you think the chairmen made these statements?

▶ **Online and Data Questions**
www.worthpublishers.com/ball

11. The text Web site has data from the Ball–Sheridan study on inflation targeting. One variable is the standard deviation of output growth, which measures the instability of output.

    a. In theory, how might inflation targeting affect output stability? (*Hint*: One could argue for either positive or negative effects.)

    b. What do the Ball–Sheridan data say about this issue? Compare the standard deviation of output growth before and after the early 1990s in countries that adopted inflation targets and countries that didn't.

12. The text Web site links to "Inflation Targeting for the United States?" a 2005 article by economist Marvin Goodfriend, and to a comment on the article by Donald Kohn, then the vice chair of the Fed. Goodfriend supports inflation targeting and Kohn opposes it. Write a brief essay saying which side you agree with and why. Have events since 2005 bolstered Goodfriend's or Kohn's arguments?

Monetary Policy and Exchange Rates

Saul Loeb/AFP/Getty Images

May 25, 2010: U.S. Treasury Secretary Timothy Geithner and Chinese Premier Wen Jibao meet in Beijing. The dollar–yuan exchange rate was one topic of conversation.

Recent U.S. presidents have not commented on the policies of the Federal Reserve, but they have talked about the policies of another central bank: the People's Bank of China. They have urged the bank repeatedly to allow the value of the Chinese currency, the yuan, or renminbi (literally, people's currency), to increase.

After meeting with Chinese leaders in 2007, President Bush said, "I emphasized to the delegation that we will be watching very carefully as to whether or not they will appreciate their currency." In 2010, President Obama echoed his predecessor: "The renminbi is going to go up and it's going to go up significantly. We are going to be paying attention over the next several months to make that determination."

Why do China's leaders want a weak yuan? How does the People's Bank keep the currency weak? Why do U.S. leaders care? Can they force China to change its policy?

Central banks and governments care about exchange rates because movements in these rates create risk for firms engaged in foreign trade and for owners of foreign assets. Exchange rate fluctuations also interfere with policymakers' efforts to stabilize aggregate output and inflation. Consequently, we examine first *why* many central banks try to stabilize exchange rates.

We then discuss *how* central banks influence exchange rates. Their tools include interest rate changes, foreign exchange interventions, and controls on capital flows. Sometimes countries cooperate in controlling exchange rates, but sometimes friction occurs, as it has between China and the United States.

We will see that every exchange rate policy has pluses and minuses. As a result, exchange rate policies are controversial the world over. Some central banks tolerate substantial fluctuations in exchange rates, while others try to keep them fixed. An extreme version of fixed rates is a currency union, such as the euro area. Countries in a currency union adopt a common money, making it impossible for exchange rates among the countries to change.

17.1 EXCHANGE RATES AND STABILIZATION POLICY

The relationship between monetary policy and exchange rates is complex. Sometimes changes in policy cause changes in exchange rates. An increase in interest rates by the central bank causes a fall in net capital outflows (capital outflows minus capital inflows). As a result, the currency appreciates. Such exchange rate movements are part of the transmission mechanism through which monetary policy affects the economy.

▶ Figure 13.7 charts the monetary transmission mechanism.

On the other hand, many movements in exchange rates are *not* caused by central banks. They can arise, for example, from shifts in the confidence of asset holders or changes in commodity prices. Such events can destabilize the economy, so central banks are likely to react to them. Shifts in monetary policy can be responses to exchange rate movements as well as causes of these movements.

Exchange Rates and Aggregate Expenditure

Let's discuss how a shift in exchange rates might affect an economy and how the central bank might respond. In this example, the underlying shock to the economy is a change in the confidence of asset holders.

▶ The analysis that follows draws on the theory of real exchange rate fluctuations in Sections 6.4–6.5 and on the theory of aggregate expenditure in Section 12.2.

Initially, the country of Boversia has a corrupt, inefficient government. But then an election brings better leaders to power. The economic outlook for Boversia improves, making Boversian assets more attractive to savers around the world. Higher confidence reduces Boversia's net capital outflows (NCO).

Figure 17.1A shows the effects of the confidence shift on Boversia's equilibrium real exchange rate (ε) and net exports (NX). In this graph, NX and NCO are measured in units of the local currency, the bover. The fall in net capital outflows means the NCO curve shifts to the left. The real exchange rate rises, and net exports fall. Net exports fall because a higher real exchange rate makes Boversian goods more expensive relative to foreign goods.

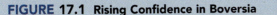

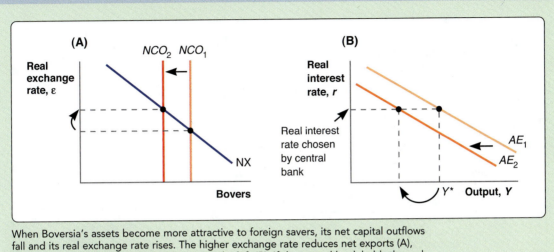

FIGURE 17.1 Rising Confidence in Boversia

When Boversia's assets become more attractive to foreign savers, its net capital outflows fall and its real exchange rate rises. The higher exchange rate reduces net exports (A), shifting the aggregate expenditure curve to the left (B). If the central bank holds the real interest rate constant, output falls.

The fall in net exports affects the aggregate expenditure (AE) curve, as shown in **Figure 17.1B**. Net exports are one of the four components of spending, along with consumption, investment, and government purchases. So the fall in net exports reduces aggregate expenditure for any given real interest rate (r). The AE curve shifts to the left.

Suppose for now that Boversia's central bank holds the real interest rate constant. In this case, the shift in aggregate expenditure reduces output. We assume that output was initially at potential (Y^*), so the AE shift pushes it below potential. Notice the irony: when people become more confident in Boversia's future, the short-run effect is a recession.

Confidence in economies can fall as well as rise. A decrease in confidence produces the opposite scenario from Figure 17.1. The NCO curve shifts to the right, reducing the real exchange rate, and the AE curve shifts to the right, raising output.

As usual, output movements affect inflation through the Phillips curve. When a rise in confidence causes a recession, the inflation rate falls; when lower confidence causes an economic boom, the inflation rate rises. Generally, shifts in confidence and the resulting changes in exchange rates destabilize both output and inflation.

Offsetting Exchange Rate Shocks

Central banks often try to stabilize the economy. When the AE curve shifts, policymakers adjust the real interest rate to keep output at potential. Such actions have side

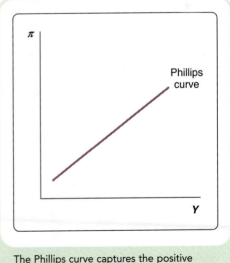

The Phillips curve captures the positive short-run relationship between output and inflation.

FIGURE 17.2 **Rising Confidence and Output Stabilization**

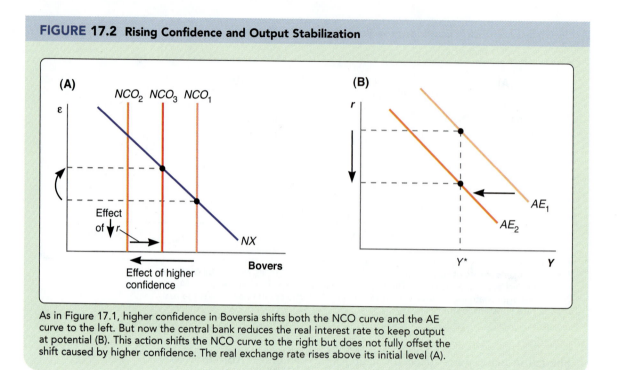

As in Figure 17.1, higher confidence in Boversia shifts both the NCO curve and the AE curve to the left. But now the central bank reduces the real interest rate to keep output at potential (B). This action shifts the NCO curve to the right but does not fully offset the shift caused by higher confidence. The real exchange rate rises above its initial level (A).

effects on exchange rates. **Figure 17.2** examines these effects using our example of increased confidence in Boversia.

The figure is easiest to understand if we start at the right, with Figure 17.2B. Remember that the appreciation of the bover has reduced net exports, shifting the AE curve to the left. The central bank offsets this shock by reducing the real interest rate, and output remains constant.

The central bank's action also affects the exchange rate, as shown in Figure 17.2A. Higher confidence in Boversia has shifted the NCO curve to the left from NCO_1 to NCO_2. The lower interest rate works in the opposite direction: it makes Boversian assets less attractive, raising net capital outflows. The NCO curve shifts to the right from NCO_2 to NCO_3.

Notice that the rightward shift in the NCO curve is smaller than the leftward shift caused by higher confidence in Boversia. Thus, the real exchange rate ends up above its initial level. The central bank *could* push the exchange rate down farther by reducing the interest rate more. But this is not necessary to keep output at potential.

To see this point, think about the different components of aggregate spending. The exchange rate ends up higher than its initial level, so net exports are lower. However, the central bank has reduced the interest rate, raising consumption and investment. Higher consumption and investment balance lower net exports, keeping output constant despite the higher exchange rate. **Figure 17.3** summarizes these effects.

As usual, our theoretical analysis only approximates reality. We've ignored problems with stabilization policy such as time lags and uncertainty about

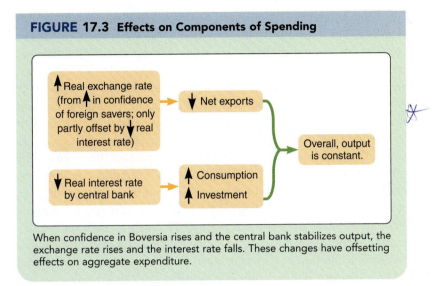

FIGURE 17.3 Effects on Components of Spending

When confidence in Boversia rises and the central bank stabilizes output, the exchange rate rises and the interest rate falls. These changes have offsetting effects on aggregate expenditure.

policy effects. Because of these problems, real-world central banks can dampen the effects of exchange rate shifts on output but not offset them perfectly. Fluctuations in exchange rates inevitably cause some instability in output.

How important are exchange rates for monetary policy? The answer varies across countries, depending on their levels of foreign trade. Trade is especially important for small countries, where exports may account for half of GDP or more. Changes in exchange rates have big effects on these economies, and central banks react to them strongly.

Foreign trade is less important in the United States, where exports are around 15 percent of GDP. When the Fed chooses interest rates, exchange rates are a secondary factor: central bankers focus more on developments in the domestic economy. One can often ignore exchange rates in analyzing U.S. policy, but this is impossible for many countries. The next case study discusses a central bank that pays a lot of attention to exchange rates.

CASE STUDY

Canadian Monetary Policy

Canada has a high level of foreign trade: imports and exports are each about 40 percent of GDP. More than half of Canada's trade is with the United States. Foreign trade makes exchange rates important for Canada's economy, especially the rate between the U.S. and Canadian dollars. The Bank of Canada responds strongly to changes in this rate.

One example comes from the early 2000s. Canada experienced a fall in net capital outflows, the type of event portrayed in Figure 17.1. The underlying cause was declining confidence in the United States, where the economy was slowing. U.S. assets became less attractive to Canadians, so less capital flowed out of Canada.

As predicted by Figure 17.1, the fall in net capital outflows raised Canada's exchange rate. The Canadian dollar rose from 0.62 U.S. dollars in January 2002 to 0.83 in November 2004. This appreciation reduced Canada's net exports, threatening to cause a recession.

The Bank of Canada responded with low interest rates. Over 2003–2005, the bank kept the nominal rate between 2 and 3 percent; inflation was around the same level, so the real rate was near zero. As in Figure 17.2, low interest rates kept output near potential despite the high exchange rate.

In 2005, the bank's governor, David Dodge, explained the rationale for low interest rates. They were needed "to provide support for domestic demand [i.e., consumption and investment] to offset the additional drag we expect from net exports." The drag on net exports was the strong currency. Dodge's statement fits perfectly with Figure 17.3, which analyzes the different components of spending.

This example illustrates a general pattern. Recall that, outside of financial crises, U.S. monetary policy is broadly captured by a Taylor rule: the Fed adjusts interest rates based on output and inflation. Researchers find that this rule does not fit Canada. Instead, the Bank of Canada responds to output, inflation, *and* the exchange rate. One study finds that, on average, a 1-percent rise in the Canadian dollar produces an interest rate cut of 0.2 percentage points.[*]

[*] This estimate is from Gergana Danailova-Trainor, *Open Economy Policy Rules*, Johns Hopkins University dissertation, 2004.

17.2 COSTS OF EXCHANGE RATE VOLATILITY

So far, we have assumed that central banks seek to stabilize aggregate output and inflation. They respond to movements in the exchange rate only because this variable affects output and inflation. In reality, central banks also care about exchange rates for other reasons. Fluctuations in exchange rates harm the economy directly.

Exchange Rates and Risk

▶ Table 6.1 summarizes the winners and losers from a currency appreciation.

An appreciation of a country's currency hurts some parts of its economy and helps others. The appreciation benefits individuals and firms that import goods, because imports become less expensive. Exporters are hurt because their products become more expensive for foreigners. Owners of foreign assets are also hurt, because these assets become less valuable in domestic currency. All the effects of an appreciation work in reverse when a depreciation occurs: importers lose and exporters and foreign-asset holders gain.

Over time, a country's exchange rate sometimes rises and sometimes falls. So for any firm or asset holder, the effects of exchange rate changes are sometimes good and sometimes bad. Overall, exchange rate fluctuations create risk. An exporter can see its profits rise or fall, depending on what happens to exchange rates. Similarly, buying foreign assets means gambling on exchange rates. Firms and asset holders dislike this risk.

Firms and asset holders can reduce risk by trading futures contracts for currencies. However, delivery dates in these contracts are seldom more than 6 months in the future. This means it's difficult to hedge against exchange rate movements that last more than 6 months. For example, if the dollar appreciates over several years, U.S. exporters are inevitably hurt.

Risk and Global Economic Integration

One way a firm can reduce its exchange rate risk is to trade less with foreigners. It can seek suppliers in its own country, so its costs don't fluctuate with exchange rates. It can focus on producing for the domestic market rather than expanding its business overseas. The greater the volatility of exchange rates, the greater the incentives to reduce exchange rate risk. Thus volatile exchange rates reduce international trade.

Most economists think this effect is very harmful. International trade lets countries specialize in producing goods for which they have a comparative advantage. In addition, imports provide competition for domestic firms, encouraging them to become more efficient. Trade links help new technologies spread around the world. For all these reasons, international trade boosts economic growth. When exchange rate volatility reduces trade, it hurts growth.

Volatile exchange rates also reduce international capital flows. Savers can avoid exchange rate risk by purchasing assets in their own country. This incentive to buy domestic assets prevents savings from flowing to the countries where they would be most productive.

For example, suppose a developing country badly needs new factories. American savers can finance this investment by purchasing securities from the country's firms. If the factories are productive, everyone benefits: Americans earn high returns on the securities, the local firms earn profits, and the developing economy grows. But none of this happens if exchange rate risk deters Americans from buying foreign securities.

17.3 EXCHANGE RATE POLICIES

We have seen that exchange rate fluctuations harm economies. As a result, many central banks try to stabilize exchange rates. Some even fix exchange rates at a constant level. Central banks use several different methods, summarized in **Table 17.1**, to control exchange rates. Choosing among these methods is controversial: each one has drawbacks.

TABLE 17.1 Exchange Rate Policies and Their Pitfalls

Policy Tool	Drawback
interest rate adjustments	May destabilize output
Foreign exchange interventions	Questionable effectiveness
Capital controls	Impede efficient flow of savings
Policy coordination	Countries unlikely to agree

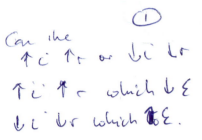

Can the
↑ i ↑ r or ↓ i ↓ r
↑ i ↑ r which ↓ ε
↓ i ↓ r which ↑o ε.

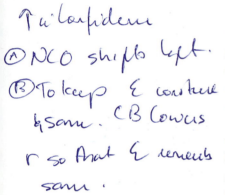

↑ in confidence
Ⓐ NCO shifts left.
Ⓑ To keep ε constant
& same. CB lowers
r so that ε remains
same.
But Y < Y*

Interest Rate Adjustments

The central bank can raise the real exchange rate by increasing the real interest rate, or lower the exchange rate by decreasing the interest rate. Therefore, if some event causes the exchange rate to change, the central bank can reverse this movement by adjusting the interest rate. But there's a catch. The interest rate adjustments needed to stabilize the exchange rate often differ from those that stabilize output and inflation. As a result, central banks face trade-offs between exchange rate stability and their other goals.

Recall our example of increased confidence in Boversia. If the central bank doesn't respond, the real exchange rate rises and output falls below potential (see Figure 17.1). Policymakers can stabilize output by reducing the real interest rate. However, this action only *partly* reverses the rise in the exchange rate. The exchange rate remains above its initial level (see Figure 17.2).

If Boversia's central bank wants to prevent *any* change in the exchange rate, then it must reduce the interest rate by more than it does when stabilizing output. **Figure 17.4** shows this case. The larger interest rate cut offsets fully the effect of the confidence shift on net capital outflows, stabilizing the exchange rate (Figure 17.4A). The larger interest rate cut also pushes output *above* potential (Figure 17.4B).

The initial shock in Figure 17.4 is a rise in confidence. If confidence falls, then the process works in reverse. Stabilizing the exchange rate requires a large *increase* in the interest rate, one that pushes output *below* potential. The general lesson is that stabilizing the exchange rate makes output less stable. Output fluctuations also destabilize inflation through the Phillips curve.

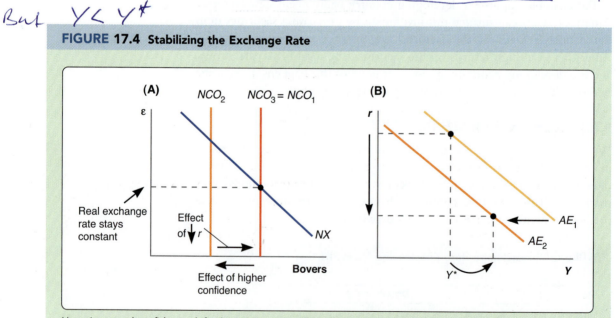

FIGURE 17.4 Stabilizing the Exchange Rate

Here, increased confidence shifts the NCO curve to the left, but the central bank lowers the interest rate enough to reverse the shift completely. The real exchange rate doesn't change (A). The lower interest rate pushes output above potential despite the inward shift of the AE curve (B).

FIGURE 17.5 A Domestic Shock and Output Stabilization

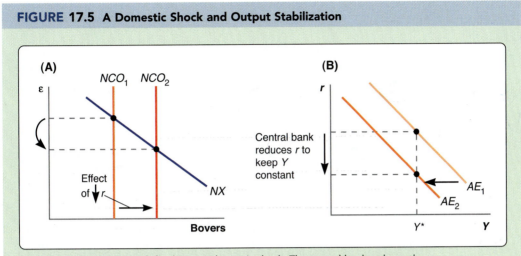

Here, Boversia's AE curve shifts due to a domestic shock. The central bank reduces the real interest rate to keep output constant (B). The lower interest rate shifts the NCO curve to the right, reducing the real exchange rate (A).

Many kinds of economic shocks create trade-offs between exchange rate stability and output stability. In **Figure 17.5**, we assume that Boversia's AE curve shifts to the left because of some domestic shock—say, a tax increase or a fall in consumer spending. This shock has no direct effect on net capital outflows. The central bank can keep output stable by reducing the real interest rate (Figure 17.5B). But this action raises net capital outflows and reduces the exchange rate (Figure 17.5A). If the central bank desires a constant exchange rate, it must keep the interest rate constant and let output fall below potential.

Central banks would like to eat their cake and have it, too. They want to stabilize exchange rates without choosing interest rates that destabilize output and inflation. Consequently, policymakers look for alternative ways to influence exchange rates.

Foreign Exchange Interventions

Central banks sometimes try to influence exchange rates through **foreign exchange interventions**—purchases or sales of foreign currencies. The central bank trades its own currency for a foreign one, or vice versa.

To make interventions possible, central banks hold **international reserves**. These are stocks of liquid assets denominated in foreign currencies, such as bonds issued by foreign governments. As of 2010, the U.S. Federal Reserve owned about $130 billion of such assets, denominated mainly in euros and yen.

Figure 17.6 shows the relationships between foreign exchange interventions and international reserves. If a central bank trades its own currency for a foreign one, it uses the proceeds to increase its reserves. For example, the Fed might trade dollars for euros and use the euros to buy European bonds.

Foreign exchange interventions purchases and sales of foreign currencies by central banks

International reserves liquid assets held by central banks that are denominated in foreign currencies

Sale of Foreign Currency.

A) Sell foreign assets.

B) International reserves ↓

FIGURE 17.6 Foreign Exchange Interventions and International Reserves

Central bank trades its currency for foreign currency... → ...uses foreign currency to buy foreign assets → International reserves increase

OR

Central bank sells foreign assets for foreign currency... → ...trades foreign currency for own currency → International reserves decrease

↑ M_S when sell dollars for euros

↓ Dollar Price.

↓ Dollar Depreciates.

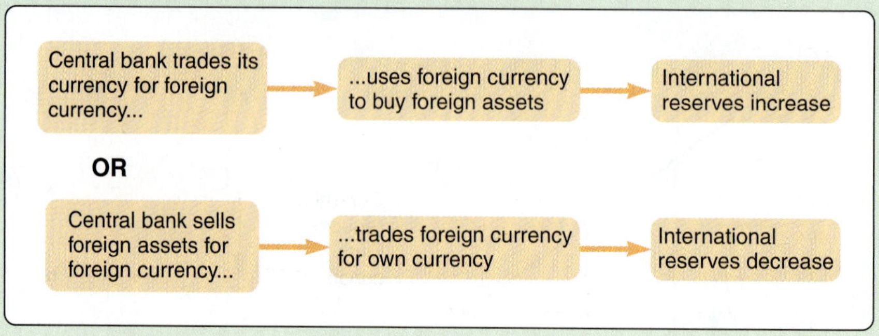

To perform the opposite intervention, a sale of foreign currency, the central bank must first sell some of its foreign assets. The Fed might sell European bonds for euros and then trade the euros for dollars. In this case, the Fed's international reserves fall.

Effects of Interventions Foreign exchange interventions affect exchange rates because they shift the supply and demand for currencies. If the Fed sells dollars for euros, the supply of dollars increases, reducing the price of the dollar: the dollar depreciates. If the Fed buys dollars, the demand for dollars increases and the dollar appreciates.

We can capture the effects of interventions with our graph of net exports and net capital outflows. **Figure 17.7A** shows what happens if Boversia's central bank buys foreign currency. It uses the foreign currency to purchase

Buy foreign currency + to NCO.

↳ NCO shifts right.

FIGURE 17.7 Interventions and the Exchange Rate

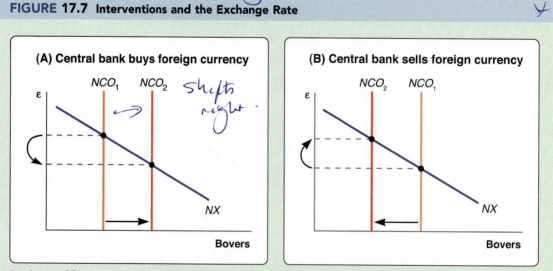

(A) Central bank buys foreign currency

NCO_1 NCO_2 *shifts right.*

ε

NX

Bovers

(B) Central bank sells foreign currency

NCO_2 NCO_1

ε

NX

Bovers

Purchases of foreign currency by the central bank raise net capital outflows and reduce the real exchange rate (A). Sales of foreign currency have the opposite effects (B).

foreign assets, which adds to capital outflows. The NCO curve shifts to the right, reducing the real exchange rate. Conversely, in **Figure 17.7B**, a sale of foreign currency shifts the NCO curve to the left and raises the exchange rate.

Why Intervene? Central banks can control exchange rates by adjusting interest rates, but the side effects on output may be undesirable. The motive for foreign exchange interventions is to escape this dilemma. Interventions allow policymakers to stabilize output and the exchange rate at the same time.

Suppose once again that a rise in confidence shifts Boversia's NCO curve to the left. The central bank can keep the exchange rate constant by reducing the interest rate, but this policy pushes output above potential (see Figure 17.4). The rise in output is unwelcome because, through the Phillips curve, it raises inflation.

The central bank can do better with a foreign exchange intervention, as shown in **Figure 17.8**. When the NCO curve shifts to the left, the central bank buys foreign currency and builds up its international reserves. This action shifts the NCO curve back to the right, preventing a change in the exchange rate (Figure 17.8A).

In this example, the AE curve doesn't shift (Figure 17.8B). Because the intervention prevents the exchange rate from moving, net exports don't change, and aggregate expenditure is unchanged at a given interest rate. With a fixed AE curve, the central bank can keep output constant by holding the real interest rate constant. Its policies stabilize the exchange rate without creating an inflationary boom.

FIGURE 17.8 Interventions and Exchange Rate Stabilization

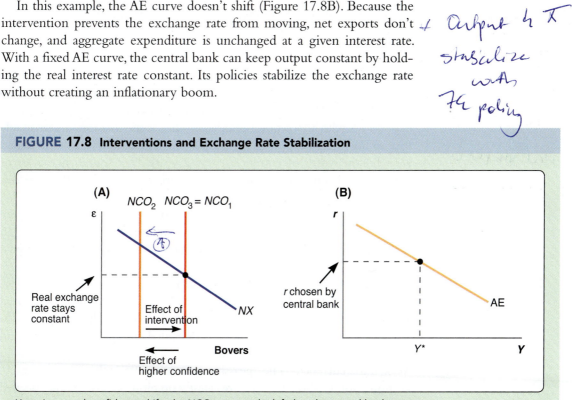

Here, increased confidence shifts the NCO curve to the left, but the central bank reverses the shift by purchasing foreign currency. The exchange rate does not change (A). The AE curve does not move and the central bank holds the interest rate constant, so output does not change (B).

▶ Section 14.4 discusses the long Japanese recession of the 1990s and early 2000s.

 Chapter 18 describes how the most recent financial crisis began in the United States then went global.

Who Intervenes? Some countries intervene heavily in foreign exchange markets. For example, the Bank of Japan sold yen repeatedly during 2003 and 2004 in an effort to hold down the currency's value. The sales totaled $315 billion worth of yen, close to 10 percent of Japan's annual GDP. Policymakers wanted a weaker yen to stimulate net exports and help the economy escape its protracted slump.

A number of central banks, including those of Mexico and South Korea, intervened in foreign exchange markets in 2008–2009: they bought their own currencies in an effort to increase the currencies' values. These central banks were responding to falling confidence in their economies as the financial crisis spread around the world. Falling confidence caused increases in net capital outflows that pushed exchange rates below the levels that policymakers desired.

By contrast, some central banks rarely intervene in currency markets. The Federal Reserve traded currencies frequently in the 1970s and 1980s, but since then it has largely abandoned the practice. As of 2010, the Fed had not intervened since 2000. The same is true of the European Central Bank.

Why don't the Fed and ECB intervene more often? The answer is that they doubt the effectiveness of interventions. We've seen that, in theory, these actions affect exchange rates. Yet many economists argue that the effects are small, so interventions are not useful in practice. The next case study lays out this debate.

CASE STUDY

Do Interventions Work?

Economists who are skeptical of interventions argue that they are small relative to the foreign exchange market. We saw, for example, that Japan traded $315 billion worth of currencies over 2 years. That sounds like a lot of money, but total transactions in currency markets exceed $1 trillion per *day*. Interventions are a tiny fraction of these transactions.

Interventions shift the NCO curve, as shown in Figure 17.8. However, the size of interventions suggests that the shifts are slight and the effects on exchange rates are small. Interventions can't offset major shocks such as capital flight, as we've assumed up to now.

This reasoning leads many observers to dismiss interventions as useless. For example, in 2007 the Reserve Bank of New Zealand was worried about an appreciation of the New Zealand dollar. In June, reports *The Economist* magazine, the Reserve Bank "decided enough was enough—and let rip with the pea-shooter. It intervened in foreign exchange markets to weaken the currency." The "pea-shooter" quip reflects the view that interventions don't work. In *The Economist*'s opinion, New Zealand needed lower interest rates if it wanted a weaker currency.[*]

Yet not all economists dismiss interventions. Some suggest that interventions can change exchange rates even if they are small. One theory is that interventions signal central banks' desire to adjust exchange rates. These signals lead people to expect future actions—such as changes in interest rates—that will affect exchange rates. Expectations of future exchange rate movements affect current rates.

Others suggest that interventions can trigger self-fulfilling expectations. When people see a central bank buy a currency, they infer that the currency is likely to appreciate. This belief raises demand for the currency, and it does appreciate. This effect can be sizable even if the intervention itself is small.

Motivated by this debate, researchers have tried to measure the effects of foreign exchange interventions. This work includes a 2006 paper by Rasmus Fatum and Michael Hutchinson of the University of California, Santa Cruz.[†] Fatum and Hutchinson studied interventions in the market for yen over the period 1990–2000. They examined 43 episodes when a central bank traded yen for U.S. dollars or dollars for yen. The central bank was usually the Bank of Japan but occasionally the Fed.

For each of the 43 episodes, Fatum and Hutchinson examined the path of the dollar-yen exchange rate in the 5 days after the intervention. They judged the intervention a "success" if the exchange rate moved in the direction intended by the central bank. A sale of yen was a success if the yen depreciated over the next 5 days; a purchase was a success if the yen appreciated.

Fatum and Hutchinson found that 31 of the 43 interventions were successes; only 12 were failures. This success rate would be unlikely if interventions had no effects. Fatum and Hutchinson concluded that interventions do influence exchange rates.

The debate over interventions continues. One compromise position is that interventions affect exchange rates for periods of a few days, as Fatum and Hutchinson found, but don't influence longer-term movements in rates.

* See *The Economist*, "New Zealand Defends Its Currency," www.economist.com, June 14, 2007.
† See Rasmus Fatum and Michael Hutchinson, "Effectiveness of Daily Foreign Exchange Market Interventions in Japan," *Journal of International Money and Finance*, 25 (May 2006): 199–219.

Capital Controls

Policymakers also influence exchange rates through **capital controls**. These regulations reduce the flow of savings across countries. Some capital controls restrict capital inflows: they make it harder for foreigners to buy a country's assets. Other controls restrict outflows: they make it harder for a country's residents to buy foreign assets.

Both governments and central banks impose capital controls, and the regulations take many forms. Purchases of certain assets may require government approval or be subject to taxes or forbidden entirely.

The motives for capital controls also vary. Some countries restrict capital outflows to force savers to purchase domestic assets. This provides domestic firms with more funds for investment. Countries sometimes restrict capital inflows for political reasons. They think that foreign ownership of certain assets symbolizes outside domination of their country. For this reason,

Capital controls regulations that restrict capital inflows or outflows

FIGURE 17.9 **Capital Controls and the Exchange Rate**

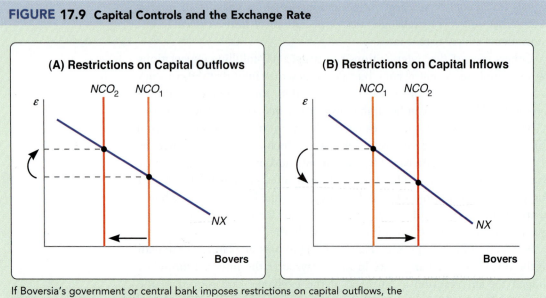

If Boversia's government or central bank imposes restrictions on capital outflows, the NCO curve shifts to the left and the exchange rate rises (A). Restrictions on capital inflows have the opposite effects (B).

Mexico's constitution limits foreign ownership of real estate or natural resources.

Effects on Exchange Rates For our purposes, a key function of capital controls is to influence exchange rates. Suppose Boversia imposes new regulations that reduce capital outflows. As shown in **Figure 17.9A**, the NCO curve shifts to the left, raising the real exchange rate. In **Figure 17.9B**, restrictions on capital inflows shift the NCO curve to the right, reducing the exchange rate.

Countries use capital controls for the same reason that they use foreign exchange interventions: to ease the trade-off between output and exchange rate stability. If a change in confidence shifts the NCO curve, capital controls can shift it back to its initial position. This stabilizes the exchange rate without an interest rate adjustment that would destabilize output.

An example occurred during the East Asian crisis of 1997–1998, when asset holders lost confidence in countries such as South Korea, Thailand, and Indonesia. These countries' NCO curves shifted to the right, reducing their exchange rates. In most cases, the central bank responded by raising interest rates sharply. These actions dampened the exchange rate movements but also caused recessions. In Indonesia, for example, the unemployment rate rose to 20 percent.

Malaysia was also hit by capital flight, but it responded differently from its neighbors. In 1998, the government imposed restrictions on capital outflows. Foreigners who owned Malaysian securities were forbidden to sell them for 12 months. Nobody could transfer funds from Malaysian bank accounts to foreign accounts or take significant amounts of cash out of the country.

 We discuss the effects of the East Asian crisis on interest rates in Section 4.2 and the effects on exchange rates in Section 6.5.

These rules prevented Malaysia's net capital outflows from rising. Therefore, the exchange rate did not fall, and the central bank did not need to raise interest rates. Indeed, when the government announced the capital controls, it also fixed the exchange rate 10 percent *above* its previous level. At the same time, the central bank reduced its interest rate target from 9.5 percent to 8 percent to stimulate aggregate spending.

These policies appear to have helped the economy. Malaysia was in a recession in 1998, but it recovered quickly after it began its new policies— unlike the neighboring countries that raised interest rates.

The Critique of Capital Controls Many economists think capital controls are a bad idea. Restrictions on capital inflows make it harder for a country's firms to finance investment. Restrictions on outflows prevent savers from earning high returns on foreign assets. In general, capital controls impede the flow of savings to the countries where savings are most productive.

Economists question capital controls even when they seem to benefit the economy in the short run, as in Malaysia. Critics argue that controls hurt the economy in the long run by reducing foreign investment. Foreigners won't put money in a country if the government might prevent them from taking it back out. These ideas have persuaded many countries to abolish capital controls. For example, the U.S. government used to tax Americans who bought foreign assets, but this policy ended in 1974.

Many developing countries still employ capital controls. India, for example, limits the quantity of foreign assets that a resident can buy in a year. It also limits the interest that foreigners can earn on Indian corporate bonds, discouraging purchases of the bonds. Many economists advise India to loosen its capital controls, but it's not clear whether this will happen.

Critics of capital controls gained ammunition from events in Thailand in December 2006. Thailand's central bank was trying to slow an appreciation of its currency, the baht. On December 18, it announced a restriction on capital inflows. Foreign savers who bought Thai assets were required to deposit 30 percent of their funds with the central bank at zero interest.

This action shook confidence in Thai assets. It stopped the rise in the currency, but it also caused a stock market crash: the Thai market fell by 12 percent when the deposit requirement was announced. Fearing further instability, the central bank quickly reversed course. On December 20, it removed the deposit requirement for most foreign savers.

Policy Coordination

Exchange rate policies inherently involve many countries. If one country acts to strengthen its currency against others, then the other currencies weaken. So countries care about one another's policies. Exchange rates are a perennial topic of discussion among officials of different countries.

In some periods, countries have cooperated on exchange rate policy. A famous example is the "Plaza Agreement," signed in 1985 at the Plaza Hotel in New York. At the time the dollar was very strong, causing a trade deficit in the United States. This deficit created political pressures for import restrictions, which America's trading partners feared. To reduce the deficit, European countries and Japan agreed to work with the United States to weaken the dollar.

Another episode of cooperation occurred in 2000, when the euro was near its all time low of 0.85 dollars. The European Central Bank, the Fed, and the Bank of Japan tried to boost the euro's value by simultaneously purchasing the currency. However, these actions did not have much effect on exchange rates. The failure of the interventions in 2000 helps explain why the Fed and ECB haven't intervened since then.

In recent years, the United States has not coordinated exchange rate policies with other countries. Given the questionable effectiveness of interventions, exchange rate adjustments require changes in interest rates. Most central banks, including the Fed, want complete freedom in setting interest rates. They don't make exchange rate agreements because such commitments would constrain their choices of interest rates.

Policymakers still discuss exchange rates at international meetings and lobby one another in speeches. The next case study discusses a country whose exchange rate policy is frequently criticized by outsiders.

CASE STUDY

The Yuan

China's economy has grown rapidly since the 1990s, to emerge in 2010 as the world's second largest economy, replacing Japan. China's growth is in part the result of growing exports. To promote exports, Chinese policymakers have worked to hold down the value of their currency, the renminbi, or yuan. A weak yuan makes Chinese goods inexpensive in foreign markets.

China has controlled its exchange rate through two sets of policies. One is restrictions on capital inflows. Before 2002, foreigners were not allowed to buy Chinese securities. The government has loosened this rule, but only slightly: only a handful of foreign financial institutions can buy the country's securities. Foreign banks are not allowed to lend in China.

China's other method for keeping the yuan weak is foreign exchange interventions. The Bank of China has sold large quantities of yuan and accumulated international reserves. As of 2010, its reserves were $2.4 trillion and climbing. Over half were dollar-denominated assets, such as U.S. Treasury bonds.

These policies have succeeded in keeping the yuan weak. From 1994 to 2005, China's nominal exchange rate was fixed at 0.121 dollars per yuan. The People's Bank allowed the currency to appreciate to 0.146 in 2008 but then fixed it again at that level. Economists estimate that the yuan's value would be 30 to 40 percent higher if it were determined in currency markets with no capital controls or central bank interventions.

As China's economy has grown, the country has become a major trading partner of the United States. A weak yuan means a stronger dollar, which hurts U.S. industries that export or compete with Chinese imports. One such industry is steel. For decades this industry's fortunes have been tied to exchange rates (see the Case Study in Section 6.2). In recent years the dollar–yuan rate has been crucial, because China has become a major steel producer, accounting for more than 40 percent of world output. The effects of the weak yuan on top of a deep recession reduced U.S. steel output from 100 million tons in 2004 to 58 million tons in 2009.

Business leaders and members of Congress complain bitterly about Chinese policy. In 2010, Senator Charles Schumer (D–New York) said, "China's currency manipulation would be unacceptable even in good economic times. At a time of 10 percent unemployment, we simply will not stand for it." Senator Schumer has proposed legislation that would retaliate for China's currency policy with tariffs on imports from China.

In June 2010, China announced that it intended to relax its control of the exchange rate, allowing it to respond to "market supply and demand." China's critics were not persuaded, however, that the yuan would appreciate significantly. Scott Paul, director of the Alliance for American Manufacturing, said, "I'll believe it when I see it," and suggested, "China's announcement is nothing more than a cynical ploy in the wake of mounting congressional pressure." As of fall 2010, Senator Schumer was still pressing for sanctions against China.*

Online Case Study: An Update on China's Currency Policy

* See *The Economist*, "The Yuan Unpegged," www.economist.com, June 24, 2010; and Rebecca Christie and Ian Katz, "Geithner Welcomes China's Yuan Move," www.bloomberg.com, June 20, 2010.

17.4 FIXED EXCHANGE RATES

We've seen that central banks have several methods for controlling exchange rates but that each has drawbacks (see Table 17.1 on page 525). Consequently, most central banks allow exchange rates to change over time in response to economic shocks. That is, they choose **floating exchange rates**.

However, this policy is not universal. Some central banks choose **fixed exchange rates**: they maintain a constant exchange rate between their currency and another one. Denmark, for example, has a national currency, the krone; it does not use the euro. But Denmark's central bank fixes the value of the krone at about 0.13 euros.

Which is better—fixed exchange rates or flexible rates? This question perennially provokes controversy. One motive for fixed rates is to promote international trade and capital flows. As discussed in Section 17.2, exchange rate risk deters trade and capital flows; fixed exchange rates eliminate this risk.

Floating exchange rate policy that allows the exchange rate to fluctuate in response to economic shocks

Fixed exchange rate policy that holds the exchange rate at a constant level

TABLE 17.2 A Fixed Exchange Rate: Pros and Cons

Pros	Cons
Promotes trade and capital flows	Loss of independent monetary policy
Controls inflation	Danger of speculative attacks

This point is just the start of the debate. We examine several arguments, summarized in **Table 17.2**, for and against fixed exchange rates. But first, let's discuss the mechanics of *how* a central bank fixes an exchange rate.

Mechanics of Fixed Exchange Rates

Suppose the central bank of Boversia decides to fix the value of its currency, the bover. It chooses an exchange rate of 0.5 U.S. dollars per bover (or 2.0 bovers per dollar). How does the central bank maintain this exchange rate?

First, it promises to trade currencies at the chosen rate. If people want to buy bovers, the central bank provides the bovers in return for dollars. It uses the dollars to build up its international reserves. If people want to sell bovers, the central bank uses its reserves to buy them.

The central bank's purchases and sales of bovers are foreign exchange interventions. Notice, however, that the central bank does not choose the interventions. It acts passively, supplying whatever amounts of currency people want at the fixed exchange rate.

We have seen that foreign exchange interventions have limited effects on exchange rates. Thus a fixed exchange rate must be backed up by more powerful tools: interest rate adjustments or capital controls. These policies are the real basis of fixed rates.

To see this, suppose Boversia is hit with capital flight. People sell large quantities of bovers, which normally would push down the exchange rate. At first the central bank can maintain the fixed rate by purchasing bovers with its reserves of dollars. But these reserves are limited and are likely to run out during an episode of capital flight.

When the central bank runs out of reserves, it faces a choice. If it wants to maintain the fixed exchange rate, it must curb capital outflows through higher interest rates or capital controls. If it doesn't adopt these policies, it must let the exchange rate fall.

Devaluation and Revaluation

A fixed exchange rate is a fixed *nominal* rate, such as 0.5 dollars per bover. The exchange rate that matters for the economy is the *real* rate. The relation between the real rate, ε, and the nominal rate, e, is given by Equation (6.1):

$$\varepsilon = \frac{eP}{P^*}$$

where P is the domestic price level and P^* is the foreign price level. In the Boversia example, P is Boversia's price level and P^* is the U.S. price level.

A fixed nominal exchange rate does not imply a fixed real rate. Instead, the behavior of the real rate depends on the price levels P and P^*. Suppose

P grows more rapidly over time than P^*; in other words, the domestic inflation rate exceeds the foreign inflation rate. This means the ratio P/P^* rises. With a fixed nominal exchange rate (a fixed e), the rise in P/P^* raises the real rate, ε. Conversely, if P rises more slowly than P^*, the real exchange rate falls.

These changes in real exchange rates can be harmful. A rise in a country's real exchange rate reduces its net exports, which can cause a recession. A fall in the real exchange rate makes imports more expensive, hurting the country's consumers.

To address these problems, countries with fixed exchange rates occasionally change the rates. They adjust nominal rates to offset the effects of inflation on real rates. Suppose again that Boversia fixes its nominal exchange rate against the dollar and assume its inflation rate exceeds U.S. inflation. P/P^* rises over time, raising the real exchange rate. At some point, Boversia's central bank may cut the nominal exchange rate to push the real rate back down. For example, it might reduce the nominal rate from 0.5 dollars per bover to 0.4.

When a country has a fixed exchange rate, a decrease in this rate is called a **devaluation**. Boversia devalues its currency if it reduces the exchange rate from 0.5 to 0.4. An increase in the exchange rate is a **revaluation**. A devaluation or revaluation is a significant, discrete change. After the change, the exchange rate is fixed at its new level.

Devaluation resetting of a fixed exchange rate at a lower level

Revaluation resetting of a fixed exchange rate at a higher level

Loss of Independent Monetary Policy

Let's now return to the pros and cons of fixed exchange rates. We've already discussed one benefit: fixed rates encourage international trade and capital flows (see Table 17.2). The costs arise from the policies needed to control the exchange rate. These policies must include either capital controls or interest rate adjustments, and each option has costs.

We'll focus on countries without capital controls: those that use interest rates to influence exchange rates. We saw in Section 17.1 that stabilizing exchange rates can conflict with stabilizing output and inflation. A decision to fix the exchange rate means that exchange rate stability always takes precedence. As a result, the central bank loses its normal ability to stabilize the economy.

Recall the case of an adverse expenditure shock, such as an increase in taxes, that does not directly affect the exchange rate (see Figure 17.5). The central bank could keep output constant by decreasing the interest rate, but this would also decrease the exchange rate. If the central bank is committed to a fixed exchange rate, it must hold the interest rate constant and allow a recession to occur.

Sometimes a fixed exchange rate requires that the central bank change the interest rate. Policymakers must offset shocks that would otherwise cause exchange rate fluctuations. In particular, they must adjust the interest rate when foreign interest rates change.

Consider again Boversia's fixed exchange rate against the dollar. If the Federal Reserve raises the U.S. interest rate, U.S. assets become more attractive. Normally, higher demand for U.S. assets would raise net capital outflows from Boversia, reducing the exchange rate. To prevent this outcome, Boversia's central bank must raise the domestic interest rate; in effect, it must mimic the Fed's action. This prevents U.S. assets from becoming more attractive compared with Boversian assets, so net capital outflows and the exchange rate don't change.

The upshot is that the Federal Reserve determines interest rates in Boversia as well as in the United States. The Fed sets rates based on U.S. economic conditions, so its policies may be inappropriate for Boversia. Say the U.S. experiences an economic boom at the same time Boversia is in a recession. The Fed is likely to raise interest rates to slow the U.S. economy and prevent inflation from rising. Unfortunately, this action also triggers an interest rate increase in Boversia, worsening that country's recession.

Controlling Inflation

Many economists cite the loss of independent monetary policy as a disadvantage of fixed exchange rates. However, supporters of fixed rates argue that some countries benefit from the loss of policy independence.

To understand why, recall the argument for monetary rules in Section 16.3. In theory, discretionary monetary policy stabilizes the economy, but in practice it may do more harm than good. A monetary rule prevents incompetent or politically motivated policy.

A fixed exchange rate can be interpreted as one kind of monetary rule. The interest rate must be set to keep the exchange rate constant, so the central bank cannot adjust policy as it chooses. This prevents mischief. Specifically, fixed exchange rates can prevent high inflation. If Boversia fixes its exchange rate against the dollar, its monetary policy is determined by the Federal Reserve. As a result, its inflation rate will be close to the U.S. inflation rate. As long as the Fed keeps U.S. inflation low, Boversian inflation is also low.

The link between the two countries' inflation rates is complex. U.S. inflation does not directly affect Boversian inflation. Instead, differences in the two inflation rates set off a chain of effects that pushes Boversia's rate toward the U.S. rate. **Figure 17.10** outlines this mechanism. We assume that, initially, Boversian inflation exceeds U.S. inflation. With a fixed nominal exchange rate, Boversia's real exchange rate rises. The real appreciation reduces net exports, pushing output below potential. Finally, low output reduces inflation through the Phillips curve. This process continues until Boversia's inflation rate has fallen to the U.S. level, which stabilizes the real exchange rate.

Israel is one country that has used a fixed exchange rate, along with other policies, to reduce inflation. In the early 1980s, Israel financed government budget deficits by printing money, with the predictable result of high inflation. The inflation rate peaked at about 500 percent in 1985. At that point, the government cut the deficit. It also fixed the value of its currency, the shekel, against the dollar. Finally, it attacked inflation directly by

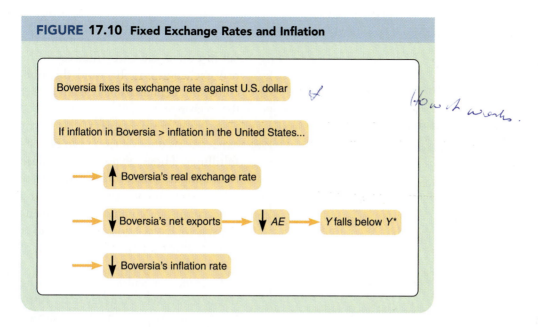

FIGURE 17.10 Fixed Exchange Rates and Inflation

How it works.

Cannot last forever.

persuading labor unions to accept smaller wage increases. This combination of policies reduced inflation quickly: Israeli inflation was less than 20 percent in 1986.

Fixed exchange rates are often temporary; countries shift policy once inflation is under control. Israel devalued the shekel in 1987 and again in 1989. Further adjustments followed, and in 2000 Israel let the currency float. It now targets inflation and does not try to control the exchange rate.

The Instability of Fixed Exchange Rates

A fixed exchange rate doesn't last forever. Eventually, as we have seen, policymakers devalue or revalue the currency or switch to a floating rate. Sometimes these shifts occur suddenly and are not entirely voluntary. They are forced on policymakers by expectations in currency markets.

Suppose again that Boversia fixes its nominal exchange rate against the dollar and that Boversian inflation exceeds U.S. inflation. The real exchange rate rises, producing the chain of effects in Figure 17.10—assuming the central bank is committed to the fixed exchange rate.

However, people may doubt this commitment. The process in Figure 17.10 is painful, because it involves a recession. At some point, the central bank may decide to stop the process by devaluing the currency. Therefore, as the real exchange rate rises, people start to think that a devaluation is likely.

This expectation triggers a series of effects, which are summarized in **Figure 17.11**. If devaluation does occur, it will hurt foreign owners of Boversian assets, as the assets will be worth less in foreign currencies. To avoid these losses, people start selling the assets. Boversia experiences capital flight.

With capital flight, the central bank quickly loses its international reserves. To maintain the fixed exchange rate, it would have to raise interest

FIGURE 17.11 The Instability of Fixed Exchange Rates

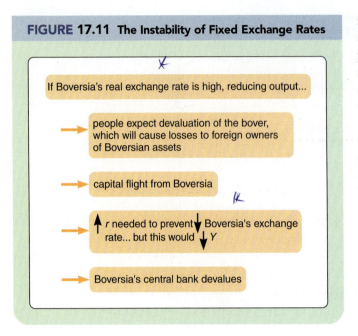

If Boversia's real exchange rate is high, reducing output...

→ people expect devaluation of the bover, which will cause losses to foreign owners of Boversian assets

→ capital flight from Boversia

→ ↑ r needed to prevent ↓ Boversia's exchange rate... but this would ↓ Y

→ Boversia's central bank devalues

▶ Section 6.6 discusses currency speculators' techniques for forecasting exchange rates.

Speculative attack
strategy of selling a currency with a fixed exchange rate to force and to profit from a devaluation

rates sharply. But this would reduce aggregate expenditure, magnifying the fall in output caused by the rise in the real exchange rate. To avoid this outcome, the central bank is likely to let the exchange rate fall.

A lesson from Figure 17.11 is that expectations of devaluation can be self-fulfilling. These expectations cause capital flight, which forces devaluation. We've seen before that self-fulfilling expectations are common in the financial system. Expectations of stock market crashes cause crashes, and expectations of bank runs cause runs.

Currency speculation increases the threat to a fixed exchange rate. Institutions such as hedge funds and investment banks try to predict movements in exchange rates and profit from them. If these speculators think Boversia will devalue, they borrow bovers and sell them for other currencies. Then, if devaluation occurs, they can repurchase the bovers for less than they sold them for. The speculators repay their loans and are left with large profits.

Currency speculators don't just predict devaluations, they help cause them. Their sales of bovers increase capital outflows from Boversia, making it more likely the central bank will devalue. The strategy of selling a currency that may be devalued is called a **speculative attack**. The word attack captures the idea that speculators try to force a policy change on the central bank.

The moral of this story is that fixed exchange rates can backfire. The goal is to stabilize exchange rates, but speculative attacks can cause large, sudden changes. Overall, exchange rates may be less volatile if they are allowed to float. The next case study discusses a famous speculative attack.

CASE STUDY

George Soros Versus the British Pound

For most of their histories, European countries had separate currencies. However, starting in 1979 most of these currencies were tied together by the exchange rate mechanism (ERM). Exchange rates were not absolutely fixed, but almost. Countries agreed on exchange rate targets and promised not to deviate from the targets by more than a few percent. Policymakers planned eventually to fix rates completely and then adopt a common European currency.

The ERM ran into problems in the early 1990s. The story starts in Europe's largest economy, Germany. East and West Germany were reunified in 1990, and the German government spent heavily to rebuild the East. High government spending caused an economic boom, raising inflation. Germany's central bank, the Bundesbank, was highly averse to inflation, so it raised interest rates to slow the economy and push inflation back down.

The rise in German interest rates threatened to raise the value of Germany's currency, the deutsche mark, against other European currencies. Equivalently, it put downward pressure on the other currencies. To prevent depreciation, many countries in the ERM needed to raise their interest rates along with Germany's. But they were reluctant, as their economies weren't booming. The United Kingdom was especially reluctant: it was in a deep recession, so higher interest rates were the last thing it needed.

This situation produced a crisis. Other countries appealed to Germany to reduce its interest rate so they didn't have to raise theirs, but Germany refused. Speculators began to think that some countries would devalue their currencies or drop out of the ERM entirely. In September 1992, speculators attacked the British pound. A hedge fund run by George Soros borrowed billions of pounds from British banks and used them to purchase deutsche marks.

Initially, the United Kingdom tried to maintain its exchange rate with higher interest rates. The Bank of England raised its interest rate target from 10 percent to 12 percent on September 16 and to 15 percent on the 17th. But the attack continued, and policymakers were not willing to raise rates further. They announced that the United Kingdom was dropping out of the ERM, and let the pound float. The exchange rate fell quickly by 10 percent, and interest rates fell below their preattack levels.

The United Kingdom's decision benefited George Soros: his profit from the speculative attack was about 1 billion dollars. (In 1995, the *Wall Street Journal* named Soros one of the eight great investors of the 20th century.) Arguably, the United Kingdom's decision also benefited its own economy. The lower interest rate and exchange rate stimulated aggregate spending, and the United Kingdom recovered strongly from its recession.

After defeating the pound, speculators attacked several other European currencies. Italy briefly raised its short-term interest rate to 30 percent but then followed the United Kingdom out of the ERM. The other ERM countries struggled to maintain the system. In July 1993, they agreed to allow larger fluctuations in exchange rates—rates could deviate from their targets by up to 15 percent. This moved the system closer to fully floating exchange rates.

These events were a setback for plans to unify Europe's currencies. However, the ERM countries eventually narrowed their exchange rate bands again, and they created the euro in 1999. By that time, Italy had rejoined the ERM, so it adopted the euro. The United Kingdom remained outside the system and retains its own currency to this day.

A Brief History of Fixed Exchange Rates

Fixed exchange rates used to be the norm, but they are less common today. Let's review some history.

▶For more on the gold standard, see Sections 2.2 and 14.2.

The Gold Standard In the late nineteenth and early twentieth centuries, most major economies were on a gold standard. Each country's currency was worth a certain amount of gold, which implied fixed exchange rates between countries. For example, a U.S. dollar was worth 0.0484 ounces of gold and a British pound was worth 0.2358 ounces. These values implied an exchange rate of $0.0484/0.2358 = 0.2053$ pounds per dollar.

This system broke down during the Great Depression of the 1930s. During that period, many countries abandoned the gold standard so they could expand the money supply. Without the gold standard, exchange rates fluctuated.

The Bretton Woods System Forty-four countries established a new system of fixed exchange rates in 1944. It was called the *Bretton Woods system* after the New Hampshire resort where the agreement was signed. Under this system, all currencies were fixed against the dollar. Fixed rates were maintained through a combination of interest rate adjustments, capital controls, and interventions.

At the time, policymakers considered fixed exchange rates essential for international trade. In the 1950s, Milton Friedman started arguing for floating rates. He thought that exchange rates should be determined by free markets, not governments. This view is common today, but most economists dismissed it during the Bretton Woods era.

Under the Bretton Woods system, currencies were sometimes devalued or revalued, and speculative attacks occurred. These events became more frequent in the late 1960s, for two reasons. First, some countries relaxed capital controls, making it harder to control exchange rates. Second, U.S. inflation rose, causing the dollar to appreciate in real terms. People started to think the United States would devalue, prompting speculative attacks on the dollar.

In 1971, a speculative attack forced an 8-percent devaluation of the dollar. Another attack produced a 10-percent devaluation in 1973—and then yet another attack began. At that point, the Bretton Woods countries let their currencies float. At the time, floating rates were meant to be temporary, but the fixed-rate system was never reestablished.

Since Bretton Woods Since 1973, the world's advanced economies have generally chosen floating exchange rates. Policymakers have decided that the benefits of fixed rates are outweighed by the loss of monetary policy and the danger of speculative attacks. Europe's exchange rate mechanism was an exception, but it was a temporary arrangement on the path to monetary union.

From the 1970s through the 1990s, many developing countries fixed their exchange rates against the U.S. dollar. However, speculative attacks forced many of these countries to abandon fixed rates, just as they had ended the Bretton Woods system. Fixed rates ended for Mexico in 1994 and for most East Asian countries during the crisis of 1997–1998. Today, most developing countries let their currencies float—although some, such as China, allow only small movements in exchange rates.

Fixed exchange rates are still common within two groups of countries. One is small countries with close links to larger economies. These countries fix exchange rates to increase integration with the larger economy. Small countries on the outskirts of the euro area, such as Denmark, fix their exchange rates against the euro. Countries in the Caribbean, such as the Bahamas, fix rates against the U.S. dollar.

The second group is oil exporters, such as Saudi Arabia and Kuwait, which also fix exchange rates against the dollar. The reason is that the price of oil in world markets is set in dollars. If Saudi Arabia's riyal floated against the dollar, changes in the exchange rate would cause changes in oil revenues as measured in riyals. Oil exporters prefer stable revenues.

17.5 CURRENCY UNIONS

A currency union is a group of countries that adopts a single money. The world's largest currency union by far is the euro area. The euro was created by 11 countries in 1999, and 17 countries used the euro at the beginning of 2011.

We can interpret a currency union as an extreme version of fixed exchange rates. Before the euro, the ERM fixed European rates, but devaluations were possible. The value of France's currency, the franc, might fall relative to Germany's deutsche mark, for example. Today, the exchange rate between German and French currency is fixed absolutely at 1.0. Both countries use the euro, and one euro in France is always worth one euro in Germany.

Why was the euro created? Has it benefited Europe's economies? Should countries elsewhere create similar currency unions? We conclude this chapter by discussing these questions.

▶ Section 2.2 compares currency unions with other extreme forms of fixed exchange rates: dollarization, in which one country unilaterally adopts another's currency, and a currency board, which issues local currency backed by foreign currency.

The Euro Area

Let's start with some background on the creation of the euro, how the euro area is expanding, and how European monetary policy is set.

The Birth of the Euro The process leading to the euro began with a 1992 agreement among the countries in Europe's exchange rate mechanism. The agreement was called the Maastricht Treaty after the Dutch city where it was signed. The ERM countries agreed to reduce fluctuations in exchange rates and eventually to fix rates. Then they would replace their national moneys with a single currency. The Maastricht Treaty said the new currency should be created by 1999. The speculative attacks of 1992 briefly set back the Maastricht process, but the euro was created on schedule on January 1, 1999.

The Maastricht Treaty determines which countries are eligible to adopt the euro. There are two requirements. First, a country has to be a member of the European Union (EU). The EU is an organization established in 1957 to promote European economic integration. Its members have agreed to remove trade barriers and capital controls, but they had separate currencies before 1999.

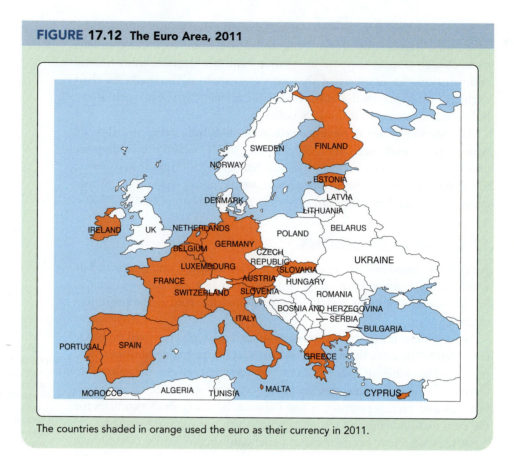

FIGURE 17.12 The Euro Area, 2011

The countries shaded in orange used the euro as their currency in 2011.

Second, a country adopting the euro has to have good economic policies, as defined by several criteria. For example, the government budget deficit has to be less than 3 percent of GDP, and inflation has to be low. The creators of the euro didn't want to share the currency with unstable economies.

Fifteen countries belonged to the EU in 1999. Two of these, Greece and Sweden, failed to meet the criteria for euro membership. Two others, Denmark and the United Kingdom, met the criteria but chose to retain their national currencies. The remaining 11 countries became the initial members of the euro area. **Figure 17.12** shows these countries, along with countries that adopted the euro later.

The Euro Area Grows In 2001, Greece satisfied the economic criteria in the Maastricht Treaty. It became the twelfth country to join the euro area.

Between 2004 and 2007, the European Union admitted 12 new members, mostly countries in Eastern Europe. These countries are eligible to adopt the euro if they meet the economic criteria. As of 2011, five of the new EU countries were using the euro: Slovenia, Slovakia, Estonia, Cyprus, and Malta. A number of others, such as Hungary and Poland, have not met the economic criteria but will likely adopt the euro if and when they do.

The United Kingdom and Denmark, which chose not to adopt the euro in 1999, have remained outside the currency union. Sweden became eligible for the euro in 2003 but did not adopt it. Both Denmark and Sweden held referendums in which a majority of citizens voted to retain their national currencies.

European Monetary Policy Monetary policy for the euro area is run by the Eurosystem, the analogue of the Federal Reserve System in the United States. The Eurosystem includes the European Central Bank (ECB) in Frankfurt and the national central banks (NCBs) of the euro countries. NCBs include Germany's Bundesbank, the Banque de France, and the Banca d'Italia.

Before the euro, the NCBs set monetary policy for their countries. Now their roles are similar to those of Federal Reserve Banks in the United States. NCBs perform central-bank functions such as processing payments and regulating banks. They also participate in making monetary policy for the euro area.

▶ Table 2.2 lists the major functions of central banks.

The ECB is run by a six-member Executive Board, the equivalent of the Fed's Board of Governors. Members of the board are chosen by agreement of the heads of state of euro countries. The president of the ECB is the chair of the Executive Board.

Monetary policy is set by the Governing Council of the Eurosystem. Again, there is a close analogy to a U.S. body, the Federal Open Market Committee. The Governing Council has 21 members: the 6 members of the ECB's Executive Board plus 15 governors of NCBs. Because more than 15 countries use the euro, NCB governors take turns on the Governing Council; governors from larger economies have more turns than those from smaller economies. The Governing Council meets in Frankfurt once a month. It sets interest rate targets for the euro area, just as the FOMC sets targets for the United States.

The Economics of Currency Unions

Do countries benefit from joining a currency union? Proponents stress that currency unions increase economic integration, while opponents focus on the loss of national monetary policy.

Economic Integration Recall the main argument for fixed exchange rates: they promote trade and capital flows between countries. As an extreme version of fixed rates, a currency union can be especially beneficial for such economic integration. Compared to a traditional fixed-rate system, a currency union has several advantages.

- *A currency union creates absolute fixity of exchange rates.* 1.0 German euros is always worth 1.0 French euros. People in Germany and France don't have to worry about speculative attacks destabilizing exchange rates. Not even George Soros could force a devaluation of one euro against another.

- *A currency union eliminates the costs of changing currencies.* Before 1999, French people visiting Germany had to trade French francs for deutsche marks. To make this transaction, they had to stand in line and pay a fee. A common currency eliminates this nuisance, encouraging people to travel and do business across national borders.

- *A common currency helps people compare prices across different countries.* Consumers can easily tell whether German goods are more or less expensive than French goods because all prices are quoted in euros. This transparency increases competition among firms in different countries, and competition increases economic efficiency.

For all these reasons, the euro's creators hoped it would increase the integration of Europe's economies and speed economic growth. Since the currency was introduced, researchers have found evidence that integration has indeed increased. Studies estimate that trade among euro area economies is 10–20 percent higher than it would be without the common currency. Capital flows have risen rapidly as individuals and institutions trade stocks and bonds across national borders.[1]

One-Size-Fits-All Policy The main drawback of a currency union is the basic problem with fixed exchange rates: the loss of national monetary policy. If each European country had its own currency and floating exchange rates, its central bank could set interest rates for the country. Instead, the ECB sets a single interest rate for the whole euro area. It can stabilize the area's economies only if the same rate is appropriate for all of them—if "one size fits all."

Critics of the euro argue that different countries need different interest rates. Within the euro area, one country may experience an economic boom at the same time another is in a recession. The first country needs an increase in interest rates to contain inflation, while the second needs lower rates to stimulate spending. The ECB can't pursue both policies at once.

The plight of Greece in 2010 illustrates the problem with one-size policy. The country's debt crisis raised interest rates and caused a deep recession, with unemployment of 12 percent. If Greece had its own currency, it could have loosened monetary policy. The value of its currency would have fallen relative to other European currencies, raising net exports and helping the economy recover. This adjustment was impossible, because Greece uses the euro.

> Greece's debt crisis is the topic of a case study in Section 4.5.

The Politics of Currency Unions

We've discussed the economic costs and benefits of currency unions. However, the decision to create the euro was more political than economic. It was part of a broader movement toward European unity.

---

[1]See Laurence Ball, "The Performance of Alternative Policy Regimes," Chapter 23 in Benjamin Friedman and Michael Woodford (eds.), *Handbook of Monetary Economics*, North Holland Press, 2011.

This movement began after World War II as European leaders sought to avoid future conflicts. They created institutions to bind countries together, such as the European Union and the North Atlantic Treaty Organization (NATO), the military alliance. A European Parliament meets in Brussels, Belgium; it has little power, but some hope that will change and Europe will move toward full political union.

Supporters of European unity favor any policy that promotes their broad goal. They pushed for the euro as one more step toward unity. When the currency was introduced, Wim Duisenberg, the ECB's first president, described the political importance of the event:

> The euro is a symbol of stability and unity. Countries from a continent which, throughout the ages, has so often been ravaged by war, have together vowed to uphold the values of freedom, democracy, and human rights. In addition to the economic and political benefits that the euro brings, it will, I believe, help to change the way in which we think about one another as Europeans. . . . The people of Europe have one more fundamentally important thing in common—their money![2]

The euro is also a political symbol for Eastern European countries seeking to adopt the currency. These countries are eager to leave behind their Communist histories and tie themselves to Western Europe. When Slovenia adopted the euro in 2007, Prime Minister Janez Jansa said, "The euro isn't important only for our economy, we expect psychological benefits. . . . we are coming closer to the most developed part of the EU and this will give confidence."[3]

Political symbolism helps explain opposition to the euro as well as support. Although some politicians dream of a united Europe, others are nationalist. For them, the euro is a threat to their countries' identity and strength.

This view is one reason why the United Kingdom opted out of the euro when it was created. Margaret Thatcher, the former prime minister, was a strong critic of the euro. In 1998, she insisted that her Conservative Party "pledge to retain the pound and so maintain control over our destiny as a nation state." In 2001, she said "I would never be prepared to give up our own currency . . . if you have a single currency you give up your independence. You give up your sovereignty. This we must never do."[4]

More Currency Unions?

Several currency unions exist outside Europe. A currency union in West Africa includes eight countries, and one in Central Africa includes six. These groups fix their exchange rates against the euro. The Eastern Caribbean has a currency union of nine small countries.

Economists and politicians have proposed new currency unions in many parts of the world, such as Latin America, East Asia, and all of Africa.

---

[2]Statement at the unveiling of euro banknotes, European Central Bank, Frankfurt, August 30, 2001.
[3]Interview with Agence France-Presse, December 25, 2006.
[4]Margaret Thatcher, article on BBC.co.uk, September 14, 1998; and speech to Conservative election rally in Plymouth, May 22, 2001.

Supporters believe the euro has been good for Europe and want the same benefits for their regions. However, there is strong opposition in many places. Much debate about currency unions is likely in the coming years.

The ultimate currency union would be the whole world. If all nations agreed, a world central bank could issue a single world currency. This idea has been advanced by Robert Mundell of Columbia University, the winner of the 1999 Nobel Prize in Economics. Most economists dismiss Mundell's idea, but a world currency could exist someday. If it does, the world will probably have a floating exchange rate against the currencies of any extraterrestrial economies we encounter.

Summary

17.1 Exchange Rates and Stabilization Policy

- Economic shocks such as shifts in asset holders' confidence cause fluctuations in exchange rates. These exchange rate movements destabilize output and inflation.

- Central banks adjust interest rates to offset the effects of exchange rates on output and inflation. Adjustment to exchange rate movements is a major part of monetary policy in countries with high levels of foreign trade, such as Canada.

17.2 Costs of Exchange Rate Volatility

- Fluctuations in exchange rates create risk for importers and exporters of goods and for owners of foreign assets.

- Exchange rate risk discourages international trade and capital flows, reducing economic efficiency and growth.

17.3 Exchange Rate Policies

- Central banks have several tools for stabilizing exchange rates, but each has drawbacks.

- A central bank can stabilize exchange rates by adjusting interest rates, but it may destabilize output in the process.

- Some central banks try to influence exchange rates through foreign exchange interventions (purchases and sales of foreign currency). The effectiveness of interventions is questionable, however.

- Some countries impose capital controls (restrictions on capital inflows or outflows). These regulations help policymakers control exchange rates, but they impede the flow of savings to countries where the savings are most productive.

- Countries sometimes coordinate their exchange rate policies, but often these policies cause frictions. Since 2000, the United States has objected openly to China's policy of keeping its currency weak.

17.4 Fixed Exchange Rates

- A central bank can fix the nominal exchange rate by committing to buy or sell its currency at the fixed rate. It supports this policy with interest rate adjustments or capital controls (or both).

- With a fixed exchange rate, policymakers sometimes devalue or revalue the currency. Often, the reason is to offset drift in the real exchange rate caused by differences between foreign and domestic inflation.

- A country with a fixed exchange rate loses its independent monetary policy. The central bank cannot adjust interest rates to stabilize output.

- A fixed exchange rate can prevent high inflation by tying a country's inflation rate to that of another country.

- Speculative attacks can cause fixed exchange rates to collapse, as in the United Kingdom in 1992.

- From 1944 to 1973, most countries had fixed exchange rates under the Bretton Woods system. Since then, most countries have adopted floating exchange rates.

17.5 Currency Unions

- A currency union is a group of countries that adopts a common money. The euro area is the world's largest currency union.

■ The primary advantage of a currency union is greater economic integration. The primary drawback is that the currency union has a single monetary policy, which may not be appropriate for all member countries, as Greece's debt crisis in 2010 illustrates.

■ The impetus for creating the euro was political: a common money symbolizes European unity.

Key Terms

capital controls, p. 531

devaluation, p. 537

fixed exchange rate, p. 535

floating exchange rate, p. 535

foreign exchange interventions, p. 527

international reserves, p. 527

revaluation, p. 537

speculative attack, p. 540

Questions and Problems

1. Suppose that firms in Boversia gain confidence in the economy, so domestic investment rises for any given interest rate. For now, assume that net capital outflows don't change. Using graphs, show what happens to output and the real exchange rate under three assumptions about Boversia's monetary policy:

   a. The central bank holds the real interest rate constant.

   b. The central bank adjusts the real interest rate to keep output constant.

   c. The central bank adjusts the real interest rate to keep the real exchange rate constant.

2. Suppose again that investment rises in Boversia. In this case, assume that higher confidence in the economy also causes a decrease in net capital outflows. Use graphs to answer the following questions:

   a. If the central bank holds the real interest rate constant, what happens to output and the real exchange rate?

   b. If the central bank wants to keep output constant, should it raise or lower the interest rate?

   c. If the central bank wants to keep the exchange rate constant, should it raise or lower the interest rate?

3. Consider the scenario in Figure 17.4: a rise in confidence causes a fall in net capital outflows, and the central bank adjusts the interest rate to keep the exchange rate constant. For this case, explain what happens to each of the components of aggregate spending: consumption, investment, government purchases, and net exports.

4. Suppose government spending rises in Boversia, shifting out the AE curve. The central bank would like to keep both output and the real exchange rate constant. Using graphs, show how policymakers can accomplish these goals through a combination of an interest rate adjustment and capital controls.

5. Compare two statements about exchange rates that Henry Paulson, Treasury secretary under President Bush, made in 2007: (1) "A strong dollar is in our nation's interest." (2) "The currency [China's yuan] needs to appreciate, and it needs to appreciate faster." Are the two statements consistent with one another? Why might the same official make both statements?

6. What is the difference between a depreciation of a currency and a devaluation of a currency? What is the difference between an appreciation and a revaluation?

7. In 2020, Boversia fixes its exchange rate at 0.5 dollars per bover. From 2020 to 2025, Boversia experiences inflation of 5 percent per year, while U.S. inflation is 2 percent per year.

   a. By how much does Boversia's real exchange rate change from 2020 to 2025?

   b. If Boversia wants to return the real exchange rate to its 2020 level, by how much should it devalue or revalue its currency in 2025?

8. Some countries have a "crawling peg" for their nominal exchange rate: they adjust it by a fixed percentage every year. For example, Boversia might reduce its exchange rate against the dollar by 3 percent per year. Why might a country adopt a crawling peg?

9. Boversia has a fixed exchange rate against the dollar. Taxes rise in the United States, reducing U.S. aggregate expenditure. The Federal Reserve adjusts the U.S. interest rate to keep output constant, and Boversia's central bank adjusts its interest rate to keep the exchange rate constant. Using graphs, show what happens to Boversia's output, interest rate, and exchange rate.

10. Under the Maastricht Treaty, a country may adopt the euro only if its government budget deficit is less than 3 percent of GDP. What is the rationale for this requirement? (*Hint*: See Section 14.2.)

11. Suppose the U.S. dollar is abolished. To replace it, each of the 12 Federal Reserve Banks issues a currency for its region. The Boston Fed issues the New England dollar, the Richmond Fed issues the Mid-Atlantic dollar, and so on. What are the costs and benefits of this change?

12. A currency board issues money backed by a foreign currency (review Section 2.2). Like a currency union, a currency board is an extreme version of a fixed exchange rate. Are speculative attacks a danger with a currency board? Explain.

▶ Online and Data Questions
www.worthpublishers.com/ball

13. On the text Web site, examine (i) the behavior of the U.S.–Canada exchange rate over 2005–2007 and (ii) the interest rate targets chosen by the Bank of Canada over the same period.

   a. Over 2005–2007, did the Bank of Canada respond to movements in the exchange rate in the manner described in the case study in Section 17.1?

   b. Economists attribute changes in Canada's exchange rate over 2005–2007 to increases in the prices of commodities that Canada exports, including oil and metals. Does this help explain the answer to part (a)? (*Hint*: See the discussion of commodity prices in Section 6.5).

14. Through Internet research, update the information in Figure 17.12. Find out which countries have joined the euro area recently or are likely to join soon. Why are these countries joining while others in the European Union are still left out?

Financial Crises

© Underwood & Underwood/CORBIS

E conomies are constantly buffeted by shocks to aggregate expenditure and inflation. Central banks usually try to stabilize their economies by adjusting short-term interest rates. As we have observed throughout this book, however, one especially devastating shock requires extraordinary responses: a **financial crisis**. Such a major disruption of the financial system can cause economic disaster if policymakers don't respond effectively.

Financial crises typically involve sharp falls in asset prices and failures of financial institutions. In the United States, a financial crisis in the early 1930s triggered the Great Depression. The U.S. crisis that started in 2007 produced a recession that by many measures was the worst since the Depression. Financial crises have also damaged economies around the world, among them Argentina's in 2001 and Greece's in 2009–2010.

Regardless of where or when they occur, financial crises are complex events; the feedbacks among different parts of the financial system and the economy make them dangerous and difficult to stop. In some periods, including the 1930s, central banks have responded passively to crises. During the most recent financial crisis, the Federal Reserve intervened aggressively to contain the damage, for example, by serving as lender of last resort to financial institutions that were cut off from other funds. The Treasury Department also aided troubled institutions by purchasing their stock.

Financial crises are complex events. To understand them, we must understand the workings of financial markets and the banking system,

During the Great Depression of the 1930s, the U.S. unemployment rate reached 25 percent. Unemployed workers struggled to find sources of income.

Financial crisis major disruption of the financial system, typically involving sharp drops in asset prices and failures of financial institutions

the behavior of the aggregate economy, and the policies of central banks. Previous chapters have discussed these topics separately; here we pull them together.

We look first at the events in a typical financial crisis and the various ways in which governments and central banks respond. Then we use this background to examine what happened in the United States starting in 2007 and to discuss some of the regulatory reforms that have been proposed and enacted in the wake of this crisis. Finally, we explore financial crises in emerging economies and the controversial role of the International Monetary Fund (IMF) in responding to them.

18.1 THE MECHANICS OF FINANCIAL CRISES

No two financial crises are exactly alike, but most share a few basic features. We first discuss what happens to the financial system in a crisis and then look at how a crisis affects the rest of the economy.

Events in the Financial System

 This discussion draws on earlier coverage of asset-price crashes (Section 3.5), bank insolvencies (Section 9.6), and bank runs (Section 10.1).

At the center of most crises are declines in asset prices, failures of financial institutions caused by insolvency or liquidity crises, or some combination of these events.

Asset-Price Declines A crisis may be triggered by large decreases in the prices of stocks, real estate, or other assets. Many economists interpret these decreases as the ends of asset-price bubbles During a bubble, people expect asset prices to rise, which causes high demand for the assets, which makes the expectations of higher prices self-fulfilling. Asset prices rise far above the present value of expected income from the assets.

Then, at some point, sentiment shifts: people begin to worry that asset prices are too high and start selling the assets, pushing prices down. Falling prices shake confidence further, leading to more selling, and so on. Asset prices may fall over periods of months or years, or a crash may occur in the course of a single day.

Insolvencies In a typical crisis, decreases in asset prices are accompanied by failures of financial institutions. An institution may fail because it becomes insolvent, that is, its assets fall below its liabilities and its net worth (capital) becomes negative. A commercial bank can become insolvent because of loan defaults, increases in interest rates, and other events. When a bank becomes insolvent, regulators are likely to force its closure.

Other kinds of financial institutions can also become insolvent. Hedge funds, for example, borrow money from banks to purchase risky assets. If the prices of these assets decline, a fund's net worth can become negative. When this happens, the fund is likely to default on its debts and go out of business.

Insolvencies can spread from one institution to many others, because financial institutions have debts to one another. Banks have deposits at other banks, lend to each other in the federal funds market, and lend to hedge funds and investment banks. If one institution fails, its depositors and lenders suffer losses, and they, in turn, may become insolvent.

Liquidity Crises Even if a financial institution is solvent initially, it can fail because it doesn't have enough liquid assets to make payments it has promised. The classic example of a liquidity crisis is a bank run. Depositors lose confidence in a bank, try to withdraw large amounts from their accounts, and exhaust the bank's reserves and liquid securities. To make the payments it has promised its depositors, the bank must sell its illiquid assets at fire-sale prices. Losses on these transactions can push it into insolvency.

Liquidity crises can also occur at nondepository institutions, such as hedge funds and investment banks. These institutions often raise funds by making short-term loans and issuing commercial paper. To stay in business, they must raise new funds continuously to pay off maturing debts. If creditors lose confidence and cut off funding, an institution can be forced into a fire sale of its illiquid assets, leading to insolvency.

Liquidity crises can spread from one financial institution to another largely for psychological reasons. If a bank experiences a run, for example, depositors at other banks start worrying about the safety of their own funds. They may start making withdrawals, thus triggering an economywide banking panic and widespread failures.

Financial Crises and the Economy

Financial crises have both direct and indirect costs. The direct costs include losses to asset holders when asset prices fall. They also include losses from financial institution failures. Owners of a failed institution lose their equity, and the institution's creditors lose funds they have lent. When a failed institution is a bank, losses also fall on uninsured depositors and the Federal Deposit Insurance Corporation (FDIC).

Although these direct costs can be large, the greatest costs from financial crises come from their indirect effects. A crisis can set off a chain of events that plunges the whole economy into a recession. **Figure 18.1** summarizes the key parts of this process.

Lending and Spending As charted in Figure 18.1, falling asset prices can lead to a sharp fall in aggregate expenditure. One reason is that asset holders suffer a loss of wealth, which leads them to reduce their consumption. Falling asset prices also shake the confidence of firms and consumers, who may interpret them as signs that the overall economy is in trouble. Uncertain of the future, they put off major decisions about spending until things settle down, and investment and consumption fall.

A fall in asset prices also makes it harder for individuals and firms to borrow. Lower prices decrease the value of borrowers' collateral and net worth, which worsens adverse selection and moral hazard in loan markets. The result is a **credit crunch**, a sharp decrease in bank lending. Some borrowers are cut off from loans or face higher interest rates.

Some of the effects in Figure 18.1 are introduced in Section 13.2, which discusses how events in the financial system affect aggregate expenditure and illustrates these effects by examining Japan's experience in the 1990s and early 2000s.

Credit crunch a sharp reduction in bank lending

FIGURE 18.1 A Financial Crisis

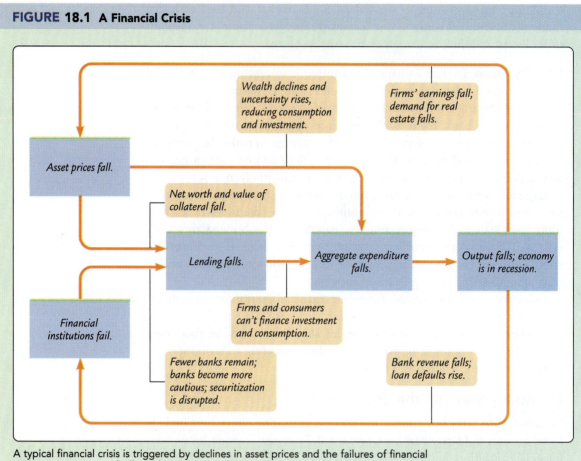

A typical financial crisis is triggered by declines in asset prices and the failures of financial institutions. A series of effects then leads to a fall in output, which reinforces the causes of the crisis.

Failures of financial institutions also cause a credit crunch. When commercial banks fail, they stop lending. Surviving banks may fear failure and become more conservative in approving loans. They may also reduce loans in order to increase their liquid assets and guard against runs. When investment banks fail, securitization falls, which reduces the funds available for bank loans.

A credit crunch means less spending by firms and individuals who rely on credit. This decrease in investment and consumption reduces aggregate expenditure, adding to the direct effect of asset-price declines. In the short run, a fall in aggregate expenditure reduces output. In this way, a crisis can cause a deep recession.

A Vicious Circle Unfortunately, that's not the end of the story. If a financial crisis causes a recession, the recession can then exacerbate the crisis. Figure 18.1 shows this feedback effect. Asset prices are likely to fall further: stock prices fall because the recession reduces firms' expected profits, for example, and real estate prices fall because of lower demand for real estate.

A recession also worsens the problems of financial institutions. Banks lose revenue because a recession reduces the demand for loans. Firms go bankrupt, increasing loan defaults. Worries about these problems make bank panics more likely. For all these reasons, bank failures rise during a recession.

Because of these feedbacks, a financial crisis can trigger a vicious circle of falling output and worsening financial problems. Once a crisis starts, it can sustain itself for a long time.

So far we've discussed the most common elements of crises. Crises often have additional wrinkles—other ways they hurt the economy and build on themselves. To see how much can go wrong, let's examine the Great Depression.

CASE STUDY

Disaster in the 1930s

In U.S. economic history, the Great Depression stands out as a unique disaster. The unemployment rate rose from 3 percent in 1929 to 25 percent in 1933, and it was still 15 percent in 1940. The Depression pushed millions of middle-class families into poverty. By comparison, the unemployment rate peaked at 10.1 percent in October 2009 as the most recent financial crisis wound down.

The depression began in the early 1930s with a financial crisis that had the classic ingredients of falling asset prices and failures of financial institutions, shown in Figure 18.1. The fall in asset prices started with a stock market crash: on October 28, 1929, the Dow Jones Index fell 13 percent. After the crash, stock prices kept falling: the Dow index fell from 365 before the crash to 41 in 1932, a decrease of 89 percent.

The stock market crash created great uncertainty about the economy, because a crash of this size was unprecedented. Uncertainty led firms and consumers to postpone major purchases, such as automobiles, so aggregate expenditure fell.

A wave of bank failures then rolled across the country from 1930 to 1933. Midwestern banks failed when farmers defaulted on loans, and these failures made people nervous about other banks. Eventually, a series of panics swept the country as depositors lost confidence and, with no deposit insurance to protect them, rushed to withdraw funds. President Franklin Roosevelt eventually ended the panics with the bank holiday of March 1933, but more than a third of all U.S. banks failed.

▶ For more on bank panics in the 1930s, see the case study in Section 10.1.

Falling stock prices and massive bank failures reduced bank lending dramatically, resulting in a credit crunch. Because firms and individuals couldn't borrow, investment and consumption fell, causing a decrease in aggregate expenditure. As is usual in crises, falling aggregate expenditure, and hence falling output, magnified the problems of the financial system, especially the stock market. With the economy depressed, firms' earnings prospects were bleak. Stock prices stayed low: it took until 1954 for the Dow Jones Index to climb back to its 1929 level.

▶The money multiplier, m, is the ratio of the money supply to the monetary base. As calculated in Equation (11.2),

$$m = \frac{(C/D) + 1}{(C/D) + (R/D)},$$ where

C/D is the currency–deposit ratio and R/D is the reserve–deposit ratio.

A special twist in this episode was a sharp fall in the money supply. Because of the bank panics, people started holding more currency, and banks increased their reserves to guard against runs. The currency–deposit and reserve–deposit ratios rose, reducing the money multiplier. The fall in the multiplier reduced the money supply by 33 percent between 1929 and 1933. The fall in the money supply reduced aggregate expenditure, reinforcing the effects of the stock market crash and lower bank lending.

The fall in the money supply also led to deflation: the aggregate price level fell by 22 percent from 1929 to 1933. Deflation in turn increased debt burdens: a given nominal debt became larger in real terms. Heavier debt caused many borrowers, especially farmers, to default on bank loans, and these defaults further weakened banks and prolonged the severe credit crunch. The depression was made "Great" because so many problems occurred at the same time.

18.2 FINANCIAL RESCUES

A financial crisis creates a vicious circle in which problems in the financial system and falling aggregate expenditure reinforce one another. Governments and central banks seek to break this cycle. They do so partly with expansionary fiscal and monetary policies, which boost expenditure. In crises, however, policy actions typically are not limited to these standard macroeconomic tools. Policymakers also take a range of actions aimed directly at reducing the problems of the financial system, especially the failures of financial institutions.

Generally, these policies involve the use of government or central-bank funds to prevent institutions from failing or to compensate individuals or firms that are hurt by failures. In popular discussion, such policies are often called *bailouts*. This umbrella term is imprecise, however, because it is used for policies that vary widely. Bailouts range from giveaways of government money to loans or asset purchases that are costless or even profitable for taxpayers. This section explores some policy actions aimed at ending a financial crisis and looks at the debate about their benefits and costs.

Liquidity Crises and the Lender of Last Resort

Liquidity crises at financial institutions, such as bank panics, are one cause of broader financial crises. A liquidity crisis can push a solvent institution into insolvency, causing it to fail for no good reason.

Fortunately, central banks have a simple solution for liquidity crises. They can make emergency loans to institutions that are running out of liquid assets, allowing them to avoid fire sales of their illiquid assets. In other words, a central bank can serve as **lender of last resort**. A borrowing institution remains solvent and repays the central bank when its liquidity crisis subsides. To ensure repayment, the central bank requires the borrower to pledge some of its assets as collateral for the loan.

Lender of last resort
central bank's role as emergency lender to financial institutions

When Congress established the Federal Reserve in 1913, the main purpose was to create a lender of last resort for U.S. banks. Unfortunately, during the bank panics of the early 1930s, the Fed underestimated the danger to the banking system and the economy and therefore did not lend to many banks. The Fed learned from this mistake and has acted quickly during more recent liquidity crises.

Deposit insurance helps prevent bank runs, thus reducing the need for a lender of last resort, but it does not eliminate the need entirely. Some banks raise most of their funds through borrowing and deposits that exceed the limit on insurance. These uninsured funds disappear quickly if depositors and lenders lose confidence in a bank. A lender of last resort is needed for such an emergency.

In the United States, a bank facing a liquidity crisis can approach the Federal Reserve and request a *discount loan*, which the Fed approves if it judges that the bank is solvent and can post sufficient collateral. The Fed lends simply by crediting the bank's account. Discount loans are available only to commercial banks and savings institutions, financial institutions that fit the definition of "bank": they accept deposits and make loans.

At times, however, the Fed has stretched its role as lender of last resort by providing liquidity to other financial institutions. After the terrorist attacks of September 11, 2001, for example, the Fed encouraged banks to lend to securities firms facing liquidity crises; in turn, the Fed promised to lend any necessary funds to the banks. As we discuss later in this chapter, the Fed lent money directly to securities firms during the financial crisis of 2007–2009.

▶ Review Chapter 11 for more on Federal Reserve lending to banks.

Giveaways of Government Funds

When a central bank acts as lender of last resort, it helps a solvent institution facing a liquidity crisis. The loan prevents the institution from failing and is repaid with interest. Ultimately, there is no cost to the central bank, the government, or taxpayers.

Not all financial institution failures are caused by liquidity crises. Sometimes an institution simply loses money, so its assets fall below its liabilities and it becomes insolvent. Normally, this causes the institution to fail and default on its debts. In some cases, however, policymakers intervene. Instead of lending to an institution, the government or central bank gives money away. It may give funds to the failing institution to restore its solvency and keep it in business. Alternatively, it may let the institution fail but compensate other individuals and institutions that are hurt by the failure.

Deposit insurance commits the government to paying part of the costs of bank failures. The FDIC compensates depositors for their losses up to some limit. Today, few economists question the desirability of deposit insurance, at least in countries with effective bank regulation. The controversial issue is whether compensation should extend beyond promised insurance payments. When a bank fails, should the government protect uninsured depositors and creditors? Should it aid failing institutions with no insurance guarantees, such as investment banks and hedge funds?

The Pros and Cons of Giveaways When the government gives away funds beyond required insurance payments, its purpose is to prevent the problems of an insolvent financial institution from spreading. If one institution fails, it defaults on debts to other institutions, and their losses can cause them to fail. A rash of failures can produce a financial crisis and push the economy into a recession. The government can prevent this outcome by preventing the first institution from failing or by compensating other institutions for losses from the initial failure.

Such government intervention has two sorts of costs. The first is the direct costs of payments from the government. These costs are ultimately borne by taxpayers. The second cost is a worsening of moral hazard, the problem that financial institutions may misuse the funds they raise.

▶ Section 10.3 analyzes the moral hazard problem in the context of deposit insurance.

In particular, the prospect of government aid makes it more likely that institutions will take excessive risks, lose money, and become insolvent. Normally, an institution's creditors and uninsured depositors monitor what happens to their money and cut off funds if the institution misuses them. But if the government intervenes when institutions face failure, everyone comes to expect protection from losses. Nobody has incentives to monitor, so institutions can easily raise funds to finance gambles. These institutions earn a lot if the gambles succeed, and if they lose, the losses fall largely on taxpayers.

When any given institution is in danger of failing, it's hard to know how badly the failure would damage the financial system. It's also hard to gauge how much a government rescue will increase moral hazard in the future. Because of these uncertainties, economists differ sharply on the desirability of government intervention.

Too Big to Fail Historically, decisions about whether to rescue an insolvent financial institution have been influenced strongly by the institution's size. A large institution has more links to other institutions than a small one does. It is likely to borrow heavily, and if it is a bank, it is likely to hold deposits from other banks. Consequently, regulators fear that the failure of a large institution threatens the financial system, whereas the failure of a small institution is relatively harmless. In other words, some financial institutions are deemed **too big to fail (TBTF)**.

Too big to fail (TBTF) doctrine that large financial institutions facing failure must be rescued to protect the financial system

The term TBTF was coined by a congressman after the rescue of Continental Illinois Bank in 1984, an episode discussed in the following case study.

CASE STUDY

The Continental Illinois Rescue

Before 1984, the U.S. government had never extended significant aid to an insolvent financial institution beyond promised payments on deposit insurance. That changed when Continental Illinois, then the nation's seventh-largest commercial bank, ran into trouble. Continental had lent heavily to energy companies and to the governments of developing countries, and both groups defaulted during a worldwide recession in the early 1980s. In May 1984, Continental was on the brink of failure.

Regulators feared that the failure of Continental Illinois would have widespread effects. More than 2000 smaller banks had accounts at Continental. For 66 of these banks, deposits at Continental exceeded their total capital; for another 113, the deposits were more than half of their capital.

Regulators feared that many of these banks would fail if they lost their deposits, shaking confidence in the financial system. The Comptroller of the Currency, the head regulator of national banks, said after the crisis that Continental's failure would have caused "a national, if not international, financial crisis the dimensions of which were difficult to imagine."[*]

Policymakers acted aggressively to save Continental. Despite the bank's insolvency, the Fed lent it $3.6 billion to keep it in operation. The FDIC promised to protect all of Continental's creditors and depositors, waiving the usual limit on insurance. Eventually, the FDIC bought Continental from its shareholders, added capital, and sold it to Bank of America. In the process, the FDIC lost about $1 billion.

These actions were controversial at the time, and they remain so. Critics stress the moral hazard problem and argue that policymakers overstated the risks from a failure of Continental. The debate over treating some institutions as too big to fail continued in the years after the Continental rescue and intensified during the financial crisis of 2007–2009.

[*] Todd Conover, testimony before House Banking Committee, September 19, 1984.

Risky Rescues

The potential failure of a large financial institution creates a dilemma for policymakers. Letting the institution fail and default on its debts can damage the financial system, but preventing this outcome is costly for taxpayers and creates moral hazard. Policymakers wrestled with this dilemma repeatedly during the most recent financial crisis.

Looking for a compromise between inaction and giveaways of government funds, they developed two new ways to aid troubled financial institutions. Unlike loans to solvent institutions facing liquidity crises, these new policies expose taxpayers to a risk of losing money. On the other hand, unlike traditional giveaways of government funds, they *may not* cost the government anything and might even earn money. Let's discuss these policies, risky loans and equity injections, and the rationales for using them.

Risky Loans In this type of rescue, the central bank moves beyond its traditional role as lender of last resort, in which it makes riskless loans to solvent institutions. When the central bank makes risky loans to prevent failures of financial institutions, it is not certain the loans will be paid back.

In some cases, the Fed has taken on risk by lending to institutions that might fail. In September 2008, for example, it lent $85 billion to the insurance conglomerate American International Group (AIG). Losses on *credit default swaps*, derivatives with payouts triggered by defaults on other securities, had left the company near bankruptcy. The Fed loan prevented AIG from defaulting immediately on debts to other institutions, but it meant the Fed was on the hook for $85 billion if, as many feared, AIG declared bankruptcy later.

In other cases, the Fed has taken on risk by lending against collateral of uncertain value. In March 2008, it lent $29 billion to JPMorgan Chase to finance the takeover of the investment bank Bear Stearns, accepting as collateral some of Bear's holdings of subprime *mortgage-backed securities* (MBSs). The decline in value of these very MBSs had pushed Bear to the brink of bankruptcy. Crucially, the loan to JPMorgan was made *without recourse*: if the value of the collateral declined further, the Fed would be entitled only to the collateral, not the $29 billion it had lent. The Fed stood to lose if the subprime crisis worsened.

During the crisis of 2007–2009, many economists and politicians criticized the Fed for risking money on troubled financial institutions. Fed officials argued, however, that the risks were modest. Part of their rationale was that the Fed's actions would ease the financial crisis, which in turn would reduce the risk that its debtors would default or that the value of their collateral would fall.

In other words, by agreeing to accept some of the potential losses from the financial crisis, the Fed hoped to prevent these losses from occurring. This strategy was similar to the logic of deposit insurance: by agreeing to bear the costs of a harmful event (bank runs), the government makes the event less likely.

Equity Injections A financial institution becomes insolvent when its capital (equity) falls below zero. It can restore solvency and stay in business if it raises new capital by issuing stock. If an institution is troubled, however, individuals and private firms may not be willing to buy its stock. This problem is the rationale for **equity injections**, or purchases of stock, by the government. The U.S. Treasury Department pursued this rescue policy in 2008 and 2009.

In buying the stock of a financial institution, the government provides the institution with capital to ensure its solvency. Like any purchaser of stock, the government receives an ownership share in the institution and it takes on risk. If the institution ultimately fails, or if it requires further assistance to survive, the government can lose money. On the other hand, the government can earn a profit on behalf of taxpayers if the institution recovers and its stock price rises. Equity injections are controversial because opinions vary on the government's likely gains or losses.

Government purchases of stock are also controversial because they deviate from a financial system based on free markets. Critics argue that the behavior of government-owned institutions may be influenced by politics. In 2008, for example, the Treasury imposed restrictions on executive pay as a condition for purchasing stock. Many voters supported such restrictions, believing that executives who had played a role in the financial crisis should

For context on the Fed's risky loans, see the case studies in Section 5.1, on JPMorgan Chase's purchase of Bear Stearns, and Section 5.6, on AIG's troubles with credit default swaps.

Equity injection purchases of a financial institution's stock by the government

▶ The equity injections of 2008–2009 had one historical precedent: purchases of bank stock during the 1930s by the government-owned Reconstruction Finance Corporation.

not receive huge salaries and bonuses. Critics argued that high pay was needed to retain the most talented executives and that the government should not interfere with the market forces that determine salaries.

18.3 THE U.S. FINANCIAL CRISIS OF 2007–2009

The Great Depression of the 1930s showed how a financial crisis can have devastating macroeconomic repercussions. For many years after World War II, however, no such crisis caused an economic upheaval in the United States. Bank failures during the savings and loan crisis of the 1980s cost the government $150 billion and embarrassed regulators, but the episode had modest effects on the overall economy. In the 1990s and into the 2000s, failures of financial institutions were rare. Many economists believed that U.S. bank regulation was effective at preventing excessive risk taking and keeping the financial system safe.

More generally, the 1990s and early 2000s were a period of economic stability in the United States. The high inflation of the 1970s and the deep recession caused by the disinflation of the 1980s joined the Great Depression in the history books. Economists often referred to the 1990s and 2000s as the "Great Moderation" because of its low inflation and steady output growth.

▶ The case study in Section 12.4 reviews the history of the U.S. economy since 1960.

Over 2007–2009, everything changed. The United States experienced a 55-percent fall in the stock market, the failures of some of the country's most prestigious financial institutions, and a disruption in lending throughout the economy. The worst recession since the 1930s pushed the unemployment rate from less than 5 percent in 2007 to more than 10 percent late in 2009.

As with any disaster, controversy abounds about what events were critical and who deserves the blame. With hindsight, however, we can see that a series of adverse events played central roles in the financial crisis. **Figure 18.2** summarizes the timeline of these events and also shows the unprecedented responses of the government and Federal Reserve to the crisis. Some economists have bitterly criticized these actions; others think they saved the economy from an even worse fate—a collapse that could have rivaled the 1930s for the worst economic disaster in U.S. history.

The Subprime Crisis and the First Signs of Panic

In 2006 and 2007, the house price bubble of the early 2000s began to deflate, producing a surge of defaults on subprime mortgages. New Century Financial and Ameriquest, large finance companies that specialized in subprime mortgages, declared bankruptcy in April and August 2007, respectively. Other financial institutions that held securities backed by subprime mortgages suffered billions of dollars of losses, leading firms such as Citigroup and Morgan Stanley to fire their chief executives in 2007.

For more on the subprime mortgage fiasco, see the case study in Section 8.4.

Yet few saw the subprime crisis as a threat to the entire financial system or the economy. In mid-2007, economists estimated that financial institutions might lose a total of $150 billion on subprime mortgages—not pocket change, but not a lot compared to the U.S. annual GDP of $14 trillion.

Text continues on p. 564.

FIGURE 18.2 The U.S. Financial Crisis and Its Aftermath, 2007–2010

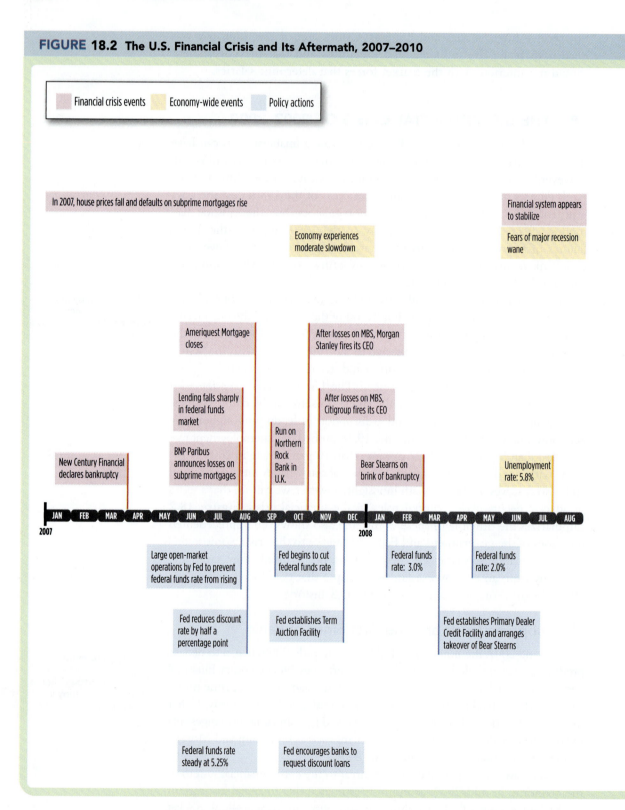

FIGURE 18.2 (continued)

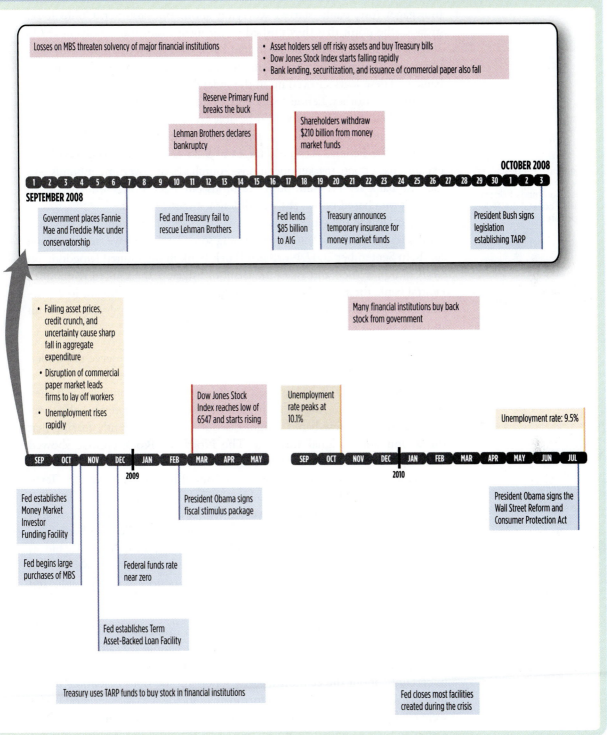

Losses on MBS threaten solvency of major financial institutions

- Asset holders sell off risky assets and buy Treasury bills
- Dow Jones Stock Index starts falling rapidly
- Bank lending, securitization, and issuance of commercial paper also fall

Reserve Primary Fund breaks the buck

Lehman Brothers declares bankruptcy

Shareholders withdraw $210 billion from money market funds

OCTOBER 2008

SEPTEMBER 2008

Government places Fannie Mae and Freddie Mac under conservatorship

Fed and Treasury fail to rescue Lehman Brothers

Fed lends $85 billion to AIG

Treasury announces temporary insurance for money market funds

President Bush signs legislation establishing TARP

- Falling asset prices, credit crunch, and uncertainty cause sharp fall in aggregate expenditure
- Disruption of commercial paper market leads firms to lay off workers
- Unemployment rises rapidly

Many financial institutions buy back stock from government

Dow Jones Stock Index reaches low of 6547 and starts rising

Unemployment rate peaks at 10.1%

Unemployment rate: 9.5%

SEP OCT NOV DEC JAN FEB MAR APR MAY **2009**

SEP OCT NOV DEC JAN FEB MAR APR MAY JUN JUL **2010**

Fed establishes Money Market Investor Funding Facility

President Obama signs fiscal stimulus package

President Obama signs the Wall Street Reform and Consumer Protection Act

Fed begins large purchases of MBS

Federal funds rate near zero

Fed establishes Term Asset-Backed Loan Facility

Treasury uses TARP funds to buy stock in financial institutions

Fed closes most facilities created during the crisis

The Liquidity Crisis of August 2007 Warning signs of the economic disaster to come showed up in the summer of 2007. As losses on subprime mortgages rose, banks started worrying about one another. Could losses grow to the point that they pushed major institutions into insolvency? On August 9, the huge French investment bank BNP Paribus announced large losses on subprime mortgages, news that ratcheted up the fears of U.S. bankers. These fears showed up in the federal funds market, in which banks lend to one another. Lenders suddenly became scarce, because banks questioned whether borrowers would be able to repay their loans.

▶ Section 11.4 describes how the Federal Reserve uses open-market operations to control the federal funds rate.

On August 9 and 10, the scarcity of lenders pushed the federal funds rate far above the Federal Reserve's target of 5.25 percent. The Fed used large, expansionary, open-market operations—purchases of government bonds—to increase bank reserves and push the funds rate back down. On August 10 alone, it purchased bonds at three different times of the day.

Banks around the world remained worried about one another's solvency for the rest of 2007 and into 2008, causing some banks to have trouble raising funds. In September 2007, Northern Rock Bank in the United Kingdom ran short of liquid assets and asked the Bank of England, the United Kingdom's central bank, for a loan. News of this request caused depositors to lose confidence in Northern Rock, producing the United Kingdom's first bank run in more than a century.

▶ The case study in Section 10.1 describes the Northern Rock bank run, which is pictured on p. 285.

The Fed's Response In the United States, the Federal Reserve responded to the disruption of interbank lending by vigorously playing its role as lender of last resort. It encouraged banks to request discount loans if they needed cash, and on August 16 it reduced the discount rate by half a percentage point. Yet few banks sought discount loans, apparently fearing that this action would signal weakness. The Northern Rock episode showed that requesting help from the central bank could backfire.

The low level of discount lending prompted the Fed to create the Term Auction Facility (TAF) in December 2007. Under this program, the Fed lent to banks through auctions. Every 2 weeks, it provided a predetermined level of loans (typically between $25 billion and $75 billion) to banks that submitted the highest interest rate bids. Banks were more eager to bid in these auctions than to take out traditional discount loans, because the Fed took the lead in lending. Also, participation in auctions was not publicized as widely as were requests for discount loans.

Effects on the Economy Late 2007 also saw a moderate slowdown in the U.S. economy. Falling housing prices reduced people's wealth, leading to lower consumption. Consumption and investment were also dampened by uncertainty about the economy, partly reflecting the signs of trouble in the financial system and partly the unfortunate coincidence that world oil prices were rising. Concerned about these developments, the Federal Reserve began easing monetary policy to boost aggregate expenditure. Between August 2007 and January 2008, it reduced its target for the federal funds rate from 5.25 percent to 3.0 percent, as charted in Figure 18.2.

Bear Stearns and the Calm Before the Storm

The next unpleasant surprise was the near failure of investment bank Bear Stearns, where losses on massive holdings of subprime mortgage–backed securities mounted as the prices of these securities fell over 2007. In March 2008, rumors spread that Bear might become insolvent, and these fears produced a liquidity crisis. Bear relied heavily on short-term borrowing to fund its asset holdings, and much of this funding disappeared as lenders lost confidence in the firm. As Bear Stearns ran out of liquid assets, its lawyers prepared to file for bankruptcy.

On March 16, Bear Stearns's predicament produced the first financial rescue of the crisis: the Fed's risky loan to JPMorgan Chase to purchase Bear. The Fed acted out of fear—first, that Bear's failure would hurt other institutions that had lent it money; and second, that a blow to confidence would trigger liquidity crises at other investment banks.

Some economists, however, saw the Fed's fears about Bear Stearns as overblown. They criticized the rescue for the risk that the Fed took on and the moral hazard created by saving Bear's creditors from losses. In April 2008, former Fed official Vincent Reinhart called the Bear Stearns rescue "the worst policy mistake in a generation."

Shortly after the Bear Stearns deal, the Fed made other efforts to head off problems in the financial system and economy. It once again reduced its target for the federal funds rate, to 2.0 percent at the end of April 2008. The Fed sought to prevent liquidity crises by expanding its role as lender of last resort. In March, it established the Primary Dealer Credit Facility (PDCF), which offered loans to *primary dealers* in the government securities market. Primary dealers, which trade with the Fed when it performs open-market operations, include the largest investment banks as well as commercial banks, so investment banks also became eligible for emergency loans from the Fed.

After the Bear Stearns rescue, no major shocks hit the financial system for six months. Over the summer of 2008, fears about the solvency of financial institutions receded, and policymakers grew hopeful that the economic damage from the financial drama would be modest. In June, Fed Chair Ben Bernanke said, "The risk that the economy has entered a substantial downturn appears to have diminished over the last month or so."

Disaster Strikes: September 7–19, 2008

Over the course of two weeks in September 2008, optimism about the economy vanished as the financial crisis erupted. Bad news arrived at a dizzying pace, detailed at the top right in Figure 18.2.

Fannie and Freddie Face Insolvency Mounting losses on mortgage-backed securities threatened the solvency of Fannie Mae and Freddie Mac, the government-sponsored enterprises that purchase a large share of U.S. mortgages. On September 7, the government took Fannie and Freddie into conservatorship. Under this arrangement, the Treasury promised to cover Fannie and Freddie's losses with public funds so they wouldn't default on

▶ Section 8.3 recounts the history of Fannie Mae and Freddie Mac.

bonds they had issued. Default would have caused catastrophic losses to commercial banks and other financial institutions that held trillions of dollars of Fannie's and Freddie's bonds. Their bankruptcies would also have disrupted mortgage lending, because many banks made loans with the expectation of selling them to Fannie or Freddie for securitizing.

The government received stock that gave it 80 percent ownership stakes in Fannie and Freddie. Nonetheless, the Treasury's action was in essence a pure giveaway of government funds. It was clear that Fannie and Freddie were insolvent and that the government would be giving them more money than their stock was worth. As of 2010, the Fannie and Freddie rescues had cost the government more than $200 billion.

Lehman Brothers' Bankruptcy Next came the event that many now consider the key blow to the financial system: investment bank Lehman Brothers declared bankruptcy on September 15. Like Bear Stearns, Lehman had taken large losses on subprime MBSs—to the brink of failure. And once again, the Federal Reserve sought to arrange a takeover, in this case by the British bank Barclay's. But the deal fell through at the last minute, in part because of objections from British bank regulators.

It is unclear whether the Fed or the Treasury could still have saved Lehman. Ben Bernanke and then-Secretary of the Treasury Henry Paulson have said they did not have the legal authority to provide funds to Lehman after the Barclay's deal fell through. Critics contend that policymakers could have done something and that they misjudged the harm of letting Lehman fail. The Fed and the Treasury may have hesitated about acting aggressively because of the earlier negative reaction to the Bear Stearns rescue. A new rescue would have sparked harsh criticism that policymakers were worsening moral hazard yet again.

Lehman's failure shocked financial markets. The firm had been a pillar of the U.S. financial system since 1850, and it was the largest U.S. firm in any industry ever to file for bankruptcy. Everyone on Wall Street knew that Lehman was in trouble in September 2008, but many presumed that, like Bear Stearns, the firm would be taken over by a healthier institution.

Bankruptcy meant that Lehman defaulted on its borrowings from other financial institutions. Few people knew exactly how much Lehman owed or what institutions were its creditors, so fears arose that many institutions could suffer losses that threatened their solvency. In addition to the direct effects of Lehman's defaults, the failure of such a prestigious firm suggested that *any* financial institution could fail.

The events that followed Lehman's failure were sufficiently dire that it was the last big institution to declare bankruptcy throughout the crisis. Seeking to stem the financial panic, the Fed and the Treasury acted aggressively to save other institutions from Lehman's fate.

The Rescue of AIG Policymakers' new activism began on September 16, the day after the Lehman bankruptcy. AIG, the giant insurance conglomerate, was the next institution in line to fail until the Fed made an emergency loan of

$85 billion. In explaining this action, Ben Bernanke said that a failure of AIG "could have resulted in a 1930s-style global financial and economic melt-down, with catastrophic implications for production, income, and jobs."

A bankrupt AIG would have defaulted on the $20 billion of commercial paper that it had issued. In addition, it would not have made promised payments on the credit default swaps it had sold on subprime mortgage-backed securities. As a result, other institutions would not have been compensated for losses on the MBSs. Individuals and businesses that had purchased insurance policies from AIG would have seen their insurance coverage disappear suddenly.

The Money-Market Crisis A final episode in the September 2008 debacle involved money-market mutual funds (MMMFs). MMMFs hold Treasury bills (short-term government bonds) and commercial paper (short-term corporate bonds) and sell shares to savers. The funds generally yield low returns but are considered safe, because their assets have short maturities and low default rates. Since money-market funds were invented in the 1970s, almost nobody who put a dollar in a money-market fund ended up with less than a dollar. Many people came to view money-market funds as similar to bank accounts, which also yield low but safe returns.

The day of the AIG rescue, however, one large money-market fund, the Reserve Primary Fund, *broke the buck*: the value of a share in the fund, which originally cost $1, fell to 97 cents. The reason was simple: the fund owned large quantities of Lehman Brothers' commercial paper, which had plummeted in value when Lehman declared bankruptcy the day before. Suddenly, people were reminded that a money-market fund is *not* a bank account with a guaranteed return. And unlike bank deposits, government insurance does not cover shares in money-market funds.

The result was a run on MMMFs. In two days, September 17 and 18, panicked holders of money-market shares withdrew $210 billion from the funds, reducing total assets by approximately 22 percent. This outflow slowed on September 19, when the Treasury Department announced it would temporarily offer insurance to money-market funds. But confidence remained shaky, and the funds' assets slipped further over the next few months.

A Flight to Safety The quick succession of crises at major institutions created panic. Nobody knew what shock would come next, when the crisis would end, or how devastating it would be for the economy. This atmosphere led to a *flight to safety*. Financial institutions became fearful of any assets that appeared risky, including stocks, the bonds of corporations without top credit ratings, and securities backed by any kind of bank loans. Institutions dumped these assets and bought those they considered safest: 3- and 6-month Treasury bills. T-bills were considered safe, because it was unlikely that the government would default on its debt over the next 6 months, even in a financial crisis.

We can see some effects of the flight to safety in **Figure 18.3**, which shows data from financial markets during the latter half of 2008 through early 2009.

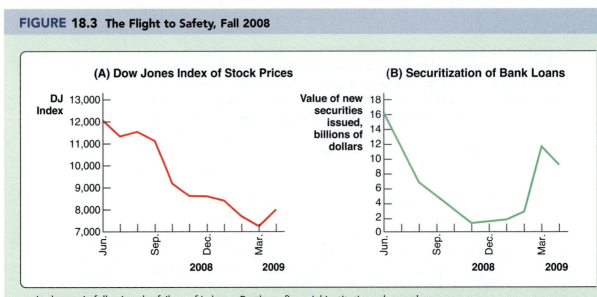

FIGURE 18.3 The Flight to Safety, Fall 2008

In the panic following the failure of Lehman Brothers, financial institutions dumped any assets that appeared risky, causing a sharp fall in stock prices (A), a collapse in securitization of bank loans (B), and higher interest rates on corporate bonds with moderate default risk (C). A surge in the demand for Treasury bills, a safe asset, pushed the interest rate on T-bills near zero (D).

Sources: finance.yahoo.com, Securities Industry and Financial Market Association, and Federal Reserve Bank of St. Louis.

Starting in September 2008, the Dow Jones Index of stock prices plummeted for 6 months (Figure 18.3A). Securitization fell dramatically as demand for securitized loans disappeared (Figure 18.3B). The prices of BAA-rated corporate bonds (bonds with moderate default risk) fell, which implied a sharp rise in their interest rates as measured by yield to maturity (Figure 18.3C). In contrast, the flight to Treasury bills pushed their prices up, and their interest rates fell almost to zero (Figure 18.3D).

An Economy in Freefall

Much of the financial crisis played out in the Wall Street area of lower Manhattan and in Washington, D.C., where financial institutions and policy-makers grappled with the crisis. In the fall of 2008, however, the problems of Wall Street spread to Main Streets across the country, plunging the economy into a deep recession.

The story followed the broad pattern outlined in our basic model of a financial crisis, Figure 18.1 on page 554, and in our review of the Great Depression of the 1930s. The stock market plunge and the accelerating decline in housing prices reduced consumers' wealth. The dramatic news from the financial system hit consumer confidence hard: from September to November 2008, the University of Michigan's survey of consumer confidence revealed one of the largest drops in the survey's 60-year history. Falling wealth and falling confidence caused a contraction in consumption spending.

FIGURE 18.3 (continued)

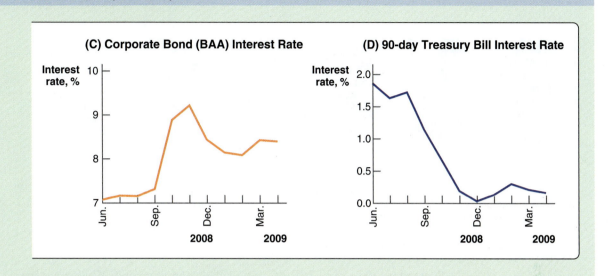

Financial panic also caused a credit crunch with many dimensions. Banks became fearful of lending because losses on mortgages had reduced their capital, meaning further losses could push them into insolvency. With financial institutions fearful of securities backed by bank loans, investment banks stopped securitizing auto loans, credit-card debt, and student loans. Because they could not sell loans to securitizers, banks had fewer funds to lend. Finally, the rise in interest rates on risky corporate bonds made investment projects too costly for many firms. With both investment and consumption falling, aggregate expenditure fell, and a deep recession began.

Some economists think the run on money-market mutual funds following on the heels of the Lehman Brothers failure was one of the most damaging events of the crisis. It set off a chain of effects, summarized in **Figure 18.4**. Money-market funds needed to make large payments to panicked shareholders, and this depleted the cash they would normally have used to purchase new commercial paper from corporations. Across the country, companies far removed from finance—including industries such as manufacturing—suddenly had difficulty selling commercial paper.

The purpose of commercial paper is to cover firms' short-term needs for cash. For example, firms use commercial paper to cover production costs, such as wages and materials, while they wait for revenue to come in from selling their output. The sudden breakdown of the commercial paper market in

FIGURE 18.4 The Money-Market Crisis, Fall 2008

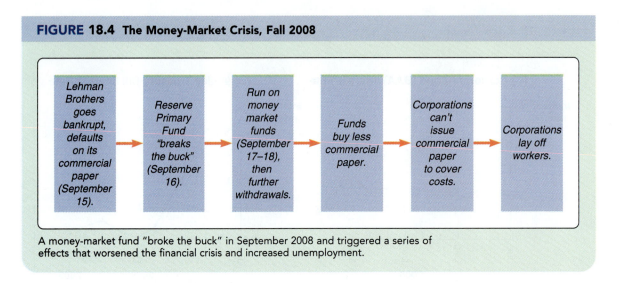

A money-market fund "broke the buck" in September 2008 and triggered a series of effects that worsened the financial crisis and increased unemployment.

September 2008 caused firms around the country to join Wall Street in panicking.

Businesses feared that they wouldn't have enough cash to pay their bills. They responded by slashing costs, which required sharp reductions in output and layoffs of workers, the last link in Figure 18.4. The unemployment rate started rising, adding yet another channel from the financial crisis to aggregate expenditure: consumption fell among laid-off workers and those who feared they might be laid off next.

Through the end of 2008 and into 2009, the financial crisis was in full swing. The deteriorating economy had feedback effects on the financial system: it caused stock and housing prices to continue to fall, and it caused more borrowers to default on bank loans, increasing banks' risk of insolvency. In this vicious circle, the worsening problems of the financial system pushed aggregate expenditure even lower and caused unemployment to rise rapidly.

The Policy Response

As the financial crisis accelerated in late 2008, so did the response of policymakers. Worries about excessive government interference in the economy were swept aside as the Federal Reserve and the Bush and Obama administrations took unprecedented actions to stave off disaster (see Figure 18.2 on pages 562–563).

The TARP On October 3, 2008—18 days after Lehman's failure—President Bush signed an emergency act of Congress establishing the Troubled Asset Relief Program (TARP). The TARP committed $700 billion of government funds to rescue financial institutions.

The initial plan behind the TARP was for the government to purchase "troubled assets," primarily subprime mortgage-backed securities. After the program was established, however, the Treasury decided to use most of the funds for equity injections: instead of purchasing the assets of financial institutions, it purchased shares in the institutions themselves. In late 2008 and early 2009, the Treasury became a major shareholder in most of the country's large financial institutions, ranging from Citigroup to Goldman Sachs to AIG.

Federal Reserve Programs Before the Lehman panic, the Fed had already sought to support the financial system with the Term Auction Facility and the Primary Dealer Credit Facility. In the fall of 2008, the Fed added half a dozen new programs, most with the bureaucratic title, "facility," in their names and ugly acronyms. (This flurry of activity was reflected in the title of a speech by Fed Governor Kevin Warsh: "Longer Days and No Weekends.") The goals of the Fed's programs included repairing the commercial paper market, rejuvenating securitization, and pushing down interest rates on mortgages. Specific actions included the following:

- In October 2008, the Fed established the Money Market Investor Funding Facility (MMIFF). This program addressed the disruption of the commercial paper market after the run on money-market funds. Under the MMIFF, the Fed lent money to banks that agreed to purchase commercial paper from money-market funds. This arrangement helped the funds ensure that they could raise cash if their shareholders demanded it. In turn, as funds became less worried about withdrawals, they became more willing to buy commercial paper from corporations.

- In November, the Fed established the Term Asset-Backed Loan Facility (TALF). Under this program, the Fed lent to financial institutions such as hedge funds to finance purchases of securities backed by bank loans. The goal was to ease the credit crunch by encouraging the securitization process, which broke down during the post-Lehman panic. The Fed accepted the securities purchased under the program as collateral, and its loans were without recourse, which meant the Fed took on the risk that the securities would fall in value.

- Also in November 2008, the Fed began purchasing prime mortgage-backed securities issued by Fannie Mae and Freddie Mac. The goal was to drive down interest rates on these securities and ultimately reduce rates on the prime mortgages behind the securities. Over a year, the Fed bought more than a trillion dollars' worth of prime MBSs. Studies estimate that these purchases reduced mortgage rates by 0.3 or 0.4 of a percentage point. The Fed hoped that lower rates would increase the demand for housing and help slow the fall in U.S. housing prices.

Through the text Web site follow the link to a page on the Fed Web site, Credit and Liquidity Policies, which catalogs the full range of Fed responses to the financial crisis.

Monetary and Fiscal Policy Policymakers also sought to counter the economic downturn with the traditional tools of monetary and fiscal policy. From September to December 2008, the Federal Reserve cut its target for the federal funds rate from 2 percent to a range from 0 to 0.25 percent. This near-zero range was still in place at the end of 2010.

When President Obama took office in January 2009, stimulating the economy was a top priority. The next month, Congress passed a fiscal package, the Economic Recovery and Reinvestment Act, which allocated about 5 percent of GDP to tax cuts, spending on infrastructure, and aid to state governments.

The Aftermath

Economists and policymakers will long debate the wisdom of Fed and Treasury actions during the financial crisis and of the fiscal stimulus. Whatever the role of these policies, the financial system started returning to normal in 2009. Yet the broader economy remained troubled.

The Financial Crisis Eases One sign that the financial system was beginning to recover was stock prices. The Dow Jones Index hit a low of 6547 in March 2009 and then rose 65 percent over the following 12 months. Fears of further financial institution failures waned, and such institutions as Goldman Sachs and Citigroup, which had lost billions of dollars in 2008, returned to profitability in 2009.

As the financial crisis eased, so did the need for the Federal Reserve's emergency lending programs. Borrowing under the TAF, PDCF, and other programs dwindled over 2009, and the Fed quietly ended them early in 2010. Many financial institutions bought back the stock they had sold to the government under TARP. In the end, the government made money on many of these transactions, selling back the stock at higher prices than it paid.

Much of the money that the Fed and the Treasury poured into the most troubled institutions, including AIG, Fannie Mae, and Freddie Mac, will probably never be recouped. But overall, the direct costs of financial rescues proved modest relative to the economic damage, in terms of lost output and high unemployment, which the financial crisis caused. A government audit of TARP in 2010 estimated that it will eventually cost taxpayers $40 billion, a small fraction of the $700 billion spent.

Unemployment Persists After rising from under 5 percent before the crisis to 10 percent in late 2009, unemployment stayed high. In October 2010, the unemployment rate was 9.6 percent, and economic forecasters predicted rates of 8 to 9 percent into 2011 and beyond.

Because the unemployment rate stayed high, more and more people found themselves jobless for long periods. In October 2010, workers who had been unemployed more than half a year accounted for 3.9 percent of the labor force, up from 0.8 percent 3 years earlier.

In most models of economic fluctuations—including the AE/PC model used in much of this book—a recession causes a short-run rise in unemployment, but in the long run unemployment returns back to an unchanged natural rate. Since World War II, most U.S. recessions have followed this pattern. For example, unemployment rose from 6 percent in 1980 to over 10 percent in 1982 then fell to 7 percent in 1984 and to 6 percent in 1987.

The most recent financial crisis and recession, however, may have longer-lasting effects on the unemployment rate. Theories of *hysteresis* posit that a prolonged recession can leave permanent scars on the labor force, making workers less employable and raising the natural rate of unemployment. Time will tell whether the aftermath of the financial crisis leads to a more prominent role for hysteresis in analyses of U.S. unemployment.

▶ Section 12.5 discusses the concept of hysteresis in unemployment.

Constraints on Macroeconomic Policy With high unemployment lingering, you might think that policymakers would seek to reduce it through expansionary fiscal or monetary policy. But in 2009–2010, economic policy was severely constrained. The combined effects of the recession and fiscal stimulus spending pushed the 2009 government budget deficit to about 10 percent of GDP, by far the highest level since World War II. The deficit exacerbated a long-term problem of rising government debt, a trend resulting from the costs of Social Security, Medicare, and Medicaid. Some economists and political leaders advocated for more stimulus spending, but most believed that the government couldn't afford it.

Starting in December 2008, monetary policy was constrained by the fact that the Fed's target for the federal funds rate was close to its lower bound of zero. A zero nominal rate was not low enough to produce the increase in aggregate expenditure needed to reduce unemployment, and it was impossible to reduce the federal funds rate further. In other words, the United States was stuck in a **liquidity trap**: the Fed's usual tool of interest rate cuts was not available to promote economic recovery.

▶ Section 14.4 analyzes the U.S. liquidity trap in detail and describes the Fed's efforts to stimulate aggregate expenditure despite it.

Liquidity trap situation in which output is below potential at a nominal interest rate of zero (a real interest rate of $-\pi$), eliminating the central bank's usual ability to raise output and inflation; also, *zero-bound problem*

Increased Moral Hazard Another legacy of the crisis is the precedent set by government rescues of financial institutions. Economists and political leaders agree that these actions have worsened moral hazard, potentially setting the stage for increased risk taking and future crises. Thus, a consensus emerged favoring new government regulation to protect the financial system and the economy.

18.4 THE FUTURE OF FINANCIAL REGULATION

The crisis of 2007–2009 sparked intense debate about government regulation of financial institutions. How can the government prevent future crises or at least minimize the damage they inflict on the economy? Although many economists and political leaders advocate reform, there is little consensus on *what* new regulations are desirable.

This section outlines the major ideas for financial reform set forth in these debates. The Dodd-Frank Act—formally, the Wall Street Reform and Consumer Protection Act—that President Obama signed into law in July 2010 implements some of these ideas.

We can classify many proposals for financial reform within four broad categories:

1. Increased regulation of nonbank financial institutions

2. Policies to prevent institutions from becoming too big to fail

TABLE 18.1 Financial Reform Proposals

Problem	Proposed Reforms
Nonbank financial institutions are insufficiently regulated.	Impose regulations similar to those for commercial banks: restrictions on assets, capital requirements, supervision.
	Give a government agency resolution authority over failing institutions.
Some institutions are considered too big to fail.	Limit size of institutions.
	Tie capital requirements to size.
	Limit scope of institutions.
Financial institutions have incentives to take too much risk.	Require security issuers to have skin in the game.
	Reform rating agencies.
	Restrict executive pay.
Multiple regulators lead to gaps in regulation.	Consolidate agencies that regulate financial institutions.
	Create new agency to oversee existing agencies and address systemic risk.
	Tighten regulation of financial holding companies.

3. Rules that discourage excessive risk taking

4. New structures for regulatory agencies

Table 18.1 lists the major reform proposals in each category.

Regulating Nonbank Financial Institutions

Commercial banks are heavily regulated in the United States. To reduce the risk of bank failures, regulators restrict the assets that banks can hold, impose capital requirements, and subject banks to frequent examinations to be sure they are not taking on too much risk. Nonbank financial institutions, such as investment banks, hedge funds, and insurance companies, do not face the same regulations. As a result, they have been able to engage in riskier behavior. They have held low levels of capital and high levels of risky assets, such as subprime mortgage–backed securities.

Why are banks and nonbank financial institutions treated differently? Part of the justification for bank regulation is the existence of government deposit insurance. The government is committed to compensating depositors if a commercial bank fails, so it has an interest in preventing risky behavior that might lead to failure. At the same time, deposit insurance makes risky behavior more likely, because it eliminates depositors' incentives to monitor banks. By contrast, nonbank institutions have no deposits, so the government has not promised to pay anyone if, say, an investment bank fails. Without insurance, lenders to nonbank financial institutions have incentives to monitor their behavior.

The financial crisis has led economists and policymakers to question this traditional thinking. The crises at investment banks such as Bear Stearns and Lehman Brothers and at insurance giant AIG revealed that lenders had not monitored them well enough to prevent excessive risk taking. Further, the absence of insurance did not mean the government could be indifferent to these institutions' failures. The aftermath of the Lehman bankruptcy showed that the failure of an investment bank can potentially have significant adverse repercussions. To keep the financial crisis from getting worse, the government reasoned that it had to rescue other institutions even though it was not obligated to them for any insurance payments.

To prevent this situation from recurring, many economists argue that the types of regulations previously reserved for commercial banks should be extended to nonbank financial institutions. In the future, institutions such as investment banks and hedge funds may be required to hold more capital and fewer risky assets, and regulators may scrutinize their activities more closely.

Not surprisingly, financial institutions generally dislike the idea of greater regulation, because restrictions on risky activities limit their profit-seeking opportunities. In addition, financial institutions and some economists argue that stricter regulation could stifle financial innovation. When financial engineers create new securities, their actions may appear risky but may actually improve the functioning of the financial system.

An example is junk bonds, an innovation of the 1970s that has allowed corporations with low credit ratings to fund investment through the bond market. Securitization is another innovation that has, in some cases, benefited borrowers and asset holders. Although the securitization of subprime mortgages proved disastrous, securitization of auto loans and student loans appears to be successful. Securitization has provided funds for people to buy cars and go to school, and owners of these securities have earned healthy returns. Overly restrictive regulations could impede such innovations, making the financial system less effective in channeling funds from savers to investors.

Ideally, regulations should be strict enough to prevent excessive risk taking yet not be so restrictive that they impede productive financial innovation. Implementing this principle is difficult, however, because it is hard to predict which innovations will be successful and which will cause problems.

Another proposed regulatory reform would change how the government deals with failed financial institutions. Once again, the basic idea is to treat nonbank institutions more like commercial banks. An insolvent bank is taken over by the FDIC, which attempts to minimize the costs to taxpayers and the disruption of the economy. The FDIC can take time, for example, to find another institution that will take over the failed bank and keep the profitable parts of its business running.

In contrast, when a nonbank financial institution fails, it declares bankruptcy. This outcome may be inefficient, because it triggers a complicated legal process and increases uncertainty about the ultimate losses to creditors. Bankruptcy is also likely to bring the business of the financial institution to a halt, thus disrupting the activities of other institutions with which it does

▶ Section 10.7 describes the procedures that the FDIC follows in closing insolvent banks.

business. Bankruptcy can shake confidence in the whole financial system, as the Lehman bankruptcy revealed.

In the crisis of 2007–2009, Fed and Treasury officials felt it necessary to save financial institutions from failure with emergency loans and equity injections. Such risky rescues might become unnecessary if a regulatory agency gains *resolution authority* over nonbank institutions such as investment banks and hedge funds—the mandate to take them over when they become insolvent. Regulators could close or sell troubled institutions in an orderly fashion and potentially avoid a panic that threatens the financial system and the economy.

Addressing Too Big To Fail

Starting with Continental Illinois in 1984, policymakers have rescued institutions they deemed TBTF. Institutions such as Continental, and later Bear Stearns and AIG, had large debts to other institutions, as well as other types of commitments, such as AIG's promised payments on credit default swaps. The sheer size of these firms and their interconnectedness with other institutions meant that their failure could trigger insolvencies throughout the financial system. Failures of smaller institutions may be less likely to pose this systemic risk.

One way for regulators to address TBTF is to prevent financial institutions from becoming too large or interconnected. Possible tools include restrictions on institutions' size or restrictions on their scope.

Restricting Size Some economists suggest stricter limits on the amounts of assets or liabilities held by financial institutions. The limit on deposits at a commercial bank—currently, 10 percent of all U.S. deposits—could be reduced. In addition, limits on assets or liabilities could be extended to non-bank institutions.

Regulators could also adopt less-rigid policies. Rather than banning institutions above a certain size, they could create disincentives to growth. For example, capital requirements might be more stringent at larger institutions. The need to hold more capital would reduce the risk that large institutions will fail. It would also discourage institutions from becoming overly large in the first place, because higher capital requirements reduce an institution's return on equity.

▶Section 9.6 examines the relationship between a bank's capital and its return on equity.

▶Section 8.2 details the trend toward consolidation in the banking industry.

Such regulations would counter a half-century-long trend in which financial institutions have grown larger through mergers. This trend was facilitated by the repeal of past regulations, such as limits on interstate banking and on the number of branches a bank can have. Deregulation was motivated by a belief in economies of scale, the idea that large banks have lower costs per customer than small banks. Today, some economists argue that the danger that large banks pose to the financial system outweighs the benefits from economies of scale.

Restricting Scope Other proposed reforms would limit the scope of financial institutions by restricting the range of different financial businesses that one firm can operate. Such regulation would reduce the danger that problems in one part of an institution will hurt the other parts. For example, losses by risk-taking investment bankers would not reduce the funds available to commercial bankers for lending to individuals and businesses.

Like restrictions on institutions' size, restrictions on their scope would reverse a historical trend. The repeal of the depression-era Glass-Steagall Act in 1999 allowed commercial banks to merge with investment banks and insurance companies, creating *financial holding companies* (FHCs) such as Citigroup. Supporters of such mergers suggest that they create economies of scope: it is efficient for customers to receive a range of financial services from one institution.

Once again, the recent financial crisis has led some economists to advocate reregulation in which FHCs are required to break up or reduce their range of activities. Others believe that limits on institutions' scope are not necessary if regulation is improved along other dimensions.

Discouraging Excessive Risk Taking

In the view of most economists, excessive risk taking by financial institutions is a key cause of financial crises. In addition to extending regulation to more types of institutions and limiting their size and scope, reformers have proposed a variety of curbs on risky behavior. We briefly review three ideas.

Requiring "Skin in the Game" Some financial reformers propose that institutions that arrange risky transactions should take on some of the risk themselves: these firms should be required to have "skin in the game." For example, an investment bank that securitizes loans should have to hold a certain amount of the securities it creates. Behind this idea is the view that before the financial crisis, buyers of subprime mortgage-backed securities were unaware of how risky the securities were. Requiring skin in the game gives financial institutions a disincentive to create overly risky products.

Reforming Rating Agencies This idea, too, arises from the belief that buyers of subprime MBSs did not understand their risks. Before the financial crisis, rating agencies such as Moody's and Standard & Poor's gave many subprime MBSs the highest possible rating, AAA. These ratings greatly understated the securities' riskiness, so institutions, such as pension funds, that thought they were purchasing safe assets ended up suffering large losses.

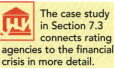 The case study in Section 7.3 connects rating agencies to the financial crisis in more detail.

Critics suggest that one reason this happened stemmed from the way rating agencies earn money: they are hired and paid by the issuers of the securities they rate. Raters are likely to get more business if they inflate the grades they assign. This conflict of interest would shrink through implementing a new source of revenue for rating agencies—a tax on financial institutions is one idea—or by having regulators review the agencies' ratings.

Reforming Executive Compensation Executives at many financial institutions receive annual bonuses of millions of dollars if profits for the year are high. This practice encourages them to take high-risk gambles that may yield high returns in the short term. (Executives aren't required to pay millions of dollars if the gambles fail.) Recall that in 2008 the Treasury Department imposed limits on executive compensation as a condition for equity injections under the TARP. Some economists and Congress members think that such limits should exist all the time; others object to the government, rather than the market, regulating pay at private firms.

Changing Regulatory Structure

▶ Section 10.4 describes how the regulatory structure that governs U.S. commercial banks evolved. Logic had nothing to do with it.

The U.S. system of financial regulation is complex. A mixed bag of federal and state agencies regulates commercial banks. At the federal level alone, some are regulated by the Office of the Comptroller of the Currency (OCC), some by the Federal Reserve, and some by the FDIC. Until 2010, the Office of Thrift Supervision regulated savings institutions.

Investment banks are regulated at the federal level by the Securities and Exchange Commission (SEC). The Federal Reserve has sometimes resisted calls to restrict risk taking by investment banks on the grounds that they are the SEC's responsibility. Yet the SEC has not focused on ensuring the solvency of nonbank financial institutions. Rather, its main objective has been to curb securities market participants from engaging in illegal activities, such as insider trading and the falsification of accounting information by companies that issue stock.

Many economists argue that gaps and inconsistencies in regulation enabled the risky behavior that produced the most recent financial crisis. Some believe the government should abolish existing regulatory agencies and consolidate their responsibilities within one new agency. An alternative is to preserve existing agencies but add one that coordinates regulation. The creation of such an agency, the Financial Services Oversight Council (FSOC), was a centerpiece of the 2010 regulatory reforms. The FSOC will monitor the entire financial system for threats to stability, not just individual institutions for insolvency risk.

One gap in current regulation involves financial holding companies, such as Citigroup and JPMorgan Chase, with units in diverse businesses. The Federal Reserve is responsible for regulating FHCs but in the past has largely confined itself to reviewing FHC mergers with and acquisitions of other institutions. Different units of FHCs are regulated by different agencies—commercial banking units by various bank regulators, investment banking by the SEC, and insurance businesses by state insurance commissions. As we have discussed, problems in one unit of an FHC can hurt other units. In the future, the Federal Reserve may take responsibility for monitoring risky activities in all parts of a financial holding company.

CASE STUDY |

The Financial Reforms of 2010

In July 2010, Congress passed the Dodd-Frank Act and President Obama signed it into law.* Almost all Democrats supported the act, and almost all Republicans opposed it. Democrats hailed the act as the foundation for a healthy financial system; Republicans predicted it would reduce efficiency and innovation at financial institutions.

The act puts into practice some of the reform ideas discussed in this section. Its most important provisions include the following:

- The Financial Services Oversight Council coordinates financial regulation, as described in the preceding section. The Secretary of the Treasury chairs the council, which includes representatives from the Federal Reserve, SEC, FDIC, OCC, a new Consumer Financial Protection Bureau, and other agencies.

- A new Office of Credit Ratings examines rating agencies annually and publishes reports on their performance.

- The FDIC gains authority to take over and close a nonbank financial institution if its troubles create systemic risk. Costs to the FDIC will be financed through fees paid by financial institutions. Most failures, those that do not endanger the financial system, will still trigger traditional bankruptcy proceedings.

- Financial holding companies that own banks are prohibited from sponsoring hedge funds, a step toward separating banks and securities firms.

- Issuers of certain risky securities, including mortgage-backed securities, must have skin in the game: they must retain at least 5 percent of the default risk on such securities.

The Dodd-Frank Act also empowers the Financial Services Oversight Council and the Federal Reserve to issue additional regulations, including stricter capital requirements and supervision of nonbank financial institutions. The FSOC and Fed can also force a large FHC to break up if it poses a grave threat to the financial system. The Office of Credit Ratings has the right to issue new regulations governing rating agencies.

In the coming years, we will see how aggressively the FSOC, Fed, and Office of Credit Ratings use their new authority, whether the Dodd-Frank reforms change the behavior of financial institutions, how effective they are in preventing crises, and what further changes in regulation occur.

> **Online Case Study:**
> An Update on Financial Regulation

* For more on the Dodd-Frank Act, see David Huntington, "Summary of Dodd-Frank Financial Regulation Legislation," Harvard Law School Forum on Corporate Governance and Financial Regulation, blogs.law.harvard.edu/corpgov/, posted July 7, 2010.

18.5 FINANCIAL CRISES IN EMERGING ECONOMIES

We have emphasized financial crises in the United States, but crises occur all over the world. They are especially common in *emerging-market economies*—countries in the middle of the world income distribution (not as rich as the United States but not as poor as many African countries). Crises occurred in Mexico in 1994, many East Asian countries in 1997–1998, Russia in 1998, and Argentina in 2001–2002. Over 2008 and 2009, the U.S. financial crisis spread around the world, and many emerging economies were hit hard.

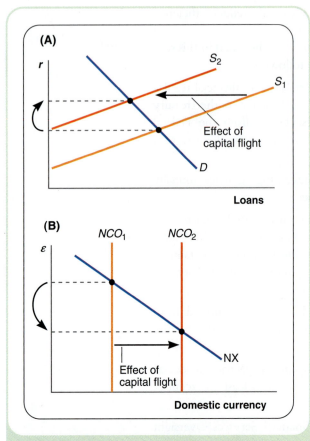

Capital flight reduces the supply of loans, increasing the real interest rate (A). It also raises net capital outflows, decreasing the real exchange rate (B).

Emerging-economy crises have much in common with U.S. crises, including bank failures and asset-price declines. However, they also have another key element: **capital flight**, a sudden decrease in net capital inflows (NCI) that occurs when foreign savers lose confidence in an economy. Capital flight creates additional channels in the vicious circle of a financial crisis.

Causes and Consequences of Capital Flight

Capital flight implies a sharp fall in the demand for a country's assets that reduces asset prices. In foreign exchange markets, a fall in net capital inflows—equivalently, a rise in net capital outflows (NCO)—reduces the real exchange rate. In the country's loan market, the supply of loans falls, raising the real interest rate.

Causes of Capital Flight Various events can shake confidence in an economy, triggering capital flight. Financial crises often involve one or more of the following:

■ *Government debt.* Rising debt levels create fears that the government will default, so foreign financial institutions stop buying government bonds. Foreigners also worry that default will hurt the economy, so they stop buying corporate securities.

■ *Political risk.* Political instability can bring bad governments to power or produce armed conflicts that disrupt the economy. Signs of instability make a country's assets more risky and can spark capital flight.

■ *Banking problems.* Loans to a country's banks from foreign banks are one kind of capital inflow. This source of funds is cut off if domestic banks encounter trouble, such as threats to their solvency from defaults on loans they have made.

Contagion Just as a bank run can trigger runs at other banks, capital flight can spread from one country to others in a process called **contagion**. When asset holders see that one country's exchange rate and asset prices have fallen, they worry that the same thing could happen in countries in the same region or in countries with similar problems. Capital flight hits these countries as asset holders try to sell before prices fall.

For example, in July 1997, the East Asian financial crisis began in Thailand when capital flight caused the value of the Thai baht to collapse. In the

Capital flight sudden decrease in net capital inflows that occurs when foreign savers lose confidence in an economy

Contagion spread of capital flight from one country to others

▶For more on the East Asian crisis, see Sections 4.2 and 6.4.

following months, capital flight spread to countries including South Korea, Indonesia, and the Philippines, driving down exchange rates and raising interest rates throughout the region.

Capital Flight and Financial Crises

Capital flight is often part of a broader financial crisis. It interacts with the basic causes of crises summarized in Figure 18.1 on page 554. One typical cause—banking problems—can trigger capital flight. At the same time, capital flight causes declines in asset prices, another key feature of crises.

The increases in interest rates caused by capital flight are often dramatic; in South Korea, for example, short-term rates jumped from 12 percent in November 1997 to 31 percent in December 1997. Higher interest rates cause investment to fall sharply. In addition, lower confidence in the economy works to reduce both consumption and investment.

The currency depreciation caused by capital flight also has deleterious effects. In emerging economies, foreign loans to the government and to domestic banks and firms are usually made in U.S. dollars, so many debts are fixed in dollars. When the exchange rate falls, each dollar costs more in local currency, so debt levels rise when measured in local currency. Higher debts hurt the economy by worsening the problems of banks and pushing corporations into bankruptcy. Higher government debt increases fears of default, worsening capital flight.

In sum, capital flight adds a number of channels through which financial crises reduce aggregate expenditure and build on themselves. The vicious circle becomes more vicious, and emerging economies rarely escape a deep recession. The following case study recounts a particularly traumatic financial crisis.

CASE STUDY

Argentina's Financial Crisis, 2001–2002

Argentina has a long history of economic crises. For decades, a central problem has been large government budget deficits. The government has sometimes financed deficits with bank loans or bonds, but at other times it has not been able to borrow. In these periods, it has financed deficits with seignorage revenue—by printing money. Rapid money growth causes high inflation, which in turn hurts economic efficiency and long-run growth.

In the 1980s, Argentina's budget deficits produced annual inflation rates in the hundreds of percent. The situation deteriorated at the end of the decade, with inflation above 2000 percent per year in both 1989 and 1990. In 1991, a new president, Carlos Menem, decided that Argentina needed major reforms. His government attacked the budget deficit with spending cuts and higher taxes. It sought to make the economy more productive by privatizing government-owned industries and eliminating barriers to international trade.

The government's most radical action was to create a currency board, an extreme form of a fixed exchange rate. The currency board set the value of an Argentine peso at 1.0 U.S. dollar and held dollar reserves to back all the pesos it created. Policymakers believed that the fixed exchange rate would

> This discussion draws from material on budget deficits and inflation (Section 14.2), currency boards (Section 2.2), and fixed exchange rates and speculative attacks (Section 17.4).

bring inflation down to U.S. levels. They also thought they could keep the exchange rate fixed permanently, because their reserves would thwart speculative attacks. No matter how many pesos speculators sold, the currency board would have enough dollars to buy them.

Initially, Menem's policies were highly successful. Inflation fell to 25 percent in 1992 and 4 percent in 1994. At the same time, output grew rapidly. Confidence in Argentina's economy soared, and capital flowed into the country. Foreign financial institutions started buying Argentine government debt, which they had shunned in the 1980s. But then several problems developed:

- Budget deficits started to rise again. This resulted largely from spending by the governments of Argentina's provinces, which the national government could not control.

- The real exchange rate rose, as typically happens when a country fixes the nominal rate to reduce inflation. Argentina's real exchange rate is $e\,(P/P^*)$, where e is the nominal exchange rate, P is Argentina's price level, and P^* is the foreign (U.S.) price level. As shown in **Figure 18.5**, the real exchange rate rose 60 percent over 1991–1993, because e was fixed and P/P^* rose: although Argentina's inflation was falling, it exceeded U.S. inflation. The rising real exchange rate reduced Argentina's net exports, slowing output growth and raising unemployment.

FIGURE 18.5 Argentina's Exchange Rate 1991–2007

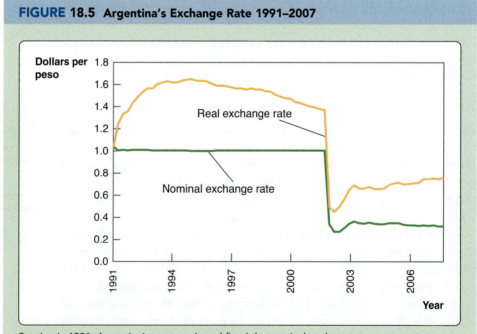

Starting in 1991, Argentina's currency board fixed the nominal exchange rate at one peso per dollar. Argentina's inflation exceeded U.S. inflation over 1991–1993, so its real exchange rate rose. The nominal and real exchange rates collapsed with the end of the currency board in 2002.

Source: International Monetary Fund

■ In 1994, Mexico endured a financial crisis triggered by rising government debt and political unrest. That crisis produced contagion. Capital flight occurred throughout Latin America, including Argentina, pushing up interest rates and reducing consumption and investment. Combined with the fall in net exports, lower consumption and investment produced a recession in the mid-1990s.

As usual in a financial crisis, all these problems reinforced one another. In the late 1990s, the recession reduced tax revenue, worsening the problem of budget deficits. The currency board precluded expansionary monetary policy: policymakers could not create additional pesos, because they did not hold enough U.S. dollars to back them.

Without monetary stimulus, the recession deepened, and the unemployment rate rose above 15 percent. Capital flight increased because of worries about rising government debt and a possible end to the currency board. In 1999, Fernando de la Rua replaced Carlos Menem as president, but it made little difference for the deteriorating economy.

In late 2001, Argentina's problems spiraled out of control. In October, the government defaulted by failing to make promised payments on its debt. November brought a banking crisis. Argentina's banks had been weakened by the long recession and by losses on their holdings of government bonds. Fearing bank failures, and with no deposit insurance, Argentines rushed to withdraw their money.

The government's response to the bank panic was drastic: it imposed a limit on withdrawals. A depositor could withdraw only 250 pesos (the equivalent of $250) in cash per week. This policy provoked a political crisis. The long recession left many Argentines furious at the government, and being denied access to their money was the last straw. Riots and looting erupted in December 2001: 26 people died and President de la Rua resigned. In January 2002, an interim president, Eduardo Duhalde, ended the currency board.

The immediate economic consequences were disastrous. As shown in Figure 18.5, the value of a peso fell from its fixed level of $1 to 27 cents in 2002. This exchange rate collapse caused a spike in import prices, reducing living standards for Argentine consumers. It also caused a huge rise in the peso values of dollar-denominated debts, leading to a wave of corporate bankruptcies. Output fell by 15 percent from 2000 to 2002, and unemployment rose above 20 percent.

At the time, some economists predicted a long depression for Argentina. However, the fall in the exchange rate

December 19, 2001: Looters steal merchandise from a supermarket in Buenos Aires during Argentina's financial crisis.

AP Photo/Daniel Luna

set the stage for a more-rapid-than-expected recovery. It made Argentine goods cheap relative to foreign goods, and exports boomed. From 2003 to 2007, output grew rapidly and unemployment fell below 10 percent. During this period, the government also managed to reduce budget deficits, the problem underlying Argentina's history of instability.

Recent Crises

The panic following the failure of Lehman Brothers triggered not only the U.S. financial crisis of 2007–2009 but also a global flight to safety. Financial institutions sold any assets that appeared risky, including many in emerging economies, where assets are generally considered risky because the economies are less stable than advanced economies. Countries in eastern Europe and Asia, for example, experienced capital flight and sharp recessions.

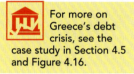

For more on Greece's debt crisis, see the case study in Section 4.5 and Figure 4.16.

In 2009–2010, a financial crisis struck Greece, which is sometimes categorized as an emerging economy because its income is low by Western European standards. The trigger for this crisis was Greece's rising government debt. Fearing default, asset holders around the world dumped Greek debt, pushing up the interest rates that Greece had to pay on new debt. The rate on 10-year Greek bonds rose from 4.7 percent in May 2008 to 8.0 percent 2 years later.

High interest rates and falling confidence pushed Greece into a severe recession. In August 2010, the unemployment rate was 12 percent and appeared to be headed higher. Making matters worse, Greek policymakers could not support their economy with traditional policy tools. They could not pursue expansionary fiscal policy because that would worsen the problem of rising debt; indeed, Greece's government was trying to cut its spending. Policymakers could not pursue expansionary monetary policy because Greece uses the euro as its currency. Monetary policy for all euro countries is set by the European Central Bank, so Greece has no independent policy tool to wield against recession.

As Greece's government struggled to make debt payments, Europeans worried that the crisis would worsen dramatically if the government actually defaulted. In addition to wrecking Greece's economy, a default could produce contagion, shaking confidence in euro area countries such as Spain and Portugal that also have high debt levels. In the fall of 2010, uncertainty hung over Europe's economies.

The Role of the International Monetary Fund

International Monetary Fund (IMF) institution that lends to countries experiencing financial crises

When financial crises threaten the United States, the Federal Reserve and Treasury Department try to contain them. When emerging economies experience crises, governments and central banks often don't have the resources to respond. In particular, they lack foreign currency needed to pay debts set in dollars. Therefore, countries in crisis often seek help from the **International Monetary Fund (IMF)**, an institution that lends to countries experiencing financial crises.

The IMF was established in 1944 to oversee the Bretton Woods system of fixed exchange rates among 44 nations, including the United States and other leading economies. That system ended in the 1970s, and since then aiding countries in financial crises has been the IMF's primary function. Most of the world's countries are members of the IMF and contribute funds to it, but rich countries provide most of the money. A country's votes on the IMF board of directors are proportional to its financial contribution, so rich countries hold most of the power.

In recent decades, the IMF has intervened in most crises involving capital flight, including those in Argentina and Greece. As we've seen, private financial institutions are wary of lending to countries in crisis. These countries turn to the IMF for emergency loans, which are made in dollars. The IMF is sometimes called the "international lender of last resort."

Countries use IMF loans in various ways, depending on their circumstances:

- The government can use the loans to make payments on its debt, preventing default.

- If a country's banks have debts denominated in dollars, the central bank can lend them dollars to repay those debts.

- The central bank can use dollars to buy its own currency in foreign exchange markets (if, unlike Greece, the country has its own currency). Increased demand for the currency dampens the fall in the exchange rate.

Each of these actions attacks a part of the financial crisis. IMF loans are also intended to boost confidence in the economy, reducing capital flight. The overall goal is to slow down the vicious circle and hasten financial and economic recovery.

Most IMF loans have strings attached. To obtain a loan, a country must sign an economic agreement with the IMF. The country agrees to reforms that address the problems underlying its crisis. For example, a government with a high debt level may be required to cut spending. This condition was a key part of an IMF agreement with Greece in May 2010. Loan provisions may also include stricter bank regulation, monetary tightening to control inflation, or privatization of government-owned industries.

IMF loans are controversial. Some economists believe they significantly reduce the damage caused by financial crises, for example, by curbing the length of recessions. Others criticize IMF loans to countries for essentially the same reason that many criticize rescues of U.S. financial institutions by the Federal Reserve and the Treasury Department: the loans create moral hazard. Aid to countries (or companies) that get in trouble encourages other countries (or companies) to behave the same way.

Still others criticize the IMF for the conditions it imposes on loans, which can be painful. Reducing budget deficits, for example, may force governments to cut spending on antipoverty programs. The IMF argues that painful reforms are needed for long-run economic growth. But the pain, critics contend, falls disproportionately on the poor.

Summary

18.1 The Mechanics of Financial Crises

- A financial crisis typically begins with declines in asset prices, failures of financial institutions, or both. Failure can result from insolvency or liquidity crises.

- A financial crisis can fuel a credit crunch and reduce aggregate expenditure, causing a recession. The recession reinforces the causes of the crisis.

- The Great Depression was triggered by the 1929 stock market crash and bank panics starting in 1930 and exacerbated by a fall in the money supply and by deflation.

18.2 Financial Rescues

- Policymakers may seek to stem a crisis by rescuing troubled financial institutions. Rescue tactics range from riskless loans to institutions facing liquidity crises to outright giveaways of government funds.

- Risky rescues, including risky loans and equity injections, are an intermediate policy that may or may not cost the government money.

- Financial rescues are controversial because of their potential costs to taxpayers and because they increase moral hazard: firms may take on more risk, thinking the government will bail them out if they get in trouble.

18.3 The U.S. Financial Crisis of 2007–2009

- Over 2007–2009, the subprime mortgage crisis evolved into a broad financial and economic crisis in the United States. The stock market fell drastically, some of the country's most prestigious financial institutions failed or came close to failing, lending was disrupted throughout the economy, and the unemployment rate rose to 10 percent.

- In response to the crisis, the Federal Reserve pushed its interest rate target to zero. The Fed lent huge amounts of money to financial institutions, and the Treasury injected equity. Congress approved a fiscal stimulus package proposed by the Obama administration.

18.4 The Future of Financial Regulation

- The most recent crisis fostered an intense debate over government regulation of financial institutions.

- Many proposals for financial reform fall into four broad categories: increased regulation of nonbank financial institutions, policies to prevent institutions from becoming too big to fail, rules that discourage excessive risk taking, and new structures for regulatory agencies.

- The Dodd-Frank Act that became law in mid-2010 created the Financial Services Oversight Council to coordinate financial regulation and the Office of Credit Ratings to monitor rating agencies. The act also gives the FDIC resolution authority over nonbank financial institutions that create systemic risk, prohibits financial holding companies that own banks from sponsoring hedge funds, and requires issuers of risky securities to have skin in the game.

18.5 Financial Crises in Emerging Economies

- In addition to bank failures and asset-price crashes, financial crises in emerging-market economies typically include capital flight and sharp decreases in exchange rates.

- Capital flight adds new channels to the vicious circle of a financial crisis. Causes of capital flight include high government debt, political instability, and banking problems.

- Argentina's financial crisis of 2001–2002 included default on government debt, a bank panic, abandonment of a currency board, and a deep recession.

- Over 2009 and 2010, rising government debt triggered a financial crisis and recession in Greece. The country's use of the euro hampered policymakers' response to the crisis. Concern rose that the crisis could spread to other euro countries with high debt levels.

- The International Monetary Fund makes emergency loans to countries struck by capital flight. Most IMF loans, such as those made to Greece, require reforms that address the underlying causes of financial crises.

Key Terms

Capital flight, p. 580

Contagion, p. 580

Credit crunch, p. 553

Equity injection, p. 560

Financial crisis, p. 551

International Monetary Fund
(IMF), p. 584

Lender of last resort, p. 556

Liquidity trap, p. 573

Too big to fail (TBTF), p. 558

Questions and Problems

1. Many economists argue that the rescue of a financial institution should protect the institution's creditors from losses but not protect its owners: they should lose their equity. Supporters of this idea say it reduces the moral hazard created by rescues.

   a. Explain how this approach reduces moral hazard compared to a rescue that protects both creditors and equity holders.

   b. Does this approach eliminate the moral hazard problem completely? Explain.

2. What could U.S. policymakers have done to prevent the Great Depression or at least to reduce its severity? Specifically:

   a. What government or Fed policies might have prevented the stock market crash and bank panics that started the financial crisis? (*Hint:* Think of policies that exist today.)

   b. Once the crisis began, what could policymakers have done to dampen the effects on the financial system and economy? Explain.

3. Some Congress members think the government should not risk taxpayer money to rescue financial firms whose highly paid executives have behaved irresponsibly. Instead, the government should aid middle- and low-income people hurt by the financial crisis, such as homeowners facing foreclosure. Discuss the arguments for this position and against it.

4. In 2010, Senator Blanche Lincoln (D–Arkansas) proposed that commercial banks be forbidden to trade derivative securities. Discuss the arguments for and against this proposal.

5. Of the proposed financial reforms discussed in Section 18.4, which would have significantly dampened the financial crisis of 2007–2009 if they had been in place before the crisis? Could any of the reforms have prevented the crisis entirely? Explain.

6. Draw an expanded version of Figure 18.1 (the outline of a typical financial crisis on page 554) for emerging economy crises. Your chart should include capital flight and show how this phenomenon and its consequences interact with the other elements common to a financial crisis.

7. In the late 1990s, some economists advised Argentina to dollarize, that is, to eliminate the peso and use the U.S. dollar as its currency. Discuss how dollarization might have changed the course of events in 2001–2002.

▶ Online and Data Questions

www.worthpublishers.com/ball

8. Do some Internet research to learn what happened to Greece's financial system and economy since the fall of 2010. Has the crisis worsened or eased? Has it affected other European or non-European economies? Have events followed the typical pattern of financial crises described in this chapter?

9. In 2010, the Dodd–Frank Act authorized the Federal Reserve, Financial Services Oversight Council, and Office of Credit Ratings to issue new financial regulations, including stronger capital requirements and restrictions on risk taking by investment banks. What major regulations have been issued since Dodd–Frank was enacted?

glossary

Accommodative monetary policy Decision by the central bank to keep the real interest rate constant when a supply shock occurs, allowing inflation to change

Actively managed fund Mutual fund that picks stocks based on analysts' research

Adaptive expectations Theory that people's expectations of a variable are based on past levels of the variable; also, *backward-looking expectations*

Adverse selection The problem that the people or firms that are most eager to make a transaction are the least desirable to parties on the other side of the transaction

After-tax real interest rate ($\hat{r}$) The interest rate adjusted for both taxes and inflation: $\hat{r} = (1 - \mu)r - \mu\pi$

Aggregate expenditure (AE) Total spending on an economy's goods and services by people, firms, and governments

Aggregate expenditure (AE) curve The negative short-run relationship between the real interest rate and output

Aggregate expenditure/Phillips curve (AE/PC) model Theory of short-run economic fluctuations that assumes a negative relationship between the interest rate and output (the AE curve) and a positive relationship between output and inflation (the Phillips curve)

Aggregate price level An average of the prices of all goods and services

Appreciation Rise in a currency's price in terms of foreign currency

Asset allocation Decisions by individuals or institutions about what assets to hold

Asset-price bubble Rapid rise in asset prices that is not justified by changes in interest rates or expected asset income

Asset-price crash Large, rapid fall in asset prices

Asymmetric information Situation in which one participant in an economic transaction has more information than the other participant

Balance sheet Financial statement that summarizes an entity's assets, liabilities, and net worth at a given date

Bank Financial institution that accepts deposits and makes private loans

Bank charter Government license to operate a bank

Bank examination Visit by regulators to a bank's headquarters to gather information on the bank's activities; part of bank supervision

Bank panic Simultaneous runs at many individual banks

Bank run Sudden, large withdrawals by depositors who lose confidence in a bank

Bank supervision Monitoring of banks' activities by government regulators

Barter System of exchange in which goods and services are traded directly, with no money involved

Basel Accord 1988 agreement that sets international standards for bank capital requirements

Behavioral finance Field that uses ideas from psychology to study how deviations from rational behavior affect asset prices

Bid–ask spread Gap between the prices at which a dealer buys and sells a security

Bimetallism Monetary system in which money is backed by both gold and silver

Bond (*fixed-income security*) Security that promises predetermined payments at certain points in time. At *maturity*, the bond pays its *face value*. Before that, the owner may receive *coupon payments*

Bond-rating agencies Firms that estimate default risk on bonds

Broker Firm that buys and sells securities for others

Budget deficit A negative level of public saving

Budget surplus A positive level of public saving

Business cycle Short-run (year-to-year) fluctuations in an economy's output and unemployment

Call option An option to buy a security

Call report Quarterly financial statement, including a balance sheet and income statement, that banks must submit to regulators as part of bank supervision

CAMELS ratings Evaluations by regulators of a bank's insolvency risk based on its capital, asset quality, management, earnings, liquidity, and sensitivity

Capital *See* **net worth**

Capital controls Regulations that restrict capital inflows or outflows

Capital crunch A fall in capital that forces banks to reduce lending

Capital flight Sudden decrease in net capital inflows that occurs when foreign savers lose confidence in an economy

Capital gain Increase in an asset holder's wealth from a change in the asset's price

Capital inflows Funds provided to a country's investors by foreigners

Capital loss Decrease in an asset holder's wealth from a change in the asset's price

Capital outflows Funds provided to foreign investors by a country's savers

Capital requirements Regulations setting minimum levels of capital that banks must hold

Capital structure Mix of stocks and bonds that a firm issues

Central bank Institution that controls an economy's money supply

Centrally planned economy *(command economy)* System in which the government decides what goods and services are produced, who receives them, and what investment projects are undertaken

Circuit breaker Requirement that a securities exchange shut down temporarily if prices drop by a specified percentage

Classical theory of asset prices The price of an asset equals the present value of expected income from the asset.

Collateral An asset of a borrower that a bank can seize if the borrower defaults

Commercial bank Institution that accepts checking and savings deposits and lends to individuals and firms

Commodity money Valuable good that serves as the medium of exchange

Community bank Commercial bank with less than $1 billion in assets that operates in a small geographic area

Community Reinvestment Act (CRA) Law from 1977 that requires banks to lend in low-income areas

Compensating balance Minimum checking deposit that a borrower must maintain at the bank that has lent it money

Conservative policymaker Central bank official who believes it is more important to keep inflation low than to stimulate output

Consumption multiplier Effect of income on consumption that magnifies changes in aggregate expenditure

Contagion Spread of capital flight from one country to others

Core deposits Banks' inexpensive sources of funds (checking deposits, savings deposits, and small time deposits)

Countercyclical monetary policy Adjustments of the real interest rate by the central bank to offset expenditure shocks and thereby stabilize output

Covenant Provision in a loan contract that restricts the actions of the borrower

Credit crunch A sharp reduction in bank lending

Credit default swap (CDS) Derivative with payouts triggered by defaults on certain debt securities

Credit rationing Refusal of a bank to lend to a borrower at any interest rate

Credit risk *(default risk)* The risk that loans will not be repaid

Credit score Numerical rating capturing a person's likelihood to repay loans based on her credit history

Credit union Not-for-profit bank owned by its depositor members, who are drawn from a group of people with something in common

Currency board Institution that issues money backed by a foreign currency

Currency–deposit ratio (C/D) Ratio of currency in circulation to checking deposits

Currency union Group of countries with a common currency

Dealer Firm that buys and sells certain securities for itself, making a market in the securities

Dealer market OTC market in which all trades are made with dealers

Default Failure to make promised payments on debts

Deflation Sustained period of negative inflation

Deposit insurance Government guarantee to compensate depositors for their losses when a bank fails

Depreciation Fall in a currency's price in terms of foreign currency

Derivatives Securities with payoffs tied to the prices of other assets

Devaluation Resetting of a fixed exchange rate at a lower level

Direct finance Savers provide funds to investors by buying securities in financial markets

Discretionary policy Monetary policy that is adjusted at each point in time based on the judgment of the central bank

Discount loan Loan from the Federal Reserve to a bank made at the bank's request

Discount rate Interest rate on discount loans

Disinflation Monetary policy of reducing inflation by temporarily raising the real interest rate

Diversification The distribution of wealth among many assets, such as securities issued by different firms and governments

Dividend Payment from a firm to its stockholders

Dollarization Use of foreign currency (often U.S. dollars) as money

Double coincidence of wants Condition needed for barter: each party to a transaction must have something the other wants

Economic boom Period when actual output exceeds potential output

Economic growth Increases in productivity and living standards; growth in real GDP

Economic risk Risk arising from fluctuations in the economy's aggregate output

Economies of scope Cost reductions from combining different activities

Efficient markets hypothesis (EMH) The price of every stock equals the value of the stock, so no stock is a better buy than any other

Electronic communications network (ECN) OTC market in which financial institutions trade securities with one another directly, rather than through dealers

E-money Funds in an electronic account used for Internet purchases

Equity *See* **net worth**

Equity injection Purchases of a financial institution's stock by the government

Equity ratio (ER) Ratio of a bank's capital to its assets; ER = capital/assets

Eurodollars Deposits of dollars outside the United States

Ex ante real interest rate ($r^{\text{ex ante}}$) Nominal interest rate minus expected inflation over the loan period; $r^{\text{ex ante}} = i - \pi^{\text{expected}}$

Exchange A physical location where brokers and dealers meet to trade securities

Expectations theory of the term structure The n-period interest rate is the average of the current one-period rate and expected rates over the next $n - 1$ periods.

Expenditure shock Event that changes aggregate expenditure for a given interest rate, shifting the AE curve

Explicit inflation target A rate or range that a central bank announces as its long-run goal for inflation

Ex post real interest rate ($r^{\text{ex post}}$) Nominal interest rate minus actual inflation over the loan period; $r^{\text{ex post}} = i - \pi^{\text{actual}}$

Federal Deposit Insurance Corporation (FDIC) Government agency that insures deposits at U.S. commercial banks and savings institutions

Federal funds Loans from one bank to another, usually for one day

Federal funds rate Interest rate that banks charge one another for one-day loans of reserves, or federal funds; also *overnight interest rate*

Federal Open Market Committee (FOMC) Body that sets the Fed's targets for the federal funds rate

Federal Reserve System (the Fed) Central bank of the United States

Fiat money Money with no intrinsic value

Finance company Nonbank financial institution that makes loans but does not accept deposits

Financial crisis Major disruption of the financial system, typically involving sharp drops in asset prices and failures of financial institutions

Financial holding company (FHC) Conglomerate that owns a group of financial institutions

Financial institution *(financial intermediary)* Firm that helps channel funds from savers to investors

Financial market A collection of people and firms that buy and sell securities or currencies

Fiscal policy The government's choice of taxes and spending

Fisher equation The nominal interest rate equals the real rate plus expected inflation: $i = r + \pi^e$

Fixed exchange rate Policy that holds the exchange rate at a constant level

Floating exchange rate Policy that allows the exchange rate to fluctuate in response to economic shocks

Floating interest rate Interest rate on a long-term loan that is tied to a short-term rate

Forbearance Regulator's decision to allow an insolvent bank to remain open

Foreign exchange interventions Purchases and sales of foreign currencies by central banks

Free-rider problem People can benefit from a good without paying for it, leading to underproduction of the good; in financial markets, savers are free riders when information is gathered

Futures contract Agreement to trade an asset for a certain price at a future point in time

Future value Value of a dollar today in terms of dollars at some future time; $1 today = $(1 + i)^n$ in n years

Gordon growth model Theory in which a stock price P is determined by an initial expected dividend, the expected growth rate of dividends, and the risk-adjusted interest rate: $P = D_1/(i - g)$

Government-sponsored enterprise (GSE) Private corporation with links to the government

Hedge fund Variant of a mutual fund that raises money from wealthy people and institutions and is largely unregulated, allowing it to make risky bets on asset prices

Hedging Reducing risk by purchasing an asset that is likely to produce a high return if another of one's assets produces low or negative returns

High-yield spread Difference between interest rates on BBB and AAA corporate bonds with 10-year maturities

Hyperinflation Inflation of more than 50 percent per month (or roughly 13,000 percent per year)

Hysteresis Theory that the short-run path of a variable, such as unemployment, affects its long-run level, such as the natural rate of unemployment

Implicit inflation target An inflation level that policymakers seek without a formal announcement

Income statement Financial statement summarizing income, expenses, and profits over some time period

Index fund Mutual fund that buys all the stocks in a broad market index

Indirect finance Savers deposit money in banks that then lend to investors

Industrial loan company (ILC) Financial institution that performs many functions of a commercial bank; may be owned by a nonfinancial firm

Inflation-indexed bond Bond that promises a fixed real interest rate; the nominal rate is adjusted for inflation over the life of the bond

Inflation rate Percentage change in the aggregate price level over a period of time

Initial public offering (IPO) Sale of stock when a firm becomes public

Inside lag Time between a shock and the policy response

Insider trading Buying or selling securities based on information that is not public

Insolvency Liabilities exceed assets, producing negative net worth

Interest Payment for the use of borrowed funds

Interest rate risk Instability in bank profits caused by fluctuations in short-term interest rates

Interest rate smoothing Central banks' practice of moving interest rates through a series of small changes

Interest rate targeting Approach to monetary policy in which the central bank chooses a level for the nominal interest rate and adjusts it when economic conditions change. The central bank sets the money supply at the level needed to hit the interest rate target.

International Monetary Fund (IMF) Institution that lends to countries experiencing financial crises

International reserves Liquid assets held by central banks that are denominated in foreign currencies

Inverted yield curve Downward-sloping yield curve signifying that short-term interest rates exceed long-term rates

Investment bank Financial institution that serves as an underwriter and advises companies on mergers and acquisitions

Investment multiplier Effect of firms' earnings on investment, which magnifies fluctuations in aggregate expenditure

Investors People who expand the productive capacity of businesses

Junk bond Corporate bond with an S&P rating below BBB

Law of one price Theory that an identical good or service has the same price in all locations

Lender of last resort Central bank's role as emergency lender to financial institutions

Letter of credit A bank's guarantee, in return for a fee, of a payment promised by a firm

Leverage Borrowing money to purchase assets

Liabilities Amounts of money owed to others

Line of credit A bank's commitment to lend up to a certain amount whenever a borrower asks

Liquidity Ease of trading an asset for money

Liquidity preference theory The nominal interest rate is determined by the supply and demand for money.

Liquidity risk The risk that withdrawals from a bank will exceed its liquid assets

Liquidity trap Situation in which output is below potential at a nominal interest rate of zero (a real interest rate of $-\pi$), eliminating the central bank's usual ability to raise output and inflation; also *zero-bound problem*

Loanable funds theory Real interest rates are determined by the supply and demand for loans

Loan guarantee Government promise to pay off a loan if the borrower defaults

Loan shark Lender that violates usury laws and collects debts through illegal means

Long-run monetary neutrality Principle that monetary policy cannot permanently affect real variables (variables adjusted for inflation)

M1 The Federal Reserve's primary measure of the money supply; the sum of currency held by the nonbank public, checking deposits, and traveler's checks

M2 Broad measure of the money supply that includes M1 and other highly liquid assets (savings deposits, small time deposits, and retail money-market mutual funds)

Margin requirements Limits on the use of credit to purchase stocks

Market risk Risk arising from fluctuations in asset prices

Medium of exchange Whatever people use to purchase goods and services

Microfinance (*microlending*) Small loans that allow poor people to start businesses

Modigliani–Miller theorem (MM theorem) Proposition that a firm's capital structure doesn't matter

Monetarists School of economists who believe that monetary policy has strong effects on the economy and that policy should be set by a rule

Monetary aggregate Measure of the money supply (M1 or M2)

Monetary base (*B*) Sum of currency in circulation and bank reserves ($B = C + R$); the Federal Reserve's liabilities to the private sector of the economy

Monetary policy Central banks' management of the money supply

Monetary-policy rule A simple rule or formula that tells the central bank how to run policy

Monetary transmission mechanism Process through which monetary policy affects output

Money Class of assets that serves as an economy's medium of exchange

Money-center bank Commercial bank located in a major financial center that raises funds primarily by borrowing from other banks or by issuing bonds

Money demand Amount of wealth that people choose to hold in the form of money

Money multiplier (m) Ratio of the money supply to the monetary base; $M = mB$

Money supply Total amount of money in the economy

Money targeting Approach to monetary policy in which the central bank chooses a level for the money supply and adjusts it when economic conditions change

Moral hazard The risk that one party to a transaction will act in a way that harms the other party

Mortgage-backed securities (MBSs) Securities that entitle an owner to a share of payments on a pool of mortgage loans

Municipal bonds Bonds issued by state and local governments

Mutual fund Financial institution that holds a diversified set of securities and sells shares to savers

NAIRU Acronym for *nonaccelerating inflation rate of unemployment*, the unemployment rate that produces a constant inflation rate; another name for the natural rate of unemployment, U^*

National bank Bank chartered by the federal government

Natural rate of unemployment (U^*) Normal or average level of unemployment

Net capital inflows Capital inflows minus capital outflows

Net capital outflows (NCO) Capital outflows minus capital inflows

Net exports (NX) Exports minus imports

Net worth (equity or capital) Difference between assets and liabilities

Neutral real interest rate (r^n) The real interest rate that makes output equal potential output, given the aggregate expenditure curve

Nominal exchange rate (e) Price of one unit of a currency in terms of another currency

Nominal GDP The total value of all final goods and services produced in an economy in a given period

Nominal interest rate (i) Interest rate offered by a bank account or bond

Nonaccommodative monetary policy Decision by the central bank to adjust the interest rate to offset a supply shock and keep inflation constant

Off-balance-sheet (OBS) activities Bank activities that produce income but are not reflected in the assets and liabilities reported on the balance sheet

Okun's law Relation between output and unemployment over the business cycle: the output gap falls by 2 percentage points when unemployment rises 1 point above the natural rate; $(Y - Y^*)/Y^* = -2(U - U^*)$

Open-market operations Purchases or sales of bonds by a central bank

Option The right to trade a security at a certain price any time before an expiration date

Order flow In a dealer market, the difference between total buy orders and sell orders over some period

Output gap ($\tilde{Y}$) Percentage difference between actual and potential output; $(Y - Y^*)/Y^*$

Outside lag Time between the policy response to a shock and its effects on the economy

Over-the-counter (OTC) market Secondary securities market with no physical location

Pawnshop Small lender that holds an item of value as collateral

Payday lender Company that provides cash in return for a postdated check

Payments system Arrangements through which money reaches the sellers of goods and services

Phillips curve (PC) The positive short-run relationship between output and inflation; also, the negative short-run relationship between unemployment and inflation

Ponzi scheme Swindle in which an asset manager falsely claims to earn high returns and pays clients who ask for cash by raising money from new clients

Potential output (Y^*) The normal or average level of output, as determined by resources and technology

Predatory lending Unfair lending practices aimed at poor and uninformed borrowers

Present value Value of a future dollar in terms of today's dollars; $1 in n years = $\$1/(1 + i)^n$ today

Price–earnings ratio (P/E ratio) A company's stock price divided by earnings per share over the recent past

Primary markets Financial markets in which firms and governments issue new securities

Principal–agent problem Moral hazard that arises when the action of one party (the agent) affects another party (the principal) that does not observe the action

Printing money Financing government budget deficits by selling bonds to the central bank

Private equity firm Financial institution that owns large shares in private companies; includes takeover firms and venture capital firms

Private loan Loan negotiated between one borrower and one lender

Private saving Saving by individuals and firms

Public company Firm that issues securities that are traded in financial markets

Public saving Saving by the government (tax revenue minus government spending)

Purchased funds Banks' expensive sources of funds (borrowings and large time deposits)

Purchasing power parity (PPP) Theory of exchange rates based on the idea that a currency purchases the same quantities of goods and services in different countries; implies that real exchange rates are constant over time

Put option An option to sell a security

Quantity equation of money Relationship among the money supply, velocity, and nominal GDP: $MV = PY$

Random walk The movements of a variable whose changes are unpredictable

Rate of return Return on a security as a percentage of its initial price; rate of return = $(P_1 - P_0)/P_0 + X/P_0$

Rate-sensitivity gap Difference between rate-sensitive assets and rate-sensitive liabilities

Rational expectations Theory that people's expectations of future variables are the best possible forecasts based on all available information

Real exchange rate (ε) Measure of the relative prices of domestic and foreign goods ($\varepsilon = eP/P^*$)

Real gross domestic product (real GDP) The measure of an economy's total output of goods and services

Real interest rate (r) Nominal interest rate minus the inflation rate; $r = i - \pi$

Recession Period when actual output falls below potential output

Regional bank Commercial bank with assets above $1 billion that operates in one geographic region

Repurchase agreement (repo) Sale of a security with a promise to buy it back at a higher price on a future date

Reserve–deposit ratio (R/D) Ratio of bank reserves to checking deposits

Reserve requirements Regulations that set a minimum level for banks' reserve–deposit ratios

Reserves Vault cash plus banks' deposits at the Federal Reserve

Return Total earnings from a security; the capital gain or loss plus any direct payment (coupon payment or dividend); return = $(P_1 - P_0) + X$

Return on assets (ROA) Ratio of a bank's profits to its assets; ROA = profits/assets

Return on equity (ROE) Ratio of a bank's profits to its capital; ROE = profits/capital

Revaluation Resetting of a fixed exchange rate at a higher level

Risk-adjusted interest rate Sum of the risk-free interest rate and the risk premium on an asset, $i^{safe} + \varphi$

Risk premium (φ) Payment on an asset that compensates the owner for taking on risk

Safe interest rate (i^{safe}) Interest rate that savers can receive for sure; also known as *risk-free rate*

Sarbanes–Oxley Act Federal legislation that strengthens the requirements for information disclosure by corporations

Savers People who accumulate wealth by spending less than they earn

Savings institution Type of bank created to accept savings deposits and make loans for home mortgages; also known as savings banks or savings and loan associations (S&Ls)

Secondary markets Financial markets in which existing securities are traded

Securities and Exchange Commission (SEC) U.S. government agency that regulates financial markets

Securities firm Company whose primary purpose is to hold securities, trade them, or help others trade them; includes mutual funds, hedge funds, brokers and dealers, and investment banks

Securitization Process in which a financial institution buys a large number of bank loans, then issues securities entitling the holders to shares of payments on the loans

Security Claim on some future flow of income, such as a stock or bond

Seigniorage revenue Revenue the government receives from printing money

Shoe leather costs Inconveniences that result from holding less money when inflation is high

Sovereign debt Bonds issued by national governments

Specialist Broker–dealer who manages the trading of a certain stock on an exchange

Speculation Using financial markets to make bets on asset prices

Speculative attack Strategy of selling a currency with a fixed exchange rate to force and to profit from a devaluation

State bank Bank chartered by a state government

Stock (*equity*) Ownership share in a corporation

Stock market index An average of prices for a group of stocks

Store of value Form in which wealth can be held

Stored-value card Card issued with a prepaid balance that can be used for purchases

Structured investment vehicle (SIV) Company created by a bank as a means of holding assets off its balance sheet, thus allowing it to circumvent capital requirements

Subprime lenders Companies that lend to people with weak credit histories

Superregional bank Commercial bank with assets above $1 billion that operates across most of the United States

Supply shock, ν Event that causes a major change in firms' production costs, which in turn causes a short-run change in the inflation rate

Suspension of payments Refusal by a bank to allow withdrawals by depositors

Sweep program Banking practice of shifting funds temporarily from customers' checking accounts to money-market deposit accounts

Takeover firm Private equity firm that buys entire companies and tries to increase the companies' profits

Taylor rule Formula for adjusting the interest rate to stabilize the economy: $r = r^n + a_y \widetilde{Y} + a_\pi (\pi - \pi^T)$

Technical analysis Set of methods for forecasting prices in financial markets based on the past behavior of prices

Term premium (τ) Extra return on a long-term bond that compensates for its riskiness; τ_n denotes the term premium on an n-period bond.

Term structure of interest rates Relationships among interest rates on bonds with different maturities

Thrift institutions (thrifts) Savings institutions and credit unions

Time-consistency problem Situation in which someone has incentives to make a promise but later to renege on it; because of these incentives, others don't believe the promise

Too big to fail (TBTF) Doctrine that large financial institutions facing failure must be rescued to protect the financial system

Trade-weighted real exchange rate Weighted average of a country's real exchange rates, with weights proportional to levels of trade

Transaction costs Costs in time and money of exchanging goods, services, or assets

Transparency Providing clear, detailed information about policymaking to the public

Undervalued asset Asset with a price below the present value of the income it is expected to produce

Underwriter Financial institution that helps companies issue new securities

Unemployment rate (U) Percentage of the labor force without jobs

Unit of account Measure in which prices and salaries are quoted

Usury law Legal limit on interest rates

Vault cash Currency in banks' branches and ATMs

Velocity of money Ratio of nominal GDP to the money supply ($V = PY/M$); shows how quickly money moves through the economy

Venture capital (VC) firm Private equity firm that buys shares in new companies that plan to grow

Yield curve Graph comparing interest rates on bonds of various maturities at a given point in time

Yield to maturity Interest rate that makes the present value of payments from a bond equal to its price

Zero bound Limit on the nominal interest rate; a central bank cannot reduce i below zero, which limits its ability to stimulate the economy

index

Note: Page numbers followed by f indicate figures; those followed by n indicate notes; those followed by t indicate tables.

Key Equations

(3.1) **FUTURE VALUE** $1 today $= \$(1+i)^n$ in n years

(3.2) **PRESENT VALUE** $1 in n years $= \dfrac{\$1}{(1+i)^n}$ today

(3.6) bond price $= \dfrac{C}{(1+i)} + \dfrac{C}{(1+i)^2} + \cdots + \dfrac{C}{(1+i)^{T-1}} + \dfrac{(C+F)}{(1+i)^T}$

(3.9) **AN ASSET'S RATE OF RETURN** rate of return $= \dfrac{(P_1 - P_0)}{P_0} + \dfrac{X}{P_0}$

(3.10) **REAL INTEREST RATE** $r = i - \pi$

(3.11) **EX ANTE REAL INTEREST RATE** $r^{\text{ex ante}} = i - \pi^{\text{expected}}$

(3.12) **EX POST REAL INTEREST RATE** $r^{\text{ex post}} = i - \pi^{\text{actual}}$

(4.1) **FISHER EQUATION** $i = r + \pi^e$

(4.3) **EXPECTATIONS THEORY OF THE TERM STRUCTURE**

$$i_n(t) = \frac{1}{n}[i_1(t) + Ei_1(t+1) + \cdots + Ei_1(t+n-1)]$$

(4.4) **THE EXPECTATIONS THEORY WITH A TERM PREMIUM**

$$i_n(t) = \frac{1}{n}[i_1(t) + Ei_1(t+1) + \cdots + Ei_1(t+n-1)] + \tau_n$$

(6.1) **REAL EXCHANGE RATE** $\varepsilon = \dfrac{eP}{P^*}$

(6.4) $NX = NCO$

(11.2) $m = \dfrac{(C/D) + 1}{(C/D) + (R/D)}$

(11.3) $M = mB$

(12.1) **OKUN'S LAW** $(Y - Y^*)/Y^* = -2(U - U^*)$

(12.2) $Y = AE = C + I + G + NX$

(12.3) **ADAPTIVE EXPECTATIONS** $\pi^e = \pi(-1)$

(12.4) **OUTPUT PHILLIPS CURVE** $\pi = \pi^e + \alpha(Y - Y^*)/Y^* \quad (\alpha > 0)$

(12.5) **UNEMPLOYMENT PHILLIPS CURVE** $\pi = \pi^e - 2\alpha(U - U^*)$

(12.8) **THE PHILLIPS CURVE WITH A SUPPLY SHOCK** $\pi = \pi^e + \alpha(Y - Y^*)/Y^* + \nu$

(14.1) **QUANTITY EQUATION OF MONEY** $MV = PY$

(15.1) **THE TAYLOR RULE** $r = r^n + a_y \widetilde{Y} + a_\pi(\pi - \pi^T)$